JUDGES

The second edition of *Judges on Trial* articulates the rules, assumptions and practices which shape the culture of independence of the English judiciary today. Enhanced by interviews with English judges, legal scholars and professionals, it also outlines the factors that shape the modern meaning of judicial independence. The book discusses the contemporary issues of judicial governance, judicial appointments, the standards of conduct on and off the bench, the discipline and liability of judges and the relationship between judges and the media. It is accessible to an international audience of lawyers, political scientists and judges beyond the national realm.

SHIMON SHETREET holds the Greenblatt Chair of Public and International Law at the Hebrew University of Jerusalem, Israel. He is the author and editor of many books on the judiciary. He is President of the International Association of Judicial Independence and World Peace and the leader of the International Project on Judicial Independence and the Mt Scopus International Standards of Judicial Independence 2008. Between 1988 and 1996 he served as Member of the Israeli Parliament and was a cabinet minister under Yitshak Rabin and Shimon Peres.

SOPHIE TURENNE is a fellow and lecturer in Law at Murray Edwards College, University of Cambridge, where she teaches comparative law, constitutional law and European law. She was one of a number of experts who took part in an OSCE–ODIHR Research Project, which led to the publication in 2010 of the *Kyiv Recommendations on Judicial Independence in Eastern Europe, South Caucasus and Central Asia*. She will act as General Reporter on the topic of judicial independence at the nineteenth International Congress of Comparative Law in Vienna (July 2014).

CAMBRIDGE STUDIES IN CONSTITUTIONAL LAW

The aim of this series is to produce leading monographs in constitutional law. All areas of constitutional law and public law fall within the ambit of the series, including human rights and civil liberties law, administrative law, as well as constitutional theory and the history of constitutional law. A wide variety of scholarly approaches is encouraged, with the governing criterion being simply that the work is of interest to an international audience. Thus, works concerned with only one jurisdiction will be included in the series as appropriate, while, at the same time, the series will include works which are explicitly comparative or theoretical – or both. The series editors likewise welcome proposals that work at the intersection of constitutional and international law, or that seek to bridge the gaps between civil law systems, the US, and the common law jurisdictions of the Commonwealth.

JUDGES ON TRIAL: THE INDEPENDENCE AND ACCOUNTABILITY OF THE ENGLISH JUDICIARY

SECOND EDITION

SHIMON SHETREET
and
SOPHIE TURENNE

CAMBRIDGE
UNIVERSITY PRESS

CAMBRIDGE
UNIVERSITY PRESS

University Printing House, Cambridge CB2 8BS, United Kingdom

Cambridge University Press is part of the University of Cambridge.

It furthers the University's mission by disseminating knowledge in the pursuit of education, learning and research at the highest international levels of excellence.

www.cambridge.org
Information on this title: www.cambridge.org/9781107629370

© Shimon Shetreet and Sophie Turenne 2013

This publication is in copyright. Subject to statutory exception and to the provisions of relevant collective licensing agreements, no reproduction of any part may take place without the written permission of Cambridge University Press.

First published by Elsevier 1976
Second edition Cambridge University Press 2013

A catalogue record for this publication is available from the British Library

Library of Congress Cataloguing in Publication data
Shetreet, Shimon.
Judges on trial : the independence and accountability of the English judiciary / By Shimon Shetreet and Sophie Turenne. – Second edition.
pages cm.
ISBN 978-1-107-01367-4 (Hardback) – ISBN 978-1-107-62937-0 (Paperback)
1. Judges–Great Britain.   2. Judicial power–Great Britain.   I. Turenne, Sophie.   II. Title.
KD7285.S54 2013
347.41′014–dc23   2013009534

ISBN 978-1-107-01367-4 Hardback
ISBN 978-1-107-62937-0 Paperback

CONTENTS

FOREWORD

Professor Shetreet's seminal work on judicial independence published in 1976 provided a systemisation of the rules and practices that safeguarded the independence of the judiciary of England and Wales at a time when the office of Lord Chancellor was of central importance. A detailed historical survey underpinned that systemisation. Lord Scarman was right to commend it in his preface to that edition. My well-thumbed copy is a measure of its use by me in the period from 2003.

That period began with the decision in June 2003 first to abolish, but then only to reform, the office of Lord Chancellor, and to create a Supreme Court and a new system for judicial appointments. The legislative changes in the Constitutional Reform Act to give effect to those decisions came into effect in 2006. Although as with many major reforms, the changes are still evolving, this is an excellent time to take stock and provide a systemisation of the new system. A second edition is not only needed, but most welcome. The stated aim is to make explicit the rules, assumptions and practices in force within our judiciary in consequence of the changes.

Underpinning that aim is a detailed exposition of the way in which the judicial system operates. Subjects that might not at first sight appear important are explained in such a way that their significance becomes apparent. The flexibility of case assignment (or listing) is assessed in comparison to the principles applicable in Germany. As the authors perceptively observe, that flexibility is accepted because of the culture of trust that underpins our judicial system.

Old issues are carefully re-analysed in the light of some changes that antedate the 2003 decisions. Although judges have always given lectures that have, with a greater or lesser degree of self-restraint, addressed matters of controversy, until 1987, the Kilmuir rules constrained judges from speaking in other circumstances, particularly to the media. The authors analyse the changes that have occurred and tentatively conclude that the applicable principle is one of free but circumspect speech guided by long-standing constitutional culture. Although principles of judicial conduct have long rested on Magna Carta, the judicial oath and accepted practice, in 2002 detailed rules were for the first time set out in the *Guide to Judicial Conduct*. These required and receive critical evaluation – for the most part favourable.

The changes initiated in 2003 are subjected to critical appraisal; again matters that might not seem very significant are carefully considered – one of the nine chapters is devoted to the structure and governance of the judiciary. The role of the Judicial Appointments Commission is also carefully examined. Whilst applauding its creation as a step taken towards greater judicial independence, it rightly subjects to critical examination the need for greater diversity, the concept of a judicial career and the role of training in supporting progression and mobility.

Many fundamental questions are asked. For example, whether the safeguards in the Constitutional Reform Act will in fact safeguard the judiciary from political pressure or interference, whether there are sufficient checks and balances to govern the inherent tension between judicial independence and accountability and whether the balance between the fundamental values of a justice system are, in the context of diminishing resources, properly balanced with efficiency and performance. Although no specific answers are given, the detailed research and clear explanations of the system contain clear pointers to realistic answers.

Like Lord Scarman in 1976 I would unreservedly commend this new edition to anyone who wishes to understand the role of the judicial branch of the state, what its independence and accountability actually entail and what remains to be done to foster its continued constructive role in the good governance of the state. *Judges on Trial* remains the apt title.

Sir John Thomas
President of the Queen's Bench Division
June 2013

Postscript from the authors (July 2013): since he wrote this Foreword, Sir John Thomas was appointed Lord Chief Justice of England and Wales, with effect from 1 October 2013.

ACKNOWLEDGMENTS

Judicial independence, as a core condition for a democratic state, engages all of civil society. The first edition of Shetreet's *Judges on Trial: a Study of the Appointment and the Accountability of the English Judiciary* (1976, North-Holland Publishing Company) was the first book in which the corpus of rules, assumptions or standards, and practices that shape the culture of independence within the English judiciary were made explicit. Thirty-seven years later, our aim is to offer a distinctive contribution to the modern meaning and practice of the vexed notion of 'judicial independence'. This book provides a systematic discussion of the requirements of judicial independence and accountability, buttressed by interviews with leading judges and jurists. The text takes into account developments until mid-January 2013, when the book was presented for publication. It has been possible to acknowledge further events, until the end of April 2013, but only in the footnotes. We have been involved in the International Project of Judicial Independence (of the International Association of Judicial Independence, sponsored by the Hebrew University and the University of Cambridge) of which Professor Shetreet is the general coordinator and Dr Turenne is a member. We drew on this project in the course of writing this book, as well as on the publications that accompany the regular meetings of scholars involved with this project. Our sincere thanks go to those participants.

Professor Shetreet expresses his gratitude to the University of Cambridge Faculty of Law for his appointment as a Herbert Smith Visiting Professor in 2008, and his revisit to the university in 2010. He is also grateful to Clare College, Cambridge, for his appointment as Senior Academic Visitor in the years 2008, 2010 and 2011 (Michaelmas Term). In addition, Professor Shetreet expresses his gratitude to the Hebrew University, to the Faculty of Law at the Hebrew University of Jerusalem and to the Harry and Michael Sacher Institute of Comparative Law at the Hebrew University of Jerusalem, for supporting the project of writing this book.

Dr Turenne owes a debt of gratitude to a large number of people who have facilitated this research. She gives hearty thanks to John Bell for being available when needed and his helpful comments on ideas or drafts, and to Anja Seibert-Fohr for enabling her stay, and the fruitful discussions which followed, at the Max Planck Institute in Heidelberg in 2011. This research was partly funded by Murray Edwards College, Cambridge. Albertina Albors-Llorens, Paola Filipucci, Isabelle Guinard and Eleanor O'Gorman were true supporters; her partner, Jonathan, and her parents lived through the writing process with her and kept her son, Jérôme, away from her desk – but they all offered welcome distractions too. Dr Turenne dedicates this work to the memory of her grandmother, Estelle Bénazéraf. Carolyn Fox, Finola O'Sullivan and Richard Woodham, from Cambridge University Press were most efficient and reliable in overseeing the publishing process.

We wish to express our deep gratitude to all the judges and senior jurists who gave generously of their time. Their help increased our understanding of the contemporary issues of the English judiciary. Sophie Briant, the Honourable Mr Justice Hickinbottom, Her Honour Judge Isobel Plumstead, the Right Honourable Lord Justice Beatson, the Right Honourable Lady Hallett, the President of the Queen's Bench Division, the Right Honourable Sir John Thomas, Robin Auld, Lord Phillips and the late Lord Bingham deserve particular mention. Any deficiencies are entirely our own.

TABLE OF CASES

UK

Parliamentary cases

European Court of Human Rights

Court of Justice of the European Union

Australia

Bahamas

Barbados

Belize

Ceylan

Canada

Republic of Ireland

Singapore

South Africa

St Lucia

Trinidad and Tobago

US

TABLE OF LEGISLATION

Australia

Ireland

New Zealand

ABBREVIATIONS

ABA	American Bar Association
AIJA	Australian Institute of Judicial Administration
AJCL	American Journal of Comparative Law
Am Pol Sci Rev	American Review of Political Science
BIICL	British Institute of International and Comparative Law
Cardozo L Rev	Cardozo Law Review
CJA	UK Commission for Judicial Appointments
CJQ	Civil Justice Quarterly
CLJ	Cambridge Law Journal
CLP	Current Legal Problems
CRA	Constitutional Reform Act 2005
Crim LR	Criminal Law Review
CYELS	Cambridge Yearbook of European Legal Studies
DCA	UK Department for Constitutional Affairs
Denning LJ	Denning Law Journal
ECHR	European Convention on Human Rights
ECtHR	European Court of Human Rights
EHRLR	European Human Rights Law Review
FLR	Family Law Reports
HLR	Harvard Law Review
HoC	House of Commons
HoL	House of Lords
HRA	Human Rights Act 1998
ICLQ	International and Comparative Law Quarterly
Ir Jur	The Irish Jurist
Israel LRev	Israel Law Review
JLS	Journal of Law and Society
JPN	Justice of the Peace
J Pub Teach Law	Journal of of the Society of Public Teachers of Law
Jud	Judicature
LJ	Lord Justice/Lady Justice
LQR	Law Quarterly Review

LRB	London Review of Books
LS	Legal Studies
MLR	Modern Law Review
NLJ	New Law Journal
OJLS	Oxford Journal of Legal Studies
PL	Public Law
Pol Quart	Political Quarterly
Pol Sc Quart	Political Science Quarterly
Sydney L Rev	Sydney Law Review
UBC Law Rev	University of British Columbia Law Review
U Chi JIL	Chicago Journal of International Law
U Ill L Rev	University of Illinois Law Review
YLJ	Yale Law Journal

1

Introduction

1.1 Judicial independence is an essential pillar of liberty and the rule of law; 'without a judiciary which can and will administer law fairly and fearlessly between the parties, no other guarantee given to the litigants by the law is likely to be of value'.[1] The many requirements of judicial independence can be found in international and domestic foundational texts.[2] Yet its modern meaning and practice is as unique as the character of each judiciary is, fashioned by checks and balances generated through history by various stakeholders in the judiciary. The protagonists in the story of judicial independence most noticeably comprise the executive

[1] J.A. Jolowicz, 'Angleterre', in M. Cappelletti and D. Tallon (eds.), Fundamental Guarantees of the Parties in Civil Litigation (Milan: Giuffrè, 1973), p. 121; Montreal Universal Declaration on the Independence of Justice, Preamble.

[2] Art. 10 Universal Declaration of Human Rights; Art. 14 International Covenant on Civil and Political Rights; the Montreal Universal Declaration on the Independence of Justice, 1983; Basic Principles on the Independence of the Judiciary, adopted by the United Nations General Assembly, GA Res. 40/32 of 29 November 1985, para 5, UN GAOR, 40th Session, Supp. No. 53, at 205 (UN Doc A/40/53 (1985)) and GA Res. 40/146 of 13 December 1985, para. 2, UN GAOR 40th Session, Supp. No 53, at 254, UN Doc A/40/53 (1985); International Commission of Jurists, 'The Rule of Law and Human Rights: The Judiciary and the Rule of Law' 1959–62. The Montreal Universal Declaration on the Independence of Justice builds upon The Syracuse Draft Principles on the Independence of the Judiciary 1981 ('the Syracuse Principles'), the Independence of the Judiciary in the LAWASIA Region: Principles and Conclusion, 1982 ('the Tokyo Principles') and The International Bar Association Code of Minimum Standards of Judicial Independence, 1982 ('the New Delhi Standards'); the Bangalore Principles; Beijing Statement of Principles of the Independence of the Judiciary in the LAWASIA Region, 1995. See also Committee of Ministers, Council of Europe, 'On the Independence, Efficiency and Role of Judges' (1994) Recommendation No R (94 12, adopted by the Committee of Ministers on 13 October 1994, 518th meeting of the Ministers' Deputies, Principle I, s2(d); Consultative Council of European Judges, Council of Europe, 'On Standards Concerning the Independence of the Judiciary and the Irremovability of Judges', (2001) CCJE, OP. No 1, (23 November 2001) and 'On the Principles and Rules Governing Judges' Professional Conduct, in Particular Ethics, Incompatible Behaviour and Impartiality' (2002) CCJE, OP. No 3 (19 November 2002)'; Council of Europe, European Charter on the Statute of Judges (1998).

and the legislature. In England and Wales,[3] they also include a number of autonomous bodies with statutory powers, such as the Judicial Appointments Commission. Judicial independence depends thus to a significant extent on the constitutional relations external to the judiciary, such as the relationship between Parliament and the government.[4] It is also a significant component of government culture to the extent that it must be supported by the political climate and social consensus.[5] The political leadership and the legal elite must work together to develop a culture of judicial independence underlined by some significant guidelines. This process is of necessity gradual and ongoing.

The checks and balances regarding the judiciary create, however, a continuous tension between judicial independence and the public accountability of judges in a democracy.[6] This tension, in turn, reflects a line of demarcation for the judicial power of the state, according to the principles of parliamentary sovereignty and separation of powers.[7] This means that the model of judicial accountability adopted in a given society determines, to a large extent, the independence of the judiciary.[8]

In this book, we examine the requirements of judicial independence and accountability in England, in the light of the process of constitutional

---

[3] The United Kingdom has three separate legal jurisdictions: England and Wales; Northern Ireland, and Scotland. While references to Northern Ireland and Scotland may occasionally be made, the judiciary of England is the primary subject of our study. England and Wales currently share a single legal jurisdiction, but note the debate on whether Wales should be a separate legal jurisdiction, Welsh Government, 'Consultation Document. A Separate Legal Jurisdiction for Wales', WG-15109 (27 March 2012); Welsh Government, 'A Summary of Consultation Responses. A Separate Legal Jurisdiction for Wales', WG-16277 (17 August 2012).

[4] V. Bogdanor, *The New British Constitution* (Oxford: Hart, 2009), pp. 282–4.

[5] For this reason, other important political, legal events or controversies are occasionally referred to in this book, but we do not consider the whole legal system; topics such as legal aid and the legal profession are only incidentally considered.

[6] Lord Hailsham, 'The Independence of the Judicial Process' (1978) 13 Israel LRev 1, 8–9; J. Beatson, 'Judicial Independence and Accountability: Pressures and Opportunities' (2008) *Judicial Review* 1, G. Canivet, M. Andenas and D. Fairgrieve (eds), *Judicial Independence and Accountability* (London: BIICL, 2006); S.B. Burbanks and B. Friedman (eds), *Judicial Independence at the Crossroads: An Interdisciplinary Approach* (Thousand Oaks, California: Sage Publications, 2002).

[7] W. Blackstone, *Commentaries on the Laws of England* (1765), vol. I, ch. 7, p. 258; R. Masterman, *The Separation of Powers in the Contemporary Constitution* (Cambridge University Press, 2010).

[8] M. Cappelletti, 'Who Watches the Watchmen? A Comparative Study on Judicial Responsibility' (1983) 31 AJCL 1; S. Shetreet and J. Deschenes (eds.), *Judicial Independence: The Contemporary Debate* (Boston: M. Nijhoff, 1985), pp. 570–5.

reform which started with the Human Rights Act 1998. The conceptual requirements of judicial independence and the necessary elements for maintaining a culture of judicial independence are closely related.[9] Our analysis develops through a series of studies of the judiciary as an institution and as a collective:[10] thus we look at judicial governance, judicial appointments, the mechanisms for monitoring judges and the standards of conduct on and off the bench, as well as the relationship between freedom of expression, judges and public confidence in the courts. These topics constitute case studies of the interactions between judges and a range of actors, such as the Lord Chancellor/Secretary of State for Justice or the Judicial Appointments Commission for England and Wales and Parliament. We consider the judiciary as a social organisation within a context of expectations set by legal norms and by other institutions. Our premise is that the historical political context is a major determinant in the interpretation of the principle of judicial independence within a legal system.[11]

In keeping with the first edition of the book, our approach combines a theoretical with a practical analysis buttressed by interviews with judicial office holders and 'stakeholders' in the judiciary. We interviewed more than twenty-five judicial office holders and a similar number of stake-holders in the judiciary, including legal practitioners, scholars, retired judges and others involved in the appointment or monitoring of judges.

---

[9] This is the approach adopted by the International Association of Judicial Independence and its International Project of Judicial Independence conducted by a research group of international jurists – to which the authors belong, which approved the *Mt. Scopus Approved Revised International Standards of Judicial Independence*, 2008 (hereafter Mt. Scopus) available at www.jiwp.org.

[10] J. Bell, *Judiciaries within Europe, A Comparative Review* (Cambridge University Press, 2006), p. 4; Thomas LJ, 'The Position of the Judiciaries of the United Kingdom in the Constitutional Changes', Address to the Scottish Sheriffs' Association (Peebles, 8 March 2008); Lord Phillips, 'Judicial Independence' – Commonwealth Law Conference (Nairobi, Kenya, 12 September 2007); for other perspectives, see C. Guarnieri and P. Pederzoli, *The Power of Judges: A Comparative Study of Courts and Democracy* (Oxford University Press, 2002); P. Derbyshire, *Sitting in Judgment. The Working Lives of Judges* (Oxford: Hart, 2011).

[11] Bell, *Judiciaries within Europe*, 355, R.A. Macdonald and H. Kong, 'Judicial Independence as a Constitutional Virtue', in A. Sajo and M. Rosenfeld (eds), *The Oxford Handbook of Comparative Constitutional Law* (Oxford University Press, 2012), p. 831; P.H. Russell, 'Towards a General Theory of Judicial Independence', in P.H. Russell and D.M. O'Brien (eds), *Judicial Independence in the Age of Democracy* (Charlottesville/London: University of Georgia, 2001), p. 1; C.M. Larkins, 'Judicial Independence and Democratization: A Theoretical and Conceptual Analysis' (1996) 44 *American Journal of Comparative Law* 605.

The judges interviewed included judges from all benches and other judicial office holders, such as tribunal judges. The questions addressed selected general issues with some additional questions specific to the role and knowledge of the interviewees. The interviews were used to support and shape the analysis of the literature considered, from judicial statistics to the existing academic discussions on judicial independence, including judicial writings.[12]

Individual and collective or institutional independence

1.2 Judicial independence must be secured both at the institutional level and at the individual level for judges to be protected from threats to their personal or professional security that may influence their official duties.[13] The collective and individual aspects of judicial independence are embedded in the English judicial oath to do justice – 'I will do right by all manner of people, after the law and usages of this realm, without fear or favour, affection or ill will'.[14] Institutional or collective independence may be undermined by fear or favour, when 'affection or ill-will' jeopardises the independence of the individual judge. Either way, impartiality is central to the independence of the individual judge. 'Justice must be rooted in confidence: and confidence is destroyed when right-minded people go away thinking: "The judge was biased".'[15] It is *the* fundamental principle of justice both at common law and under Article 6 of the European Convention on Human Rights (ECHR):[16] accordingly, impartiality is a fundamental guarantee of justice at common law and is enshrined in Article 6 of the European Convention on Human Rights.

---

[12] Publicly available but internal documents to the judiciary, contacts and personal recommendations helped us define a varied list of interviewees, with some narrowly involved in judicial governance and others familiar with judges but external to them. Interviews were conducted under the Chatham House Rule, ensuring that any statement made in an interview would not be attributed to the interviewee in the book; for that reason, even though we make a judicious use of non-attributed quotations, a list of interviewees is not included in this publication. Approximately half of the interviews lasted one hour, with the other half lasting significantly longer; in practice the discussion of the topics considered in Chapters 3, 4 and 8 took most of the interview time.

[13] Mt. Scopus, ss. 2.2, 2.12 and 2.13.

[14] Senior Courts Act 1981, s. 10(4); Promissory Oaths Act 1868.

[15] *Metropolitan Properties Ltd* v. *Lannon* [1969] 1 QB 577. See also Arts. 41 and 47 Charter of Fundamental Rights of the European Union.

[16] *AWG Group* v. *Morrison Ltd* [2006] EWCA Civ 6, para. 6 [Mummery LJ].

But the independence of the individual judge rests upon two concepts. It first entails a substantive independence, independence in the conduct of the judicial business – the judge's core activity being to decide cases and, in the case of higher courts, to give judgments that may constitute precedents. Individual judges are subject to no other authority for their decisions than the appeal courts. A basic requirement for maintaining public confidence in the legal system is the court's duty to provide a reasoned judgment for its decisions.[17] Once a judge has decided what the applicable legal principle is, he may not discard it through personal dislike or belief that the principle might soon be changed by Parliament or overruled by the higher courts, or through a sense that the judgment might cause popular outrage. Instead he must apply the law as it is understood to be and leave it to the higher courts or the legislature to decide to effect any change.[18] It is to some extent a myth that judges do not change the common law; instead they find more accurate ways of expressing it, so that some previous cases are not overruled but rather distinguished or 'better explained'.[19]

Further guarantees of individual and substantive independence include relieving judges of personal civil liability for acts performed in the course of their judicial duties. Since the seventeenth century, judges of the High Court and above have enjoyed exemption from civil liability for anything done or said by them in the exercise of their judicial function, and provided that they acted in good faith. Circuit and district judges, in certain circumstances, may be liable in tort for actions beyond their jurisdiction. The exclusion of civil liability for judicial acts is granted as a matter of public policy, 'not so much for [the judges'] own sake as for the sake of the public, and for the advancement of justice, that being free from actions, they may be free in thought and independent in judgment, as all who administer justice ought to be'.[20] A fear of being

---

[17] *English* v. *Emery Reimbold and Strick Ltd* [2002] 1 WLR 2409 (CA), para. 12.

[18] See Lord Lowry's statement in *C* v. *DPP* [1996] AC 1. In that case, the House of Lords refused to abolish a long-established common law defence in criminal law for very young defendants on the ground that it had become obsolete, and Parliament duly did so instead in Crime and Disorder Act 1998, s. 34.

[19] Bell, *Judiciaries within Europe*, 337; T. Etherton, 'Liberty, the Archetype and Diversity: A Philosophy of Judging' [2010] PL 727; Lord Reid, 'The Judge as Law Maker' (1972) 12 J Pub Teach Law 22.

[20] *Garnett* v. *Ferrand* (1827) 6 B & C 611, 625 [Lord Tenterden CJ], adopted by the Court of Appeal in *Sirros* v. *Moore* [1975] QB 118, 132 [Lord Denning MR]; *Arthur JS Hall and Co* v. *Simons* [2002] 1 AC 615.

sued could influence a judge's decision; the judicial immunity thus protects the independence of the judiciary and the integrity of the judicial process. The only 'fear' a judge has in making a decision is rather that of being overruled on appeal.[21]

Second, the independence of the individual judge involves some personal independence in the sense that the terms and tenure of the judicial office are adequately secured. Thus the Act of Settlement 1701 established judicial tenure during good behaviour to senior judges and gave them protection from unilateral removal by the Crown. Personal independence is characterised by judicial appointment during good behaviour terminated at retirement age, and by safeguarding an adequate judicial remuneration and pension against the executive's discretion. Thus, executive control over the judges' terms of service, such as remuneration or pensions, is inconsistent with the concept of judicial independence. Rules of judicial conduct at the same time pursue the similar aim of excluding the judge from financial or business entanglements which are likely to affect (or rather to seem to affect) him in the exercise of his judicial functions.

A further dimension of judicial independence transcends the distinction between substantive and individual independence of judges. Internal independence of judges demands that individual judges be free from unjustified influences, not only from entities external to the judiciary, but also from within. Judges need safeguards for their independence from peers or more senior judges in the discharge of their official duties.[22] But a judge cannot rely on internal independence as a shield against guidance from other judges who are responsible for court administration. It may be argued that internal independence only applies to the substantive and procedural aspects of adjudication, however the distinction between an

---

[21] However, the possible impact of this concern on decision making should not be underestimated, especially in areas where the law is overly complex, as is the case with sentencing. One recorder has freely told members of his Inn that when he started to sentence criminals, he would try to avoid sentencing them to prison for fear of being corrected on appeal. He only changed his practice when he actually did find himself forced to sentence a defendant to prison for supplying prohibited drugs, upon which he noticed that the defendant and his family seemed remarkably pleased at the sentence, and he later gingerly inquired of his clerk whether he thought that they might have been expecting a longer prison sentence.

[22] Cappelletti, 'Who Watches the Watchmen?', 7–9; J. Beatson, 'Reforming an Unwritten Constitution' (2010) 126 LQR 48; R v. UK [1997] 24 EHRR 221 and R v. Spear [2003] 1 AC 734; Mt. Scopus, s. 9.

administrative action and a purely adjudicative action which is a form of dispute resolution may not be straightforward.[23]

Until the Constitutional Reform Act 2005 (CRA), judges were appointed by and managed within the Lord Chancellor's Department. For as long as the judiciary was under the leadership of the Lord Chancellor, independence from political authorities was the main defining factor for judicial independence, and the independence of the English judiciary would appear mostly a characteristic of individual judges.[24] Judicial independence has been a matter of legal culture, solidly resting upon conventions developed over times. Yet England, where the first phase of judicial independence began over 300 years ago, also provides a vivid illustration of the mutual impacts of domestic and international law and jurisprudence. Cultures of judicial independence are built on both the domestic and international fronts, and in their more advanced stages reinforce each other. Article 6(1) of the ECHR provides the right to be tried by an impartial and independent tribunal established by law. This, in the case law of the European Court of Human Rights, placed an emphasis on a formal separation of powers between the judiciary and the executive.[25] In combination with personal tensions within the Cabinet in England and Wales, it led to the abolition of the Lord Chancellor's position as head of the judiciary. Parliament enshrined in the CRA the obligation for government ministers to 'uphold the continued independence of the judiciary'.[26] A wider duty is placed upon the Lord Chancellor and Secretary of State (two distinct government offices to which one

---

[23] Cappelletti, 'Who Watches the Watchmen', 7–9.

[24] R. Stevens, *The English Judges: Their Role in the Changing Constitution*, rev. edn (Oxford: Hart, 2005); Lord Irvine, *Human Rights, Constitutional Law and the Development of the English System* (Oxford: Hart, 2003), p. 205.

[25] Human Rights Act 1998, s. 1(3) sch. 1 incorporates the European Convention on Human Rights into UK law; *Procola* v. *Luxembourg* (1995) 22 EHRR 193; *McGonnell* v. *UK* (2000) 30 EHRR 289; *Findlay* v. *UK* (1997) 24 EHRR 221, para. 52; *R (Brooke)* v. *Parole Board* [2008] EWCA Civ 29, paras. 78–80.

[26] CRA, s. 3 provides: (1) the Lord Chancellor, other Ministers of the Crown and all with responsibility for matters relating to the judiciary or otherwise to the administration of justice must uphold the continued independence of the judiciary ... (5) the Lord Chancellor and other Ministers of the Crown must not seek to influence particular judicial decisions through any special access to the judiciary; (6) the Lord Chancellor must have regard to (a) the need to defend that independence; (b) the need for the judiciary to have the support necessary to enable them to exercise their functions; (c) the need for the public interest in regard to matters relating to the judiciary or otherwise to the administration of justice to be properly represented in decisions affecting those matters.

person is appointed) to 'have regard' to both 'the need to defend' the independence of the judiciary and 'the need for the public interest in regard to matters relating to the judiciary or otherwise to the administration of justice to be properly represented in decisions affecting those matters'.[27]

The impact of the formal separation of powers on judicial independence, under the CRA, is substantial. The Lord Chief Justice has become head of the judiciary but he is not a politician, nor a member of the Cabinet or a Speaker in the House of Lords as had been the Lord Chancellor before. Instead the Lord Chief Justice is chosen by a specially appointed committee, convened by the Judicial Appointments Commission. The creation of a new Judicial Appointments Commission also greatly reduced the role of ministers in judicial appointments. Full-time members of the judiciary are excluded from the House of Commons and from the House of Lords. Equally, by statute, no Member of Parliament can be appointed to the Judicial Appointments Commission. Yet, while the formal recognition of the principle of separation can only support the culture of judicial independence, the continuation of judicial independence is not a matter of course; it is subject to continuous challenges.

Judicial governance

1.3 The type of judicial governance and leadership over the organisation of the judiciary will influence its susceptibility to external influence. In England and Wales, judicial independence is not understood as self-government in the sense of judges having control of and managing judicial appointments, career progress or termination of office, in addition to running the administration of justice.[28] Indeed, Lord Bingham observed that 'many judges resented what they perceived as an administration breathing down their necks treating them as pawns on a bureaucratic chess board'.[29] This can otherwise be described as greater scrutiny of public services in light of the new public management values of effectiveness, efficiency and economy, which developed in the 1980s

---

[27] CRA, s. 3(6).

[28] Lord Woolf, 'The Rule of Law and a Change in the Constitution' (2004) CLJ 317. Compare with the experience in the United States regarding executive control over court administration: until 1939 the central responsibility for court administration at the federal level was vested in the Attorney General; in 1939 the responsibility went to the judiciary, see 28 USCA § 605.

[29] T. Bingham, *The Business of Judging* (Oxford University Press, 2000), p. 67.

and coincided with the growth in size (and budget) of the judicial system. The tensions were formally resolved in the 2004 Concordat, a soft law agreement of constitutional importance between the Lord Chancellor and the Lord Chief Justice. The Concordat set out the principles and practices supporting the transfer of functions to the Lord Chief Justice in relation to the administration of justice.[30]

The senior judiciary thereby negotiated a shared leadership structure in the administration of justice, through the executive agency of the Ministry of Justice, today known as Her Majesty's Courts and Tribunals Service. The Concordat emphasises both the need for cooperation and the dividing lines between the judicial business and the responsibilities of the Lord Chancellor for the provision of financial, material or human resources:[31] the judiciary and the executive have distinct functions but they must work together in a proper relationship as a part of the overall government of the country. A system of consultation and joint decision making between the Lord Chief Justice and Lord Chancellor characterises their 'close working relationship'.[32] The judicial system is thus defined by the association of an independent judiciary with the Courts and Tribunals Service, which provides for the administrative infrastructure supporting the conduct of the courts' and tribunals' business.

The Lord Chief Justice now exercises some considerable responsibilities in respect of the judiciary and of the business of the courts of England and Wales. This is done with the assistance of the Judicial Executive Board, a small cabinet with the general responsibility for judicial administration, and through a number of delegations to senior judges. The Senior Presiding Judge, in particular, acts as a point of liaison between the judiciary, the courts and government departments, and oversees the work of Presiding Judges of the circuits. The Senior President of Tribunals is at present a separate judicial office with similar responsibilities to the Lord Chief Justice. More than 200 full-time equivalent civil servants now report directly to the Lord Chief Justice;[33] senior

---

[30] HL Committee on the Constitution, 'Relations between the executive, the judiciary and Parliament' (2006-07, 151) para. 13; HL Committee on the Constitution, 'Meetings with the Lord Chief Justice and Lord Chancellor' (2010-11, 89) Q. 11. On 'concordats' as soft-law instruments, see R. Rawlings, 'Concordats of the Constitution' (2000) 116 LQR 257.

[31] Concordat, para. 19; see the text reproduced in Appendix 6, Report from the Select Committee on the Constitutional Bill, Volume I, HL Paper No. 125-I (24 June 2004).

[32] Lord Woolf's response to the Lord Chancellor's statement to the House of Lords on 26 January 2004 announcing his agreement on the Concordat with the judiciary.

[33] Judicial Office Business Plan 2012-2013, p. 20.

judges have private offices and jurisdictional teams; the Judicial College
and the Office of Judicial Complaints fall within the remit of the Lord
Chief Justice's responsibilities. The new governance arrangements under
the CRA therefore map out a new regime of accountability, with the exact
terms of this regime left open.

Although the CRA puts on a statutory footing most of the Concordat,
the principle of separation of powers enshrined in the CRA did cast a
light on the 'politically-charged process' of obtaining resources.[34] The
judicial system has been reconceived as a public service which must meet
reasonable public expectations within necessarily finite resources.[35] The
approach adopted to adjust demand and supply for judicial services has
been to request courts to do more with less, and such efficient judicial
management has relied upon the development of the organisation of
justice. The drive for efficiency and economy in the conduct of judicial
business entails greatly increased managerial responsibilities upon judges,
relating to caseload, deployment and the allocation of particular cases.

However, the organisation of justice also determines the way in which
judges relate to each other and achieve a sense of collective independence.[36] The traditional sense of social responsibility that the judiciary
imparts to individual judges is a strong instrument for ensuring its
independence, and interference with the judiciary as a whole is likely to
have a negative impact on the sense of independence of individual judges.
The wider range of tasks now allocated to the judiciary requires that the
concept of judicial independence is not confined to the personal and
substantive independence of the individual judge, but also extends to the
independence of the judiciary as a whole. The concept of institutional or
collective independence of the judiciary calls for scrutiny of the range of
activities which support the judicial role of decision making.[37] It requires
greater judicial involvement in the administration of justice, including
the preparation of budgets for the judicial system. The degree of judicial
engagement ranges from consultation, sharing responsibility with the
executive (or the legislature) to exclusive judicial responsibility. Though
it is generally accepted that judges cannot claim independence from

---

[34] J. Mackay, 'The Role of the Lord Chancellor in the Administration of Justice', Earl Grey
Lecture, University of Newcastle, 24 February 1990.
[35] A. Zuckerman, 'Civil Litigation: a Public Service for the Enforcement of Civil Rights'
(2007) 26 CJQ 1.
[36] Mt. Scopus, ss. 2.12 and 2.13.
[37] S. Shetreet, 'The Administration of Justice: Practical Problems, Value Conflicts and
Changing Concepts' (1979) 13 UBC Law Rev 52, 57–62.

required and necessary guidance and supervision in the administration of justice, the aggregate work of the courts and tribunals requires vigilance about the daily interactions between administrative and judicial actions. Justice may require time and, for public confidence to be maintained, the values of efficiency and economy in the conduct of judicial business must be reconciled with procedural fairness.

Discipline and removal of judges

1.4 The power to remove and discipline judges directly affects individual judges and the judiciary as a collective and institution. Tenure of judicial office is a fundamental tenet of judicial independence; however judges from the High Court and above hold office subject to a power of removal by the Queen on an address presented to her by both Houses of Parliament. It is important to recognise that this mechanism aims to protect senior judges from executive interference but also gives Parliament a 'sacrificial' tool of accountability.[38] Removal of judges below the level of the High Court on grounds of misbehaviour is by the Lord Chancellor with the concordance of the Lord Chief Justice.[39] Perceived inability is not grounds for removal.

The grounds for disciplinary procedures express some self-imposed standards of judicial conduct. They reflect the values and history that shape the way in which judges perceive their role. They have also emerged from the parliamentary debates regarding complaints against judges for improper conduct. The more homogeneous and narrow the judiciary was, the less need there was to write standards down as everyone assumed knowledge of the rules learnt at the Bar. The increasing size and greater diversity of the judiciary, the greater the need to issue guidelines, and the publication of a *Guide to Judicial Conduct* in 2002 constructs standards of judicial conduct as a defining component of public trust in the judiciary. The *Guide* introduces in broad terms the six principles developed under the Bangalore Principles of Judicial Conduct: judicial independence, impartiality, integrity, propriety (and the appearance of propriety), equality of treatment to all before the courts, and competence and diligence.[40] In addition, the *Guide*

---

[38] V. Bogdanor, 'Parliament and the Judiciary: The Problem of Accountability', Third Sunningdale Accountability Lecture, 2006.

[39] Senior Courts Act 1981, s. 11; CRA, s. 33.

[40] Judge's Council of England and Wales, *Guide to Judicial Conduct*, rev. version 2011 *Guide to Judicial Conduct*, see also, UK Supreme Court, *Guide to Judicial Conduct*, 2009; The

introduces guidance on personal relationships and perceived bias as well as on activities outside the courts, in relation to the media, for example, or after retirement. The *Guide*'s section on propriety is effectively a checklist of potential activities each of which is capable of a possible reprimand or even removal: from having to accept a level of public scrutiny higher than that normally experienced by the average citizen, to financial probity and the need to avoid all possible potential or actual conflicts of interest.

Core to the *Guide* is the idea that judges must strive to maintain and enhance the confidence of the public, the legal profession and litigants, in the impartiality of the judge and of the judiciary.[41] It is, however, also a valid principle that no party may choose its tribunal whether by insisting on a particular judge or by objecting to one without sufficient cause.[42] This must be balanced against the principle that judges should show sensitivity to a party who may still nurse a genuine (though baseless) reservation about, for example, a judge's relationship with a firm of solicitors who has instructed his opponent. The Court of Appeal has always played an important disciplinary role in maintaining high standards of judicial behaviour in court. It consistently upholds the fundamental requisite that justice must not only be done but must also manifestly be seen to be done.[43] Rightly so, as one judge's manner of conducting a trial or adjudicating a dispute may have consequences when the outcome is taken to appeal. Whether it reverses the judgment, quashes the conviction, reduces the sentence or changes the judgment in any manner, the disapproval and condemnation of the misconduct may restore the public confidence in the courts, which might otherwise have been impaired. This disciplinary power of the court has a restraining and preventive effect on judges.

The effectiveness of the standards of judicial conduct rests upon a combination of individual voluntary compliance, peer pressure (informal sanctions) and legally imposed sanctions (reprimand, suspension or

Bangalore Draft Code of Judicial Conduct 2001 adopted by the Judicial Group on Strengthening Judicial Integrity, as revised at the Round Table Meeting of Chief Justices held at the Peace Palace, The Hague, 25–26 November 2002).

[41] *Guide to Judicial Conduct*, para. 3.1 and s. 7; the *Guide* refers to the common law for guidance on bias in particular. The guidance applies to fee-paid as well as full-time and part-time judges.

[42] S. Sedley, 'When Should a Judge Not Be a Judge?' (2011) 33 LRB 1, 9.

[43] *Goold* v. *Evans & Co* [1951] 2 TLR 1189, 1191 [Denning LJ]; *Brassington* v. *Brassington* [1962] P 276, p. 282; *Hobbs* v. *CT Tinling & Co Ltd* [1929] 2 KB 1, 48.

removal) following a formal complaints procedure before the Office for Judicial Complaints, a newly established body under the CRA. In addition, until that constitutional settlement, the power to discipline was in the hands of the Lord Chancellor, also the head of the judiciary, albeit that few judges have had charges established against them. The formal handling of complaints about the personal conduct of judges is now dealt with under a new regulatory framework introduced in the CRA.[44] The power to discipline judges is shared between the Lord Chief Justice and the Lord Chancellor, and follows an investigation from the Office for Judicial Complaints, thus placing safeguards upon the use of their disciplinary power.

The option of making a complaint to the Office for Judicial Complaints is an additional and separate remedy to launching an appeal. Only by appealing can a litigant hold out any hope of reversing a decision by the judge or of affecting the outcome of the case. Equally, only by making a complaint via the Office for Judicial Complaints might he see an official acknowledgement of the misconduct of an identified judge accompanied by a sanction. There is yet potential overlap between the two remedies. Bad behaviour in court, such as falling asleep or displaying impatience with one party or showing that the outcome has been decided before the end of the trial, can both trigger an appeal and also an application to the Office of Judicial Complaints (either by one of the parties or by the Presiding Judges of the court). Equally, an egregious decision to hear a case in which the judge has an apparent interest may trigger both an appeal and complaint. Yet judges can take steps to make their decisions appeal-proof, for example by making it clear that they have had regard to all the factors to which the law requires them to have regard when finding facts.[45] While one may hope that the appeal procedure will be sufficiently rigorous to provide remedies where misconduct is in play, having a procedure for complaints to the Office of Judicial Complaints might be thought to be a necessary addition to ensure judicial account-ability even in cases where there is apparent overlap in jurisdiction.

---

[44] Under CRA 2005, s. 115, 'the Lord Chief Justice may, with the agreement of the Lord Chancellor, make regulations providing for the procedures that are to be followed in: (a) the investigation and determination of allegations by any person of misconduct by judicial office holders; (b) reviews and investigations (including the making of applications or references) under ss. 110–12 [CRA 2005]; the Judicial Discipline (Prescribed Procedures) Regulations 2006 and the Office for Judicial Complaints, *The System for Handling Magistrates' Conduct, Pastoral and Training Matters*, April 2006, para. 1.2.1.

[45] M. Friedland, *A Place Apart: Judicial Independence and Accountability in Canada* (Ottawa: Canadian Judicial Council, 1995), p. 157.

Public confidence

1.5 The media acts as a powerful check upon the judiciary by reporting the courts' activities; media reporting supports the principle of open justice which, in turn, feeds public confidence in the courts. The judicial system and judges should not be immune from fair criticism, so long as it is done in good faith and in good taste, and judges should use sparingly the extreme measure of contempt of court to address criticism of the courts. Public trust[46] in the courts and the judiciary, however, is also reliant upon an accurate reflection of the professional character of judicial business. One should be aware of the dangers that lie in undue popular pressures on judges. Excessive popular pressure and irresponsible journalists hungry for sensational pieces may put judges in an unbearable position. It may threaten the independence of the judges who often have to act against popular wishes to protect dissenters and members of minority groups. It is no surprise that it is the vulnerable and outcast members of society who stand to gain from the human rights protection introduced by the Human Rights Act 1998, and it is no surprise that it is members of these groups who have been readiest to invoke the Act.[47] Most prominently, senior judges have struck down central aspects of the government's efforts to detain or monitor terrorist suspects whom the Crown Prosecution Service does not wish to prosecute.[48] The recent tensions that have developed between executive and judiciary have to be kept in proportion for public confidence to be maintained in the independence of the judiciary and the integrity of government.[49]

The need for an 'outward-looking' English judiciary, increasingly engaging with the media, is evident. In practice, the provision of information about judges and the judicial system has multiplied. The traditional right to a public hearing and the right of access to information has been enhanced by solutions for new media, specific press rules, and an

---

[46] We consider public opinion to the extent that it constitutes a defining factor behind some of the constitutional changes, such as the creation of the Judicial Appointments Commission and the need to have regard to diversity in appointments, and to the extent that the judiciary shows greater awareness of it, for example the Office of Lord Chief Justice having now developed a more efficient communications strategy with the media and so forth.

[47] T. Bingham, 'The Human Rights Act' (2010) 6 EHRLR 568, 569.

[48] *A* v. *Secretary of State for the Home Department* [2004] UKHL 56; *Secretary of State for the Home Department* v. *AF* [2009] UKHL 28.

[49] A. Bradley, 'Relations between Executive, Judiciary and Parliament: an Evolving Saga?' [2008] 4 PL 470, 488.

unprecedented amount of judicial statistics or documents relating to the role and functions of courts and judges. This greater transparency of the courts' functioning and judicial workings increases public accountability and responsiveness. It is another sign that judges' obligations are to inform public knowledge and understanding about the law and its application.[50] It should be encouraged as a form of social accountability that does not compromise judicial independence. Rather, it gives 'space and peace of mind to judges to work according to the best possible professional and legal standards in conducting hearings and writing judgments'.[51]

But the projection of a positive image of the judiciary and the judicial system in the media remains unfinished business. Media reporting on the judiciary tends – appropriately – to focus on the possibility of a miscarriage of justice. The extra-judicial activities of judicial office holders will however also be scrutinised. Their published views in particular may trigger issues of bias which may influence the image of the judiciary as an institution and a collective. Whether and to what degree a judge should pursue certain extra-judicial activities – such as conducting political inquiries – is a matter of legal culture. The concern for public confidence in the court imposes restrictions on the behaviour of judges even outside the courtroom. In England, judges get involved on their own initiative in their local communities. Upon appointment they are expected to give up all activities with political flavour, such as membership of Parliament, and it is almost axiomatic that full-time judges should not engage in political controversy. Exposure on internet social networks or blogs may yet blur the distinction between the private and public spheres for judges.

Judicial appointments and judicial career

1.6 An aspect of maintaining public confidence in recent times has been the overt concern for diversity in the composition of the judiciary, as in all other areas of public life. This had been part of the drive for the constitutional reform in 2005. The English judiciary is made up of separate groups of judges: the circuit and district benches, and the High Court bench. A Queen's Counsel who wished to enter the judiciary would either be a part-time recorder then circuit judge, or he would be directly appointed to the High Court bench. Before 1971 solicitors had no access to the bench; there were only 2,500 barristers. The legal profession was

[50] P. Langbroek, International Journal for Court Administration, editorial, April 2011.
[51] *Ibid.*

small and getting references through what is known today as 'secret soundings' was the accepted norm. Although that appointment process based on consultation was praised for appointing individuals on merit, it was also perceived as encouraging self-replication, with judges being from a narrow social elite.[52] As alluded to above, the narrow social background of the judiciary and the under-representation of women, as well as black and Asian minorities, has long been the source of heated public debate. Public confidence in the courts is enhanced by broad reflection in the judiciary of all social strata, ethnic groups and geographical regions in a given country. There is currently a sense of urgency in promoting in effective ways the appointment of individuals from under-represented groups to the bench.

In addition, the judiciary has grown in size and complexity with the merging of administration of tribunals (with distinct tribunal benches) and of the magistracy into one single administrative entity, Her Majesty's Courts and Tribunals Service. The traditional perception of a single cadre for the judiciary – the High Court and above – is thus under strain, though it is inappropriate to characterise the English judiciary as a hierarchically integrated professional corps, unlike its counterparts on the European continent. But we do refer, in this book, to judicial office holders in the most inclusive way (including tribunal members and magistrates) and when we refer to the 'senior judiciary', we mean the High Court judges and above.[53] It is fair to say at once that some interviewees were more discomfited than others by accepting that magistrates are part of the 'judicial family', suggesting that this current discourse is not one to which many professional judges subscribe.

A most significant constitutional change under the CRA is thus the creation of the Judicial Appointments Commission. The Judicial Appointments Commission has sought to remove political patronage from the appointments system. The requirements of merit and good character for appointment to the Bench are underpinned by the principles of transparency, independence from politics and a concern for a fair reflection of society in the appointment process. Transparency in particular supports the prioritisation of merit and a fairer reflection of society.[54]

---

[52] J.A.G. Griffith, *The Politics of the Judiciary*, 5th edn (London: Fontana, 2010), pp. 18–22.

[53] CRA, s. 109(4).

[54] See J. Limbach et al., Interrights Report on 'Judicial Independence: Law and Practice of Appointments to the European Court of Human Rights', May 2003; *Montréal International Declaration of Independence*, Art. 2.13.

Parliament also requires the Judicial Appointments Commission to have regard to the need to encourage diversity in the pool of applicants. However, the concern for diversity plays a role primarily in collecting a pool of diverse candidates for judicial appointments.[55] A shift from a focus on individual appointments to the concept of a judicial career was recommended in 2010 by an Advisory Panel to the Lord Chancellor, with the aim of achieving greater diversity within the judiciary.[56] It was later clarified that this was not a call for a career judiciary, where judges are appointed after graduating from university and trained for the bench, but rather a call to the legal profession to bring about further changes in its composition.

Constitutional adjudication

1.7 The judiciary is a branch of the government beyond being a dispute-resolution institution. Democratic accountability demands some fit between the model of constitutional review chosen and the method of judicial appointments, in order to account for an unelected court acting as guardian of the constitution over an accountable political branch.[57] The development of the English model of constitutional adjudication appears distinct from its European counterparts or the United States. The European model, adopted by several countries, including Germany and Italy, entrusts the power of constitutional review not to the ordinary court system, but rather to specialist constitutional courts. These courts meet requirements of democratic accountability by providing for special procedures for selection of their members. Those procedures are usually more political than the ordinary system appointment procedures, which are primarily based on judicial career. By contrast, the American model promotes the accountability of judicial power by giving all courts the power of constitutional review, but circumscribing that power by ensuring democratic input into the federal and state systems of judicial appointments.[58]

---

[55] CRA, s. 64(1).

[56] Report of the Advisory Panel on Diversity, 2010, panel chaired by Baroness Julia Neuberger; S. Turenne, 'Decisions, Decisions: the Best Case Scenario', *The Guardian*, 11 October 2011.

[57] We recognise that the rationale for judicial independence needs to be differentiated in different levels or types of courts, with a greater emphasis on the democratic legitimacy of high-level judges who often take politically or socially far-reaching decisions.

[58] Within the European model there is, however, considerable variety in the constitutional review structures with constitutional courts, constitutional councils or other tribunals

In the English context, constitutional adjudication relates to courts reviewing whether Acts of the UK Parliament or governmental measures are compatible with the ECHR or European Union law. A declaration of incompatibility is 'the nearest that English judges come to a constitutional review'.[59] It does not invalidate the law but invites the government to decide whether to amend the law or to remedy the incompatibility by registering a formal derogation from the ECHR. Twenty-seven declarations of incompatibility have been made since 2000.[60] This, however, does not include some occasions where the courts have avoided a declaration only by controversially stretching their interpretation of the legislation. Constitutional adjudication can also refer to devolution matters, when the legislation of the three devolved assemblies (Wales, Scotland and Northern Ireland) is referred to the UK Supreme Court.[61] The English declaratory model of constitutional adjudication, like that of Sweden, is situated between the European tradition of constitutional courts (with a separate appointment process) and the American model (based on political appointments of judges).[62]

The English judiciary's international reputation for impartiality and probity has greatly contributed to London being a leading commercial centre.[63] Multinational corporations will be attracted to invest and will engage in international trade in jurisdictions where they have confidence in the impartiality and independence of the courts. In the public sphere, following the realisation of the public that the ordinary administrative

exercising constitutional review powers in some countries, while others rely on constitutional chambers within the supreme court, see S. Shetreet, 'Models of Constitutional Adjudication', in *Essays in Honour of Konstantinos D. Kerameus* (Athens/Brussels: Ant. N. Sakkoulas/Bruylant, 2009), p. 1259; M. Rosenfeld, 'Constitutional Adjudication in Europe and the United States: Paradoxes and Contrasts', in G. Nolte (ed.), *European and United States Constitutionalism* (Cambridge University Press, 2005), p. 197; M. Shapiro and A. Stone Sweet, *On Law, Politics, and Judicialization* (Oxford University Press, 2002); D. Rousseau (ed.), *La Question prioritaire de constitutionalité* (Paris: Lextenso, 2010).

[59] J. Bell, 'United Kingdom: Constitutional Courts as Positive Legislators', in A.R. Brewer Carias (ed.), *Constitutional Courts as Positive Legislators. A Comparative Law Study* (Cambridge University Press, 2011), p. 809.

[60] Ministry of Justice, 'Responding to human rights judgments. Report to the Joint Committee on Human Rights on the Government's response to human rights judgments 2010-11', Cm 8162 (HMSO, September 2011), p. 5.

[61] *Starrs* v. *Ruxton* 2000 JC 208 (appointment of temporary judges ('sheriffs') held contrary to judicial independence).

[62] J. Resnik, 'Judicial Selection and Democratic Theory: Demand, Supply, and Life Tenure' (2005) 26 Cardozo L Rev 579, 593-4.

[63] Stevens, *The English Judges*, p. 82

and political institutions are failing to solve issues, judicial redress has been sought where these institutions have failed. The executive can also sometimes refrain from resolving certain matters, thus avoiding the political price of the decision. This shifts the questions to the courts in order to secure a judicial resolution of disputes that are economic or political in nature.[64] Thus, as Parliament became overburdened, so judges have taken on more creative roles both in court and in pre-legislative institutions such as the Law Commission.[65]

The constitutional role of the courts in protecting the rule of law through the development of judicial review and the advent of the Human Rights Act 1998 have, however, exposed the political impact of judicial decisions to the wider community. The increasing readiness of the courts to intervene in administrative decision making has led to a significant development of the principles of review[66] in recent decades. This follows the development of broad statutory powers of the executive and the perception that ministerial responsibility to Parliament falls short of adequately protecting citizens against a misuse of executive powers.[67] The advent of constitutional adjudication under the Human Rights Act 1998 has strengthened the position of the judiciary yet it also exacerbated the opportunities for politicians and judges to come into conflict, under the courts' obligation to declare legislation incompatible if it does not admit of a reading compatible with the ECHR.[68] Judges can also disapply national law on the ground of incompatibility with European Union law.

The aggregate work of the judiciary as a collective entity has come under scrutiny beyond the legal community as a consequence not only of that increase in judicial power. The development of accountability for resources within the public service has also brought to light the great range of activities that support the judicial role of deciding cases. English judges, whose independence was mostly an individual attribute, now share with continental judges the constraints of a bureaucratic institution such as the Courts and Tribunals Service. The existence of a formal appointment process and a regulatory framework for judicial conduct, as well as the greater emphasis on training certainly constitute foundation

---

[64] N. Stephen, 'Judicial Independence – A Fragile Bastion', in Shetreet and Deschenes (eds.), *Judicial Independence*, 529, 543.

[65] Bell, *Judiciaries within Europe*, 353.

[66] J. Jowell, 'Restraining the State: Politics, Principle and Judicial Review' (1997) 50 CLP 189.

[67] *R v. Secretary of State for the Home Department, ex p. Fire Brigades Union* [1995] 2 AC 513, 567 [Lord Mustill].

[68] Human Rights Act 1998, s. 3.

stones towards the professionalisation of the judiciary. This is done in the English way, where the skills and wealth of experience acquired as a legal practitioner are a prerequisite for entry to the bench.

But still, the independence of the judiciary must be reinforced. The measurement of courts' and tribunals' performance, judicial conduct and judicial appointments are, since the CRA, subject to close monitoring. The use of parliamentary questions and debates and the appearance of judges during Select Committee inquiries as well as reports to Parliament have multiplied in recent years. Parliamentary accountability is likely to develop in order to build support for judicial independence against the executive. The first overt step was observed in 2012 when the English candidates for the seat in the European Court of Human Rights were questioned by MPs in addition to ministers, although the final decision was made by the European institutions in Strasbourg itself. Constitutional arrangements are as yet not settled and further changes to the constitutional position of the judiciary are not to be excluded. Nonetheless, the culture of judicial independence is strong.

Judicial independence is a cornerstone of Britain's constitutional arrangements,[69] and it has predominantly been a matter of conventions and practices rather than legal rules. These conventions and practices respond to the organisational structure of the judiciary; they relate to the legal community of academics, lawyers and lay judges, and to the wider community that includes the political community and public opinion. Our aim is to make explicit the rules, assumptions and practices in force within the English judiciary today. The case study of judicial independence in England shows the multiple influences upon the culture of judicial independence, from the institutional structure of the judiciary, the constitutional conventions and statutes which safeguard the independence of the judiciary, the standards of judicial conduct adopted by the judiciary on and off the bench, to the legal developments relating to judicial independence in the courts' case law.

---

[69] Lord Irvine, 'Parliamentary Sovereignty and Judicial Independence: Keynote Address', in J. Hatchard and P. Slinn (eds.), *Parliamentary Supremacy and Judicial Independence: A Commonwealth Approach* (London: Cavendish Publishing, 1999) p. 167.

2

Constitutional steps towards judicial independence

Introduction

2.1 The history of judicial independence has been well documented by Robert Stevens.[1] With the purpose of setting the constitutional background to this work, we sketch, over the centuries, the position of the judiciary in relation to the executive and Parliament, before considering the further step towards judicial independence under the Constitutional Reform Act 2005 (CRA) and the consequences of the Human Rights Act 1998 (HRA). A sense of the existing strains allows us to understand better the concern that the Lord Chancellor's duty to preserve the independence of the judiciary should be put on statutory footing in the CRA.

I. History

2.2 Our brief historical account focuses upon the emergence of the foundations of the modern judiciary in the events of the seventeenth century. In the sixteenth and seventeenth centuries, judges were an integral part of the royal administration and, at the direction of the Crown, performed many administrative duties.[2] To Tudor and early Stuart men the distinction between judicial and administrative duties would have been rather obscure. Holdsworth's observation that the Chancery was 'a branch of the civil service as well as a judicial court'[3] applied in varying degrees to many institutions that we now refer to as

---

[1] R. Stevens, *The Independence of the Judiciary. The View from the Lord Chancellor's Office* (Oxford: Clarendon Press, 1993); *The English Judges: Their Role in the Changing Constitution*, rev. edn (Oxford: Hart, 2005).

[2] W.J. Jones, *Politics and the Bench* (London: Allen & Unwin, 1971), pp. 18–19, 21–2, 51–2; A.F. Havighurst, 'The Judiciary and Politics in the Reign of Charles II' (1950) 66 LQR 62, 65–6; W. Holdsworth, *History of English Law*, vol. I, 2nd edn (1937), p. 273, vol. IV, p. 75.

[3] Holdsworth, *History*, vol. V, p. 245.

'courts of law'.[4] As long as the King and Parliament did not come into conflict and did not look to the courts of law for support in the struggle for power, the independence of the judges was not an important issue.[5] Thus, under the Tudors, the issue of judicial independence did not give rise to difficulties. During this period the judges undoubtedly were not independent: they were under strict royal control and the Crown enjoyed their cooperation. Since judges were not sought by the sovereign of the day to be instruments in political struggles, this harmonious cooperation met with popular approval.[6] Similarly, because judges were outside the sphere of politics, very few were removed for political reasons during this period, even though they held office at the King's (or Queen's) pleasure.[7]

In the seventeenth century the situation changed. The King and Parliament no longer worked harmoniously together, and in the struggle for power both the Crown and Parliament appealed to the law for support. The determination of individual cases that came before the courts required the demarcation of the boundaries of parliamentary privilege and of royal prerogative. The judges thus became so important to the political struggle that both Crown and Parliament began to exercise every available form of control over the judiciary. At this juncture of history the independence of judges became an important issue.

A.   Royal control over judges

2.3 With respect to control over the judiciary, the advantage lay with the Crown, which could exercise this control in various ways. The primary and most extreme form of control was removal from office. The judges held their offices at the King's pleasure and could be removed by the Crown without cause. In the seventeenth century the power of removal was frequently exercised by the King to ensure that those who

---

[4] W.J. Jones, *Politics and the Bench* (London: Allen & Unwin, 1971), 18.

[5] S.R. Gardiner, *A Student's History of England*, vol. I, pp. 1–2 (London: Longman, Greens and Co, 1890); A. Harding, *Social History of English Law* (Harmondsworth: Penguin, 1965), pp. 252–3.

[6] Holdsworth, *History*, vol. V, 347.

[7] Chief Justice Cholmley and Montague were dismissed at the accession of Mary; another judge was imprisoned for his religious principles; Elizabeth is suspected of having removed a judge (Robert Manson) on political grounds: E. Foss, *The Judges of England* (London: Longman, Brown, Green, and Longmans, 1857), vol. V, pp. 343–4, 370–3; 527–8; Gardiner, *A Student's History*, vol. II, 7–8. Holdsworth describes this case as a 'doubtful instance': Holdsworth, *History*, vol. V, 346.

did not submit to the royal command would no longer remain on the bench. The dismissal of Chief Justice Coke by James I in 1616 for his refusal to submit to Royal intervention in the *Case of Commendams*[8] foreshadowed a long series of removals of judges for political reasons.[9] A secondary form of control was suspension. Thus, Sir Edward Coke had been suspended from office in June 1616 before he was finally removed in November 1616.[10] Further, not all the judges held office during pleasure. The Barons of the Exchequer, unlike their brethren in the Court of Common Pleas and the King's Bench, held their office during good behaviour.[11] Likewise, for some time in the seventeenth century other judges also held office during good behaviour. If displeased, the King might merely forbid them to sit in court,[12] thereby in actuality suspending them from office.

The King did not always resort to the powers of removal and suspension. Less extreme measures for securing judicial subservience were available. Despite the *Case of Prohibitions*,[13] in which Coke affirmed Bracton's dictum that the King was subject to the law and custom of England, the Crown would attempt to interfere with the ordinary course of justice.[14] In the *Case of Commendams*[15] Chief Justice Coke and the rest of the judges refused to obey a royal order not to proceed to judgment

---

[8] *Colt and Glover* v. *Bishop of Coventry*, 80 ER 290 (KB) (1616).

[9] For an analysis of the prolonged conflict between James I and Sir Edward Coke, see C.D. Bowen, *The Lion and the Throne: The Life and Times of Sir Edward Coke 1552-1634* (Boston: Little, Brown, 1957). See also, for other examples of the exercise of removal: Foss, *The Judges*, vol. VI, 291, 322-4, vol. VII, 4, vol. VIII, 201; C.H. McIlwain, 'The Tenure of English Judges' (1913) 7 Am Pol Sci Rev 217, 222; for an account of the removals of Charles II and James II, see A.F. Havighurst, 'James II and the Twelve Men in Scarlet' (1953) 69 LQR 522.

[10] Foss, *The Judges*, vol. VI, 118; J. Campbell, *Lives of the Chief Justices* (London: John Murray, 1849), vol. I, pp. 288 and 292.

[11] *Coke's Institutes*, vol. IV, p. 117. After 1631, Barons were also appointed during pleasure, McIlwain, 'Tenure of English Judges', 219-21; E. Haynes, *Selection and Tenure of Judges* (Littleton, Co: Rothman & Co., 1944), p. 77.

[12] See *John Walter's Case*, Coke Reports, vol. III, 203 (1630); Foss, *The Judges*, vol. VI, 216, 372; *John Archer's Case* (1672); Foss, *The Judges*, vol. VII, 52-3.

[13] *Prohibitions Del Roy* Mich 5 Jacobi 1; (1608) 77 ER 1342.

[14] See Jones, *Politics*, 137; Coke also denied that the King was entitled to change the common law or to create any new offence by proclamation, see the *Case of the Proclamations*, 12 Co Rep 74; (1610) 77 ER 1352; *Fuller's Case* (1607) 77 ER 1322. Sir Edward Coke also indicated that lower courts would lose their immunity from suit if they acted outside their jurisdiction, see the *Marshalsea Case*, 10 Co Rep 68b; (1613) 77 ER 1027.

[15] *Case of Commendams, Colt & Glover* v. *Bishop of Coventry & Lichfield* 80 ER 290 (KB) (1616).

until they had spoken with the King. Thereupon they were summoned before King James I, and all the judges, except Coke, were forced into submission.[16] But in some cases the attempted interference with judicial proceedings was successfully resisted by the judges.[17]

Likewise, the control of the Crown over the judiciary was exercised by consulting the judges on the legality of a proposed course of action. The result was that the judges were often called upon to take part in cases in which they had already committed themselves by the delivery of an extra-judicial opinion. In the sixteenth century the Crown consulted the judges when the law appeared to be doubtful, and generally their opinions were followed.[18] In the seventeenth century the judges were asked by the Crown to render extra-judicial opinions sustaining disputed royal prerogatives and regarding pending cases.[19]

As a subsidiary form of royal control over the judiciary, a judge would be transferred from one judicial office to another. Threat of transfer could be used either to persuade the judge to submit to the royal wishes or to punish him for previous behaviour that was unsatisfactory to the Crown.[20] Moreover, under the fiscal system then in existence, judges' salaries and pensions were paid directly by the King out of the royal revenue and were, of course, dependent upon his discretion. Similarly, the promotion of judges depended upon the King's discretion. Royal control over judicial remuneration and promotion was therefore not devoid of significance.[21]

---

[16] H. Broom, *Constitutional Law Viewed in Relation to the Common Law and Exemplified by Cases* (London: W. Maxwell, 1866), pp. 147–8.

[17] Broom, *Constitutional Law*, pp. 147–8: under the Tudors, judges also resisted royal interference with the judicial process; Holdsworth, *History*, vol. V, 348; Brooke LJ, 'Judicial Independence – Its History in England and Wales', in H. Cunningham (ed.), *Fragile Bastion. Judicial Independence in the Nineties and Beyond* (Sidney: Judicial Commission of New South Wales, 1997), pp. 94–5.

[18] Holdsworth, *History*, vol. V, 348.

[19] Gardiner, *A Student's History*, vol. II, 277; T.P. Taswell-Langmead, *English Constitutional History*, 10th edn by T.F.L. Plucknett (London: Sweet and Maxwell, 1946), pp. 392n, 430–1; E.C.S. Wade, 'Consultation of the Judiciary by the Executive' (1930) 46 LQR 169, 181–2. The practice of consulting the judges and eliciting extra-judicial opinions did not come to an end until the second half of the eighteenth century, when it fell into desuetude, see Broom, *Constitutional Law*, 151.

[20] For example, the transfer of Coke from the office of Chief Justice of the Common Pleas to that of Chief Justice of the King's Bench in 1613 after the *Case of Commendans*, see D.J. Medley, *A Student's Manual of English Constitutional History* (Oxford: Blackwell, 1894), p. 488.

[21] W.E. Hearn, *The Government of England: its Structure and its Development*, 2nd edn (London: Longmans, Green & Co., 1886), p. 79.

The choice of the form of control to be exercised in a particular case depended on the importance of the royal interest at stake, and the degree of independence and resistance demonstrated by the judges. It seems that the Crown first offered favours in the hope of influencing the judges to respond favourably to the royal wishes. Sometimes, however, the judges demonstrated an independent stand and were not tempted by the royal smile and favour 'to take a broad view of the extent of their master's prerogative'.[22] Likewise, the royal interest at stake was sometimes too important to be put at the slightest risk. In those instances the Crown had to resort to the more extreme measures of suspension and removal, partly because Parliament succeeded in cutting down royal control over the judges and partly because there was no confidence that less extreme measures would be effective. However, royal control over judges was exercised at the cost of political repercussions. As Gardiner observed:

> From henceforth [the Crown] could no longer expect to obtain that moral support which it had hitherto received from the decisions pronounced from the Bench by the judges who were, comparatively at least with the men who held office subsequently to Coke's disgrace, independent of the favours and the anger of the Crown.[23]

B.   Coke versus Bacon

2.4 It was the struggle between the Crown and Parliament in the early Stuart period that gave rise to the conflict between Coke and Bacon on the duties and functions of the judges. Bacon expressed the view that the judges were lions 'but yet lions under the throne, being circumspect that they do not check or oppose any points of sovereignty'.[24] Thus: 'it was a happy thing in a state when Kings and states do often consult with Judges and again when judges do often consult with the King and state'. In short, he believed that the judges' function was not merely to declare the law but to support the government.[25]

Coke, however, claimed that judges must impartially expound and apply a supreme law which governs the royal prerogatives, parliamentary

---

[22] T.R.S. Anson, *The Law and Custom of the Constitution*, 3rd edn (Oxford: Clarendon, 1907), vol. I, p. 30.

[23] Gardiner, *A Student's History*, vol. III, 27.

[24] F. Bacon, 'Essays: Of Judicature', in J. Spedding, R. Ellis. and D. Heath (eds.), *Works of Francis Bacon* (New York: Hurd and Houghton, 1861 reprint), vol. VI, pp. 506 and 510.

[25] Anson, *The Law and Custom*, vol. I, 30.

privilege, and the rights of the individual.[26] Coke believed that in passing their judgments, the judges were under no duty to consult the King when their decisions affected the powers of the Crown. As history has shown, it is Coke's view that has prevailed,[27] and in *Bonham's Case* he went on to say that a 'repugnant' act of Parliament can be 'controlled' by the courts. Coke probably meant to express a belief that there are some fundamental principles of English law which Parliament should not violate. He did not propose a judicial review of legislation in violation of the fundamental laws but advocated the strictest interpretation of statutes which appeared to alter them.[28]

C.   Parliamentary control over judges

2.5 In the face of strong Royal influence over the judges, Parliament, in turn, sought to exercise its own control over the judiciary. Those who gave decisions which Parliament deemed inconsistent with parliamentary privilege or with the rights of the people and those who were guilty of misconduct in the discharge of their judicial functions were either impeached or called before Parliament to defend and explain their decisions or alleged misconduct. Parliamentary action against judges was in the main motivated by political considerations. Judicial activities were labelled 'illegal', 'contrary to fundamental laws' or 'corrupt', but in effect the judges were proceeded against by Parliament to protect the political interests at stake and to curb royal powers.[29] Thus, in 1680, Lord Chief Justice William Scroggs of the King's Bench was impeached by the Commons for illegal and arbitrary behaviour in court and charged also for having 'traitorously and wickedly endeavoured to subvert the fundamental laws'. Though the Lords refused to impeach him, he was removed from the bench.[30]

Similarly, impeachment proceedings were initiated against the judges who delivered the opinion in the *Ship Money* case in 1637, upholding the power of the King to levy indirect taxation for ships without the consent of Parliament.[31] In 1698 the Lords summoned Chief Justice

---

[26] *The Case of Prohibitions* 77 ER 1342 (1607); *Dr Bonham's Case* 77 ER 638 (1608); see above para. 2.3.

[27] Harding, *Social History*, 260.   [28] *Ibid.*   [29] See generally Havighurst.

[30] (1680–1692) 2 Parl. Deb., 1, 22–5.

[31] *R v. Hampden* (1637) 3 State Trials 825; D.L. Keir, 'The Case of Ship Money' (1936) 52 LQR 546; 3 Howell's State Trials 1260; J. Hatsell, *Precedents of Proceedings in the House of Commons, with Observations* (London: Printed for L. Hansard and Sons, 1818), vol. IV, pp. 139 et seq.

Holt and asked him to give reasons for his decision in *R v. Knollys*.[32] In that case, it was held that the court had the right to determine the existence of a privilege claimed by the House of Lords. Holt refused to comply with the demand of the Lords, and categorically stated that the Lords had no power to interfere with a decision of the court unless it came before them on appeal. The Lords dared not commit Holt and escaped an embarrassing situation by adjourning. Whether or not this interference was warranted, the public strongly supported Holt.[33]

Parliament did not confine its efforts to questioning and impeaching judges for past behaviour. In 1629 the House of Commons attempted to persuade the Barons of the Exchequer to change their minds on a particular matter. The King protested at this attempt, insisting that judges should not be so approached.[34]

D.   Legislation to secure judicial independence

2.6 Parliament not only proceeded against judges for allegedly encroaching upon its privilege and favouring the Crown, but also passed legislation aimed at the elimination of royal interference with the judicial process.[35] In passing this legislation, Parliament was motivated less by a commitment to judicial independence than by the political consideration of curbing royal powers. Whatever the motives behind it, such legislation contributed to strengthening the independence of the judges. The Act establishing the judicial oath provided that the judges should swear that they would not receive any fee or present from a party to a case before

---

[32] *R v. Knollys* (1695) I Ld. Raym. 10; 91 ER 904.

[33] Campbell, *Lives*, vol. II, 148–152. For further discussion of Parliamentary inquiry into legal proceedings and impeachment proceedings against judges see Jones, *Politics*, 75–7, 137–43. In particular, see the Commons investigation into the conduct of Chief Justice Kelynge in 1667, who fined one jury for disobeying his directions and on other occasions imprisoned juries who delivered verdicts contrary to his directions, 9 Commons Journal 4, 18, 20, 29, 35–7; 6 Howell's State Trials 992–1019; Campbell, *Lives*, vol. I, 509–510 (1849); the impeachment of Sir Richard Watson for improperly charging a jury; (1680–1692) 2 Parl. Deb., 15; Hatsell, *Precedents*, vol. IV, 128; the questioning of Justice Pemberton by the House of Commons about the opinion of the Court in two important constitutional cases, 10 Commons Journal 210, 213, 217, 224 (1688–1693); J. P. Kenyon, *The Stuart Constitution* (Cambridge University Press, 1996), p. 445.

[34] See Jones, *Politics*, 53, 169.

[35] For example, 2 Edward III c.8, I Statutes at Large 425; II Richard II c.10, 2 Statutes at Large 297.

them except from the King who paid their salaries. Nor were they to give counsel when the King was party, and further they would not regard any letter or message from the King with relation to any point pending before them.[36] This and other legislation also played an important role in improving the standards of judicial behaviour, as well as in reducing royal influence over the judges and the judicial process.

It was not until the second half of the seventeenth century that Parliament touched the heart of the problem: judicial tenure. In January 1640 the Lords presented a petition to Charles I, praying that judges should hold office during good behaviour,[37] and in June Charles I conveyed to Parliament 'that the judges hereafter shall hold their places, *quam diu se bene gesserint*'.[38] For some thirty years all judges' patents were during good behaviour. Writers have disagreed as to the exact periods prior to the Act of Settlement in which judges held office during good behaviour, but it is generally admitted that after 1688 all judges were appointed during good behaviour.[39]

In 1669 Charles II substituted 'during pleasure' for 'during good behaviour' in the judges' patents, as did James II. As has briefly been shown, they frequently exercised their power of removal to dismiss judges from office on political grounds. In 1680 the House of Commons summoned several judges who had been removed and questioned them about the circumstances of and motives for their removal.[40] In the same year a resolution to draw up a bill providing that thereafter judges should hold their office during good behaviour was passed by the Commons,[41] but nothing came of it. Earlier in 1673 the Commons debated a bill, which failed to become law, providing that judges should hold office during good behaviour.[42] In 1691 'an Act for ascertaining the commissions and salaries of judges'

---

[36] See also 20 Edward III c.4, 2 Statutes at Large 17; 20 Edward III c.l, 2 Statutes at Large 22; c.2; c.3, 2 Statutes at Large 22–3.

[37] 4 Lords Journal 130 (12 January 1640); McIlwain, 'Tenure of English Judges', 222; A.F. Havighurst, 'The Judiciary and Politics in the Reign of Charles II' (1950) 66 LQR 62, 65.

[38] Lords Journal 132 (15 January 1640).

[39] McIlwain, 'Tenure of English Judges', 222–4; Lord Birkenhead, *Points of View* (London: Hodder and Stoughton, 1922), vol. II, pp. 159–61; H. Cecil, *Tipping the Scales* (London: Hutchinson, 1964), p. 26; Holdsworth, *History*, vol. I, 195 n. 2; Havighurst, 'The Judiciary', 65. For the period prior to 1688, we are inclined to believe that the period suggested by Lord Birkenhead and Professor Havighurst (1640–1668) is accurate.

[40] 9 Commons Journal 683 (17 December 1680).

[41] 9 Commons Journal 308 (13 February 1673).

[42] M.A. Thomson, *A Constitutional History of England. 1642–1801* (London: Methuen, 1938), p. 282.

was passed by both Houses[43] but failed to receive the royal assent, the apparent reason being that salaries were to be charged out of the royal revenue without obtaining the prior approval of the Crown.[44]

E.   The Act of Settlement 1701

2.7 Security of judicial tenure was finally established in 1701 by the Act of Settlement,[45] which provided that 'judges' commissions be made *quam diu se bene gesserint* and their salaries be ascertained and established, but upon the address of both houses of Parliament it may be lawful to remove them'. Even after the Act of Settlement, however, the independence of the judges of the Crown was still incomplete. Their commissions ceased on the death of the reigning King, and their salaries were still inadequately established, as no step had been taken to implement the command of the Act of Settlement that they 'be ascertained and established'.[46] By an Act passed in the reign of Queen Anne,[47] it was provided that the commissions of the judges should continue six months after the death of the reigning sovereign unless the new King chose to remove the judge before the expiration of that period. This measure did not cure the deficiency, since it was still within the unlimited discretion of the new monarch either to remove the judges before the six months were over or not to reappoint them after that period.[48]

Since the Acts of Anne did not spell out the patents of judges but rather spoke of 'patent or grant of any office or employment, either civil or military', it is not clear whether these Acts applied to the judges.[49]

---

[43] 10 Commons Journal 678 (February 1691).

[44] Hearn, *The Government*, 82; for another possible reason, see H. Hallam, *The Constitutional History of England from the Accession of Henry VII to the Death of George II*, 5th edn (London: John Murray, 1846), vol. II, p. 357.

[45] It was originally resolved that judges should be removable on the address of either House of Parliament, but it was later amended to both Houses, Hallam, *Constitutional History*, vol. II, 358; see generally Stevens, *The English Judges*.

[46] Lord Sankey LC, 90 HL Deb, 77 (23 November 1933).

[47] 1 Ann. Statute I c.8, 10 Statutes at Large 415; 6 Ann. c.7, II Statutes at Large.

[48] In fact, in 1714 and 1727 a number of judges failed to be reappointed on the accession of George I and George II and other judges were removed from office before the six months had expired, McIlwain, 'Tenure of English Judges', 224; Thomson, *A Constitutional History*, 282; Foss, *The Judges*, vol. VIII, 99; Hearn, *The Government*, 82; but see Campbell, *Lives*, vol. V, 149.

[49] See Holdsworth, *History*, vol. X, 434. Campbell doubts whether legislation was needed to provide that the judges' patents should not cease at the death of the King, arguing that this method of removing a judge was excluded by the Act of Settlement, Campbell, *Lives*, vol. V, 149.

Whether the Acts of Anne applied to the judges and whether the Act of Settlement excluded their removal at the death of the King, remain merely academic questions for the issue was expressly settled by the Act of 1760 passed in the first year of the reign of George III.[50] Upon accession, George had earnestly suggested in a speech before Parliament that the commissions and salaries of judges be better safeguarded.[51] The Act subsequently provided that judges should continue to hold office 'during good behaviour', rather than *quam diu se bene gesserint* and notwithstanding the demise of the monarch. This clause was only the first of the many re-enactments of the original provision in the Act of Settlement establishing judicial tenure during good behaviour and providing that a judge may be removed upon an address of both Houses. Nevertheless, while subsequent legislation introduced some changes in the wording of the clause, the meaning of the clause remained unchanged. The present formulation of the clause is found in the Senior Courts Act 1981 and the Tribunals, Courts and Enforcement Act 2007: all judges of the High Court and of the Court of Appeal as well as the Senior President of Tribunals hold office 'during good behaviour', until retirement age subject to a power of removal by His Majesty on an address by both Houses of Parliament.[52] A similar provision applies to the UK Supreme Court Justices.[53]

2.8 Developments since the Act of Settlement have further secured the independence of the judiciary. An Act of 1760 first established judicial salaries, and provided that they should be made a permanent charge upon the Civil List.[54] In 1799 legislation established judicial pensions.[55] Only in the nineteenth century did judges' remuneration take the form of comprehensive salaries coupled with a prohibition against supplementing it. Until then judicial salaries were supplemented by additional sources of income such as judicial fees, presents, profits arising out of sale of offices, allowances for robes and loaves of sugar. The additional

---

[50] 1 George III c.23, 23 Statutes at Large 305.
[51] 28 Commons Journal 1094; The King's words were recited in the preamble to the Act.
[52] Senior Courts Act 1981 (formerly known as the Supreme Court Act 1981), s. 11(2); sch. Tribunals, Courts and Enforcement Act 2007, sch. 1, para. 6.
[53] CRA, s. 33.
[54] 1 Geo. III, c.23 (1760), 23 Statutes at Large 305; on judicial salaries, see below paras. 4.43 and 7.30.
[55] 39 Geo. III, c.110, s.7 (1799).

sources of income were eliminated in a very long, gradual evolution extending over three centuries.[56]

F.   Judgment on the judiciary of the Stuart period

2.9 The Whig historians passed a severe verdict on the bench under the Stuarts. It seems, however, that the judiciary under the Stuarts was not as subservient as has been generally suggested and that the quality of the judges at that time was higher than is generally believed.[57] Even 'Bloody Judge Jeffreys' has been defended, on the ground that the judges regarded themselves as a branch of the royal administration and sincerely believed in the theory of monarchy which, until the appalling political blunders of James II, was supported by the majority of Englishmen. It has also been suggested that the achievement of judicial independence should not be attributed to the efforts of the Opposition, who frequently acted in this matter from purely political motives.[58] While some have argued that the severe verdict of the great Whig historians on the judicial bench under Charles II and James II remains,[59] it seems that a scrutiny of the role of the judiciary in the constitutional struggle preceding the Glorious Revolution and the Act of Settlement leave serious doubts as to the validity of the prevailing view on the judiciary of the Stuart period.

G.   Crown, Parliament and judges after 1700

2.10 The introduction of good behaviour tenure for judges did not create an independent judiciary at the stroke of a pen. The judiciary, having been for so long a branch of the executive and at the storm centre of affairs during the Stuart era, could not immediately and entirely be removed from the entanglements of politics. Parliamentary attempts at

---

[56] Holdsworth, *History*, vol. I, 252–3; T. Mathew, *For Lawyers and Others* (London: Hodge, 1938), pp. 71–87; Cecil, *Tipping the Scales*, 209–30; Lord Sankey LC, 90 HL Deb., 75 et seq. (23 November 1933).

[57] G. Keeton, 'The Judiciary and the Constitutional Struggle 1660–88' (1962) 7 J Pub Teach Law 56; Jones, *Politics*, 18–19, 147–8.

[58] According to Keeton, 'it was the fact that the reaction to the excesses of James II came from the nation as a whole, irrespective of political belief, that made possible the evolution of the modern conception of the function of the judiciary', Keeton, 'The Judiciary and the Constitutional Struggle', 67.

[59] R.F.V. Heuston, *Lives of the Lord Chancellors (1885-1940)* (Oxford: Clarendon Press, 1964), p. 39.

exerting political pressure on the bench continued even after the Act of Settlement[60] and more than a century passed before the modern concept of judicial independence as we know it today emerged. The King and his ministers also sought to put pressure on judges concerning pending cases long after the Act of Settlement. In 1770, two members charged in Parliament that a minister tampered with a judge, and the King sent the judge a letter which he returned unopened.[61] There is also evidence that in 1767 politicians tampered with the integrity of judges by giving them lottery tickets which they sold openly.[62] The influence of the Crown on the bench did not pass away with the Act of Settlement. Having been for so long a branch of the executive, judges had strong tendencies to support the Crown.[63]

The judges in the eighteenth century and in the first half of the nineteenth century were charged with having been overly zealous in enforcing the repressive measures of the legislature against political opponents. As one writer put it, 'the sternest upholder of authority could not have accused the judges of any undue predilection for liberty of opinion'.[64] Campbell and Erskine May suggested that the laws of libel were administered by the judges in such a way as to leave little room for free speech, and trials conducted in such a manner as to persuade the juries to convict those who stood on trial for expressing criticism of the government.[65]

---

[60] The story of the attempt to question Chief Justice Holt about his decisions in *Ashby* v. *White* (1705) 2 Ld. Raym. 938, 92 ER 126, and *Paty's Case* ((1705) 2 Ld. Raym. 1105, 92 ER 232) and his strong resistance is an instructive illustration. (These cases dealt with the courts' determination of Parliamentary privilege.) Lord Campbell, however, who also relates the story, argues that no such proceedings ever took place: Campbell, *Lives*, vol. II, 164–5.

[61] (1765–1771) Parl. Hist. 1228–9, 1295. There is good reason to believe that the charges were not unfounded, see Foss, *The Judges*, vol. VIII, 412.

[62] Cecil, Tipping the Scales, 19.

[63] In light of this, Hallam suggested that 'we should look upon them with some little vigilance, and not come hastily to a conclusion that, because their commissions cannot be vacated by the Crown's authority they are wholly out of reach of its influence', Hallam, *Constitutional History*, vol. II, 358. See also Hearn, *The Government*, 86–8; Medley, *A Student's Manual*, 490; Lord Brougham, *Present State of the Law: the Speech of Henry Brougham, Esq, MP, in the House of Commons on Thursday February 7 1828* (London: Henry Colburn, 1828), p. 20 where he quotes his famous speech before the Commons in 1828: 'Whenever a question comes before the Bench, whether it is upon prosecution of libel or upon any other matters connected with politics, the counsel at their meeting take for granted that they can tell pretty accurately the leaning of the court, and predict exactly enough which way the consultation of the judges will terminate.'

[64] Medley, *A Student's Manual*, 490.

[65] Campbell, *Lives*, vol. VI, 516–17; the story is also told of Chief Justice Ellenborough who presented the draft of a letter of resignation after failing to persuade the jury to convict in

The Whiggish view on the judges of the eighteenth and early nineteenth centuries, as reflected in the preceding passages, should be read with a degree of scepticism. In the Stuart era it was easier to blame the judges for the difficulties than to admit that the whole system had failed.[66] In the eighteenth and early nineteenth centuries, it was similarly easier to put the responsibility for the suppression of free speech upon the judges than simply upon the law of libel which they had to apply. For the purpose of this study it may be pointed out that judicial independence in this period was in the process of gradual evolution, as were other concepts of modern British government, such as Opposition and Cabinet.

This takes us to another aspect of judicial association with the executive. In the eighteenth century and at the beginning of the nineteenth century there were several instances of judges who served as members of the Cabinet and took an active part in the political arena on the side of the Crown. Lord Hardwicke kept the office of Chief Justice of the King's Bench for about four months after he had entered the Cabinet as Lord Chancellor (from February to June 1737).[67] Chief Justice Mansfield served as a minister in the Cabinet for some nine years (1757–1765). This appointment did not pass without criticism;[68] yet, half a century later Chief Justice Ellenborough was appointed to the Cabinet. Lord Ellenborough's appointment to the Cabinet was severely condemned in the press and in Parliament as unconstitutional conduct. However, the government was strong enough to defend the appointment, for a resolution of censure was decisively rejected in both Houses of Parliament.[69] In defending the appointment, Lord Erskine, then the Lord Chancellor, correctly argued that there was nothing unconstitutional in summoning the Chief Justice to the Privy Council and further pointed out that the word Cabinet was unknown to the law and constitution. Likewise, the precedent set by Lord Mansfield was heavily relied upon.[70] To Lord Campbell, Lord Erskine's arguments appear to be based on 'mere formality and in complete disregard of the practice'.[71] As has been shown by

---

the trial of Howe in 1817, Erskine May, *The Constitutional History of England*, edited and continued by F. Holland (London: Longman, Greens, 1912), pp. 75–6.

[66] Jones, *Politics*, 32.

[67] Holdsworth, *History*, vol. XII, 244; Campbell, *Lives*, vol. V, 39–40; A. Todd, *On Parliamentary Government in England: its Origin, Development and Practical Operation* (London: Longmans, Green & Co., 1867–69), vol. II, p. 157.

[68] Campbell, *Lives*, vol. III, 188.   [69] *Ibid.*, 186.   [70] Campbell, *Lives*, vol. VI, 584–5.

[71] *Ibid.*, 686.

Foord,[72] Cabinet and Opposition developed only in the nineteenth century. Lord Erskine, therefore, was right when he argued in 1805 that 'Cabinet' was then unknown to the law of the constitution.

Whether or not the service of judges in executive positions was inconsistent with the concept of judicial independence, as it was then understood, there is little doubt that the severe criticism in the press and Parliament of Lord Ellenborough's serving in an executive position helped in establishing the proposition that judges should not sit in the Cabinet. No subsequent case of a judge serving as a Cabinet minister is recorded. Common law judges were excluded from the House of Commons in 1805, but the Master of the Rolls continued to sit in the Commons until the passing of the Supreme Court of Judicature Acts 1873 and 1875, which excluded all superior judges from sitting in the House of Commons. Before the Judicature Acts, the disqualification of the judges from the House of Commons rested on the law and custom of Parliament.[73]

II.   The Constitutional Reform Act 2005

2.11 Elsewhere in this book we document the continuing struggles between the judiciary and the executive over salaries and pensions and other matters. It is difficult to identify moments of crises in the twentieth century; such anomalies as undoubtedly persisted, such as the fact that the Lord Chancellor was at the same time a Cabinet minister, member of the House of Lords and able to sit in the House of Lords in its judicial capacity, caused surprisingly few difficulties in practice. As far as public confidence was concerned, the greater concern was almost certainly the lack of transparency in judicial appointments which lay in the gift of the Lord Chancellor but which went to white men from the same privileged backgrounds.

Reform, when it came, arrived almost overnight. It was not prompted by any particular crisis or alleged scandal. The Labour government announced the formal separation of powers between the judiciary and the other two branches of government without consultation with the judiciary or any planning of its profound consequences on judicial

---

[72] A. Foord, *Her Majesty's Opposition 1714–1830* (Oxford University Press, 1964).
[73] For historical accounts of disqualification of judges from the House of Commons, see Hatsell, *Precedents*, 3rd edn (1796), vol. II, 26–9; Birkenhead, *Points of View*, vol. II, 151–7.

governance and accountability. In June 2003, a government press release stated plans to abolish the office of the Lord Chancellor, to separate the most senior judges who used to sit as members of the House of Lords into a new Supreme Court of the UK, and to establish a new system for judicial appointments in England and Wales. No draft Bill was published at the time of the press release. It seems that the move was informed by the tensions within the Cabinet between Lord Irvine, the then Lord Chancellor, and the Prime Minister Tony Blair, and the press release was accompanied by a Cabinet reshuffle leading to the departure of Lord Irvine.[74] Commentators criticised the proposals variously as having been written on the back of an envelope, or the product of policy making on the hoof.[75] Some intense parliamentary debate followed in both Houses: the Conservative Opposition in the House of Lords moved a successful amendment to the Loyal Address after the Queen's Speech, calling on the government 'to withdraw their current proposals and to undertake meaningful consultation with Parliament and the senior judiciary before proceeding with legislation', and the House of Commons Constitutional Affairs Committee set up a major inquiry and report into it.[76] At the second reading of the Constitutional Reform Bill in March 2004, the House of Lords relied upon a procedure that had not been used for decades and referred the bill to a special committee with powers to take evidence and amend the bill before recommitting it to a Committee of the whole House.[77] 'Carried over' to the 2004–05 session, the bill was modified in significant ways in both Houses before receiving royal assent five days before Parliament was prorogued for the 2005 general election. In due course, then, the CRA effected the changes

---

[74] Lord Irvine only learnt of the constitutional reform a week before it was announced, see his paper submitted to the HL Committee on the Constitution, 'The Cabinet Office and the Centre of Government', HL 30, 2009–2010, Evidence 81–4; Lord Windlesham, 'The Constitutional Reform Act 2005: Ministers, Judges and Constitutional Change: Part 1' [2005] PL 806; Lord Windlesham, 'The Constitutional Reform Act 2005: The Politics of Constitutional Reform: Part 2' [2006] PL 35.

[75] A. Le Sueur, 'The Conception of the UK's New Supreme Court', in A. Le Sueur (ed.), *Building the UK's New Supreme Court* (Oxford University Press, 2004), p. 4; see also Lord Steyn, 'The Case for a Supreme Court' (2002) LQR 382.

[76] A. Le Sueur, 'From Appellate Committee to Supreme Court: A Narrative', in L. Blom-Cooper, B. Dickson and G. Drewry (eds.), *The Judicial House of Lords 1876–2009* (Oxford University Press, 2009), chapter 5; House of Commons Constitutional Affairs Committee, 'Judicial Appointments and a Supreme Court (Court of Final Appeal)' HC 2003–04, 48.

[77] Various Lords took part in the debates and Lord Hoffman voted against the government, see Le Sueur, 'From Appellate Committee to Supreme Court: A Narrative'.

announced in 2003 through a belated consultation process. The legislation provided that the Lord Chancellor need only 'appear to the Prime Minister to be qualified by experience'[78] but also that he had the duty to preserve the independence of the judiciary.[79]

All three elements of the reforms – the transfer of the role of head of the judiciary to the Lord Chief Justice, the creation of the UK Supreme Court and the establishment of a new Judicial Appointments Commission, are essential elements of the constitutional settlement in England and Wales today. They are considered in detail in the rest of this book to the extent that they help us 'unpack'[80] the meaning of judicial independence in England and Wales today. We consider at length the transfer to the Lord Chief Justice of the Lord Chancellor's main responsibilities in relation to the judiciary in our third chapter; the role of the Judicial Appointments Commission in our fourth chapter, and the impact of the creation of the UK Supreme Court in our ninth chapter on constitutional adjudication. We shall also consider the creation of the new Ministry of Justice, the minister for which also acts as the Lord Chancellor for statutory purposes but sits in the House of Commons. The Ministry, as we shall see, took over a collection of responsibilities from other ministries: it encompasses responsibility for judges (taken over from the Department for Constitutional Affairs) and for prisons (taken over from the Home Office) and this curious amalgamation sparked concerns among judges about the possible budgetary arrangements in the new Ministry, as we shall see in Chapter four.

III.   The impact of the Human Rights Act 1998

2.12 We should, at this point, introduce the Human Rights Act 1998, which has been the origin of the majority of criticism of judges, from both politicians and the media, in recent years. Until the HRA came into force on 2 October 2000, the ECHR was not incorporated into UK domestic law, even though the UK had been a leading contributor to the process that led to adoption, by the Council of Europe, of the ECHR in 1950. The HRA thus brought in a recalibration of the relationship between the individual and the state.[81] It makes specified rights under the

---

[78] CRA, s. 2.   [79] CRA, s. 3.

[80] Stevens, *The Independence of the Judiciary*, introduction.

[81] T. Bingham, 'The Human Rights Act' (2010) *European Human Rights Law Review* 568, 570; N. Bamforth, 'Parliamentary Sovereignty and the Human Rights Act 1998' [1998] PL

ECHR (Convention rights) part of national law, thereby giving individuals the right to bring some claims under the European Convention directly in UK courts. Significantly, acts – including decisions – of public authorities are said to be 'unlawful' under section 6(1) HRA if they violate a Convention right, and it was for that reason that the Act took so long to come into force. All public authorities were thought to need time to absorb the implications of the Act. Chief among them was the judiciary: courts are themselves 'public authorities' and might act unlawfully if they pass judgments that amount to violations of any incorporated Convention right – albeit that the Act makes clear that the only remedy for any judicial unlawful act would lie on appeal to a higher court.

The Act does not allow for the possibility that Parliament too might act 'unlawfully' in passing or declining to pass any legislation, but it provides that the minister of the Crown in charge of a bill in either House of Parliament is required, before the second reading, either to make a statement that 'in his view' the provisions of the bill do not infringe the Convention or to make a statement that although he was unable to make a statement of compatibility, the government nevertheless wished to proceed with the bill.[82] Parliamentary sovereignty is carefully preserved by confining the courts to a declaration of incompatibility[83] in cases where compatibility with the Convention cannot be achieved by interpretation, however, where 'it is possible to do so', the courts must interpret a statutory provision in order to render its meaning compliant with the Convention rights; and that exercise in interpretation may involve 'reinterpretation'.[84] Similarly acts of public authorities which violate Convention rights are not 'unlawful' if they are required under primary legislation that cannot be reinterpreted.[85]

A declaration of incompatibility does not affect the validity or effectiveness of the incompatible legislation. Thus, despite the House of Lords' decision that their detention violated Articles 5 and 14 of the ECHR, the suspected international terrorists remained in Belmarsh prison awaiting new legislation.[86] The political impact of declarations of incompatibility, however, compensates for the lack of legal remedy. Parliament tends

---

572; Stevens, *The English Judges*, 129–36; White Paper, 'Rights Brought Home: The Human Rights Bill' (Cm 3782, 1997).
[82] HRA, s. 19(1).   [83] HRA, s. 4.   [84] HRA, s. 3(1).   [85] HRA, s. 6(2).
[86] *A v. Secretary of State for the Home Department* [2005] 2 WLR 87.

to enact or approve amending legislation to address the incompatibility. If this becomes a convention, it would reduce the gap between a system which has full judicial review of legislation (a power to strike down incompatible legislation) and the UK's compromise solution.[87]

2.13 The future of the HRA is in some doubt.[88] It seems safe to say that opposition to the Act is partly a matter of power. Although the Labour government passed the Act, Labour ministers (especially successive Home Secretaries) were quick to deride judges for adverse decisions under the Act when in power. The tendency for the Act to be used as a trump card in certain judicial review cases is one reason for its unpopularity for any party in government. One chief effect is that claimants in judicial review may ask the judge for a higher degree of scrutiny of an executive decision if the decision interferes with one of their Convention rights – as will be the case when, for example, people stand to be deported, denied (or forcibly given) medical treatment, rehoused or have their children taken into care. In particular, the Home Office, whose system for dealing with immigration was famously said by one of its former ministers while he held office in 2006 (John Reid) to be 'unfit for purpose', is thought to have its errors and inefficiencies exposed much more clearly in deportation cases: here, the applicant is able to rely on his right to a family life in Article 8 ECHR to force the ministry to give timely and coherent reasons for its decisions.

However, to Conservative eyes too, the basic rights which the Act affords to individuals are contentious. Thus in 2011 the present Home Secretary derided at the Conservative Party Conference a decision in which an immigrant was given leave to remain under Article 8 ECHR on the basis that he had a cat. In the furore which resulted from the Home Secretary's anecdote (during which it emerged, on reading the judgment, that the ownership of the cat had not been a significant reason for the decision but was mentioned as an aside) the Prime Minister supported the Home Secretary. The new Justice Secretary, Chris Grayling, a non-lawyer, has now suggested that withdrawal from the ECHR might feature in the Conservative Party's election manifesto for the next general election in 2015.

---

[87] D. Feldman, 'The Impact of the Human Rights Act 1998 on English Public Law', Keynote address delivered at the conference 'European Influences on Public Law: 5 Years of the Human Rights Act 1998 in English Law and Recent Developments in France', BIICL, London (7 October 2005), para. 8.

[88] Commission on a Bill of Rights, 'A UK Bill of Rights? The Choice Before Us', vol. I (December 2012); C. O'Cinneide, *Human Rights and the UK Constitution* (London: British Academy Policy Centre, 2012).

2.14 This takes us to the arguments in opposition to the HRA. Claims that have been made of the HRA are (i) that it allows or even requires judges to pronounce on political matters; (ii) that section 3 HRA effectively allows senior judges to rewrite primary legislation when they hold that it is necessary and yet 'possible' to do so in order to avoid incompatibility with a Convention right; and (iii) that judges may be required to impose in England and Wales rules which derive rather from the authority of the various judges in the European Court of Human Rights in Strasbourg.

In relation to the first criticism, it is difficult to find examples where judges have relied on essentially political arguments in making decisions under the Act. Whether a person's rights are affected by executive action or inaction is a question of law, and questions of proportionality of executive interference and public policy are also familiar to them from cases of judicial review and negligence (among other areas of domestic law). Judges, unlike politicians, work within a legal framework where they can only give opinions which may seem to have a political element where such opinions are required, and when they do so, they must give reasons for their decisions, and those reasons must address the arguments that are made to them. Reasons, rather than status, are the foundation of their authority.[89] Judges are accountable through the reasoning in their decisions, with the appeal mechanism as a check upon their decisions. Lord Bingham, in the Belmarsh case, considered that it was 'wrong to stigmatise judicial decision-making as in some way undemocratic' since 'the function of independent judges charged to interpret and apply the law is universally recognised as a cardinal feature of the modern democratic state, a cornerstone of the rule of law itself;[90] giving effect to rights not to be imprisoned on discriminatory criteria only supported the rule of law.

Moreover, the willingness of judges to find violations under the Act depends on the issue at stake. In the Belmarsh case, the House of Lords was willing to apply a high standard of scrutiny in relation to the alleged discrimination against foreign nationals under Article 14 ECHR, but it was deferential to the government in its assessment of an emergency threat to the life of the nation, notwithstanding its own clear scepticism.

---

[89] D. Feldman, 'Human Rights, Terrorism and Risk: the Roles of Politicians and Judges' [2006] PL 364, 375; 'The Impact of the Human Rights Act 1998 on English Public Law', n. 87 above.

[90] A v. Secretary of State for the Home Department [2004] UKHL 56, para. 42 [Lord Bingham].

Their Lordships have been just as astute not to use the Act as a vehicle for reviewing the legality of the Iraq War, remarking that such an inquiry would be better served by legal and other historians.[91]

Besides, some matters have been left to the courts for resolution. Thus, rights of privacy under Article 8 ECHR have been successfully asserted in favour of some applicants in cases of media intrusion under the cloak of the remedy for breach of confidence,[92] while it was clear that this remedy, which states must provide in recognition of the Strasbourg jurisprudence, was not likely to be afforded by the government, whose relationship with the media is a regular subject of (negative) comment. Similarly, their Lordships held that Article 8 ECHR required a suicidal person who needed assistance to die to be able to ascertain the likelihood that a family member who might assist her would be prosecuted.[93] This was necessary to give a remedy to people who find themselves trapped in this invidious situation, since Parliament is unwilling to legislate in the area of euthanasia.[94] Yet the legislature welcomed this solution, and a few years after the decision, a House of Commons debate ended favourably to those who supported the Director of Public Prosecutions' new guidelines which resulted from the decision.[95]

The courts may also return the matter to the political domain for resolution. When the House of Lords held that detention of foreign suspects of terrorism was incompatible with Articles 5 and 14 of the Convention, the government responded with control orders, which for some time were thought to be compatible with the Convention – the main doubts about their inherent compatibility with Article 6 ECHR came first from Strasbourg.[96] When the courts decide that some persons cannot be extradited because they would not receive a fair trial abroad, typically efforts are made to negotiate with the requesting state to ensure that a trial would meet minimal Convention standards. When the House

---

[91] In *R* v. *Prime Minister* [2008] UKHL 20, the House of Lords declined to rule that compliance with Art. 2 ECHR required the Prime Minister to order a public inquiry into the legality of the Iraq War which had led to the death of the applicant's son. It was thought to be too remote from the cause of death of the soldiers concerned and such a wider declaration would be better delivered 'in the history books'.

[92] *Campbell* v. *MGN Ltd* [2004] UKHL 22.

[93] *R (Purdy)* v. *Director of Public Prosecutions* [2009] UKHL 45.

[94] *Ibid.*, paras. 57–9 [Lady Hale].

[95] *Hansard*, HC, vol. 542, cols 1363–1440, 27 March 2012.

[96] *A and others* v. *UK*, Application No. 3455/05, 19 February 2009.

of Lords decided that the Home Secretary does not act as an impartial or independent tribunal when deciding the minimum term a murderer should spend in prison,[97] the government responded with legislation which set statutory minimums for certain types of cases.[98] Now that the courts have declared, following the lead of Strasbourg,[99] that blanket bans on prisoners voting are incompatible with the Convention, it is expected that legislation will similarly specify which categories of prisoner will automatically forfeit the vote.

The second argument, that judges have a de facto power to rewrite offending legislation, is also exaggerated. The common law itself prohibited torture, recognised some freedom of expression, rights against arbitrary detention and gave effect to fair trial rights and so much else that is incorporated in the ECHR. Before the Human Rights Act came into force, the House of Lords gave effect to a journalist's right of freedom of expression (in the context of investigating a possible miscarriage of justice) in striking down secondary legislation that seemed to deny him access to interview the prisoner in question. Yet still parliamentary sovereignty was preserved, as Lord Hoffmann explained in *ex parte Simms*:

> In the absence of express language or necessary implication to the contrary, the courts ... presume that even the most general words were intended to be subject to the basic rights of the individual. In this way, the courts of the UK, though acknowledging the sovereignty of Parliament, apply principles of constitutionality little different from those which exist in countries where the power of the legislature is expressly limited by a constitutional document.[100]

This also means that Parliament can legislate contrary to fundamental principles of human rights provided that, through the use of explicit language, it is willing 'to accept the political cost'.

Allan accordingly rejects the claim that section 3 HRA authorises an interpretative approach that would otherwise be unprecedented and illegitimate. He instead argues that judges have a 'continuing responsibility to bring [a] provision into harmony with present expectations and constitutional needs'. Legal interpretation is as much a matter of construction, highly sensitive to context, as it is a matter of 'instruction',

---

[97] *R (Anderson)* v. *Secretary of State for the Home Department* [2002] UKHL 46.
[98] Criminal Justice Act 2003, sch. 21.   [99] *Hirst* v. *UK (No. 2)* [2005] ECHR 681.
[100] *R* v. *Secretary of State for the Home Department, ex parte Simms* [2000] 2 AC 115 [Lord Hoffmann].

where some substantive judgments come into play. The 'instruction' comes from the common law principles and presumptions which clarify the meaning of a particular statute.[101] Allan suggests that section 3 HRA 'reproduces a fundamental feature of the common law constitution; for the common law also recognises basic constitutional rights and requires their protection against unjustified encroachments'. This seems to be the better explanation of the leading case *Ghaidan*, where the court considered that homosexual partners were afforded the various protections of the Rent Act 1977, despite the statute's implicit requirement that partners must be 'of the opposite sex'.[102] This robust interpretation accords with what must now be regarded as the common law's evolved understanding of the intolerability of discrimination on the grounds of sexual orientation. This decision is accepted for what it is – the removal of an outdated discriminatory provision in the 1970s which no contemporary politician would seek to defend.[103]

Similarly, the decision in the House of Lords that the Special Immigration Appeals committee could not receive evidence which was procured by torture by foreign agents (thus striking down secondary legislation to the opposite effect) was based on common law and not on the HRA.[104] If this is right, then the HRA itself does not give the judges significant extra power to reinterpret legislation; such interpretative powers have already been assumed at common law without courting political controversy.

The third argument is that the Strasbourg judges have themselves extended the scope of the Convention beyond that which was intended in the 1950s, or that they have been interpreting it according to a continental style of reasoning, and that it is inappropriate that our judges should follow their interpretations of the Convention. Yet section 2 HRA only requires English courts to 'take account of' the Strasbourg jurisprudence. As was said in *R (Ullah)* v. *Special Adjudicator*,[105] 'the duty of national courts is to keep pace with the Strasbourg jurisprudence as it

---

[101] T.R.S Allan, 'Human Rights Act in Constitutional Perspective' (2006) 59 CLP 27, p. 36.
[102] *Ghaidan* v. *Godin-Mendoza* [2004] UKHL 30, para. 30 [Lord Nicholls].
[103] Whether the reach of s. 3 HRA goes beyond that of the principle of legality is the subject of extensive debate, but see *Ghaidan* v. *Godin-Mendoza* [2004] UKHL 30, 32–3 [Lord Nicholls], 49 [Lord Steyn]; *(Wilkinson)* v. *Inland Revenue Commissioners* [2005] 1 WLR 1718, para. 17 [Lord Hoffman]; *HM Treasury* v. *Ahmed* [2010] UKSC 2, paras. 11–138 [Lord Phillips].
[104] *A* v. *Secretary of State for the Home Department* [2005] UKHL 71.
[105] [2004] UKHL 26.

evolves over time: no more, but certainly no less'. Where a Strasbourg decision has been made in apparent ignorance or misunderstanding of an English legislative scheme, the English courts have felt free to depart from it. Thus, between 2009 and 2011, there was uncertainty about whether the reception of hearsay evidence would result in an unfair trial within the meaning of Article 6 ECHR, if that evidence would have decisive effect. This was said to be so by the Fourth Section of the European Court in *Al-Khawaja and Tahery* v. *UK*.[106] To some extent, this was a peculiarly English difficulty, because there is no facility for both parties to arrange to put questions to witnesses before a trial in England, when many European countries have such facilities and thus the prohibition on 'decisive' hearsay evidence was less problematic for them. But the Supreme Court, applying section 2 HRA, decided to depart from the Strasbourg ruling and held that there were sufficient safeguards elsewhere in the legislative scheme to enable any such evidence if the judge thought that an unsafe verdict might result from admitting the evidence.[107] When the issue returned to the Grand Chamber of the European Court of Human Rights, the decision of the Fourth Section of the European Court in *Al-Khawaja* was largely reversed.[108]

More often, however, English courts do follow Strasbourg jurisprudence as they do not strongly disagree with it. Thus, the House of Lords had itself doubted whether Article 8 ECHR was engaged by the wish of a person to know whether someone who might assist her suicide would be pros-ecuted;[109] but when Strasbourg accepted the argument, it followed suit.[110] However, as already noted, this decision enabled it to solve in some compromised way the problem of prosecutions for minor acts in eutha-nasia which Parliament was unwilling to face. For the purpose of our discussion, this suffices to show that English judges do not import a jurisprudence of a foreign court; rather, they recognise it as a fuller articulation of many of the norms of the common law and apply its rulings where it does not disturb the considered development of English law.

Our suggestion, then, is that the judiciary, in the main, have used the powers of reinterpretation of statutes and of declaring acts of public

---

[106] *Al-Khawaja* v. *UK* (2009) 1 EHRR 49.
[107] *R* v. *Horncastle and others* [2009] UKSC 14.
[108] *Al-Khawaja* v. *UK* [2011] ECHR 2127.
[109] *Pretty* v. *Director of Public Prosecutions and Secretary of State for the Home Department* [2001] UKHL 61.
[110] *Pretty* v. *UK* (2002) 35 EHRR 1.

authorities to be unlawful under the HRA in cases where the Convention rights confirm or go only incrementally beyond the values of the common law itself.

IV. Constitutional adjudication

2.15 The independence of the judiciary is conceived within the realm of boundaries between the courts and Parliament, yet these boundaries are subject to 'whether the courts and Parliament neatly complement each other, whether there is competition or rivalry between them, and, in the event of disagreement, how it may be resolved'.[111] Constitutional adjudication, in the sense of reviewing the compatibility of an Act of Parliament against a national constitution, is not, however, unknown to the Law Lords sitting in the Judicial Committee of the Privy Council. It has, from time to time, considered a range of constitutional matters, from death row cases[112] to matters pertaining to judicial independence. Lord Diplock thus affirmed in *Hinds* v. *The Queen* the 'outstanding public importance' of judicial independence as a safeguard of the judicial determination of each individual citizen's civil and criminal responsibilities,[113] while, in *Suratt* v. *Attorney General of Trinidad and Tobago*[114] views differed on the degree of protection from outside influence of the office holder of a particular jurisdiction that is required by the principle of judicial independence.

The Privy Council had also had, since 1998, jurisdiction in relation to devolution matters.[115] This competence was transferred to the UK Supreme Court, which therefore has appellate jurisdiction and special statutory powers to consider referred questions, including questions by the relevant law officer or ministers of the devolved entities. This is akin to constitutional adjudication to the extent that the UK Supreme Court is ready to review the distribution of powers between the UK and the national Parliaments of Scotland, Wales and Northern Ireland. While

---

[111] A. Bradley, 'The Sovereignty of Parliament – Form or Substance ?', in J. Jowell and D. Olivier (eds.), *The Changing Constitution*, 7th edn (Oxford University Press, 2011), pp. 34 and 37.

[112] *Reyes* v. *The Queen* [2002] UKPC 11; *R* v. *Hughes* [2002] UKPC 12; *Fox* v. *The Queen* [2002] UKPC 13; *Benjamin* v. *Trinidad and Tobago* [2012] UKPC.

[113] *Hinds* v. *The Queen* [1977] AC 195, 210, 221-G [Lord Diplock].

[114] [2007] UKPC 55.

[115] See the Scotland Act 1998, the Northern Ireland Act 1988 and the Government of Wales Act 2006.

the impact of devolution on the courts is a matter that falls outside the remit of this book, Lady Hale's comment that 'the UK has become a federal state with a Constitution regulating the relationships between the federal centre and the component parts'[116] bears relevance to our setting, in this chapter, of the constitutional landscape in which the English judiciary operates. The decision of the UK Supreme Court in *AXA General Insurance Ltd v. Lord Advocate*,[117] in particular, engaged with the question of judicially reviewing the legislative powers of the Scottish Parliament on the alleged grounds of incompatibility with a Convention right and irrationality. Having found that devolved legislatures, unlike the Westminster Parliament, are not sovereign legislatures, Lord Hope, giving the leading judgment, and addressing the issue as one of principle,[118] stated that:

> It is not entirely unthinkable that a government which has that power may seek to use it to abolish judicial review or to diminish the role of the courts in protecting the interests of the individual. Whether this is likely to happen is not the point. It is enough that it might conceivably do so. The rule of law requires that the judges must retain the power to insist that legislation of that extreme kind is not law which the courts will recognise.[119]

In addition, Lord Reed rightly suggested that devolved legislatures, in the absence of express contrary provision in the devolution Acts, cannot legislate incompatibly with fundamental rights, whether or not enshrined in the ECHR, or the rule of law, or confer on another body the power to do so.[120]

While generally the Acts of the Scottish Parliament are not amenable to common law judicial review, Lord Hope's judgment provides the basis for the constitutional jurisdiction of the Supreme Court in exceptional circumstances.[121] The necessary reliance upon the democratic process justifies such narrow jurisdiction: in the words of Lord Bingham, 'the democratic process is liable to be subverted if, on a question of political or moral judgment, opponents of an Act achieve through the courts what they could not achieve through Parliament'.[122] In the context of tensions

---

[116] Lady Hale, 'The Supreme Court in the UK Constitution', *Legal Wales* (12 October 2012).

[117] [2011] UKSC 46; see also *Martin v. HM Advocate* [2010] UKSC 10.

[118] *AXA General Insurance Ltd v. Lord Advocate (Scotland)* [2011] UKSC 46, para. 48.

[119] *Ibid.*, 46, 51; *R (Jackson) v. Attorney-General* [2005] UKHL 56.

[120] *AXA General Insurance Ltd v. Lord Advocate (Scotland)* [2011] UKSC 46, para. 152 [Lord Reed]; *R v. Secretary of State for the Home Department ex parte Simms* [2000] 2 AC 115.

[121] C. Himsworth, 'Case Comment' [2012] PL 205, 213.

[122] *R (Countryside Alliance) v. Attorney General* [2007] UKHL 52, para. 45.

about the boundaries of judicial action in relation to the Westminster Parliament, this is a pointed marker of the courts' jurisdiction with regard to the conceivable abolition of judicial review by Parliament, be it Westminster or a devolved legislature. Judicial review affords the protection of the rule of law and cannot be lightly interfered with. Yet, shortly before this book was completed, the Prime Minister suggested that he had plans to restrict the opportunity for judicial review. If taken forward, in the absence of a written constitution protecting it, it would create 'islands of power immune from supervision and restraint'.[123]

Conclusions

2.16 In the absence of a written constitution, constitutional reform in the UK is, by necessity, piecemeal in nature. The various steps taken towards judicial independence are no different. Gradually Parliament won its battle with the Crown so that the judges should be free from royal influence and patronage. But having won this freedom, the judges proved mostly resistant to being under the patronage of Parliament, or more accurately the governing party which holds the majority in Parliament. Any arrangements whereby judges would sit in Parliament, let alone Cabinet, were criticised and during the nineteenth century Parliament would be pressed into passing legislation guaranteeing judicial salaries and tenure and barring them from political office. By the late twentieth century, politicians who wished to influence the judiciary would be more likely to use the media for their purposes, and this trend has become most apparent since the passing of the HRA, since when it has not always been clear whether ministers have meant to attack the legislation itself or the judges who would reach adverse decisions on account of it.

Despite the complaints that may be justly levelled at the way in which the reforms in the CRA were presented and implemented, it remains the case that the reforms were to enhance separation of powers and transparency in appointments. Whether the CRA safeguards judges from political pressure or interference is perhaps an ambitious question, for this is rather to be determined by the maturity and integrity of politicians, and the robustness of the senior members of the judiciary. This theme too runs through the rest of this book.

---

[123] *Kirk v. Industrial Court* (NSW) (2010) 239 CLR 531, para. 55 [French CJ, Gummow, Hayne, Crennan, Kiefel and Bell JJ).

3

The structure and governance of the English judiciary

Introduction

3.1 This chapter comprises four sections. First, we set out an overview of the structure of the courts and tribunals. Second, we consider the judicial hierarchy of those courts, with some observations on tribunals. Third, we examine the recent transfer of judicial governance by civil servants to the partnership with the judiciary and Her Majesty's Courts Service (HMCS, recently relabelled HMCTS (Her Majesty's Courts and Tribunal Service) to reflect the inclusion of tribunals). Fourth, we discuss three particular administrative responsibilities which are now transferred to judges, namely decisions on deployment and case assignment given to senior judges and the increased emphasis on case management for all trial judges.

Laws are of little value if the legal system does not provide an efficient method for enforcing them and obtaining redress for their violation. This requires an efficient organisation of the judiciary and an efficient judicial process, characterised by consistency and constancy. In this respect, the Concordat[1] and the Constitutional Reform Act 2005 (CRA) vest in the Lord Chief Justice some considerable responsibilities in respect of the judiciary and of the business of the courts of England and Wales. This may explain why for most judges interviewed the administration of justice was seen as one the main areas where changes had deeply affected the judiciary. The Lord Chief Justice exercises these responsibilities by delegation,[2] thereby formalising the existing hierarchy and leadership positions within the judiciary and reflecting specific arrangements for

---

[1] See the text of the Concordat reproduced in Appendix 6, Report from the Select Committee on the Constitutional Bill, vol. I, HL Paper No. 125-I (24 June 2004).

[2] It was not intended that the Lord Chief Justice should exercise all these powers and functions personally, and thus the organisation of the judiciary was adjusted to support the various transferred responsibilities, Evidence to HL Select Committee on the Constitutional Reform Bill, 2004, HL Paper 125-II, cols. 218, 233.

judicial governance. These structures and practices determine the way in which judges relate to each other and achieve a sense of collective independence.[3] The Senior President of Tribunals is at present a separate judicial office with similar, but not identical, responsibilities to the Lord Chief Justice.

While judges did not play a major role in supervising the conduct of business of the courts before the CRA came into force, the managerial trend seems unavoidable. It seems to be accepted now that 'Judges today have to be far more business-like and professional than ever before', as Lady Justice Hallett noted in 2011,[4] and the dual leadership structure of the administration of justice, in partnership with HMCTS, reflects the more managerial roles allocated to judges in recent times. Decisions taken by judges in the exercise of their judicial office can affect the use of courts' resources. If the judge decides that a case is to be transferred to another court because something has gone wrong in the judicial process – for example, there has been a suggestion of interference with jurors – this can have a financial impact on the HMCTS's resources and other agencies involved in the justice system. It is not simply a matter of the judges being aware of the economic impact of their decisions; it is also about their having the last word where the interests of justice are at stake, so that the more costly route in a case may be insisted upon when it seems truly necessary. Lord Chief Justice Judge commented that 'the public rightly sets great store in an efficient, effective and impartial justice system – with an independent judiciary at its heart'.[5] It is part of our argument in this chapter that judicial independence does not exclude managerial accountability for delivering a public service of justice.

I.   The structure of courts and tribunals

3.2 The courts of law are the most visible feature of the English legal system,[6] and tribunals have also gradually become a regular feature. The

---

[3] J. Bell, *Judiciaries within Europe, A Comparative Review* (Cambridge University Press, 2006), pp. 21, 26, 359–60, 368.

[4] Lady Justice Hallet, 'How the Judiciary is Changing', in Judicial Appointments Commission (ed.), *Judicial Appointments: Balancing Independence, Accountability and Legitimacy* (2010), p. 94; J. Resnik, 'Managerial Judges' (1982) 96 HLR 374.

[5] Judicial Office, 'Judicial Business Plan 2010–2011'.

[6] See, for a thorough grasp of the English legal system, S.H. Bailey, J.P.L.Ching and N.W. Taylor, *Smith, Bailey and Gunn on the Modern English Legal System*, 5th edn (London: Sweet and Maxwell, 2007).

courts' and tribunals' structure is set out below, with two charts available in Annex 1 to this book. The greatest volume of cases is dealt with by the lower judiciary and tribunals, who rely greatly upon part-time judges at this level.

A.   Courts

3.3 The judiciary is traditionally divided into corps. Lay magistrates sit in magistrates' courts and the closely allied youth courts. Tribunal members sit in tribunals. District judges and circuit judges hear a mixture of 'first instance' civil and criminal cases, including presiding over jury trials in the Crown Court. Judicial reviews and appeals on points of law from magistrates' courts are heard in the High Court. Then there is the Court of Appeal which comprises a civil and criminal division and from either division there may be an appeal to the UK Supreme Court.

The magistrates' court is the lowest court of criminal jurisdiction and they deal with the great majority of criminal cases – summary motoring, indictable and youth proceedings. They initially decide early issues in criminal procedure; whether police can hold suspects for further questioning after the statutory 36-hour period expires; whether police may search people's houses, and whether people facing charges should be given bail; they may impose anti-social behaviour orders (ASBOs), and they license pubs and strip clubs and so forth. There were 25,170 serving magistrates in England and Wales in 2012, and 1.62 million criminal proceedings were completed in magistrates' courts in 2011 (excluding adult breaches).

County courts deal with about 1.5 million claims a year, with a majority of civil cases (by contrast with family claims).[7] The civil cases typically relate to debt, repossession of property and personal injury, whereas the family cases relate to divorce or separation.[8] There is at least one circuit judge (known as county court judges before 1971) in some of these county courts, and they generally hear cases which are worth over £25,000 or have greater importance or complexity.[9] District judges

[7] Annual Tribunals Statistics, 1 April 2011 to 31 March 2012, published 28 June 2012, p. 21.
[8] The county court judiciary, established in 1846, was long known as the 'poor man's court', as a route for local judges and small claims, P. Polden, *A History of the County Courts 1846–1971* (Cambridge University Press, 1999), p. 1.
[9] Circuit judges sometimes have an appellate jurisdiction as well, see, e.g., Part 30 of the Family Procedure Rules 2010.

(known as registrars before the Courts and Legal Services Act 1990), who are assigned to county courts, will hear other cases but they also case-manage proceedings, deal with repossession matters, and make contested and uncontested assessments of damages.

The civil court judge is not to be confused with the stipendiary magistrate who also has the title of district judge (magistrates' court) and whose judicial culture has more in common with lay magistrates. The district judge (magistrates' court) has been said to perform the same work as thirty-two lay (and thus part-time) magistrates, though the role of the magistracy is one that is well recognised.[10] A district judge is likely to sit in any case potentially involving legal difficulty or publicity.

Appointment as a circuit or district judge is an entry-level position traditionally characterised by the greater diversity in the profile of judges, by comparison with judges from the High Court and above. There were ninety-four women out of 548 circuit judges (14 per cent) in 2010, and a low number of solicitors. Entry to the lower judiciary is attractive, with almost 1,500 applications for the last selection exercise for the post of district judges in 2012, with twenty-eight positions available. The attraction of such posts is similar across judiciaries: they provide a mid-career move bringing a more predictable and less strenuous workload compared with private practice.[11] In addition, the efforts of the Judicial Appointments Commission to widen the pool to black and Asian minority ethnic candidates and women have been particularly successful at this level. At the level of district judges, the Judicial Shadowing Scheme is an equally successful initiative from the Lord Chief Justice. It provides legal practitioners with a genuine interest in judicial appointment an insight into the role and experience of being a judge.[12]

3.4 The High Court and the Court of Appeal are generalist courts, a distinguishing factor from many European jurisdictions – and a relevant consideration in considering facilitating deployment or stints of work

---

[10] P. Seago, C. Walker and D. Wall, 'The Development of the Professional Magistracy in England and Wales' [2000] Crim LR 631.

[11] Bell, *Judiciaries within Europe*, 310; A. Clarke, 'Soliciting Justice' (1999) 96 *Law Society Gazette* 28.

[12] The Advisory Panel on Judicial Diversity strongly supports it as a way of encouraging diversity within the judiciary. From 2006 to 2012, the scheme received 1,121 applications to shadow a district judge (Civil), the highest number compared to requests to shadow any other type of judge. In 2011–12, the scheme received 505 requests for work shadowing and out of those, 327 requests were to shadow a district judge (Civil, Family, Magistrates).

from the lower courts to the High Court.[13] This said, judges are appointed to one of the three divisions of the High Court: Queen's Bench, Chancery or Family, and many judges are deployed to some specialised courts within each division, such as the Administrative Court,[14] which hears judicial review cases, or the Commercial Court, the Technology and Construction Court and the Admiralty Court in the Queen's Bench; or the Companies Court, the Bankruptcy Court or the Patent Court in the Chancery Division.

There were 16,600 proceedings started in the Queen's Bench Division in 2010, the majority of which (11,800) were issued at the High Court District Registries around the counties, against 4,900 issues at the Royal Courts of Justice in London.[15] The existence of High Court centres in the provinces requires judges of the High Court to spend time 'on the circuit' away from home, a substantial factor in particular mitigating against attracting women to the High Court.

Some statistics can be briefly mentioned in distinguishing the type of work done at the High Court. It received 11,200 applications to apply for permission to apply for judicial review in the Administrative Court in 2011 and 1,220 were granted.[16] The majority of these applications, as in previous years, concerned asylum and immigration matters and this has highlighted the scarcity of judges expert in immigration laws. There were 571 appeals/applications disposed of in the Administrative Court during 2011, with 396 applications for judicial review dealt with during that year. The transfer of reconsideration applications to the Upper Tribunal in 2010 resulted in a steep reduction in appeals and applications received by the Administrative Court. The Administrative Court is also competent to hear appeals by way of case stated where received. There were, in 2011, 79 such appeals, 73 per cent of which were appeals from magistrates' courts, most of which relate to criminal matters – which shows the broad scope of 'administrative' law in England and Wales.

The Chancery Division deals with technical law relating to land and property, taxation, competition disputes, intellectual property, contract, professional negligence and generally business and industry matters

---

[13] See below, para. 3.34.

[14] Practice Direction (Administrative Court: Establishment) [2000] 4 All ER 1071.

[15] Ministry of Justice, 'Judicial and Court Statistics', 28 June 2012.

[16] *Ibid.*, 64–5; V. Bondy and M. Sunkin, 'The Dynamics of Judicial Review Litigation: the Resolution of Public Law Challenges Before Final Hearing' (London: The Public Law Project, 2009); see also M. Sunkin et al, 'The Positive Effect of Judicial Review on the Quality of Local Government' [2010] *Judicial Review* 337.

(e.g. partnership). There were more than 35,000 proceedings started in the Chancery Division in 2011 and more than 12,000 applications filed at the Bankruptcy Court in 2011. In 2011, fifty-two appeals were disposed of out of ninety-one appeals set down for hearing by the Chancery Division.[17]

The Family Division of the High Court is one of the three levels of courts, with the county courts and family proceedings courts (which are part of the magistrates' courts) dealing with family matters; High Court judges will take on the most complex family work.[18]

The Crown Court, by contrast, is a unitary court, but is currently based at seventy-six centres across England and Wales. High Court judges sit in the more serious criminal cases.[19] They sat in 2 per cent of all trial cases dealt with in the Crown court in 2011.[20] Circuit judges (who have had criminal jurisdiction at the Crown Court since 1971) sat in 89 per cent of all trial cases dealt with in the Crown Court in 2011, and recorders, who deal with the less complex or serious cases, in 9 per cent of all trial cases dealt with in the Crown Court that year. In 2011, 148,000 cases were received in the Crown Court, and 91,910 cases were committed/sent for trial to the Crown Court that year. There were 93,960 disposals of cases committed/sent for trial in 2011 (in light of the outstanding caseload). Some 42,981 cases were committed to the Crown Court for sentence in 2011; 13, 359 appeals were made against magistrates' decisions.

Since the passing of the CRA, the High Court, the Court of Appeal and the Crown Court are considered as the senior courts of England and Wales.[21]

---

[17] Ministry of Justice, 'Judicial and Court Statistics 2011', 54–5.

[18] Most matters are dealt with under the Children Act 1989 in all three levels of courts. There were 29,500 public law applications involving children made by local authorities in 2011, against 109,700 private law applications involving children, which usually follow a breakdown in their parents' relationship: Judicial and Court Statistics 2011, 21–2.

[19] Ibid., 44. The Crown Court has jurisdiction to deal with the cases sent for trial by magistrates' courts in respect of 'indictable only' offences (i.e. those which can only be heard by the Crown Court); 'either way' offences committed for trial (i.e. those which can be heard in either a magistrates' court or the Crown Court); defendants committed from magistrates' courts for sentence; and appeals against decisions of magistrates' courts.

[20] For the purpose of trial in the Crown Court, offences are divided into classes of seriousness, according to directions given by the Lord Chief Justice, with the concurrence of the Lord Chancellor, since 6 June 2005. High Court judges sat in 27% of all Class 1 cases compared to only 2% in each of Class 2 and Class 3 cases: Judicial and Court Statistics 2011, 44.

[21] Senior Courts Act 1981, as amended by CRA (c. 4), ss. 59, 148, sch. 11 para. 26(1).

3.5 In the Court of Appeal, the Criminal and the Civil Divisions hear appeals from the High Court, Crown Court and county courts. The great bulk of the Criminal Division's work is appeals against the sentence imposed in the Crown Court (5,623 appeals in 2011 out of 7,475 applications), the remaining being appeals against conviction (1,535 in 2011).[22] Most of these applications for permission are considered by a single judge (4,600 in 2011), they would otherwise be considered by one Lord Justice of Appeal assisted by one or two High Court judges.

The Civil Division hears appeals mainly against decisions of the High Court and county courts and certain other courts such as the Patents Court. In the Court of Appeal Civil Division, a total of 3,758 applications were filed or set down and 3,709 disposed of in 2011. The Civil Division saw more than 1,200 appeals filed in 2011 and disposed of 1,180 appeals on civil matters.[23] The growing work comes from the Asylum and Immigration Tribunal (a quarter of the appeals in 2011), followed by appeals from the county courts on non-family matters, and appeals from the Administrative Court of the High Court Queen's Bench Division. Courts of two or three judges are normally constituted from the Master of the Rolls and the Lords Justices.

3.6 The UK Supreme Court is a United Kingdom institution. Even though it was created without consultation, its existence is grounded on its quasi-federal nature. The UK Supreme Court Justices also serve as members of the Privy Council, a supreme court for a number of members of the Commonwealth.[24] It assumes, in other words, the jurisdiction of the House of Lords under the Appellate Jurisdiction Acts 1876 and 1888, and it also has jurisdiction in relation to devolution matters under the Scotland Act 1998, the Northern Ireland Act 1988 and the Government of Wales Act 2006.[25] Its workload is yet minimal in comparison with many other supreme courts – between April 2011 and March 2012 it heard sixty-nine appeals and gave eighty-five judgments:[26] it concentrates on appeals on points of law general public and constitutional importance.

---

[22] Ministry of Justice, 'Judicial and Court Statistics 2011', 62–3.   [23] Ibid., 64.

[24] For a recent, and critical, analysis, see P. O'Connor QC, 'The Constitutional Role of the Privy Council and the Prerogative, a JUSTICE Report' (2009).

[25] See paras. 2.12, 2.15 and 2.16 and, generally, L. Blom-Cooper, B. Dickson and G. Drewry (eds), The Judicial House of Lords 1876–2009; A. Paterson, The Law Lords (London: Macmillan, 1982); L. Blom-Cooper and G. Drewry, Final Appeal: A Study of the House of Lords in its Judicial Capacity (Oxford: Clarendon Press, 1972).

[26] The Supreme Court Annual Report and Accounts 2011–2012, HC 26.

B.   Tribunals

3.7 Tribunals deal with a growing number of claims. HMCTS managed 739,600 receipts or claims to all tribunals during 2011–12, with 732,600 cases disposed of that year.[27] The three largest tribunals in terms of volume of claims are the Social Security and Child Support Appeals (47,700 receipts in 2011–12); the Employment Tribunals (31,800 receipts) and Immigration and Asylum (24,300 receipts).

There are about 5,000 judicial office holders in tribunals, including those within Employment Tribunals in England and Wales and their Scottish counterpart, and the Employment Appeal Tribunal. Until recently, government bodies would set up tribunals to adjudicate between citizens and themselves in respect of their decisions that might affect citizens as individuals. They might deal with matters as disparate as tax, immigration and parking appeals. Substantial structural reform of the tribunal system was proposed in the Leggatt Review of Tribunals in 2001[28] and given effect by the Tribunals, Courts and Enforcement Act 2007. The Tribunals Service was formed as an executive agency of the Ministry of Justice, with responsibility for the unified administration of the tribunals system. The Tribunals, Courts and Enforcement Act 2007 Act extends the guarantee of judicial independence under the CRA to the Senior Presidents of Tribunals and to most tribunals.[29] Tribunals are thus now a central part of the justice system. Tribunal members themselves, whether lay members or professional judges, are regarded as members of the 'judicial family' and appointments are subject to the Judicial Appointments Commission's procedures, while disciplinary matters fall within the remit of the Office of Judicial Complaints. Tribunal members are also required to take the oath of allegiance and the judicial oath before the Senior President of Tribunals.[30]

The Leggatt Review was not the first occasion on which the essentially judicial nature of tribunals was recognised, notwithstanding the relatively informal procedures and substantial law involvement. The Committee on Administrative Tribunals and Enquiries (the Franks Committee) had

---

[27] Annual Tribunals Statistics 2011–2012, 28 June 2012, p. 3.

[28] A. Leggatt, 'Review of Tribunals, Tribunals for Users, One System, One Service', HMSO (2001).

[29] Tribunals, Courts and Enforcement Act 2007, s. 1. The duty, under the CRA, on the Lord Chancellor and other ministers to 'uphold the continued independence of' the court judiciary is extended to the tribunal judicial offices listed in sch. 14 of the CRA.

[30] Tribunals, Courts and Enforcement Act 2007, sch. 3 para. 10.

argued in 1957 that tribunals should be fully integrated into the civil justice system: 'In all these cases Parliament has deliberately provided for a decision independent of the Department concerned ... and the intention of Parliament to provide for the independence of tribunals is clear.'[31] It considered that tribunals had certain 'practical' advantages over courts as providers of administrative adjudication. Tribunals, it has generally been argued, can provide administrative justice more quickly, cheaply, accessibly, flexibly, informally and expertly.[32] But from the 1970s onwards, the increasing emphasis on alternative dispute resolution, for example, is thought to have reduced the comparative advantages of tribunals over lower civil courts.

In the early part of the twenty-first century, the coming into force of the Human Rights Act 1998 (HRA) has had a significant impact on the way tribunals are organised. It became a matter of concern that tribunals, most of whose case work would involve determining litigants' civil rights or obligations, would not be regarded as sufficiently 'independent' for the purposes of Article 6(1) of the European Convention on Human Rights (ECHR) if those of its members who had to hear alleged complaints about administrative blunders were themselves paid out of the budget of the same ministry. The fact that the tribunals would typically hear cases in the same building as their sponsoring department was in itself far from ideal. However, the merger under HMCTS means that a number of tribunals may suffer from a relative lack of resources due to becoming only a small part of the Ministry of Justice. The Employment Tribunal and the Employment Appeal Tribunal remain outside this system; however, they are served by the Tribunals Service and are led by the Senior President of Tribunals. Presumably the issue of independence raised under Article 6(1) ECHR is not a pressing one here because employment tribunals hear cases where neither side is allied to the executive.

Aside from concerns about independence, the Leggatt Review of Tribunals made recommendations which set the foundations for the Tribunal system to be 'independent, coherent, professional, cost-effective and user-friendly'.[33] It suggested the creation of a new, independent

---

[31] Committee on Administrative Tribunals and Enquiries, Cmnd. 218 (London: HMSO, 1957), para. 128.

[32] G. Richardson, 'Tribunals', in D. Feldman (ed.), *English Public Law* (Oxford University Press, 2004), ch. 20; H.W. Wade and C.F. Forsyth, *Administrative Law*, 10th edn (Oxford University Press, 2009), p. 773; *Cooke* v. *Secretary of State for Social Security* [2001] EWCA Civ 734.

[33] Leggatt, 'Review of Tribunals', para. 1.

tribunal service to take over the management of the tribunals from their sponsoring departments, and the creation of a composite, two-tier tribunal structure, under the leadership of a senior judge. These recommendations reflect the view that the provision of external and independent review is central to the role of tribunals. In response, in 2004, a government White Paper promoted the development of a new approach to administrative justice, in order to strengthen access to redress within the administrative justice field.[34] Two years later the larger tribunal systems were transferred from their parent departments such as the Department for Work and Pensions (for the Appeals Service, now Social Security and Child Support Appeals) and Department of Health (for the Mental Health Review Tribunal) to the newly created Tribunals Service.

In addition, the Tribunals, Courts and Enforcement Act 2007 acts upon a 'logic of judicialisation'[35] with a radical reform of the tribunal system. The Act restructured the existing tribunal jurisdictions into a two-tier model, the First-tier tribunal and the Upper Tribunal, which has now absorbed over thirty individual tribunals in addition to taking on a number of new jurisdictions.[36] The establishment of the Upper Tribunal brought a welcome rationalisation of the confused network of appeal routes which tribunal claimants had to negotiate under the present law, and the introduction of a common set of procedural rules across the tribunal system, as proposed by Leggatt, has been a strong unifying element of tribunals.

The majority of tribunals' adjudication process involves the resolution of disputes between (typically) citizens and the state arising out of

---

[34] See the government's response to the Leggatt review in the White Paper, 'Transforming Public Services: Complaints, Redress and Tribunals', Cm 6243 (2004). The problems of access to redress in this field have been illustrated by Hazel Genn's 2006 Report, 'Tribunals for Diverse Users' (DCA Research Series 1/06, Department for Constitutional Affairs, London, 2006); see also the Consultation Paper No. 187, 'Administrative Redress: Public Bodies and the Citizen', 3 July 2008; T. Cornford, 'Administrative Redress: the Law Commission's Consultation Paper' [2009] PL 70.

[35] P. Cane, 'Judicial Review in the Age of Tribunals' [2009] PL 479, conclusion. See, for an overview of tribunals, W. Wade and C. Forsyth, *Administrative Law*, 10th edn (Oxford University Press, 2009), ch. 24.

[36] See Annex 1 for a relevant chart; Tribunals, Courts and Enforcement Act 2007, ss. 3 and 7. The jurisdictions of these tribunals are organised into 'chambers' within the Upper First-tier Tribunal and the Upper Tribunal with a senior judicial leader (Chamber President) for each Chamber. There are still some tribunals outside the scope of that reform, such as the Parking and Traffic Appeals Service (Parking Adjudicators), for practical reasons mainly, relating to the complexity of the organisation.

administrative decision making.[37] There are, therefore, two sets of institutions performing administrative adjudication: courts have inherent jurisdiction via judicial review while tribunals have selected statutory jurisdiction. Judicial review is of last resort, with courts discouraging applicants who have a choice between review by a tribunal and review by a court, from opting for the latter. Thus, courts, as of last resort, remain a necessary component of the administrative justice system.

The Tribunals and Courts Enforcement Act 2007 also created the role of Senior President of Tribunals, whose task it is to 'lay before Parliament matters concerning tribunal members and the administration of justice by tribunals'.[38] The Senior President is concerned with high-level matters while Tribunal and Chamber Presidents are responsible for the day-to-day administration of their chamber or tribunal. They work closely with the Chief Executive of Tribunals, particularly on the budget; perhaps due to being historically located within the administrative branch of the government, tribunal judges have a tradition of working closely with tribunals' administrators. Tribunal representatives are also closely involved in judicial governance.[39] The Senior President of Tribunals is nonetheless responsible to the Lord Chancellor and is required to report to him.[40] He is required to cover matters in relation to relevant tribunal cases, and the Annual Report produced in 2012 details the 'interesting cases' and the 'use of judicial review powers' for various chambers, thus drawing attention to changes or tensions in the substance of the law in a way that goes beyond the report presented from time to time by the Lord Chief Justice.

The 2007 Act also substituted for the previous Council on Tribunals a new Administrative Justice and Tribunals Council, with lay and legal members (lay members forming the majority), and the Parliamentary Commissioner for Administration a member *ex officio*. It is a permanent advisory body whose duty it is to keep under review the administrative justice system as a whole, and the tribunal organisation and procedure.[41]

---

[37] G. Richardson and H. Genn, 'Tribunals in transition: resolution or adjudication?' [2007] PL 2007 119; C. Harlow and R. Rawlings, *Law and Administration*, 2nd edn (London: Butterworths, 1997).

[38] Tribunals, Courts and Enforcement Act 2007, sch. 1 para. 13.

[39] The Senior President attends the Judicial Executive Board as a full member, and the Judges' Council. There is a Tribunals Committee of the Judges' Council, which includes representatives of the First-tier judges and members, nominated through the Tribunal Judges' Forum. Tribunal judges are also represented on the Judges' Council committees.

[40] Tribunals Courts and Enforcement Act 2007, s. 43.

[41] Tribunals, Courts and Enforcement Act 2007, sch. 7.

It is meant to be more influential than the previous Council.[42] A draft order abolishing the new Council, however, has now been laid before Parliament under the Public Bodies Act 2011.[43] The Public Administration Select Committee and the Justice Select Committee have questioned the resources and expertise of the Ministry of Justice to take on some of the Council's functions, but to no avail.[44] In particular, the Justice Select Committee rightly suggests that 'greater accountability to ministers is not appropriate in this instance because of the extent to which the administrative justice and tribunal system deals with disputes between the citizen and the executive'.[45]

3.8 It has been suggested that the persistence of the division of administrative jurisdiction between tribunals and the High Court might be explained by the long-held view that in certain areas and on certain issues, only judges of superior courts have the status to stand up effectively to central government.[46] But one may point to the presence of High Court judges in the tribunal system: in 2012, the heads of three out of the four chambers in the Upper Tribunal were High Court judges. This introduction of the post of 'tribunal judge' has increased the flexibility in deploying judges, allowing bridges between the court and the tribunal systems. One may recall that the unified tribunal system's aim, under the Leggatt review, was to acquire 'a collective standing to match that of the Court System and a collective power to fulfil the needs of users in the way that was originally intended'.[47] Indeed, the Upper Tribunal has a supervisory function of the principles developed under the various specialists jurisdictions, and it is seen as having the potential to be a force of administrative justice.[48] It is a 'superior court of

---

[42] Wade and Forsyth, *Administrative Law*, 782.

[43] Draft Public Bodies (Abolition of Administrative Justice and Tribunals Council) Order 2013, 18 December 2012, see s. 11(1) Public Bodies Act 2011.

[44] Justice Committee, 'Eighth Report, Scrutiny of the draft Public Bodies (Abolition of Administrative Justice and Tribunals Council) Order 2013' (March 2013); Public Administration Committee, 'Twenty First Report of Session 2010–12, Future oversight of administrative justice: the proposed abolition of the Administrative Justice and Tribunals Council', HC 1621 (February 2012); Justice Committee, 'Fifth Report of Session 2012–13, Draft Public Bodies (Abolition of Administrative Justice and Tribunals Council) Order 2013', HC 927 (January 2013).

[45] Justice Committee, 'Eighth Report, Scrutiny of the draft Public Bodies (Abolition of Administrative Justice and Tribunals Council) Order 2013' (March 2013), para. 25.

[46] Cane, 'Judicial Review'.   [47] Leggatt, 'Review of Tribunals', para. 8.

[48] It has limited statutory review jurisdiction under Tribunals, Courts and Enforcement Act 2007, ss. 15–17; see A. Leggatt, 'Review of Tribunals', para. 6.32; T. Buck, 'Precedent in

record'[49] and in 2011, the Supreme Court ensured that, though strictly defined, judicial review would be available against unappealable decisions of the Upper Tribunal, thus clarifying some essential features of the relationship of the Upper Tribunal with the higher courts.[50]

C. Prosecutors

3.9 There is still a much greater distance between prosecutors and the judiciary in England than in some continental countries, where both are seen as arms of the state and may be trained for their roles at a very early stage of their careers. Some major developments reflect the growing power of public prosecutors, however, and create the possibility of tension with the judiciary. England did not even have a professional public prosecutorial service in the 1970s. The office of the Director of Public Prosecutions existed but he only had the power to consent (or not to consent) to prosecuting certain types of cases under statute and to advising on particularly sensitive cases that might be referred to him. For the main part, the police would instruct solicitors, who would then instruct counsel, about cases which they thought should be prosecuted. By virtue of the Prosecution of Offences Act 1985,[51] the Crown Prosecution Service was set up with the task of making final charging and prosecution decisions in relation to all cases with which the police previously dealt. By late 2012 the Director of Public Prosecutions had some 7,000 staff working nationally in distinct areas, dealing with around one million prosecutorial decisions each year, a tenth of which result in prosecutions. Once employed by the Crown Prosecution Service – as opposed to remaining independent counsel who may simply be instructed by the Crown Prosecution Service to advise on individual

---

Tribunals and the Development of Principles' (2006) 25 CJQ 458; Wade and Forsyth, *Administrative Law*, 781; R. Carnwath, 'Tribunal Justice – a New Start' [2009] PL 48; E. Laurie, 'Assessing the Upper Tribunal's Potential to Deliver Administrative Justice' (2012) PL 288.

[49] Tribunals, Courts and Enforcement Act 2007, s. 3(5).

[50] *R (Cart)* v. *UT* [2011] UKSC 28; *Eba* v. *Advocate General for Scotland (Scotland)* [2011] UKSC 29; see also *R (Jones)* v. *First-tier Tribunal (Social Entitlement Chamber)* [2013] UKSC 19; E. Laurie, 'Assessing the Upper Tribunal's Potential to Deliver Administrative Justice' (2012) PL 288.

[51] Prosecution of Offences Act 1985, s. 1(1); A. Sanders, 'Prosecutions in England and Wales' in J.-P. Tak (ed.), *Tasks and Powers of the Prosecution Services in the EU Member States*, Vol. I (Nijmegen: Wolf Legal Publishers, 2004).

cases or to present them in court – they are, unlike judges, civil servants, and so must follow and apply internal policies.

Crown prosecutors are appointed on account of legal aptitude and experience though some non-legally qualified case workers are employed by the Crown Prosecution Service too. Training is provided on CPS policies upon appointment. The decision to prosecute must be taken in the light of the duty to drop cases which are likely to fail, with the aim that fewer cases would come to court only to be stopped by the judge for lack of evidence. A first Code for Crown Prosecutors was promulgated in order to ensure consistency across the service and, since then, the Crown Prosecution Service has bound itself only to prosecute a case which it thought it was more likely than not to prove in court and the prosecution of which could be said to serve the public interest.[52] It is often said too that the role of the prosecutor is to seek just outcomes, not to achieve convictions at all costs.[53] This can affect the way in which cases are presented in court – prosecutors should alert the court to authorities that favour the defendant if they appear to have been overlooked – and there remains a prohibition on arguing for a particular form of sentence upon conviction.

It is the police who take the initial decision to investigate offences and to arrest suspects. Once the decision to prosecute has then been taken by a Crown prosecutor on the basis of evidence supplied by the police, the fate of the defendant is mainly in the hands of the judiciary. This is evident at the outset, when the defendant is charged, because he is then summoned to appear at the magistrates' court and it is they – not the police or the prosecutor – who decide whether the defendant shall remain at liberty pending trial, and if so, under what conditions. Consideration of this distinction led to the Supreme Court case of *Assange*[54] in 2012, which concerned the procedural steps that must be satisfied in England in order to extradite a suspect to another European country under the European Arrest Warrant. The Extradition Act 2003 only

---

[52] See now the sixth version of the Code (February 2010).

[53] Para. 2.4 of the Code provides that 'Prosecutors must always act in the interests of justice and not solely for the purpose of obtaining a conviction' and, under para. 3.5, 'Prosecutors must make sure that they do not allow a prosecution to start or continue where to do so would be seen by the courts as oppressive or unfair so as to amount to an abuse of the process of the court.' On the 'quasi-judicial' and 'quasi-executive' responsibilities of the public prosecutor, see J. Rogers, 'Restructuring the Exercise of Prosecutorial Discretion in England' (2006) 26 OJLS 775.

[54] *Assange v. The Swedish Prosecution Authority (Rev 1)* [2012] UKSC 22.

permitted the extradition where the request from the other country had been approved by a 'judicial officer' in that country, and the question was whether a public prosecutor (in Sweden, in this case) could be said to be regarded as a 'judicial officer' for the purposes of the English legislation. The Supreme Court held by a 5:2 majority that the Swedish Prosecutor was a judicial authority, because it is common on the Continent for the public prosecutor to assume a judicial role in deciding such important matters as detention before trial; the English Act should be read with this common understanding in mind, having regard to practice in the other member states.[55]

3.10 After charge, the prosecutor's core decisions relate to deciding who should be charged with what offence. The prosecutor may still decide to add or to drop some charges. It is rare for the courts to entertain judicial review of a decision to prosecute, reasoning that this would involve satellite litigation and that defendants can generally be expected to 'make their point' at the criminal trial itself.[56] Irregularities by the prosecutor may more conveniently be challenged as an abuse of process in the criminal court, when the trial starts. This may occur if, for example, the prosecutor has reneged on a promise, but it will not succeed if the defendant simply wishes to argue that there was no public interest in the prosecution. It is settled law that even if the judge considers the case to be trivial and unworthy of the attention of the courts, he may not stay the case merely on account of his own disapproval or contrary view of the public interest. If he were to have this power, then juries might start to entertain the (arguably, prejudicial) notion that any case which is put to them for adjudication does have the approval of the judge as well as the prosecutor.[57]

The judiciary is not involved in plea bargaining, that is, where the defendant may indicate a willingness to plead guilty to a lesser offence than one for which he has been charged, in return for a more serious charge being dropped, before the trial starts.[58] But after the defendant has

---

[55] However, the two dissenters thought that, in the absence of any provision defining the term, the interpretation of 'judicial officer' in an English Act of Parliament had to be read in accordance with its ordinary English meaning, which precluded the validity of authorisation by a public prosecutor.

[56] *R v. Director of Public Prosecutions, Ex parte Kebeline and others* [1999] UKHL 43.

[57] *DPP v. Humphreys* [1977] AC 1.

[58] The judge may, however, elect to give the defendant an indication of the maximum length of sentence he would receive if he were to plead guilty, *R v. Goodyear (Karl)* [2005] EWCA Crim 888.

formally pleaded guilty or not guilty to a particular charge, control of the case passes altogether from the prosecutor to the court. Charges can only be withdrawn, added or amended with the approval of the court.

3.11 Two possible sources of tension between the public prosecutor and the judiciary may arise from prosecutorial decisions not to prosecute 'in the public interest'. First, the prosecutor may be thought to be usurping the role of the judiciary if he considers some arguably serious cases not to be worthy of prosecution. With this in mind, the Code for Crown Prosecution cautions that, even if the public interest assessment seems finely balanced, it may be prudent to prosecute and to allow the judge to decide what weight should be given in sentencing to the various mitigating factors that may be present. Yet the advent of conditional cautions in the Criminal Justice Act 2003 has encouraged prosecutors to divert cases of some seriousness from the courts, by offering the defendant a condition of being cautioned (and thus, a condition of not being prosecuted instead) if they consider that the condition in question might meet the sort of outcome which the judge or magistrate would have wanted. This may include payment of a financial penalty as a condition for avoiding prosecution in the courts. It is assumed that, where the defendant accepts a penalty by way of conditional caution, the right to a fair trial under Article 6 ECHR is not breached because the defendant thereby waives his right to an independent tribunal. The extent of conditional cautioning may be questioned; the Divisional Court has, on judicial review, quashed a decision of the Crown Prosecution Service to administer a conditional caution on the basis that the offence was so serious that any decision short of prosecution was irrational.[59]

The second source of tension may come from decisions by prosecutors effectively to decriminalise certain acts by not prosecuting them 'in the public interest', even though the law laid down by the courts clearly holds that the alleged acts are criminal. In the leading case in England[60] it was held that if the Director of Public Prosecutions is minded not to prosecute minor cases of assisted suicide in the public interest then he must openly declare his policy so that others may make informed decisions about their own prospects of being prosecuted, should they choose to offend. It is not clear how influential this case will be; it was decided on

---

[59] R (Guest) v. Director of Public Prosecutions [2009] EWHC 594 (Admin).
[60] R (Purdy) v. Director of Public Prosecutions [2009] UKHL 45; J. Rogers, 'Prosecutorial Policies, Prosecutorial Systems, and the Purdy Litigation' [2010] Crim LR 543–4.

the basis that assisted suicide itself engages the victim's right to a private life under Article 8 ECHR. But it may influence a culture whereby many parts of the criminal law will need to be studied according to two sources – the substantive law as declared by the judges, and the policy decisions of the Crown Prosecution Service regarding certain types of criminality because these decisions will signify in greater detail the likelihood of prosecution in practice.

Another source of tension comes from the Attorney General's duty to superintend the discharge of the duties of the Director of Public Prosecutions, the Director of the Serious Fraud Office, and the Director of the Revenue and Customs Prosecutions Office[61]; he also oversees the functions of the Director of Public Prosecutions for Northern Ireland. The Attorney General, however, may face a fundamental conflict of interest in deciding whether or not to pursue a prosecution in the public interest. By convention, and in order to guard against the risk of 'instrumentalisation of criminal justice', the Attorney General acts independently of the government in making his decision.[62] In practice, this convention, like all constitutional conventions, ends by those involved just ceasing to respect it. It is arguable that the current convention fails to support the political independence of the administration of justice: the perceptions of a lack of independence and of political bias risk an erosion of public confidence in the office.[63] Thus, public controversy followed the decision to drop a Serious Fraud Office investigation into allegations that Saudi officials were bribed to win an order for a British arms firm. The media speculation was that the Attorney General changed his mind about his decision whether or not to prosecute as a direct result of political pressure from Downing Street.[64]

One may doubt whether it would be appropriate that an Attorney General (as a member of the executive) should have the legal right to stop a prosecution, for the same reason that it can be abused. The need for

---

[61] Prosecution of Offences Act 1985, s. 3(1); Attorney General's Office, 'Protocol between the Attorney General for England and Wales and his Prosecuting Departments' (July 2009), paras. 2.2–2.4, 2.6 and 4.3.

[62] J. Spencer, Evidence 106, HC Constitutional Affairs Committee, 'Constitutional Role of the Attorney General. Fifth Report of Session 2006–07' (HC 306, 2007).

[63] HC Constitutional Affairs Committee, 'Constitutional Role of the Attorney General', para. 54.

[64] See, on this subject and others (such as the 'cash for honours' investigation and allegations of political pressure to amend legal advice on the war in Iraq), HC Constitutional Affairs Committee, 'Constitutional Role of the Attorney General'.

reform of the role and responsibilities of the Attorney General was highlighted by the House of Commons' Constitutional Affairs Committee:
'Allegations of political bias, whether justified or not, are almost inevitable
given the Attorney General's seemingly contradictory positions as an
independent head of prosecutions, his or her status as a party political
Prime Ministerial appointment, and his or her political role in the formulation and delivery of criminal justice policy.'[65]

D.   Court estate

3.12 Quality of justice relates partly to the services provided by court staff in
terms of reception or waiting areas etc. The lack of building maintenance
has been a problem[66] and in 2003 the Judge's Council reminded the
government of the already urgent problems which were not being addressed
because of a lack of resources, citing leaking roofs in courts across the
country, and the fact that the Commercial Court was very poorly housed.
A brand new Commercial Court opened in December 2011 in London,
encompassing the Chancery Division of the High Court, the Admiralty and
Commercial Court, and the Technology and Construction Court.

The principle of local justice is an important one and access to justice
within reasonable travelling distance is essential. In a context of financial
cuts, the principle of efficiency of resources seems to prevail. Estates
integration, with magistrates' courts and county courts sharing premises,
or rationalisation has been pursued in order to lower running costs by
merging and closing courts, on the ground that this was disposal of
underused or outdated courthouses. Thus in December 2010 the closure
of ninety-three magistrates' courts and forty-nine county courts and the
merger of various local justice areas were announced, with the first courts
closing in April 2011. The move was presented also as an opportunity to
reinvest for modernisation in other magistrates' and county courts. To
date, 129 courts have closed.

An efficient use of judicial resources is, however, relevant to the
principle of access to justice. To that purpose the Crime and Courts Bill
2012 creates a unitary County Court and a unitary Family Court.[67]

---

[65] HC Constitutional Affairs Committee, 'Constitutional Role of the Attorney General',
      para. 56.
[66] Lord Chief Justice, 'The Review of the Administration of Justice in the Courts' (HC 448,
      2008), pp. 48–50.
[67] Crime and Courts Bill 2012, cl. 17.

In effect, it lifts the geographical boundaries on county courts, allowing for a better allocation and transfer of cases between court centres. It also provides for a maximised use of judicial and administrative resources in the courts, as the new courts will sit at various locations, and will operate in a way similar to the way in which the High Court and the Crown Court operate. While this should reduce waiting times, it is likely to limit the local presence of county courts, as they become hearing centres with reduced court staffing. District judges will be based in trial centres and deployed to smaller courts as necessary. It also builds on pilot projects with centralised telephone contact with the county courts, identifying the most common queries and thus addressing the customer needs more effectively and efficiently.[68]

The judiciary have supported the reform in principle and practice, with judges supervising work at the centres. Moves to increase e-working, and the ability of parties to conduct business electronically must be encouraged.

II. Judicial figures with administrative roles

3.13 The long-standing perception of the judiciary as a collection of individuals rather than a collective entity explains the rather informal governance structure of the judiciary, traditionally based upon the idea that individual judges in their judicial capacity must be free from any interference. In practice, however, there has always been a sense of hierarchy with an oversight of the administration of justice This hierarchy became more and more apparent as the judiciary grew in size and the senior judges gradually expanded their administrative responsibilities. The rushed announcement of the separation of powers between the judiciary and the Lord Chancellor meant that no one was given much time to anticipate the needs created by the transfer of a vast range of responsibilities to the Lord Chief Justice under the CRA. We examine, in this section, how the existing positions of leadership within the judiciary absorbed the delegations of responsibilities from the Lord Chief Justice arising from the CRA. The Lord Chief Justice is assisted by the Judicial Executive Board, a small cabinet with the general responsibility for judicial administration. The Senior Presiding Judge acts as a point of liaison between the judiciary, the courts and government departments,

---

[68] HMCS Annual Report and Accounts 2010–11, HC 1281, p. 10.

and oversees the work of Presiding Judges. The Presiding Judges and the Family Division Liaison Judges and Chancery Supervising Judges have a general oversight of the courts' administration on the circuits, while the Resident and Designated Civil and Family Judges also provide leadership to the judiciary within their court centre or group of courts. The Judges' Council is a sounding board rather than an institution of governance,[69] but must be mentioned here for its influential working parties. The Senior President of Tribunals is at present a separate office and will be briefly considered.

A.   The leadership from the Lord Chief Justice

3.14 The CRA transferred the role of head of the judiciary from the Lord Chancellor to the Lord Chief Justice, who is chosen by a specially appointed committee convened by the Judicial Appointments Commission. Under the CRA, the Lord Chancellor is responsible for the administrative functioning of the courts, while the Lord Chief Justice has responsibility for the judicial function of the courts, which comprises the deployment of individual judges, their welfare, training and guidance, and the judicial business of the courts (including the allocation of work within the courts). The Lord Chief Justice shares responsibility with the Lord Chancellor for the provision of the complaints and disciplinary system for the judiciary.[70]

A 'quiet revolutionary step' has been the 'mini-Concordat', whereby the Judicial Office for England and Wales was created to support the Lord Chief Justice and other members of the senior judiciary in their administrative – and constitutional – role. The Judicial Office builds on the pre-existing small private offices of the Lord Chief Justice, the Master of the Rolls and President of the Family Division. It has regularly grown in size since it was established in 2006, as the professionalisation of the judiciary develops further and the administrative responsibilities of

---

[69] Bell, *Judiciaries within Europe*, 322.

[70] The Lord Chief Justice exercises these responsibilities through the Judges' Council and the Judicial Executive Board, a committee that comprises senior members of the judiciary. The Mt. Scopus Standards, like the IBA Standards, support the shared responsibility model as the best approach for the administration of lower courts in parliamentary systems of government, see Mt. Scopus, paras. 2.13 and 2.14. It is not appropriate for the executive to be involved or to have responsibility over judicial matters or judicial functions, see Mt. Scopus, paras. 2.9, 2.12.

the judiciary keep on expanding.[71] Thus, when Lord Philips became Lord Chief Justice in 2005, he had one person on his staff, against seventy people when he left in 2008. As noted by one interviewee, the CRA was a shock to most people in that respect too. The Judicial Office now supports the Senior President of Tribunals too.

3.15 The Judicial Office is currently divided into groups reflecting the key functions assumed by the Lord Chief Justice: a first group relates to Strategy, Communications and Governance; a second to Human Resources for the Judiciary (created in October 2011, with the transfer of some judicial human resources functions from the Ministry of Justice to the Judicial Office); the Judicial College (replacing the Judicial Studies Board) forms the third group; Corporate Services constitute a fourth. Resources are agreed with the Permanent Secretary of the Ministry of Justice. A fifth group is concerned with senior judicial support through Private Offices and Jurisdictional Teams. The Judicial Office includes administrators, legal advisers and communication or human resources experts. A sixth function was acknowledged with the addition of the Office of Judicial Complaints to the Judicial Office in 2011.

The function of communication is key to the Judicial Office, as the Lord Chief Justice is responsible for representing the views of the judiciary to Parliament, to the Lord Chancellor and to ministers connected to the administration of justice generally.[72] This marks the formal separation of the judiciary from the executive; one may wonder how, in the past, the Lord Chancellor's Office dealt with the judiciary wanting to circulate views that may have been critical of the government through its Press Office (as it was then known). The Judicial Office also ensures good internal communications within the judiciary.

B. The Judicial Executive Board

3.16 Although, until 2005, the general responsibility for judicial administration lay formally with the Lord Chancellor, in practice the Heads of Division of the High Court[73] took responsibility for the assignment of judges to various duties. They were also responsible for the orderly

---

[71] Lord Chief Justice, 'The Judicial Studies Board Lecture 2010', Inner Temple (17 March 2010).
[72] Judicial Office, 'Judicial Office Business Plan 2013–2014'; see below, paras. 8.12 and 8.15–8.18.
[73] The Master of the Rolls, the Vice-Chancellor of the High Court (now known as Chancellor of the High Court) and the President of the Family Division.

running of the scheduling of cases (the cause lists). The Lord Chief Justice would also maintain close contacts with the Presiding Judges of the circuits in order to deal with matters affecting the divisions of the High Court. There were informal meetings between the Heads of Division, and the Judicial Executive Board created in 2005 derives from those informal meetings. They progressively included the Deputy Chief Justice, the Vice-President of the Queen's Bench Division, the Deputy Heads of Family and Civil Justice, the Judge in Charge of Modernisation and the Senior Presiding Judge. There were no regular meetings but the meetings solved numerous issues, such as filming court proceedings and orders restricting the reporting of proceedings. They would also be the place to discuss appointments to the High Court and Court of Appeal, in parallel with regular meetings with the Lord Chancellor on judicial appointments.[74]

The Judicial Executive Board meets monthly and comprises ten members: the Lord Chief Justice, the Heads of Division (The Master of the Rolls, the President of the Queen's Bench Division, the President of the Family Division and the Chancellor of the High Court (the revised title of the Vice-Chancellor)), the Vice-President of the Queen's Bench Division, the Chairman of the Judicial College, the Senior President of Tribunals, the Senior Presiding Judge and the Chief Executive of the Judicial Office. As a supervisory board, it enables the Lord Chief Justice to make policy and executive decisions. It is a small cabinet where policy is made on issues such as judicial deployment, appointment to non-judicial roles or appointments criteria. It also manages the relationship with the executive, with HMCTS and with Parliament, and approves, in agreement with the Ministry of Justice, the budget for the Judicial Office, which provides the administrative support for the Judicial Executive Board.

C. The leadership from senior judges

3.17 The engagement between judges and the courts' administrative staff goes back to 1971, when a centralised administration of justice was introduced.[75] Two (sometimes three) High Court judges were appointed on each circuit to have a general oversight of the courts' administration, as a constitutional safeguard of the position of judges on the circuits.

---

[74] Lord Mackay, 'The Lord Chancellor in the 1990s', inaugural Mischon Lecture at University College London (6 March 1991), para. 28.
[75] See below, para. 3.32.

These judges are now known as Presiding Judges.[76] They manage the deployment of individual judges and the judicial business of the courts (including the allocation of cases on their circuit), for the Crown Court, the High Court outside the Royal Courts of Justice and the county courts.

As the Lord Chief Justice gained new responsibilities under the CRA, Heads of Divisions and the Presiding Judges have accordingly expanded theirs, supported by the newly created Circuit Judicial Secretariats. They assist the Lord Chief Justice in discharging his responsibility for general supervision of judges, in relation to welfare and guidance (facilitating mentoring, training or guidance on career development) and discipline. They also have responsibility for the deployment and the welfare of district judges (magistrates' courts). Finally, they also advise the Senior Presiding Judge on the needs for judicial appointments below the level of the High Court.

The Senior Presiding Judge, appointed from the Lord or Lady Justices of Appeal, oversees the work of Presiding Judges. He or she acts as a point of liaison between the judiciary, the courts and government departments and is also a board member of HMCTS and thus the overarching link between the Administrative Court staff and judges. A Deputy Senior Presiding Judge, appointed from High Court judges now assists him. It is no coincidence that this position was created after the CRA, in response to the increased workload of the Senior Presiding Judge. We were told that the Senior Presiding Judge currently spends 90 per cent of his time on administration, away from court sittings. This is for a limited period of three years, as it would be, in the words of one interviewee, unpopular among the judiciary to spend more time effectively as a civil servant.

3.18 Family Division Liaison Judges and Chancery Supervising Judges have similar responsibilities for the Family and Chancery jurisdictions to those of Presiding Judges, though they are accountable to the Head of the Queen's Bench division and the Head of the Chancery Division respectively. The appointment of those managerial judges is largely a matter of who happens to be available at the time a vacancy opens up. The position requires a substantial number of days away from sitting in court, and it is not necessarily perceived as a promotion. Interviewees presented this responsibility as a substantial imposition, and a former Presiding Judge mentioned a minimum of two hours daily spent on administrative tasks while she was acting as a Presiding Judge.

---

[76] Courts and Legal Services Act 1990, s. 72. There are two Presiding Judges per circuit and they serve for a term of four years.

3.19 Resident and Designated Civil and Family Judges, under the overall responsibility of the Presiding and Family Division Liaison Judges, also provide leadership to the judiciary within their court centre or group of courts. They are in charge of the allocation and despatch of the business of the court, the deployment of judges and they deal with matters relating to welfare and guidance (facilitating mentoring, training or guidance on career development). They liaise with the Circuit/Regional Director and Area Director from HMCTS to discuss issues such as staff appointments[77] and numbers, budgetary and accommodation issues, deployment and sitting days, the timeliness of and accuracy in the drawing up of orders.

Resident Judges of the Crown Court similarly deal with the monitoring of various matters: the volume of work coming into court, the trials that are not heard when listed, the delays and the disposal rates for trials; the efficient use of jury service (a matter obviously specific to their court); on the one hand, witnesses who are called to testify but in the end are not required and, on the other hand, the amount of time such witnesses have to wait before being called.[78]

3.20 At all levels, these managerial judges are expected to work in collaboration with courts' managers to improve the efficiency and economy of the system. They need adequate administrative support, as emphasised by the Lord Chief Justice in 2008.[79] While there are reports of improvement since then, some have further questioned the replication of tasks between the Ministry of Justice and the judiciary.

D.   The Judges' Council

3.21 The Judges' Council was set up under the Judicature Act 1873 and continued to function until 1981. It was chaired by the Lord Chancellor and all the judges of the Supreme Court were members. The then Lord Chief Justice, Lord Lane, set up a new Judges' Council in 1988, chaired by the Lord Chief Justice, with an exclusive membership of the more senior judges. It was set up with the purpose of marking the separation of the judiciary from Parliament, specifically from the House of Lords, which

---

[77] In particular the appointment, transfer or removal of the court manager, listing officer, diary manager and case progression officer at the court or courts for which they are responsible.
[78] Lord Chief Justice, 'The Review', para. 5.35.   [79] Ibid., para. 4.11.

was a traditional forum for judges to express their views. The Judges' Council's composition and structure was further renewed in 2002 and 2006.[80] It acts today as an eighteen-member body representing the views and interests of all parts of the judiciary, including the Magistrates' Association and tribunals. It is still chaired by the Lord Chief Justice. The Lord Chief Justice and the Senior Presiding Judge of the UK Supreme Court serve *ex officio*; the usual period of membership for the other members is three years. There are no direct elections to the Council. Each level of the judiciary has its own association or council[81] where elections are held and the officers of those associations or councils (or their delegates) serve on the Judges' Council.

Though the English judiciary lacks any union activity, the Judges' Council traditionally transmits the collective views of the judiciary. It played a substantial role in negotiations between the Lord Chief Justice and the Lord Chancellor on the Concordat. It informs and advises the Lord Chief Justice and has discussions with the Lord Chancellor in relation to the financing of the courts[82] and other issues relating to the judiciary as a whole, such as judicial welfare and the promulgation and updating of guidelines on judicial conduct. It also publishes an annual report. It is separate from the Judicial Appointments Commission, although it also selects the three judicial members of the Commission.[83]

The Judges' Council is particularly effective through its working groups, such as, e.g., a working group on performance and efficiency in the operation of the courts, which allow judges to influence the development of the law and of the judicial institution. To a great extent, it is a sounding board rather than an institution of governance,[84] and this justifies its wide membership. It is unlikely that the English will follow the Spanish and French models of judges' associations based on political allegiance,[85] however the diversity of activity between judges at different

---

[80] Thomas LJ, 'The Judges' Council' [2005] PL 608.

[81] The Council of Circuit Judges, the Association of District Judges and the Magistrates' Association, the Association of District Judges, the Forum of Tribunal Organisations, the Council of Appeal Tribunal Judges.

[82] Under para. 24 of the 2004 Concordat, the Council meets with the Chief Executive of Her Majesty's Court Service (now HMCTS) to provide judicial input on resources.

[83] CRA, sch. 12, para. 7(7).   [84] Bell, *Judiciaries within Europe*, 322.

[85] These are more like their German counterparts as voluntary associations with some interest in professional education, see Bell, *Judiciaries within Europe*, 322. In 2004 the Council became a member of the European Network of Judges' Councils, an organisation set up 'to promote judicial independence and to analyse and exchange information on issues of common interest such as case management, judicial conduct and judicial functions'.

levels may require structures additional to the Judges' Council to channel views more effectively and indeed, a High Court Association has recently been created.

III.   The judicial partnership with HMCTS

3.22 The engagement between the administrative staff from HMCTS and the judiciary pre-dates the CRA, though the current terms of governance of HMCTS are the result of the conflict that arose following the creation of the Ministry of Justice in 2007. It was clear in 1971 that the 'antiquated'[86] system for criminal trials had to be reformed, and a unified Court Service for all courts other than the magistrates' courts and House of Lords and a centralised administration of justice were introduced under the Courts Act 1971. The small secretariat of the Lord Chancellor was converted into a department of state employing around 10,000 civil servants. The Court Service became an executive agency of the Lord Chancellor's Department in 1995. It was, in 2005, replaced by Her Majesty's Courts Service (HMCS),[87] which took over the unified management of the criminal, family and civil courts, as agreed under the 2004 Concordat. One interviewee described the creation of HMCS as 'trouble avoidance' from the government in shifting responsibilities to an agency. HMCS also gained responsibility for the administration of the magistrates' courts.[88]

The Ministry of Justice then became responsible for criminal justice, prisons and penal policy, three areas formerly within the remit of the Home Office. It also took responsibility for courts services and legal aid, previously within the remit of the Department for Constitutional Affairs. As a result, the Lord Chancellor has to balance the cost of maintaining prisons with the courts budget. This concern led senior judges, during 2007, to negotiate with the government for greater autonomy over the

---

[86] G. Lane, 'Judicial Independence and the Increasing Executive Role in Judicial Administration', in S. Shetreet and J. Deschenes (eds.), *Judicial Independence: The Contemporary Debate* (Leiden: M. Nijhoff, 1985), p. 525.

[87] Courts Act 2003, s. 2(1); Framework Agreement dated 1 April 2005. Some have argued that the change was aimed primarily at improving criminal justice, A. Reeves, *The Path to Justice: A Review of the County Court System in England and Wales* (Brighton: Emerald Publishing, 2006), p. 80.

[88] Until then, the circuit courts only managed the Crown Court and magistrates' courts committees managed magistrates' courts. The Courts Act 2003 abolished the magistrates' courts committees.

disposal of the resources for the administration of justice, with dual leadership over HMCS (now HMCTS) as a result.[89] The partnership structure adopted for HMCTS also explains why judges today are managers of the judicial process. The purpose of a more expedient, effective and efficient handling of court cases arises partly from the competition between the Ministry of Justice and other departments for its budget, and partly from the liberalisation of services and the reduction of the public sector in England and Wales as in many states, which led to pressures on the judicial process to abide by economic performance standards.[90] But it has also gained growing acceptance from the judiciary under the steer from the Council of Europe and the European Court of Human Rights, which assert the importance of a more efficient handling of judicial business as a way to strengthen the rule of law in Europe.

A. The Court Service

3.23 The objectives of HMCTS include providing the supporting administration for a fair, efficient and accessible courts and tribunal system; supporting an independent judiciary in the administration of justice; and continuous improvement of performance and efficiency across all aspects of the administration of the courts and tribunals.[91] In practical terms, HMCTS provides the support necessary for the day-to-day business of the courts and tribunals. It deals with the operation of court facilities and the treatment of court users, and provides the administrative system, the staff and the infrastructure (IT, buildings). It is similar to a special agency for the courts such as that in Spain or Sweden.[92] Judicial governance thus operates within the HMCTS framework. The Lord Chancellor remains under the duty to provide the infrastructure supporting the administration of justice,[93] and the Chief Executive of HMCTS is under a duty to ensure that all of its activities are in accordance with that agreement.

---

[89] Her Majesty's Courts Service Framework Document, Cm. 7350 (2008).

[90] R. Jagtenberg and A. De Roo, 'From Traditional Judicial Styles to Verdict Industries Inc', in N. Huls, M. Adams and J. Bomhoff (eds.), *The Legitimacy of Highest Courts' Rulings* (The Hague: TMC Asser Press, 2009), p. 301.

[91] Her Majesty's Courts and Tribunal Service, Framework Document 2011, Cm 8043 (2011).

[92] J. Bell, 'Sweden's Contribution to the Governance of the Judiciary', in M. Andenas and D. Fairgrieve (eds.), *Tom Bingham and the Transformation of the Law. A Liber Amicorum* (Oxford University Press, 2009), p. 221.

[93] Courts Act 2003, s. 1.

Prior to the Concordat, there is evidence of some formal structures where judges and civil servants worked together: the IT board created in 2001 on which a judge of the Court of Appeal served as the 'Judge in Charge of Modernisation', is the first example of a close working relationship between civil servants and senior judges, with its frustrations and achievements.[94]

3.24 There was once a long-standing dispute between the Parliamentary Ombudsman and the Lord Chancellor's Department (as it was then) as to whether the Parliamentary Commissioner was competent to review allegations of maladministration against court staff. It was argued that the courts were outside its jurisdiction, as a separate and independent body. Unlike his predecessor Lord Hailsham, however, Lord Mackay did not object to the scrutiny of his department by the Parliamentary Ombudsman, or the Parliamentary Home Affairs Committee. The Courts and Legal Services Act 1990 clarified that court staff actions were within the remit of the Parliamentary Ombudsman, unless they were under judicial instruction.[95] The Parliamentary Ombudsman noted in 2002, however, that it could be difficult to distinguish between an administrative and a judicial action.[96]

Her Majesty's Inspectorate of Court Administration was created in 2005 and abolished in 2011.[97] The Inspectorate, though sponsored by the Ministry of Justice, provided an independent review of the administration of the Crown Court, county courts and magistrates' courts, but was not to 'inspect persons making judicial decisions, or exercising any judicial discretion'.[98] It sought to contribute to the improvements in performance and service provision to users. The government justified its abolition by the fact that the landscape in which the Inspectorate operated has changed considerably since its inception in 2005, and that HMCTS now has robust audit methods and management information processes in place, which negates the need for independent inspection. External audit by the National Audit Office completes the scrutiny of HMCTS.

---

[94] Brooke LJ, 'Courts Modernisation and the Crisis Facing our Civil Courts', 7th ILAS Annual Lecture (24 November 2004).

[95] Courts and Legal Services Act 1990, s. 110.

[96] Parliamentary Ombudsman, Annual Report 2000–2001, HC 5 (2001–2002), p. 38.

[97] Public Bodies Act 2011, sch. 1.

[98] Her Majesty's Inspectorate for Court Administration, 'Annual Report 2006–2007' (2007), p. 9.

3.25 On 1 April 2011, Her Majesty's Courts Service and the Tribunals Service were brought together into one integrated agency, Her Majesty's Courts and Tribunals Service.[99] Some interviewees described it as a 'Leviathan'. The integrated agency has led to some financial savings and to a reduction in staff numbers, as part of the cuts in public expenditure in all parts of the public sector. Since 2011 HMCTS has been responsible for managing all courts (including the magistrates' courts) and tribunals, except the UK Supreme Court. The Supreme Court has its budget provided by the Ministry of Justice, but it has operational autonomy.[100]

B.   Dual leadership

3.26 The Ministry of Justice funds HMCTS and the Lord Chancellor reports to Parliament on the administration of justice and spending. The argument stands, therefore, that the budget for the courts may partly depend on sentencing policy – the more people in prisons, the less money there is for the courts. Additional pressure comes from expenditure on legal aid and legal services. The judiciary has now, however, secured a position of greater influence in the administration of the court system and its resourcing. This acts upon, to some extent, the transfer of the role of head of judiciary from the Lord Chancellor to the Lord Chief Justice under the CRA.[101] The traditional consultation process has been put on a basis that reflects the new constitutional settlement, so that the judiciary has a greater voice in the strategic decision making on the administration of the courts.

---

[99] Her Majesty's Courts and Tribunal Service, 'Framework Document 2011', Cm 8043 (2011). The Court Service has had 4 management structures over about 10 years. Some 10 years ago, one would talk about circuits. Then the court management structure was divided into counties in order to reduce management costs. Four years later, there are regions with 3 counties included per region and one regional manager. The administrator in charge of circuits is currently known as the regional administrator.

[100] The judicial committee of the House of Lords drew its budget from that of the legislature. Under CRA, s. 50(1)(b) the Lord Chancellor must ensure that the UK Supreme Court is provided with such resources as he thinks are appropriate for the Court to carry on its business; the Supreme Court Chief Executive must ensure that the Court uses those resources to provide an efficient and effective system to support the Court in carrying on its business, CRA, s. 51. The Chief Executive of the Court must carry out his or her functions in accordance with any directions given by the President of the Court, CRA, s. 48(4).

[101] CRA, s. 7.

The operation of the HMCTS (as it is now) is no longer controlled by the Ministry of Justice but it is not fully autonomous either.[102] HMCTS is jointly accountable to the Lord Chief Justice and the Lord Chancellor on matters of its governance, financing and operation. The Lord Chancellor and Lord Chief Justice jointly agree the aims, priorities and funding for HMCTS.

Day-to-day governance of the HMCTS is delegated to a board with an independent chairman. Senior judges sit as board members of HMCTS,[103] ensuring that the Chief Executive and directors are aware of concerns from the wider judiciary, including judicial salaries and the needs of the courts. The monthly meetings of the board deal with issues such as performance of HMCTS against targets, the budget or the needs of the estate, which all affect and depend to some extent on the way the business of the courts is conducted by the judiciary.

The Concordat aimed for an early engagement of the judiciary with the (today) Ministry of Justice and HMCTS 'at strategic level, including issues on resource plans and bids'.[104] This provides a necessary safeguard to the interests of the judiciary, as the Lord Chancellor stopped acting as head of the judiciary. Judges and the Ministry of Justice need to cooperate to get the best possible outcome: judges are responsible for delivering an efficient public service of justice and the executive finances the judicial branch of government and the public service of justice.[105] The reality of such cooperation varies within each court, depending on the level of interactions and the mutual understandings between judges and HMCTS staff as to what is needed to achieve justice in an efficient and economic way. Thus, the report on the Inspection of Leeds Magistrates' Court, published in March 2008, highlighted administrative failings for which judges had no responsibility.[106] In practice, judges have had a greater input into defining the Court Service's objectives since 2005. Thus, in 2006, HMTCS aimed for justice being done 'as quickly as possible'. Since

---

[102] The budget is still allocated by Parliament to the Ministry of Justice and then by the latter to HMCTS.

[103] The responsibilities of the board include giving advice and, where necessary, direction to HMCTS (having been given direction by the Lord Chief Justice and Lord Chancellor); ensuring a strong working relationship between staff of HMCTS and the judiciary at all levels and ensuring that the planning, performance and financial management of the agency is carried out efficiently and effectively and with openness and transparency, Framework Document 2011, para. 4.1.

[104] Concordat, para. 20.   [105] Lord Chief Justice, 'The Review', 16.

[106] See Criminal Justice Joint Inspection, 'Leeds Magistrates' Court. A Report on the Resulting and Warrant Withdrawal Procedures Used at Leeds Magistrates' Court' (March 2008).

2008, a 'timely access' to justice has been the preferred formula. This reflects a greater awareness of the tension between speedy delivery of justice and the quality of justice itself.

C. Shared administration in question

3.27 In many judicial systems, resources for the judicial system are under the responsibility of the executive and Parliament, on the ground that the executive ultimately decides on the allocation of resources, with the judiciary's involvement in the allocation process. But the full transfer of administrative responsibilities to judges has also been considered in England. In 2003 the Judges' Council argued for the running of the court system to be fully entrusted to the judiciary or to a body independent of the executive of which the judges are active members. Reference was made to the federal courts of the United States and to Australia, where the judiciary carry part of the responsibility for the running of the court system.[107] Similarly, in Ireland, Scotland or Denmark today, the administration of justice is separate from the executive and lies fully in the hands of the judiciary. Scotland must negotiate its budget directly from the Treasury. In all cases, an institutionalised separation of powers is argued for. However, while the Irish equivalent of HMCTS employs roughly 900 people, HMCTS employed 21,000 people in April 2011. It would seem difficult then to transpose that solution to the English judiciary.

At the heart of the discussion lies the provision of resources for the courts and judicial system. In the past, discussions between senior members of the judiciary and representatives of the Court Service and the Lord Chancellor would determine the allocation of resources for the administration of justice, and the Lord Chancellor's Department would then negotiate with the Treasury. The results of these discussions would be added up to find the total public expenditure. The allocation of resources to the administration of justice was then one part of overall government expenditure. Attempts to limit public expenditure led to a change in the process, as an overall total was agreed first with the Treasury before being divided between ministries. This system created an 'even more intense'[108] competition for resources between the

[107] 'Judges' Council Response to the Consultation Papers on Constitutional Reform' (November 2003), para. 57.

[108] Lord Mackay, The Administration of Justice (London: Stevens & Sons/Sweet & Maxwell, 1994), Hamlyn Lectures, p. 20.

ministries. In addition, following the public management revolution in the 1980s, the Lord Chancellor's Department applied 'The Financial Management and Value for Money' regimes to courts, introducing budgetary discipline and efficiency monitoring. The Lord Chancellor's Office thereby gained some of the aspects of a conventional ministry of justice.[109]

Lord Browne-Wilkinson expressed his concern, in 1987, that judges be appropriately involved in budget setting.[110] He called for greater judicial autonomy over the use of the resources made available for the administration of justice. However, unless it is taken to its extreme, that is, there are 'no courtrooms, staff, books, pay, not even a palm tree' (per Lord Mackay), views differ on when questions of resources fetter the independence of the judiciary.[111] The Lord Chancellor has responsibility for the provision of all kind of resources, whether financial, material or human resources.[112] Whether this duty is legally enforceable is a question that has not arisen yet, though at least one judge interviewed thought that extremely insufficient resources would lead to the 'atomic option' of deferring the matter to Parliament for its ultimate say.[113]

Lord Phillips was also concerned, in 2011, that the UK Supreme Court's independence could be undermined by having its annual budget dependent on what the Ministry of Justice could be persuaded to give each year.[114] The Lord Chancellor, Kenneth Clarke, responded that the Supreme Court had to be accountable for its budget. Accountability or effectiveness in using resources and judicial independence go hand in hand, as stated by Lord Chief Justice Judge in 2010: 'Times change, and however they do change, for the purposes of the judiciary, our independence and effectiveness must be reinforced.'[115] There is some basis to Lord Phillips's concerns, however. Following the decision of *Cadder* v. *HM Advocate*, in which the UK Supreme Court held that questioning detained suspects without access to legal advice before a police interview breached Cadder's rights, the Scottish Justice Secretary threatened to end

---

[109] In terms of public expenditure and manpower, the Ministry of Justice is one of the largest government departments, with about 76,000 people in February 2012 (including those in the Probation Service, and 21,000 employees of HMCTS).

[110] N. Browne-Wilkinson, 'The Independence of the Judiciary in the 1980s' [1988] PL 44, 53; Lord Ackner, *The Erosion of Judicial Independence* (John Stuart Mill Institute, 1997).

[111] Lord Mackay, *The Administration of Justice*, 15.   [112] Concordat, para. 19.

[113] See also HL Committee on the Constitution, 'Meetings with the Lord Chief Justice and Lord Chancellor (2010–11)', 89, Q11.

[114] See CRA, s. 50.   [115] Judicial Office, 'Business Plan 2010–2011'.

the Scottish funding for the Supreme Court, stating 'He who pays the piper, as they say, calls the tune.'[116]

The 'corporate independence' of the Court is currently under discussion between the government and the Supreme Court. This follows a call from Lord Phillips, in his capacity as Law Lord, for the Lord Chancellor to relinquish his right to appoint the UK Supreme Court Chief Executive.[117] The Chief Executive would be accountable to the UK Supreme Court President and to Parliament only.[118] This would increase the separation of powers from the executive without diminishing accountability to Parliament.

Lord Philips's speech may also reflect a concern about the loyalty of the court administrators. The majority of judges interviewed praised the civil servants working in courts, but some noted that some civil servants came to courts with an agenda. They were sometimes referred to as 'delivery managers' and it was suggested that they should not be appointed for life. Yet, good interactions between court administrators and judges are necessary for the partnership between the executive and the judiciary to work effectively: the Senior Presiding Judge, the resident judges and the court administrators need to trust each other to work together.

3.28 The call for greater autonomy illustrates a growing discrepancy between the traditional understanding of judicial independence as individual independence of the judge, and the reality of judicial adjudication being considered as a public service for the enforcement of rights.[119] Under the latter conception, judges are subject to accountability requirements of efficiency and transparency similar to any other public service. The challenge lies in strengthening judicial self-governance as a means towards independence, while enhancing judicial accountability. Indeed,

---

[116] *Cadder v. HM Advocate* [2010] UKSC 43.

[117] CRA, s. 48(2) provides that the Lord Chancellor must appoint the Chief Executive after consulting the President of the Court; *Hansard*, HL, col. 649 (4 December 2012), cols. 1488–1500 (18 December 2012). Discussions between the government and the UK Supreme Court are now concluded. The Crime and Courts Bill will amend the CRA 2005 so that the president of the UK Supreme Court, rather than the Lord Chancellor, is made responsible for the appointment of the Chief Executive. It will be no longer necessary for the Chief Executive to agree the staffing structure of the court with the Lord Chancellor; see *Hansard*, HL, col. 835 (25 March 2013).

[118] CRA, s. 54; Lord Falconer, *Hansard*, HL, col. 1237 (14 December 2004).

[119] Cf. the call from the Council of Europe for greater autonomy of the judiciary in the administration of justice: Council of Europe, 'Allegations of Politically-Motivated Abuses of the Criminal Justice System in Council of Europe Member States', Resolution 1685 (2009), para. 5.4.1.

the benefits of having judges chairing a body that many judges today describe as a Leviathan seems questionable. It would be a change in the constitutional arrangements, and an even greater imposition of administration on judges. Additional resources would be needed to support the Lord Chief Justice.[120] In such configuration, the judiciary would go to Parliament to negotiate its budget and would be directly involved in the intense political discussions about resources. This does not seem desirable. Besides, although judicial independence and judicial self-government are often linked, the latter does not necessarily follow from the former. Judicial independence does not in itself require full institutional autonomy, even though it requires checks and balances. Thus, the judiciary must have a satisfactory input into the decision-making process and that judicial input must be set on a statutory basis in order to preserve separation of powers and judicial independence. But the Ministry of Justice's involvement also constitutes one check upon court efficiency, and it prevents the corporatism that might arise from a fully insulated judiciary.

D.   Performance management as 'quality management'

3.29 The potential impact of HMCTS on the conduct of judicial business may be gleaned from the 'Lean Programme', introduced in 2008 as a pilot in two courts in Liverpool and Birmingham, and now at the heart of how HMCTS operates, looking for efficient and cost-effective services. Described as a 'working simpler program',[121] it is based on the *European Foundation for Quality Management Excellence* model (EFQM), a non-prescriptive framework for driving organisations towards excellence in performance. EFQM was adopted from the inception of HMCS. Activities and court procedures are timed and timeliness targets can be set as a result. The Lean Programme aims at introducing greater flexibility in the use of resources, so that staff can be borrowed from one court to help an overburdened court; or funding for additional sitting days can be allocated where necessary to reduce the increasing workload and reduce delay.[122]

---

[120] I. Judge, 'The Judicial Studies Board Lecture 2010', Inner Temple (March 2010).

[121] P.M. Langbroek (ed.), 'Quality Management in Courts and in the Judicial Organisations in 8 Council of Europe Member States', CEPEJ (2010/3), CEPEJ Studies no. 13, p. 33.

[122] HMCS, 'HMCS Annual Report and Accounts 2010–11' (HC 1281, 2011), p. 9.

This 'fundamental change to [HMCTS] working culture'[123] can also be seen as 'quality management', with a greater transparency and accountability of HMCTS, and a greater consistency of courts services across England and Wales as a consequence.[124] Quality is understood in a quantitative way, with the measure of the resources and time needed for numerous courts' activities. The core procedural activities of the court justify this approach: filing a case, procedures to manage and hear cases, and procedures to pronounce judgment.[125] Statistics deal with the workload, capacity and time taken for cases to come to trial. The Key Performance Indicators in 2010–11 are thus setting targets against, for example, the proportion of days overall jurors sit on trial during their period of service before the Crown Court; the reduction of the average time taken from charge to disposal for adult charged cases before magistrates' courts; community penalties within a certain period of time following the relevant failure to comply with a court order; increasing the volume of defended small claims completed otherwise than by a hearing (settlement); the percentage of care and supervision cases that achieve a final outcome for the child; maintaining the 'very satisfied' element of the HMCTS court user survey above a certain level.[126]

The performance standards are agreed by the Lord Chancellor and the Lord Chief Justice though the HMCTS Board. They do not bind the independent judiciary in deciding individual cases, but, as outlined above,[127] judges have been involved in the administration of justice since the Courts Act 1971 with the creation of the position now known as Presiding Judge. They are expected to be managers of the judicial process, and they account to the Lord Chief Justice for their managerial position. Presiding Judges and Resident Judges scrutinise performance statistics for their court centres and work with them to find ways of improving performance.[128]

---

[123] Ibid.

[124] F. Contini and R. Mohr, *Judicial Evaluation: Traditions, Innovations and Proposals for Measuring the Quality of Court Performance* (Saarbruken: VDM Verlag, 2008), pp. 36–42.

[125] G.Y. Ng, *Quality of Judicial Organisation and Checks and Balances* (Antwerp: Intersentia, 2007), p. 133.

[126] HMCS Annual Report and Accounts 2010–2011, pp. 12–13, cf. L. Glanfield and T. Wright, *Model Key Performance Indicators for NSW Courts* (Sydney: Justice Research Centre, Law Foundation of NSW, 2000).

[127] Paras. 3.22 and 3.27.

[128] Lord Chief Justice, 'The Lord Chief Justice's Report 2010–2012', para. 36.

3.30 Importantly, a proper monitoring and evaluation of the courts' standards depends upon an accurate and transparent system of data collection. Statistics are thus expected to be crude. In 2008, however, the Lord Chief Justice noted the lack of data in some parts of the business, and some inconsistency between the figures collated and published centrally and locally held data.[129] The accuracy has improved, with statistics now available in a systematic manner on criminal and civil courts, the judiciary and some associated offices in England and Wales, such as the Judicial Committee of the Privy Council.

Since 2005 the courts' performance has been monitored monthly by Courts Boards.[130] The information is discussed at local level, and at regional level, by the HMCTS Performance Committee, consisting of area performance managers, chaired by a regional director. It reports to the HMCTS Executive Committee, itself accountable to the HMCTS Board, which includes judges in its membership. The statistics are perceived by the judiciary as a way to assess future needs for judges, staff and court buildings,[131] with practical tools being developed, such as a new system for determining the optimum staffing required to meet the demand in courts and therefore determine the financial allocation to each court; or another system for forecasting the number of court sitting days.[132]

3.31 The centralisation of judicial administration, however, has meant that public servants from the Lord Chancellor's Department are involved in the listing as judges themselves, to the great concern of Lord Lane in 1997:

> The bureaucratic machinery for running the courts is so huge that it is in danger of swamping (albeit unconsciously) the proper powers of judges. We are in danger of allowing the administrative tail to wag the judicial dog. Inevitably, as the bureaucratic machine becomes larger and larger, those who operate it will cease to have, as the staff did in times gone by, loyalty towards the judge and the court; they will unconsciously have their first loyalty to what they regard as the service which is the bureaucratic machine ... However in that division of loyalty, however understandable it may be, lies the danger. It is essential that judges remain in control of their courts, in control of their listing, in control of the allocation of judges. Any serious encroachment by the executive on this territory can spell the end of independence.[133]

---

[129] Judiciary of England and Wales, 'The Lord Chief Justice's Review of the Administration of Justice in the Courts' (March 2008), p. 25.

[130] Courts Act 2003, s. 5(5).   [131] 'The Lord Chief Justice's Review', 25.

[132] HMCS, 'HMCS Annual Report and Accounts 2010–11', 6.

[133] Lane, 'Judicial Independence', 528.

The concern for loyalty appeared as the operation of the Court Service gradually became shaped by the new public management revolution, as noted above.[134] Under the new public management principles, performance management is key, and so are the values of efficiency, effectiveness and economy of the judicial system. Yet the search for efficiency in the administration of justice, if it improves productivity in some ways, can affect the way judges work, beyond a more managerial role being attached to the judicial function. We mentioned in our introduction Lord Bingham's comment that 'many judges resented what they perceived as an administration breathing down their necks treating them as pawns on a bureaucratic chess board'.[135] The Lord Chancellor himself had acknowledged those tensions by inviting, in November 1994, the Chief Executive of the Court Agency and the Agency staff to work closely with judges, as well as consulting them before any major in-year change in resource allocation was decided. This was to be formally resolved with the shared leadership structure in the administration of HMCTS previously discussed.

The quality of court staff is one of several elements fundamental to the effective and efficient operation of the courts. According to the Lord Chief Justice in 2008, the 'overall picture . . . is one that does give rise to concern'.[136] The pressure on staff to perform well created low morale and a high turnover of staff was noted at the time.[137] Interviews with judges have also emphasised the importance of good interactions between judges and staff for a court to run efficiently.

3.32 The European Commission for the Efficiency of Justice (CEPEJ), a body created by the Council of Europe, has developed a 'checklist' for scrutinising the quality of their judicial process – presented as no more than an introspection tool for policy makers, court managers, court presidents, judges and other judicial practitioners.[138] It invites them to

---

[134] Note also Lord Woolf, *Access to Justice: Final Report to the Lord Chancellor on the Civil Justice System in England and Wales* (London: HMSO, 1996).

[135] Lord Bingham, 'Judicial Independence', Judicial Studies Board Annual Lecture (5 November 1996), pp. 67–8.

[136] Judiciary of England and Wales, 'The Lord Chief Justice's Review', 20.

[137] *Ibid.*, 22–3, 26.

[138] CEPEJ, 'European Judicial Systems Edition 2012 (2010 Data): Efficiency and Quality of Justice', CEPEJ Studies no. 18 (Strasbourg: Council of Europe, 2012). National models are also developed, e.g., the 'Quality model' of the Finnish Court of Appeal of Rovaniemi or the 'Rechtspraaq model' in the Netherlands; the scrutiny of the court workings was initiated in the United States with the creation of the *Trial Court Performance Standards*.

review, in particular, the management of activities ranging from the preparation of cases to the final decision making by a judge and its execution, for example the allocation of cases between judges, court hearings and case management itself. It also invites reflection upon the means available for the adequate operation of the courts, assessing whether sufficient financial resources are there to support the use of information and communication technology (court management information systems, electronic files, electronic data exchange, video conferencing).

The European checklist is premised on the ground that the administration of justice is not simply about delivery of a service; as a *sui generis* public service, justice produces social links[139] and individuals are entitled to demand an adequate level of protection for their rights, just as they are entitled to demand an adequate health or transport service. As for any other public service, then, good management is required for justice to be delivered.[140] The benchmarks for assessing the quality of the judicial process, however, are based upon quantitative factors that relate essentially to the resources used in terms of expenditure and staff numbers, and to the number of cases concluded and the processing time needed for handling and deciding cases. They do not apply to the judicial decision itself, and they do not reflect the complexity of cases and specialism of the law.[141] Does greater efficiency in quantitative terms necessarily lead to greater 'quality' of justice? The answer goes both ways. A speedier process supports better quality of justice – 'justice delayed is justice denied'. But efficiency constraints may equally have a detrimental impact on judicial behaviour: judges may become more strategic and, for example, rely to a greater extent on the facts as presented by the Crown Prosecution Service in order to gain time. Similarly, the development of alternative dispute resolution allows courts to deal more accurately with more complex cases but this assumes a consistent practice between courts of filtering cases through alternative dispute resolution. A fine

---

[139] CEPEJ, 'Checklist for Promoting the Quality of Justice and the Courts' (Strasbourg: Council of Europe, 2008), p. 2.

[140] Judicial adjudication has been argued to be a public service for the enforcement of rights, A. Zuckerman, 'Civil Litigation: a Public Service for the Enforcement of Civil Rights' (2007) 26 CJQ 1; H. Fix-Fierro, *Courts, Justice and Efficiency: A Socio-Legal Study of Economic Rationality in Adjudication* (Oxford: Hart, 2004); M. Fabri, J.P. Jean, P. Langbroek, H. Pauliat, *L'Administration de la Justice en Europe et l'Evaluation de sa Qualité* (Paris: Montchrestien, 2005).

[141] 'Lord Chief Justice's Report 2010–2012', para. 56.

tuning of these efficiency requirements is thus required for public confidence in the judicial process to be sustained.

IV.   Deployment, assignment and case management

3.33 Deployment and assignment are subject to the principle of internal independence, while case management illustrates the extent of the involvement of judges in an efficient judicial system.

A.   Deployment

3.34 Judicial deployment maximises the use of judicial resources in the courts and tribunals. The judicial business varies in volume and in the nature of cases brought before each court. It is therefore necessary to regularly review and modulate the number and identity of judges in each court, as they have different skills and different areas of knowledge, in order to ensure that cases can be brought to trial in the most effective and time-efficient manner.[142] Judicial deployment is also subject to the principle of internal independence. Transfer must be possible for the best administration of justice, but it cannot be unlimited or unchecked for fear that it may be exercised as a means of control over the judiciary: a judge should not be moved to another court for taking a decision that has created controversy, or fear that he would do so. We are not aware that this has happened in England. One safeguard for internal independence, however, might be provided by the dual leadership between the Lord Chief Justice and Lord Chancellor: this is where the Lord Chancellor may provide an independent yet authoritative view.[143]

The Lord Chancellor, in consultation with the Lord Chief Justice, sets the geographical and functional jurisdictional boundaries of courts.[144] The Lord Chief Justice is responsible for the posting and roles of individual judges within that framework.[145] He maintains some appropriate arrangements for the deployment of judges to courts and tribunals (subject to having regard to the responsibilities of the Senior President of Tribunals).[146] The transfer of power from the Lord Chancellor to the

---

[142] This is a matter of debate within the judiciary, see Judicial Working Group, 'Justice Outside London' (2006).
[143] J. Beatson, 'Reforming an Unwritten Constitution' (2010) 126 LQR 48.
[144] Concordat, para. 26.   [145] *Ibid.*, paras. 26–7 and 29–30.
[146] CRA 2005, s. 7(2).

Lord Chief Justice reflects the need for the head of the judiciary to deploy judges free from executive influence. Similarly, the Senior President of the tribunals assigns judges and members to the chambers of the First-tier Tribunal and Upper Tribunal.[147]

Deployment is equally a matter of efficiency of resources, and so real and effective consultation between the Lord Chief Justice and Lord Chancellor is required on this matter.[148] The Lord Chief Justice is responsible, after consultation with the Lord Chancellor, for determining which individual judge should be assigned to which division, circuit, district, or county court.[149] In practice, numerous statutes dealing with court jurisdiction specify which judicial office holders may sit in that court. The Vice-President of the Queen's Bench Division coordinates with the Heads of Division the deployment of High Court judges. He had done so in practice before 2005 but formally the deployment and transfer of judges was then for the Lord Chancellor. Senior judges can generally be transferred without their consent,[150] though a High Court judge can only be moved with his consent within one division or from one division to another.[151]

Below the High Court, the Lord Chancellor's power, prior to the CRA, was in practice exercised by the Court Service in consultation with Presiding Judges. The latter now have the responsibility for the deployment of circuit and district judges and, in practice, the circuit judicial secretariat consults judges and HMCTS on the needs of the courts in the circuit. The workload, sitting patterns, performance pressures and judges' preferences feed recommendations as to changes in deployment.[152] Interviewees emphasised that judicial deployment to courts was not

---

[147] Tribunals, Courts and Enforcement Act 2007, sch. 4.

[148] Concordat, para. 28.

[149] The introduction of a unitary County Court under the Crime and Courts Bill will reduce the role of the Lord Chief Justice in this respect, see Crime and Courts Bill 2012, cl. 17.

[150] Senior Courts Act 1981, s. 9(1) and (3).

[151] Senior Courts Act 1981, s. 5(2); a High Court judge's consent is not necessary for his assignment to sit in the Court of Appeal nor is a Lord Justice's consent necessary for his assignment to sit in the High Court. See also R.E. Megarry, *Miscellany-at-Law. A Diversion for Lawyers and Others* (London: Stevens and Son, 1956), p. 10 (transfer of Sir Ford North from the Queen's Bench Division to the Chancery Division). Until 1944 a judge could be transferred from one division to another at the executive's discretion, see the Supreme Court of Judicature (Consolidation) Act 1925, s. 4(2), as amended by the Supreme Court of Judicature (Amendment) Act 1944, 7 & 8 Geo. VI, c. 9, s. 1.

[152] Thomas LJ, 'The Judicial and Executive Branches of Government: a New Partnership?' (2006) 63 *Amicus Curiae* 3.

rigid: it is possible to move judges within one circuit but making changes from one circuit to another, for example from Leicester to Northampton, would be harder, given some practical implications for witnesses, for instance.

The senior district judge (Chief Magistrate) has responsibility for the deployment of district judges (magistrates' courts) and liaises with the senior judiciary and Presiding Judges on those matters – it is ultimately a delegated responsibility of the Lord Chief Justice.

The deployment of judges to particular levels of courts other than their usual level, as noted in the previous paragraph, is the responsibility of the Lord Chief Justice after consultation with the Lord Chancellor. A list of suitable judges, to be agreed with the Judicial Appointments Commission,[153] is drafted by the Lord Chief Justice, from which list the circuit judges and recorders can be selected to sit in the High Court. Outside this pool, the Senior President of Tribunals can also be requested to sit. The Crime and Courts Bill 2012 introduces some new flexibility in the deployment of judges across different courts and tribunals of equivalent or lower status,[154] thus bringing a clearer sense of mobility between courts and tribunals. Under the bill, circuit judges may act in the Court of Appeal (Criminal Division), under a process managed by the Judicial Appointments Commission in concurrence with the Lord Chief Justice.[155] High Court judges and Court of Appeal judges may sit at the Family Court and the county court in addition to the Crown Court where they can already be deployed.[156] Certain tribunal judges may sit in a magistrates' court; certain Crown Court and deputy district judges would be allowed to sit in an employment tribunal, and district judges and circuit judges could sit in the Employment Appeal Tribunal.[157] The Bill thus acts upon the unified structure of the tribunals system under the Tribunals, Courts and Enforcement Act 2007, by allowing for moves between the courts and tribunals systems. It creates a clearer sense of career progression within the judicial ranks, helping suitable judicial office holders to apply and be recognised. It is a noticeable step in

---

[153] As acknowledged in the Concordat (para. 39), there is a range of nominations to various posts, both permanent and temporary, which are very similar to deployment issues. For example, particular judges may be nominated to deal with specific areas of business, such as patents cases.

[154] Crime and Courts Bill 2012, cl. 19 and sch. 13.

[155] Crime and Courts Bill 2012, cl. 19.   [156] Crime and Courts Bill 2012, cl. 13 s. 1(1).

[157] Crime and Courts Bill 2012, sch. 13 s. 4(1).

supporting judicial career development, itself an important factor in increasing judicial diversity.[158]

3.35 Increased flexibility in judicial deployment to magistrates' courts had already been obtained under the Courts Act 2003, which allows district judges (magistrates' courts) to sit as Crown Court judges and gives judges of the higher courts all the powers of Justices of the Peace.[159] The Crime and Courts Bill 2012 enlarges the range of judges who have powers of Justice of the Peace to senior judges, certain tribunal judges, district judges and deputy district judges, as well as members of a panel of chairmen of employment tribunals.[160] This follows a research paper from the Ministry of Justice in 2011 which suggested that district judges could be deployed on the more complex, serious or lengthy cases (though defining those can be difficult) where their training and experience is an advantage.[161] There seems also to be data evidence, however, that district judges may be more likely than magistrates to use custodial sentences for comparable cases, so that any strategic deployment may influence the sentencing outcomes.[162]

3.36 The deployment of judges must be considered in relation to the number of judges. Until 1968 the number of judges at all levels was fixed by statute and could be increased or decreased by legislation only. Since the Administration of Justice Act 1968, the executive has control over the increase in the number of judges.[163] Consultation of the Lord Chief Justice is expected before the Lord Chancellor determines the overall number of judges required, including the number required for each

---

[158] Advisory Panel (Baroness Neuberger Chairwoman), 'The Report of the Advisory Panel on Judicial Diversity 2010', March 2010.

[159] Courts Act 2003, ss. 25–26, ss. 65–66; Senior Courts Act 1981, s. 8.

[160] Crime and Courts Bill 2012, sch. 13, s. 5(1).

[161] See the Lord Chancellor's Department Working Party (Lord Venne convenor), 'The Role of the Stipendiary Magistracy' (1996).

[162] Ipsos MORI, 'The Strengths and Skills of the Judiciary in the Magistrates' Courts' (London: Ministry of Justice Research Series 9/11, 2011), pp. 62–3; see the 'Response from the Judicial Policy Committee of the Magistrates' Association', January 2012.

[163] Senior Courts Act 1981, s. 2(4) (Court of Appeal); the resolution must be approved by Parliament. The Maximum Number of Judges Order 2008, Order 2008 No. 1777, increased the number of judges at the Court of Appeal from 37 to 38; for the High Court, see Senior Courts Act 1981, s. 4(4). There is no statutory maximum number for circuit judges; their number is to be determined by the Lord Chancellor with the concurrence of the Minister for the Civil Service: Courts Act 1971, s. 16. See, for district judges (magistrates' courts) and deputy district judges (magistrates' courts) Courts Act 2003, ss. 22–26. CRA, s. 23 regulates the number of UK Supreme Court justices.

division, jurisdiction and region and the number required at each level of the judiciary.[164] The number of divisions of the High Court can be reduced or increased by an Order in Council.[165] However, since the CRA, the executive no longer has discretion to fill vacancies at the level of the High Court and above: the duty falls to the Lord Chancellor unless the Lord Chief Justice indicates that he is happy to leave the vacancy unfilled.[166]

The Lord Chancellor's power to assign certain judges to sit beyond their retirement age or to continue hearing a specific case beyond their retirement has also been transferred to the Lord Chief Justice, with a requirement for the concurrence of the Lord Chancellor, since it may have significant implications for resources.[167]

The statutory cap on the number of judges at the High Court in particular is an important drive towards efficiency in deployment.[168] While there is no fear that the executive would attempt to pack the courts or otherwise use its control over the number of judges as a means of control over the judiciary, the combination of a capped number of judges and increasing administrative pressure is likely to make the judicial job less attractive, and one senior judge drew attention to the possibility 'that we create a job where we end up dead, diseased or too tired!'.

B.   Case assignment

3.37 Case assignment, or case allocation, is a judicial responsibility.[169] The Lord Chief Justice is responsible, after consultation with the Lord Chancellor, for deciding the level of judge appropriate to hear particular classes of case (including the issuing of Practice Directions in that regard).[170] In practice, the judge in charge of each court decides how and by whom each case will be heard, and district judges play a crucial role here. Thus, the Presiding Judges of the circuits have the overall

---

[164] Concordat, para. 29.   [165] Senior Courts Act 1981, s. 7.

[166] CRA, s. 77 (Court of Appeal), s. 68 (Lord Chief Justice and Heads of Division), s. 86 (High Court).

[167] Concordat, para. 42.

[168] The Maximum Number of Judges Order 2003, 2003 no. 775, increased the number of judges from 106 to 108. The Crime and Courts Bill 2012 provides for the existing statutory limits on the number of High Court judges and judges of the Court of Appeal to be calculated on the basis of full-time equivalents to take account of part-time working, Crime and Courts Bill 2012, sch. 12.

[169] Concordat, para. 36.   [170] Concordat, para. 37.

responsibility for listing on each circuit/region, allocating the work between judges or particular courts and deciding the priorities for hearing cases, listing cases before particular judges.[171]

The Lord Chief Justice also issues authorisations or 'tickets' to individual judges to hear specified cases or classes of cases at a certain court level.[172] This relies upon training or experience judges might have in a particular subject – thus a Crown Court judge can be 'ticketed' to try murder, rape and fraud cases, and similar procedures apply at the Technology and Construction Court. Having the appropriate ticket allows the judges to hear those specified cases in courts within their assigned geographic area, beyond their own court. Ticketing is a decision made internally within the judicial structure and without any external interference.

In England, the assignment is, in practice, made by the listing officer. One recurrent concern is to balance the caseload between judges; this takes the form of allocating cases to the judge available rather than weighting the case as can be done in some other countries. Listing reviews can happen in order to equalise work, introduce greater flexibility and reduce waiting time across the circuit in specialist courts in some areas.[173] In practice, the day-to-day listing is dealt with by listing officers from the Court Service (e.g., the Listing Officer in the Crown Court), who ensure that the various judges with the relevant tickets are available to hear cases. The decisions are made largely around time assessments – how long is the case going to be in the court diary and when it is going to start? The needs of the case – whether expert evidence is allowed, and the balance between, e.g., family and civil law cases – are also relevant factors for listing.

Another consideration at play is the principle of continuity, so that the same judge stays with the case: some judges will be sitting away on the

---

[171] Courts and Legal Services Act 1990, s. 9. Each circuit court centre has a resident judge, normally the senior judge, in charge of the criminal listing in the Crown Court, following guidance or directions issued by the Lord Chief Justice and by the Senior Presiding Judge – and subject to the supervision of Presiding Judges under para. IV. 33 of the Consolidated Practice Direction. In the Magistrates' Court, the judicial members of the Justices' Issues Forum for each area are responsible for determining the listing practice in that area.

[172] In relation to judges assigned to particular cases, the level of judiciary to which a judge belongs and his or her experience or specialisation ('ticketing') will determine the level or type of work he or she can undertake. Numbers, criteria and levels for the authorisation are decided by the Lord Chief Justice after consultation with the Lord Chancellor, Concordat, para. 38.

[173] Judiciary of England and Wales, 'The Lord Chief Justice's Review', 19.

circuit and may not be available in a timely manner, with a hearing being delayed as a consequence. Similarly, the case may also be delayed because the length of the case may have been underestimated by the listing officer, leading it to be adjourned and rescheduled. The shortage of space within courts may compound the delay. A judge who takes over a case from another is generally bound by any pretrial rulings already made by his predecessor.

Efficient listing is also an administrative priority. Listing officers are accountable for making the most efficient use of the courtrooms. The judge must actively manage cases to further serve the overriding objective of dealing with cases justly and at proportionate cost.[174] Listing is thus one area where managerial accountability and the integrity of the judicial process may clash. Indeed, HMCTS performance targets can have an impact on case listings because only certain elements of performance are measured. Thus, if a court is below its targets for small claims in civil litigation, a listings manager could file more small claims, causing a distortion in the overall disposal of all the cases. In practice, barristers might raise unhappiness with the judge about a particular listing, leaving the judge as arbiter, though it seems that many judges tend to back up their listing office.

3.38 The type of proceedings shapes the practice and responsibilities of judges and listing officers, as do case management or the availability of alternative dispute resolution. In criminal proceedings, where the accused stands trial depends partly on the type of offence he or she is accused of and their age. Lord Steyn clarified that fairness requires the court to consider a triangulation of interests in a criminal case, 'taking into account the position of the accused, the victim and his or her family, and the public'.[175] Prior to the 2005 Criminal Procedure Rules (set up following Lord Justice Auld's 2003 review of criminal courts), the practice and procedure in criminal courts were governed by some fifty sets of rules and almost 500 individual regulations. The Criminal Procedure Rules provide guidance on case management through the whole of the criminal process, thus providing greater consistency through courts.[176]

---

[174] Rule 1.1(1), Civil Procedure Rules 1998, SI 3132/1998, as amended by Rule 4, Civil Procedure (Amendment) Rules 2013, SI 2013/262 (L. 1); J. Sorabji, 'The Road to New Street Station: Fact, Fiction and the Overriding Objective' (2012) *European Business Law Review* 23, p. 77.

[175] *Attorney General's Reference No. 3 of 1999* [2000] UKHL 63.

[176] Courts Act 2003, s. 69(4). In 2010 the Committee began a practice of consolidation of the Rules every October, at the start of the legal year, with amendments made each April,

Judges then play an effective role in listing and exercise an extensive managerial role at the plea and case management hearing which takes place in every Crown Court case.[177]

In relation to tribunals, expertise, performance in existing judicial office(s), track record, potential and/or appraisal are relevant factors for assignment.[178] In general, the allocation of cases by the Tribunal President will follow the specialisation of judges. Specialisation by ticket is also a defining principle for case allocation within the tribunals. Priority is given to efficiency of listing:

> The power to assign between chambers and tribunals exists primarily to allow the work of the tribunals to be dealt with in the most efficient and effective manner possible. The starting point for this policy, and decisions made under it, is therefore business need – that is, the power to assign is to be used where the chamber or tribunal would benefit from the extra help which assignment can bring.[179]

In family proceedings and family court proceedings, where magistrates have a broad jurisdiction,[180] the Justice's clerks and legal advisers (formerly known as court's clerks) to the magistrates have a quasi-judicial role,[181] deciding in some cases whether cases are transferred up to the county court.[182] Before the Commercial Court, settlement rates are high and therefore the listing office will 'overlist' or overbook the Court, bearing in mind the substantial paperwork often required for cases coming before

---

in order to make the Rules predictable and to increase the modernisation of the criminal justice system, see 'Lord Chief Justice's Report 2010–2012', paras. 46–9.

[177] The Crown Court Manual, May 2005. The CPR apply to the criminal division of the Court of Appeal, the Crown Court and all magistrates' courts in England and Wales.

[178] Senior President of Tribunals, 'Assignment. Senior President's Policy Statement' (2009), para. 23. 'Assignment' is the statutory term used to describe the function of locating a judge or member within the tribunal structure by placing him or her in a chamber. 'Ticketing' is a non-statutory term used to describe the function of authorising a judge or member to undertake a defined category of judicial work within a chamber. 'Cross-ticketing' is an expression sometimes used to describe authorising a judge or member, who is ticketed to undertake work within one jurisdiction in a chamber, to undertake work in a different jurisdiction in that chamber: Senior President of Tribunals, Annual Report 2012, p. 32.

[179] Senior President of Tribunals, 'Assignment. Senior President's Policy Statement' (2009), para. 23; courts judges will come into the tribunals system if they bring some particular expertise not otherwise available, or which is not available at the right level, *ibid.*, paras. 4–5.

[180] Magistrates' Courts Act 1980, s. 65.

[181] Practice Direction (Justices: Clerk to Court) [2000] 1 WLR 1886.

[182] See, e.g., stage II of 'The Protocol for Judicial Case Management in Public Law Children Act Cases' (June 2003) (2003) 2 FLR 719.

the Commercial Court. For many years, insufficient courtroom space and outdated technology were also taken into account in listing.

Listing of cases to come before the Court of Appeal is marked by the large (and rising) number of applications for appeal made by litigants in person. Litigants in person generally take up more court time, both in case management hearings and at final hearings.[183] The lack of proper IT is also noticeable.

3.39 These informal rules contrast with the principles embedded in the German constitution.[184] Under that system, the heads of court make proposals for case assignment (and also for the allocation of judges within the court), but the actual decision is made annually by the local Judicial Council. The criteria established by that Council for case assignment are binding and heads of courts are liable, in principle, to disciplinary measures for not following them. The informal exchange of cases between judges in England is thus unacceptable in Germany. There the constitutional right to 'the legal judge' drives the management plan for the courts, rather than the value of efficiency of resources as in England.

The English flexibility, however, may be better seen as a structured discretion which takes into account factors others than the human resources issue. The clerk will undertake the distribution of cases, with the aim, in particular, of avoiding judge shopping as far as possible. Cases are allocated on a random basis at the UK Supreme Court, although either the President or Deputy President will sit on most cases and, in specialist areas, other judges with particular expertise may be selected. The difference between the German and the English approaches seems rather one of emphasis. The plans for case assignment reflect an emphasis on process in Germany, that is, the need to define the jurisdictional competence which shapes the right to a fair trial. In the common law tradition, the emphasis is on the trial itself, such that the judge conducting the hearing cannot generally leave the trial once a case starts. The English system of allocation could be abused in theory but this does not happen in practice. This illustrates a culture of trust within the

---

[183] Civil Justice Council (Working Group), 'Access to Justice for Litigants-in-Person (or self-presented litigants). A Report and Series of Recommendations to the Lord Chancellor and to the Lord Chief Justice' (November 2011).

[184] Article 101 I 2 Grundgesetz; M. Fabri and P.M. Langbroek, *Is There a Right Judge for Each Case? A Comparative Study of Case Assignment in Six European Countries* (Antwerp: Intersentia, 2007).

judiciary such that the values of impartiality and internal judicial independence are strongly internalised. The interviewees questioned on this matter did not see the need to display them through policies on case assignment similar to those adopted in Germany.

As we now consider case management, we should note that case management and listing are both organisational matters, however listing uniquely affects the autonomy of the judicial process. It must therefore remain under judicial control.

C. Case management

3.40 In 2003 Richard Susskind described management as 'anathema to the business of judging' for many judges,[185] because it imposed constraints, procedures and standards to which, it was thought, judges as independent and impartial arbiters should not be subject. One judge recalled in interview how judges would look at him 'with glazed eyes' when he would talk about 'managing' budget in the years 2000–07. Case management requires judges to work actively with parties to litigation in order to bring each particular case to trial in a speedy, cost-effective and just manner. Judges can be active in making sure that a case is not taking an unreasonable time. The introduction of case management in the civil justice system and, at a later stage, into criminal cases, following Lord Woolf's report on access to justice in 1996, was a major trigger for the change in attitudes and the greater involvement of judges in the administration of the justice system.[186] Also, in that year, section 35 of the Criminal Procedure and Investigations Act 1996 allowed judges to give pretrial rulings so that decisions on difficult points of law could then be appealed immediately, an improvement on the previous situation where the point could only be appealed, if at all, after the full trial had finished (further interlocutory appeals by the prosecution were introduced in the Criminal Justice Act 2003). Elsewhere, such as at the Commercial Court, it had long been recognised that the judges had a responsibility for the definition of the essential issues in a case before the trial.[187]

---

[185] R. Susskind, 'Management and Judges', in M. Saville and R. Susskind (eds.), *Essays in Honour of Sir Brian Neill: The Quintessential Judge* (London: LexisNexis UK, 2003), p. 53.

[186] A. Clarke, 'The Woolf Reforms: A Singular Event or an Ongoing Process?', in D. Dwyer (ed.), *The Civil Procedure Rules Ten Years On* (Oxford University Press, 2009), 33.

[187] Thomas, 'The Judicial and Executive Branches', 6.

The Judicial Studies Board recognised in 2004 that case management was a specific skill that might require training.[188] The increasing involvement of judges in the pretrial management of cases can be seen in other jurisdictions too, on both sides of the Atlantic. Thus a French report[189] highlighted in 1997 the need for a more efficient use of the courts, and a similar managerial trend can be seen in the United States.[190] Judges retain some flexibility in their management of the case under the Civil Procedure Rules, of the 'overriding objective of enabling the court to deal with cases justly'.[191] This allows for a suitable balance between the value of efficiency in the administration of justice and the value of procedural fairness, a balance necessary to sustain the public confidence in the courts. Case management aims to prevent abuse from the publicly funded court system but procedural fairness must be preserved, and the parties' perspectives are not to be distorted by the search for economic efficiency.[192]

3.41 The Senior Presiding Judge acts mainly to oversee a consistent approach between the courts on processes. By way of example, the scheme 'Criminal Justice, Simple, Speedy and Summary Justice' was launched in 2007 by the judiciary, in the magistrates' courts, where adjournments and delay often occurred. It aimed to reduce the number of unnecessary hearings in cases of low-level criminal activities (such as drink driving or burglary), and reduce the overall time taken for such cases to reach their conclusion.[193] This required the police, the Crown Prosecution Service, the courts and defence lawyers to work together to attain maximum efficiency. The project was extended up towards the Crown Court and into the youth criminal justice system. It is now followed up by a joint initiative, 'Stop Delaying Justice', led by

---

[188] Criminal Case Management Framework, July 2004.

[189] J.M. Coulon, *Réflexions et Propositions sur la Procédure Civile, Rapport au Garde des Sceaux* (Paris: La Documentation Française, 1997).

[190] A.T. Kronman, *The Lost Lawyer, Failing Ideals of the Legal Profession* (Cambridge, Mass.: The Belknap Press of HUP, 1993); O. Fiss, 'The Bureaucratization of the Judiciary' (1983) 92 YLJ 1442.

[191] CPR, r 1.1 (1), 1998, SI 3132/1998, as amended by Rule 4, Civil Procedure (Amendment) Rules 2013, SI 2013/262 (L. 1).

[192] See also H. Genn, *Judging Civil Justice* (Cambridge University Press, 2010), pp. 172–3: 'The post-Woolf judge in the civil courts is an active case manager [who must] balance values of efficiency, equality, expedition, proportionality and careful allocation of the scarce resources of the court.'

[193] Lord Chief Justice Judge, 'Summary Justice in and out of Court, The Police Foundation's Harry Memorial Lecture', speech given at Drapers' Hall, London (7 July 2011).

magistrates and district judges working together, which aims to ensure that trials are fully case managed at the first hearing and disposed of at the second hearing. It was also up to the Senior Presiding Judge to initiate schemes in 2010–11 to ensure that guilty pleas would be made at the earliest opportunity and early plea arrangements are now being rolled out nationally in courts across the country.[194]

In parallel, alternative dispute resolution mechanisms have been introduced to reduce the number of cases coming to courts. Judges can redirect litigants, after a first screening of their case, to an external mediator. This illustrates a global trend towards incitement or mandatory referral to mediation outside the courts, a trend also encouraged as a means to save costs to the justice system and the parties.[195] Alternative dispute resolution concerns the simple disputes, leaving the more complex cases to courts. Awareness about mediation as an alternative means of resolving family disputes is particularly emphasised; thus applicants for legal aid can be exempted from Family Mediation Information and Assessment sessions in certain circumstances only.[196] Lord Neuberger MR (as he was then) referred to 'the insidious idea that litigation is actually a bad thing; and that other, more consensual means of resolving disputes are necessarily good things'; alternative mechanisms such as mediation, with its emphasis on resolution rather than rights, 'cannot be the norm, or approach the norm'.[197] Access to court should remain the main event as a matter of fundamental right; people cannot be forced to mediate as a means of saving costs in the administration of justice.[198]

Interviewees pointed to the government's tendency to see the courts as businesses; and a concern about the cost of access to justice was tangible. In the context of this study, suffice it to mention that the Legal Aid, Sentencing and Punishment of Offenders Act 2012 enacted a series of

---

[194] HMCS, 'HMCS Annual Report and Accounts 2010–11', p. 9; Lord Chief Justice's Report 2010–2012, para. 37.

[195] Genn, *Judging Civil Justice*, 68.

[196] H. Genn et al., 'Twisting Arms: Court-Referred and Court-Linked Mediation under Judicial Pressure', Ministry of Justice Research Series 1/07 (May 2007). Another example would be the pilot scheme launched in 2012 to extend the Court of Appeal's mediation scheme to personal injury and contract disputes under a certain value, in order to avoid the extra costs and demands of a full Court of Appeal hearing.

[197] Lord Neuberger MR, 'Swindlers (including the Master of the Rolls?) Not Wanted: Bentham and Justice Reform', Bentham Lecture (2 March 2011), paras. 41, 43–4; Genn, *Judging Civil Justice*, 122–5.

[198] Genn, *Judging Civil Justice*.

recommendations made by Lord Justice Jackson in 2009, in his review of the costs of civil litigation. The abolition of the recoverability of a number of add-on costs (such as referral fees), for example, is expected to reduce costs and provide a more level playing field for litigation.[199]

3.42 Costs and delays are seen as paramount criteria of quality – or rather, lack of quality – of judicial proceedings. The speed and timeliness of the judicial process is a matter of right, with delays of judicial proceedings being legally relevant at common law and under Article 6(1) ECHR. In the criminal context, under Article 6(1) ECHR, the reasonable time requirement limits the state of uncertainty of the defendant, and a violation of the reasonable time requirement can occur in the absence of prejudice caused by trial or judicial delay. The length of the delay, the reasons given by the prosecutor for that delay and the efforts made by the accused to assert his rights are all relevant factors to determine whether the delay was 'unreasonable'. The remedy for a violation will not, however, be that the trial is stopped for abuse of process, unless irredeemable prejudice has been caused by the delay.[200] In the European Court of Human Rights' case law, the question, under Article 6(1) ECHR, whether the fairness of the trial has not been nor would be compromised by the delay in proceedings, is answered according to each case's circumstances.[201]

The House of Lords in *Porter* v. *Magill*[202] adopted a similar approach in civil proceedings. The right to a determination of a person's civil rights within a reasonable time does not require the complainant to show the prejudice caused by the delay. A lack of resources and chronic under-funding of the legal system generally cannot be an excuse for unacceptable delays, yet, as Lord Bingham explained, 'there is nothing in the Convention jurisprudence [that] requires courts to shut their eyes to the practical realities of litigious life even in a reasonably well-organised system'.[203] Thus some exceptional circumstances could justify an excessive lapse of time. Excessive delay can make a judicial decision unsafe and it may be unfair or unjust to let it stand, thus leading to a retrial.[204]

---

[199] Lord Chief Justice's Report 2010–2012, para. 70; Jackson LJ, 'Review of Civil Litigation Costs: Final Report' (Belfast: TSO, 2009).

[200] *Attorney General's Reference (No. 2 of 2001)* [2003] UKHL 68; *Attorney General's Reference (No. 1 of 1990)* 95 Cr App R 296.

[201] *Konig* v. *Federal Republic of Germany* (1978) 2 EHRR 170; *Deumeland* v. *Germany* (1986) 8 EHRR 448; *Spiers (Procurator Fiscal)* v. *Ruddy* [2007] UKPC D2.

[202] [2001] UKHL 67.   [203] *Procurator Fiscal* v. *Watson and Burrows* [2002] UKPC D1.

[204] *Cobham* v. *Frett* [2001] 1 WLR 1775; *Habib Bank Ltd* v. *Liverpool Freeport (Electronics) Ltd* [2004] EWCA Civ 1062; *Jervis* v. *Skinner* [2011] UKPC 2 (Bahamas).

The speedy administration of justice – or at least, one that is not unduly delayed – is thus a matter of right. It follows that judges should be active in drawing attention to unreasonable delays of which they are aware. In *CDC2020* v. *Ferreira*,[205] Brooke LJ addressed the procedural difficulties met by the appellant in seeking to file a notice of appeal. In that case, the Central London County Court's delays were prejudicial to the marketing of a small residential development. Lord Justice Brooke noted that the Central London County Court 'now has a bad reputation for misfiling documents and failing to record telephone messages'. He referred to the 'very high turnover of staff' and stated that 'HM Court Service professes itself unable, with the resources currently provided to it, to correct the position to any significant extent'.[206] Unusually, he also requested that a copy of the judgment be sent to the relevant director within HM Court Service and to the Master of the Rolls as head of Civil Justice, adding:

> Somehow a way must be found of ensuring that the Central London County Court provides a service of the quality that litigants in that court and their legal advisers, and the staff, lawyers and judges of the Court of Appeal should be entitled to expect from those whose business it is to serve the courts and the members of the public who use them.[207]

Delays, late pleas in criminal courts and adjourned trials in all the courts were highlighted by the Lord Chief Justice in 2008.[208] Of course, delays can sometimes be unavoidable, due to the complexity of some cases, with some lengthy pretrial proceedings or a prolonged preparation of criminal prosecutions on account of compliance with duties of disclosure; or because of the heavy workload of judges, and/or the justified absence of witnesses and other parties. Praising the 'true professionalism' of (now) HMCTS, the Lord Chief Justice emphasised the need for the increase in workload to be matched by increases in judicial and administrative resources.[209] In the current tight financial climate, that is not an approach that is likely to be adopted in the coming years. The emphasis is rather upon improvements in the timeliness of the court processes, by reducing the length of trials, the number of late guilty pleas and the number of unnecessary hearings.[210]

---

[205] [2005] EWCA Civ 611.   [206] *CDC2020* v. *Ferreira* [2005] EWCA Civ 611, para. 43.
[207] *Ibid.*, para. 45.
[208] Judiciary of England and Wales, 'The Lord Chief Justice's Review', 23, 27, 29, 34.
[209] *Ibid.*, 19–23.   [210] Lord Chief Justice's Report 2010–2012, paras. 36–7.

Delays in judicial proceedings are not normally attributable to the judge, but judges are very occasionally responsible for delays in then giving judgments. A strong judicial policy aims for a prompt delivery of judgments, with senior judges monitoring delays. All judges sitting in family disputes should deliver judgment within one month, and judges sitting in civil cases within two months. Judges must inform the Senior Presiding and Liaison Judges about any delay, and explain the reasons for it. Judgments which have been outstanding for more than three months are monitored by senior judges.[211] A grievance procedure is in place and the decision can be appealed on the ground of an unreasonable delay, as noted above, under Article 6 ECHR. We shall revisit this in our Chapter 5 on standards of conduct on the bench.[212]

Conclusions

3.43 Lord Woolf referred to 'a close working relationship' between the judiciary and the executive, 'a special quality of our justice system which, in the interests of the public, it is important to preserve'.[213] Their partnership is characterised by a system of consultation and joint decision making between the Lord Chief Justice and Lord Chancellor in a range of areas such as court management.[214] It is difficult to assess the partnership of the judiciary with the Ministry of Justice since it was not entered into at times of severe financial cuts across all public services. The idea that that Lord Chancellor 'insulated' judges from a political process of resources allocation' belongs to an era that was already long gone when the CRA came into force. The greater scrutiny in the light of the new public management values of effectiveness, efficiency and economy coincided with the growth in size (and budget) of the judicial system. It had already contributed to an increase in administrative responsibilities upon judges with a designated leadership role. This only made more visible the need for renewed mechanisms of accountability.

It is similarly challenging, or too early, to assess the impact of the financial cuts on the conduct of judicial business, though it seems that in times of crisis, IT, building maintenance and training are most likely to suffer.

---

[211] F. Gibbs, *The Times*, 10 February 2009.   [212] At para. 5.24.

[213] Thomas LJ, 'The Judicial and Executive Branches', 3.

[214] The Concordat was established following discussions between the Judges' Council, senior judges and the Department for Constitutional Affairs (DCA, as the Lord Chancellor's Department had been briefly rebranded).

The increasing difficulty courts experience in coping with caseloads is, in practice, a global trend, in both common law and civil law countries. In England, in an attempt to match demand and supply for judicial services, courts have been requested to do more with less. The search for performance and efficiency in the administration of justice applies across all aspects of the administration of the courts and tribunals, signalling that judges fall within this remit, provided that they are not concerned in their judicial capacity. This has resulted in the implementation of numerous standards, such as timeliness of a trial, which justify the measuring and monitoring of the judicial process with the aim of improving court efficiency. The management of the judicial process illustrates how the exercise of judicial responsibilities constitutes a daily interaction and engagement with HMCTS, which has set up a monitoring and evaluation system rather similar to those applying to many European judiciaries or to the Australian and Canadian judiciaries. A large amount of data on the day-to-day business of the courts supports HMCTS's framework for court administration, and this has helped to make courts more accountable, responsive and user friendly over a wide range of activities. It has led to a more formal structure for judicial governance. It also made clear, however, that judges had to be closely involved in the longer-term planning of the administration of justice, though some have suggested that the role of HM Treasury in the modernisation of courts could rather act as a brake on modernisation.[215]

Nevertheless, one may wonder whether, under the HMCTS regime, the judiciary is treated much differently from any executive agency. We noted the increased managerial responsibilities that some judges have in their division or circuit, relating to courts' caseload, deployment and the allocation of cases. Many of the judges interviewed believed that, though the current system did not emasculate (sic) them, it had had a profound impact on the judiciary as it endeavoured to reconcile the values of procedural fairness with efficiency and economy in the conduct of judicial business. While HMCTS sets out agency standards, senior judges have a duty to make an effective use of their mandate to propose standards or targets, in order to ensure the fine tuning of procedural fairness with efficiency and economy in the conduct of judicial business. The balance must be maintained between these fundamental values of the justice system, so that the focus on efficiency and performance

---

[215] H. Brooke, 'Courts Modernisation and the Crisis Facing our Civil Courts', 7th ILAS Annual Lecture (24 November 2004).

standards is not excessive. The managerial drive also requires vigilance as to the daily interactions between administrative and judicial actions. As observed with listing, court officials may be caught between their obligations as civil servants and their duty of loyalty to the judges who hear the cases.

England spends slightly less than average on courts, legal aid and prosecution services compared to other European countries,[216] yet quality of justice cannot be measured 'simply in terms of speed and cheapness, or by how many cases we can persuade to go elsewhere'.[217] Adequate resources to support the administration of justice must be seen positively, as the way to vindicate rights and enforce obligations through adjudication.

[216] CEPEJ, 'European Judicial Systems Edition 2012 (2010 Data): Efficiency and Quality of Justice', ch. 2, esp. p. 55.
[217] Genn, *Judging Civil Justice*, 76–7.

4

Judicial appointments

Introduction

4.1 In any system, the methods of appointment have direct bearing on both the integrity and independence of the judges. Weak appointments lower the status of the judiciary in the eyes of the public and create a climate in which the necessary independence of the judiciary is liable to be undermined. Similarly, political appointments that are seen by the public as not based on merit may arouse concern about the judge's independence and impartiality on the bench. The quality of judicial appointments depends upon the process and standards applied by the appointing authorities, yet every appointment system has its limitations. It is difficult to predict what sort of judge a man or a woman will be and irreversible mistakes in judicial appointments are bound to occur, even when the method of appointment is fair and efficient and the standards are high, as they are in England. Such errors in selection apply equally to appointing persons who were unfit for occupying a judicial office as well as failing to appoint a person who might have been a good judge.

In this chapter, we consider the principles which shape the selection process and criteria. Professional competence and integrity are a universal requirement for appointment to the bench, and are encompassed in the English requirement of 'merit and good character'. This requirement is underpinned, however, by the principles of transparency, independence from politics, a concern for a fair reflection of society in the appointment process and proper judicial accountability. Transparency, in particular, supports the prioritisation of merit and a fairer reflection of society. In England, the lack of diversity in the composition of the judiciary is noticeable at the level of the High Court and above, and the policies adopted to encourage diversity within the judiciary (from the 'trickle up' policy to the 'need to have regard to diversity') should not compromise the requirement of merit for judicial appointment. The Judicial Appointments Commission, which now recommends all appointments to the Lord Chancellor, can only have regard to the need to encourage diversity in the pool of applicants.[1] This duty aims to address the persistent criticism of the judiciary that the judges have been white, male and upper middle class, privately educated Oxbridge graduates and barristers.[2] We shall discuss whether this criterion and the lay involvement in the Judicial Appointments Commission is sufficiently robust and whether the Lord Chancellor should have the power to decline any of its recommendations.

The principles mentioned above inform the design of a judicial appointments process in a constitutional democracy, however only the historical and constitutional context can explain developments and justify certain trends.[3] So we start this chapter with a brief survey of practice before the Constitutional Reform Act 2005 (CRA) set up the Judicial Appointments Commission.

I. The appointment process and its criteria

4.2 We consider the dominant role of the Lord Chancellor in the appointments process prior to the CRA before examining the role of the Judicial Appointments Commission since then. While merit has been the 'touchstone for appointability'[4] since the 1860s, its interpretation did not exclude improper political considerations until the Lord Chancellorships of Lords Loreburn and Haldane.[5] Eligibility for the court and tribunals judiciary relies upon some statutory qualifications, combining 'merit' and 'good character' with experience of legal practice and some non-statutory qualifications, which aim to tailor the job description to the specific needs of the court at issue.

A. The Lord Chancellor

4.3 The office of the Lord Chancellor has always been anomalous under the traditional theory of separation of powers. Before the CRA, the Lord

---

[1] CRA, s. 64(1).

[2] J. Bell, *Judiciaries within Europe, A Comparative Review* (Cambridge University Press, 2006) 314.

[3] HL Committee on the Constitution 2012.

[4] Lord Clarke, 'Selecting Judges: Merit, Moral Courage, Judgment and Diversity' (2009) 5 *High Court Quarterly Review* 49.

[5] R. Stevens, *The English Judges: Their Role in the Changing Constitution*, rev. edn (Oxford: Hart, 2005), pp. 12–21.

Chancellor combined within his role the three functions of government: judicial, executive and legislative. By tradition he was head of the judiciary and exercised judicial powers; he was a member of the Cabinet, having executive functions and being subject, like all other ministers, to the doctrine of collective responsibility for the acts of the government; and he was also the Speaker of the House of Lords, taking a leading part in the legislative proceedings of the House and frequently defending and expounding government policy. As a member of the Cabinet, he came into office when his party gained power and, like the other ministers, held office at the pleasure of the prime minister. His office would (and still does) come to an end when his party left power or when the prime minister dismissed him.

Save for a few exceptions,[6] the appointment of the Lord Chancellor was always political in nature. Usually, when forming his Cabinet, the prime minister would take as Lord Chancellor a barrister of high standing who had rendered services to his party or at least had been in sympathy with its views and policies. The common pattern was service as an MP, Solicitor General, or Attorney General[7] (sometimes service as a minister), then Lord Chancellor. It was unlikely that the man chosen on political grounds to hold the Great Seal would not be 'of the highest standing and eminence in the profession'.[8] In practice, the prime minister always selected for the office of Lord Chancellor men who enjoyed the confidence of both the dominant party and the Bar.[9]

The constitutional anomalies in the light of the principle of separation of powers were seen as theoretical rather than having a practical impact. Following the institution of the Appellate Committee of the House of Lords shortly after the Second World War and the change of hours of legislative sittings of the House of Lords, it became increasingly rare

---

[6] Like Lord Sankey, Lord Maugham (1933–39) and Lord Simonds (1951–54) had not been active in party politics and both were Law Lords when they were chosen to go to the Woolsack.

[7] For a survey of Attorneys General and Solicitors General who later became Lord Chancellors, see J.L.J. Edwards, *The Law Officers of the Crown: a Study of the Offices of Attorney-General and Solicitor-General with an Account of the Office of the Director of Public Prosecutions of England* (London: Sweet & Maxwell, 1964), ch. 15; see also Toulson LJ, 'Judging Judicial Appointments', Pilgrim Fathers Lecture, Plymouth (3 December 2009), p. 9.

[8] R.F.V. Heuston, *Lives of the Lord Chancellors (1885–1940)* (Oxford: Clarendon Press, 1964), xxi.

[9] G. Coldstream, 'Judicial Appointment in England' (1959) 43 *Journal of the American Judicial Society*, 41, 44.

for the Lord Chancellor to participate in the hearing of appeals in the House of Lords, for he usually presided over the legislative sitting of the House at the same time that appeals were heard before the Appellate Committee.

Under the CRA, the post of Lord Chancellor is combined with that of Minister of Justice. He now sits in the House of Commons instead of the House of Lords – he must now be elected directly by his constituents. He is no longer head of the judiciary, and so his own legal prestige is less important. Under section 2 CRA, the prime minister can now appoint anyone whom he deems to be 'legally qualified' for the role and, in September 2012, for the first time in the modern era, a non-lawyer Conservative MP, Chris Grayling, became Lord Chancellor.

4.4 The method of appointment of the superior judges – High Court and above – was, until the CRA, a matter of practice and convention.[10] The Lord Chancellor played the decisive role in the selection of the higher judicial officers who were appointed by the Queen upon the advice of the prime minister. In his capacity of President of the High Court, the Lord Chancellor was responsible for the appointment of High Court judges. He was also responsible for the appointment of ordinary High Court judges ('puisne judges'), circuit judges, recorders, deputy judges, stipendiary magistrates and lay magistrates, who were appointed by the Queen upon his advice.[11]

Under the supervision of the Permanent Secretary, the Lord Chancellor's Department used to maintain records of potential candidates for the High Court and for the lower judicial offices.[12] At any given time the Lord Chancellor's Office had a list of qualified candidates who could be considered for judicial vacancies. The Lord Chancellor's staff also processed the applications for Queen's Counsel, which enabled them to follow up the advancement of leading members of the Bar from among whose ranks judges were drawn. In the process of selection of High Court

---

[10] The Supreme Court of Judicature Act 1873 provided that judges were to be appointed 'in the same manner as heretofore' and the following legislation followed this spirit.

[11] The role of the Queen in the selection of judges has always been limited to issuing the letters patent upon the advice of the Lord Chancellor, though George V tried to convince Prime Minister Lloyd George that his choice of F.E. Smith for the office of Lord Chancellor was not wise – see the letters sent on behalf of His Majesty to the Prime Minister in Lord Birkenhead, *The Life of F.E Smith, First Earl of Birkenhead* (London: Eyre & Spottiswoode, 1960), 332.

[12] Stevens, *The English Judges*, 58.

judges, the Lord Chancellor, with the assistance of his permanent secretary, would consult with the senior judiciary and the Bar.[13]

In the wake of an unprecedented resignation of a High Court judge after a little more than two years on the bench, Lord Hailsham, then Lord Chancellor, stated in Parliament that when he interviewed judges, he would tell them that he 'regard[ed their] irremovability by Parliament as one reason for treating the career as a permanent one and that they should approach the Bench with the enthusiasm of a bridegroom approaching marriage, or of a priest approaching priesthood'.[14] To modern eyes, this speech also betrays the assumption that the Lord Chancellor would be approaching male candidates.

In July 1993, following a review of the judicial appointments system, the then Lord Chancellor Lord Mackay started to introduce open competition procedures for judicial vacancies below the High Court. His aim was to enlarge the field for selection and to make judicial appointment procedures more transparent. Specific job descriptions were attached to vacancies and interviews of candidates were required for all but the appellate courts' positions. Members of the Bar who wished to be considered for appointment filed applications accompanied by three letters of recommendation from judges and leading barristers who knew them well. The steady increase in the number of judicial appointments made it difficult for the Lord Chancellor to have personal knowledge of all the persons considered for appointment, and the role of the permanent secretary and the Lord Chancellor's staff in the process of selection grew with time. Independent inquiries were conducted to learn more about the character and professional ability of the applicant. At a later stage, applicants were interviewed by senior officials of the Lord Chancellor's Office, usually sitting with one of the Presiding Judges to whose circuit the appointed judge was to be assigned. Upon completing the examinations, inquiries and interviews, recommendations were submitted to the Lord Chancellor, who made the ultimate choice.

It was rare for the Lord Chancellor to involve himself in appointments to lower courts. It took only a few weeks to appoint someone. High standards in appointments were achieved through the practice of appointing judges

---

[13] See Lord Hailsham, in 312 HL Deb, 1317–18 (19 November 1970): 'Indeed, I always have [the closest consultation] with heads of Divisions on any matter of importance affecting judicial patronage'.

[14] In a letter to an American lawyer, see M Erskine, 'The Selection of Judges in England: A Standard for Comparison' (1953) 39 *American Bar Association Journal* 279.

from a small pool of candidates who shared a common professional background, and were known by professional repute to those making and advising on appointments. In addition, upon arrival in office in 1997, Lord Irvine introduced public advertisement for High Court vacancies arising after 1 October 1998, although the Lord Chancellor reserved his right to recommend the appointment of persons who had not applied. The changes made by the Lord Chancellor's' Department to the selection process of the lower judiciary were thus extended to the High Court appointments.

The criticisms of the process (for all levels of appointment) centred not so much on the quality of appointments, nor the confidentiality of consultation or the references of candidates. Rather the process was challenged because it served to persuade candidates to apply by a 'tap on a shoulder'. The appointment thus heavily depended on the visibility of the individual to the judges through social and professional networks.[15] The Bar played a significant role in the process of selection and should be credited (or held responsible, as the case may be) for the quality of the appointments. The Law Society would have no part in the process, believing it to be a waste of their and their members' time as only barristers were considered to be eligible. Thus, while this consultation process could be praised for appointing individuals on merit, it was perceived as encouraging self-replication, with judges coming from a narrow social elite.[16]

Yet, as a branch of government, the judiciary cannot be composed with a total disregard for the make-up of society.[17] The perception of judicial fairness is linked to a judiciary fairly reflective of society.[18] Women began to enter the English judiciary in 1965, later than in a number of European countries.[19] As the entry rate into the Bar and into the solicitor's profession has reached equality between men and women,

[15] Report on Judicial Appointments and QC Selection, Main Report (1999), (the 'Peach Report'), 5.

[16] J.A.G. Griffith, *The Politics of the Judiciary*, 5th edn (London: Fontana, 1997), pp. 18–22.

[17] S. Shetreet, 'The Normative Cycle of Shaping Judicial Independence in Domestic and International Law: The Mutual Impact of National and International Jurisprudence and Contemporary Practical and Conceptual Challenges' (2009) 10 U Chi JIL 275.

[18] Under Art. 2.13 of the Montreal Declaration, 'the process and standards of judicial selection shall give due consideration to insuring a fair reflection by the judiciary of the society in all aspects'. One speaks of 'reflection' of society as the principle of impartiality excludes judges from 'representing' the views of a particular constituency or community.

[19] C. McGlynn, 'The Status of Women Lawyers in the United Kingdom', in U. Schultz and G. Shaw (eds.), *Women in the Worlds' Legal Professions* (Oxford: Hart, 2003), ch. 9.

the 'trickle' policy considered in the (1999) Peach Report has not come to fruition. Similar concerns about the low number of ethnic minority candidates for judicial appointment have been raised. The need to sustain public confidence in the courts led to the establishment of the Judicial Appointments Commission, with a duty to have regard to the need to encourage diversity in the pool of applicants.[20]

B. The Judicial Appointments Commission

4.5 JUSTICE called for a judicial nominating commission in 1972.[21] The idea of a Judicial Appointment Commission as an advisory or executive body was regularly mooted until the Peach Report in 1999 recommended a Commissioner for Judicial Appointments who would continuously audit the appointment procedures. But the first three annual reports, special investigations and responses to consultations by the first Commissioner for Judicial appointments, Sir Colin Campbell, only resulted in more criticisms of the existing system[22] and in 2003, a consultation paper from the government gave the impulse for reform:

> 19. The fundamental problem with the current system is that a Government minister, the Lord Chancellor, has sole responsibility for the appointments process and for making or recommending those appointments. However well this has worked in practice, this system no longer commands public confidence, and is increasingly hard to reconcile with the demands of the Human Rights Act.
>
> 20. In the same way, the central role successive Lord Chancellors have played in the selection of judges has taken up much of their time. This has inevitably diverted their attention from the core business of administering the justice system, and in particular running the courts.
>
> 21. The time has now come for a radical change to the judicial appointments system to enable it to meet the needs and expectations of the public in the 21st century. Any system which is introduced must, in addition to ensuring quality, also guarantee judicial independence. A Commission will provide a guarantee of judicial independence, will make the system for appointing judges more open and more transparent, and will work to

---

[20] CRA, s. 64(1).

[21] K.E. Malleson, 'Modernising the Constitution: Completing the Unfinished Business' (2004) 24 LS 119, 120.

[22] K.E Malleson, 'Rethinking the Merit Principle in the Judicial Appointments Process' (2006) *Journal of Law and Society* 126; 'Creating a Judicial Appointments Commission: Which Model Works Best?' [2004] PL 102.

make our judiciary more reflective of the society it serves. A Commission will also free the Department to focus on its core responsibilities.[23]

The case was reinforced by the creation, in 2002, of a Judicial Appointment Board in Scotland and the creation of the framework for establishing a judicial appointment commission in Northern Ireland.

4.6 The Judicial Appointments Commission, launched in April 2006, is a permanent public body sponsored by the Ministry of Justice. The Commission consists of fifteen members appointed for relatively short part-time terms of five years, with a maximum of ten years of service. Those members comprise six lay people, five judges (taken from the different levels of court), one solicitor, one barrister, and two lay judges (one magistrate and one tribunal member).[24] The three most senior judicial members are appointed by the Judges' Council. The other members are appointed by open competition independent of the executive. No member can be appointed to the Judicial Appointments Commission if he or she is employed in the civil service, in order to ensure full independence of the Judicial Appointments Commission. The composition of the Judicial Appointments Commission ensures a judicial and public input into the appointment of judges, and it removes the possibility of political influence. The strong legal presence is mitigated by the fact that the chair of the Commission is a lay member. In addition, the lay members must never have been practising lawyers. Currently former senior public office holders occupy the lay seats, and this may merit further discussion.

The Commission is responsible for recommending candidates for most judicial offices in England and Wales outside the Supreme Court, including all appointments to the High Court and below.[25] For the more senior judicial posts – Lord Chief Justice, other heads of division and Lords Justices of Appeal, ad hoc selection panels are appointed by the Judicial Appointments Commission following statutory criteria.[26]

---

[23] UK Department for Constitutional Affairs, 'Constitutional Reform: a New Way of Appointing Judges', report CP 10/03 (July 2003), pp. 17–18.

[24] CRA, sch. 12.   [25] CRA, ss. 85–94.

[26] CRA, ss. 67–84. The heads of division are the Lord Chief Justice, the Master of the Rolls, the President of the Queen's Bench Division, the President of the Family Division and the Chancellor of the High Court. Amendments to the Crime and Courts Bill have recently been tabled. If adopted, the Lord Chief Justice would be interviewed and appointed by a panel of five, chaired by the chairman of the Judicial Appointments Commission. The majority of members would be lay people rather than judges, 'for the first time in the job's history', see F. Gibbs, 'Top Judge Could Be a Woman as Decision Goes to Lay Majority', *The Times*, 12 March 2013.

The Judicial Appointments Commission's role for appointments to the UK Supreme Court is limited to having one Commission member sitting as one of the five members of the selection panel.[27]

Appointments to tribunals are also mainly made through the Commission, even for the few tribunals left outside the new tribunals structure.[28]

The CRA also established a Judicial Appointments and Conduct Ombudsman to investigate complaints from candidates for judicial office about the way in which their application was handled as well as procedural matters.[29]

4.7 The Commission determines its own selection process subject to the statutory requirements that selection must be solely on merit; the person selected must be of good character, and the Commission must have regard to the need to encourage diversity in the range of persons available for judicial selection.[30] This duty primarily lies in developing and collecting a pool of diverse candidates, and its success is dependent upon the legal professions' own efforts to retain their best talents among women and ethnic minorities, as we shall discuss below. The selection process consists broadly of the following steps: advertising and applications are followed by shortlisting and the shortlisted candidates attend a selection day for assessment. The assessment is made in a panel report, which is part of the information presented to the Commission. The latter then proceeds to statutory consultation before sending a report with a single recommendation to the Lord Chancellor, who can accept, reject or invite reconsideration of that recommendation.

The selection exercises are widely advertised and, following an assessment of good character upon reception of the applications, the shortlisting of candidates is undertaken on the basis of written evidence (including the candidate's application form and references) or on the basis of tests designed to assess the candidate's ability to perform in a judicial role.

For those tests, the Judicial Appointments Commission uses various (alternative or combined) methods. For all positions, a paper sift (references and application form) is required. For specialist and the most

---

[27] CRA, ss. 26–31 and sch. 8.

[28] Tribunals, Courts and Enforcement Act 2007, Schs. 2–4 (First-tier and Upper Tribunals).

[29] In 2011–12, only 7 cases out of 647 complaints concerned the handling of applications for judicial appointment, and the Ombudsman noted the 'generally very good' investigation processes for complaints from the Commission, Judicial Appointments and Conduct Ombudsman, Annual Report 2011–2012, p. 8.

[30] CRA, ss. 63–64.

senior appointments, there is more likely to be only one paper sift followed by a panel interview. However for large selection exercises (below senior circuit judge), the paper sift will only be considered after qualifying tests, consisting of case studies, have been used to shortlist candidates. The qualifying tests are considered as a more objective system since there is less reliance on references than when a paper sift is used. In addition, the large exercises will involve a selection day that is likely to involve a combination of role-play exercises and a formal interview. Interviews and role-play exercises in particular make the appointment process more transparent, as they make the background of the applicants as apparent as their abilities.

Some of our interviewees considered that the overwhelming number of applications justified the introduction of a paper sift and a qualifying test. The tests and the selection exercise materials themselves have been developed as 'equality-proof', in collaboration with an advisory group consisting of members of the Bar Council, the Law Society, and CILEX (the Chartered Institute of Legal Executives) and through 'dry runs'. Interviewees familiar with the work of the Commission noted that setting up qualifying tests had been a steep learning curve, and one interviewee acknowledged that tests are better designed today.

All interviewees expressed reservations on the qualifying test, on the basis that some top barristers failed the entry test, and that the tests were still not conducive to judicial diversity. One interviewee commented: 'Perhaps they failed because they didn't prepare but they are very busy people. If they failed the exam, it must be a bad exam.' Candidates now seem better prepared. Some other interviewees considered the qualifying test 'clunky' or inappropriate for full-time appointments, on the assumption that part-time judicial experience is the main prerequisite for full-time appointments. Others expressed their fear that the qualifying test might exclude diverse candidates. If the qualifying test requires 'judge craft', then this might be a recipe for judicial cloning. Many of our interviewees thought that the qualifying test had nothing to do with the ability of making judgments and some claimed that there was some evidence of a lack of correlation between having done a good test and doing well as a judge.

One recordership exercise was criticised for requiring some knowledge of the criminal process or proceedings (a recordership requires three weeks a year of hearing criminal cases), thus preventing civil or commercial practitioners from success. The examples of questions given to us, however, did not necessarily support these criticisms. One selection exercise apparently included the following scenario: someone tells you in your capacity of judge that the jury has an argument. They want a cigarette break. What do you do? The right answer seems to be that the judge should give them the cigarette break but ask them to leave all papers and mobile phones behind, and give them instructions about what they can or cannot do. Does one really have to go to training or to practice in the criminal courts to answer this? Another question required the candidates to say what they would do if they were to hear a case from counsel with whom they, as a judge, had had an affair. The answer given to us was that the judge has to disclose the fact to the other side.

Either way, our interviewees drew different conclusions from their criticisms of the qualifying test. Some reported that the appointment process seemed to be designed for people who spend time in courts, when the establishment of the Judicial Appointments Commission was set to go beyond the old boys' network for appointments. Others thought that the qualifying test had led to some unsatisfactory appointments because (they suggested) it had nothing to do with the ability to make judgments, though they acknowledged that bad appointments existed under the previous regime of appointments too.

Some thought that the best barristers would not apply. A selection exercise for a recordership in one circuit in 2010 attracted 1,200 applications for 120 places. Of those applicants, 800 failed the first round of the competition, and 300 were interviewed. There are large numbers of applicants who apply repeatedly, and who are required to take a different test for every application, which proves very costly in terms of time and money. For this reason, the process is likely to be modified in the near future. Parallels have been made with the process of appointment to the Civil Service, where a baseline test can be taken which remains valid for a few years with a handful of selected candidates then taking a role-play or further exercises specifically tailored to the position they have applied for. This would act in place of the qualification test.

References are always sought, either before the paper sift, or after the qualifying test. Although there is no formal requirement that a referee should be a judge, a number of potential applicants to a judicial post indicated in a recent survey their belief that, in practice, one needs a reference from a High Court judge to be successful.[31] The suggestion, during debates leading to the CRA, of giving the Lord Chief Justice a power of veto on appointments was not adopted. This prevents judicial

---

[31] Judicial Appointments Commission, 'Barriers to Application for Judicial Appointment Research' (2009), p. 3.

corporatism, though many contacts exist with the senior judiciary before appointments are made at senior level.

4.8 The timeline of the appointments process could be improved. The time elapsing between the offer of appointment and the judge commencing office can be two years, with no certainty as to when the successful candidate will get a position because (depending on which position is sought) none might be available yet. In addition, the Commission is dependent on the Ministry of Justice promptly informing them that a vacancy has to be filled, and some delays from the Ministry of Justice have been noted. Time is then needed for the Ministry of Justice, the Judicial Office and the Judicial Appointments Commission to agree upon the non-statutory criteria for eligibility to a particular post. This timeline undoubtedly has an impact on careers which have to be put on hold pending appointment. The Constitution Committee rightly pointed, in 2012, to the need for greater certainty and a shorter time lapse between the offer of appointment and the judge commencing office.[32] For a long time, however, there was no tool for forecasting the needs and vacancies within the judiciary, and HMCTS has taken the credit for having provided such a tool in 2011. Under the old system of appointments, the Senior President would have been the one with the necessary knowledge of personnel and vacancies with the support of the court officials.

4.9 The transfer of judicial selection to an independent Commission formally ensures a non-executive bias in the selection process. The prime minister plays a formal role in the process, thus limiting the danger of any future party politicisation of the system. For the same reason, the Lord Chancellor's role is reduced to that of providing a safeguard against the appointment of unqualified candidates, in the unlikely event that any should be recommended.[33] For all appointments, the Lord Chancellor then receives a report and a single recommendation from the independent selection panel involved. He can accept or reject this, or he can invite a reconsideration.[34] The Commission may also decide that none of the applicants was suitable for appointment and

---

[32] HL Committee on the Constitution Report, 2012, para. 125.

[33] K.E. Malleson, *The Legal System*, 3rd edn (Oxford University Press, 2007), p. 212.

[34] CRA, ss. 26(3), 70, 71, 73 and 90. The panel will generally consist of 3 people: a panel chair who has been appointed following the Nolan Principles on Appointments to Public Offices, an independent lay member and a judicial member, who provides the necessary technical expertise and legal knowledge. He or she is generally drawn from the jurisdiction to which the appointment relates.

decline to make a recommendation, and in such case the Lord Chancellor can ask the Commission to reconsider that decision.[35]

The Lord Chancellor has therefore not been removed from the decision-making process. However, if he rejects the nominee, he can only do so on the ground that the person is not suitable for the post, and he must give reasons in writing for doing so.[36] This is an important safeguard against the abuse of ministerial discretion,[37] but it is not clear which reasons will be regarded as 'legitimate', and the only fallout from any unsatisfactory decision would seem to be at a political level, since the Commission cannot reselect a candidate who has been rejected.

The Lord Chancellor can also require the Commission to reconsider a selection but only if there is not enough evidence that the person is suitable for the office concerned or there is evidence that the person is not the best candidate on merit.[38] Reasons must also be given in writing in this case. Between 2007 and 2010, only a handful of recommendations, out of about 3,000 put forward to the Lord Chancellor, were not approved. Thus, in 2010, the (then) Lord Chancellor Jack Straw asked for reconsideration of the panel's recommendation for the post of President of the Family Division. This led to the delayed appointment of Sir Nicholas Wall as head of the Family Division, as the Commission resubmitted his name. There was speculation by the press that the Lord Chancellor had sought to block that appointment following critical and public comments from that candidate about the resources of the family courts.[39] One judge interviewed cited this example as evidence of the Commission's willingness to 'wrestle' with the executive to support the independence of the judicial selection process.

Although some judicial consultation remains,[40] the revised processes for selection mark 'a significant extension of professionalism in judicial appointments and a greater recognition of a career'.[41] This model, under which the executive makes selection after receiving recommendations from an appointments commission, applies in Canada, South Africa, and several American states, though in each there are fine differences, such as whether the

---

[35] CRA, ss. 88(2) and 93.
[36] CRA, s. 91(1).   [37] Malleson, 'Judicial Appointments in England and Wales', 46–7.
[38] CRA, s. 91(2).
[39] But see the former Lord Chancellor, Jack Straw, 'Judicial Appointments', Hamlyn Lecture, Inner Temple (4 December 2012).
[40] CRA, ss. 27, 71, 80, 88(3) and 94(3).
[41] Bell, *Judiciaries within Europe*, 313. See also Lord Judge LCJ, 'Diversity Conference' (11 March 2009).

commission recommends one name in particular or a list of approved names from which the executive may choose one. (By contrast, in South Africa, the executive is required to appoint those nominated by the commission.)

4.10 The Crime and Courts Bill transfers to the Commission the selection of deputy High Court judges.[42] While the selection of deputy High Court judges applies to judges who have already been registered on the list of judges to the High Court,[43] sitting as a deputy High Court judge appears, in practice, to be a required step for appointment to the High Court bench. This extension of remit is therefore a welcome development as it will bring transparency and openness to a process of approval which is largely in the hands of the Heads of Division.

4.11 The Crime and Courts Bill 2012 also transfers the Lord Chancellor's decision-making power to the Lord Chief Justice in relation to appointments below High Court appointments and appointments to tribunals.[44] The former Lord Chancellor Kenneth Clarke suggested that his lack of knowledge of the candidates for these positions had made his role 'largely ceremonial and ritualistic'.[45] It is hoped that the transfer will, in practical terms, make the appointments process faster. It is also suggested that the gap left by the executive should be filled by the presence of lay members representative of the civil society in appointment panels. They are expected to convey a fresh viewpoint and challenge the judicial input as appropriate. Some have doubted the influence of the lay members, and have suggested that the substantial judicial input, through consultation and the influence of judicial members of the Commission, creates a risk of the Commission 'cloning the existing judiciary' in terms of skills and experience'.[46] Undoubtedly judges are in a strong position to assess the professional ability and potential of those who are considered for appointment to the bench, and the lack of significant progress towards increasing diversity within the senior judiciary has been seen by many as

---

[42] Crime and Courts Bill 2012.   [43] See above, paras. 3.39 and 3.40.

[44] Crime and Courts Bill 2012, sch. 12.

[45] Evidence to the Lords Committee on the Constitution inquiry on judicial appointments, p. 15.

[46] R. Hazell, 'Britain's Constitutional Reforms: Trivial or Transforming?', Transcript of Anthony Simpson Memorial Lecture (2009). Yet the European Charter on the Statute of Judges 1998 (Art. 1.3) requires, in respect of every decision affecting the selection, recruitment, appointment, career progress or termination of office of a judge, 'the intervention of an authority independent of the executive and legislative powers within which at least one half of those who sit are judges elected by their peers following methods guaranteeing the widest representation of the judiciary'.

evidence that this risk of cloning has become reality. In particular, retaining consultation with existing judges, albeit in a modified and limited form, maintains the advantage given to candidates already visible to existing judges, most of whom are barristers.

There is no essential reason, however, why lay members should not be able to resist the views of judicial members. If sufficiently robust, they can demand that the judicial members articulate to their own satisfaction their reasons for preferring a candidate if they are not obvious from the paperwork, so as to avoid judicial corporatism. The difficulty is rather that there are no criteria for the qualifications required of the lay members, though there is a procedure of public appointments by advertisement. The practice relating to the selection of the lay members constitutes a path for influence on the appointment process and, as such, requires greater attention. While the secrecy of deliberations makes the degree of judicial influence in appointment commissions a matter of speculation, we have come across anecdotal evidence that the insiders' knowledge – the judicial experience – speaks volume during deliberations, and some have argued that judges had a 'pivotal role' in the appointment process at the UK Supreme Court in particular, where consultation with the senior judiciary is significant.[47] One interviewee involved in senior judicial appointments noted that the judicial members had, by definition, a head start on the non-judicial members. Evidence from other legal systems with a substantial judicial presence in the appointment commission further suggests that appointments are frequently made on the basis of seniority rather than on strict merit.[48] This is where lay members need to be able to bring individual expertise and broader perspectives, as representatives of civil society. The notion of 'merit' is broad enough that non-judicial members should feel as competent as judges to assess many of the key features of merit.

4.12 In 2008 the Parliamentary Joint Select Committee expressed its disappointment with the lack of measurable progress towards increasing diversity within the judiciary. Similarly, the Constitution Committee observed in 2012 that it shared the widespread impatience to see early progress made on improving the numbers of women and BAME (black, Asian and minority ethnic) judicial appointments. Even so, the

---

[47] A. Paterson and C. Paterson, 'Guarding the Guardians? Towards an Independent, Accountable and Diverse Senior Judiciary' (London: CentreForum, 2012), p. 28.
[48] Bell, *Judiciaries within Europe*.

Improvements

Commission raised the number of women High Court judges to seventeen with five women being appointed between 1 April 2008 and June 2009, the highest number ever. More women and black and minority ethnic candidates are applying for judicial roles than before the Judicial Appointments Commission was set up; more women are also being selected under the Judicial Appointments Commission than before.

As in Canada and the United States, the Commission has made considerable efforts to widen the pool of applicants. 'Encouragement to apply' is permitted, but, as is usual with all types of employment, then followed by submission to an open and standardised assessment process. While some interviewees rejected it as a possible return to the 'tap on the shoulder', there was a consensus that some good candidates had been lost with the new appointment process, and that consideration led others to be broadly supportive of such encouragement to apply. Some interviewees thought that it would be acceptable for circuit leaders to issue encouragement, but not judges in a higher position of authority. With a clear judicial reluctance to adopt anything that might be seen as the old 'tap on the shoulder', the attention naturally turns to the legal professions. One interviewee suggested that the heads of chambers had a role to play in encouraging the members of the chambers to apply; it would seem more difficult to persuade the heads of law firms to do the same in the light of their strong reluctance to let their partners develop some part-time judicial experience.[49]

There is also a broad consensus from our interviewees that some robust selection procedures have been set to meet the Commission's statutory duty to appoint on merit and to ensure that the procedures are fair to all. Both some of our interviewees and the Law Society observed that 'the fact that the complaints against those processes are in the main coming from white male Oxbridge educated barristers (who are no longer guaranteed appointment) would suggest that the [Judicial Appointments Commission] has succeeded'.[50]

C. Merit

4.13 The Judicial Appointments Commission is required, under the CRA, to select people of good character solely on the basis of merit.[51] 'Merit' builds on a range of different skills and qualities, in addition to

---

[49] See below, para. 4.23.
[50] Written Evidence before Committee on the Constitution, Autumn 2011.
[51] CRA, s. 63(2) and (3); Malleson, 'Rethinking the Merit Principle in Judicial Selection'.

the intellectual capacity necessary to become a judge. It had traditionally been defined by reference to success in the courtroom as an advocate.[52] Lord Falconer acknowledged in 2011 that merit was still defined in that way by many in the legal profession and this naturally favours Queen's Counsel (QCs).[53] Applying its statutory duty to encourage diversity in the range of applicants, however, the Judicial Appointments Commission has widened the definition of 'merit', which relies upon five qualities and abilities: intellectual capacity;[54] personal qualities;[55] an ability to understand and deal with people fairly;[56] authority and communication skills;[57] and efficiency.[58] It reduced the relevance of 'advocacy skills', as opposed to 'communication skills'. The Commission's main concern was to remove barriers and to ensure that the definition of merit did not unfairly favour one group over another. The third criterion noted above, the 'ability to understand and deal fairly' was also amended following the recommendation of the Advisory Panel to the Lord Chancellor on Judicial Diversity in 2010, to the extent that it now requires from candidates 'an awareness of the diversity of the communities which the courts and tribunals serve and an understanding of differing needs'.[59]

The publication of disaggregated selection criteria provides for greater transparency by allowing candidates to be assessed against a common set of standards for a particular position.[60] But the balancing of the values

---

[52] H. Cecil, *The English Judge* (London: Stevens and Sons, 1970).

[53] HL Committee on the Constitution, 'Twenty-Fifth Report – Judicial Appointments', March 2012, para. 84.

[54] This refers to a 'high level of expertise in your chosen area or profession', the 'ability quickly to absorb and analyse information', an 'appropriate knowledge of the law and its underlying principles, or the ability to acquire this knowledge where necessary'.

[55] The personal qualities expected are 'integrity and independence of mind', 'sound judgement', 'decisiveness', 'objectivity', the 'ability and willingness to learn and develop professionally', and the 'ability to work constructively with others'.

[56] The 'ability to understand and deal fairly' is understood as 'an awareness of the diversity of the communities which the courts and tribunals serve and an understanding of differing needs', the 'commitment to justice, independence, public service and fair treatment', and the 'willingness to listen with patience and courtesy'.

[57] The 'authority and communication skills' refer to an 'ability to explain the procedure and any decisions reached clearly and succinctly to all those involved', the 'ability to inspire respect and confidence', the 'ability to maintain authority when challenged'.

[58] Efficiency requires the 'ability to work at speed and under pressure' and the 'ability to organise time effectively and produce clear reasoned judgments expeditiously (including leadership and managerial skills where appropriate)'.

[59] Advisory Panel on Judicial Diversity, 'Report', recommendation 20.

[60] S. Evans and J. Williams, 'Appointing Australian Judges: A New Model' (2008) 30(2) *Sydney Law Review* 295, 295–7.

that are implicit in the concept of merit depends on the weight given to each criterion. For example, is the third criterion, the 'ability to understand and deal fairly' (which includes an awareness of the diversity of the communities served) given the same weight as the fourth one, 'authority and communication skills'? The glittering factors for a man and a woman may not be the same. One interviewee pointed out: 'for a man, he might be a Queen's Counsel having had a wife at home taking care of his children'. Women practitioners will not have the same experience as men when they come back from having raised a family and cannot fully catch up with that. This should be borne in mind when assessing merit in individual cases.

4.14 The lack of significant changes in the composition of the judiciary at senior level has led to the perception that serving judges appoint in their own image. The action suggested by the Advisory Panel on Judicial Diversity in 2010, endorsed by the Constitution Committee in 2012, seems to be adequate and necessary to overcome any such tendency: all selection panels should be gender- and, wherever possible, ethnically diverse, and members should undertake diversity training.[61]

Nevertheless, diversity and merit are distinct considerations, and should remain so in the appointment process. Lord Carswell emphasised: 'you might have A, B and C: you cannot call them equal, but they are all very appointable, though they have different qualities, but one fills a need for a particular skill and will therefore be appointed. A particular skill is taken into account but this is not called merit.'[62] The challenge lies in enhancing the value of diversity in the appointment process without undermining the notion of merit. A diverse background shapes the skills, knowledge and experience of one individual and it may be difficult to distinguish the added value of a particular skill, knowledge and experience from the characteristic of diversity. Baroness Hale has persuasively argued that:

> In disputed points you need a variety of perspectives and life experiences to get the best possible results. You will not get the best possible results if everybody comes at the same problem from exactly the same point of view. You need a variety of dimensions of diversity. I am talking not only about gender and ethnicity but about professional background, areas of

[61] Advisory Panel on Judicial Diversity, 'Report', recommendations 31, 41 and 43, and Committee on the Constitution Report 2012, paras. 87–8.
[62] Lord Carswell, Oral Evidence, Q 303.

expertise and every dimension that adds to the richer collective mix and makes it easier to have genuine debates.[63]

Equality and diversity, from a regulatory perspective, are primarily about ensuring processes and setting and enforcing standards that facilitate fair and open access to the bench. The Commission's duty to have regard to diversity applies to the range of persons available for selection, not at the level of the selection itself. Although the UK Association of Women Judges noted the Commission's hesitation to suggest the adoption of quotas, there does not seem to be any appetite for mandatory quotas, that is, appointment to the bench according to certain proportions.[64] Quota systems, in any event, vary in mechanisms and impact according to complex and context-specific factors. One should also beware of the assumption that a greater number of women in the judiciary may promote different views from the judiciary as it is currently composed. This is unlikely to be necessarily the case where women connected to legal, political and economic elites come to power, as demonstrated by studies on the representation of women in Parliament.

4.15 There have been recommendations that the 'tipping provision' or 'tie-breaker' contained in section 159 of the Equality Act 2010 applies to the appointments process. This was endorsed by Lord Neuberger, then Master of the Rolls, and can be found in the 2012 Crime and Courts Bill. The application of section 159 would allow the appointment authority to give priority, among candidates of equal merit, to the one who comes from an underrepresented group.[65] 'Merit', however, is an open-ended standard. Unless the components of 'merit' are disaggregated into

---

[63] Oral Evidence before the Committee on the Constitution, 2012, Q 220; see also Q 216, written evidence by Baroness Hale, para. 2; evidence by Sir Thomas Legg, para. 17, and by Lord Mance, paras. 10–11.

[64] See the Oral Evidence from Lord Judge CJ Q 188; Q 252 (Hallett LJ), Q 266 (Association of Women Solicitors), Q 333 (Baroness Prashar).

[65] Under s. 159, between two equally qualified individuals for a recruitment or promotion exercise, the individual with a protected characteristic may be chosen over the individual without that characteristic, where those with the protected characteristic are under-represented in the relevant activity. The 8 protected characteristics listed under the Equality Act 2010 are age, disability, gender reassignment, pregnancy and maternity, race, religion or belief, sex and sexual orientation. However, under Equality Act 2010, s. 159(6), the positive action provisions in s. 159 cannot be used to do anything that is prohibited by or under another enactment. Yet s. 63(2) CRA states that, for judicial appointments, selection must be solely on merit. Section 159 thus does not currently apply to judicial appointments, and the adoption of the Crime and Courts Bill would

objective selection criteria which are applied in a consistent way, the notion becomes 'almost wholly subjective, allowing each decision maker to construct his or her own features which are significant'.[66] It also makes the finding of 'equal merit' between candidates a subjective matter and potentially limits the impact of section 159. It has been suggested that, in practice, appointments panels fairly rarely found candidates of equal merit. Baroness Neuberger, Lord Phillips and Lord Judge CJ also doubted whether two candidates are ever truly equal.[67] In that context, section 159 would make little impact. Yet it seems likely, as suggested by some other senior judges,[68] that section 159 could have some use. In particular, in large selection exercises, it may not be possible to rank every candidate in strict order of merit and so a number of candidates may be considered to be of equal merit,[69] thus allowing section 159 to come into play. If there is to be a 'trickle up' effect from making more appointments at the lowest levels, this may prove to be one viable long-term strategy.

Alternatively, on the basis that a number of individuals will be equally capable and suitably qualified, some would support a 'merit threshold': once a set plateau of skills and capability has been reached, preference would be given to the candidate from an underrepresented group.[70] This, however, may lead to the perception that the most meritorious judge may not be appointed due to considerations of diversity. It should be rejected, as it can only weaken confidence in the quality of the judiciary.

One may wonder whether the achievement of diversity targets should be regulated. Unlike quotas, targets would not be mandatory: they would be goals towards which the Judicial Appointments Commission would aim. For example, as suggested by the UK Association of Women Judges, there could be a target of at least 30 per cent of the full-time judiciary

---

clarify that, between two candidates of equal merit, the Judicial Appointments Commission would be able to prefer one for the purpose of increasing diversity.

[66] Evans and Williams, 'Appointing Australian Judges', 297.

[67] Oral Evidence, Q 224, Q 183, Q 184. The Chairman of the Judicial Appointments Commission also said that the large numbers of woman and Black, Asian and Ethnic Minorities' representatives appointed since 2006 made s. 159 unnecessary: Oral Evidence from Christopher Stephens, 2011, question 364, p. 386.

[68] Oral Evidence Q 377 (Lord Chancellor), Q 98 (Goldring LJ), Q 240, (Hallett LJ), Q 240 (Lord Neuberger MR).

[69] Committee on the Constitution, paras. 98–101.

[70] Lord Falconer, the Director of JUSTICE, and the Chair of the Black Solicitors Network; contra, Oral Evidence, Q 71 (District Judge Tim Jenkins), Q 86 (Goldring LJ), Q 240 (Lord Neuberger MR), Q 303 (Lord Woolf), written evidence by the Association of HM District Judges, and by the Judicial Executive Board.

being female by 2020, in order to create a 'critical mass' of women judges, encouraging other women to apply.[71] Lord Judge CJ has rightly emphasised that in truth targets could easily turn into a quota system.[72] They should be opposed for that reason, as potentially undermining the notion of merit, and the independence of the appointments process.[73] If targets are considered in the near future, they would need to be set with great care, on the basis of better data than that which is currently available.[74]

4.16 So we would argue that the notion of merit is not to be watered down either directly or indirectly by the needs for diversity. Instead fifty-three recommendations were made by an Advisory Panel to the Lord Chancellor in 2010, to improve the diversity of the judicial applicants across various areas.[75] They include the following: (i) ensuring that lawyers from all backgrounds recognise early on in their career that becoming a judge could be a possibility for them; (ii) more effort by the legal professions to promote diversity at all levels and to support applications from talented candidates from all backgrounds; (iii) better information on the career paths available; (iv) these career paths must promote opportunities across the courts and tribunals as one judiciary; (v) providing a variety of means for potential applicants for judicial office to understand what the role involves and to gain practical experience and build confidence; (vi) open and transparent selection processes that promote diversity and recognise potential, not just at the entry points to the judiciary but also for progression within it to the most senior levels.[76] The House of Lords Constitution Committee, in 2011, urged the implementation of these recommendations, and the Crime and Courts Bill 2012 already addresses the issue of mobility and progression through the judicial ranks.[77]

D. Legal practising experience

4.17 In 2004 the (now defunct) Department of Constitutional Affairs consulted on means of increasing diversity among the judiciary in the UK. They concluded that the qualifications required to serve as a judge

---

[71] Figure suggested in written evidence by UK Association of Women Judges, [16].
[72] Oral Evidence Q 188; Advisory Panel on Judicial Diversity, 'Report', recommendation 5.
[73] See the Joint Committee on the Draft Constitutional Renewal Bill, para. 141.
[74] Committee on the Constitution Report 2012, para. 107.
[75] Advisory Panel on Judicial Diversity, 'Report'.   [76] Ibid., 19.
[77] See above, paras. 3.34 and 3.35.

were a barrier to a broader judiciary and recommended that they be varied, in particular by shortening the period of legal practice demanded before seeking office. In response, the Tribunals, Courts and Enforcement Act 2007 introduced various changes to the eligibility rules for judicial office.[78] The possession and use of rights of audience for a specified period was discontinued as the basic test, as it led to the perception that advocacy skills were a prerequisite for appointments.[79] The newly introduced test is based on possession of a relevant qualification and legal experience for a specific period.[80] The number of years for which the qualification has been held and the experience gained was reduced, and eligibility was extended to other legal professional groups than barristers or solicitors, such as those holding a qualification awarded by CILEX or an authorised body designated for the purposes of the Courts and Legal Services Act 1990.[81] Relevant experience in law is broadly construed to include any 'law-related activity', including, for example, teaching or researching law.[82]

4.18 The statutory qualifications are based on the years of experience in advocacy, with a greater number of years required according to the status of the Court.[83]

Eligibility for appointment as a Lord Justice of Appeal requires the candidate to either satisfy the judicial-appointment eligibility condition on a seven-year basis or to be a judge of the High Court.[84] Since 1990, the criteria for appointment as a circuit judge or recorder are either holding the position of district judge or an equivalent judicial appointment for at least three years, or having a general right of audience in the Crown Courts or county courts (i.e., having advocacy experience of at least seven years).[85] Direct entry is common at all levels in the judiciary below that of the Court of Appeal.

Recorder is a fee-paid part-time judicial role held by practising lawyers. The function of the fee-paid part-time post is both to fill a need

---

[78] Tribunal, Courts and Enforcement Act 2007, ss. 50–52.

[79] S.H. Bailey, *Smith, Bailey and Gunn on the Modern English Legal System* (London: Sweet & Maxwell, 2007), paras. 4.023 and 4.029.

[80] Courts and Legal Services Act 1990, s. 71.

[81] Courts and Legal Services Act 1990, ss. 27–28; Tribunals, Courts and Enforcement Act 2007, s. 51. In the case of CILEX or any other authorised body, the qualification in relation to a particular judicial office is specified in an order from the Lord Chancellor.

[82] Tribunals, Courts and Enforcement Act 2007, s. 52(2)–(5).

[83] Senior Courts Act 1981, s. 10(3)(a), (b) and (c); Courts and Legal Services Act 1990, s. 71; County Courts Act 1984, s. 9.

[84] Senior Courts Act 1981, s. 10(3) (b).

[85] Courts and Legal Services Act 1990, s. 71 and sch. 10.

and to provide a training ground for potential full-time judges, in so far as circuit judges need to have held a judicial appointment for at least three years. However, holding a fee-paid part-time judicial post is difficult for solicitors who, unlike barristers, are not self-employed, and must obtain the agreement of their partners to taking unpaid time off to sit as a judge. The tenure in office of a recorder came under scrutiny following the decision of the High Court of Justiciary that Scottish temporary sheriffs, appointed by the Lord Advocate, now a member of the Scottish government, were insufficiently independent of the executive for compliance with the requirements of Article 6 ECHR.[86] As a result, since 2000, part-time appointments are for no less than five years, and reappointment will be automatic (where appointments are renewable) unless on limited and specific grounds. Although security of tenure existed in practice, the revised arrangements established some formal safeguards of independence.[87]

A five-year general qualification[88] is required for the position of district judge or deputy district judge. The latter is a part-time appointment. A distinctive feature of the English system is its reliance on members of the legal profession acting as part-time judges – nearly 60 per cent of judicial posts are part time.

4.19 The CRA is unclear on who may define the non-statutory eligibility criteria. There is a tension between the Lord Chancellor and the Judicial Appointments Commission who jointly consider what is appropriate. On the one hand, the Judicial Appointments Commission, keen to encourage diversity, aims to ensure that the non-statutory criteria are kept to a minimum, given their potential to narrow the pool of potential candidates. On the other hand, since the Lord Chancellor is responsible for the administrative functioning of the courts, the Lord Chancellor considers himself best placed to determine their needs in consultation with the Lord Chief Justice. It is argued by the Lord Chief Justice that the Judicial Appointments Commission, like a recruitment agency, must respond to the needs of the client's business; and 'those needs must be judged and

---

[86] *Starrs v. Procurator Fiscal, Linlithgow* [2000] HRLR 191; *Millar v. Procurator Fiscal, Elgin* [2000] UKPC D4; [2002] 1 WLR 1615; *Clancy v. Caird (No. 1)* 2000 SC 441; [2000] HRLR 557.

[87] Bailey, Smith, Bailey and Gunn, 239.

[88] That is, a right of audience in relation to any class of proceedings in any part of the Supreme Court or all proceedings in county courts or magistrates' courts: Tribunals, Courts and Enforcement Act 2007.

articulated by the business, not the recruitment agency'.[89] This is likely to be a continuing source of tension.

II. A fair reflection of society

4.20 Here we discuss further aspects of the struggle for a more diverse judiciary. The duty of the Commission to have regard to the need for a more diverse judiciary ensures equal opportunities for all and supports the confidence of the public and the legal profession in the judiciary. A fair reflection of society matters not in the individual case brought to court, where what essentially matters is a judge who listens and who will take the parties' interest at heart. But a fair reflection of society is necessary on a cohort basis, to sustain public confidence in the judiciary.[90] A diverse judiciary will approach the task of judging from the varied perspectives of its judges; that judges bring to bear their different life experiences enriches collective decision making.[91] As stated by L'Heureux-Dubé and McLachlin JJ, 'The reasonable person does not expect that judges will function as neutral ciphers; however, the reasonable person does demand that judges achieve impartiality in their judging.'[92]

4.21 Attention has therefore turned to the pool of candidates available for selection. Judges have traditionally come from the senior Bar which is itself lacking in diversity. Outreach is taking place so that more judicial appointments are to be made from amongst other more diverse pools, such as that of solicitors, who are more diverse at all levels, or that of employed barristers and candidates from CILEX too. Some of our interviewees also pointed to the government lawyers, prosecution lawyers and in-house counsel as an obviously diverse yet untapped pool of candidates for judicial appointments. It is likely that, for as long as judges are not

---

[89] See the Joint Parliamentary Scrutiny Committee on the Draft Constitutional Renewal Bill, The Draft Constitutional Renewal Bill, Report, vol. 1 (2008), para. 174. The Committee confirmed that the Lord Chancellor should be given the power to determine non-statutory eligibility criteria.

[90] Art. 2.15 Mt. Scopus; K. Malleson, *The New Judiciary* (Aldershot: Ashgate Press, 1999), p. 111.

[91] See Dobbs J, 'Diversity in the Judiciary', Lecture at Queen Mary University of London (17 October 2007).

[92] *R* v. *S. (R.D.)* [1997] 3 SCR 484, para. 38 [L'Heureux-Dubé and McLachlin JJ]; M. Minow, 'Stripped Down Like a Runner or Enriched by Experience: Bias and Impartiality of Judges and Jurors' (1992) 33 *William and Mary Law Review* 1201.

regularly appointed from these pools, most interested candidates would naturally assume that they would not get through the process.[93]

The lack of diversity of the judiciary is a recurrent issue. Henry Cecil already criticised the lack of diversity within the judiciary in 1970.[94] Abel, Stevens and Griffiths also raised some powerful criticisms.[95] The lack of diversity is now being grappled with by Parliament, the judiciary and the Judicial Appointments Commission. But the reasons for the lack of significant changes in the composition of the judiciary are distinct: they differ per underrepresented group – the lack of solicitors is not explained by the same reasons which explain the lack of women on the bench. Diversity issues must be further nuanced in the light of substantial changes taking place at the level of the lower judiciary.

A.   Queen's Counsel as judges

4.22 High Court judges are mainly chosen from Queen's Counsel ('Silks') with years of experience in oral advocacy. From the eighteenth century onwards, selection as a Queen's (or King's) Counsel became a recognition of professional eminence.[96] Queen's Counsel were retained to conduct court work on behalf of the Crown, this until 1920 when permission was not needed before accepting a brief to appear against the Crown. They are traditionally selected from barristers although it is now open to employed barristers and solicitors. Selection was made upon consultation; Gareth Williams QC (as he then was) described it in 1992 as based on 'the Franz Kafka school of business management'.[97] Becoming a QC has been the traditional pathway to the judiciary and the Silk appointment system was criticised for the same reasons that the judicial appointment system was. A report of the Office of Fair Trading[98] in 2001 pointed out that the (then) existing system, administered by the Lord Chancellor's Office and based on secret soundings, was distorting

[93] Lord Falconer before the Committee on the Constitution, Oral Evidence Q 157.

[94] Cecil, The English Judge.

[95] B. Abel-Smith and R. Stevens, Lawyers and the Courts. A Sociological Study of the English Legal System, 1750–1965 (London: Heinemann Educational Books, 1967).

[96] Elizabeth I appointed the first group of Queen's Counsel, including Francis Bacon, to assist the Attorney General in giving legal advice to the monarch, W. Holdsworth, History of English Law,, vol. VI, pp. 472–3.

[97] The Times, 27 September 1993, cited by D. Pannick, 'Why the Silk's Purse Won't Survive' [2001] PL 439.

[98] OFT, March 2001, paras. 270–9.

competition among junior and senior barristers and did not apply the objective standards that would make it a genuine quality accreditation scheme.[99] A debate followed at the Bar; given the traditional connection between QCs and the judiciary, the future of the rank of QC became part of the proposals for constitutional reforms made by the Secretary of State for Constitutional Affairs in 2003, alongside the creation of a Supreme Court and the establishment of a Judicial Appointments Committee. A new more transparent process, with selection based on a 'competency framework' by a panel independent from the government, was agreed between the Law Society and the Bar Council in 2004, and approved by the Lord Chancellor and Secretary of State for Constitutional Affairs.

Among QCs today 11 per cent are women; among senior partners of solicitors' firms, the proportion of women is less than 25 per cent. Those are the eligible pools from which senior appointments are made.[100] While the attrition rate of women is a vexing issue, statistics show a recent trend towards greater diversity in terms of gender and ethnicity upon entry at the Bar. In 2010, 53 per cent of those called to the Bar were women; 43 per cent were individuals from BAME backgrounds.[101] In addition, at the Criminal Bar at least, there is little expectation that practitioners will have an Oxbridge background.

B.   Solicitors as judges

4.23 The path to eligibility of solicitors for judicial offices has not been smooth. In 1938 solicitors became eligible as chairmen of quarter sessions, and in 1949 as stipendiary magistrates. They became indirectly eligible for appointment as recorders or circuit judges in 1971, as a result of a compromise.[102] The Courts Act 1971 also gave some powers promptly used by the Lord Chancellor to direct that solicitors may appear

---

[99] OFT, 278; Sir Colin Campbell, Stevens 1993.
[100] Christopher Stephens, Oral Evidence, Committee on the Constitution.
[101] The General Council of the Bar of England and Wales and the Bar Standard Boards, 'Bar Barometer 2012: Trends in the profile of the Bar' (London: the General Council of the Bar of England and Wales, November 2012). In 2010–11, however, 49% of calls to the Bar were women, and 44% were of individuals from BAME backgrounds, *ibid.*, pp. 39–41.
[102] 313 HL Deb., 1652 et seq. (17 December 1970); L. Blom-Cooper, 'The Judiciary in an Era of Law Reform' (1966) 37 *Political Quarterly* 378; Lord Goodman, 288 HL Deb. 616 (29 January 1968). Cf. B. Abel Smith and R. Stevens, *In Search of Justice* (London: Allen Lane, 1968), p. 190.

and conduct proceedings in the Crown Court.[103] A solicitor had to serve as a recorder for five years before becoming eligible for appointment as a circuit judge.[104] Such a ban on direct appointment to the circuit and the High Court was removed by Lord Mackay in 1990.[105] Solicitor-advocates, defined by their higher rights of audience, were expressly encouraged to consider the bench, and Michael Sachs was the first solicitor appointed to the High Court in 1993. Since then, only three other solicitors have been appointed to the High Court: Lawrence Collins in 2000, Henry Hodge in 2004 and Gary Hickinbottom in 2008. Lawrence Collins then became Lord Justice of Appeal in 2007, and a Law Lord in 2009.

Several arguments have been raised about the entry of solicitors to the bench.[106] It was argued in 1970 that the Bar was too small, with 3,000 members, to remain the exclusive source for judicial appointments, especially in the light of the rapidly increasing number of judicial appointments in the higher and the lower levels of the judiciary.[107] Yet only practising barristers with maturity and experience of advocacy before the higher courts were seen as qualified to try cases. The lack of background in litigation was once considered to make solicitors, all things being equal, less likely to be qualified for higher judicial appointment, though it has always been admitted that the appointment of some solicitors could be justified from time to time. The high quality of the English judiciary has long been perceived as relying upon choosing judges from among the leading barristers, who have had large experience in litigation and who have absorbed the Bar's traditions of independence and integrity.[108] But this is 'a thin basis for denying the entire solicitors' branch of the profession and the public the advantage of wider choice in selecting judges'.[109] Nonetheless, 'it is fair

---

[103] Courts Act 1971, s. 12.   [104] Administration of Justice Act 1973, s. 15.

[105] Courts and Legal Services Act 1990, s. 17 (solicitor-advocates). Until 1993 the only solicitors who had reached the High Court were those solicitors transferring to the Bar, see the Lord Chancellor, 312 HL Deb., 319 (19 November 1970).

[106] 235 HL Deb. 954–2 (23 November 1961) 288 HL Deb., 612–19 (Goodman), 636–9 (Gardiner), (29 January 1968); 312 HL Deb., 1279 (Fletcher), 1280–281 (Dilhorne), 1295–97 (Goodman), 1304 (Denning), 1318–22 (Hailsham) (19 November 1970); 313 HL Deb. 1362 et seq. (19 December 1970). For an exhaustive examination see JUSTICE, 'The Judiciary. The Report of a JUSTICE Sub-committee' (Chairman: Peter Webster QC, 1972), paras. 9–20.

[107] The Beeching Commission, Cmnd. 4153 (1969), (1969).

[108] Lord Gardiner, 'Two Lawyers or One?' (1970) 23 CLP 1, 19; Cecil, *The English Judge*, 14–15.

[109] M. Zander, 'Book Review', 35 MLR 104, 105 (1972); Lord Goodman, *Hansard*, HL, vol. 288, col. 616 (29 January 1968).

to say that the absolute integrity and high quality of the superior judges have been closely connected with the modern ethos of practice at the Bar'.[110] Concerns about the professional competence of some solicitor-advocates have also regularly been raised.[111] In response, solicitor-advocates have themselves expressed concern that 'judicial appraisal' may form part of the quality assurance process overseen by the Legal Services Commission.

Recent encouragements from the Commission and the Lord Chief Justice to apply have not been effective. In December 2010, the Lord Chief Justice, Igor Judge, admitted before the House of Lords' Constitution Committee that the recent increased efforts from the judiciary had been unsuccessful as solicitors aged thirty-eight to forty-five had not been enabled to apply for appointment as a recorder or a district judge.[112] The Judicial Appointments Commission's ten-year analysis of the appointment of solicitor candidates shows that solicitors are performing better at entry- and mid-level positions under the new appointments regime than under the previous methods of appointment.[113] But the number of solicitors applying has hardly changed for most roles over the past ten years, and has even dropped for High Court positions. In addition to prejudices against solicitors, the geographical and jurisdictional flexibility of the senior judiciary can be difficult for solicitors. A highly paid solicitor with aspirations to the High Court or the Supreme Court (Lord Collins is a former head of litigation at City firm Herbert Smith) would need to take time out of practice for a part-time appointment at around the age of 40, when most solicitors are at their fee-earning peak. A fee-paid judicial office thus entails a significant drop in salary. One of the High Court judges who was once a City

---

[110] S.A. de Smith, *Constitutional and Administrative Law* (Englewood Cliffs, NJ: Prentice Hall, 1971), 369.

[111] *QiuYeu* (unreported) Southwark Crown Court, see (2009) *Law Society Gazette*, 21 May 2009, 22 May 2009 and 17 March 2010. There Gledhill J in open court, at the conclusion of a criminal trial, gave his critical views on the ability of some of the solicitor-advocates appearing before him; for a similar debate in Scotland following *Woodside (Alexander)* v. *HM Advocate* [2009] HCHAC 19 (HCJ), see R. S. Shiels, 'Professional Conduct and the Solicitor Advocate' (2009) *Criminal Law Review*, 794.

[112] Lord Chief Justice, Unrevised transcript of evidence taken before The Select Committee on the Constitution, Evidence Session No. 1, Questions 1–32, 15 December 2010. Oral Evidence before the Committee on the Constitution, Lord Neuberger MR (Q 250) and Lady Justice Hallett (Q 254). 'Judicial Selection and Recommendations for Appointment Statistics', England and Wales, April 2010 to September 2010, Statistics bulletin.

[113] January 2010.

solicitor noted how he would work weekends and use annual leave to ensure that sitting did not reduce his billable hours.[114]

The reluctance of City firms to allow their partners to hold part-time judicial posts is well known. It has been suggested that an application to the bench from a solicitor showed disloyalty to the law firm, and becoming a recorder was once reported as committing 'career suicide'.[115] A part-time judicial office can seem impossible for those juggling the demands of practice and family life. The length of time between the offer of appointment and the judge commencing office, and the lack of certainty as to when the successful candidate will get a position also exacerbate the difficulties of solicitors in applying to the bench. At best, for some of the bigger City firms, a part-time judicial appointment is equivalent to pro bono work – a part of their corporate social responsibility activities – but even that requires a significant cultural change within the solicitors' profession.[116]

A further development is that a significant part of the business of the top private law firms is in commercial arbitration between companies who prefer their services in dispute resolution to the length and expense which they anticipate if they proceed through the courts. It is an important matter for discussion, but outside the remit of this book, as to how the judiciary can benefit from the expertise of these solicitors.

4.24 Legal executives face similar barriers. There were 24,509 Legal Professional Associates – effectively paralegals of all sorts – in 2001 and 51,250 Legal Professional Associates in 2009, an increase of 109 per cent. Among legal executive lawyers, 75 per cent are women and more than 13 per cent are of black or minority ethnicity. It is reasonable to assume that some of these associates could undertake low-level work, and changes introduced by the Tribunals, Courts and Enforcement Act 2007 made Fellows of CILEX, which trains these legal professionals, eligible to apply for selected judicial roles, such as that of deputy district judge. Associate prosecutors are trained by CILEX and many are supervised employees of the Crown Prosecution Service conducting simple prosecutions, for example road traffic matters. Nonetheless it remains to be seen how many will succeed in rising up to (yet alone beyond) the level of district judge.

---

[114] See also Lord Collins, Written evidence before the Committee on the Constitution, paras 7–10; Lady Justice Hallett, Oral Evidence Q 254.

[115] Oral Evidence before the Committee on the Constitution, Baroness Pashar (Q 314); H. Genn.

[116] F. Gibb, 'Lord Judge: Recession could Harm Judicial Diversity', *The Times* (12 March 2009); Committee on the Constitution Report 2012, para. 125.

C. Women on the bench

4.25 The role of women in the judiciary is unfortunately rather limited. The first full-time female judge was Elizabeth Lane who became a county court judge in 1962 before moving to the High Court in 1965, much later than in a number of European countries.[117] There were two women at the High Court in 1974 out of seventy-five judges, against sixteen out of 108 today.[118] Lady Hale became the first and so far only female Lord of Appeal in Ordinary in 2004. Today there are four women out of thirty-eight judges at the Court of Appeal. Three women sat on the circuit (as against over 200 men) in 1973, against 101 out of 680 circuit judges today.[119] In comparison, women Justices of the Peace comprised more than a third of the total number of lay justices (over 19,000) in 1974; they constituted 51 per cent of the serving magistrates in 2012.[120]

In 1973, only 13 per cent of newly admitted solicitors were women and 10 per cent of those called to the Bar.[121] Many voices have criticised the senior judiciary for being insufficiently representative of society,[122] with the danger of losing public confidence in the courts as a result. In a renewed awareness in the 1990s, the senior judiciary acknowledged the need to increase the number of women on the bench and the issue came before Parliament in 1996.[123] By 2000, despite the size of the judiciary in England and Wales increasing tenfold from 300 in 1970 to 3,000 in 2000, the percentage of women appointed to the bench had not grown substantially.[124]

Action was taken to give effect to the senior judiciary's declarations of good will. Both Lord Chancellors Mackay (1987–97) and Lord

---

[117] Bell, *Judiciaries within Europe*, 315.

[118] Rose Heilbron was the first woman to sit as a recorder in 1956 before appointment to the High Court in 1974.

[119] Two of the three were former county court judges who had become circuit judges under the Courts Act 1971.

[120] 822 HL Deb. 467, 168 (5 August 1971); Judicial Statistics, 'Serving magistrates by HMCTS region, England and Wales' (31 March 2012).

[121] McGlynn, 'Status of Women Lawyers', 95.

[122] E.g., M. Berlins and C. Dyer, *The Law Machine* (London: Penguin, 2000), p. 71.

[123] Lord Taylor, 'The Judiciary in the Nineties', The Richard Dimbleby Lecture (30 November 1992); HoC Home Affairs Committee, 'Report on Judicial Appointment Procedures', 1996.

[124] L. Barmes and K. Malleson, 'The Legal Profession as Gatekeeper to the Judiciary: Design Faults in Measures to Enhance Diversity' (2011) 74 MLR 245.

Falconer (2003–07) actively encouraged women to apply for QC and junior judicial posts. A method of selection was introduced in 2003 which was shown to reduce bias in the selection of certain district judges.[125] The CRA, as noted above, requires the Judicial Appointments Commission to have regard to diversity at the level of the selection pool. In spite of these efforts, a 2008 survey showed that the proportion of women in the senior judiciary (High Court and above) had only marginally progressed since 2003, with representation of women of 6.8 per cent in 2003 against 9.6 per cent in 2008.[126]

The loss of younger women from the legal profession has been a significant factor in the low number of women judges.[127] For a long time barriers to women's success would exist at each point in their careers at the Bar, from obtaining a pupillage to getting clerks to assign work to them.[128] Women solicitors also experienced difficulty in their day-to-day professional activities.[129] The difficulties are lesser today with the entry rate into the Bar having reached equality between men and women, and clerks being of a different generation and having a different mindset towards women. The argument of an inevitable time-lag between the introduction of equal opportunities measures and their implementation through changes in social attitudes is nonetheless becoming increasingly less persuasive.[130] As a result, the legal profession has regularly been invited to bring about changes in its composition at the very top, a matter to which we return when considering the appointments to the Supreme Court.

---

[125] G. Healy, G. Kirton, M. Ozbilgin, M. Calveley, C. Forson, F. Oikelome and A. Tatli, *Assessment Centres for Judicial Appointments and Diversity* (Research Report for the Department of Constitutional Affairs, 2006); C. Thomas, *Judicial Diversity and the Appointment of Deputy District Judges* (London: CJA, 2006).

[126] Equality and Human Rights Commission, 'Sex and Power' (2008), p. 9.

[127] McGlynn, 'Status of Women Lawyers'.

[128] Berlins and Dyer, *The Law Machine*, 41; H. Kennedy, *Eve Was Framed: Women and British Justice* (London: Vintage, 1993, revised edn 2005); R. Hazell, *The Bar on Trial* (London: Quartet, 1978).

[129] See, for example, the letter of Vera M. Brown (1972) 116 *Solicitors' Journal* 81–2, in which she protests against the identification of lady solicitors as secretaries, both by the profession and by laymen.

[130] Joint Parliamentary Scrutiny Committee on the Draft Constitutional Renewal Bill, 'The Draft Constitutional Renewal Bill. Report' (HC 551-I and HL 166-I, 2008), para. 197; Barmes and Malleson, 'The Legal Profession as Gatekeeper to the Judiciary: Design Faults in Measures to Enhance Diversity', 270.

D. Legal academics as judges

4.26 Appointment of legal academics as judges is rare.[131] It is generally thought that the legal academic is not qualified for appointment directly as a trial judge, with control of a jury, if he were to take the usual starting position of recorder. The traditional and recommended route to the bench for academics starts with tribunals: most tribunals are essentially fact-finders[132] but in a less formal environment, and forensic experience can thus be gained there. Recordership can then be acquired, before applying to the High Court. Conversely it has always been accepted, at least in principle and taking into account one conception of 'merit', that legal academics could be appointed to the House of Lords or Supreme Court, because they would deal with 'pure law' or principles there, and indeed their background would equip them particularly well to deal with some academic points of law and questions of social policy.

However, the barriers between the academic and judicial professions remain stark and such an appointment is not expected in the near future. Many of the judges interviewed thought that it would be difficult to 'parachute' academics into the Court of Appeal, and some thought that the tendency of top academics to specialise in particular parts of the law may be a disadvantage on the bench where there is little possibility of hearing cases regularly in a discrete area. Academics are permitted to choose their own areas of specialism but flexibility may be of more value in the judiciary. The greater mobility under the Crime and Courts Bill 2012,[133] however, with wider opportunities to be deployed to the High Court, would seem to surmount that objection. It supports the concept of progression through the ranks and increased diversity.

E. CPS and government lawyers

4.27 The eligibility of lawyers from the Government Legal Service and Crown Prosecution Service (CPS) is a matter of debate; the composition of these groups is far more diverse than the rest of the legal profession. Government lawyers are eligible to sit as deputy district judges

---

[131] Recent past and present full-time academics now in full-time judicial office include Baroness Hale, Lord Justice Buxton, Lord Justice Kay, Lord Justice Beatson, Mr Justice Cranston, and Lord Justice Elias; B. Hale, 'Equality and the Judiciary: Why Should We Want More Women Judges?' [2001] PL 489.

[132] Not all: the Social Security Commission is about pure law.

[133] See paras. 3.34 and 3.35.

(magistrates' courts), civil recorders and fee-paid tribunal judges, except in matters which involve their own department, because they would not be seen as independent – yet these matters are those in which they are most experienced and skilled. The problem, reinforced by some interviewees, is most acute in relation to the lawyers from the CPS: they are in principle eligible for recorder or deputy district judge posts but the fact that most prosecutions are brought by the CPS limits the opportunities to sit on criminal cases, and the lack of part-time judicial experience makes a full-time salaried judicial position less likely.[134]

More thought might be given to what constitutes a true conflict of interest. Doubts have thus been raised that the current sitting limitation for CPS lawyers could be justified since somebody at the referral Bar who does nothing but prosecution work can be a recorder in that area and sit on criminal cases.[135]

While it remains necessary to avoid conflicts of interest, there may be an argument in favour of relaxing the requirement to have acted as a fee-paid judge and for the Judicial Appointments Commission to find alternative means of testing their abilities. CPS lawyers could also sit as part-time judges away from the geographic area in which they work as prosecutors. This is problematic too, however, given the increasing number of formerly prosecuting agencies now under the CPS umbrella. Responsibility for the numerous prosecutions brought for benefit fraud by the Department for Work and Pensions, for example, has now been transferred to the CPS. While this amalgamation brings greater consistency in public prosecutions, it entails that more persons are CPS employees, and more prosecutions are brought by the CPS. This must be read against the House of Lords' judgment that even a juror who is an employee of the CPS cannot sit on a case brought by the CPS as it would infringe the principle *nemo iudex in sua causa*.[136]

F.   The tribunals judiciary

4.28 Before the Tribunals, Courts and Enforcement Act 2007 came into force, members of tribunals would be appointed by the relevant Secretary

---

[134] Committee on the Constitution, Committee on the Constitution, Twenty-Fifth Report. Judicial Appointments (7 March 2012), paras. 126–32.
[135] *Ibid.*, para. 130.   [136] *R* v. *Abdroikov* [2007 1 WLR 2679.

of State. There was no consistent practice between departments, although a common set of the main rules for appointments was produced by a team of tribunals' representatives and lawyers from the Ministry of Justice following the Leggatt Review. The establishment of the Judicial Appointments Commission thus introduced significant changes and consistency in appointments procedures. Interviewees were prompt to acknowledge that the systemic changes following the Leggatt Review and the Tribunals, Courts and Enforcement Act 2007 had raised the profile of tribunals. Some interviewees emphasised the value of appraising part-timers and the existence of mentors, the greater diversity among tribunal judges, as well as the fact that it was hard work and that a bad part-timer would not last long in the post.

The merger of courts and tribunals within HMCTS in 2011 has led to a greater interplay between them. Judicial moves between courts and tribunals are simply a matter of work assignment and it is also conceivable that some tribunal members and lower court judges may be trained together in the near future. The deployment of some tribunal judges to the High Court under the Crime and Courts Bill, as noted earlier,[137] illustrates a possible career progression. The Bill's impact may be restricted, however, as many tribunals are still specialist tribunals, and the expertise gained in a particular social matter may not be sufficient for advancement to the High Court. It would seem desirable to further develop progression through tribunals too.

One may also recall the recent case of *R (Cart)* v. *UT*,[138] where the UK Supreme Court clarified the circumstances in which the unappealable decisions of the Upper Tribunal are amenable to judicial review in the High Court. It held that permission for judicial review should be granted if the claim raises an important point of principle or some other compelling reason to review the case. This could be seen as evidence that the immigration tribunals can contribute to the development of the law, something that would not have been accepted ten to fifteen years ago, when there was a much greater variety between adjudicators. As one interviewee observed, however, an alternative explanation, equally valid, is that the workload in tribunals is such that the legal issues remain 'floating' and have to be solved by courts.

---

[137] See above, paras. 3.34 and 3.35.
[138] *R (Cart)* v. *UT* [2011] UKSC 28; [2012] 1 AC; *R (MR (Pakistan))* v. *UT (Immigration & Asylum Chamber) & SSHD* [2011] UKSC 28.

III.   Judicial mobility and progression

4.29 Each bench is perceived as requiring different skills. In this context, promotion 'up the ranks' may not be taken for granted, even for post-holders who are thought to be doing very well in their present post. Instead, it may be thought, promotion should only naturally work within the same bench itself (e.g. one may be promoted to be the Presiding Judge of a certain Division, although some interviewees rejected the idea that this could be seen as a promotion). Indeed, the fact that each post must be subject to competition substantially dilutes the expectation that 'good performers' will be promoted as a matter of course. We have noted that the Crime and Courts Bill strengthens the transparency and openness of the process by transferring within the remit of the Judicial Appointments Commission the selection of deputy High Court judges.[139]

With the adoption of the Crime and Courts Bill, judicial appointments are open to competition up to the level of the High Court, Court of Appeal and again at the UK Supreme Court. At the level of the Court of Appeal, the candidates are effectively promoted from the High Court. Some have suggested that appointments to the Court of Appeal could be open to competition from outside the High Court. Some stark differences, however, between the two appellate courts explain the High Court preference. The Supreme Court gives judgment in about sixty cases per year, a number markedly small in comparison with the caseload of the Court of Appeal.[140] The Supreme Court is widely perceived as dealing with 'pure law' and as such most interviewees did not consider the lack of judicial experience as a disqualification in itself for appointment. The Court of Appeal requires some criminal work, and part-time experience as a High Court judge in this field ensures that the appointee is immediately operational.

Judicial appraisal has rightly been suggested as a way to enhance career progression. The Judicial Appointments Commission supports appraisal as evidence of the candidates' performance,[141] and appraisal is also one of

---

[139] Crime and Courts Bill 2012, Senior Courts Act 1981 s. 9(2CA), as inserted by para. 49, see above, para. 4.16.

[140] Ministry of Justice, 'Judicial and Court Statistics 2011'; G. Drewry and L. Blom-Cooper, The House of Lords and the English Court of Appeal', in Blom-Cooper, Dickson and Drewry (eds), *The Judicial House of Lords 1876–2009*, p. 48.

[141] Thus the Judicial Appointments Commission, in collaboration with the Association of Her Majesty's District Judges, developed a process of using appraisal information in the reference process for the District Judge Selection Exercise in 2011, which will be adapted

the suggestions made by the Advisory Panel on Judicial Diversity, in order to enhance the structure of judicial careers.

Some informal mechanisms for accountability and promotion existed before the CRA, with informal discussions taking place between judges within a circuit or at district court level. These discussions would eventually shape the views of the Senior Presiding Judge when deciding about appointments. An appraisal scheme administered and operated by the judiciary would be desirable. Yet it raises a dual concern of undue interference with judicial decisions and of abdication of responsibility when promotions are heavily based on appraisals by peers.[142] There is currently no comprehensive system for appraisal for courts or tribunals.[143] The appraisal system is rather 'patchy' for tribunals, but appraisal also applies to deputy district judges: the district judge will sit with a deputy district judge once a year. Judicial appraisal is a costly exercise: a judge has to take a day out of sitting to appraise another. Unlike tribunals, the judiciary never had a budget in place for appraisals, and the recent financial cuts make the development of appraisal unlikely.

Judicial appraisal needs to be finely tuned to be meaningful. There was a broad consensus among interviewees that appraisal should apply to part-time judges, such as recorders. Many interviewees thought that full-time judges who are working with each other need not be appraised. Horizontal appraisal, between colleagues, within a collegiate court is not appropriate. One suggestion would be to involve recently retired judges in appraisals. The factors to be considered during an appraisal also need to be carefully drafted. The Tribunals' Protocol for appraisals lists 'number of appeals' as one element of the appraisal.[144] It can only be one factor among others since the appeal could be triggered by a genuinely difficult issue rather than, for example, excessive sentencing from a judge. But this should not undercut the potential relevance of the factor; some judges are systematically appealed against because they do seem to

---

for the 2013 District Judge (Civil) Exercise, 'Evidence from the Judicial Appointments Commission to the Senior Salaries Review Body' (September 2012), para. 16; K. Malleson, 'Judicial Training and Performance Appraisal: The Problem of Judicial Independence' (1997) 60 MLR 655.

[142] Bell, *Judiciaries within Europe*, 24.

[143] A pilot recorder scheme of appraisal on the Northern circuit built on an appraisal scheme developed at District Court level in Wales but, though it went well, it had to stop due to lack of funding.

[144] Judicial Studies Board, 'Appraisal Standards and Appraiser Competences in Tribunals', December 2009.

indulge in excessive sentencing, and nothing happens in practice as a result. Indeed, a proper appraisal system may make a particular impact at Crown Court level. In 2011, 72 per cent of case law showed guilty pleas: so it is problematic if significant numbers of trial judges are regularly over-sentencing without any form of appraisal. Sentences take effect immediately in England and the offender may have served his sentence by the time that his appeal against it might be heard.

Interviewees noted how the judicial sentencing guidelines from the Sentencing Council had improved judicial performance, with some pointing to the need to ensure that the guidelines were followed – appraisal would be helpful in this regard. Sentencing based on the guidelines has become a complicated exercise and requests for appeal from the Attorney General have increased on the basis that judges do not tick all the boxes required under the sentencing guidelines. Some interviewees also considered the appraisals done by courts' user groups or, for example, counsel. Many had in mind a legal magazine survey, giving out names which were then picked up by the media. The survey of judges was not systematic, however, and the views of everyone in London and in the courts outside London would have been required. More to the point, one needs only one strong bitter view to distort the survey.

While both mentoring and appraisal support career progression by bringing in principles of conduct on a one-to-one basis, mentoring is a personal development tool when appraisal can be used for promotion. If appraisal is taken into account for promotion purposes, however, a judicial appraiser would seem necessary to safeguard judicial independence. Promotion is now decided by the Judicial Appointments Commission. There is a need for differentiated methods of selection between the appointment of a candidate to the position of judge for the first time, at whatever level of the judicial hierarchy, and the promotion of a judge up the judicial ladder.[145] This would support the development of a fast-track appointments system, so that those willing to gain entry at a senior level can be brought in to the judiciary on the basis of their judicial experience and achievements. A fast-track is desirable subject to maintaining a fair and open appointment process based on merit.

---

[145] L. Blom-Cooper, 'The Age of Judicial Responsibility: The Retirement and Resignation of Appellate Court Judges', in S. Shetreet and C. Forsyth (eds.), *The Culture of Judicial Independence: Conceptual Foundations and Practical Challenges* (Leiden: M. Njihof, 2012).

4.30 Training can also be raised as one element supporting the professionalism and career progression of the English judiciary. The first judicial sentencing seminar took place in the Royal Courts of Justice in the 1960s; it lasted one day. In 1979, a systematic structure for judicial training, the Judicial Studies Board, was created, providing a type of pupillage, with trainees sitting alongside a more experienced judge, and an induction programme with annual refresher courses.[146] In 2010 the Judicial Studies Board became a Judicial College; the content of judicial education remains the responsibility of judges themselves, with the aim of promoting a culture of self-development among judges. The recognition that all judges need regular training further departs from the long-established view that the art of judging was seen to be acquired almost 'by osmosis' during a judicial career. The focus is on practical skills and ethical standards, more than on updates on the law. Financial constraints, however, limit the impact of training.

4.31 We should also mention the salaried part-time working scheme now operating both in the courts and tribunals, up to but excluding the High Court.[147] It is not clear yet whether the extra flexibility in working hours will prove sufficiently attractive to those in private practice, in particular those with childcare responsibilities. One senior judge interviewed doubted the impact of this scheme, noting that the fractional posts available to district judges seemed to have been taken by male judges near retirement. This could mean that there are not enough female lawyers high enough up the ranks to be considered for those positions, or that male judges are to be preferred for whatever reason for those fractional posts. Following criticisms that opportunities for fractional working should be available at all levels of the judiciary, the Crime and Courts Bill 2012 provides for part-time appointments at the High Court and above, with the aim of increasing the number of those with childcare responsibilities there.[148]

---

[146] Cf. for other European judiciaries, G. Di Frederico (ed.), *Recruitment, Professional Evaluation and Career of Judges and Prosecutors in Europe* (Bologna; IRSIG-CNR, 2005); CEPEJ, 'European Judicial Systems Edition 2012 (2010 Data): Efficiency and Quality of Justice'.

[147] The first cadre of circuit judges commenced salaried part-time sittings during 2005–06, with a steady increase of judicial office holders into the scheme since then. The right to request flexible working is provided in the Employment Rights Act 1996, s. 80F (as inserted by the Employment Act 2002, s. 47(1) and (2)).

[148] The Bill introduces a reference to the full-time equivalent number of judges to the statutory number of judges in the High Court, Court of Appeal and UK Supreme Court, Crime and Courts Bill 2012, sch. 12.

The Judicial Appointments Chairman has argued that salaried part-time working in the High Court would be transformational,[149] and it was recommended by the Constitution Committee; it certainly supports the idea of career progression between the lower and senior ranks with a consistent policy of flexible working. While many judges seem to believe that part-time working would be difficult to accommodate within the senior judiciary, given the long trials which can take place, at least one senior judge interviewed concurred with the Lord Chief Justice that it is possible to organise sitting patterns for High Court judges who have caring responsibilities, so that during, for example, half-term school holidays they can be at home.[150] The acceptance of career breaks was also seen as a further step, not yet achieved either within the judiciary or the legal professions, towards increasing the number of women within the judiciary.

The Lord Chief Justice has now expressed his support in the Crime and Courts Bill for more flexible deployment of tribunal judges and, subject to business need, for measures to enable more flexible working patterns in the High Court and above.

IV.   The UK Supreme Court

4.32 The United Kingdom has still never had an ethnic minority Law Lord and has only one Law Lady. One issue, therefore, is whether consideration of greater diversity at the UK Supreme Court would lead to the dilution of the 'merit' principle, at the heart of appointments to the highest Court in the land. Another matter of debate is the strengthening of the democratic accountability through a possible political input in the appointment process.

A.   The appointment process

4.33 Applicants to the UK Supreme Court must have held high judicial office for at least two years, or must satisfy the judicial-appointment eligibility condition on a fifteen-year basis, or have been a qualifying

---

[149] Oral Evidence, question 364.

[150] For a word of caution on part-time arrangements in senior courts, see Oral Evidence from Lord Carswell (Q 296), Lord Woolf (Q 297); Lord Mackay (Q 144) and the Oral Evidence from the Lord Chief Justice (Q 189).

practitioner for at least fifteen years.[151] The importance of representations of the different legal systems within the United Kingdom justifies the requirement that, between them, the Supreme Court Justices 'will have knowledge of, and experience in, the law of each part of the United Kingdom', thus building upon the convention that two members from the House of Lords were from Scotland and one from Northern Ireland.[152]

The appointment process relies upon an ad hoc Selection Commission of five members, convened by the Lord Chancellor when a vacancy arises.[153] It is chaired by the President of the Court and includes the Deputy President of the Supreme Court and three other members drawn respectively from the Judicial Appointments Commission, the Judicial Appointments Board for Scotland and the Northern Ireland Judicial Appointments Commission.[154] The potential conflict of interest in relation to the President and Deputy President of the Court has been widely criticised, and the fact that the President of the UK Supreme Court chairs the panel appointing his/her own successor has also been recognised as inappropriate. Both are due to disappear under the Crime and Courts Bill 2012.[155]

Supreme Court appointments must be on merit and remain subject, under the CRA, to some consultation with the senior judges, the Lord Chancellor, the First Ministers of Scotland and Wales, and the Secretary of State for Northern Ireland.[156] The consultations with senior judges prior to the shortlisting of candidates create potential conflicts of interest since they might themselves have applied for those posts.[157]

The ad hoc Selection Commission must submit a report to the Lord Chancellor which must state who has been selected and who was consulted.[158] The Lord Chancellor is then required to consult with the same persons as the Commission.[159] The first minister in Scotland and the first

---

[151] CRA, s. 25(1) as amended by ss. 50–52 of the Tribunals and Enforcement Act 2007. High judicial office includes High Court judges of England and Wales, and of Northern Ireland; Court of Appeal judges of England and Wales, and of Northern Ireland; and judges of the Court of Session.

[152] CRA, s. 27(8). The Committee on the Constitution noted that this is not comparable to the appointment of an individual from an underrepresented group, Committee on the Constitution Report 2012, para. 92.

[153] CRA, sch. 8.   [154] CRA, s. 27.

[155] CRA, ss. 27 and 27A as amended or inserted by the Crime and Courts Bill 2012, sch. 12, paras. 4 and 5.

[156] Ibid.   [157] Paterson and Paterson, 'Guarding the Guardians?', 29.   [158] CRA, s. 28.

[159] Ibid.

minister for Wales and the Secretary of State for Northern Ireland are also to be consulted. If the Lord Chancellor is content with the recommendation made by the Commission, he forwards the person's name to the prime minister who, in turn, sends the recommendation to the Queen. The Lord Chancellor can reject a recommendation of the Commission but only on the grounds that the person 'is not suitable for the office concerned'. The Commission is then not permitted to reselect that candidate.[160] The Lord Chancellor can also require the Commission to reconsider a selection if (a) there is not enough evidence that the person is suitable for the office concerned, (b) there is evidence that the person is not the best candidate on merit, or (c) there is not enough evidence that if the person were appointed the judges of the court would between them have knowledge of, and experience of practice in, the law of each part of the United Kingdom. Reasons must be given in writing by the Lord Chancellor to the Selection Commission for rejecting or requiring reconsideration of a selection.[161]

B.   The appointment authorities

4.34 Currently the panel includes two members of the Supreme Court itself, and three representatives from the three jurisdictions in the United Kingdom, who do not have to be lay persons. It is suggested that the Selection Commission itself should be expanded specifically to include lay persons and preferably with a greater diversity and ethnicity mix. Experience from other countries tends to show that the more diverse the panel, the more diverse the appointments.[162] The presence of some senior academic lawyers and/or senior representatives of the legal profession would make the commitment to seeking diversity demonstrably visible and more effective. As noted above, Supreme Court decisions normally resolve higher questions of law, and academics, even if themselves removed from the tumult of litigation, can have an expert view on how convincing some applicants are in their judgments.

Another feature of the English model limits undue political interference: the Lord Chancellor currently exercises a power of veto over the recommendation of the Selection Commission rather than a choice.[163] However, under the Crime and Courts Bill 2012, the Lord Chancellor

---

[160] CRA, s. 30.   [161] CRA, s. 30.   [162] Bell, *Judiciaries within Europe*.
[163] The German position is relevant as there a veto power can be exercised by the executive, see J. Bell, Written Evidence before Parliament, 2004 and *Judiciaries within Europe*.

may sit (but not chair) as a member of the Selection Commission for the appointment of the President of the Supreme Court.[164] In such case, he would lose his power of veto.[165] He would, however, retain the right to ask the appointing commission to reconsider its chosen candidate.[166]

One may doubt whether it is appropriate for the Lord Chancellor to sit as a member of the selection commission for the office of the UK Supreme Court President.[167] If, however, this proposal becomes law, the closer involvement of the Lord Chancellor may be accommodated with greater safeguards against any improper political influence. One such safeguard exists in Germany, the first place to have a public list of eligibility. Whether people are included on this list is something which can be (and is) challenged in the courts, and the choice of people for appointment from the list can equally be challenged. Thus, a German judge was able (successfully) to challenge the nomination of a member of the Green party to the *Bundesgerichtshof* on the ground that he was better qualified (a view which was shared by the judges in the *Bundesgerichtshof* itself). The right of applicants or disappointed colleagues to challenge decisions may be a sufficient safeguard against improper political decisions.[168]

C.   Merit and diversity

4.35 Many politically significant decisions are taken at the level of the Court of Appeal and UK Supreme Court. Here individuals are needed with experience in reasoning on points of principle and policy of the

---

[164] See CRA 2005, s. 27(1)(c), as inserted by the Crime and Courts Bill, sch. 12, paras. 4 and 5. Under sch. 12 Crime and Courts Bill, the details of the selection process for appointments to the UK Supreme Court will be removed from the CRA 2005. They will instead be set out in secondary legislation, with a power conferred to the Lord Chancellor to make regulations about membership and procedures for the selection process, see CRA 2005, s. 27A, as inserted by the Crime and Courts Bill, sch. 12, paras. 4 and 5. Consultation with the three heads of judiciary in each of the UK's legal jurisdictions will be required before making regulations, and the regulations will be subject to affirmative resolution procedure, see CRA 2005, s. 27A, as inserted by the Crime and Courts Bill, sch. 12, paras. 4 and 5.

[165] See CRA 2005, ss. 27 and 27A, as amended or inserted by the Crime and Courts Bill, sch. 12, paras. 4 and 5.

[166] CRA 2005, ss. 27 and 27A as amended or inserted by the Crime and Courts Bill, sch. 12, paras. 4 and 5.

[167] Constitution Committee, 'Second Report Crime and Courts Bill [HL]' (June 2012), paras. 15–17.

[168] J. Bell, 'Memorandum', in Select Committee on Constitutional Reform Bill, 'First Report. Written Evidence', vol. II, HC 125-II (24 June 2004); D.P. Kommers, 'The German Judiciary', In P.H. Russell and D.M. O'Brien (eds), *Judicial Independence in the Age of Democracy* (Charlottesville/London: University of Georgia, 2001) p. 131.

highest importance. More than 50 per cent of litigation brought to the Supreme Court is public law litigation.[169] Should a candidate of equal merit to another candidate but with great public law experience be preferred? The answer to this argument is provided by the English judicial culture. Traditionally, one of the many strengths of the English judiciary has been that, when promoted to the High Court, judges would gain a breadth of experience and move from one type of case to the other – even though some areas, such as intellectual property, are seen as needing particular expertise. The expectation would be that accession to the Court of Appeal might lead to promotion to the UK Supreme Court, because it is a sign of the candidate's perceived versatility.

This is not to say that time served in the High Court or Court of Appeal is a necessary stage for justices of the UK Supreme Court. It is rather that, once we recognise that appointments to the UK Supreme Court or Court of Appeal could come from outside the Court of Appeal or the High Court, then the importance of the candidate's specific individual expertise to the collective composition of the Court may become decisive. Guidance from the Lord Chancellor on the notion of merit may assist the panel in concerns for the collective needs of the UK Supreme Court.[170] Lord Phillips further suggested, though did not endorse, one amended statutory test for 'merit' in Supreme Court appointments, as follows: 'The Commission must select that candidate who will best meet the needs of the court, having regard to the judicial qualities required of the Supreme Court Justice and to the current composition of the court.'[171] The guidelines for questioning for nomination to the South African Constitutional Court treat diversity as 'a component of competence'; diversity 'is not an independent requirement superimposed on the constitutional requirement of competence'.[172]

---

[169] Lord Phillips, Evidence before the Committee on the Constitution, Autumn 2011.

[170] CRA, s. 27(9). Under the Crime and Courts Bill 2012, before issuing any guidance to Selection Commissions, the Lord Chancellor will consult the senior judge of the UK Supreme Court. Then guidance will be subject to Parliamentary scrutiny, see CRA 2005, s. 27B, inserted by the Crime and Courts Bill, sch. 12, para. 6. Further, under the Crime and Courts Bill 2012, s. 159 of the Equality Act 2010 will apply to UK Supreme Court Appointments, see Crime and Courts Bill, Pt. 2, sch. 3; HL, Deb., col. 834 (25 Mar 2013).

[171] HL Select Committee on the Constitution, 'Judicial Appointments', Twenty-Fifth Report (7 March 2012), para. 91.

[172] Judicial Services Commission, 'Guidelines for questioning candidates for nomination to the Constitutional Court', p. 5; F. du Bois, 'Judicial Selection in Post-Apartheid South Africa', in K. Malleson and P. H. Russell (eds.), *Appointing Judges in an Age of Judicial Power. Critical Perspectives from Around the World* (University of Toronto Press, 2006), p. 281.

In many other European countries, it is taken for granted that a broad range of experience and expertise in the court sharpens the quality of decision making, and the appointments at constitutional court level reflect a mixture of judicial and non-judicial experience.[173] It seems right that having more female and ethnic minority judges would improve the reasoning, even if not necessarily the outcome, in some decisions.[174] This applies to the UK Supreme Court which hears appeals in panels and to the Court of Appeal which holds hearings in smaller panels.

To take but one example from many, while her peers speak about restricting the defence of duress for criminals who knowingly keep the company of violent people,[175] it is Baroness Hale alone who points out that many such 'criminals' could be previously law-abiding partners of violent men who force them to assist them in their ventures, or to help them cover up their own crimes. One does not have to be a woman to note this point, and not all women will agree with all of her views; but there can be little doubt that her gender enables or even empowers Baroness Hale to share certain wider insights about the potential implications of Supreme Court decisions. Baroness Hale commented, having been outvoted 4:1 on another case, that it could be that the 'physical differences between men and women lead them to have different views of what dignity means in this context. So it is not surprising that women take a different view.'[176]

Similarly, suitably qualified judges from ethnic minorities might, for example, have their own views about how far the police should be allowed in certain designated areas to stop and search anyone for items which may be connected to terrorism. Such a decision was taken by the (then) House of Lords despite a recognised concern that such powers might be used disproportionately against ethnic minorities, in the form of 'racial profiling'.[177] Notably, this decision was overturned by the European Court of Human Rights.[178]

---

[173] C. Thomas, 'Judicial Diversity in the United Kingdom and Other Jurisdictions: A Review of Research, Policies, and Practices' (The Commission for Judicial Appointments, 2005); Advisory panel on judicial diversity, 'Report'.

[174] R. Hunter, C. McGlynn and E. Rackley, *Feminist Judgments: From Theory to Practice* (Oxford: Hart Publishing, 2010); E. Rackley, *Women, Judging and the Judiciary. From Difference to Diversity* (London: Routledge-Cavendish, 2012).

[175] *R v. Hasan* [2005] UKHL 22; [2005] 2 AC 467.

[176] *McDonald Citation*, The Times, 15 October 2011; see also *R v. J* [2005] 1 AC 562 and *R v. G* [2008] UKHL 37.

[177] *R (Gillan) v. Metropolitan Police Commissioner* [2006] UKHL 12.

[178] *Gillan and Quinton v. UK* (2010) 50 EHRR 45.

Lord Sumption's appointment demonstrates that the weight given to academic[179] and intellectual ability might depend upon the judicial role that is being sought. In respect of selection for the Supreme Court, this is particularly significant on account of its relevance to the development of general principles. Further, on that basis, a legal academic or law commissioner relatively unused to litigation and the conduct of trials might be a potential candidate for the Supreme Court.[180] Testing the applicant's aptitude would then involve a review of his or her most significant legal works, perhaps with an eye on whether they typically suggest solutions to common problems.

D.   The role of Parliament

4.36 One often-mooted answer to the problem of diversity is that the appointments to the Supreme Court should be overseen by a parliamentary committee made up of members from a representative spectrum of political parties. Some also argue that the lack of input from the legislature in the appointment process amounts to an unacceptable lack of democratic accountability.[181] Answering to Parliament for the way in which Supreme Court justices are selected, including their awareness of the benefits of greater diversity, constitutes a necessary check on the judiciary. But it does not follow that any individual appointment should be called into question via pre- or post-appointment hearings. However, while the UK Supreme Court appointment system enhances the protection from partisan politics, it falls short of constituting a corporate process of appointments. It has been described as the 'least accountable' system in the common law world because of the lack of elected politicians in the commission's membership, and the lack of devices to enhance transparency.[182] It is arguable that some form of parliamentary involvement in the appointment process of Supreme Court justices would generate a greater political legitimacy of the Supreme Court. This would appear desirable in a context of expanded review of executive and legislative action. Also, the public understanding of the appointment process would be further improved, and the public may indeed become more interested in learning of the powers of the Supreme Court. That

---

[179] For the sake of clarity, Lord Sumption had not been a legal academic.
[180] Lord Clarke, 'Selecting Judges', para. 29.
[181] Paterson and Paterson, 'Guarding the Guardians?'; Mt. Scopus, para. 4.2.
[182] P. Russell, 'Conclusion', in Malleson and Russell (eds.), *Appointing Judges*, 430–1.

would give the media an extra opportunity to educate the public about issues of legal policy, such as judges' approaches to the scope of review under the Human Rights Act 1998, which might be thought to act as a sort of counterbalance to the feeding of inaccurate information from some tabloid newspapers.

Confirmation hearings, however, were rejected by the Joint Select Committee on the Draft Constitutional Renewal Bill in 2008, on the basis that the balance achieved under the CRA made further reforms of the appointment process premature.[183] Concerns were expressed about the risk of politicising the judicial appointments process. It has also been argued that 'the involvement of Parliament would add little, if any, value to the process, be a drain on, or subject to, parliamentary time and resources, and be liable to delay the overall appointments process'.[184] Perhaps another reason would be distrust of the media. Tabloid reporting, which is typically exaggerated in order to excite its readership, may be thought unlikely to contribute helpfully to ascertaining judicial merit, and most would think it to be for the better that such newspapers do not currently involve themselves in campaigns as to who should be appointed to the top judicial positions. Different views may be found in countries where the influence of the media on public life is regarded as healthier.

The House of Lords Select Constitution Committee, in 2012, was opposed to giving Parliament a greater involvement in the judicial appointment process, concluding:

> We are against any proposal to introduce pre-appointment hearings for senior members of the judiciary. However limited the questioning, such hearings could not have any meaningful impact without undermining the independence of those subsequently appointed or appearing to pre-judge their future decisions. In the United Kingdom, judges' legitimacy depends on their independent status and appointment on merit, not on any democratic mandate.
>
> We agree that post-appointment hearings of senior judges would serve no useful purpose. There may be an exception in the case of the Lord Chief Justice and the President of the Supreme Court who undertake leadership roles for which they can properly be held to account.

---

[183] Joint Committee on the Draft Constitutional Renewal Bill, 'The Draft Constitutional Renewal Bill', Report, vol. 1 (2008), para. 164.

[184] Ministry of Justice, 'The Governance of Britain: Analysis of Consultations', Cm 7342-III (2008), para. 175. The deterrent effect of appointment hearings on potential candidates was also considered.

Parliamentarians, acting in that capacity, should not sit on selection panels for judicial appointments. There is no useful role that parliamentarians could play in Judicial Appointments that could not be played by lay members on selection panels. It would not be possible to choose one or two parliamentarians without recourse to political considerations and in so doing it would be difficult to maintain the appearance of an independent judicial appointments process.[185]

A number of points made in this passage must be developed. First, the Constitution Committee rejects the suggestion that some parliamentary Select Committee could hold pre- or post-appointment hearings of the judicial appointees.[186] Critics would emphasise that few interesting questions can be legitimately asked or that questions would be asked which should not be asked for fear of attacking judicial independence or compromising judicial impartiality.[187] Nonetheless, supporters of confirmation hearings have relied in particular upon the Canadian Supreme Court appointment process to defend their case. It is argued that 'beyond the necessary restrictions, Canadian Supreme Court nominees have answered informatively on a broad range of topics . . ., from the qualities that qualify them for the post to the broad relationship between the judiciary and the other branches of state'.[188] The one judge interviewed supporting confirmation hearings, however, took distance from the Canadian system on the ground of its politicisation.

One might consider the American president's power to select Supreme Court justices, which is exercised with the 'advice and consent' of the Senate. In the summer of 2010, for four days, Sonia Sotomayor answered questions from the Senate Judiciary Committee, before her nomination was subject to a vote in the Senate. The *New York Times* thus commented: 'Despite 583 questions from senators amid wall-to-wall news media coverage, her hearing may prove to be as notable for what the country did not learn about her as much as for what it did.'[189] This would support the view that her appointment had been secured during the

---

[185] HL Select Committee on the Constitution, n. 91, pp. 61–2.

[186] Ministry of Justice, 'The Governance of Britain: Judicial Appointments', Consultation Paper CP 25/07, Cm. 7210 (2007), p. 48; see also HL Select Committee on the Constitutional Reform Bill, Minutes of Evidence given by Robert Hazell (6 April 2004).

[187] See the Oral Evidence from Lady Justice Hallett, Lord Irvine and Lord Justice Goldring.

[188] Paterson and Paterson, 'Who's Guarding the Guardians?'; the distinctive social and cultural context singles out the Judicial Appointments Commission from South Africa, where the majority of members of the Appointments Commission are politicians, and where the notion of merit has been modified to integrate ethnical considerations.

[189] Cited by R. Smith, 'Judging the Judges' (2009) 159 NLJ 1154.

consultation that must have preceded the candidate's nomination, in a way which may not be too dissimilar to the consultation process for appointments to the highest court of the UK.

One key difference between the two processes is that the American legislature is part of the consultation process. It might then be further argued that, in the English context, the Westminster system would place the confirmation hearings in the hands of the executive, as it forms the dominant part of the legislature. Indeed, even if such a panel were drawn from a cross-section of political parties, the readiness of recent government ministers publicly to attack judgments which they found unwelcome creates an uneasy background to any political involvement in individual appointments. It follows that the Crime and Courts Bill provision for greater involvement of the Lord Chancellor in appointments to the most senior judiciary in England and Wales is unnecessary and has the potential to reintroduce political patronage.

The House of Lords Constitution Committee also states that 'in the United Kingdom, judges' legitimacy depends on their independent status and appointment on merit, not on any democratic mandate'. Indeed, judicial legitimacy refers to the acceptance of the court by the parties, the citizens and society at large, and there are several different sources of constitutional judicial legitimacy. Legitimacy justifies public trust in the court on the basis of various factors, such as the selection of judges, their independence and the reasoning supporting the court's judgments.[190]

4.37 Most of the European judicial appointment institutions recognise that those who have political responsibility are among those best placed to undertake such scrutiny of candidates for judicial appointments,[191] and various states from the Commonwealth have a legislative input into the process. The variations of legislative involvement reflect a specific balance between distinct values such as impartiality, separation of powers, accountability, transparency and the requirement of a fair representation of civil and/or political society in the composition of the judiciary. In brief, differing cultures of judicial independence shape the selection processes and criteria, and the English model of appointments

---

[190] J.E. Soeharno, 'From Rechtsstaat to Ruler in the Rule of Law: an Inquiry into the Increased Role of the Judiciary', in A. van Hoek et al. (eds.) *Multilevel Governance in Enforcement and Adjudication* (Antwerp: Intersentia, 2006), p. 157.

[191] Bell, 'Memorandum'.

must be assessed in the English constitutional settings, so that each trait of the appointment process should be seen as one part of a whole.[192]

Certainly, any openly political bias can be highly corrosive of the merit principle in judicial appointment. Some of our interviewees were concerned that MPs would allow their own politics and beliefs to influence their decision, for example if candidates offered different views relating to euthanasia (one interviewee remarked that in this area the democratic system was already usurped by having so many Bishops in the House of Lords). Many agreed that a fair reflection of society is a legitimate goal which can achieved within the requirements of maintaining the professional quality and the moral integrity of the judiciary. For this purpose, however, it was thought that greater clarity on criteria and responsibilities of the lay members, with a greater gender and ethnic mix, should be set. Interviewees were keen to have a cross-section of talents, strong and independent lay members who must be able to challenge the judicial members of the panels beyond asking them for reasons for their views.

V. Judicial appointments to the European Court of Human Rights and to the Court of Justice

4.38 Judicial selection for international courts and tribunals is traditionally a matter for the state, and the appointment processes accordingly greatly vary between states. Public trust in these courts depends upon, among other factors, the selection of judges and their independence.[193] But as a matter of general observation on international courts, it is not always clear in some states whether the most able and independent judges have been appointed, and in the case of the most able judges, whether this has been because of, or in spite of, the selection process, which is not universally well advertised nor free from political influence.[194] Of particular interest, in the context of this book, is the English appointment system for the Court of Justice of the European Union in Luxembourg and for the European Court of Human Rights in Strasbourg. Both Courts have had a profound impact on domestic law, and

---

[192] S. Shetreet, 'On Assessing the Role of Courts in Society' (1980) 10 *Manitoba Law Journal* 355, 399–402.

[193] P. Mahoney, 'The International Judiciary: Independence and Accountability' (2008) 7 *The Law and Practice of International Courts and Tribunals* 313; H. Ruiz-Fabri and J.-M. Sorel (eds), *Indépendence et impartialité des juges internationaux* (Paris: Pédone, 2010).

[194] R Mackenzie et al (eds), *Selecting International Judges: Principles, Process, and Politics* (Oxford University Press, 2010) 2.

domestic judges take into consideration and apply their jurisprudence on a daily basis.[195] Judicial selection for both Courts has recently been subject to reforms, with a much-needed greater emphasis on transparency and judicial skills as criteria for appointments.

To many, the Court of Justice's case law fosters integration more efficiently than the inter-governmental arrangements/the Treaties themselves.[196] The principles of direct effect and primacy of European Union law[197] are the cornerstones of an ever-maturing European constitutional order. Individuals have benefited from the judicial development of legal obligations that can be enforced against the member states, so that this 'new legal order' is yet more than an international legal regime which would create obligations enforceable solely among the participating states themselves.[198] The Court of Justice recruits one judge for every member state, who serves one renewable term of six years. Candidates are first selected at a national level. Their selection is then discussed by the Council of Ministers, who would be expected to appoint them unanimously, 'by common accord'. Until the Lisbon Treaty, the Court had no formal say in the selection process. The subject of judicial selection was perceived as an 'unfinished, and almost unstarted, business':[199] candidates seemed to be endorsed by the Council without discussion and national procedures could be seen as lacking transparency or guarantees of independence from executive influences.[200]

---

[195] See, e.g., the comment from the Immigration & Asylum Chamber President that his Chamber 'has had to consider how the decision of the CJEU in Case 34/09 *Ruiz Zambrano* (8 March 2011) applied to cases where a non citizen parent faces removal either with or from a UK citizen child', the Senior President of Tribunals' Report for 2012, pp. 18–19.

[196] The analysis of judicial appointments to the Court of Justice of the European Union relies in part upon excerpts from S. Turenne, 'AG's Opinions or Separate Opinions? Judicial Engagement at the CJEU' (2011–2012) 14 CYELS 723.

[197] European Communities Act 1972; Case 26/62 *Van Gend en Loos* v. *Nederlandse Administratie der Belastingen* [1963] ECR 1 and Case 6/64 *Costa* v. *ENEL* [1964] ECR 585; *Thoburn* v. *Sunderland City Council* [2003] QB 151.

[198] The European legal order is short of a federal state but is more than an international organisation of independent sovereigns, A.-M. Burley and W. Mattli, 'Europe before the Court: A Political Theory of Legal Integration' (1993) 47 *International Organization* 41.

[199] Lord Mance, 'The Common Law and Europe: Differences of Style Or Substance and Do They Matter?', Presidential Address to the Holdsworth Club of the University of Birmingham, 26 November 2006, p. 10.

[200] Lord Mance, 'The Composition of the European Court of Justice', talk given to the UK Association for European Law, 19 October 2011, p. 8.

Under Article 255 of the Treaty on the Functioning of the European Union (TFEU), however, an advisory panel was created, appointed by the Council. It comprises seven national and European judges and lawyers, chosen from among former members of the Court of Justice and the General Court, members of national supreme courts and lawyers of recognised competence, one of whom is proposed by the European Parliament. The panel gives an opinion on the candidates' suitability to perform the respective duties of Judge and Advocate General of the Court of Justice.[201] The introduction of a screening panel with a dominant judicial presence is a breakthrough towards the emancipation from a purely political appointment process, at least at the level of the Council. Though it does not have a power of veto, the panel's practice to enquire about the national selection process is a welcome scrutiny and encouragement of independent judicial selection procedures at state level. This can only develop greater independence and transparency of the appointment process, and the promotion of merit,[202] a key component of any court's persuasive authority.

The advertising for the post of UK judge, in the last round of selection in 2011, appeared on the Judicial Appointments Commission's website. But the competition is overseen by the Foreign and Commonwealth Office, on merit and in accordance with the Equality Act 2010. The latest appointee to the Court of Justice was recommended to the government following a selection and interview process, with the interview panel comprising lay, judicial and legal members.

Under Article 252 TFEU, appointees to the Court must be 'persons whose independence is beyond doubt and who possess the qualifications for selection to the highest judicial offices in their respective countries or who are jurisprudents of recognised competence'. The potential needs for particular expertise in a field are not specified in the judicial recruitment process, yet it seems to be commonly accepted that the Court would benefit from more judges with experience in criminal cases and, interestingly, the appointed judge, Christopher Vajda QC, is an expert in competition law and European law and has also sat as a recorder within the Crown Court for the past eight years – which fits in with the current needs of the Court of Justice.

---

[201] See the panel operating rules, the Council Decisions of 25 February 2010 (2010/125/EU) and (2010/124/EU).

[202] J. Limbach et al., *Judicial Independence: Law and Practice of Appointments to the European Court of Human Rights* (London, Interights, 2003).

In practice, the chosen judges and Advocates General support the process of European integration.[203]But the lack of data on the processes of the Court of Justice – where there is no separate judgment – makes it difficult to assess the variations in reasoning between judges within the Court and any possible correlation with the judicial selection process. In international courts, legal cultures (starting with whether judges have been practitioners or academic scholars before being appointed), policy preferences and career incentives appear to be the three grounds behind variations in judicial reasoning.[204] Some note a trend among member states towards appointing professional judges and general judges from constitutional or public law courts,[205] though the Court's Annual Report for 2010 shows a professorial bias among Advocates General, with far more diverse backgrounds for judges.

The short tenure of six years might lead to judges being concerned about their reappointment, and the advisory panel cannot prevent an inappropriate or politically motivated non-renewal of the mandate of a judge, but the single-voice judgment style adopted by the Court at least ensures that governments do not know the opinions of their national judge.[206]

4.39 By comparison with the Court of Justice of the European Union, the European Court of Human Rights interprets and applies the European Convention on Human Rights (ECHR). When domestic courts deal with a case under the Human Rights Act 1998 (HRA), they are required to take into consideration any relevant Strasbourg case law.[207] The UK Supreme Court has recently clarified that:

> where ... there is a clear and constant line of decisions whose effect is not inconsistent with some fundamental substantive or procedural aspect of our law, and whose reasoning does not appear to overlook or misunderstand some argument or point of principle, we consider that it would be wrong for this Court not to follow that line.[208]

---

[203] F. Bruinsma, 'A Socio-Legal Analysis of the Legitimacy of Highest Courts', in N. Huls, M. Adams and J. Bomhoff (eds), *The Legitimacy of Highest Courts' Ruling. Judicial Deliberations and Beyond* (The Hague: T.M.C. Asser Press, 2009) 61.

[204] E. Voeten, 'The Politics of International Judicial Appointments. Evidence from the Court of Human Rights' (2007) 61 *International Organization*, 669.

[205] D. Edward, evidence to the House of Lords, *The Treaty of Lisbon: an Impact Assessment*, 10th Report of Session 2007–2008; HL Paper 62-II, vol. II Evidence, Q132.

[206] Turenne, 'AG's Opinions or Separate Opinions?'.   [207] HRA, s. 2(1).

[208] See *Manchester City Council* v. *Pinnock* [2010] UKSC 45, para. 48; *R (Ullah)* v. *Special Adjudicator* [2004] UKHL 36, para. 20 [Lord Bingham]; *R* v. *Horncastle* [2009] UKSC 14; *Al-Khawaja* v. *UK* (2009) 49 EHRR 1; *Al-Khawaja* v. *UK* [2011] ECHR 2127.

In addition, the European Court of Human Rights' judgments bind the UK as a matter of international law.[209] In the context of acrimonious tensions following the European Court's judgment on prisoners' voting rights, the UK concerns have focused on the qualification and experience of judges, judicial independence and transparency of selection.[210]

Judges appointed now have a single non-renewable nine-year term.[211] Under Article 21(1) ECHR, 'The judges shall be of high moral character and must either possess the qualifications required for appointment to high judicial office or be jurisconsults of recognised competence'. In practice, member states submit a list of three candidates to the Parliamentary Assembly of the Council of Europe. In 2012, the shortlist for the UK judge was compiled by a five-person panel, comprising two senior judges, including a Scottish judge, a representative of the Judicial Appointments Commission of Northern Ireland, one legal adviser from the Ministry of Justice and one legal adviser from the Foreign and Commonwealth Office. The shortlist was considered by the Advisory Committee established by the Committee of Ministers of the Council of Europe, which meets to assess whether the national shortlists name candidates who meet the criteria for appointments set out by the Council of Ministers.[212] Interviews were conducted by a sub-committee on the election of judges to the Court from the Parliamentary Assembly of the Council of Europe. They made some confidential recommendations available to all members of the Assembly before they voted to elect one of the three UK candidates. The names and CVs of the shortlisted candidates were also published on the website of the Council of Europe. The national shortlist of three names must generally include at least one member of the under-represented sex (defined as the sex which makes up less than 40 per cent of the Court).[213] The member states are also 'invited

---

[209] Art. 46 ECHR.

[210] *Hirst v. UK (No. 2)*, Application No. 74025/01; see Report published in May 2011, Dr. Başak Çalı, Anne Koch and Nicola Bruch.

[211] Protocol No. 14 to the ECHR.

[212] See the panel operating rules, Resolution CM/Res (2010) 26 of 10th November 2010.

[213] Council of Europe Parliamentary Assembly, Resolutions 1366 (2004), Recommendation 1649 (2004) and Resolutions 1426 (2005) and 1627 (2008); Advisory Opinion on certain legal questions concerning the lists of candidates submitted with a view to the election of judges to the European Court of Human Rights, 12 February 2008.

to ensure that the selection bodies/panels (and those advising on selection) are themselves as gender-balanced as possible'.[214]

However the English selection process is an ad hoc one, and in the aforementioned context of heavy criticism of the European Court, 'a group of MPs from the three main political parties' met the appointments candidates for 'confidential discussions', in the words of one of the MPs, after they were shortlisted, with the aim of 'improving democratic account-ability'.[215] One can express concern at such informality, not to mention the lack of discussion in Parliament itself about these confidential discussions. We do not know what was passed on from this meeting to the UK members of the Council of Europe Parliamentary Assembly. This casual and self-invested approach to selection to a high judicial office does not enhance the independence of the appointment process, nor does it do any good to democratic accountability. It is all the more regrettable that the final outcome saw the defeat of the candidate with the most high-profile human rights agenda among those shortlisted. The absence of reference to this intervention by MPs in a letter previously sent by the Ministry of Justice to the Joint Committee on Human Rights detailing the appoint-ment process also shows that the Ministry of Justice was bypassed in this process. It shows the need for a formalisation of the appointment process so that it falls squarely under the remit of an independent body – such as the Judicial Appointments Commission, so that only they send on any documents or views to the Council of Europe Parliamentary Assembly.

4.40 In both cases, while the ad hoc procedures in place in England have always ensured open competition in practice, their ad hoc nature leaves room for a politicised process in the nomination of candidates, as illustrated by the ad hoc 'confidential discussions' with the candidates for the European Court of Human Rights. Transparency and independ-ence may be strengthened, and the adoption of an advisory panel for appointments to both courts is a step in that direction; it also paves the way for the authority of states in the selection process to diminish.[216] This is not to exclude any political input in the appointment process on the basis of the sensitive nature of the decisions taken by both courts, but to require transparency in the way that any political influence is wielded.

---

[214] Council of Europe Parliamentary Assembly, Recommendation 1646 (2009), 'Nomin-ation of candidates and election of judges to the European Court of Human Rights', para. 5.
[215] *The Guardian*, 22 May 2012.   [216] Mackenzie et al., *Selecting International Judges*, 8–9.

VI.   Judicial remuneration

4.41 English judges are among the highest paid public officials.[217] The differentiation in the remuneration of particular posts is based on a job weight assessment. The current salary structure is divided into ten salary groups (with uniformity within those groups), according to the level of the court and the significant managerial, advisory and administrative responsibilities exercised within the court.[218] Although an independent review body, the Senior Salaries Review Body,[219] reviews judicial salaries and makes recommendations, the government annually decides the judicial pay structure and the level of remuneration. A prominent member of the Judicial Sub-Committee thus recalled: 'The Lord Chancellor would plead poverty; the Judges need'; the Review Body's role seems to be 'to square the circle'.[220]

Underlying the whole question of judicial remuneration, however, is that of the independence and integrity of the judiciary and the consequent need to secure the independence of judges from not only political but also financial pressure and entanglements. Judicial independence thus requires that judicial remuneration should be guaranteed by law.[221] Judges are paid out of the Consolidated Fund which means that

---

[217] As of 1 April 2012, the annual salary of the Lord Chief Justice was fixed at £239,845, the Master of the Rolls and the President of the UK Supreme Court at £214,165; the Justices of the UK Supreme Court, the Chancellor of the High Court, the Deputy President of the Supreme Court, the Lord Justice Clerk, the President of the Family Division, the President of the Queen's Bench Division and the Justices of the UK Supreme Court at £206,857; the Senior President of Tribunals at £203,643; the Lord Justices of Appeal at £196,704; the High Court judges at £172,753; circuit judges and some Upper Tribunal judges at £128,296; see the full list in Review Body on Senior Salaries, 'Thirty-Fourth Report on Senior Salaries 2012', Report No. 79, Cm 8297.

[218] The criteria put forward for the determination of judicial remuneration were once as varied as they were disputed, see 525 HC Deb., 1059 (23 March 1954); 716 HC Deb., 639 (14 July 1965); 800 HC Deb., 1566 (30 April 1970); 808 HC Deb., 1487 (16 December 1970); 313 HL Deb., 1339 (15 December 1970).

[219] C. 15 Administration of Justice Act 1973. The first Review Body, the Top Salaries Review Body, was established in 1971 and became known as the Review Body for Senior Salaries in 1993, see R. Stevens, *The Independence of the Judiciary. The View from the Lord Chancellor's Office* (Oxford: Clarendon Press, 1993), p. 134.

[220] M. Beloff, 'Paying Judges: Who, Whom, Why, How Much?'(2006) 18 *Denning Law Journal* 1, 24.

[221] International Covenant on Civil and Political Rights, Art. 14, General Comment No. 32, para. 19; Principle I.2b.ii, Recommendation (94) 12 of the Committee of Ministers of the Council of Europe; the Consultative Council of European Judges of the Council of Europe, Opinion No. 1, para. 62.

their salaries are immune from challenge by backbenchers and cannot be reduced other than by statute itself.[222] They may be increased by administrative action. Safeguards must be in place if they are to be decreased. Moreover, the financial reward should be commensurable with the dignity of their profession and burden of responsibilities.[223] Individuals of suitable character, ability, experience and motivation will only be attracted to the judicial office if the total reward for judicial posts decided by government shows that the judiciary is valued.[224] Judicial office no doubt has its attractions, but they alone may not, without adequate remuneration, ensure the high standard of the judiciary. While it is doubtful if very large salaries are necessary to secure integrity,[225] judges should be free from financial anxieties. The legal system cannot function properly in the absence of judges with the necessary levels of skill, knowledge and motivation, and it must anticipate the challenges of attracting the best practitioners who will normally be taking a pay cut upon entry to the bench. Similar safeguards must be set in relation to pensions, which are a critical part of a judge's remuneration package.

A.   The role of the Review Body on Senior Salaries

4.42 The government annually decides the judicial pay structure and the level of remuneration upon guidance from an independent review body, the Review Body on Senior Salaries, which examines whether the pay structure and level of remuneration are well suited to the needs of the judiciary. The Review Body has remit over all full-time and part-time salaried judicial office holders in the courts and tribunals[226] of the United Kingdom. The fee-paid judiciary members are not part of its standing remit although many fees are set by reference to the salary for the corresponding full-time post.[227]

---

[222] Senior Courts Act 1981, s. 12 provides that judges' salaries shall be set by the Lord Chancellor in conjunction with the Minister for the Civil Service. Section 12(3) specifies that 'Any salary payable under this section may be increased, but not reduced, by a determination . . . under this section.'

[223] Principles I.2b.ii and III.1.b, Recommendation (94) 12 of the Committee of Ministers of the Council of Europe.

[224] Review Body on Senior Salaries, 'Thirty-Fourth Report', 1.28.

[225] J.R. Spencer, *Jackson's Machinery of Justice*, 8th edn (Cambridge University Press, 1989), p. 274.

[226] Review Body on Senior Salaries, 'Review of Tribunals' Judiciary Remuneration 2008', Report No. 66.

[227] Coroners remain outside the Review Body on Senior Salaries' remit. Despite being judicial office holders, they are not considered to be members of the courts' judiciary.

4.43 Although judges ought not to set how much they should be paid, they ought to have an input into the determination of their remuneration. Some competing considerations shape various models for decision making on judicial remuneration. Thus, the legislature, as in Australia or Belgium,[228] could decide the budget. A legislative process can be cumbersome though. Alternatively, the Court Service could be responsible for its own budget, including judicial remuneration, within the limits of the sum allocated to it by the legislature. This was rejected in the course of the discussions leading to the Constitutional Reform Act 2005.[229] The executive could also decide on judicial remuneration without a third-party intervention as in Sweden; but the executive is a frequent client of the courts, and the independence of the judicial process requires that at least the executive should not alone set the judicial salaries. A further possibility would be to adjust salaries by reference to a particular index, as in some Australian states, or by reference to the average wage, as in Israel, though this may not provide sufficient leverage in increasing or decreasing salaries in some appropriate circumstances.[230]

In this context, the institution of the Review Body appears as a good compromise, by acting as the interface between the government and the judiciary. As one interviewee said, 'it works for those who are not unionised'. An independent review body is also the solution adopted in New Zealand or South Africa among other jurisdictions.[231] As stated by the Canadian Supreme Court in *Provincial Judges Reference*, independent judicial compensation commissions, the functional equivalent to the English Review Body, are required in order 'to avoid the possibility of, or the appearance of, political interference through economic manipulation'.[232] The existence of a review body avoids negotiations between

---

They are appointed by individual local authorities and paid in a different way. The post of Chief Coroner created in 2012, falls however under the Review Body's remit since only High Court or circuit judges are eligible for this post, see Review Body on Senior Salaries, 'Thirty-Fourth Report', 4.26; Coroners and Justice Act 2009.

[228] S. Shetreet and J. Deschenes (eds.), *Judicial Independence: The Contemporary Debate* (Leiden: M. Nijhoff, 1985), p. 672.

[229] N. Browne-Wilkinson, 'The Independence of the Judiciary in the 1980s' [1988] PL, 44.

[230] Beloff, 'Paying Judges'.

[231] Remuneration Authority Act 1977 (NZ); Judges' Remuneration and Conditions of Employment Act No. 42 2001 (South Africa).

[232] Reference re Remuneration of Judges of the Provincial Court of Prince Edward Island; Reference re Independence and Impartiality of Judges of the Provincial Court of Prince Edwards Island; *R* v. *Campbell*; *R* v. *Ekmecic*; *R* v. *Wickman*; *Manitoba Provincial Judges Assn.* v. *Manitoba (Minister of Justice)* [1997] 3 SCR 3 (hereafter Provincial Judges

judges and the executive, which may create a perception of undue influence in the course of bargaining for an agreement.[233] In practice, in Canada as in England, the judiciary makes representations to the Review Body since judges are not unionised and no collective bargaining takes place.

The advice of the Review Body is not binding upon the executive.[234] The Review Body's assessments have generally led them to suggest increases in judicial salaries – including a 40 per cent rise in 1990, which was rejected by the government as unaffordable. In recent years the government has felt it necessary to reject similar recommendations and has sometimes staged the increases proposed.[235] Thus, in 2009, for the fourth year running, the pay increase suggested by the Review Body (approximately 2.6 per cent) was not implemented in full.[236] In 2010–12, against a background of a long recession followed by severe pressure on public finances, the Review Body did not suggest any increase.[237] As a result, in 2012, the value of the take-home pay of circuit judges, for example, fell by 15.9 per cent.[238]

Not only is the judiciary highly dependent on the Review Body's assessments, but there is also no parliamentary debate on judicial salaries.[239] Despite some heated debates over the years, the relatively low public profile of the judges tends to put them at a disadvantage in fighting the government's decisions not to accept the advice of the

---

Reference), para. 133. The Court grounded its solution on the unwritten constitutional principle of judicial independence and the guarantee of an independent and impartial tribunal under s. 11(d) Charter of Rights. The majority dismissed their previous judgment in *Valente* v. *The Queen* [1985] 2 SCR 673 as obiter; see also *Beauregard* v. *Canada* [1986] 2 SCR 56, para. 77; Re Public Sector Pay Reduction Act (1996) 20 DLR 449.

[233] Provincial Judges Reference, para. 188.

[234] Judicial salaries in point of law are determined by the Lord Chancellor with the agreement of the Treasury, CRA, s. 34(2).

[235] Staging in 2002 caused 'unanimous disapproval and even resentment', SSRB, Cm 5718, para. 4.5. There have been two staged pay rises since 2006.

[236] Yet the SSRB noted, in its 2011 Report, that the opportunities for progression within the judiciary are significantly fewer than for the other public sector groups, and that the judiciary does not benefit from the performance-related pay which exists in the other public sector 'senior salary' groups.

[237] Review Body on Senior Salaries, 'Thirty-Fourth Report', ch. 4.

[238] Applying a similar formula to other judges shows that the take-home pay for district judges fell by 16.5%; for High Court judges by 17%; and for Court of Appeal judges by 18.5%, Review Body on Senior Salaries, 'Thirty-Fourth Report', Appendix C, 76; Lord Chief Justice's Report 2010–2012, para. 18.

[239] Because judges are paid out of the Consolidated Fund, Senior Courts Act 1981, s. 12.

Review Body on Senior Salaries. By comparison, the Canadian Supreme Court held in *Provincial Judges Reference* that, if the government departs from the recommendations made by the relevant Canadian commission, it must be prepared to give reasons for its decisions, if necessary through judicial review.[240] In the context of rising litigation on judicial remuneration, the Canadian Supreme Court limited the scope of that judgment by holding, in *Bodner*,[241] that the government's failure to justify its decision by a certain standard of rationality would generally lead to the matter being returned to the government for consideration, and also to the adoption of a lower standard of rationality than the standard usually applied for the application of Charter rights.[242] The Court accepts as justifications reasons relating to the public interest, broadly understood. It primarily aims at screening out purely political considerations or discriminatory reasons.[243]

Yet the near constant litigation on judicial remuneration since the *Canadian Provincial Judges Reference* and the *Bodner* judgments[244] shows that the institution of a review body in itself is not sufficient to establish a dispute-resolution mechanism between the judiciary and the executive on matters of judicial pay. The explanation may lie in the key distinction that the principle of an independent compensation commission was unilaterally imposed by the Canadian courts themselves, not by the legislature.

---

[240] The Court, however, left questions of institutional design of the commission to the government that would establish it, *Provincial Judges Reference*, paras. 133–5, 147 and 167. Proposals for changes in judicial remuneration must be put forward to the commission, see *Mackin* v. *New Brunswick (Minister of Finance)*; *Rice* v. *New Brunswick (Minister of Finance)* [2002] 1 SCR 405, paras. 42–9.

[241] *Provincial Court Judges Association of New Brunswick* v. *New Brunswick (Minister of Justice)*; *Ontario Judges Association et al* v. *Ontario (Management Board)*; *Bodner* v. *Alberta*; *Conférence des juges du Québec* v. *Quebec (Attorney General)*; *Minc* v. *Quebec (Attorney General)* [2005] 2 SCR 286 (hereafter *Bodner*).

[242] The court 'should avoid issuing specific orders to make the recommendations binding unless the governing statutory scheme gives them that option', *Bodner*, para. 44. The standard of rationality is not the standard applying under s. 1 of the Charter but simply a requirement that there is a legitimate reason why the government has chosen to depart from the recommendation of the commission, *Bodner*, paras. 25–6. The 'totality of the process' must also have been respected so that the purpose of preserving judicial independence and depoliticising the setting of judicial remuneration has been achieved, *Bodner*, paras. 31 and 83. In *Bodner*, the Court upheld the decisions of three out of the four provinces whose judicial remuneration had been challenged.

[243] Reference re Secession of Quebec [1998] 2 SCR 217.

[244] A. Dodek and L. Sossin (eds.), *Judicial Independence in Context* (Toronto: Irwin Law, 2010), pp. 25–93.

B. Increasing and decreasing judicial salaries

4.44 Since 1832, when a High Court judge's salary was reduced from £5,500 to £5,000, judicial salaries have not been decreased without the consent of the judiciary,[245] although Gladstone unsuccessfully attempted further reduction in the 1870s,[246] and a further battle was needed to ensure that cuts were not included in the National Economy Act 1931.[247] But until 1965, salaries of the High Court judges could be increased too only by statute, and judges proved less successful in campaigning for statutory increases than they had been in campaigning against proposed decreases. In 1951, Lord Goddard complained in the House of Lords, in the course of the debates on the increase in the salaries of county court judges, that 'one cannot pick up a newspaper nowadays without discovering that someone has received a rise. Everybody gets a rise except the judges.'[248] In the course of the debates on the increase of judicial salaries in 1965, it was alleged that judges exerted pressure on the Lord Chancellor to take the necessary steps for increasing judicial salaries, and that the Lord Chancellor, in turn, exerted pressure on the government to pass the proposed increases unchanged.[249]

Under the Judges' Remuneration Act 1965, the more expedient procedure of delegated legislation was introduced for this purpose by Order in Council, subject to an affirmative resolution in each House of Parliament. A similar procedure had already been introduced for the increase of the salary of county court judges in 1957.[250] Parliament thus began to delegate its legislative authority to increase judicial remuneration to the executive in 1965. Since 1973 increases in the salary of the High Court judges may be determined by the Lord Chancellor with the consent of the Minister for the Civil Service[251] without the need for an Order in

---

[245] 2 & 3 Will. IV, c.116, s.1 (1832); The Judges' Remuneration Act 1954, 2 & 3 Eliz. II, c.27 (£8,000) provided for the first salary increase since 1832 for High Court judges.

[246] B. Abel-Smith and R. Stevens, *Lawyers and the Courts* (London: Heineman, 1967), p. 127.

[247] W. Holdsworth, 'Constitutional Position of the Judges' (1932) 48 LQR 25; Heuston, *The Lives*, 513–19.

[248] 211 *Law Times* 104 (1951).

[249] 716 HC Deb., 1987, 2012, 2098, 2099 (22 July 1965); 808 HC Deb., 1510 (16 December 1970).

[250] See the Judicial Offices (Salaries) Act 1952 for the increase in judicial remuneration to county court judges and the Judicial Offices (Salaries and Pensions) Act 1957. County Courts Act 1984, s. 6(1) (amended by Courts and Legal Services Act 1990, s. 125(3), sch. 18, para. 42).

[251] The functions of the Minister for the Civil Service in relation to salaries were transferred to the Treasury in 1973, Administration of Justice Act 1973.

Council.[252] This has in effect applied to High Court judges the procedure for increasing the salaries of the circuit judges.[253] The Administration of Justice Act 1973 also recognised the role of the Top Salaries Review Board (now the Review Body on Senior Salaries) in making (non-binding) recommendations to the Lord Chancellor.

But salaries of the higher judiciary can still only be decreased by statute.[254] Unlike removal of a judge by address, which requires a resolution of both Houses of Parliament, reduction of judicial salaries by any amount may be done by the House of Commons alone invoking the money bill procedure under the Parliament Act 1911. The decrease of salaries by statute for the higher and lower judiciary appears unsatisfactory and indeed, the principle that judges' pay should not be diminished while they hold office is reflected in many constitutions and laws of other jurisdictions, many of them being common law-based jurisdictions, such as the United States, India, Australia, Canada, Ghana, Ireland, New Zealand and Singapore.[255] Other non-common law jurisdictions such as Japan or Brazil also adopted that principle.[256]

Nonetheless an economic crisis may justify a legislative cut of the salaries of all state officials, including judges.[257] In such a situation, the Venice Commission considers that the reduction of judicial salaries need not be regarded as a breach of the principle of the independence of judges.[258] According to the Commission, it may rather be seen as a token of solidarity and social justice, demanding of judges a proportional

---

[252] Administration of Justice Act 1973, s. 9; Senior Courts Act 1981, s. 12; for UK Supreme Court Justices, see CRA, s. 34.

[253] Courts Act 1971, s. 18(2).

[254] Senior Courts Act 1981, s. 12(3); ss. 9(1) and (3) Administration of Justice Act 1973, s. 9 (1) and (3) (s. 9(3) as amended); CRA., s. 34

[255] Art. 111.1, US Constitution and *United States* v. *Will* (1980) 449 US 200, 218–19; Art. 125, the Constitution of India (1949); Commonwealth of Australia Constitution Act 1900, s. 72(ii); for Canada, see the British North America Act 1807, s 100 and W.R. Lederman, 'The Independence of the Judiciary', 1956 *Canadian Bar Review* XXXIV 1139, 1163; Art. 35.5, Irish Constitution, see *McMenamin* v. *Ireland* (1994) in *Law Reports Monthly*, vol. 2, 377 (Geoghan J). For New Zealand, Constitution Act 1986 Part IV, s. 24; The Constitution of the Republic of Singapore 1996, s. 98(8).

[256] Art. 95, III, The Constitution of the Federation of the Republic of Brazil 1988.

[257] Provincial Judges Reference, para. 184.

[258] The Venice Commission (The European Commission for Democracy through Law), 'Report on the Independence of the Judicial System. Part 1: Judges' (Council of Europe, CDL AD (2010)004), para. 46. Cf. Israel, where a reduction in judicial salaries may be made only if it does not solely apply to the public sector salaries, see S. Shetreet, *Justice in Israel: A Study of the Israeli Judiciary* (Leiden: M. Nijhoff, 1994), pp. 160–1.

responsibility for eliminating the consequences of the economic and financial crisis of their country, by putting on them a burden equal to that for other public officials. Nonetheless, the general principle highlighted above, that remuneration must be commensurate with the dignity of a judge's profession and his or her burden of responsibility, continues to apply, and the Venice Commission must be approved in stating that:

> If the reduction does not comply with the requirement of the adequacy of remuneration, the essence of the guarantee of the stability of conditions of judge's remuneration is infringed to a degree that the basic aim, pursued by that guarantee, i.e. a proper, qualified and impartial administration of justice is threatened, even leading to a danger of corruption.[259]

This translates into various desirable safeguards. The reduction of the judicial remuneration should, first, not be aimed specifically at judges; it must be part of a reduction in pay across the public sector which applies to the senior public officers whose salary is compared with the judicial salary. Moreover, the judicial remuneration cannot be reduced in a greater proportion than that of the other senior public officers whose salary is comparable, on pain of violating the principle of equality established as a general principle of law.[260] Finally, the cuts should be limited in time.

Nevertheless, the prohibition of a reduction of judicial salary has been abandoned in Sweden, Belgium, the Netherlands and, very recently, Ireland. The amendment of the Irish Constitution,[261] approved by referendum in 2011, shows that there is no such thing as a constitutional bar to the reduction of salaries, as it put an end to the principle that the reduction of judicial remuneration was prohibited during the currency of office.[262] This was done in the context of the long-running economic crisis which started in 2008 and led to a reduction of public sector pay as well as setting a levy on pension contributions made by the public sector.[263] The

---

[259] Venice Commission, Opinion No. 598/2010 CDL-AD(2010) 038, para. 20.

[260] Consultative Council of European Judges, 'Situation report on the judiciary and judges in the different member states', CCJE (2011) 6, 18 January 2012, para. 17.

[261] The Twenty-Ninth Amendment of the Constitution (Judges' Remuneration) Bill 2011 (No. 44 of 2011).

[262] See the new Art. 35.5.3, Irish Constitution; *McMenamin* v. *Ireland* [1994] 21 LRM 368, 377 [Geoghan J]; *O'Byrne* v. *Minister of Finance* [1959] IR 1, 38, where the Supreme Court held that a requirement that a judge pays income tax on the same basis as other citizens could not be said to be an attack on judicial independence.

[263] The Financial Emergency Measures in the Public Interest (No. 2) Act 2009 (a reduction in public sector pay).

referendum was prompted by the dispute between the judiciary and the Irish government about the application of the pay cut and the levy to the judiciary. The Irish Attorney General had advised the government that the Irish constitution prevented the application of those measures to the judiciary. In response, the government encouraged the judges to voluntarily contribute to their pensions under a scheme specially set up in 2010 (125 out of 147 judges did so). One interviewee alluded to the fact that the Irish government did say that it would publish the names of those who volunteered and those who did not. Either way, a judicial memorandum from July 2011 called for an independent adjudication on what the judicial reductions should be, with an express reference to the Canadian decision of *Provincial Judges Reference*, which, as noted above, held that judicial independence requires an independent review body to make recommendations on the appropriate level of judicial remuneration.[264] Following some selected leaks in the press the judiciary decided to put the document in its entirety on its website. The document was eventually withdrawn at the request of the government, and the referendum announced. The Irish new constitution provision, however, fails to contain sufficient safeguards to ensure that the reduction of judicial salaries remains exceptional. While it does require the reduction to be proportionate to the reduction applying to a 'comparator class' from the public sector, the new provision does not define the comparator class; nor does it define the public interest behind the reduction.

C.   An adequate judicial remuneration

4.45 Judges must receive sufficient remuneration to secure true economic independence.[265] According to the Venice Commission, the level of remuneration should be determined in the light of the social conditions in the country and compared to the level of remuneration of higher civil servants.[266] The remuneration should also be based on a general standard and rely on objective and transparent criteria. This is the case in England and Wales, where the Review Body is, under its terms of reference, to have regard to the funds available to departments as set out in the government's departmental expenditure limits.[267] While

---

[264] See para 4.38.
[265] Art. 13, Universal Charter of the Judge; European Charter on the Statute of Judges, para. 8.
[266] Venice Commission, 'Report on the Independence of the Judicial System', 46.
[267] Review Body on Senior Salaries, 'Thirty-Fourth Report', 3.

affordability may be taken into account, it ought not to bind the Review Body, however, which is to have equal regard to the need to recruit, retain and motivate suitably able and qualified people to exercise their different responsibilities.[268] This may explain why one interviewee described the Review Body's decisions between 2010 and 2012 not to suggest any general increase in remuneration as 'a pusillanimous stance'. In addition, increases in judicial salaries are set within the rate permitted by the general prices and incomes policy as laid down by the proper bodies, this in light of the rise in the cost of living and the state of the economy.[269]

Importantly, the Review Body has regard to many other top salaries in the public sector and it has regard to a broad comparability between the judiciary and two other main public sector groups, the senior civil service and the senior officers in the armed forces. Although a direct link between the salaries of the higher judiciary and those of top civil servants has been denied by some,[270] it cannot be denied that the level of remuneration of comparable positions in government service is a relevant factor. Practitioners may be attracted away from judicial office if the differential in salary is too great to be balanced by the advantages of judicial office other than financial remuneration.[271] Salaries should be increased at a rate equivalent at any rate to that paid elsewhere in the public sector and, in practice, some of the increases in judicial salaries have been advocated on that ground.

Comparisons with other public sector groups, however, are limited by the judiciary's constitutional position. Judges must not only be independent, but must be seen to be independent. Although having high salaries in order to avert suspicions of judicial corruption is a moot point in England, where the culture of judicial independence is strong, the link between unacceptably low pay and corruption remains significant in other jurisdictions.[272] Instead, the concern about judicial remuneration

---

[268] Ibid.
[269] Ibid., 1.7–1.22; The Consultative Council of European Judges of the Council of Europe, Opinion No. 1, para. 62.
[270] 800 HC Deb., 1567 (30 April 1970); 808 HC Deb., 257 (8 December 1970) 1507 (16 December 1970).
[271] In 1970 Sir Henry Fisher resigned from the High Court after only two years on the bench to take up a business appointment; financial considerations apparently played an important role in his decision, see (1970) 114 Solicitors' Journal 593.
[272] J.C. Wallace, 'Resolving Judicial Corruption', in C. Das and K. Chandra (eds.), Judges and Judicial Accountability (Delhi: Universal Law Publishing Company, 2003), pp. 86–101.

in England and Wales is one of quality of recruitment and retention. The English tradition of judicial independence depends, in the words of Lord Bingham, 'on the willingness of the most successful practitioners at the height of their careers to accept appointment to the judicial Bench'.[273] Our interviewees raised the prospect of seeing the high status and prestige enjoyed by the judiciary diminishing, leading in due course to appointments from less-well-qualified candidates. The remuneration of judges has to correspond to the dignity of the profession,[274] and judicial remuneration reflects the prestige which society accords judges. Yet, while a relatively low judicial remuneration may affect quality of justice and is therefore undesirable, it need not threaten judicial independence.

The Review Body acknowledges that if pay is too low, then sooner or later the remit groups will start to suffer from inadequate numbers, quality or performance, and possibly all three.[275] Thus its role must be to set an 'acceptable minimum level' of salary.[276] It is suggested that at least judicial salaries should be assessed not only in formal but also in real terms. Freezing salaries at times of high rates of inflation may indirectly interfere with independence, though there is no suggestion that the government has sought to influence the judges either collectively or individually in this way. Moreover, while holding office, judges may not, by convention, take up any other engagement for further remuneration and they may not return to practise at the Bar upon leaving the bench.[277] The government should not abuse its position, in effect, as a quasi-monopoly employer. Public sector pay for comparable groups including the judiciary should not be held down for political reasons, such as 'setting an example', or because there is no problem with retention since judges would find it hard to switch careers.[278]

Some interviewees mentioned their dilemma in taking a salary cut upon entry from the Bar and the financial sacrifice involved for those at the top of their field, especially in commercial practice, is well

---

[273] Bingham, 'Judicial Independence', 66. Cf. the testimonies of Stephen Breyer and Samuel Alito, Associate Justices, Supreme Court of the United States, before the House Committee on the Judiciary, Subcommittee on the Courts, the Internet and Intellectual Property, Oversight Hearing on 'Federal Judicial Compensation', 19 April 2007 and the Supreme Court's 2007 Year-end Report on the Federal Judiciary (2008).

[274] Venice Commission, 'Report on the Independence of the Judicial System', 46.

[275] Review Body on Senior Salaries, 'Thirty-Fourth Report', 1.28.

[276] Provincial Judges Reference, paras. 193–6.   [277] See above, para. 4.37.

[278] Review Body on Senior Salaries, 'Thirty-Fourth Report', 1. 29.

documented.[279] Interviews reinforced that point, though the financial cut was also generally accepted as part of the public service aspect of their appointment. Judicial salaries have long been below what the most senior and successful practitioners, both barristers and solicitors, expect to earn.[280] However, the differential between judicial salaries and practice has greatly increased over the last twenty years, with an estimate in 2008 that practitioners at the top end of commercial practice regularly earned more than £500,000 per year as compared with the High Court salary.[281] Moreover, people in general are having children at an older age and there is a higher rate of divorce and remarriage, with significant financial commitments continuing longer and to an older age than perhaps was the case thirty years ago. A drop in income upon appointment to the High Court may thus become more difficult to contemplate.[282]

Yet it is difficult to assess the claim that the judicial salary may have deterred good practitioners from applying to the High Court since High Court judges are appointed through advertisement and open competition rather than by invitation. The Review Body mentions some genuine recruitment difficulties in 2012 in respect of a small number of posts in the 'senior judiciary'.[283] By comparison, some recent evidence suggests that although solicitors appointed as judges typically have come from among the higher earners among solicitors with sixteen to thirty-five years of post-qualification experience, most of the solicitors among the group of solicitors with between sixteen and thirty-five years of experience would have received a pay rise if appointed to the judiciary.[284] Taking the value of the pension into account, some judicial posts, in the lowest salary band, typically district judges, will continue to be attractive.[285] The Review Body acknowledged, however, that the

---

[279] H. Genn, 'The Attractiveness of Senior Judicial Appointment to Highly Qualified Practitioners', Report to the Judicial Executive Board of England and Wales (December 2008), pp. 11, 18–19.

[280] Joshua Rozenberg wrote in 1994 that 'The real problem is not that judges earn too little but that lawyers earn too much', *The Search for Justice* (London: Hodder and Stoughton, 1995), p. 92.

[281] Genn, 'The Attractiveness of Senior Judicial Appointment', 18–19. The High Court salary was £165,900 against £172,753 in 2012.

[282] *Ibid.*

[283] Review Body on Senior Salaries, 'Thirty-Fourth Report', 1.27; *Report of the Review Body of Senior Salaries in 2002*, Cm 5389-11, para. 4.26.

[284] Review Body on Senior Salaries, 'Thirty-Fourth Report', 1.26.

[285] *Ibid.*, 4.6 and Appendix G.

quality of recruits may fall, rather than the numbers, as the best people perceive the relative decline in reward and choose to make their careers elsewhere.[286]

Judicial remuneration, furthermore, may not be the only factor that militates against application to or acceptance of judicial appointment. 'A distaste for going out on circuit, increasing control by the civil service, a sense that in terms and prestige "fings ain't what they used to be", and constraints on lifestyle' are some further factors.[287] Solitude and the requirement to sit outside one's specialist field, especially in criminal courts, are additional deterring factors.[288] Conversely, a judicial appointment still has its attractions unrelated to salary or which can be said to mitigate the drop in income, such as the opportunity to make the decision, which includes the possibility of contributing to the development of the law and policy and in some cases, the opportunity to 'do good' or to 'do justice'; a different kind of intellectual challenge or interest, including the opportunity to hear a variety of cases, to hear high-quality cases and to pursue particular areas of law; less or a different kind of stress as compared with practice, for example the relentlessness of advocacy; the status and prestige or professional acknowledgement of one's quality as a lawyer; public service ethic, in the sense that, having been successful at the Bar, it would be appropriate to 'give something back' to society.[289]

The Review Body on Senior Salaries conducts major reviews of the judicial pay structure every four to five years. Those major reviews are essential as, relying on independent job evaluation exercises, they acknowledge the changes in job weight at different levels over time. The salary structure takes into account, for example that, at circuit level, some judges are responsible for the allocation of criminal, civil or family judicial work, in addition to dealing with procedural matters and giving general advice and guidance to the other judges.

4.46 The Review Body also suggested in 1997 that performance-related pay 'would involve systems of management and appraisal whose

---

[286] *Ibid.*, 1.26.   [287] Beloff, 'Paying Judges', 35.

[288] Genn, 'The Attractiveness of Senior Judicial Appointment', 12.

[289] D. Pannick, *Judges* (Oxford University Press, 1987), p. 20. Michael Beloff QC cites Sir Peter Bristow, writing in a memoir (*Judge for Yourself* (London: Kimber, 1986), p. 25: 'You would fairly be said to be relieved of financial worry with your bottom placed firmly on the consolidated fund. To those who all their working lives had to pay their taxes in arrears, PAYE [Pay As You Earn tax code system] came as an enormous blessing', Beloff, 'Paying Judges', 26; Genn, 'The Attractiveness of Senior Judicial Appointment', 9–10.

authority and efficiency would be controversial and which could be seen to challenge the principle of judicial independence'.[290] However judicial appraisal is now openly debated and not seen as incompatible with judicial independence in principle,[291] and judicial management is no more anathema to the judiciary.[292] In 2012 the Review Body simply acknowledged that, to a limited extent, in the judiciary, the main reward for performance may be through promotion rather than differential pay.[293] Or, as Michal Beloff QC emphasised, 'all judges at the same level are equal; some are clearly more equal than others; but that inequality should be reflected in their promotion, not their pay'.[294] The Review Body further recognised 'the arguments that performance-related pay would be both wrong in principle and impractical for the judiciary'.[295] The Universal Charter of the Judge provides a stronger view that the remuneration must not depend on the results of the judge's work.[296]

While the cost or practicality of judicial appraisal have not yet been sorted, the judges' managerial responsibilities are clearly defined and, in 2010, the Review Body consulted the Lord Chief Justice over additional remuneration for some of those with additional responsibilities, including the management or supervision of others of the same group. The Lord Chief Justice considered that it would be inherently unfair for some of those judges to be paid and others not to be paid for those roles.[297] While these additional duties are seen as a 'huge imposition' by the 'managerial' judges themselves, they also often involve these judges taking time out of court and thus other judges are required to take on a greater share of the normal judicial business.[298] If managerial duties give rise to some additional remuneration, the greater workload that falls upon others as a result of taking time out of court may also lead to some additional remuneration. There is also a strong view, reflected in our interviews too, that uniform pay rates help to maintain collegiality.[299] Thus, the Court of Appeal judges rejected in 2002 a system of payment for additional responsibility, as they felt that it would create a climate of

---

[290] SSRB, Cm 3451 1997, para. 22.   [291] See above, para. 4.29.

[292] See above, para. 3.40.

[293] Review Body on Senior Salaries, 'Thirty-Fourth Report', 1.33.

[294] Beloff, 'Paying Judges', 29.

[295] Review Body on Senior Salaries, 'Thirty-Fourth Report', 1.33.

[296] Art. 13 of the Universal Charter of the Judge.

[297] Lord Chief Justice, 'Letter to the Senior Salaries Review Body', 19 October 2010.

[298] *Ibid.*

[299] See also the SSRB 2011 Report on Senior Salaries, Report no. 77, Com. 8026.

competition to the detriment of the collegiate atmosphere.[300] Selection of judges for many additional duties is a matter of judicial deployment, not one of promotion. An additional remuneration for managerial judges would require a far more formal selection procedure which would be likely to slow down the current system. The impact on collegiality and efficiency of justice would be substantial. In a broader picture, however, any additional remuneration for managerial judges in the form of a performance bonus, combined with other recent measures such as greater flexibility in deployment across jurisdictions and pressure towards judicial appraisal, would be construed as yet another illustration of a greater career structure.

D.   Judicial pensions

4.47 There is no privilege or taxable benefit as such in addition to salary and pension. Full-time and part-time judges can only claim travel and subsistence expenses incurred in the course of their judicial duties. The time when judges sitting in the Crown Court were accommodated in the Judges' lodging at public expense and were provided with cooks and butlers free of charge has long gone. Magistrates benefit from similar arrangements to judges for travel and subsistence expenses to which they would not otherwise be entitled.[301] An allowance may be available to compensate for loss of earnings which would otherwise have been received. The amount that may be claimed for financial loss allowance is subject to an upper limit to the extent that many people who act as magistrates do so at their own financial loss.

Full-time judges and salaried part-time judges are entitled to pensions on retirement.[302] The judge's pension is his benefit, with its value to an average member of the judiciary amounting to about 35 per cent of salary.[303] It is a significant part of a judge's remuneration package. The position which applied broadly to all judges, until January 2012, was that they each had a non-contributory pension for themselves and a scheme to which they had to contribute for their dependants' benefits.[304] Most

---

[300] Lord Chief Justice, 'Letter'.   [301] Justices of the Peace Act 1997, s. 10.

[302] Depending on whether the individual judge was appointed before or after 1 April 1995, a judicial pension is payable under either the 1981 Judicial Pensions Act or the Judicial Pensions and Retirement Act 1993; for the UK Supreme Court, see CRA, s. 37.

[303] Judicial Pensions Scheme Resource Accounts 2006–07 HC 73; Review Body on Senior Salaries, 'Thirty-Fourth Report', 4.12.

[304] The Pensions (Increase) Act 1971.

VI. JUDICIAL REMUNERATION

appointees to the bench will have been earning much more than a judge receives by way of salary, and the assurance of substantial entitlements on retirement reduces the impact of the financial cut taken upon entry to the bench. Changes or freezes in judicial salaries have, of course, a knock-on effect on pensions (as has economic crisis upon interest rates).

The European Charter on the Statute for Judges states that the level of the retirement pension must be as close as possible to the level of their final salary as a judge[305] and in England and Wales, the amount of the pension is linked to salary and depends upon the period of service. A maximum pension of one-half of the final salary of a judge is payable after twenty years as a judge.[306] In broad terms, members of the judiciary pay a contribution of between 1.8 and 2.4 per cent of salary to accrue a final salary pension for their dependants' benefit at the rate of 1/40th for each year of service up to twenty years. This follows a long-running tax dispute between the judiciary and the government,[307] the outcome of which was to maintain (though not to improve) the value of the judicial remuneration package. Judges made representations to the Lord Chancellor when the government's Finance Act 2004 introduced changes in the tax treatment of pensions,[308] which were bound to have an adverse impact on the judicial pension benefits when they came into effect in 2006. Evidence provided in 2004 to the Senior Salaries Body revealed the risk, outlined by the Lord Chief Justice and the Permanent Secretary to the Department of Constitutional Affairs, that 'a significant number of judges' might resign before the Finance Act 2004 came into force in order to avoid the new tax regime.[309] Following protests from the judiciary, with a continuing threat of resignation from senior judges,[310] the Lord Chancellor secured a different arrangement, whereby the value of judicial remuneration packages would be maintained under the Judicial Pensions

---

[305] Art. 6.4 of the European Charter on the Statute of Judges. A retirement pension should also be guaranteed.

[306] Judicial Pensions and Retirement Act 1993, s. 3 raised the period of service for a full pension from 15 to 20 years. The retirement age was also prospectively lowered to 70.

[307] The pensions tax regime came into force on 6 April 2006. The judicial pension scheme now allows judges to keep their money in a non-tax-exempt private scheme, but judicial pensions no longer attract the preferential tax treatment afforded to tax-approved schemes, i.e., a tax-free lump sum benefit payable on retirement or following the death of a judge and tax relief on contributions.

[308] It introduced a £1.5m cap on the amount of tax-free money allowed in a pension fund.

[309] Twenty-seventh report on Senior Salaries, Report no. 59, Cm 6451 (February 2005), para. 4.11.

[310] F. Gibbs, 'Judges Threaten to Resign over Pension Losses', *The Times*, 6 October 2005.

Scheme.[311] There is now a new non-pensionable lump sum payment on a judge's retirement and a reduction in the pension contribution rates payable by judges for their dependants' benefit.

It is to be noted that the pension cut was raised at a time when Home Secretaries – David Blunkett and Charles Clarke – had clashed with the judiciary over individual judgments and the anti-terror legislation proposals. In the course of the dispute, the Lord Chief Justice pointed out that, since the judges' pensions were statutory, judges were 'excluded from opportunities available to other professionals to take action to protect themselves against the new legislation'[312] and that the new legislation breached the legitimate expectation that they had entertained in accepting judicial appointment. We have noted this in relation to judicial salaries already: the judiciary is at a disadvantage in challenging the government's departure from the Review Body's recommendations. The convention that judges cannot return to practice further limits the room for judicial manoeuvre.

Pensions were again a matter of debate in Parliament in February 2011 when the government argued that judges, like any other public service pension scheme members, should begin to contribute towards their own pensions. There is no express prohibition on alteration or reduction in the terms of the pension. Nonetheless, in the context of a freeze in judicial pay, as argued by Lord Falconer and Lord Woolf, the introduction of contributions from the judge to his or her personal pension leads to a total reward reduction without any commensurate increase in the benefits obtained. Lords Mackay, Falconer and Woolf raised the principle that a serving judge shall not have his terms of service adversely affected without his consent during his term of service as part of the rule of law and an internationally recognised principle.[313] The assumption that the judicial contribution to pensions would have no impact on recruitment and retention of judges was also questioned.

But none of their Lordships' points is reflected in the Pensions Act 2011. The Act makes provision for judges to make contributions to their pensions, as elsewhere in the public sector.[314] One interviewee emphasised how anything they might say might turn against them: 'The press

[311] Judicial Pensions Scheme, 'Resource Accounts 2005–06', HC 1463 (20 July 2006), p. 4.
[312] Gibbs, 'Judges Threaten to Resign over Pension Losses'.
[313] HL Deb., 623–8 and 634 (15 February 2011); Art. 13 of the Universal Charter of the Judge; the European Charter on the Statute of Judges, para. 8.
[314] Pensions Act 2011, s. 34.

hates us. What could we say about pensions when people lose their jobs?' Another interviewee mentioned some 'considerable growls of opinion which suggest that we should go for judicial review, and as far as we can on this. And the tone of the private emails I receive about this ... Quite a number of judges have threatened to resign now.'[315] The Irish referendum on the constitutional bar to the reduction of salaries was referred to by a number of interviewees, with one of them commenting with humour, on the voters' 75 per cent approval of the reduction of salaries, that 'The judges were very pleased that they got 25 per cent of the voters to support them, given their image.'

In addition, under the new section 9A of the Judicial Pensions and Retirement Act 1993 (introduced by the Pensions Act 2011), the appropriate minister may, by regulations made with the concurrence of the Treasury, make provision for and in connection with requiring contributions to be made towards the cost of judicial pensions. In other words, the level of judicial contributions is not fixed and it is open to the executive to increase the level of contributions of existing judges currently in office. In a context where governmental criticisms of the courts have been rife, this new power given to the executive without any further details cannot be welcome. As suggested by Lord Falconer, it is for future governments 'a classic tool with which to interfere with judicial independence'.[316] It might be possible to say that a decision to exercise that power was taken in response to a set of decisions unfavourable to the government.[317] It also blurs the specificity of the judiciary, now assimilated to the public sector at large by the government, as it justifies the legislative change on the ground that the current judicial pension scheme was 'a bit of an anomaly among public sector pensions'.[318]

4.48 Fee-paid part-time judges have no entitlement to a judicial pension on retirement pro rata to the pension of full-time circuit judges. The

---

[315] This was also reported in *The Times* in January 2012, stating that 'the action group was started by High Court masters but has snowballed to include judges at all but the most senior levels, including High Court cost judges, tribunal and employment judges, district and circuit judges'.

[316] HL Deb., 627–8 (15 February 2011).   [317] HL Deb., 628 (15 February 2011).

[318] HL Deb., 331 (14 July 2011). In addition, under the Pensions Act 2011, the government's use of a different market indicator (the consumer prices index instead of the retail prices index) to uprate public sector pensions from April 2011 is also likely to reduce the value of judicial pensions; the Review Body estimated that the judicial pension is likely to be worth almost 25% less after 20 years of uprating by the consumer prices index, Review Body on Senior Salaries, 'Thirty-Fourth Report', 12.

long-running claim to the contrary by a retired recorder Dermod O'Brien pitched the judiciary against the government on pensions obligations. O'Brien claimed that under European law, as a 'worker', he should be entitled to a pension, and his arguments were favourably received by the Court of Justice of the European Union. In 2012, in a preliminary ruling following a reference from the UK Supreme Court,[319] the Court of Justice of the European Union held that the European Framework Agreement on part-time work[320] precluded, for the purpose of access to the retirement pension scheme, national law from establishing a distinction between full-time judges and part-time judges remunerated on a daily fee-paid basis, unless such a difference in treatment was justified.[321] The Court of Justice commented that the Ministry of Justice could not solely differentiate between a fee-paid part-time judge and a full-time judge on the basis that a recorder is paid on a daily basis and retains the opportunity to practise as a barrister. It emphasised that budgetary considerations alone cannot justify the unequal treatment.[322] It also considered as a 'crucial factor' that part-time and full-time judges performed essentially the same activity.[323]

In accordance with the principles laid down by the Court of Justice, the Supreme Court held in 2013 that O'Brien was a part-time worker, and that the Ministry of Justice had not justified the difference of treatment between a fee-paid part-time judge and a full-time or salaried judge for the purpose of access to the retirement pension scheme.[324]

Before the Court of Justice, judicial independence had also been raised to justify the removal of judges from the scope of the European Framework Agreement on part-time work. That argument was roundly – and rightly, in our view – rejected by the Court of Justice of the European Union, following Advocate General Kokott's Opinion. She held that independence in terms of the essence of an activity was not in itself an

---

[319] *O'Brien v. Ministry of Justice* [2010] UKSC 34.
[320] Directive 97/81 and the Part-time Workers Regulations.
[321] C-393/10 *Dermod Patrick O'Brien v. Ministry of Justice*, 1 March 2012.
[322] Joined Cases C-4/02 and C-5/02 *Schönheit and Becker* [2003] ECR I-12575, para. 85, and Case C-486/08 *Zentralbetriebsrat der Landeskrankenhäuser Tirols* [2010] ECR I-3527, para. 46.
[323] C-393/10 *Dermod Patrick O'Brien v. Ministry of Justice*, para. 62.
[324] The Supreme Court rejected, inter alia, the budgetary considerations raised by the Ministry of Justice: 'Sound management of the public finances may be a legitimate aim, but that is very different from deliberately discriminating against part-time workers in order to save money', *O'Brien v. Ministry of Justice* [2013] UKSC 6, para. 67.

appropriate criterion for excluding a professional category from the scope of the European Framework Agreement on workers. She also distinguished between independence in judicial activities and the external conditions of a judge's activity, which were at issue in the case of *O'Brien*.[325] In that respect, the House of Lords' decision in *Percy v. Board of National Mission of the Church of Scotland* applies.[326] Here the House of Lords held that judges are nevertheless subject to some organisation of their work, even though this can be managed by the judges themselves with a greater degree of flexibility. Judges are not self-employed persons. Advocate General Kokott doubted that the rights granted by the Framework Agreement in general, and an entitlement to a retirement pension in particular, could jeopardise the essence of the independence of a judge; 'on the contrary, an entitlement to a retirement pension strengthens the economic independence of judges, and thus ultimately also the essence of their independence'.[327]

4.49 In a written ministerial statement in July 2012, the Lord Chancellor recognised that the judicial pension scheme is 'a critical element of the remuneration offered to the judiciary', continuing: 'Nevertheless we must ensure that the pensions provided are fair, sustainable and affordable.'[328] Discussions with the judiciary are continuing on reform proposals that 'will ensure that the pension provision for judges compares fairly with that offered to others in the public service'.[329] There is much to be said for the informal representations made by the judiciary over judicial remuneration. The Review Body plays a constitutional role as an interface between the judiciary and government by setting some objective criteria for job assessment and comparability with the public and private sector. The Canadian Supreme Court rightly emphasised the virtues of independence, objectivity and effectiveness of the Canadian equivalent to the Review Body on Senior Salaries. It has a standing structure – it is not

---

[325] Opinion of Advocate General Kokott in Case C-393/10 *Dermod Patrick O'Brien* v. *Ministry of Justice*, delivered on 17 November 2011, paras. 47–51.

[326] *Percy* v. *Board of National Mission of the Church of Scotland* [2005] UKHL 73, para. 45 [Lady Hale].

[327] Opinion of Advocate General Kokott in Case C-393/10 *Dermod Patrick O'Brien* v. *Ministry of Justice*, delivered on 17 November 2011, para. 50.

[328] Lord Chancellor, 'Written ministerial statement, Reform of Judicial Pensions', 17 July 2012.

[329] See the Lord Chancellor's 'Written ministerial statement, Reform of Judicial Pensions', 5 February 2013: the new pension scheme, with increased contributions, will apply to all serving judiciary other than those who are within 10 years of pension age at 1 April 2012 (around 75% of judges were within 10 years of retirement age at 1 April 2012).

an ad hoc body – but its authority must be doubted in the light of the government departing from its recommendations for four years in a row.

We noted that, under the Pensions Act 2011, it is open to the executive to increase the level of contributions of existing judges currently in office. If the judicial terms of appointments are changed after judges have taken an appointment, they will not be able to regain the former high earnings that they had before they became a judge. While some may have a limited sympathy for high earners, the judges are entitled to be treated fairly and to have confidence that, once they have taken an appointment, the rules of the game will not change adversely towards them.[330] Even more important, the discretionary power given to the executive is a tool that could interfere with judicial independence. Ultimately however, judges are paid large enough salaries to render them free from the risk of judicial corruption, and the culture of judicial independence is evidently strong. Yet, while judicial remuneration remains high, the cumulative effect of the freeze in salary and a substantial change in the judicial pension at a time of high inflation, in addition to the increased judicial workload, is likely to cause judicial retention and recruitment problems in a mid-term perspective, to the detriment of quality of justice in a durable way.[331] The Review Body recently expressed the concern 'that the morale and motivation of the judiciary is being adversely affected by the deterioration, both relative and absolute, in their terms and conditions'.[332]

Conclusions

4.50 The appointments system must be placed in the context of the English machinery of justice. Before 1971 solicitors had no general right of audience and there were 2,500 barristers. The legal profession was small and getting references through what is known today as 'secret soundings' was the accepted norm. That system became unsustainable as the judiciary grew in size, as the Bar grew in numbers and as solicitors became solicitor-advocates. Most of our interviewees strongly defended the Judicial Appointments Commission, which has removed political patronage from the appointment system and brought in the value of transparency necessary to the culture of judicial independence. It has also

---

[330] HL Deb., 624 (15 February 2011).
[331] Review Body on Senior Salaries, 'Thirty-Fourth Report', 4.16; Lord Chief Justice's Report 2010–2012, 1.6.
[332] Review Body on Senior Salaries, 'Thirty-Fourth Report', 4.16.

enhanced the value of professionalism, with greater complexity in the criteria used to assess 'merit' and substantial lay involvement. Our interviewees agreed that the executive plays a legitimate role in the process of appointment, especially at senior level, but the majority rejected a greater involvement of the Lord Chancellor in the appointment process as proposed by the Crime and Courts Bill 2012. The concern for a non-partisan process – as well as a concern for costs of any confirmation hearings in Parliament – prevailed.

In addition, while the lack of flexibility of speed in appointments was regretted by many interviewees, the lack of administrative efficiency of the Department for Constitutional Affairs (the predecessor to the Ministry of Justice) was also recalled by many. The overall view was that the standard of appointments made by the Judicial Appointments Commission was not greatly dissimilar to those that would have been made before the establishment of the Judicial Appointments Commission, with most appointments, certainly at the level of the senior judiciary, considered as very good by our interviewees. The House of Lords Constitution Committee has recently supported the existing appointments model and recommended some limited changes to the process, including the increase in size of the UK Supreme Court selection commissions, with greater lay representation. It would seem wise to retain the constitutional balance established under the CRA, so that the Lord Chancellor retains his current limited veto power, as 'the guardian of the process with a long-stop responsibility'.[333]

Challenges remain for the Judicial Appointments Commission. Many interviewees thought that some of the best practitioners were not applying under the new regime of appointments, a point taken on board by the Judicial Appointments Commission. The Commission has not yet been conspicuously successful in enhancing the diversity of the judiciary, and there seems to be some pessimism as to whether it will succeed. This reflects the wider difficulties in the legal profession that too few women and ethnic minority lawyers hold senior positions, and there is the additional problem that working in the High Court may not be attractive for a mother with children of school age. The itineraries for circuit judges may be reconsidered so as to take account of these caring responsibilities.[334] Another deterrent is the desirability of fee-paid part-time judicial experience, which constitutes in practice the first step towards obtaining

---

[333] Lord Falconer, Evidence before the Committee on the Constitution, Autumn 2011.
[334] UK Association of Women Judges, Written Evidence, para. 11.

a salaried full-time position, but can be difficult for many applicants with family commitments. Part-time fee-paid judicial work tends to entail working from time to time as required, rather than working to a set number of reduced hours.[335] Outstanding academics could also be invited to join the judiciary, and not necessarily at the junior end in tribunals.

We noted the shift from a focus on individual appointments to the concept of a judicial career recommended in 2010 by an advisory panel to the Lord Chancellor, with the aim of achieving greater diversity within the judiciary.[336] However the stage for entry into a judicial career seems unclear. We do not propose a move towards a system where judges are appointed after graduating from university and trained for the bench, and indeed some countries which use such a system (such as France) have been looking at the English model and perceiving benefits from judges having had lengthy legal experience as practitioners. A clearer sense of progression and mobility within the judicial ranks, however, as can be found in most other professions, can help suitable candidates already on the benches to apply and be recognised – albeit this is a long-term goal which may involve appraisals or other measures of a judge's acumen.

A forthcoming challenge for the Judicial Appointments Commission is to oversee appointments to the European Court of Justice and the shortlisting process for the English judge at the European Court of Human Rights. It has nowhere been explained why the international status of these courts should require political input or input of any other kind as the Judicial Appointments Commission is already able to provide. Perhaps as the Judicial Appointments Commission, still a very new body, gains in authority over time, it will have sole responsibility for appointing English judges to the European courts, with limited input from the executive.

---

[335] HL Committee on the Constitution Report 2012, para. 113.
[336] Advisory Panel on Diversity, 'Report'.

5

Standards of conduct on the bench

Introduction

5.1 The principle of impartiality underlies the judicial oath to do justice 'without ... affection or ill-will'. Lord Bingham explained:

> A judge must free himself of prejudice and partiality and so conduct himself, in court and out of it, as to give no ground for doubting his ability and willingness to decide cases before him solely on their legal and factual merits as they appear to him in the exercise of an objective, independent, and impartial judgment.[1]

It would be possible to devote pages to similar statements of principle and to some extent English lawyers can be forgiven for doing so. Judicial impartiality is said to be '*the* fundamental principle of justice'[2] both at common law and under Article 6 of the European Convention on Human Rights (ECHR): 'justice should not only be done, but should manifestly and undoubtedly be seen to be done'.[3]

It is well known that a judge must be impartial in two senses; he must neither be actually biased towards a party in the case, nor must he appear to be biased to the (hypothetical) fair-minded observer. Should either be the case, then he must disqualify himself. Devlin LJ observed that 'Bias is or may be an unconscious thing and a man may honestly say that he was not actually biased and did not allow his interest to affect his mind, although, nevertheless, he may have allowed it unconsciously to do so'.[4]

---

[1] T. Bingham, 'The Judge as Lawmaker', in *The Judge* (Oxford University Press, 1981), p. 3, also in *The Business of Judging* (Oxford University Press, 2000). W. Lucy, 'The Possibility of Impartiality' (2005) OJLS 25, 3.

[2] *AWG Group v. Morrison Ltd* [2006] EWCA Civ 6, para. 6 [Mummery LJ].

[3] *R v. Sussex Justices, ex parte McCarthy* [1924] 1 KB 256 [Lord Hewart]; *Brown v. Stott* [2001] 2 WLR 817 [Lord Steyn]; *Amjad and others v. Steadman-Byrne* [2007] EWCA Civ 625, para. 16 [Sedley LJ].

[4] *R v. Barnsley Licensing Justices, ex parte Barnsley and District Licensed Victuallers' Association* [1960] 2 QB 167, 187 [Devlin LJ].

To the extent that the fair-minded person would guess that this might happen, the judge must recuse himself. Even in cases where some cause for apparent bias is present but the threshold is not met, a judge would be wise to recuse himself in any event, although there may be practical considerations and the possibility of waiver by the parties affected to take into account. This affords a flexibility in practice which may achieve more than if the rules for disqualification were to be enshrined in statute, as occurs in the United States.[5] In England, the two categories of actual and apparent bias are developed by case law, accompanied only by a number of statutory prohibitions against certain types of adjudications.[6]

Besides looking to the common law for guidance, the *Guide to Judicial Conduct* provides that judges should strive to maintain and enhance the confidence of the public, the legal profession and litigants, in the impartiality of the judge and of the judiciary; and it offers some 'signposts' for guidance, noting the overlap with the common law rules on bias.[7] It is accepted, for example, that any significant financial interest from a judge, or a member of the judge's family, to the knowledge of the judge, in the outcome of the case will disqualify the judge.[8] There is also consensus to say that a judge, or a barrister or solicitor when he sits ad hoc as a member of a tribunal, should not sit on a case to which a near friend, close relative or client is a party. Beyond this, a real appearance of bias can apply to the judge knowing someone involved in the case as a friend, foe or family member, or generally when the judge can be found to have an association or social interest in a matter indirectly connected with an issue raised before the court. The standards of impartiality, which shape the threshold for a successful allegation of bias, are thus high, higher as

---

[5] J. Frank, 'Disqualification of Judges' (1974) 56 *Yale Law Journal* 605; *Laird* v. *Tatum* (1972) 93 S. Ct. 7.

[6] H.W. Wade and C.F. Forsyth, *Administrative Law*, 10th edn (Oxford University Press, 2009), ch. 13; Justices Jurisdiction Act 1742; Public Health Act 1875, s. 258; *R* v. *Lee ex parte Shaw* (1882) 9 QBD 394; *R* v. *Henley* [1892] 1 QB 504; *R* v. *Pwlheli Justices ex parte Soane* [1948] 2 All ER 815; Licensing Act 1964, ss. 21–22 but see *R (Chief Constable of Lancashire)* v. *Crown Court at Preston* [2001] EWHC 928 (Admin) [2002] 1 WLR 1332 regarding compliance with Art. 6(1) ECHR; Factories Act 1961, s. 164(7).

[7] *M* v. *Islington LBC* [2002] 1 FLR 95. The guidance applies to fee-paid as well as full-time and part-time judges. *Guide to Judicial Conduct*, 3.1 and s. 7.

[8] *Guide to Judicial Conduct*, 3.8. 'Judge's family' is defined under the Bangalore Principles as '... a judge's spouse, son, daughter, son-in-law, daughter-in-law, and any other close relative or person who is a companion or employee of the judge and who lives in the judge's household' and 'Judge's spouse' includes: 'a domestic partner of the judge or any other person of either sex in a close personal relationship with the judge", cited by the *Guide to Judicial Conduct*, 5.2.

time goes by, set by the indispensable requirement of public confidence in the administration of justice.[9]

Interviewees noted that appeals on the basis of apparent bias have recently sharply increased. This does not seem to us to imply a rise in unsatisfactory practices governing judicial disqualification, for the Court of Appeal would rather err on the side of caution, considering in one case, for example, that, even where the allegation of apparent bias cannot be sustained, the judge should have recused himself for the avoidance of doubt.[10] In some such cases though, the trial judge may have been right to be resolute in insisting on hearing a case: it is also a valid principle that no party may choose its tribunal whether by insisting on a particular judge or by objecting to one without sufficient cause.[11] Inevitably, in borderline cases this must be balanced against the principle that judges should show sensitivity to parties who may still nurse an understandable and genuine (if exaggerated) unease about the judge's impartiality.

Two core distinctions can be made at this early stage. First, claims of bias must be distinguished from issues relating to the independence of the court from the parties. The European Court of Human Rights noted the close relationship between the concepts of independence and impartiality in *Findlay* v. *UK*:

> The Court recalls that in order to establish whether a tribunal can be considered as 'independent', regard must be had inter alias to the manner of appointment of its members and their term of office, the existence of guarantees against outside pressures and the question whether the body presents an appearance of independence.
>
> As to the question of 'impartiality', there are two aspects of this requirement. First, the tribunal must be subjectively free from personal prejudice or bias. Secondly, it must also be impartial from an objective viewpoint, that is, it must offer sufficient guarantees to exclude any legitimate doubt in this respect. The concepts of independence and objective impartiality are closely linked.[12]

---

[9] *Lawal* v. *Northern Spirit Ltd* [2003] UKHL 35, para. 22 [Lord Steyn].

[10] *Drury* v. *BBC and another* [2007] All ER (D) 205. The difference between suggestions of bias and of lack of independence has been recognised in the context of prison disciplinary hearings, where the High Court was more concerned to exercise review in the case of apparent bias, since lack of institutional independence on the part of the prison governor was regarded as an unavoidable evil of a system which required quick resolution of minor incidents, *R (King)* v. *SSJ* [2010] EWCA Crim 2522.

[11] S. Sedley, 'When Should a Judge Not Be a Judge?' (2011) 33 LRB 1, pp. 9–12.

[12] *Findlay* v. *UK* (1997) 24 EHRR 221, para. 73; *Porter* v. *Magill* [2001] UKHL 67; [2002] 2 AC 357, para. 88.

The judicial oath supports a distinction between independence and bias. Independence is undermined by fear or favour.[13] Independence refers to the institutional separation of power of the judicial branch from the legislature and executive branches, and to the structural independence of the judge from the party to the dispute. The detailed consideration of the structures of the decision-making bodies involved determines institutional independence; where independence is lacking, then it does not matter which judge sits on the tribunal. By contrast, bias depends on the individual judge himself and his earlier dealings with the parties, other statements made that relate to the case and his own personal interests, which may be furthered by a particular outcome, as considered later in this chapter.[14]

Suggestions of bias should also be distinguished from *non iudex in sua causa* (No one should be judge in his or her own cause).[15] This doctrine relates to judges who are institutionally connected to one of the parties. Thus, the House of Lords in *R* v. *Abdroikof* decided that a member of the Crown Prosecution Service (CPS) may not sit as a juror in a case brought by the CPS, though he might sit in a case brought by an independent agency.[16] This comes as no surprise on account of *iudex*: it is not a case where independence is lacking because there are no conceivable adverse consequences for the juror whatever the outcome, and it may be quite clear that there is no bias if he knows none of the parties, including any of the prosecutors involved.

5.2 The first part of this chapter is thus concerned with the common law test for bias and the process that leads to recusal. In the second part of the chapter, we illustrate the disciplinary role of the Court of Appeal on broader fair trial principles rather than because (as is the case in the first part of this chapter) the judge should have recused himself at the outset of the trial. The judicial manner of conducting a trial or

---

[13] Sedley, 'When Should a Judge Not Be a Judge?'.

[14] *R (Alconbury Developments Ltd)* v. *Secretary of State for the Environment* [2003] 2 AC 295; *Tsfayo* v. *UK* (2004) 39 EHRR SE22; *R(A)* v. *Croydon LBC* [2009] 1 WLR 2557; *De-Winter Heald* v. *Brent LBC* [2010] 1 WLR 990; cf. *R (L)* v. *Secretary of State for Justice* [2009] EWCA Civ 2416, where the test in *Porter* v. *Magill* [2001] UKHL 67 was applied by Laws LJ in dismissing the application, though the question was one of independence, Laws LJ referring to the lack of 'current or past hierarchical or institutional connection with any individual potentially implicated in the circumstances of the claimant's attempted suicide', para. 47.

[15] See *Dr Bonham's Case*; *Earl of Derby's Case* (1613) 77 ER 1390.

[16] *R* v. *Abdroikov* [2007] 1 WLR 2679.

adjudicating a dispute may have consequences when the outcome is taken to appeal. In this regard, the Court of Appeal plays an important role in maintaining high standards of judicial behaviour in court.[17] The Court of Appeal has been active in criticising judges for hostile questioning of a client giving evidence, or for constant interruption of counsel's cross-examination of a witness. The party offended or prejudiced, and the public at large, might otherwise be tempted to attribute misconduct of a particular judge to the judiciary as a whole. The disapproval and criticism of the appellate court eliminates such danger and restores the scales of justice to their proper balance.

However, beyond the outcome of a case itself, the formal handling of complaints about the personal conduct of judges is dealt with under a new regulatory framework introduced in the Constitutional Reform Act 2005 (CRA).[18] The Lord Chief Justice and the Lord Chancellor drew up the Judicial Discipline (Prescribed Procedures) Regulations 2006 under which the Office of Judicial Complaints was created, as had been anticipated in the Concordat. The option of making a complaint to the Office for Judicial Complaints is an additional remedy to launching an appeal; but the two remedies are fundamentally different. Only by appealing can a litigant hold out any hope of reversing a decision by the judge or of affecting the outcome of the case. Equally, only by making a complaint via the Office for Judicial Complaints might he see official acknowledgement of the misconduct of an identified judge accompanied by a sanction. Sanctioning a judge is not formally the purpose of the appeal process,[19] although, where the Court of Appeal does record criticism (usually[20] politely expressed) of the trial judge, the judgment will be sent

---

[17] *Goold* v. *Evans & Co* [1951] 2 TLR 1189, p. 1191 [Denning LJ]; *Brassington* v. *Brassington* [1962] P 276, 282; *Hobbs* v. *Tinling* [1929] 2 KB 1, 48.

[18] Under s. 115 CRA, 'the Lord Chief Justice may, with the agreement of the Lord Chancellor, make regulations providing for the procedures that are to be followed in (a) the investigation and determination of allegations by any person of misconduct by judicial office holders; (b) reviews and investigations (including the making of applications or references) under ss. 110–112 [CRA 2005].

[19] Lord Widgery LCJ suggested that reprehensible behaviour of a High Court judge should not normally be mentioned in judgments but referred to him or to a Presiding Judge of circuit, F. Lawton, 'Judging the Judges', *The Times*, 14 July 1998.

[20] L.J. Blom-Cooper and G. Drewry, *Final Appeal: A Study of the House of Lords in its Judicial Capacity* (Oxford: Clarendon Press, 1972), pp. 86–7. This not always the case. Ex-Technology and Construction Court judge Mr Justice Seymour's judgment in *Co-op* v. *ICL* was found 'unfair' and his views lacking in any 'commercial sense whatsoever', *Co-operative Group (CWS) Ltd* v. *International Computers Ltd* [2003] EWCA Civ 1955, para. 39 and conclusions; in another case, although the decision was upheld, the

to the judge concerned,[21] and where there is any reason for concern about the conduct of the judge it is sent to the Presiding Judges in his or her area.[22]

There is some overlap between these categories. Bad behaviour in court, such as falling asleep or displaying impatience with one party or showing that the outcome has been decided before the end of the trial, can both trigger an appeal and also an application to the Office of Judicial Complaints (either by one of the parties or by the Presiding Judges of the court). The *Guide to Judicial Conduct* reflects this overlap by referring to principles of judicial ethics and to common law jurisprudence, and our analysis thus starts with a clarification of the *Guide's* status.

I.   A written code of conduct

5.3 Judicial standards of conduct foster a culture of judicial independence by providing an idealised account of the conduct expected from judges in their relationships with the public, with the legal system and with the legal profession. Notwithstanding their importance for the judiciary itself, the traditional English attitude towards judicial standards of conduct was 'that the less definition attempted, the better; that if you pick judges who know how to behave, then all will be well as if you do not, no amount of analysis of ethical problems will help'.[23] Judges were guided by conventions, traditions, practices and understandings which have been established over the years. Such attitudes prevailed until this new millennium. Much has changed in a short period of time. Judicial standards of conduct are now expressly construed as a defining component of public trust in the judiciary, and we

---

judge's adverse findings as to a company's intentions and honesty were said to be 'entirely wrong', 'unjustified and [they] should not have been made', *Vogon International Ltd* v. *Serious Fraud Office* [2004] EWCA Civ 104, paras 29 and 31. Judge Seymour was redeployed in 2005 to hear non-Technology and Construction Court cases; Lord Hoffman strongly criticised one of Eady J's judgments, *Jameel* v. *Wall Street Journal Europe SPRL (No. 3)* [2007] 1 AC 359, paras. 57–8, shortly afterwards counterbalanced by the tribute paid by the Court of Appeal to the judgment of Eady J and his handling of the case in *McKennitt* v. *Ash* [2006] EWCA Civ 1714, paras. 81 and 88. See also M. Friedland, *A Place Apart: Judicial Independence and Accountability in Canada* (Ottawa: Canadian Judicial Council, 1995), p. 157.

[21] See, e.g., *Gardiner Fire Ltd* v. *Jones* [1998] All ER (D) 474.

[22] A successful appeal to a higher court does not of itself provide a basis for criticism of a trial judge, though see Judicial Communications Office Statement, Statement 120606/06, 11/06/2006.

[23] J. Thomas, *Judicial Ethics in Australia*, 3rd edn (Chatswood NSW: LexisNexis Butterworths, 2009), p. v; S. Sedley, 'Judicial Ethics in England' [2003] 29 *Legal Ethics* 6.

need to consider the standards to which members of the judiciary may be held. Thus Lord Bingham commented that 'the practice of appointing judges from a small pool of candidates, sharing a common professional background, and known personally or by professional repute to those making and advising on appointments, has enabled much [on legal ethics] to be taken for granted'.[24] Since full-time judges are difficult to remove prior to the statutory age, one might add that if standards cannot be defined, then one could not but place the strongest emphasis on appointment, and yet every appointment system must have its limitations.

Until 2002 the written canons of judicial conduct were the Magna Carta 1215 ('To none will we sell, to none deny or delay right or justice') and the judicial oath ('I will do right by all manner of people, after the law and usages of this realm, without fear or favour, affection or ill will'). In 2002 came a third canon, the *Guide to Judicial Conduct* (revised in 2011). It was essentially drafted in response to international and national texts, which have emphasised the need to set some appropriate standards of judicial conduct, so that the impartiality and the independence of judges can be demonstrably seen.[25] It provides a useful reminder that the traditional understanding of judicial independence as the insulation from the executive, or judicial self-governance, is not an end in itself. It rather serves the most favourable conditions under which the judge may decide in an impartial way, *sine spe ac metu* (without fear or hope).[26] In 2009 the UK Supreme Court adopted its own, rather similar, *Guide to Judicial Conduct*. But the *Guide* can also provide an answer to the growth in numbers of judges at the lower levels and the resulting greater complexity of the judiciary. Indeed, most disciplinary proceedings so far have concerned magistrates. Thus the *Guide*, even though it says nothing surprising to lawyers, nonetheless has an important advisory role to play.

As mentioned in our Chapter 1, the *Guide to Judicial Conduct* broadly follows the six principles asserted in the Bangalore Principles of Judicial Conduct: judicial independence, impartiality, integrity, propriety (and

---

[24] T. Bingham, *The Business of Judging. Selected Essays and Speeches* (Oxford University Press, 2000), p. 69.

[25] See Art. 6(1) ECHR and the First Principle of the Bangalore Principles of Judicial Conduct; *Guide to Judicial Conduct*, para. 1.2; cf. Murray Gleeson CJ, 'Foreword', in The Council of Chief Justices of Australia, *Guide to Judicial Conduct*, 2nd edn (Melbourne: Australasian Institute of Judicial Administration Inc., 2007).

[26] G. di Frederico, 'Independence and Accountability of the Judiciary in Italy. The Experience of a Former Transitional Country in a Comparative Perspective', in A. Sajo and R. Bentch (eds), *Judicial Integrity* (Leiden: Brill, 2004), p. 15.

the appearance of propriety), equality of treatment to all before the courts, competence and diligence. As the Bangalore principles do, the *Guide* introduces guidance on personal relationships and perceived bias as well as on activities outside the courts, in relation to the media for example, or after retirement. The *Guide* ranges over questions of morality and detailed prescriptions of proper professional behaviour, including matters of etiquette.

It is arguable that most of the guidance contained in the *Guide* is declaratory of existing conventions or standards of judicial conduct which must be followed. The duty to follow such guidance derives from the oath taken upon judicial appointment, which requires the judge to follow 'the law and usages of the realm'.[27] It is not, however, a contractual duty, for judges are not considered to be 'persons in Her Majesty's Service', but are rather statutory officers.[28]

II.   Judicial impartiality: procedure, disclosure and waiver

5.4 We now examine the mechanics of dealing with the possibility of bias. In this area, the judge needs to be seen to be proactive from the start; he should not be waiting for the parties to raise the issue. If a judge realises, before the hearing, that a case in his list is one in which he should not sit for any (sufficient) reason, as discussed below, he must recuse himself. Ordinarily he would arrange for another judge to take the case, which would be done informally by the judge's clerk. There is no need to consult the parties in clear-cut cases where recusal is required, because the matter is not formally dependent upon the parties' objections. Indeed it would be wrong to do so, since he would effectively be asking one of the parties to waive their right to a fair trial (such a waiver would be ineffective anyway: mere disclosure of a cause of bias does not avoid an objection to a judge who, in the light of the matter disclosed, clearly ought not to hear the case).[29]

Disqualification for apparent bias is not a discretionary matter for the judge. Thus, tempting though it may be in such cases for the parties to reason that, since they trust the only judge available, they might disregard

[27] Guide to Judicial Conduct, 2.2–2.3; Guide to Judicial Conduct (UK Supreme Court), para. 2.2; Guide to Judicial Conduct (Australia), 1.1.

[28] On that basis judges argued that they should not be subject to salary cuts under the National Economy Act 1931; their resistance prevailed and the cuts did not apply to them, see paras. 4.41, 4.44, 7.31.

[29] *Helow v. Secretary of State for the Home Department* [2008] 1 WLR 2416, 58.

a factor which gives rise to apparent bias, that temptation must be resisted, even in the event of possible inconvenience, such as finding another suitable judge: 'Efficiency and convenience are not the determinative legal values: the paramount concern of the legal system is to administer justice, which must be, and must be seen by the litigants and fair-minded members of the public to be, fair and impartial. Anything less is not worth having.'[30] Where Article 6(1) ECHR applies, it is unlikely that the rule against bias gives way to necessity.[31]

At the other end of the scale, if the judge is aware of a factor which, on proper examination, could not possibly found a case of real or apparent bias, then he should continue the case and need not even disclose the factor to the parties. The general practice on disclosure is further reflected in *Laurence* v. *Thomas*:

> Judges should be circumspect about declaring the existence of a relationship where there is no real possibility of it being regarded by a fair-minded and informed observer as raising a possibility of bias. If such a relationship is disclosed, it unnecessarily raises an implication that it could affect the judgment and approach of the judge. If this is not the position no purpose is served by mentioning the relationship.[32]

If the judge is put on notice that he should not sit due to a potential conflict of interest, he should make inquiry of the full facts and make disclosure in light of them – assuming that he does not consider the facts sufficient to require disqualification.[33] As we will see below, many cases of apparent bias can be argued either way on the known facts and it is vital that all borderline cases are the subject of argument. Thus the passage from *Laurence* v. *Thomas* continues:

> On the other hand, if the situation is one where a fair-minded and informed person might regard the judge as biased, it is important that disclosure should be made. If the position is borderline, disclosure should be made because then the judge can consider, having heard the submissions of the parties, whether or not he should withdraw. In other situations disclosure can unnecessarily undermine the litigant's confidence in the judge.[34]

---

[30] *AWG Group* v. *Morrison Ltd* [2006] EWCA Civ 6, para. 29 [Mummery LJ].

[31] *Kingsley* v. *UK* (2002) 35 EHRR 177; at common law, *Dimes* v. *Proprietors of Grand Junction Canal* (1852) 3 HLCas 759; *Great Charte* v. *Kennington* (1730) 2 Str. 1173.

[32] *Laurence* v. *Thomas* [2003] QB 528, para. 64.

[33] *Locabail (UK)* v. *Bayfield Properties Ltd* [2000] QB 451, para. 26 B–D; Guide to Judicial Conduct, 3.12.

[34] *Laurence* v. *Thomas* [2003] QB 528, para. 64.

In addition, the very fact of disclosure can be a 'badge of impartiality', showing that the judge has 'nothing to hide and [was] fully conscious of the factors which might be apprehended to influence ... her judgment'.[35] In practical terms, an appeal in a borderline case on the basis that the judge should have recused himself seems more likely to succeed if the judge had not thought the factor even to merit disclosure. The *Guide to Judicial Conduct* summarises the practice:

> Disclosure should of course be made to all parties and, save when the issue has been resolved by correspondence before the hearing, discussion between the judge and the parties as to what procedure to follow should normally be in open court, unless the case itself is to be heard in chambers. The consent of the parties is a relevant and important factor but the judge should avoid putting them in a position in which it might appear that their consent is sought to cure a ground of disqualification. Even where the parties consent to the judge sitting, if the judge, on balance, considers that recusal is the proper course, the judge should so act. Conversely, there are likely to be cases in which the judge has thought it appropriate to bring the circumstances to the attention of the parties but, having considered any submissions, is entitled to and may rightly decide to proceed notwithstanding the lack of consent.

Practical difficulties arise where the arguable conflict of interest becomes apparent at short notice upon the opening of the case. Although the judge may not consider the facts sufficient to require recusal, disclosure should still be made so that the judge can consider, having heard the submissions of the parties, whether he should withdraw.[36] It is generally the case that the parties will agree that the trial must continue. But it should be possible for the judge to recuse himself at this point and for the case to be transferred to another judge. When a matter comes to light later in the course of the hearing, it is sufficient for the judge to disclose only what he then knows. There is no obligation on him to make inquiry, but if further inquiry is made and some relevant facts are discovered then he would be obliged to disclose them.[37]

In *AWG Group Ltd* v. *Morrison*,[38] on the eve of a eve of six-month trial with 250 trial bundles, the trial judge realised that one of the witnesses had been known to him for thirty years as a long-standing family acquaintance.

---

[35] *Davidson* v. *Scottish Ministers (No. 2)* [2005] 1 SC (HL) 7, 19 [Lord Bingham], 54 [Lord Hope].
[36] *Taylor* v. *Lawrence* [2003] QB 528, 61–5.
[37] *Locabail (UK)* v. *Bayfield Properties Ltd* [2000] QB 451, 26 B–D.
[38] *AWG Group* v. *Morrison Ltd* [2006] EWCA Civ 6.

The defendants sought to have the judge stand down. The judge accepted a suggestion from the claimants that they would call other witnesses instead of that one. This was because there was a grave concern to see that a long and complex trial was not postponed. There was not any suggestion of actual bias or personal interest. In spite of this, the Court of Appeal held that the judge should have recused himself as he had known one of the parties' potential witnesses socially for some thirty years, and the withdrawal of that particular witness would not in practice remove his friend's interest in the case from the events. Where the judge's impartiality is questioned, the appearance is just as important as the reality of the matter.[39] Mummery LJ emphasised that concerns about inconvenience, costs and delay were irrelevant to the crucial question of the real possibility of bias and automatic disqualification at trial of the judge.[40]

The judicial oath also creates a presumption of impartiality and justifies, at least in part, a high threshold for displacing the presumption of impartiality.[41] If the judge considers that there is no bias (real or apparent), he may however take into account the practicalities of finding another judge, who is available and equally able to deal with the matters under trial. He might also consider whether one of the parties has some other motive for seeking his recusal. Note the remarks of Gleeson CJ, McHugh, Gummow and Hayne JJ in *Ebner*:

> In a case of real doubt, it will often be prudent for a judge to decide not to sit in order to avoid the inconvenience that could result if an appellate court were to take a different view on the matter of disqualification. However, if the mere making of an insubstantial objection were sufficient to lead a judge to decline to hear or decide a case, the system would soon reach a stage where, for practical purposes, individual parties could influence the composition of the Bench. That would be intolerable.[42]

Similarly the *Guide to Judicial Conduct* provides:

> A judge is entitled to keep in mind his general duty to try the cases in his or her list and the listing burden and delay which may be occasioned by a recusal. Moreover, it must be recognised that the urgency of the

---

[39] R v. *Bow Street Stipendiary Magistrate, ex parte Pinochet Ugarte (No. 2)* [2001] 1 AC 119, 139 [Lord Nolan].

[40] *AWG Group* v. *Morrison Ltd* [2006] EWCA Civ 6, 29 [Mummery LJ].

[41] Guide to Judicial Conduct, 7.2; R v. *S (RD)* [1997] 3 SCR 484, para. 117; *In re Medicaments and Related Classes of Goods (No. 2)* [2000] EWCA Civ 350, 700, para. 83.

[42] *Ebner* v. *Official Trustee* (2000) 205 CLR 337, para. 20.

situation may be such that a hearing is required in the interests of justice notwithstanding the existence of arguable grounds in favour of disqualification.[43]

There is no specific procedure for attacking the qualification of the judge if he chooses to try the case himself, except going to the Court of Appeal after he delivers his judgment. In that case, bias would only be raised as a ground for appeal. However, following the *Pinochet (No. 2)* decision,[44] Lord Irvine (then Lord Chancellor) suggested that future decisions on potential bias in the House of Lords (now Supreme Court) should be collectively taken, with the panel of judges addressing the issue of bias before the hearing, and the Law Lord in the chair making the final decision.[45]

While this would seem appropriate before the Supreme Court, and was indeed received favourably by some senior judges, we need to consider whether this would also be desirable before the lower or appellate courts. It may seem strange that the judge himself should be making such decisions, however on balance we suggest that the regulation of recusal processes would seem to be satisfactorily overseen by trial judges them-selves, though if they have the ready opportunity to consult other judges, then so much the better. Moreover, a judge is likely to be cautious in continuing the trial in a case of doubt; it is in the nature of a trial judge to fear being corrected on appeal. However, plausible allegations of actual bias, which are comparatively rare, should be dealt with by another judge.

5.5 There are limited possibilities of waiver. It is not possible to waive the right to a different tribunal if it is the case that the present tribunal is affected by either real or apparent bias. The issue of waiver only arises in cases where the judge has concluded that there is an arguable case of bias, though he is minded to think it insufficient to require recusal. Counsel of the party potentially affected may then waive his right to argue the point. The person who is said to have waived must have acted 'freely and in full knowledge of the facts',[46] and the full relevant facts must be confined to the essential facts allowing the litigant to understand the nature of the

---

[43] Guide to Judicial Conduct, 3–14.

[44] *R v. Bow Street Metropolitan Stipendiary Magistrate, ex parte Pinochet Ugarte (No. 2)* [2001] 1 AC 119.

[45] K. Malleson, 'Judicial Bias and Disqualification after Pinochet (No 2)' (2000) 63 MLR 119.

[46] *R v. Bow Street Metropolitan Stipendiary Megistrate, ex parte Pinochet Ugarte (No. 2)* [2001] 1 AC 119, 137 [Lord Browne-Wilkinson]; J. Goudkamp, 'Judicial Bias and the Doctrine of Waiver' (2007) 26 CJQ 310, 327.

case.[47] A waiver must also be made clearly and unequivocally.[48] Lord Bingham of Cornhill observed:

> In most litigious situations the expression 'waiver' is used to describe voluntary, informed and unequivocal election by a party not to claim a right or raise an objection which it is open to that party to claim or raise. In the context of entitlement to a fair hearing by an independent and impartial tribunal, such is in my opinion the meaning to be given to the expression.[49]

In *Jones v. DAS Legal Expenses Insurance Co Ltd*, the Court of Appeal provided some guidance on the relevant protocol at the start of the hearing:

> The options open to the parties should be explained in detail. Those options are, of course, to consent to the judge hearing the matter, the consequence being that the parties will thereafter be likely to be held to have lost their right to object. The other option is to apply to the judge to recuse himself. The parties should be told it is their right to object, that the court will not take it amiss if the right is exercised and that the judge will decide having heard the submissions. They should be told what will happen next. If the court decides the case can proceed, it will proceed. If on the other hand the judge decides he will have to stand down, the parties should be told in advance of the likely dates on which the matter may be re-listed.[50]

There must also be a fair opportunity for the parties to reach an unpressurised decision.[51] In addition, the waiver of a Convention right must 'not run counter to any important public interest'[52] and must be accompanied by 'minimum guarantees commensurate to its importance', such as the services of a lawyer.[53] Although there may be only a few minutes at the start of a hearing for the parties to consider their options, the judge must ensure that the party is not rushed into agreeing to the case continuing. This is particularly important in the case of a litigant in

---

[47] *Jones v. DAS Legal Expenses Insurance Co Ltd* [2003] EWCA Civ 1071, para. 36.

[48] *Locabail (UK) v. Bayfield Properties Ltd* [2000] QB 451, para. 15; *R v. Secretary of State for the Home Department ex parte Fayed* [2001] Imm AR 134, para. 120.

[49] *Millar v. Dickson* [2002] 1 WLR 1615, para. 31.

[50] *Jones v. DAS Legal Expenses Insurance Co Ltd* [2003] EWCA Civ 1071, para. 35.

[51] *Smith v. Kvaerner Cementation Foundations Ltd (Bar Council intervening)* [2006] EWCA Civ 242, para. 29; *Millar v. Dickson* [2001] UKPC D4, para. 31; *D v. Ireland* ECtHR No. 11489/85, (1986) 51 DR 117.

[52] *McGonnell v. UK* (2000) 30 EHRR 289, para. 44.

[53] *Pfeifer and Plankl v. Austria*, ECtHR, A 227 (1992) 14 EHRR 692, para. 37.

person, and the Court of Appeal provided some guidance on the matter in *Jones* v. *DAS Legal Expenses Insurance Co Ltd*:

> The parties should always be told that time will be afforded to reflect before electing. That should be made clear even where both parties are represented. If there is a litigant in person the better practice may be to rise for five minutes. The litigant in person can be directed to the Citizens Advice Bureau if that service is available and if he wishes to avail of it. If the litigant feels he needs more help, he can be directed to the chief clerk and/or the listing officer. Since this is a problem created by the court, the court has to do its best to assist in resolving it.[54]

The point that a waiver (or tacit acceptance) must be unpressurised has been taken at Strasbourg too. In *McGonnell* v. *UK*,[55] where the Royal Court of Guernsey had authoritatively ruled that the executive role exercised by the Deputy Bailiff of Guernsey did not affect his independence, the Court held that it was not unreasonable for the applicant not to have raised the matter of bias at the national level, and so he could not be said to have failed to exhaust his domestic remedies.

The time between the disclosure and an immediate waiver and a subsequent objection to the waiver is relevant. In *Jones* v. *DAS Legal Expenses Insurance Co Ltd*, the chair informed the claimant – a litigant in person – that her husband was a barrister and was occasionally instructed by the respondents; the claimant waived objection. The claimant later wished to raise objection. The Court of Appeal was left 'with a nagging doubt' that the claimant had been 'hustled into' his decision to waive objection. However, he had had ten weeks to mull over the disclosure since the trial had unexpectedly to be adjourned before starting again, and 'any handicap he may have suffered by having been so suddenly confronted with making a decision on the first morning had evaporated'.[56] He had, ten weeks after the initial disclosure, waived his right to objection.

Once appropriate disclosure has been made, and a party raises no objection to the judge hearing or continuing to hear a case, that party 'cannot thereafter complain of the matter disclosed as giving rise to a real danger of bias. It would be unjust to the other party and undermine both the reality and appearance of justice to allow him to do so.'[57]

---

[54] *Jones* v. *DAS Legal Expenses Insurance Co Ltd* [2003] EWCA Civ 1071, 35 (i)–(vi).
[55] *McGonnell* v. *UK* (2000) 30 EHRR 289, para. 55.
[56] *Jones* v. *DAS Legal Expenses Insurance Co Ltd* [2003] EWCA Civ 1071, para. 38.
[57] *Locabail (UK)* v. *Bayfield Properties Ltd* [2000] QB 451, para. 26.

Nevertheless, intervening at the time of what seems to be a manifestation of bias may not be an easy task for counsel who must choose between not raising the matter and thereby losing a possible ground for appeal, or raising the matter and adding to the costs and loss of time by aborting proceedings and having the case transferred to another judge. Needless to say, the general public confidence in the judges' impartiality may tilt the balance one way or the other. Counsel may also wish to stay on good terms with the judge before whom he may appear in many future cases, and if he wishes to argue the point, counsel's further obligation is to present full information including additional costs incurred by the trial adjournment, and information as to when the trial could take place before another judge.[58]

Appeal on the question of bias remains possible, where the point was contested and lost at trial, or where the (full) evidence of it arose so late that there was little alternative but to complete the trial, or where a supposed waiver was made under undue pressure.

III. Actual and apparent bias

5.6 Actual bias, sometimes labelled predetermination in the judicial context, automatically disqualifies the judge, however cases of actual bias are rarely alleged; the proof of actual bias is difficult. One example of actual bias can be seen in *R v. Bingham Justices ex p. Jowitt*,[59] where the divisional court of the Queen's Bench quashed the conviction of the defendant in a speeding case. In announcing his conviction, the justices' chairman said that, where there was a conflict of evidence between a constable and a member of the public, 'my principle in such cases has always been to believe the evidence of the police officer'. But rarely would a judge or other tribunal express such opinions. A more likely scenario is that, at an early stage of a case, a judge will admit or reveal certain preconceptions about how he views the main issues, and the question is then whether those preconceptions will truly prevent him from changing his mind should the evidence of arguments of counsel warrant it. Such cases are often argued on the basis of apparent bias,[60] though in so far as

---

[58] *Smith v. Kvaerner Cementation Foundations Ltd (Bar Council intervening)* [2006] EWCA Civ 242, paras. 37–8.

[59] *R v. Bingham Justices ex parte Jowitt* (1974) QBD; for a recent allegation, see *Red River UK Ltd v. Sheikh* [2009] EWHC 3257 (Ch).

[60] *Southwark LBC v. Jiminez* [2003] EWCA Civ 502, para. 25.

they relate to comments actually made by the judge at the start of the case, treating such cases as ones of arguable actual bias would ideally attract the safeguard already suggested, that the matter of the judge's bias be automatically referred to another judge.

In spite of being treated together in some cases, the difference between apparent bias and actual bias (sometimes labelled 'predetermination' in this context) has been recognised.[61] Beatson J (as he was then) distinguishes them in these terms:

> Predetermination is the surrender by a decision-maker of its judgment by having a closed mind and failing to apply it to the task. In a case of apparent bias, the decision maker may have in fact applied its mind quite properly to the matter but a reasonable observer would consider that there was a real danger of bias on its part. Bias is concerned with appearances whereas predetermination is concerned with what has in fact happened.[62]

Nevertheless, there are times in any trial and in any pretrial review where a judge is entitled to express a preliminary view.[63] There is nothing wrong in a judge indicating the way he may be thinking on a particular point, provided that this is a provisional view only and that it does not appear that this is a concluded view.[64] Thus, in *El-Farargy* v. *El-Farargy*, which concerned a matrimonial property dispute, the Court of Appeal held that, in the light of the husband's appalling forensic behaviour, 'no observer sitting at the back of his court could have been surprised that he had formed a "prima facie" view nor even that it was "a near conviction"'. The Court continued: 'A fair-minded observer would know, however, that judges are trained to have an open mind and that judges frequently do change their minds during the course of any hearing.'[65] Good practice therefore requires leaving the parties in no doubt that preliminary views,

---

[61] *R* v. *Secretary of State ex parte Kirkstall Valley* [1996] 3 All ER 304, 319 [Sedley J]; *R. (Persimmon Homes)* v. *Vale of Glamorgan Council* [2010] EWHC 535 (Admin), para. 116; for cases treating the concepts together, see *R (Georgiou)* v. *Enfield LBC* [2004] EWHC 779 (Admin), para. 31 [Richards J]. *National Assembly of Wales* v. *Condron* [2006] EWCA Civ 1573 [Richards LJ]; *R (Lewis)* v. *Redcar and Cleveland BC Longmore* [2009] EWHC 954; T. Endicott, *Administrative Law* (Oxford University Press, 2009), p. 177.

[62] *R (Persimmon Homes)* v. *Vale of Glamorgan Council* [2010] EWHC 535 (Admin), para. 116 [Beatson J].

[63] *El-Farargy* v. *El-Farargy* [2007] EWCA Civ 1149.

[64] *Southwark LBC* v. *Jiminez* [2003] EWCA Civ 502, para. 38 [Peter Gibson LJ].

[65] *El-Farargy* v. *El-Farargy* [2007] EWCA Civ 1149, paras. 26–7.

particularly if they are expressed trenchantly,[66] are only provisional and the judge remains open to persuasion.

The Court of Appeal nonetheless allowed the appeal on the second ground of apparent bias, finding certain comments of the judge unacceptable. Ward LJ stated:

> There is a world of difference between saying: 'If he chose to depart never to be seen again' and gratuitously adding 'if he chose to depart on his flying carpet never to be seen again'. Likewise it would have been unexceptional to say that the Sheikh would be present 'to see that no stone is unturned', without glibly adding 'every grain of sand is sifted'. The judge could well make the point that he did not know what lines of communication were available to Saudi Arabia or wherever the Sheikh may be yet once again there was no need for the uncalled-for addition of 'at this I think relatively fast-free time of the year'. Without the additional words, the judge was making fair points but the incidental injections of sarcasm were quite unwarranted.
>
> The third example is the worst. Mr Cayford quite clearly did not understand why the judge had interrupted his submission that the Sheikh's case was not entirely clear by commenting that the affidavit was 'a bit gelatinous'. He did not understand the interruption because he would not have appreciated that, as Mr Randall correctly submits, the judge was setting himself up to deliver the punch line to his joke, 'a bit like Turkish Delight'.[67]

In *Brassington* v. *Brassington*, the Court of Appeal observed:

> There are moments when a court may well feel that an indication of the court's point of view may be valuable and helpful to the parties. But such an intervention is always fraught with dangers. To a judge's mind it is axiomatic that any view which he may hold before the conclusion of the case is merely provisional, and that if any evidence or argument subsequently appears which makes his present view of the case untenable he will abandon that view. But litigants often do not appreciate this. They may mistake a provisional view for a concluded prejudgment.[68]

More recently, in *Amjad* v. *Steadman-Byrne*,[69] the issue was whether there were only two persons in a car at the time of a car accident. But at trial, during a lunch break, the district judge saw counsel in chambers and expressed the view that he could not see how the defendant could

---

[66] *Southwark LBC* v. *Jiminez* [2003] EWCA Civ 502, para. 39.
[67] *El-Farargy* v. *El-Farargy* [2007] EWCA 1149, paras. 28–9.
[68] (1962) pp. 276, 282 (Trial judge: Mr Commissioner Gallop, QC).
[69] *Amjad* v. *Steadman-Byrne* [2007] EWCA Civ 625.

win; he then observed that it was 'flavour of the month' for insurers to prosecute claimants with 'Asian sounding names'.[70] The district judge also observed that D worked for the police and that such persons always think they are right. The Court of Appeal had little difficulty in quashing the verdict.

In *Ezsias* v. *North Glamorgan NHS Trust*,[71] appeal was made against a finding of bias from an employment tribunal chairman, sitting alone during a pre-hearing review. During the pre-hearing review, on Ezsias' prospects for success, the chairman said, inter alia: 'I am of the opinion that the claim not merely has "little prospect of success" but that it has no reasonable prospect of success' and 'I would go further and say that I have no doubt that it is bound to fail'. In the document drafted as the outcome of that meeting, the lack of 'reasonable prospect of success' from Ezsias was again asserted by the chairman. The Court of Appeal held the document 'on its face plainly and unequivocally suffused with a concluded view as to Mr Ezsias's prospects of success'.[72] Although it was submitted that, at a second hearing, the chairman had explained that the first document only expressed an interim opinion, both Elias J and the Court of Appeal found that the way the chairman expressed herself in the first document made the position irretrievable. The chairman's subsequent explanation was enough to acquit her of actual predetermination but it could not displace the perception of a closed mind which any fair-minded and informed observer would have formed.

Here the trenchant views expressed by the chairman during the pre-hearing review were not expressly stated at the time as preliminary views and, even if her earlier ruling had been described as provisional at the time, the forceful way in which the chairman's conclusion was expressed would still have led the fair-minded and well-informed observer to the conclusion that there was very little prospect of the chairman shifting from her original view. It is suggested that the same result should have been reached if the case had been presented as one of actual bias. Similarly, during an adjournment of the inquest concerning the sinking of *The Marchioness*, the coroner was reported as describing some of the relatives of the deceased as 'unhinged' and 'mentally unwell', which indicated a real possibility of unconscious bias. A new coroner was ordered to resume the decision-making process.[73]

---

[70] *Ibid.*, para. 4.   [71] *Ezsias* v. *North Glamorgan NHS Trust* [2007] EWCA Civ 330.
[72] *Ibid.*, para. 18.
[73] *R* v. *Inner West London Coroner ex parte Dallaglio* [1994] 4 All ER 139.

5.7 Since the nineteenth century, a real likelihood of bias would lead to quashing of a judicial determination[74] and the courts often invalidated judicial decisions on the ground of the reasonable suspicions of the party aggrieved, without having made any finding that a real likelihood existed. The common law test was adjusted in *In re Medicaments and Related Classes of Goods (No. 2),*[75] where a member of a tribunal had applied for employment with one of the principal expert witnesses in a case before her. The emphasis was no longer on the perspective of the party aggrieved, but that of the fair-minded observer. The Court of Appeal held that a fair-minded observer would consider that she was likely to favour the evidence given by them and to consider them a more reliable source of expert opinions if it was a firm that she wished to be employed by. Lord Phillips gave judgment for the court:

> The court must first ascertain all the circumstances which have a bearing on the suggestion that the judge was biased. It must then ask whether those circumstances would lead a fair-minded and informed observer to conclude that there was a real possibility, or a real danger, the two being the same, that the tribunal was biased.[76]

This effectively confirmed Lord Goff's earlier attempt to reformulate the test in *R. v. Gough,* as

> having ascertained the relevant circumstances, the court should ask itself whether, having regard to those circumstances, there was a real danger of bias on the part of the relevant member of the tribunal in question, in the sense that he might unfairly regard (or have unfairly regarded) with favour, or disfavour, the case of a party to the issue under consideration by him.[77]

In *Porter v. Magill,*[78] a 'modest adjustment' to the test enunciated in *R v. Gough* was endorsed, such that the question, as laid by Lord Hope, is now 'whether the fair-minded and informed observer, having considered the facts, would conclude that there was a real possibility that the [decision maker] was biased'.[79] As one judge suggested in the course of our interview, this could be translated as 'if this objection was raised in

[74] *Metropolitan Properties Co (FGC) Ltd* v. *Lannon* [1969] 1 QB 577.

[75] *In re Medicaments and Related Classes of Goods (No. 2)* [2001] EWCA Civ 350.

[76] *In re Medicaments and Related Classes of Goods (No. 2)* [2000] EWCA Civ 350, 85.

[77] *R* v. *Gough* [1993] AC 646, 670.   [78] *Porter* v. *Magill* [2001] UKHL 67.

[79] *Ibid.,* para. 103; *Kataria* v. *Essex Strategic Health Authority* [2004] EWHC 641, para. 46 (Admin) [Stanley Burton J]; *Lawal* v. *Northern Spirit* [2003] UKHL 35; *Gillies* v. *Secretary of State for Work and Pensions* [2006] UKHL 2.

Parliament, what would Parliament's answer be?'. As ever, any doubt in the matter should be resolved in favour of disqualification.[80]

Lord Steyn later acknowledged that the 'public perception of the possibility of unconscious bias is the key'[81] and the English test of bias in *Porter* v. *Magill* is now regarded as having converged with the test adopted in Canada, Australia and New Zealand and Scotland.[82] It is also in line with the objective requirement for impartiality contained in Article 6 ECHR.[83] The Strasbourg Court ascertains whether the judge or tribunal offered guarantees sufficient to exclude any legitimate doubt in respect of his impartiality: 'It must be determined whether, quite apart from the judge's personal conduct, there are ascertainable facts which may raise doubts as to his impartiality. In this respect even appearances may be of a certain importance.'[84]

5.8 The fair-minded observer is expected to adopt a balanced approach as 'a reasonable member of the public [who] is neither complacent nor unduly sensitive or suspicious'.[85] He is 'neither naïve or complacent nor unduly suspicious or cynical'.[86] In *Helow* v. *Secretary of State for the Home Department*,[87] Lord Hope fleshed out the idealised fair-minded observer as:

> The sort of person who always reserves judgment on every point until she has seen and fully understood both sides of the argument ... The 'real possibility' test ensures that there is this measure of detachment ... Then there is the attribute that the observer is 'informed'. It makes the point that, before she takes a balanced approach to any information she is given, she will take the trouble to inform herself on all matters that are relevant. She is the sort of person who takes the trouble to read the text of an article as well as the headlines. She is able to put whatever she has read or seen

[80] *Locabail (UK) Ltd* v. *Bayfield Properties Ltd and another* [2000] QB 451, para. 10.
[81] *Lawal* v. *Northern Spirit* [2003] UKHL 35, para. 14.
[82] *Merrabux* v. *Attorney General of Belize* [2005] 2 AC 513, para. 22.   [83] Para. 14 A–B.
[84] *Hauschildt* v. *Denmark* (1990) 12 EHRR 266, paras 46 and 48; *De Cubber* v. *Belgium* (1984) Series A no. 86, 13–14, 24; *Findlay* v. *UK* (1997) 24 EHRR 221, para. 73; *Pullar* v. *UK* (1996) 22 EHRR 391. The subjective test applied by the European Court of Human Rights is directed to the identification of actual bias, on the basis of the judge's personal conviction in a given case, see *R.* v. *Abdroikov* [2007] 1 WLR 2679, para. 16 [Lord Bingham]. The tribunal must be subjectively free from personal prejudice or bias.
[85] *R* v. *Abdroikov* [2007] 1 WLR 2679, para. 15 [Lord Bingham]; *Johnson* v. *Johnson* (2000) 201 CLR 488, 53 [Kirby J], cited in *Lawal* v. *Northern Spirit* [2003] UKHL 35, para. 14 [Lord Steyn] and in *Gillies* v. *Secretary of State for Work and Pensions* [2006] 1 WLR 781, paras. 17 [Lord Hope] and 39 [Lady Hale].
[86] *Bolkiah* v. *State of Brunei Darrussalem* [2007] UKPC 62, para. 16 [Lord Bingham].
[87] *Helow* v. *Secretary of State for the Home Department* [2008] 1 WLR 2416.

into its overall social, political or geographical context. She is fair-minded, so she will appreciate that the context forms an important part of the material which she must consider before passing judgment.[88]

In questioning the judge's impartiality to the eyes of that notional observer, it is reasonable to expect the observer to be aware of the law and the functions of those who play a part in its administration.[89] He does not come to the matter as a stranger or complete outsider and to have a reasonable working grasp of how things are usually done,[90] for example, a specific decision-making process. In adopting the perspective of a fair-minded observer, the Court will take account of an explanation given by the tribunal and assume that the hypothetical observer is also aware of that explanation.[91]

It is important not to suppose that the fair-minded observer is so well informed about judicial procedures and the likely financial, social and private lives of judges that his conclusions on the matter of apparent bias will be exactly the same as those held by the judiciary itself. In spite of this, the forensic manoeuvring[92] that goes with the notion of a fair-minded observer means that the notional observer sometimes appears as rather omniscient.[93] Indeed, in considering all the evidence,[94] the court also includes those circumstances apparent to the court upon investigation,[95] in addition to the circumstances or material facts which were available – even if not actually known – to the complainant or hypothetical observer at the original hearing. In *Virdi* v. *Law Society*, the Court of Appeal rejected the claim of the appellant solicitor against a

---

[88] *Ibid.*, paras. 1–3.   [89] *Lawal* v. *Northern Spirit* [2003] UKHL 35, paras. 21–2.

[90] *Bolkiah* v. *State of Brunei Darussalem* [2007] UKPC 62, 16.

[91] *In re Medicaments and Related Classes of Goods (No. 2)* [2000] EWCA Civ 350, para. 67.

[92] G. Hammond, *Judicial Recusal: Principles, Process and Problems* (Oxford: Hart Publishing, 2009), p. 52.

[93] *Meerabux* v. *Attorney General of Belize* [2005] UKPC 12; [2005] 2 AC 513; M. Elliott, 'The Appearance of Bias, the Fair-Minded and Informed Observer, and the "Ordinary Person in Queen's Square Market"' (2012) CLJ 247; A. Olowofoyeku, 'Bias and the Informed Observer: A Call for a Return to Gough' (2009) 68(2) CLJ 388.

[94] *R* v. *Gough* [1993] AC 646, 670 [Lord Goff]; *R* v. *Inner West London Coroner ex parte Dallaglio* [1994] 4 All ER 139, 151 [Brown LJ]; *Porter* v. *Magill* [2001] UKHL 67, 103 [Lord Hope]; *Flaherty* v. *National Greyhound Club Ltd* [2005] EWCA Civ 1117, para. 27 [Scott Baker LJ]; *Gillies* v. *Secretary of State for Work and Pensions* [2006] UKHL 2, 17 [Lord Hope], and *R (Persimmon Homes)* v. *Vale of Glamorgan Council* [2010] EWHC 535 (Admin), paras. 53, 116 [Beatson J].

[95] *In re Medicaments and Related Classes of Goods (No. 2)* [2000] EWCA Civ 350, para. 83; *R* v. *Gough* [1993] AC 646, 670; *R* v. *Abdroikov* [2007] 1 WLR 2679, para. 69 [Lord Carswell], but see *Re P (a barrister)* [2005] 1 WLR 3019.

finding by the Solicitors Disciplinary Tribunal of serious professional misconduct.[96] The tribunal clerk had retired with the tribunal members when they considered their decision, and he also assisted in drafting the findings. After the hearing, the appellant found out from the tribunal's website that the clerk was an employee of the Law Society seconded to the tribunal and argued that this gave rise to apparent bias and breached Article 6 ECHR. The Court of Appeal held that there was no apparent bias on the facts of the case: the Solicitors Disciplinary Tribunal used a building not used by the Society, the Society had no control over the routine management of the Solicitors Disciplinary Tribunal, none of the clerks had ever served the Society in any other capacity and they had no routine contact with the Society other than as a nominal employer.

While a fair-minded observer might have become convinced of the impartiality of the tribunal if he or she had undertaken such painstaking research before the hearing, it is nonetheless desirable that courts and tribunals anticipate and try to avoid arrangements which might give appearances of bias to ordinary laymen. Interviewed judges told us that litigants in person are the ones who tend to question the judge's impartiality and to seek review of it. Such cases pose difficulties if there is no trusted legal expert on hand to advise the litigant that a relationship that may come as a complete surprise to him is in fact quite normal in the legal world.

When finding the facts relevant for the 'fair-minded observer' test, a court on appeal may take into account a statement from the judge as to what he or she knew at the time (such as: did he actually know that a witness before him had the power to dismiss one of his children from his job?). But the court is not bound to accept any such statement, and in any event 'no attention will be paid to any statement by the judge as to the impact of any knowledge on his or her mind'.[97] Presumably no attention should be paid to the fact that the judge had thought it unnecessary to recuse himself (as one would expect when any other type of judicial decision is being appealed). In relation to tribunals where more than one adjudicator is sitting, and complaint is being directed at one of them, it would be inappropriate for the other members of a tribunal to hear evidence in relation to another member.[98]

[96] *Virdi* v. *Law Society* [2010] EWCA 100.
[97] *Locabail (UK) Ltd* v. *Bayfield Properties Ltd and another* [2000] QB 451, para. 19 [Lord Bingham CJ, Lord Woolf MR and Sir Richard Scott V-C]; *Baker* v. *Quantum Clothing Group and others* [2009] EWCA Civ 499 (CA).
[98] *Hamilton* v. *GMB Northern Region* [2007] IRLR 391, para. 25.

5.9 The likelihood of bias is also liable to depend on what the main issues in the trial may be. This was evident in the joined cases of *R* v. *Abdroikov, R* v. *Green, R* v. *Williamson*,[99] where the House of Lords had to decide whether the presence of a serving police officer established a reasonable apprehension of bias. It was held that the mere presence on a jury of a police officer would not necessarily create such a possibility of bias as to deny the defendant a fair trial, and noted that Parliament had decided that they were in principle eligible.[100] The House emphasised that it depended on the circumstances of the case, the issues to be decided, the background of the juror in question, and the closeness of any connection which he or she might have to the case to be tried.[101] In one of the joined cases, the majority of the House (Lord Rodger and Lord Carswell dissenting) noted a crucial dispute on the evidence between the defendant and the police sergeant and considered that the instinct, however unconscious, of a police officer on the jury to prefer the evidence of a brother officer would be judged by the fair-minded and informed observer to be a real and possible source of unfairness, beyond the reach of standard judicial warnings and directions.[102] Here the profession of the juror and the issue at trial were thought to be uncomfortably close. For the general run of cases, the view of Lord Carswell, that the number and diversity of people in a criminal jury constitutes a safeguard against such prejudice or bias on the part of any one juror exercising sufficient influence to determine the outcome of the trial, is likely to hold sway.[103]

Similarly, in *R (Pounder)* v. *HM Coroner for North and South Districts of Durham and Darlington*,[104] the claimant sought judicial review of the refusal of the coroner to recuse himself from a second inquest into the death in custody of his son. The coroner had presided over the first inquest and had declined to rule on a key question of whether the physical restraint used on the deceased was lawful. That decision had been quashed on judicial review and the case remitted to him on the basis

---

[99] *R* v. *Abdroikov* [2007] 1 WLR 2679.

[100] Albeit that this was not the case in other jurisdictions such as Scotland, Northern Ireland, Australia, New Zealand, Canada, Hong Kong, Gibraltar and a number of states in the United States. Some other US states have adopted a procedure to question jurors on their occupation and allegiances.

[101] *Flaherty* v. *National Greyhound Racing Club* [2005] EWCA Civ 1117, 27 [Scott Baker LJ].

[102] *R* v. *Abdroikov* [2007] 1 WLR 2679, para. 26 [Lord Bingham].   [103] *Ibid.*, para. 67.

[104] *R (Pounder)* v. *HM Coroner for North and South Districts of Durham and Darlington* [2010] EWHC 328 (Admin).

that the matter was of such importance that it had to be considered. The claimant argued that the coroner's decided views tainted the second inquest with apparent bias. Burnett J granted the application in these terms:

> The integrity of the Coroner is not in doubt for a moment. The issue is one of perception and risk viewed from the outside ... Prudence naturally leans on the side of being safe rather than sorry. In the light of my conclusions that the Coroner has expressed his decided views on causation of the restraint and the honesty of the Serco witnesses [...] I consider that he must recuse himself from the further investigation of Adam Rickwood's death.[105]

The Court is not suggesting that coroners should routinely recuse themselves after they are asked to rehear a case on which they have already erred. Normally they would be expected to put their pride behind them and to consider the remaining matters afresh as instructed. In this case, though, the coroner had already shown such scepticism towards the line of argument that had been put before him that a fair-minded person would not expect him to have a suitably open mind on the next occasion. It may have been relevant that in coroner's courts in particular, the proceedings are inquisitorial and the coroner retains power to determine the scope of the issues: there may be more concern about remitting cases to coroners than there would be when the High Court remits criminal matters to the same magistrates to reconsider.

5.10 As can be seen, every application must be decided on the facts and circumstances of the individual case. Any reason leading to a 'real ground for doubting the ability of the judge to ignore extraneous considerations, prejudices and predilections and bring an objective judgment to bear on the issues before him'[106] gives rise to a real danger of bias. There are some further general principles, however. Under *Locabail,* no real danger of bias arises in itself from factors such as religion, ethnic or national origin, gender, age, class or sexual orientation of the judge, and, at least in the ordinary course of events, his or her social or educational background or previous political associations. The Court continued:

> Nor, at any rate *ordinarily*, could an objection be soundly based on the judge's social or educational or service or employment background or history, nor that of any member of the judge's family; or previous political

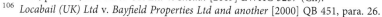

---

[105] *Ibid.,* para. 32; *Red River UK Ltd* v. *Sheikh* [2009] EWHC 3257 (Ch).
[106] *Locabail (UK) Ltd* v. *Bayfield Properties Ltd and another* [2000] QB 451, para. 26.

associations; or membership of social or sporting or charitable bodies; or Masonic associations; or previous judicial decisions; or extra-curricular utterances (whether in text books, lectures, speeches, articles, interviews, reports or responses to consultation papers); or previous receipt of instructions to act for or against any party, solicitor or advocate engaged in a case before him; or membership of the same Inn of Court, Circuit, local Law Society or chambers.[107]

We have thought it necessary to add our own emphasis to the word 'ordinarily' and we will examine typical factual scenarios below.

IV.   Typical categories of bias complaint

5.11 Bearing in mind that apparent bias is a fact-sensitive question, and recalling that all plausible concerns should be the subject of adversarial argument, we may profit from looking further at the broad categories of complaints which have featured in the case law thus far, some of which are also anticipated in the *Guide to Judicial Conduct*.

A.   Pecuniary interest

5.12 Under the *Guide to Judicial Conduct*, the existence of a significant financial interest in the outcome of the case on the part of the judge or, to the knowledge of a judge, on the part of a member of the judge's family will plainly disqualify him from hearing the case.[108] It is not material that the judge could not reasonably be suspected of having been influenced by his pecuniary interest, perhaps by reference to his great wealth. The possible appearance of bias still prevents the judge from adjudicating in that case. In *Dimes* v. *Grand Junction Canal Co*,[109] the House of Lords, after consulting the judges, set aside a decision of the Lord Chancellor granting relief to the Grand Junction Canal Company in which he was a substantial shareholder. The Lord Chancellor had not disclosed the interest to the defendant. Lord Campbell CJ said:

> No one can suppose that Lord Cottenham could be, in the remotest degree, influenced by the interest that he had in the concern, but it is of the last importance that the maxim that no man is to be a judge in his own cause should be held sacred. And that it is not to be confined to a cause in which he is a party but applies to a cause in which he has an

---

[107] *Ibid.*, para. 25.   [108] Guide to Judicial Conduct, 3.8.
[109] *Dimes* v. *The Proprietors of the Grand Junction Canal* (1852) 3 HL Cas 759.

interest ... This will be a lesson to all inferior tribunals to take care not only that in their decrees, they are not influenced by their personal interest but to avoid the appearance of labouring under such an influence.[110]

Only a 'significant financial interest', that is, one which is not too remote or speculative, will suffice to trigger automatic disqualification.[111] The *Guide to Judicial Conduct* states that:

> Such an interest may arise without the judge having an interest in the case to be tried if the case is to decide a point of law which may affect the judge in his personal capacity. In taking the decision whether to hear the case, the judge should have regard, in relation to the point of law, to the nature and extent of his or her interest, and the effect of the decision on others with whom he or she has a relationship, actual or foreseeable.

Many judges in the Chancery Division hold shares in large companies. They may also have another personal association with a corporation, such as being a board member. The Court of Appeal rejected, in *Locabail*, the strict view that a judge should disqualify himself no matter how small and trivial the pecuniary interest or shareholding in the outcome of the proceedings may be.[112] The question is whether the outcome of the case can realistically affect the judge's interest. The judge's pecuniary interest may be so small as to be incapable of influencing his decision one way or the other but any doubt should be resolved in favour of disqualification.[113] Whether the shareholding would be regarded as minor depends on the number of shares when compared with the total capital of the amount involved in the litigation; whether the company is a public or private company; and to what extent the issue under adjudication would have any effect on his interest. Automatic disqualification would thus

---

[110] *Ibid.*, 793; cf. *Clenae Pty. Ltd. and others v. Australia and New Zealand Banking Group Ltd* [1999] VSCA 35.

[111] *R v. Bristol Betting and Gaming Licensing Committee, ex parte O'Callaghan* [2000] QB 451, a companion case to *Locabail (UK) Ltd v. Bayfield Properties Ltd and another* [2000] QB 451; Guide to Judicial Conduct, 3.8.

[112] See also *R v. Rand* (1866) LR 1 QB 230, 232 [Blackburn J]; *R v. Camborne Justices, ex parte Pearce* [1955] 1 QB 41, 47 [Slade J].

[113] *Locabail (UK) v. Bayfield Properties Ltd* [2000] QB 451, para. 10; *Sigurdsson v. Iceland* [2003] ECHR IV, where a financial link between one of the parties to litigation and the judge's husband disqualified the judge as not being impartial; *Industries South Africa (Pty) Ltd v. Metal and Allied Workers' Union* [1992] 3 SA 673, 694; *Auckland Casino Ltd v. Casino Control Authority* [1995] 1 NZLR 142 (CA), see Hammond, *Judicial Recusal*, 22–5.

apply to the judge with substantial shares in a company to the extent that an outcome favourable to the company might increase the value of the shares and, accordingly, the dividend paid to the judge. Similar considerations would apply if a judge held shares as a trustee or if he was otherwise associated with a corporation.

Traditionally, judges who, on their list of cases, recognise the name of a company in which they hold shares anticipate an objection and transfer the case to another judge. Stephen Sedley notes that 'it has not been unknown for a judge, typically in the Chancery Division, to mention to the parties that he or she holds shares in one of them and to have the objection summarily waived, as often as not with a polite expression of hope that "your Lordship's shares will prosper whatever the outcome"'.[114] Such cases should be regarded as those in which the judge's interest would not necessarily seem significant to the fair-minded observer, such that a party may properly waive opportunities to take the point further.

In principle, indirect financial interests might suffice to disqualify a judge, but one imagines that in such cases the potential extent of the interest might need to be more than merely 'significant'. In *Locabail*, apparent bias had been raised against the deputy High Court judge who was a member of a firm of solicitors. The judge's firm was acting in other litigation against the claimant's husband. It was argued that if the firm succeeded in the other litigation against the husband, the firm's clients would recover more money from the claimant's husband if the claimant had lost her claim than if she had succeeded. This would increase the firm's goodwill and reputation and hence its profits, in which the judge would share. The Court of Appeal found a 'tenuous connection between the firm's success in an individual case on the one hand and the firm's goodwill and the level of profits on the other hand'. In the absence of a direct pecuniary interest, the only test applicable was the one set in *R v. Gough*, asking whether in the circumstances of the case, there was a real likelihood, in the sense of a real possibility, of bias on the part of the deputy judge.[115]

As to the judge's position as a taxpayer, the *Guide to Judicial Conduct* directs us to section 14 of the Senior Courts Act 1981,[116] under which a judge of the senior courts or of the Crown Court 'shall not be incapable of acting as such in any proceedings by reason of being, as one of a class

---

[114] Sedley, 'When Should a Judge not Be a Judge?'.
[115] *R v. Gough* [1993] AC 646, 668 [Lord Goff].   [116] Guide to Judicial Conduct, 3.9.

of ratepayers, taxpayers or persons of any other description, liable in common with others to pay, or contribute to, or benefit from, any rate or tax which may be increased, reduced or in any way affected by those proceedings'.

B.   Personal relationships

5.13 Lord Denning's proposition in *Metropolitan Properties Co (FGC)* v. *Lannon* remains:

> No man can be an advocate for or against a party in one proceeding, and at the same time sit as a judge of that party in another proceeding. Everyone would agree that a judge, or a barrister or solicitor (when he sits ad hoc as a member of a tribunal) should not sit on a case to which a near relative or a close friend is a party. So also a barrister or solicitor should not act in a case to which one of his clients is a party. Nor in a case where he is already acting against one of the parties. Inevitably people would think he would be biased.[117]

A fortiori a breach of impartiality may arise where the judge has acted as a lawyer for the applicant's opponent in other proceedings.[118] With express reference to *Locabail*, the *Guide to Judicial Conduct* reflects the current practice:

> 7.2.1 A judge should not sit on a case in which the judge has a close family relationship with a party or the spouse or domestic partner of a party.
>
> 7.2.2 Personal friendship with, or personal animosity towards, a party is also a compelling reason for disqualification. Friendship may be distinguished from acquaintanceship which may or may not be a sufficient reason for disqualification, depending on the nature and extent of such acquaintanceship.
>
> 7.2.3 A current or recent business association with a party will usually mean that a judge should not sit on a case. A business association would not normally include that of insurer and insured, banker and customer or council taxpayer and council. Judges should also disqualify themselves from a case in which their solicitor, accountant, doctor, dentist or other professional adviser is a party in the case.
>
> 7.2.4 Friendship or past professional association with counsel or solicitor acting for a party is not generally to be regarded as a sufficient reason for disqualification.
>
> 7.2.5 The fact that a relative of the judge is a partner in, or employee of, a firm of solicitors engaged in a case before the judge does not necessarily

---

[117] *Metropolitan Properties Co (FGC)* v. *Lannon* [1969] 1 QB 577, 600.

[118] *Wettstein* v. *Switzerland* [2000] ECHR 695, 47; *Walston* v. *Norway* Application no. 37272/97 ECtHR 11 December 2001.

require disqualification. It is a matter of considering all the circumstances, including the extent of the involvement in the case of the person in question.

   7.2.6 Past professional association with a party as a client need not of itself be a reason for disqualification but the judge must assess whether the particular circumstances could create an appearance of bias.

   7.2.7 Where a witness (including an expert witness) is personally well known to the judge all the circumstances should be considered including whether the credibility of the witness is in issue, the nature of the issue to be decided and the closeness of the friendship.

   7.2.8 A judge should not sit on a case in which a member of the judge's family (as defined in the *Bangalore* principles) appears as advocate.

5.14 As can be seen, a judge should not sit on a case in which a member of the judge's family (as defined in the Bangalore principles) appears as advocate.[119] The judge's family, under the Bangalore principles, comprises a judge's spouse, son, daughter, son-in-law, daughter-in-law, and any other close relative or person who is a companion or employee of the judge and who lives in the judge's household. The 'judge's spouse' refers to a domestic partner of the judge or any other person of either sex in a close personal relationship with the judge.[120] The Code of Conduct of the Bar of England and Wales endorses this practice: a barrister must not accept any instructions if to do so would cause him to be professionally embarrassed, and for this purpose a barrister will be professionally embarrassed if the matter is one in which 'whether by reason of any connection with the client or with the Court or a member of it or otherwise it will be difficult for him to maintain professional independence or the administration of justice might be or appear to be prejudiced'.[121] This confirms the end of a once well-established practice under which there was no objection to a barrister practising in a court where his father is one of several judges on the ground that it would be impossible to know beforehand which judge would try the case.[122]

5.15 In the English context, personal knowledge of counsel does not disqualify per se. Appearance of bias does not simply arise from the fact that the recorder and the counsel are in the same chambers. This understanding is reflected in the statement, in the *Guide to Judicial*

---

[119] Guide to Judicial Conduct, 7.2.8.   [120] *Ibid.*, 5.2.

[121] Art. 603(b), Code of Conduct of the Bar of England and Wales, 8th edn in force since October 2004.

[122] W.W. Boulton, *Conduct and Etiquette at the Bar*, 5th edn (London: Butterworths, 1971), pp. 37–8.

Conduct, that friendship or past professional association with counsel or solicitor acting for a party is not generally to be regarded as a sufficient reason for disqualification.[123] Judges, whether full time or part time, frequently have present or past close professional connections with those who appear before them and it has long been recognised that this, of itself, creates no risk of bias nor, to those with experience of our system, any appearance of bias.[124] The informed observer must be expected to be aware of the legal culture and traditions of this jurisdiction, in particular of solicitors and barristers being acquainted with the judge:

> Those legal traditions and that culture have played an important role in ensuring high standards of integrity on the part of both the judiciary and the profession which happily still exist in this jurisdiction. Our experience over centuries is that this integrity is enhanced, not damaged, by the close relations that exist between the judiciary and the legal profession ...
>
> It is also accepted that barristers from the same chambers may appear before judges who were former members of their chambers or on opposite sides of the same case. This close relationship has not prejudiced but enhanced the administration of justice. The advantages in terms of improved professional standards which can flow from these practices have been recognised in other jurisdictions.
>
> The informed observer will therefore be aware that in the ordinary way contacts between the judiciary and the profession should not be regarded as giving rise to a possibility of bias. On the contrary, they promote an atmosphere which is totally inimical to the existence of bias. What is true of social relationships is equally true of normal professional relationships between a judge and the lawyers he may instruct in a private capacity.[125]

This said, changes in the way that some chambers fund their expenses mean that members of some chambers share expenses on the basis of contributing a percentage of earnings. This, combined with the fact that counsel can now act under a conditional fee agreement, means that, in some cases at least, there may be grounds for arguing that a recorder should not sit in a case in which one or more of the advocates are members of his chambers.[126] For instance, where the counsel in question was acting under a conditional fee agreement, a ruling that reduced the earnings of counsel appearing before him could result in an increase of

---

[123] Guide to Judicial Conduct, 7.2.4.

[124] See, e.g., *Nye Saunders & Partners* v. *Alan E Bristow* (1987) 37 BLR 92; *Laker Airways Inc* v. *FLS Aerospace Ltd* [2000] 1 WLR 113; *Taylor* v. *Lawrence* [2003] QB 528; *Birmingham City Council* v. *Yardley* [2005] EWCA Civ 1756.

[125] *Taylor* v. *Lawrence* [2003] QB 528, para. 61.

[126] Bar Council CFA Panel, 'Conditional Fee Agreements Guidance', February 2006.

the contribution to expenses made by the recorder. Examples would be a strike-out application or an application for permission to appeal.[127]

In some cases, the potential influence of counsel may be a concern, not so much because it undermines the independence of the court, but rather because the lay person who finds himself on the tribunal may be thought likely to hold the arguments of counsel in too high regard. In *Lawal* v. *Northern Spirit Ltd*,[128] a Queen's Counsel, sitting part-time in the Employment Appeal Tribunal, subsequently appeared as counsel before an Employment Appeal Tribunal lay member with whom he had previously sat. A differently constituted Employment Appeal Tribunal (Lindsey J) had decided that there was no real possibility of bias. The majority of the Court of Appeal dismissed the appeal but the House of Lords, while also dismissing the appeal on the facts (Lindsay J's panel was not known to the advocate), made a point of principle supporting the appellant's claim: a part-time judge cannot appear before a panel consisting of any lay member with whom he has previously sat. The terms of appointment of a part-time Chairman of an Employment Appeal Tribunal bar such a person appearing as an advocate in a region to which he is assigned in his judicial capacity precisely to avoid allegations of bias.[129] Similarly, the degree of reliance placed by lay members on the recorder's view of the law requires that a recorder should not be allowed to address jurors whom in the past he has sat with, and has directed on matters of law as a part-time judge.[130] We also note that jurors should make it known to the trial judge if they recognise counsel from social or professional situations.

5.16 Social links are dealt with on a case-by-case approach.[131] Under the *Guide to Judicial Conduct*, 'past professional association with a party as a client need not of itself be a reason for disqualification but the judge must assess whether the particular circumstances could create an appearance of bias'.[132] Present professional relationships are more difficult. Lord Evershed MR once disqualified himself from sitting in an appeal because he knew the appellant, who was his anaesthetist. Lord Evershed commented: 'I have slid into unconsciousness under his care.'[133] The *Guide to Judicial Conduct* indeed recommends that judges should disqualify

---

[127] *Smith* v. *Kvaerner Cementation Foundations Ltd (Bar Council intervening)* [2006] EWCA Civ 242, paras. 12 and 17.

[128] *Lawal* v. *Northern Spirit Ltd* [2003] UKHL 35.   [129] *Ibid.*, para. 18.

[130] *Ibid.*, para. 15.   [131] *E* v. *Merchant Taylors School* [2009] EWCA Civ 1050.

[132] Guide to Judicial Conduct, 7.2.6.   [133] *The Times*, 13 March 1958.

themselves from a case in which their solicitor, accountant, doctor, dentist or other professional adviser is a party in the case.[134] More generally, the *Guide* suggests that a current or recent business association with a party will usually mean that a judge should not sit on a case.[135]

This, however, only applies to relationships with the parties themselves and not by extension to relationships solely with their representatives. In *Lawrence* v. *UK*,[136] the European Court of Human Rights dismissed as ill founded the allegation of bias from a deputy judge who had used a particular firm of solicitors for the purposes of drafting his will, when that firm was also involved in proceedings before him. The European Court confirmed the judgment of the Court of Appeal, that the use by a judge of a particular firm of solicitors for the purposes of drafting his will should not of itself give rise to any expectation, or even any suspicion, that the judge would be untrue to his judicial oath and favour another client of those solicitors in proceedings before him. Among other facts, the deputy judge did not know, when he presided over the first day of the trial, that the applicant's opponents were represented by that same firm of solicitors and that, when the trial recommenced in November 1999, he had obtained the express confirmation of both parties to the litigation that there was no objection to him continuing to hear the case. Nor could the judge be said to have a significant pecuniary interest in his dealings with the firm.

The opposite of friendship, namely animosity, may be different. Personal animosity towards a party is a compelling reason for disqualification,[137] and even animosity between the judge and a firm of solicitors or his partners may give rise to a real danger of bias as far as the client himself is concerned.[138] In *Howell* v. *Lees Millais*,[139] a judge had been in negotiations with a firm of solicitors with whom the first applicant was a partner. The judge's negotiations with the firm broke down and with some bad feeling from the judge, who expressed his

---

[134] Guide to Judicial Conduct, 7.2.3.
[135] *Ibid.*, 7.2.3. A business association would not normally include that of insurer and insured, banker and customer or council taxpayer and council.
[136] *Lawrence* v. *UK*, Application No. 74660/01 ECtHR 24 January 2002, 8–10.
[137] Guide to Judicial Conduct, 3.2.2.
[138] *Howell* v. *Lees Millais* [2007] EWCA Civ 720, 8 [Sir Anthony Clarke MR]; *Locabail (UK) Ltd* v. *Bayfield Properties Ltd and another* [2000] QB 451, 25; in relation to coroners, see *R* v. *Inner West London Coroner ex parte Dallaglio* [1994] 4 All ER 139; *R (Butler)* v. *HM Coroner for the Black Country District* [2010] EWHC 43 (Admin).
[139] *Howell* v. *Lees Millais* [2007] EWCA Civ 720.

'considerable disappointment' and complained that some of the firm's emails had been 'condescending' or 'insulting'. Although the judge was not having any contact with the partner making the first application, the applicants sought the judge's recusal a short time after when he was about to hear that application. The judge refused to withdraw from the case at the end of an acrimonious hearing. The Court of Appeal found that the judge generally was 'intemperate' in his dealings with the applicant's counsel and his behaviour 'was wholly inappropriate' as he indulged in 'extraordinary' exchanges in court. A fair-minded informed observer would conclude that there was a real possibility that the judge was biased against the firm and its partners.[140]

This led to the first complaint to the Office of Judicial Complaints against a High Court judge and resulted in a public reprimand from the Lord Chief Justice and Lord Chancellor for misconduct. The Lord Chief Justice tersely stated that 'a firm line [had] now been drawn under this matter', and that the judge had his full confidence. It may be best to regard the Court of Appeal decision in *Howell* as based on bias, but to regard the subsequent disciplinary action as based upon the intemperate nature of the comments which manifested that bias. The tone of judicial comments and exchanges in court can in itself constitute misconduct. It also seems that this was a matter of actual and not only apparent impropriety, manifested in intemperate behaviour on the bench.

C.   Preliminary views

5.17 Following the *Guide to Judicial Conduct*, the judge who has shown partisanship on topics relevant to issues in the case, or is known to have strong convictions on the matter expressed extra-judicially, by reason of public statements or other expression of opinion on such topics, may have to recuse himself, whether or not the matter is raised by the parties. We are considering mainly situations where he or she has made statements on other occasions (including other cases) which would tend to cause the reasonable-minded observer to conclude that he or she would not be able to approach the present case with an open mind. We are thus not considering those cases where the judge has already expressed a forceful view on a point of law or disputed fact which has

---

[140] *Ibid.*

arisen earlier in the same proceedings; these were examined earlier as an instance of alleged actual bias.

However, apparent bias may still be arguable where the judge has dealt adversely with the defendant before, even if he has been scrupulous not to say or do anything which suggests actual bias in the present case. In *Hauschildt* v. *Denmark*,[141] the City Court judge who presided over the trial and the High Court judges who took part in deciding the case on appeal had already dealt with the case at an earlier stage of the proceedings. They had given various decisions with regard to the applicant at the pretrial stage, including decisions concerning detention on remand. That in itself was not found sufficient by the European Court to justify fears of impartiality, but the Court still concluded apparent bias as the pretrial decisions statutorily required the conviction from the judges that there was 'a very high degree of clarity' as to the question of guilt.[142] As a result, there was little difference between the issues settled by the judges in the pretrial and trial proceedings, and the statutory requirement created a legitimate doubt as to the judges' impartiality.[143]

In England, however, a judge would not decide a bail application primarily on the basis of evidence which shows nothing more than that the defendant is likely to have committed the offence currently charged. Perhaps a more regular difficulty in England might arise in the case of repeat offenders in the magistrates' courts, who, after a while, may have appeared at some point before all the available justices in the area. There does not seem to be case law on this subject, perhaps because the priority of the defendant may simply be to avoid the harshest magistrates rather than to seek trial from an unknown magistrate. Since December 2004 it has been easier for the prosecution to admit his previous offences as evidence in any event, and so there is little to gain from seeking trial from a magistrate outside the jurisdiction.

5.18 The requirement for neutrality does not require judges to discount the very life experiences that may so well qualify them to preside over disputes.[144] As noted by the Canadian Judicial Council:

---

[141] *Hauschildt* v. *Denmark* (1990) 12 EHRR 266.   [142] *Ibid.*, para. 52.

[143] *Ibid.*, paras. 46 and 52; *Fey* v. *Austria* (1993) 16 EHRR 387; *De Cubber* v. *Belgium* (1984) Series A no. 86, pp. 13–14, 24.

[144] *R* v. *S (R.D.)* [1997] 3 SCR 484, para. 119 [Cory J]; but see *Swain-Mason and others* v. *Mills & Reeve* [2011] EWCA Civ 14, paras. 21 and 119: although allegations of bias against the judge had not been made out, given the 'strong views' expressed by the judge on the prospects of one part of the claim, and the 'strong views unfavourable to the defendants'

Rather, the wisdom required of a judge is to recognize, consciously allow for, and perhaps to question, all the baggage of past attitudes and sympathies that fellow citizens are free to carry, untested, to the grave. True impartiality does not require that the judge have no sympathies or opinions; it requires that the judge nevertheless be free to entertain and act upon different points of view with an open mind.[145]

As with personal relationships, it may be relevant to consider exactly what the real issues in the case might be. If a judge has dealt with a matter while at the Bar, he would have to disqualify himself. Thus, in one case, a judge disqualified himself from interpreting a will which he had drafted while at the Bar, for no fair-minded observer would think it easy for the judge to easily assume that he might have made an error earlier in his career and to look at the matter entirely afresh. In *R v. S.*,[146] a judge ordered the discharge of a jury in a fraud trial because of allegations of jury tampering, and he decided to continue the trial as a judge alone. Yet the judge had been involved in nine trials which were directly concerned with a fraud in which the appellant in the tenth trial was alleged to have been a central figure. The judge was 'aware of a vast body of information affecting their client of which the defence would have been ignorant', and 'some of his observations about the appellant himself in the course of his sentencing remarks were specific to and critical of the appellant'.[147] Taking these points together and in context, the appeal was allowed by the Court of Appeal on the ground that, even though actual bias could not be shown, an informed objective bystander might legitimately conclude that bias was a realistic possibility. To the extent that this may only have become apparent in the judge's sentencing remarks, this case illustrates that sometimes an effective appeal procedure is necessary as a final safeguard against apparent bias.

The further removed the cause of bias may be from the issue in question, the harder the test is to apply, and one does not expect judges to be challenged on the basis of their past clients (not least because barristers abide by the cab-rank rule and do not turn down cases which they are competent to handle). In *The Gypsy Council and others* v.

---

on another aspect of the case, and since the appeal succeeded on other grounds, the Court of Appeal ruled that 'when the trial starts again, it should be heard by a different judge'.

[145] The Canadian Judicial Council, *Commentaries on Judicial Conduct* (Cowansville, Quebec: Yvon Blais, 1991), p. 12, cited in *R v. S (R.D.)* [1997] 3 SCR 484, paras. 35 and 119.

[146] *R v. S.* [2010] 1 WLR 2511.   [147] *Ibid.*, para. 43.

UK,[148] the domestic judge (David Pannick QC) had appeared as counsel for the government in numerous previous domestic cases where the government argued that public authorities had not infringed the rights of gypsies. The Court found that no legitimate doubt on the judge's impartiality could be raised simply on that basis, when Mr Pannick's practice covered a wide range of litigation.

The *Guide to Judicial Conduct* further states that the risk of disqualification, whether of the judge's own volition or following an application, 'will seldom, if ever, arise from what a judge has said in other cases'.[149] This refers to past criticism of the conduct of a party or his lawyers by a judge in a case or to a past decision adverse to a party.[150] It may happen, however, that the courts find that there is no ground for disqualification but they take into account the availability of another judge to hear the case and conclude that, for the avoidance of doubt or any possible later objection, the judge should recuse himself.[151] Yet it is important that judicial officers discharge their duty to sit and do not, by acceding too readily to suggestions of appearance of bias, encourage parties to believe that by seeking the disqualification of a judge, they will have their case tried by someone thought to be likely to decide the case in their favour.[152] Thus, mere criticism by a party of a judge's conduct towards that party in previous proceedings does not per se constitute a ground for disqualification. In one case, one litigant in person argued that the judiciary was likely to favour arguments advanced by professional representatives over the lay person; and he criticised the one judge who had previously refused him permission to appeal in related proceedings.[153] His request to stay proceedings on that basis was rejected by the Court of Appeal. The Court emphasised the need to resist the regular temptation for a judge to disqualify himself simply because it would be more comfortable to do so, as this would in effect give a party the choice of their judge by criticising, justifiably or not, the one they did not wish to hear their case.[154]

---

[148] *The Gypsy Council and others* v. *UK*, Application No. 66336/01, ECtHR 14 May 2002.
[149] Guide to Judicial Conduct, 3.10.
[150] *Drury* v. *BBC and another* [2007] All ER (D) 205.   [151] *Ibid.*
[152] *Ansar* v. *Lloyds TSB Bank Plc* [2006] EWCA Civ 1462; cf. *Re JRL ex parte CJL* [1986] 161 CLR 342, 352 [Mason J], cited in *Locabail (UK) Ltd* v. *Bayfield Properties Ltd and another* [2000] QB 451, para. 22.
[153] *Dobbs* v. *Triodos Bank NV* [2005] EWCA Civ 468, para. 7; *Rothermere* v. *Times Newspapers Ltd* [1973] 1 All ER 1013, 1017.
[154] *Dobbs* v. *Triodos Bank NV* [2005] EWCA Civ 468, para. 7.

We may also note an earlier case, however, which concerned a libel suit by the *Daily Mail* against *The Times* for an article written by Bernard Levin, in which he attacked the *Daily Mail* for shutting down the *Daily Sketch*. *The Times* successfully asked for a trial by jury, inter alia, on the grounds that Mr Levin had been critical of the judiciary in the past and had expressed antipathy towards certain judges in a way that might cause a judge to feel resentment against him. Lord Denning MR rejected the suggestion that 'the judges, or any one of them, would be prejudiced against him', although 'no judge whom he criticised would dream of sitting on the case'.[155] Lord Denning considered, however, that 'if a newspaper has criticised in its columns the great and the powerful on a matter of large public interest – and is then charged with libel – then its guilt or innocence should be tried with a jury, if the newspaper asks for it'.[156]

There may be a working distinction between a judge's past caseload as an advocate or as a judge, and his expressed views outside his representation of clients or disposal of cases. In *Timmins* v. *Gormley*, a recorder had published extensively on personal injury topics in almost all the publications devoted to that subject, and it was submitted that there was a real danger that he was subject to unconscious but settled prejudice against insurers, and that his findings supported allegation of bias. The Court of Appeal found that the case turned on the statements made in those articles. Noting that there was nothing improper in the recorder being engaged in writing activities, the Court stated:

> It is the tone of the recorder's opinions and the trenchancy with which they were expressed which is challenged here. Anyone writing in an area in which he sits judicially has to exercise considerable care not to express himself in terms which indicate that he has preconceived views which are so firmly held that it may not be possible for him to try a case with an open mind.[157]

The Court allowed the appeal and ordered a retrial on the basis that they had to take

> a broad common sense approach, whether a person holding the pronounced pro-claimant anti-insurer views expressed by the recorder in the articles might not unconsciously have leant in favour of the claimant and against the defendant in resolving the factual issues between them.

---

[155] *Rothermere* v. *Times Newspapers Ltd* [1973] 1 All ER 1013.   [156] *Ibid.*, G.
[157] *Timmins* v. *Gormley* [2000] 1 All ER 65, para. 85; *Newcastle City Council* v. *Lindsay* [2004] NSWCA 198.

Not without misgiving, we conclude that there was on the facts here a real danger of such a result'.[158]

To similar effect, we note that one judge recused himself from presiding in a foxhunting case because he had previously condemned the activity as 'barbaric and cruel' and voted for a ban on it when he was an MP, before he was elected to the High Court in 2007.[159] He recused himself following the formal objections from lawyers who had raised the appearance of bias. This is perhaps a good example of a borderline case where recusal is wise in practice whether or not it is strictly necessary.

5.19 Apparent bias in this context can only be found on the basis of expressed views. There is no room for 'attributing' views to judges by virtue of their gender or race. If a judge is of the same or different racial group of the parties to the case, it would not require disqualification. It is too obvious to be mentioned, had it not given rise to difficulties some years ago. In 1969 the chairman of a magistrates' bench excluded a coloured woman magistrate from considering an application for bail of three white men charged with threatening behaviour in a racial riot. The Lord Chancellor advised that the chairman should not have asked the coloured magistrate to disqualify herself.[160] The same is true of juries; so there is no right (say) for a black defendant to have any number of black jurors at his trial, even if alleged racism is a live issue in the trial.[161] In fact the apparent ability of all-white juries in England to deliver fair decisions in such cases seems to be supported by recent empirical evidence.[162]

D. Membership of pressure groups

5.20 We now turn to cases where bias may be apparent from a judge's membership of a group, even if he has not made public statements about its causes. As seen with *Pinochet (No. 2)*, a judge may have to disqualify himself by reason of his association with a body that institutes or defends the suit; for here, Lord Hoffmann was on the board of Amnesty

---

[158] *Timmins* v. *Gormley* [2000] 1 All ER 65, para. 85.

[159] *The Times*, 29 July 2008. A Member of Parliament is not per se disqualified from being a judge, *Pabla Kay* v. *Finland* (2004) 42 EHRR 688.

[160] *The Times* 3 September 1969; G. Borrie, 'Judicial Conflicts of Interest in Britain' (1970) 18 AJCL 697, 708.

[161] *R* v. *Ford* [1989] QB 868.

[162] C. Thomas, 'Are Juries Fair?' (London: Ministry of Justice Research Series 1/10, 2010).

International.[163] A judge should disqualify himself if he is the chairman or a member of the board of a charitable organisation, or member of the governing body of a school which is a party to a case. Lord Evershed MR once disqualified himself from hearing an appeal on the ground that he was an *ex officio* member of the Church Commissioners for England, who were parties to the action.[164] By comparison, mere membership of, or subscription to, a voluntary association does not require disqualification. As such, mere membership does not connote any form of approval or endorsement of that which was said or done by the association's officers. Disclosure, subject to counsel's objection and argument, is likely to be sufficient. Where proceedings are brought by, for example, a Bar association as in *Meerabux v. Attorney General of Belize*,[165] mere membership of the association by the judge, as opposed to active involvement in its affairs or in the institution of the proceedings, does not trigger automatic disqualification.[166] This was clearly stated in 1889 in *Leeson v. General Council of Medical Education and Registration*, where mere membership of the Medical Defence Union was held not to be sufficient to disqualify.[167] In *Allinson v. General Council of Medical Education and Registration*, mere *ex officio* membership of the committee of the Medical Defence Union was also held to be insufficient to trigger disqualification.[168]

It seems generally to be the case that 'mere' members of a group need to have been shown to have been demonstrably active in promoting the causes of the group (as they may relate to the case) if bias is to be regarded as apparent. In *Salaman v. UK*,[169] the European Court of Human Rights considered that membership of a judge in the Freemasons in the United Kingdom did not per se raise doubts as to his impartiality where a witness or party in a case is also a Freemason. In March 1998, however, a parliamentary Select Committee inquiry led by Chris Mullin concluded that, although there had not been any evidence of impropriety or malpractice as a result of a judge being a Freemason, there was a public perception that there might be such impropriety or

---

[163] Malleson, 'Judicial Bias'.

[164] M. Hood Philips, *Constitutional and Administrative Law*, 5th edn (London: Sweet & Maxwell, 1973), p. 521.

[165] *Meerabux v. Attorney General of Belize* [2005] 2 AC 513.

[166] *Ibid.*, para. 24 [Lord Hope].

[167] *Leeson v. General Council of Medical Education and Registration* (1889) 43 Ch D 366.

[168] *Allinson v. General Council of Medical Education and Registration* (1894) 1 QB 750.

[169] *Salaman v. UK* Application No. 43505/98 ECtHR 15 June 2000.

malpractice.[170] In response, Lord Irvine LC required that, from March 1998, judges disclose their Masonic membership. Anyone being appointed for the first time to any judicial office, including coroners, was asked whether they belonged to the Freemasons and, if not, that they notified the Lord Chancellor in the event that they subsequently joined them. The rule was rescinded in November 2009 on the basis that, following Jack Straw LC, it would be disproportionate to continue with such practice when there had not been any evidence of impropriety or malpractice as a result of a judge being a Freemason. This change of attitude followed the successful challenge of similar Italian rules before the European Court of Human Rights, which found that the obligation to declare membership of a non-secret society breached the applicants' right to free association and was discriminatory.[171]

In *Helow*,[172] the House of Lords considered a challenge to the impartiality of a Lord in Ordinary on the basis of her membership of the International Association of Jewish Lawyers and Jurists. The appellant was a sympathiser with the Palestine Liberation Organization who claimed that she was 'at risk' from several sources, including Israeli agents. Her claim for asylum had been rejected by an immigration adjudicator. She was refused leave to appeal by the Immigration Appeal Tribunal and sought review of that refusal. The Court of Session judge, Lady Cosgrove, who dismissed her petition for review, was a founding member of the International Association of Jewish Lawyers and Jurists, whose magazine included articles hostile to the Palestine Liberation Organization.

It was argued that her membership of such an association 'gave the appearance of being the kind of supporter of Israel who could not be expected to take an impartial view of a petition for review concerning a claim for asylum based on the petitioners' support for the Palestinian Liberation Organisation'.[173] The appellant relied upon the principle in *Pinochet (No. 2)* extending automatic disqualification to cases where the judge's decision would lead to the promotion of a cause in which he or she was involved together with one of the parties. It was argued that the

---

[170] Report of the House of Commons Select Committee on Freemasonry in the Police and the Judiciary (the 'Mullin Inquiry').

[171] *Grande Oriente d'Italia di Palazzo Giustiniani v. Italy (No. 2)* (2007) Application No. 26740/02 ECtHR 31 May 2007.

[172] *Helow v. Secretary of State for the Home Department* [2008] 1 WLR 2416.

[173] *Ibid.*, para. 13 [Lord Rodger].

judge had not disassociated herself from the views expressed in the various articles published in the Association's journal, which she received and must have read. Her reaction to the articles was unknown, and that in itself justified the suspicion of bias.

The House of Lords dismissed the argument: there was no appearance of bias simply by reason of such membership. Contrary to *Pinochet (No. 2)*, in *Helow* the Association was not a party to or in any way concerned with the asylum proceedings concerning the appellant.[174] There was thus no reason for the judge to recuse herself. Nothing suggested that the judge had ever expressed support for the more extreme anti-Palestinian views that that Association had expressed on occasions, and a fair-minded observer would think that her membership did not imply any form of approval or endorsement of that which was said or done by the organisation's officer.

As Lord Hope remarked, had Lady Cosgrove in *Helow*

> dropped even the slightest hint on any occasion, however, informal, that she was in sympathy with what was published, the result might well have been quite different ... That case offers some reassurance to judges who like to be well informed and are observed reading the *Sun* or some other such tabloid which has taken sides on an issue which comes before them judicially. They can read what they like, so long as they do not say or do anything to associate themselves with what has been written.[175]

Notwithstanding his or her extracurricular interests, any professional judge is expected, by training and experience, to practise and display impartiality.

A similar reasoning can be found in the New Zealand Court of Appeal's judgment in *Collier* v. *Attorney General*.[176] In that case the appellant had given the appellate judges a questionnaire directed at any conflict of interest, prior discussion of the case with others, or membership of the 'Religion of Islam, Judaism, Church of Scientology, Theosophical Society, Church of Latter Day Saints, Illuminati, Orange Lodge, Druids, Skulls and Bones, Ku Klux Klan, or any society or organisation or group which requires oaths to be taken which would conflict with the judicial oath'. The Court of Appeal held: 'To invoke membership of any association listed in [these] questions as a sufficient

---

[174] *Ibid.*, para. 40 [Lord Mance].

[175] Lord Hope, 'What Happens When a Judge Speaks Out?', Holdsworth Club Presidential Address (19 February 2010), p. 8

[176] *Collier* v. *Attorney General* [2002] NZAR 257 (CA); see Hammond, *Judicial Recusal*, 51.

basis for disqualifying a Judge from sitting would also be inconsistent with the unlawful discrimination provisions of the Human Rights Act 1993 and the New Zealand Bill of Rights Act 1990.'[177]

V.   The disciplinary role of the Court of Appeal

5.21 Improper conduct of the trial judge adds 'great weight to the substance of the appeal',[178] and together with other grounds of appeal may result in the reversal of judgment in a civil or criminal case.[179] In civil cases the court has a general power to order retrial in cases where one party has not had a fair trial due to judicial misconduct. In criminal appeals, however, until 1968, the Court of Appeal seemed reluctant to accept arguments that the misconduct of the judge should affect the conviction, save in extreme cases.[180] The Court of Appeal's scrutiny of judicial misconduct was also limited for a long time by its reliance for evidence upon the transcript of the trial only,[181] when these were not easily available,[182] though, as a matter of principle, it did not exclude the admission of such evidence by witnesses.[183] Since 1968, any conviction should be quashed if the judge's conduct has rendered the conviction 'unsafe' and this word allows the appeal court to consider the fairness and propriety of the trial as well as its factual accuracy.

In *Randall* v. *R*, Lord Bingham emphasised the 'absolute' right of a criminal defendant to a fair trial:

> There will come a point when the departure from good practice is so gross, or so persistent, or so prejudicial, or so irremediable that an appellate court will have no choice but to condemn a trial as unfair and

---

[177] *Ibid.*, para. 24.   [178] *Brassington* v. *Brassington* [1962] P 276, 281.

[179] *Yuill* v. *Yuill* [1945] P 15; *Hobbs* v. *Tinling* [1929] 2 KB 1; *Jones* v. *National Coal Board* [1957] 2 QB 55.

[180] *R* v. *Hircock* [1970] 1 QB 67, where the sentence was reduced; *R* v. *McKenna* [1960] 1 QB 411. This case shows that, when the misconduct of a judge was serious or had attracted adverse publicity or invoked parliamentary action, the Court of Appeal was already likely to overcome these inhibitions and put the principles higher than the particular case; but see JUSTICE, 'Report', 48–9.

[181] *R* v. *Hircock* [1970] 1 QB 67, 70, 72–3.

[182] In the 1970s, transcripts of the court proceedings would be written by shorthand writers, but the transcript was not required by law before the county courts; the appeal would then depend on the judge's notes.

[183] Criminal Appeals Act 1968, s. 23(1)(c); *R* v. *Langham* [1972] Crim LR 457.

quash a conviction as unsafe, however strong the grounds for believing the defendant to be guilty.[184]

To similar effect, in the words of Lord Goddard, 'It may, and not infrequently does, happen that something is done in the course of a trial which is not strictly in accordance with the recognised procedures. If that is so the court must consider whether or not it is an irregularity which goes to the root of the case.'[185]

The Criminal Division of the Court of Appeal is still regarded as being prepared to tolerate minor procedural irregularities, or, in the words of Professor Spencer, 'to hold its judicial nose and uphold the conviction, if it is convinced that the defendant is really guilty, and would still have been convicted even if the procedural irregularity not taken place'.[186] Even falling asleep during the trial does not necessarily make any ensuing conviction unsafe.[187] Yet the disciplinary power of the Court still has a restraining and preventive effect on the judges. Many, if not most High Court judges or circuit judges look for promotion; frequent reversal or reprimand without reversal moves a judge away from the list of candidates for promotion. There may be some doubt whether reversals due to error of judgment in substantive law alone have this effect, for reversal of judgments in these cases may be the result of a mere difference in interpretation between the trial court and the appellate court. However, there can be little doubt that reversal or censure of a judge on the ground of his improper conduct in the trial adversely affects his chances of promotion.[188]

Even where the appeal court declines to quash a conviction on account of the judge's misconduct, it may nevertheless think it appropriate to reduce the sentence that he passed, thereby censuring in some substantial sense the judicial misconduct. Thus, if the judge has made several derogatory comments about the defendant, or about his trial tactics, during the case, then the defendant may feel that he has been sentenced more harshly than he would normally have been, and while

---

[184] *Randall v. R.* [2002] 2 Crim App R 267, 284.

[185] *R v. Furlong and others* (1950) 34 Cr App R 79, 84–5.

[186] J.R. Spencer, 'Quashing Convictions, and Squashing the Court of Appeal' (2006) 170 JPN 790–3.

[187] *R v. Betson* [2004] EWCA Crim 254 CA (Crim Div), para. 47 [Rose LJ]. In that case, falling asleep did not prevent the judge from summing up to the jury the significant features of the evidence or speeches in a comprehensive and balanced summing up.

[188] Cecil, *The English Judge*, 73–4.

not all harsh sentences are reduced on appeal (sentencing remains a matter of structured discretion) reductions may occur when the Court of Appeal is uneasy about misconduct which may seem linked to a relatively harsh sentence. Conversely, in the cases where the judge's misconduct is thought wholly to have undermined the perception of the fairness of the trial, the Court of Appeal may quash the conviction but also order a retrial, and will tend to do so where the evidence against the accused was plainly very strong.[189]

Although it ordinarily acts upon complaints of counsel raised on appeal, the Court of Appeal sometimes criticises the conduct of the judges on its own initiative. In a case relating to *The Da Vinci Code* book where a mysterious code is being sought, Mr Justice Peter Smith (a known follower of the book) produced a seventy-page ruling in which he had deliberately buried his own coded message. In upholding the judgment, Lloyd LJ observed that 'the judgment is not easy to read or to understand. It might have been preferable for him to have allowed himself more time for the preparation, checking and revision of the judgment.'[190]

We broadly categorise below the occasions on which the appeal court may make pointed criticisms of trial judges.

A. Excessive intervention

5.22 While excessive judicial intervention in the examination of witnesses does not always amount to apparent bias, it is often contended that it may vitiate the conduct of the trial. Intervention to clarify a genuine ambiguity is acceptable and may even be best practice, if the judge anticipates that the jury might be confused by the ambiguity which neither party to the case seems to be about to resolve. But questions which suggest incredulity as to what is being said by a witness are different. Here, the judge must leave it to one of the parties to undermine the evidence, resisting the temptation to 'step into the arena'[191] to do the job himself, as he is likely to have done in the past as a barrister. This

---

[189] In 1988, the power of the Court of Appeal to order a new trial widened from 'fresh evidence' to 'where it appears to the court that the interests of justice so require', Criminal Justice Act 1988, s. 43(2).

[190] *Baigent and another* v. *The Random House Group Ltd* [2007] EWCA Civ 247, para. 3.

[191] *R* v. *Hamilton* (unreported) [1969] Crim LR 486; *R* v. *Hulusi & Purvis* (1973) 58 Cr App R 378; *R* v. *Matthews* (1984) 78 Cr App R(S) 23; *R* v. *Sharp* (1998) 94 Cr App R 144.

principle was emphasised in *Almeida* v. *Opportunity Equity Partners Ltd*, where the trial judge engaged in extensive questioning of the evidence, expressing at times a high degree of scepticism and disbelief during the witness's evidence.[192] The Privy Council held that the judge's conduct was not such as to render the trial unfair, differing from the Court of Appeal on the basis that their Lordships considered that the judge's interventions were motivated 'not by partiality, but by the wish to understand the evidence (which was often obscure and inconsequential) and to push on the trial process'.[193] This case thus confirms the continuing authority of the observations of Denning LJ in 1957:

> [The Judge] must keep his vision unclouded ... Let the advocates one after the other put the weights into the scales – the 'nicely calculated less or more' – but the judge at the end decides which way the balance tilts, be it ever so slightly. The judge's part in all this ... is to hearken to the evidence, only himself asking questions of witnesses when it is necessary to clear up any point that has been overlooked or left obscure to see that the advocates behave themselves seemly and keep to the rules laid down by law to exclude irrelevancies and discourage repetition; to make sure by wise intervention that he follows the points that the advocates are making and can assess their worth; and at the end to make up his mind where the truth lies. If he goes beyond this, he drops the mantle of a judge and assumes the robe of an advocate; and the change does not become him well ... Such are our standards.[194]

Many authorities address the situation where the judge does not seek to clarify ambiguities but contributes his own views as to the truth of the evidence being heard. Thus, in *R* v. *Perren*, allowing the appeal, Toulson LJ (as he was then) reaffirmed that it is for the prosecution to cross-examine, not for the judge, and continued:

> The appellant's story may have been highly improbable, but he was entitled to explain it to the jury without being subjected to sniper fire in the course of doing so. The potential for injustice is that if the jury, at the very time when they are listening to the witness giving his narrative account of events, do so to the accompaniment of questions from the Bench indicating to anybody with common sense that the judge does not

---

[192] *Almeida* v. *Opportunity Equity Partners Ltd* [2006] UKPC 44, para. 898.
[193] *Porter* v. *Magill* [2001] UKHL 67, 103.
[194] *Jones* v. *National Coal Board* [1957] 2 QB 55, 64. This was a civil appeal, but these remarks apply to criminal proceedings too, though the jury, rather than the judge, would then be fact-finding.

believe a word of it, this may affect the mind of the jury as they listen to the account.[195]

Humphrey J put the matter in this way in R v. *Canny*:

> A prisoner is entitled to make his defence to the jury, and it is for the jury and not for the Judge to decide on its weight. The Judge has no power to stop a defence and say: 'This is an absurd defence and I will not let you put it before the jury'. When we find that the learned Judge... has really prevented the jury from trying the prisoner fairly and squarely on the evidence by repeating over and over again: 'This is an absurd defence, there is no foundation for this allegation against his wife, and the truth is, as you will find in a minute, that the prisoner did assault his wife', that is not a trial at all according to our methods and understanding. It is a mistrial.[196]

While the Criminal Procedure Rules 2005 set a general duty for judges to manage a trial actively and to avoid delays,[197] the Court of Appeal has, inter alia, continued to recognise limited powers to judges to question witnesses while parties submit evidence.[198] Trial judges are still criticised if 'they are excessive and take on the substance of cross-examination, [and] may have the potential to poison the minds of the jury against the defendant'.[199] In such cases, the convictions can be quashed and/or the judicial intervention sanctioned.[200] The prejudicial effect of the judge's intervention is decided by reference to the frequency and character of his interventions.[201] The safety of the conviction can be affected when, 'far from the judge having umpired the contest, rather he has acted effectively as a second prosecutor',[202] even when it appears that the jury would inevitably have reached the same conclusion without the judge's inappropriate interventions. For example, in 2008, the Court of Appeal quashed the defendants' convictions on the ground that the judge made excessive and prejudicial interventions during the course of the

---

[195] R v. *Perren* [2009] EWCA Cr App 348, paras. 35–6.

[196] R v. *Canny* [1945] 30 Cr App R 143, 146.

[197] Rule 3 Criminal Procedure Rules 2005; R v. *L* [2007] EWCA Crim 764, paras. 27–9.

[198] R v. *Sharp* [1994] QB 261.

[199] R v. *Harirbafan* [2008] EWCA Crim 1967, para. 3 [LJ Toulson].

[200] *Yuill* v. *Yuill* [1945] P 15, 20 [Wallington J]; R v. *Gilson* (1944) 29 Cr App R 174; R v. *Perks* [1973] Crim LR 388 (of the 700 questions asked in examination in chief, 147 came from the judge); R v. *Cain* (1936) 25 Cr App R 204 (where the trial judge himself conducted the cross-examination); R v. *Clewer* (1953) 37 Cr App R 37 (587 interventions).

[201] R v. *Perks* [1973] Crim LR 388; R v. *Cameron* [2001] EWCA Crim 562.

[202] *Michel* v. *The Queen* [2009] UKPC 41, para. 31.

evidence.[203] The judge's comments and the manner of his questioning gave the clear impression to the jury that he doubted the case for Mr Copsey, and the repeated questions of the judge were 'in the nature of cross-examination'.[204]

Senior judges remain alarmed at the number of such appeals which still come before the courts. Confronting the defendant 'on the spot' undermines the perception of the judge's partiality, and it may be that some newly appointed judges, with experience only in cross-examination, need to bear in mind their new powers in summing up the case at the end. Trial judges may be reminded that glaring holes in the defendant's account may be highlighted in the summing up of the case at the end of the trial, instead of being put to the defendant in a way which suggests disbelief. This is appropriate provided that the judge makes it clear that it is for the jury to consider what, if any, weight should be put on the purported weaknesses of the defendant's account.

B.   Defective directions

5.23 The appellate court repeatedly considers the balance of judicial summings up to juries and the permissible limits of judicial comments.[205] It gives guidance on proper directions to the jury. In addition, sample directions on particular issues are promulgated by the Judicial College (formerly known as the Judicial Studies Board). In R v. Bentley,[206] the Court of Appeal found the conviction of Bentley unsafe and allowed the appeal. Bentley had been convicted of the murder of a policeman and sentenced to death in 1952. Following the dismissal of his appeal, he was executed in 1953. His niece appealed on his behalf against his conviction by way of a reference by the Criminal Cases Review Commission.[207] Lord Bingham, on behalf of the Court, allowed the appeal on all grounds, listing the defective directions given by the trial judge (Goddard LCJ): that the trial judge had given no direction on the standard of proof, that his direction on the burden of proof had been unclear and misleading, that he had made prejudicial and unfair

---

[203] R v. Copsey [2008] EWCA Crim 2043.
[204] Ibid., para. 23; Frampton [1917] 12 Cr App R 202, 203; R v. Marr [1990] 90 Cr App R 154; Mears v. R [1993] 1 WLR 818, 922.
[205] Cohen and Bateman [1909] 2 Cr App R 197, 208 [Channell J] cited by Lord Bingham in R v. Bentley [2001] 1 Cr App R 307, para. 60.
[206] R v. Bentley [2001] 1 Cr App R 307, para. 68.   [207] Criminal Appeal Act 1995, s. 9.

comments suggesting that the police officers' bravery throughout the incident rendered the police witnesses more reliable than the defendant's and that an acquittal of the accused would undermine the reputations of the officers, that he had failed to present the case of *Bentley* adequately to the jury, and that he had failed to direct the jury adequately on constructive malice and joint enterprise.

In considering the balance of judicial summings up to juries and the permissible limits of judicial comments, Lord Bingham stated:

> It is with genuine diffidence that the members of this Court direct criticism towards a trial judge widely recognised as one of the outstanding criminal judges of this century. But we cannot escape the duty of decision. In our judgment, the summing-up in this case was such as to deny the appellant that fair trial which is the birthright of every British citizen.[208]

We might include within this category of defective directions other types of inappropriate remarks put to the jury. In *R v. McKenna*,[209] Mr Justice Stable threatened a jury that if they failed to reach a verdict in ten minutes, they would be locked up for the night. The jury retired and returned a verdict in six minutes. On appeal the convictions were quashed, notwithstanding that there was overwhelming evidence against the defendants. In the course of the judgment, the Court of Criminal Appeal said:

> It is a cardinal principle of our criminal law that in considering their verdict, concerning, as it does, the liberty of the subject, a jury shall deliberate in complete freedom, uninfluenced by any promise, unintimidated by any threat ... They still stand between the Crown and the subject, and they are still one of the main defences of personal liberty. To say to such a tribunal in the course of its deliberations that it must reach a conclusion within ten minutes or else undergo hours of personal inconvenience and discomfort, is a disservice to the cause of justice.[210]

The Court noted that 'the judge was understandably irritated by the inconvenient slowness of the jury in reaching a verdict in what he thought was a plain straightforward case'. This, however, was no excuse:

> Juries do at times take much longer than a judge may think necessary to arrive at a verdict ... and the proper exercise of the judicial office requires that irritation on these occasions must be suppressed or, at any rate, kept severely in check. To experience it is understandable; to express it in the form of such a threat to the jury as was uttered here is insupportable.

---

[208] *R v. Bentley* [2001] 1 Cr App R 307, para. 68. [209] *R v. McKenna* [1960] 1 QB 411.
[210] *Ibid.*, 422.

As the Court subscribed to the view that the evidence against all three defendants was cogent, it was with regret that they quashed the convictions. But they felt bound to do so, for 'plain though many juries may have thought this case, the principle at stake is more important than the case itself'.[211]

The fundamental principle of common law that a jury should be entitled and allowed to consider its verdict or verdicts without undue pressure was relied upon in the more recent decision of *R* v. *Mitchell*,[212] in which the Court of Appeal overturned the conviction of a General Court-Martial on the basis that the Board, sitting in Germany, having been deliberating long hours all week, reached its verdict at about 8 pm on a Saturday of a Bank Holiday weekend. At least four members of the Board had booked flights to return home to the UK to spend time with their family that weekend. Counsel for the accused raised concerns about the sitting hours and requested an adjournment, but this was refused. The Court of Appeal ruled that in this case neither the Board nor the Judge Advocate had directly exerted pressure. However, the omission to adjourn the proceedings created 'unacceptable seeds of pressure' by continuing to sit.

Judge LJ (as he then was), who gave the judgment of the court, outlined that undue pressure may arise simply from the circumstances in which the jury continued to sit, absent any judicial threats or orders. He referred to what Sir Patrick Russell, giving the judgment of the Privy Council in *De Four*, described as 'the seeds of pressure'. He said this:

> The seeds of pressure may arise without direct judicial intervention at all . . . In short, unacceptable pressure may arise from the very circumstances in which the jury is continuing to sit, leading to areas of concern exemplified, but not restricted to those noted in the judgment . . . The issue therefore is not whether the Board's verdict was produced too late in the day, or after too long a day, but whether, reasonable examination of the events of the day, in their overall context including the length of the sitting, leads to the conclusion that unacceptable pressures were or may have been created.[213]

C.   *Excessive delay in delivering judgment*

5.24 Delays in the administration of justice are a common feature of most legal systems. Various factors, such as lengthy pretrial proceedings, or the prolonged preparation of criminal prosecutions, the heavy

---

[211] *Ibid.*, 423.   [212] *R* v. *Mitchell* [2004] EWCA Crim 1665.   [213] *Ibid.*

workload of judges, and the justified absence of witnesses and other parties because of illness or otherwise, often make these delays unavoidable. Nevertheless, situations may occur where the delay is the fault of the judge hearing the case. Judgments are usually delivered *ex tempore* but they can be reserved. Lengthy delays between the last day of hearing and the delivery of judgment are not tolerated as delay in producing a judgment would be capable of depriving an individual of his right to the protection of the law.[214] Excessive delay in delivery of a judgment may require 'a very careful perusal of the judge's findings of fact and of his reasons for his conclusions in order to ensure that the delay has not caused injustice to the losing party'.[215] Thus, in a most recent such case,[216] while Lady Justice Arden apologised to the parties for the 'lamentable and unacceptable' delay in the court below, she said the function of the court in hearing the appeal was not 'to impose sanctions or investigate the reasons why the delay occurred', but to consider whether any of those findings of fact should be set aside and a retrial ordered.[217] In that case, the long delay in producing the judgment was not a good ground for allowing the appeal.

Judicial delays seemed to attain prominent attention in the late 1990s. In 1998, the Court of Appeal was asked to set aside a judgment where there had been a delay between a twenty-seven-day trial and judgment of some twenty months, time during which some of the judge's notes had been lost. The defendant's counsel had written to the judge, and told the Court of Appeal that he had considered taking out life insurance on the judge to cover lost legal costs if he died before giving his ruling. Material factual errors in the judgment were demonstrated and Peter Gibson LJ, for the Court, said:

> As the judge himself was the first to recognise, a delay of this magnitude was completely inexcusable. The plaintiff, who was not a young man, was claiming that Mr Wilson's fraudulent conduct had been causative of his financial ruin. Mr Wilson for his part was a professional man charged with serious professional misconduct amounting to fraud. Both parties were entitled to expect to receive judgment before Christmas 1994 at the very latest. The fact that they were obliged to wait another year and a quarter, even allowing for the judge's illness, is wholly unacceptable.[218]

---

[214] See above, para. 3.47; *Boodhoo* v. *AG of Trinidad and Tobago* [2004] UKPC 17, paras. 12 and 14.

[215] *Cobham* v. *Frett* [2001] 1 WLR 1775; *Rolled Steel* v. *British Steel* [1985] 2 WLR 908, para. 960.

[216] *Bond* v. *Dunster Properties Ltd* [2011] EWCA Civ 455.   [217] *Ibid.*, para. 7.

[218] *Goose* v. *Wilson Sandford* [1998] EWCA Civ 245, para. 109.

The delay had weakened the trial judge's advantage of hearing and seeing the witnesses, such that a retrial had to be ordered. Within hours of the judgment, the judge resigned.[219] In response to Peter Gibson LJ's concerns about compensation, the then Lord Chancellor, Lord Irvine, ruled in 2000 that the parties in that case should also be compensated for their legal costs.[220]

Just a few months later, the Court of Appeal considered a twenty-two months' delay between trial and judgment.[221] The appeal was nonetheless dismissed, as only a minor error in the judgment was identified on appeal. The defendant had contended that, given that delay, the judge had had insufficient recollection of the impression made by the various witnesses and of the closing submissions of defence counsel. Because of the defendant's allegations, the court wrote to the judge seeking his comments, and the judge fully accepted that the delay in delivering the judgment was not acceptable. He referred, however, to the particularly heavy burdens placed on him at the time by his judicial duties. Lord Woolf MR, handing in judgment, noted that the judge, who had been responsible for establishing the Mercantile Court in Manchester, had to some extent been 'the victim of his own success' 'in that he attracted to that court more work than he could properly handle himself. He did not draw attention to his difficulties but instead tried to take on burdens which proved to be excessive as a consequence delays occurred, such as in that case, which could not be excused'.[222]

But Lord Woolf also emphasised that:

> The fact that these delays have occurred in more than one case is not a matter which has been ignored by those who are responsible for supervising the administration of justice ... [T]he public should be assured that there have now been put in place mechanisms which will mean that if a judgment is delayed for an inappropriate time, those who have the responsibility of supervising these matters in the judiciary will be informed of this fact so that they can take steps to prevent the future occurrence of delays of the sort of which we have heard in this case.

---

[219] A highly unpopular judge, Mr Justice Harman was three times voted the profession's least favourite judge in a poll conducted by *Legal Business*. 'One young advocate was told that Chancery judges preferred a bright 'good morning, My Lord' to the more formal 'May it please your Lordship'. Apparently, Mr Justice Harman responded to this informality with 'shock, disgust and rage', and the barrister narrowly escaped contempt proceedings, *The Telegraph*, 15 May 2003.

[220] *The Independent*, 22 May 2000.

[221] *Gardiner Fire Ltd* v. *Jones* [1998] All ER (D) 474.   [222] *Ibid.*, para. 113.

His Lordship indicated that, in the normal event, it was intended that judgments of the Court of Appeal should be delivered within six weeks of the end of the hearing of the appeal.

In addition, Lord Woolf's words express a strong judicial policy aiming at maintaining high standards in the administration of justice. The problem of tardy judges was placed under the responsibility of the Lord Chancellor – and since 2005, transferred from him to the Lord Chief Justice, and the Presiding Judges of the court circuit. The 'mechanisms' referred to in his judgment included, in 2000, a meeting between the then Lord Chancellor, Lord Irvine, and senior judges, 'in order to identify the worst offenders'.[223] As part of 'good housekeeping',[224] routine deadline reminders for delivering judgments are now issued to all district, circuit and High Court judges by the Senior Presiding Judges of the circuits. All judges sitting on family disputes should deliver judgment within one month, and judges sitting on civil cases within two months, and they must inform the Senior Presiding and Liaison Judges about any delay, and explain the reasons for it.[225] Judgments which have been outstanding for more than three months are monitored by senior judges.[226] In a recent case, however, these mechanisms did not assist the parties in the case, and, as suggested by Lady Justice Arden, the Master of the Rolls, as the head of civil justice, proposed to investigate 'whether more robust and effective procedures are needed in some quarters to minimise the risk of such a problem arising in the future'.[227]

Akin to delay is the rare case of the judge who simply cannot decide the case at all. In 2008 the Law Lords refused to allow the same judge to withdraw from a case he had found too difficult to decide.[228] He then decided to recuse himself from the case, even though the parties did not request him to do so. Lady Hale said: 'If the judge is not fitted to try this case, it might be said that he is not fit to try any case in which the same problem could arise, and that would be absurd.'

---

[223] *The Independent*, 22 May 2000.
[224] F. Gibb, 'Avoiding Complaints – Keeping Judges Up to the Mark', *The Times*, 10 February 2009.
[225] *Ibid.*
[226] Judicial Communications Office, quoted by Frances Gibbs, citing Isobel Plumstead: 'There is some concern that with the increasing pressure of work on judges – resulting from the growing complexity of cases – some may be slipping behind with the delivery of their rulings. It can sometimes be difficult to arrange listing to allow time to prepare and give judgment.'
[227] *Bond v. Dunster Properties Ltd* [2011] EWCA Civ 455, para. 118.
[228] *In re B (Children) (FC)* [2008] UKHL 35.

D.   Rudeness

5.25 Rudeness may also affect the safety of a conviction if it is thought that it could materially have affected the quality of the defendant's evidence. Thus, when a judge reprimanded the defendant for speaking to a member of the public, it was alleged that the judge's behaviour had left the defendant too upset to give credible evidence to the jury moments later. The Court of Appeal observed: 'the judge was rude ("Shut your mouth and listen"), he was harsh ("How dare you speak to a member of the public"), and he was sarcastic ("You are really sorry? Yes, you will be really sorry")'.[229] It overturned the conviction relating to that count, since it could not exclude the possibility that the defendant may have given evidence more credibly had the judge dealt with the matter in a different way.

In the earlier case of *R v. Hircock*,[230] the Court of Appeal declined to interfere when, during the address to the jury of defence counsel in a criminal trial, the judge made gestures of impatience, sighed, and several times said 'Oh, God', 'and then laid his head across his arms and made groaning noises'. Although it disapproved of the conduct, the Court of Appeal held that it did not constitute sufficient ground for quashing the conviction, as the judge's conduct disparaged only the defendant's counsel, not his case. It distinguished between criticism by the judge of counsel for the defendant and criticism of the defendant himself.[231] Such distinction has been abandoned since the improper behaviour of the judge towards counsel is likely to have the same effect as that towards the defendant himself. The Court may, however, look carefully at the nature of the rudeness. A rude interruption of defence counsel on the basis that he is wasting time with irrelevant questions to prosecution witnesses may not justify quashing a conviction[232] if indeed the questions had been irrelevant. By contrast, rude interruptions while defence counsel is examining the defendant in chief may be regarded as more serious, again because there is no real distinction here between rudeness to defence counsel and to the defendant himself.

Perhaps the most difficult cases are those where the judge's manner will have distracted the jury, but not so obviously to the prejudice of the

---

[229] *R v. Tedjame-Mortty* [2011] EWCA Crim 950.

[230] *R v. Hircock* [1970] 1 QB 67, see above, para. 5.21.

[231] See C.P. Harvey, *The Advocate's Devil* (London: Stevens & Sons, 1958), pp. 50–1.

[232] *R v. Ptohopoulos* [1968] Crim LR 52.

defendant. In one case,[233] the Court of Appeal disapproved of the judge cutting counsel short in respect of his argument, without any notice that counsel was constrained in time, in circumstances where he had not had an opportunity of setting out the arguments in writing. The judge had also disallowed counsel for the defendant from making an objection on legal grounds to a question put to a witness by prosecution counsel in the absence of the witness, and exchanges became so heated that defence counsel was temporarily ejected from the court. However, prosecution counsel defused the situation by withdrawing the question. The Court concluded that both counsel and the judge were seriously at fault and did not accept that the jury would have been affected or the defendant's confidence in his counsel undermined. Ultimately, although 'the perception of impatience created by the judge was one that should not have been created',[234] and although he did not conduct the trial in a manner in which it would be expected a judge would conduct a trial, the Court concluded that overall there was no breach of the appellants' right to a fair trial.

In understanding this case, we should recall that counsel too must be courteous. In 2005 the Court of Appeal in R v. Lashley issued a reminder that:

> The remedy for an incorrect ruling is provided in this Court. It does not take the form of trying to re-embark on the argument in an endeavour to persuade the judge to a judicial rethink of a ruling that he has already given, at any rate unless and until the circumstances have changed.[235]

A judge's efforts to curb defendants' counsel had to be put in that context. Judge LJ (as he was then) spoke for the Court: 'We expect judges to be robust, and we are not troubled when counsel are oversensitive to criticism. We also recognise that from time to time judges will become impatient, sometimes unjustifiably so, without undermining the safety of the conviction.'[236] However, the convictions were quashed for lack of neutrality, since the judge's impatience had been extreme and extended to general derogatory comments about the competence of counsel, which would have damaged the defendant's confidence in the administration of justice; 'the perception of any reasonable observer present at the trial would have been similarly damaged'.[237]

---

[233] R v. Aboulkadir and others [2009] EWCA Crim 956 (20 May 2009).
[234] Ibid., para. 44.   [235] R v. Lashley [2005] EWCA Crim 2016, para. 21.
[236] Ibid., para. 48.   [237] Ibid.

The Appeal Court judgment was sent to the Presiding Judges of the relevant circuit, since Presiding Judges would, at the time, refer conduct complaints to the Lord Chancellor or the Lord Chief Justice in cases where the judge's conduct is seriously impugned. The judge, however, was not formally disciplined.

E.   Improper pressure on defendants to plead guilty

5.26 Improper pressure by the judge on defendants to plead guilty and improper remarks indicating that a defendant was sentenced more severely because he had pleaded not guilty have respectively resulted in the quashing of convictions and in the reduction of sentences. In *R* v. *Barnes*,[238] the defendant was convicted of robbery. In what the Court called 'an outburst', the judge, in the absence of the jury, commented adversely on the waste of time caused by hopeless defences and invited counsel for the defence to reconsider the position. Counsel then offered to withdraw from the case, and disclosed the advice he had given the defendant. The judge refused the services of another counsel on the ground that the other would be bound to give the same advice and he refused to adjourn the case to the next day to enable the defendant to prepare his own defence. The defendant withstood the extreme pressure to plead guilty, and maintained his plea of not guilty.

Nevertheless, the Court of Appeal held that 'it was clear that in the circumstances counsel would be gravely handicapped in conducting the defence, especially before a judge who had expressed his strong view as to the appellant's guilt, and as to the waste of time involved in fighting the case'. It being almost impossible for counsel to conduct the defence properly, the Court ruled that the conviction must be quashed: 'Just as interruptions by a trial judge making it impossible for defending counsel to do justice to the defence, will result in a conviction being quashed, so also conduct producing the same impossibility must have the same effect.'[239]

The Court also indicated that if, as a result of the pressure put upon him by the judge, the defendant had changed his plea, the Court could not have allowed his conviction to stand. If a defendant changed his plea to guilty after counsel had advised him to so plead under circumstances which suggested that this was the view of the judge, the result must be the

---

[238] *R* v. *Barnes* (1970) 55 Cr App R 100.   [239] *Ibid.*, 107.

same. So held the Court of Appeal in *R* v. *Turner*, where Parker CJ laid down rules to be followed by judges and counsel in plea bargaining.[240] As a general rule, deviation from these rules in the plea-bargaining process would result in the conviction being quashed. Before the verdict is returned, it is forbidden for a judge to indicate that a plea of not guilty would result in a more severe sentence. Even after the verdict he must not aggravate the sentence as though to give the impression that the defendant has been punished for contesting the case.[241]

The practice in *R* v. *Turner* need no longer be followed;[242] it is now possible for the defendant to seek before the trial a 'without prejudice' indication as to the likely maximum sentence he would receive if he were at that stage to plead guilty. However the procedure comes with safeguards that recognise the above points.[243] Thus, a judge must only give his indication in response to a request from the defendant and he must not indicate what the maximum sentence might be if the case were to be unsuccessfully contested. In practice, a judge might alert defence counsel to the possibility of such an advance indication, but not in such a way that presumes guilt of the defendant. It may be done clearly as a matter of routine, for example, rather than as a comment on the merits of the instant case; or it may be appropriate, for example, if it is apparent to the judge that the defendant's main concern is to avoid imprisonment, and he has already decided that he would not so sentence him if an immediate plea were offered.

F. Manifesting prejudice

5.27 A judge is not justified in the directing of a jury, or using in the course of summing up such language as leads them to think, that they must judge the facts in the way which he indicates:

> If a judge finds it necessary to intervene in the course of the examination-in-chief with questions which may seem to the jury to suggest that the evidence of the witness, although given on oath, is not to be believed, it is also necessary that the judge should remind the jury that the question of

---

[240] *R* v. *Turner* [1970] 2 QB 321, 326–7.
[241] *R* v. *Behman* [1967] Crim LR 597.
[242] *R* v. *Goodyear (Karl)* [2005] EWCA Crim 888 decides that a judge may indicate to a defendant the likely maximum sentence that would be imposed if he were to plead guilty immediately (or at least very soon, upon the receipt of legal advice) upon a supposed agreed set of facts.
[243] *Ibid.*, 53–70.

believing or not believing any particular witness is, like all other matters of
fact in a criminal trial, a question for them and not for him.[244]

As with excessive intervention in the examination of witnesses, often the
appellate court must reiterate these standards.

In *R v. Warr*, the Court of Appeal quashed the conviction and criticised
in the strongest terms a trial judge who, in directing the jury, said:

> You know perfectly well that witnesses for the defence do not always tell
> the truth. Sometimes the defendant lies in the hope of getting off ... I do
> not think you were in court a little earlier this week, or last week, when a
> man was charged with the same sort of offence as this ... The jury heard
> the evidence and did not believe a word of it and they convicted.[245]

It may be that trial judges have some positive duties to avoid a risk that juries
will be unconsciously prejudiced against defendants. In one case,[246] the trial
judge had mistakenly allowed the dock security contractors' application
for a prisoner to be handcuffed despite a lack of information and a false
assumption that there was a risk of escape from open court. The offender
submitted that the jury seeing him in handcuffs prejudiced his right to a fair
trial, and that this was sufficient to render his conviction unsafe. The Court
of Appeal held that if the information was not forthcoming the judge ought
to have asked for it. Nevertheless, the appeal was dismissed: the conviction
was not unsafe as it was obvious from the evidence that the defendant was a
several-times convicted drug dealer who dealt in class A drugs and the judge
gave an impeccable summing up to the jury.[247]

G.   *Private communications*

5.28 In principle, all communications about the case should be conducted
in public. Thorpe LJ, for the Court of Appeal, once expressed his 'misgiv-
ings as to the wisdom of the judge telephoning both leading counsel on
the eve to express his profound disquiet and irritation at the way the
parties were treating the court'.[248] A better practice, according to the
Court, would be for the judge to send the same email to each party
voicing his concerns so that there is a record of the exchange. However,

---

[244] *R v. Gilson* (1944) 29 Cr App R 174, 181 [Wrottesley J].
[245] *R v. Warr* [1969] Crim LR 331, The Times, 18 March 1969.
[246] *R v. Horden* [2009] EWCA Crim 388.
[247] *R v. Horden* [2009] Crim LR 8, 588–90.
[248] *Constantinou v. Wilmot Josife* [2010] EWCA Civ 747, para. 17.

noting the polarised positions of the parties at the start of the hearing, and following 'a profounder investigation', the Court found that the judge's allocation of costs did not exceed his ambit of discretion and did not interfere with his decision. In general, prompt disclosure of private communications with counsel at some stage before the trial is concluded may suffice to cure such irregularity provided that it does not go to the root of the case.[249]

H. Criticism and disregard of decisions of the higher courts

5.29 Higher courts in England frown upon any attempt by the lower courts to question or criticise their decisions or, even worse, to disregard them. In 1931 Mr Justice McCardie, in passing sentence on one Edward Griffith, said: 'Your record illustrates ... the unfortunate effect of unnecessary reductions of sentences of the Court of Criminal Appeal. I think that a wrong policy has been adopted in the past with respect to men who are obviously intending to commit crimes from time to time in order to obtain a livelihood.' On appeal, Lord Hewart CJ strongly criticised McCardie J for his remarks, and Avory J described them as 'a wholesale condemnation of the proceedings of the court'.[250]

In another case, the Court of Appeal criticised the judge for his 'rebellious' observations. 'With the greatest respect to Lawson J,' said Davies LJ, 'I think that those observations were out of place. It is unusual, and I am bound to say, undesirable, in my opinion, for a judge sitting at first instance – indeed, in that case in chambers – to express the opinion, though accepting that he is bound by it, that a decision, and a fairly recent decision of this court, was wrong.'[251]

The Court of Appeal itself has been criticised by the House of Lords for 'rebellious' observations. Lord Hailsham LC once rebuked the Court of Appeal for having held that *Rookes* v. *Barnard* was wrongly decided by the House of Lords, was not binding on the Court of Appeal and was 'unworkable', and accordingly judges of first instance should ignore it. Lord Hailsham said:

> I am driven to the conclusion that when the Court of Appeal described *Rookes* v. *Barnard* as decided 'per incuriam' or 'unworkable' they really only meant that they did not agree with it. But, in my view, even if this were

[249] *Constantinou* v. *Wilmot Josife* [2010] EWCA Civ 747.
[250] G. Pollock, *Mr Justice McCardie: A Biography* (London: John Lane, 1934) pp. 162–6.
[251] *Lane* v. *Wills* [1972] 1 WLR 326, 332.

not so, it is not open to the Court of Appeal to give a gratuitous advice to judges of first instance to ignore decisions of the House of Lords in this way. The course taken would have put judges of first instance in an embarrassing position, driving them to take sides in an unedifying dispute between the Court of Appeal or three members of it and the House of Lords.[252]

The then Lord Chancellor further added that

much worse than this, litigants would not have known where they stood. None could have reached finality short of the House of Lords, and in the meantime the task of advising them either as to their rights or as to the probable cost of obtaining or defending them, would have been literally quite impossible.

The Lord Chancellor observed, expressing the hope that 'it will never be necessary to say so again', that 'in the hierarchical system of courts which exists in this country, it is necessary for each lower tier, including the Court of Appeal, to accept loyally the decisions of the higher tiers'.[253]

Arguably the situation is not so clear cut, a view which was well expressed by Alec Samuels:

Is it seriously suggested that a judge cannot with reasons say that a decision is in his opinion wrong? Is the judge to become a mere negative technician? Everyone knows of instances where as a result of informal judicial criticism higher courts have changed their minds, decisions have been overruled and amending legislation has been passed. The law would be immeasurably poorer if those great masters of the common law such as Lord Atkin, Scrutton LJ and Lord Denning, and many others, had not spoken out and set everybody thinking. Judicial criticism has enabled us to see the unsoundness of Lord Devlin's categorisation in *Rookes* v. *Barnard* despite the decision of the House of Lords in *Cassell* v. *Broome*. Lawson J is a most able and highly respected judge and it will be a thousand pities if, while loyally applying the law as he finds it, he – and his judicial brethren – feels in any way inhibited from expressing a strongly held opinion on the merits.[254]

It seems that the more likely situation is that judges may freely express doubts about a ruling which binds them, though preferably obliquely. Common phrases which indicate such doubt might include an apparently unnecessary reminder that a decision is binding upon them, or a comment that the issue might be revisited by a higher court in the future. What is more important is that the lower courts make it clear that they

---

[252] *Cassell and Co Ltd* v. *Broome (No. 1)* [1972] 2 WLR 645, 653.
[253] *Ibid.*   [254] A. Samuels, 'Gagging the Judges' (1972) 122 *New Law Journal* 337.

accept that precedents are nonetheless to be followed if they cannot be distinguished, and that unhelpful cases cannot be conveniently overlooked.

We previously noted, however, that domestic courts deciding a case under the Human Rights Act 1998 are required to take into consideration any relevant Strasbourg case law,[255] and the UK Supreme Court clarified that

> where . . . there is a clear and constant line of decisions whose effect is not inconsistent with some fundamental substantive or procedural aspect of our law, and whose reasoning does not appear to overlook or misunderstand some argument or point of principle, we consider that it would be wrong for this Court not to follow that line.[256]

Can the Court of Appeal follow a ruling from the European Court of Human Rights or is it bound to follow the decision of the House of Lords/UK Supreme Court? 'In legal matters, some degree of certainty is at least as valuable a part of justice as perfection';[257] Lord Bingham thought that

> that degree of certainty is best achieved by adhering, even in the Convention context, to our rules of precedent. It will of course be the duty of judges to review Convention arguments addressed to them, and if they consider a binding precedent to be, or possibly to be inconsistent with, Strasbourg authority, they may express their views and give leave to appeal, as the Court of Appeal did here. Leapfrog appeals may be appropriate. In this way, in my opinion, they discharge their duty under the 1998 Act. But they should follow the binding precedent, as again the Court of Appeal did here.[258]

Lord Bingham insisted upon constructive collaboration between the Strasbourg court and the national courts of member states:

> The Strasbourg court authoritatively expounds the interpretation of the rights embodied in the Convention and its protocols, as it must if the Convention is to be uniformly understood by all member states. But in its

---

[255] HRA, s. 2(1). See above, para. 2.14.

[256] *Manchester City Council* v. *Pinnock* [2010] UKSC 45, para. 48; *R (Ullah)* v. *Special Adjudicator* [2004] UKHL 36, para. 20 [Lord Bingham]; *R* v. *Horncastle* [2009] UKSC 14; *Al-Khawaja* v. *UK* (2009) 49 EHRR 1; *Al-Khawaja* v. *UK* [2011] ECHR 2127.

[257] *Cassell and Co Ltd* v. *Broome (No. 1)* [1972] 2 WLR 645, 717 [Lord Hailsham].

[258] *Kay* v. *Lambeth LBC* [2006] UKHL 10, para. 43 [Lord Bingham]; *R (Purdy)* v. *Director of Public Prosecutions* [2009] EWCA Civ 92.

decisions on particular cases the Strasbourg court accords a margin of appreciation, often generous, to the decisions of national authorities and attaches much importance to the peculiar facts of the case. Thus it is for national authorities, including national courts particularly, to decide in the first instance how the principles expounded in Strasbourg should be applied in the special context of national legislation, law, practice and social and other conditions. It is by the decisions of national courts that the domestic standard must be initially set, and to those decisions the ordinary rules of precedent should apply.[259]

In these circumstances, only exceptionally would the Court of Appeal depart from a precedent set by the House of Lords.[260] The Administrative Court recently adhered to the need for the protection of legal certainty by the doctrine of precedent in *R (GC)* v. *Commissioner of the Police of the Metropolis*, where the Administrative Court felt bound to follow the House of Lords' decision that the police retention of biometric samples for an indefinite period save in exceptional circumstances was not incompatible with Article 8 ECHR.[261] By contrast, a subsequent ruling of the European Court had found that such retention was inconsistent with Article 8 ECHR.[262] However, the Administrative Court followed the alternative course of action suggested by Lord Bingham, gave permission to appeal and ordered a leapfrog appeal to the Supreme Court to determine the matter.

I. The sleeping judge

5.30 Judicial office holders 'are expected, as Sir Robert Megarry once put it, to be as wise as they are paid to look'.[263] Yet 'judicial sleepiness'[264] was for long ignored, notoriously when a prominent judge started to develop dementia, repeatedly falling asleep on the bench and being, to some

---

[259] Para. 44. Lord Irvine, 'A British Interpretation of Convention Rights' [2012] PL 237.

[260] E.g., in cases where the effect of the Human Rights Act had undermined the policy considerations that had largely dictated the House of Lords' decision, para. 45.

[261] *R (GC)* v. *Commissioner of the Police of the Metropolis* [2010] EWHC 2225 (Admin), paras. 30–5 [Lord Justice Moses]; *R (S)* v. *Chief Constable of South Yorkshire* [2004] UKHL 39.

[262] *S* v. *UK* (2009) 48 EHRR 50.

[263] Cited by Michael Kirby, 'Judicial Stress', *Annual Conference of the Local Courts of New South Wales*, 2 June 1995.

[264] There seems to have always been one sleeping judge on the Bench. Judge Dodderidge (1555–1628) became known as the 'sleeping judge' as he shut his eyes for concentrating his attention; see William Hogarth's painting *The Bench* (1758).

observers, 'visibly and distressingly half-senile';[265] in consequence of which his fellow judges wrote his judgments until he retired nine months later. As a circuit court judge said in 2006, 'It would be foolish to pretend we don't ever feel sleepy. Some judges even take smelling salts into court with them.'[266] He went on: 'It sounds nonsensical, but cases involving incidents of violence are the worst because there are often a large number of witnesses, each giving pretty much exactly the same evidence. It can be very, very soporific.'

The Court of Appeal now accepts that, when a judge sleeps or appears to be asleep, justice is not seen to be done and public confidence in the courts is damaged.[267] Thus a rape trial in Gloucester Crown Court in December 2001 had to be abandoned and a retrial ordered, when the judge fell asleep twice during the defendant's counsel's closing speech. The judge himself ordered the retrial, telling the jury: 'I am not aware that I did [fall asleep]. I think I was well aware of what he was saying to you. But if in fact I gave the impression of not listening to what he said, it would be unfair to the defendant to allow the case to go on.'[268] He was reprimanded by the Lord Chancellor in July 2002.

A disciplinary decision from 2010 from the Lord Chancellor and Lord Chief Justice shows that sleepiness which has affected a trial once can justify the immediate removal of a magistrate. The magistrate who was 'nodding off' during the first day of an assault trial at Lancaster's youth court in March 2010 was removed after an inquiry found that his behaviour 'risked bringing the magistracy into disrepute'.[269] This may seem to be a harsh decision as there was no evidence that it had happened before or would happen again. If anything, these cases emphasise the need for a thorough health check upon appointment, where any medical cause for sleepiness could be checked and treated, or acted upon as a ground for incapacity for duty. At the moment, there is a suggestion of inconsistency in how such cases are handled. The late judge Michael

---

[265] J.R. Spencer, *Jackson's Machinery of Justice*, 8th edn (Cambridge University Press, 1989) 372.

[266] Judge Michael Findlay Baker QC, quoted in *The Observer*, 11 June 2006.

[267] This was not always the case, see *R v. Langham* [1972] Crim LR 457, per Lord Widgery CJ: 'It was easy to rely on the hallowed phrase "justice must be seen to be done" in order to raise complaint over a very wide field. But, in order that justice was not seen to be done, it was necessary to point to some factor on which the doing of justice depended and then to show that that factor was not visible to those present in court.'

[268] *The Guardian*, 16 December 2003.

[269] Statement from the Office for Judicial Complaints, OJC 24/10, 20 September 2010.

Coombe fell asleep during a robbery trial in 2002 but his career survived – despite the fact that three of the defendants convicted in the trial had their sentences reduced on appeal. Similarly, Judge Gabriel Hutton hung on to his job even though he fell asleep twice during a rape trial in 2001.

Conclusions

5.31 The test for bias is now clearly set at common law and, as in Australia and other countries, the *Guide to Judicial Conduct* more explicitly outlines typical circumstances which might trigger fears or claims of bias. The course of action to be taken by a judge in responding to an application for recusal, however, is not always obvious. One suggestion might be to develop the use of Practice Directions, beyond the existing Practice Direction before the Employment Tribunal.[270] The strength of a Practice Direction cannot be underestimated: in *Southwark LBC* v. *Jiminez*, the Court of Appeal agreed with the plaintiff that the Employment Appeal Tribunal had made a material error in not complying with the Employment Appeal Tribunal Practice Direction about the conduct of the tribunal hearing.[271] Ward LJ, in *El-Farargy*, took the unusual step of including a postscript to his judgment, expressing his concern at the procedure for recusal applications:[272]

> The procedure for doing so is, however, concerning. It is invidious for a judge to sit in judgment on his own conduct in a case like this but in many cases there will be no option but that the trial judge deal with it himself or herself. If circumstances permit it, I would urge that first an informal approach be made to the judge, for example by letter, making the complaint and inviting recusal. Whilst judges must heed the exhortation in *Locabail* not to yield to a [*sic*]tenuous or frivolous objections, one can with honour totally deny the complaint but still pass the case to a colleague. If a judge does not feel able to do so, then it may be preferable, if it is possible to arrange it, to have another judge take the decision, hard though it is to sit in judgment of one's colleague, for where the appearance of justice is at stake, it is better that justice be done independently by another rather than require the judge to sit in judgment of his own behaviour.

---

[270] *Facey* v. *Midas Retail Ltd* [2000] IRLR 812; *Stansbury* v. *Datapulse Plc* UKEAT 966 98 0905, [2001] ICR 287, para. 39 H-C.

[271] *Southwark LBC* v. *Jiminez* [2003] EWCA Civ 502; *Ansar* v. *Lloyds TSB Bank Plc* [2006] EWCA Civ 1462; D. Feldman (ed.), *English Public Law* (Oxford University Press, 2004), paras. 20, 33, 36.

[272] *El-Farargy* v. *El-Farargy* [2007] EWCA Civ 1149, para. 32.

Since it is unlikely that the practice of a judge sitting in judgment on his own conduct will disappear, a Practice Direction might outline the points to take into consideration, some of which may vary from court to court, depending, for example, on the availability of other judges in each court. Most importantly, any doubt that the judge may have on impartiality should lead to withdrawal from the case. The willingness of the parties for the judge to hear the case must also be considered, though we have seen that their consent must appear to have been given without any pressure of any kind, time or otherwise, and that it must be clarified that they are content for him to hear the case rather than have to suffer an adjournment.

In the second section of this chapter, we showed how proactive the Court of Appeal was in promoting high standards of behaviour and quality of justice. The collection of examples of judicial misbehaviour in court should not undermine the reality that the standards of conduct in the exercise of the judicial office have traditionally been high and continue to be so. There is always a danger, however, that the misconduct of one isolated judge is taken to reflect the standards of behaviour of the judiciary as a whole. This in itself justifies a strong disciplinary role for the Court of Appeal in addition to the formal handling of complaints about the conduct of judges under the new regulatory framework introduced in the CRA, which brings us to our next chapter.

6

Standards of conduct in extra-judicial activities

Introduction

6.1 How much of an ordinary citizen should or can a judge be? It is only appropriate that judicial officers 'live, breathe, think and partake of opinions' in the real world, that they 'continue to draw knowledge and to gain insights from extrajudicial activities that would enhance their capacity to perform the judicial function'.[1] Yet public confidence will only be maintained if judicial office holders maintain the highest standards of probity in their professional, public and private lives.[2] In this chapter, we explore the ramifications of a changing role for the judiciary. As judges get involved on their own initiative in their local communities, some have argued that there is scope for them to do more, and that it is important that some take responsibility for projecting positive images of the judiciary.[3] Yet whether and to what degree a judge should pursue certain extra-judicial activities depends on an elaborate set of considerations. No extra-judicial activity should be so onerous or time consuming that it interferes with the judge's performance of his duties. It is almost axiomatic that full-time judges should not engage in political controversy. Upon appointment they are expected to give up all activities with a political flavour, such as holding office as a Member of Parliament. One may question the exemption of fee-paid and part-time judges from the ban on full-time judges on political activity of any kind or on any tie with political parties. Certain extra-judicial activities such as chairing public inquiries also tend to politicise the role of judges and detract from their impartial and independent status.[4] Exposure on internet social networks

---

[1] R.B. McKay, 'The Judiciary and Non-Judicial Activities' (1970) 35 *Law and Contemporary Problems* 9, 12.

[2] Baroness Prashar, Middle Temple Guest Lecture (6 November 2006), p. 10.

[3] H. Genn, evidence before the HL Committee on the Constitution, 2007.

[4] H.P. Lee, *Judiciaries in Comparative Perspective* (New York: Cambridge University Press, 2011).

or blogs may also blur the distinction between the private and public spheres for judges. Post-retirement limitations will also be examined.

I. The ban on political activities

6.2 It seems to be universally agreed that full-time judicial offices are incompatible with membership of the House of Commons.[5] Likewise upon appointment, full-time judges are expected to give up active participation in politics and avoid any political controversy. The *Guide to Judicial Conduct* provides that 'a judge must forego any kind of political activity and on appointment sever all ties with political parties'.[6]

There is more compromise in the case of part-time and fee-paid judges upon which the administration of criminal justice relies so heavily (as of April 2011 there were 1,221 recorders). They have been exempted from the statutory ban on full-time judges on political activity of any kind or on any tie with political parties. The *Guide to Judicial Conduct* reiterates the expectation that fee-paid judges nonetheless have 'the same general obligation [as full-time and part-time judges] to maintain the status and dignity of the office of judge', and that they will 'refrain from any activity, political or otherwise, which could conflict with their judicial office or be seen to compromise their impartiality'.[7]

One contemporary controversy has been the reported telephone calls from Ms Booth, days before the vital House of Commons vote for military action against Iraq, to a number of MPs to solicit their support for the government's plans to invade Iraq. A retired civil servant claimed Ms Booth's political activities were incompatible with her role as a recorder. The Lord Chancellor, Lord Irvine, ruled in 2003 that she had been acting as the prime minister's wife and as a well-known supporter and prominent member of the Labour Party, not in her capacity as a judge. According to Lord Irvine, 'in common with other part-time judicial post-holders, recorders only hold office while actually sitting judicially. This being the case, recorders are not subject to the same restrictions on political activity as full-time judges.'[8] It may be that

---

[5] House of Commons (Disqualification) Act 1975, sch. 1.
[6] Guide to Judicial Conduct, 3.3.
[7] This also applies to the European Parliament, the Scottish Parliament, the Welsh Assembly and the Northern Ireland Assembly.
[8] *The Independent*, 2 May 2003.

subsequent wording of the *Guide to Judicial Conduct* should be interpreted as a rejection of that view.

Though the number of recorders in Parliament is small, it is arguable that their dual legislative and judicial capacity may give rise to a perception of bias. The traditional view is that the risk is especially great if a Member of Parliament sits as a recorder in his own constituency. Lord Hailsham LC thus explained:

> In their own constituencies MPs and their agents are peculiarly sensitive to their popularity or otherwise. They are peculiarly vulnerable to political pressures in difficult decisions. There is always the danger that they may use the prestige of the Bench, which is great, for political advantage. On the whole it is better that they should not sit locally, and they will not in fact be appointed to sit locally. Even if none of those dangers actually existed or never actually affected decisions, I am sure that in difficult cases disappointed litigants would think that they had done so and it is better to apply the Caesar's wife criterion in such cases.[9]

This is no longer the position in law (former provisions to that effect were repealed in 1971) but there is something akin to a convention for an MP not to sit as a recorder in his own constituency. Similarly, the recorder who is also a local councillor should not sit as a recorder in the area covered by the council.[10] One may question whether merely discouraging a recorder from representing the place where he sits in his judicial function adequately ensures that in the exercise of these functions he will be removed from party politics. Situations may still arise in which justice would not be seen to be done, and a reasonable bystander may simply expect a formal separation from the political sphere. Thus, if a recorder, who is also an MP for the party in office were to try a case involving anti-government demonstrations, the public may feel that justice cannot be seen to be done. This explains why at least recorders with prominent political associations are generally expected to withdraw from any case in which their party affiliations or political views are of any relevance.[11] When making a decision as to recusal, the recorder must consider 'whether the nature and extent of the political activity would

---

[9] Lord Hailsham, 'Presidential Address' (1971) 27 *The Magistrate* 185, 186; *Hansard*, HL, vol. 331, cols. 405–407 (8 June 1972).

[10] Ministry of Justice, 'Policy, Procedure, Terms and Conditions of Service of Recorders', October 2007, para. 32.

[11] Lord Hailsham said in this context that he would like to retain 'the marriage between the practising profession and the public career of politics', *Hansard*, HL, vol. 321, col. 1311 (19 November 1970).

create a perception of unfairness in the particular case'.[12] Recorders must be alert to the risk of a perceived lack of impartiality arising from public pronouncements.[13]

It is respectfully suggested that it is today more appropriate to bar any part-time judge from membership of Parliament, on the basis of the formal recognition of separation of powers in the Constitutional Reform Act 2005 (CRA). This suggestion is gaining support in relation to lay magistrates at least. Despite the absence of a statutory prohibition on a magistrate standing for election as a Police and Crime Commissioner (PCC), the Senior Presiding Judge recently issued guidance holding that it was not permissible for magistrates to stand for such elections, inviting them to resign immediately upon announcement of their intention to do so. No judge can hold office as a PCC by virtue of his disqualification under the House of Commons Disqualification Act 1975.[14] The prohibition from standing for election as a PCC draws upon the recognition, in the CRA, that lay magistrates are judicial officeholders and therefore subject to similar constraints to judges.[15] Police and Crime Commissioners are required by statute to set local police priorities and simply campaigning for election might raise doubts about a candidate's judicial impartiality.[16]

6.3 The membership of judges in the House of Lords has been more contentious over the years. Until recently the Lord Chancellor presided over the legislative sittings of the House of Lords and was the spokesman for the government in the Upper House as well as being a member of the Cabinet, albeit that he was perceived for a long time as the least partisan of Cabinet ministers in relation to conduct of judicial business. Former Lord Chancellors took part in debates upon political questions. The Law Lords were also in a special situation as professional judges also sitting in the Upper House, though it was clearly understood by convention that the Law Lords would not become involved in politically contentious issues.[17] Similarly appeals could be heard when the House had been

---

[12] Guide to Judicial Conduct, 3.15–3.17.   [13] *Timmins* v. *Gormley* [2000] QB 451.
[14] Police Reform and Social Responsibility Act 2011, s. 66.   [15] CRA, s. 109(4), sch. 14.
[16] Several serving magistrates were selected as PCC candidates for the election in November 2012, before the guidance was issued in July 2012. The guidance was modified in that context and allowed them to campaign provided that a magistrate would undertake 'not to sit from the time of his/her selection as a candidate, and to resign if elected, he/she may resume sitting if not elected'. It was also necessary for those magistrates seeking election to conduct themselves 'in such a fashion as not to compromise their ability to return to their Bench as an independent and impartial member of the judiciary'.
[17] White Paper on House of Lords Reform, 19, s. 7.

prorogued or Parliament dissolved. Even retired Law Lords, who remain members of the House after their retirement from the bench, adhered to this established tradition of non-political activity in the chamber.

Further, judges who happened to be peers or were created peers during their period of judicial office were, until recently, members of the House of Lords. They were the Lord Chief Justice, the Lords of Appeal in Ordinary and, if peers, the Master of the Rolls and the President of the Family Division. They had the same rights as other life peers, such as the right to sit, speak and vote in the House of Lords in a legislative capacity. As we know, far-reaching reforms were introduced by the CRA; the justices of the Supreme Court hold the title 'Lord' but are not members of the House of Lords, and the same is true of other senior judicial figures. Fee-paid and part-time judges are still not formally disqualified from membership of Parliament. The Lord Chancellor is the same person as the Minister of Justice, and he is an elected politician who sits in the House of Commons. He need have no formal legal qualifications and cannot sit as a judge.

6.4 The situation under the CRA is thus one of classic formal separation of powers. Inevitably the former convention of non-political activity only established itself slowly, and in the process difficulties had been encountered. In the 1920s, the tradition was not strong enough to prevent a few Law Lords from taking part in debates on the Irish Free State Bill and some other political matters.[18] The most outspoken of all was Lord Carson, who bitterly attacked the plan for the establishment of a Free Irish State, both in debates in the House and upon a political platform in the country. That the tradition of political neutrality had not, at that time, been firmly established, we can also see from the debate following Lord Birkenhead's public censure of Carson. In that debate Carson and others attempted to establish that Law Lords, unlike other judges, could participate in political debates and even give political speeches in public meetings. Lord Finlay, Birkenhead's predecessor on the Woolsack, defended Carson, suggesting that there was no rule excluding the Law Lords from taking part in political controversy.[19] The vast majority of Lords condemned Carson for his political speech, supporting Lord Birkenhead's stand.

---

[18] *Hansard*, HL, vol. 49, col. 903 (27 March 1922), 931, 954 (29 March 1922); Lord Birkenhead, *Points of View*, vol. II (London: Hodder and Stoughton, 1922), 147–51, 183–9.

[19] *Hansard*, HL, vol. 49, col. 954 (29 March 1922).

Nonetheless, it would be wrong to be too critical of the former regime as it operated in the late twentieth century, as to do so would be to overlook some of its practical benefits. Increasingly, the Law Lords largely confined themselves to acting as technical advisers on legal points arising out of proposed legislation, and their contribution to the work of the legislature in the form of consultations off the floor was greater than their contribution by way of speeches on the floor of the House.[20] It was generally recognised that the retired Law Lords in particular might play the role of the 'resident legal expert' and they made a significant contribution to the cross-bench element in the House of Lords in the examination of legislation with a highly technical or legal content.[21] They would take part 'in debates on the administration of justice, penal policy and civil liberties, where law and politics intersect'[22] and from time to time opposed legislation and other measures which they believed constituted an executive encroachment upon the independence of the judges or the rule of law.

However, it seems that the convention that Law Lords would not become involved in politically contentious issues was less and less observed towards the end of the twentieth century and this was problematic where sitting Law Lords were involved. In 1968, Lord Avonside, a Scottish judge, accepted an invitation from the leader of the Conservative Party, which was then in opposition, to join a party policy committee to consider Conservative Party proposals for a Scottish assembly. This invoked a heated public controversy and the judge had to resign from the committee under public pressure. *The Times* defended Lord Avonside's membership of the committee, suggesting that there was no real difference between membership of a policy committee that was to consider constitutional matters and commissions of inquiry which also had political implications.[23] Yet there is still a difference between a governmental committee, with no partisan political flavour, though with a touch of controversy or political overtones, and a committee instituted by a political party to advise on party policy. Membership of a committee of a political party, whatever the subject matter considered by that committee, would result in the identification of the judge, in the eyes of the public, as a supporter of that party and an opponent of other parties. This would no doubt undermine public confidence in him and stain the whole

---

[20] G. Drewry and J. Morgan, 'Law Lords as Legislators' (1969) 22 *Parliamentary Affairs* 226.
[21] *Ibid.*, 235, 238.   [22] White Paper, cited by Lord Lester.
[23] *The Times*, 30 July and 8 August 1968.

judiciary with the taint of party politics. Moreover, *The Times* made the assumption that asking judges to act as chairmen of commissions to inquire into controversial matters is an acceptable practice. That assumption is open to question, as discussed in our next section.

Stevens has documented the role of the Law Lords well.[24] Let us mention Lord Ackner and some other Law Lords, who spoke in 1994 against the introduction by prerogative power of a new scheme to compensate the victims of violent crime.[25] By speaking against the scheme, they disqualified themselves from being members of the Appellate Committee which subsequently decided that the Home Secretary had acted unlawfully. In 1997 a Law Lord supported the Opposition on the proposal by the same Home Secretary to empower the police to use electronic surveillance without a warrant. We will never know what might have happened if a high number of sitting Law Lords had criticised a proposed law in the legislative chamber and were then called upon to decide its compatibility with the Human Rights Act (HRA) years later in the judicial chamber.

6.5 Before the CRA, if the executive failed to take a step necessary for the interests of the judges, the judges would make representation through the Lord Chancellor; since the passing of the CRA, the Lord Chief Justice speaks on their behalf, pressing for an appropriate remedy. This point was demonstrated by the examination, in previous chapters,[26] of the action taken by the judges to frustrate attempts to reduce their salaries and to ensure that their salaries be increased in accordance with the changing conditions.

II. Public inquiries

6.6 Judges have strongly opposed legislative and other measures which they believed were likely to involve the judiciary in politics or controversy. Until 1868 complaints against corrupt practices in elections were heard by Select Committees of Parliament. When it was proposed that judges should hear election petitions, the judiciary unanimously

---

[24] R. Stevens, The English Judges: *Their Role in the Changing Constitution*, rev. edn (Oxford: Hart, 2005); Law and Politics. *The House of Lords as a Judicial Body 1800–1976* (London: Weidenfeld and Nicolson, 1979); L. Blom-Cooper, B. Dickson and G. Drewry (eds), *The Judicial House of Lords 1876–2009* (Oxford University Press, 2009).

[25] Hansard, HL, vol. 552, cols. 1071–24 (2 March 1994).

[26] See above, paras. 4.38, 4.43 and 7.31.

opposed the measure. The Lord Chief Justice, Sir Alexander Cockburn, wrote to the Lord Chancellor:

> I have consulted the judges and I am charged by them, one and all, to convey to you their strong and unanimous feeling of insuperable repugnance to having these new and objectionable duties thrust upon them. We are unanimously of opinion that the inevitable consequences of putting judges to try election petitions will be to lower and degrade the judicial office, and to destroy or at all events materially impair the confidence of the public in the thoroughgoing impartiality and inflexible integrity of the judges, when in course of their ordinary duties, political matters come incidentally before them . . . We are at a loss to see how Parliament can in justice and propriety impose upon us labours wholly beyond the sphere of our constitutional duties.[27]

The objections of the judges had no effect and the legislation was passed. For all the concerns, only recently has an election court been called upon to decide that an MP should forfeit his seat on the statutory ground of making false statements about the personal character and conduct of an opponent during an election campaign.[28] The decision to do so was upheld on the facts, and the authority to do so explained precisely on the grounds that the court did not have to decide the plausibility or falsity of political statements (with due reference made to the arguments put forward to the judges in the nineteenth century), but only factual statements about a person's character, an exercise not dissimilar to their role in determining defamation cases.[29] Generally, courts otherwise prefer not to interfere with the decisions of election officers, for example to allow a candidate to present himself as a 'Literal Democrat' thus inviting confusion with the 'Liberal Democrat' candidate.[30]

Not only judges but also governments have sometimes opposed measures which might involve judges in politics. In the 1960s it was proposed to establish a Press Amalgamations Court consisting of a High Court judge as president and two lay judges, to scrutinise purchases and mergers of newspapers. Commenting on this proposal, Lord Hailsham, for the government, said that such a court was liable to involve the judiciary in politics. He pointed out that the primary function of the judges must, of course, be to retain the respect of the public for their

[27] E.S. Turner, *May It Please Your Lordship* (London: M. Joseph, 1971), pp. 200–01.
[28] Representation of the People Act 1983.
[29] *R (Woolas)* v. *Speaker of the House of Commons* [2010] EWHC 3169 (Admin).
[30] *Sanders* v. *Chichester* (1994) SJ 225.

independence – which involves not merely their actual independence of mind, but also the public's belief that they are seen to be independent in every respect.[31] Later, Lord Hailsham, as Lord Chancellor, strongly opposed a proposal to refer certain legal aspects of the British obligations on arms supply to South Africa to the Privy Council under section 4 of the Judicial Committee Act 1833. Noting that 'he could not be a party to such a constitutional monstrosity', Lord Hailsham said:

> Judges must be kept, so far as possible, out of political controversy. Obviously in the course of his ordinary judicial duties a judge, be he high or lowly, must occasionally, and will occasionally, find himself in what I might describe as the eye of the storm. He may be compelled by virtue of his office to decide a case which cannot fail to give widespread offence whichever way he decides in one way or another ... But it is altogether another thing [to assign judges] to arbitrate in a highly charged matter between the rival views of two highly political Parties.[32]

He expressed an equally strong view on inquiries by judges. At the Lord Mayor's annual dinner for the judiciary in July 1973 he said that the demand for public inquiries conducted by judges 'inevitably interferes with the process of law' and that it was impossible to safeguard the independence of the judiciary where judges are thus exposed to ordeal by public criticism, which is often the natural result of these inquiries. Such inquiries should therefore be used as a last resort.[33]

6.7 It is difficult to reconcile this once fashionable reasoning with the frequent appointment of judges to chair committees and commissions to investigate highly controversial affairs and to conduct public inquiries.[34] The tradition of appointing distinguished members of the higher judiciary as chairmen of political inquiries relies upon the fact-finding skills of judges. It is also credit to their reputation, in the public eyes, of impartiality and fairness. Yet we may only express reluctance on the use of judges to chair public inquiries.[35] It is, in practice, difficult to dissociate the figure of the appointed judge in the exercise of his judicial

---

[31] *Hansard*, HL, vol. 250, col. 939 (29 May 1963).
[32] *Hansard*, HL, vol. 317, cols. 771–2 (21 April 1971).
[33] *The Times*, 18 July 1973; *Hansard*, HC, vol. 716, cols. 644 (14 July 1965).
[34] Until the Tribunals of Inquiry (Evidence) Act in 1921 public inquiries were conducted by Select Committees of Parliament, see G. Lindell, *Tribunals of Inquiry and Royal Commissions*, Law and Policy Paper 22 (The Federation Press, 2002); see today Inquiries Act 2005, s. 10; J. Beer, *Public Inquiries* (Oxford University Press, 2011); Stevens, *The English Judge*, pp. 83–5.
[35] J. Beatson, 'Should Judges Conduct Public Inquiries?' (2005) 121 LQR 221.

functions from the figure of the judge acting as a fact finder for the purpose of a public inquiry. In the former case, he is subject to the judicial oath in determining someone's liability at law. In the latter case, he is applying his judicial skills to fact finding for the purpose of a public inquiry, outside his judicial capacity. He does not have to follow the same laws of evidence or procedures that a court or tribunal would observe,[36] in spite of the inquisitorial format adopted, for example, in Lord Scarman's Red Lion Square Inquiry in 1974. A wide range of procedures have been adopted over the years to conduct inquiries,[37] although in practice, the inquiries of the 1970s and 1980s have broadly followed the six cardinal principles recommended in 1966 by the Royal Commission on Tribunals of Inquiry, chaired by Sir Cyril (later Lord) Salmon:

1. Before any person becomes involved in an inquiry, the tribunal must be satisfied that there are circumstances which affect them and which the tribunal proposes to investigate.
2. Before any person who is involved in an inquiry is called as a witness, they should be informed of any allegations made against them and the substance of the evidence in support of them.
3. They should be given an adequate opportunity to prepare their case and of being assisted by legal advisers and their legal expenses should normally be met out of public funds.
4. They should have the opportunity of being examined by their own solicitor or counsel and of stating their case in public at the inquiry.
5. Any material witnesses they wish to call at the inquiry should, if reasonably practicable, be heard.
6. They should have the opportunity of testing by cross-examination conducted by their own solicitor or counsel any evidence which may affect them.[38]

This emphasis on the judicial character of the investigation has not prevented concern over the procedures adopted in some inquiries, in addition to criticisms of the outcomes, time and costs taken by inquiries.

---

[36] *O'Callaghan v. Mahon* [2006] IR 32, 74 [Mr Justice Hardiman]; *Canada (Commission of Inquiry on the Blood System)* [1997] 3 SCR 440; S. Sedley, 'Public Inquiries: a Cure or a Disease?' (1989) 52 MLR 469, 470.

[37] The inquiry into the Profumo affair proceeded without any legal representation or publicity until the report was published, see 'The Security Service and Mr Profumo', Cmnd 2152.

[38] Public Administration Select Committee, 'Government by Inquiry', First Report of Session 2004–05, vol. I, HC 51-I, Annex 3, (27 January 005).

In terms of length and cost, it is apposite to start with the Saville Inquiry into the events of Bloody Sunday, when thirteen civilians were killed by British soldiers. The first such report, by Lord Widgery CJ, became commonly regarded as a 'whitewash'[39] and a serious problem in bringing peace to Northern Ireland. Over a painstaking eleven years, costing some £200 million, Lord Saville reheard the evidence, and did indeed reverse most of Lord Widgery's findings, deciding that all the deceased civilians had been unjustifiably shot. The length and cost of the inquiry naturally stimulated much public debate.

For controversial outcomes and procedures, one may point to the Scott Inquiry in the 1990s, where the High Court judge Richard Scott held that the government had been blameless in allowing the sale of arms to Iraq and in apparently trying to conceal evidence of this when the sellers were prosecuted.[40] The inquiry was conducted under prerogative power, and, in a departure from the Salmon principles, the lawyers representing interested parties or witnesses were not directly involved, though they could be privately consulted. The Hutton report, in 2004, found that the death of Dr David Kelly, a scientific adviser to the government who cast doubt on the case for the invasion of Iraq, was a suicide for which the BBC rather than various members of the government was to blame.[41] The latter inquiry has been commended for the openness with which all the documents and questioning of witnesses were made available to the media and, in the process, for broadly following the Salmon six cardinal principles; but, in the view of many, this contributed all the more to the surprise when Lord Hutton expressed his own conclusions.

Happier examples, in terms of speed and outcomes, are perhaps Lord Scarman's report into the cause of rioting in London in 1981, which prompted various later reforms such as restrictions on the powers of the police to stop and search youths,[42] and Lord Taylor's report on ways to improve safety in football stadiums, which was prompted by the Hillsborough disaster in 1989.[43]

---

[39] *The Times*, 20 April 1972.
[40] Sir Richard Scott, 'Report of the Inquiry into the Export of Defence Equipment and Dual-Use Goods to Iraq and Related Prosecutions' (1996), 5 vols. In terms of outcome, the findings led to the codification of the convention of ministerial accountability.
[41] Lord Hutton, 'Report of the Inquiry into the Circumstances Surrounding the Death of Dr David Kelly C.M.G.' (2004).
[42] Lord Scarman, The Brixton Disorders, 10–12 April 1981. The Scarman Report: Report of an Inquiry (London: Penguin, 1982).
[43] Taylor LJ, 'The Hillsborough Stadium Disaster', Com 962 (1990).

In principle, there seems to be little objection to appointing judges to conduct inquiries which are essentially judicial in character and are expected to investigate particular incidents, isolate the causes, identify those responsible, and suggest methods of preventing recurrence.[44] Most importantly, they normally do not involve political controversy. The Scarman and Taylor reports seem to fall into this category. However, objections have in the past been raised against the use of judges for controversial investigations which might include the conduct of government ministers. In 1964 Lord Gardiner deplored the practice of appointing judges 'to report on the morals of ministers' and this might be thought to be borne out by the reception of the Hutton and Scott reports. Lord Widgery once suggested that we should 'draw the line where the issue was political in nature'. But that line between politics and fact is not easy to draw. Was the Profumo affair an issue political in nature, or was it essentially of a judicial character? Almost any matter, even if it were highly political, could be said to require listening to evidence and forming a conclusion. In the course of an interview with a journalist of *The Times* in August 1972, Lord Widgery said that the Londonderry inquiry was judicial in character and that judges should be prepared to take on such tasks, but as we have seen, it still proved to be both a judicial and political disaster.

We are accustomed to judicial decisions being the last word – for better or worse – and being acted on as though correct unless or until judicially overruled. The authority of the judiciary may be compromised if a member is asked to commission a report the contents of which are not duly respected by either the government or the public in the way that an ordinary decision in a court of law might be. In other words, not only does the government appoint a judge to chair an inquiry into a controversial affair, but when the judge reports on the matter, the government rejects his findings and conclusions if it suits them to do so, thereby, after the event, involving the judge himself in a bitter controversy. Thus, Mr Justice (later Lord) Devlin's response on the Nyasaland disturbances in 1959 was met with a hostile reception from the government. Commenting on this, Lord Gardiner said: 'I should have thought that if a judge is to be employed for that sort of purpose it ought to be on the footing that all the political parties agree beforehand ... that his findings of fact will be accepted; otherwise it inevitably means drawing Her Majesty's judges

---

[44] G. Zellick, 'Comment' [1972] PL 1, 2.

into matters of Party politics.'[45] Perhaps it was the intrinsic unlikelihood of returning any kind of report that would gain the usual degree of respect from all sides of the community – because of its politically sensitive nature – that should have prompted something other than a judicial inquiry in the case of the Scott and Hutton Reports. This may be a better test than simply asking whether the inquiry is of a fact-finding nature.

We thus come back to the question raised, of the judicial character of the inquiry. Under the Inquiries Act 2005, the terms of reference are set by ministerial powers. Yet the blur between the judge acting in discharge of his judicial function and the judge acting as a public servant assisting the public administration appears in Lord Saville's letter of 26 January 2005 to the Department for Constitutional Affairs (as it then was), as he was consulted on the Inquiries Bill. He thought that 'To allow a minister to impose restrictions on the conduct of an inquiry is to my mind to interfere unjustifiably with the ability of a judge conducting the inquiry to act impartially and independently of Government, as his judicial oath requires him to do.'[46] While, in order to preserve the impartiality and fairness of the inquiry, a judge acting as a public inquiry chairman should be entitled to decide on matters of procedure, it is suggested, however, that the ministerial powers to set the terms of reference of the inquiry do not per se threaten judicial independence. Sir Brian Kerr (as he then was) noted that the ministerial power to bring an inquiry to an end under the Prison Act (Northern Ireland) 1953 may affect the usefulness of the inquiry 'in that it halts the investigation on which the inquiry is embarked, but it does not alter the autonomy of the inquiry while it is taking place'.[47]

It has often been pointed out that there are other individuals besides judges whose reputation for fairness, impartiality and public standing is such that they could properly undertake those assignments.[48] It may be better to approach such persons for inquiries which are necessary but the possible conclusions of which are so likely to be so politically sensitive that they will undermine the perception of the independence of the judiciary. Thus, it was not a judge but Lord Beeching who chaired the highly successful Royal Commission on Assizes and Quarter

---

[45] *Hansard*, HL, vol. 258, col. 835 (9 June 1964).   [46] Beer, *Public Inquiries*, 1.67.

[47] *Re Wright* [2007] NICA 24, para. 29. The inquiry was carried out under the Prisons Act (Northern Ireland) 1953 rather than the Inquiries Act 2005.

[48] (1971) 121 NLJ 119.

Sessions; while Royal commissions were deemed too slow in the Salmon Report for the requirements of a public inquiry, one may point to an entirely well respected and satisfactory inquiry into the conduct of David Blunkett on the allegation that (as Home Secretary) he played a role in fast-tracking a visa application for his ex-lover's nanny. The inquiry was held not by a judge but by a senior civil servant, Sir Alan Budd.[49]

6.8 Where judges are called upon to make suggestions for law reform in the future, as they can be with inquiries, the line between law and politics is also blurred. The recent Leveson Inquiry has been tasked with making recommendations regarding regulation of the media, and the government may hide behind judicial recommendations as to the effect of legal reform.[50] On the one hand, regulation of the press involves a greater degree of legal argument (especially following the HRA) than political argument (all sides want a 'free but responsible' media). On the other hand, one recalls the earlier complaints of the misuse of judges which once prompted the *Solicitors' Journal* to write:

> The politicians are overdrawing on the capital of the judges' high reputa-
> tion for competence and impartiality in reaching conclusions by the
> judicial process of reasoning, Each time a judge is misused by being put
> up as face-saver behind whose report a government can hide in carrying
> out a policy which they shirked adopting directly, a little of the long
> esteem in which judges are held is lost and some of their authority
> undermined.[51]

There are other potential objections to judges conducting extra-judicial inquiries. Such non-judicial assignments remove from their ordinary duties judges who cannot be spared by the overburdened courts. The extraordinary length of the Saville Report effectively meant that the House of Lords was deprived permanently of an outstanding judge who would otherwise have served as one of the twelve members of the highest court in the land, and Lord Justice Leveson's services have recently been sorely missed in the Court of Appeal.

Despite the significant criticisms that can be raised on behalf of judicial independence, the traditional endorsement of judges to chair public

---

[49] A. Budd, 'An Inquiry into an Application for Indefinite Leave to Remain', HC 175 (21 December 2004).

[50] Leveson LJ, 'An Inquiry into the Culture, Practices and Ethics of the Press. Report', HC 780-I (2012).

[51] (1972) 116 Solicitors' Journal 149.

inquiries is as strong as ever.[52] The matter was not considered in the negotiations leading up to the Concordat. Under the Inquiries Act 2005, when a minister proposes to appoint as a chairman of an inquiry 'a particular person who is a judge' he must first consult the head of the relevant judiciary. By comparison, in Israel, the Chief Justice makes the appointment of any public inquiry.

Our view is that judicial inquiries should only be commissioned where the following factors are satisfied: (1) where the government has a direct interest, the Lord Chief Justice should have to add their own approval; (2) in the words of Lord Woolf, 'where the inquiry is of a highly politically sensitive nature, the Lord Chief Justice should be entitled to say not only who, but whether a judge should conduct the inquiry at all';[53] (3) (again in the view of the Lord Chief Justice) the court in which the selected judge sits will be able to continue its regular business during the anticipated period of his or her absence. It should also be clarified that the appointed judge is not acting in his or her judicial capacity, under the judicial oath, but rather in aid of public administration in an extra-judicial function, and that this does not prevent the judge from having discretion on the procedure adopted for the public inquiry.

III. Community activities

6.9 Almost any community activity, even though perfectly acceptable, may become a matter of public or political controversy. In considering whether any element of politics or controversy is present in the activity, the normal, ordinary state of things should be examined. The fact that there is a possibility of such elements arising under special circumstances is not sufficient to exclude a judge from such activities. A judge, however, should not remain any longer than necessary on a body that is likely to be involved in recurring public controversy.[54] Moreover, political involvement apart, a judge may be associated with educational, charitable and religious organisations and trusts, office in governing bodies of universities and similar institutions which are normally free of controversy.

---

[52] Ministry of Justice, 'Memorandum to the Justice Select Committee: Post-Legislative Assessment of the Inquiries Act 2005', Cm 7943 (October 2010).

[53] Lord Woolf, Written Evidence to the Select Committee on Constitutional Reform Bill, 'Supplementary Memorandum' (7 June 2004).

[54] C. Thomas, 'Judicial Diversity in the United Kingdom and Other Jurisdictions: A Review of Research, Policies, and Practices' (The Commission for Judicial Appointments, 2005), 37.

If, however, the relevant organisation happens to fall into a financial or other crisis and becomes a focus of public discussion, it would seem unsound to say that a man who has been associated with and rendered valuable service to an organisation for many years should be excluded from participating in public discussion of that organisation simply because he is a judge. But if he were to speak out in defence of his organisation, he may be accused of using his judicial position in some way.

Apart from the nature of the activities in question, the degree of association and involvement in an extra-legal community activity is to be considered. In some organisations a judge may be an active member and serve on their executive committee or as chairman. Another important consideration is time. A judge cannot participate in community activities if the time and energy required for those activities will interfere with his official functions. But a judge is always looked upon as a judge, even when he acts as an individual. Consequently, whatever he does, he is inevitably using the prestige of his office. This puts upon him a duty to avoid substantial involvement in activities which, in the public interest, do not deserve the support of the prestige of judicial office. Further, high-profile figures are not often appointed to the bench, and, for example, the decision in 2001 by Cherie Booth, a part-time judge since 1996, to become president of a children's charity, Barnardos, was seen by some as a sign that she might not consider or expect a full-time appointment to the bench.

With these observations in mind, we focus below on involvement in associations, non-profit organisations and appeals for funds.

A.   Associations

6.10 The general rule is that a judge may be a chairman of a sports association provided there is no element of business, profit or commercialisation in that association. Also, if the sport concerned is objectionable to a significant segment of the public on moral or other grounds, a judge will be expected to refrain from participation in such sports. Under this general rule a judge may be chairman of tennis, cricket or amateur rugby associations but is excluded from professional football (soccer), horse races, dog races, hare courses and the like. Professional football carries elements of profit and business. The various animal races have long since not been acceptable as they are viewed by a significant segment of the public as immoral because they present undue temptations to people to gamble and they may be cruel to animals. A judge should also avoid associating himself with an organisation that is likely to be a party or a friend to a party in a number of cases before him. Thus, a Family Division judge should not chair a family service unit, and a circuit judge should not be active in a local consumer group. We also noted earlier that membership of the Freemasons does not per se raise doubts as to a judge's impartiality where a witness or party in a case is also a Freemason,[55] and there is no obligation upon a judicial office holder to declare membership of a non-secret society.[56]

B. Non-profit organisations

6.11 Many associations with non-profit organisations are unproblematic. For example, judges often serve as trustees of art institutes. Many are actively associated with charitable organisations of any kind: for helping the poor, the old, the sick and the handicapped, or for the protection of animals. Judges are also involved in organisations which render public service such as societies for after-prison care, orphans, hospitals, medical research funds, marriage guidance and family service units. The late Lord Bingham was, for example, Chair of UK Reprieve, a charity providing legal support to prisoners as well as an active president of the British Institute for International and Comparative Law. But the judge's role should not involve active business management.[57] The *Guide to Judicial Conduct* distinguishes between active involvement in educational, charitable and religious organisations and holding high office in governing bodies of universities and similar institutions.[58] On holding such offices, the *Guide* emphasises that the management and funding structures of such organisations are 'complex, and are often the subject of public debate and political controversy'. There is thus a necessity 'to limit and regulate the nature and extent of personal involvement in contentious situations', and this would seem to highlight a new restriction in extra-judicial activities.

The restriction is well motivated. Consider Judge Callman, who became a circuit judge in 1973 and, as a governor of Birkbeck College, also became the Chair of the Investments Committee in 1995. This involved dealing with the evaporation of £6.5 million of assets invested

---

[55] See above, para. 5.50; *Salaman* v. *UK* Application No. 43505/98 ECtHR 15 June 2000.

[56] *Grande Oriente d'Italia di Palazzo Giustiniani* v. *Italy (No. 2)* (2007) Application No. 26740/02 ECtHR 31 May 2007.

[57] Guide to Judicial Conduct, 8.4.   [58] *Ibid.*, 8.4.3.

by Birkbeck in Barings Brothers Bank following the news that, due to the speculation of Nick Leeson, that bank would be forced to cease trading. He was thanked by Birkbeck College in the following terms for his role in the inquiries and negotiations that eventually led to the reinstatement of the College investments a fortnight following the news of the speculation: 'So we were more than ever glad thereafter for Judge Callman's keen analytical mind and talent for cross-examination, which made him just the right person to put eager investment managers on the spot.' Arguably there could be a concern too about the tradition of distinguished judges being appointed as university Visitors, charged with ensuring that the university's own body of law – its charter, statutes, ordinances and regulations – was properly applied by the officers of the institution. The matter is less likely to cause problems in future, however.[59]

C.   Appeals for funds

6.12 Under the *Guide to Judicial Conduct*:

> Care should be taken in considering whether, and if so to what extent, a judge's name and title should be associated with an appeal for funds, even for a charitable organisation. It could amount to an inappropriate use of judicial prestige in support of the organisation and may also be seen as creating a sense of obligation to donors.[60]

It remains permissible for judges to solicit for contributions to charities, and they may also contribute to such funds, provided that their names are not used in soliciting for other contributions. Equally, it is arguable that a judge can be involved in de minimis fund-raising activities, so long as, when fund-raising, the judge is careful to avoid using the prestige of his office. But judges should not associate themselves with a charity unless the charity is free from business influence and political controversy. Thus, in 2001 the Judges' Council wrote to judges advising them that it would be inappropriate for them to take part in 'quasi-political' events such as the Liberty and Livelihood March. Equally, judges will not associate themselves with an institution working for a controversial cause or one that renders services that are objectionable to a significant

---

[59] The establishment of a nationwide complaints system for students, run by the Office of the Independent Adjudicator for Higher Education (which became fully operational from 1 January 2005), coupled with the availability of alternative ways for members of staff to pursue grievances, means that most universities will have no future Visitors.

[60] Guide to Judicial Conduct, 8.4.2.

segment of the public. Thus, a charity that runs an abortion clinic for a minimal fee, though providing a legal and valuable social service, may not be the proper sphere of activity for a judge.

Judges may allow their names, as patrons, to be mentioned in calls for contributions, donations and bequests to charitable institutions. But they should ensure that their judicial title will be omitted. In the 1970s, some judges signed circulars addressed to individuals or companies calling for contributions, but this form of solicitation should be used cautiously as judges could be asked to sign circulars addressed to companies which can be repeat actors in litigation. Direct personal solicitation is only acceptable when done in legal circles for contributions to professional benevolent societies.

The overall position is more liberal than that in the United States, where American judges are prohibited from 'personally participating in the solicitation of funds or other fund-raising activities', but the different appointment mechanisms in particular (judicial elections) would arguably justify such prohibition.[61]

IV. Commercial activities

6.13 Holders of full-time judicial office are advised on appointment that they should discontinue any professional or business links with their former chambers or firm. All holders of judicial office, whether full- or part-time office, are advised to refrain from participating in any activity which might conflict with their judicial office. Holders of full-time judicial office are prohibited, under section 75 of the Courts and Legal Services Act 1990, from practising as barristers or solicitors and from being indirectly concerned in any such practice.

Severe restraints are also rightly placed upon the permissible scope of a judge's involvement with commercial enterprises. There is a longstanding rule that no full-time judge should hold a commercial directorship, and advice on this is provided upon appointment.[62] It applies to a directorship in any organisation whose primary purpose is profit related, whether the directorship is in a public or a private company, and whether

---

[61] Canon 4 C (3)(b), 1990 American Bar Association Model Code of Judicial Conduct. That restriction applies to charitable organisations, including those devoted to the improvement of the law, the legal system and the administration of justice.

[62] *Guide to Judicial Conduct*, 8.3.1. All full-time judges are provided on appointment with documentation which includes guidance on outside activities.

or not it is remunerated. Any person holding such a directorship is therefore expected to resign from it on appointment to judicial office. There is normally no objection to a judge holding shares in either a private or a public limited company[63] and no objection either to taking part in the management of a family estate.

However, all holders of judicial office must also have regard to the case law governing conflicts of interest, which will apply in any individual case in which the possibility arises of a conflict between the judge's private interests and those of any person or party involved in the case. By exception, it is accepted that a judge may take part in the management of family assets, including land or family businesses, and the estates of deceased close family members, whether as executor or trustee. Thus, in *Regina* v. *Bristol Betting and Gaming Licensing Committee, ex parte O'Callagham*, a joined case to *Locabail*, the Court dismissed the challenge made on the ground of judicial bias arising from the fact that the judge was a director of a company that owned rented properties and the tenants of the company included the other party involved in the case.[64] The judge was a non-executive director of what was a family property investment company, and the rent payable by the other party as tenant of the judge's company represented around 4 per cent of the total rent currently receivable by the company. A judge may also hold a directorship in a private company for this purpose or in a company formed for the management of flats of which he is a tenant.[65] The traditional reservations on outside activities remain: the management of family assets should not be complex, time consuming or contentious.

V.   Social life

6.14 In 2011 the BBC broadcasted a documentary in which Lord Hope was seen taking public transport. The Supreme Court Justices were keen to show that they were ordinary citizens. It is typical of a dual concern of judges: one is that they are no longer seen as out of touch with the community, because that is simply not the reality, and the other one is that they should more actively seek opportunities to engage with the community. Today there is no doubt that judges take public transport and have no objection based on the dignity of their function in doing so.

---

[63] A commercial partnership, such as a solicitors' partnership, would normally be treated similarly.
[64] Para. 5.12.   [65] Guide to Judicial Conduct, 8.3.2.

The use of public transport is an often-quoted example of judges being ordinary citizens, with Lady Justice Hallett again citing this example in November 2011: 'I sometimes almost despair about how judges get portrayed in the media. They don't want to get rid of the stereotype of judges because they like it. Judges travel on public transport, their homes are burgled, their children are hurt, they suffer from terrible diseases and tragedy, and the idea that they live in an ivory tower is so outdated. It really is completely unfair.'[66]

Another stereotype draws upon the judges' lodgings.[67] High Court judges are based in London but hear the most serious criminal cases outside London; the provision of special lodging is required on the ground that this enables the judges to have the privacy which is essential to their work.[68] The network of lodgings, often listed houses with extensive grounds, has now been reduced for financial reasons and HMCTS has considered the use of serviced apartments or hotels as an alternative. The isolation of the judges on circuit has been criticised,[69] though it is now mostly the requirement of being on circuit which can be criticised, as it disrupts family life for substantial parts of the year.

6.15 The *Guide to Judicial Conduct* tries to draw a fine line between over-prescribing what a judge can do outside the court and advising him to avoid pitfalls which may be relatively easy to fall into given that his professional past is likely to be as a self-employed barrister (unlike some continental systems where a judicial career is entered at a very young age). For example, attending parties hosted by legal practitioners is less likely to be appropriate if the practitioner or a member of the practitioner's firm is currently appearing before the judge, has appeared in the recent past, or is likely to appear in the near future; or if the judge's attendance will advance the practitioner's private interests.[70] Some of the *Guide to Judicial Conduct*'s guidelines can be broken down into the following categories.

First, it is understood that appointment to judicial office brings with it limitations on the private and public conduct of a judge,[71] and the standards in private life are necessarily high. Judges go to public houses (pubs) provided they are decent and not near the court. There is no

---

[66] Hallett LJ, *London Evening Standard*, 7 November 2011.
[67] S. Sedley, 'Diary', LRB, vol. 21 no. 22 (11 November 1999), p. 37.
[68] *Hansard*, HC, vol. 809, col. 279 (14 January 1971).
[69] JUSTICE, 'A Report', para. 56, p. 37; *Hansard*, HC, vol. 800, col. 1582 (30 April 1970).
[70] *Guide to Judicial Conduct*, 5.1 (3), (8) and (9).   [71] *Ibid.*, 4.1.

objection to a judge going to a respectable pub in his neighbourhood in London or near his country home and having a beer with a friend. However, a judge is not expected to be seen in pubs frequently. In the town where a Crown Court or a county court is situated judges are not expected to go to pubs or other places of that kind. Similarly, we should be surprised to learn that any judge visits strip-tease shows, brothels or casinos or entertainments of that sort. Indeed, under the *Guide to Judicial Conduct*, judges

> must avoid situations which might expose them to charges of hypocrisy by reason of things done in their private life. Behaviour which might be regarded as merely unfortunate if engaged in by someone who is not a judge might be seen as unacceptable if engaged in by a person who is a judge and who, by reason of that office, has to pass judgment on the behaviour of others.[72]

By contrast, it is desirable that, workload permitting, judges should immerse themselves in other cultural aspects of life, which would enable them to establish better contact with the world outside the courts.

Second, and as noted earlier, personal involvement in criminal proceedings gives rise to disciplinary proceedings. Conviction for an offence involving moral turpitude requires immediate suspension. The main difficulty lies in convictions of judges for traffic offences. Because Justices of the Peace try traffic offences, it is a recognised practice that a Justice of the Peace who is convicted of careless or dangerous driving or driving with too much alcohol in his blood resigns from the bench. The position with judges is less clear. In 1969 a senior judge pleaded guilty to driving a car when he had consumed alcohol in excess of the prescribed limit (at a time when this was less seriously viewed than it is today) and was fined.[73] To defend his staying on the bench, it could be said that he did not deal with criminal cases, and, therefore, the conviction for an offence of driving with too much alcohol in his blood did not affect him in his judicial functions. Though he was noticed staggering on his way to his parked car and once went to the wrong side of the road, no collision occurred nor was any damage caused.[74] He was an eminent judge and, on balance, the public interest would be adversely affected if he resigned. However, to maintain the high standards of the judiciary, it is equally arguable that he should have resigned. In Parliament, in the course of the debates on the Courts Bill, an MP referred to 'one distinguished judge

---

[72] *Ibid.*   [73] *The Times*, 1 July 1969.   [74] *Ibid.*

[who] was actually convicted of a criminal offence – only a road traffic offence, but a serious case of its kind – but did not resign. That would have been unimaginable a few years ago.' While opinion was deeply divided, the majority view was that on balance it was a wise decision to let this senior judge stay on the bench. In 1975 he was promoted to the House of Lords.

As a third category, one may question the involvement of judicial office holders in online social networks. Users of Facebook, Twitter or other online social networks rely upon them generally to stay in touch with other people with whom they have something in common. But membership of a social network creates some risks to the dignity and integrity of the office and judges must exercise caution in their use of social networks. The *Guide to Judicial Conduct* clarifies that the use of social networking is a matter of personal choice, a stance also emerging in other jurisdictions, such as the United States through the states' Judicial Ethics Committees. The *Guide* promptly warns, however, against the risks associated with social networks online, such as providing information about a judge's personal life and home address. Someone dissatisfied with the judge's decisions might undertake 'jigsaw' research and piece together information from various independent sources: 'Posting some information could put your personal safety at risk. For example your address, details of holiday plans and information about your family could be used for criminal purposes. Photographs could enable home addresses or car numbers to be identified.'[75]

The risks associated with social networks go beyond the personal security of judges. As with any public extra-judicial activity of a judge, in order to sustain public confidence, the judge must be careful to avoid saying anything which may give any impression of bias or prejudice concerning any issue, party or lawyer appearing before him or her in court. In case of doubt, it is advisable to err on the side of caution. This remains the guiding principle in finding an answer to, for example, whether it is acceptable to add a lawyer or persons who regularly appear before the judge in court (e.g., social workers), as a 'friend' on a social network, such as Facebook, Linkedin, MySpace or Twitter. That is not to say that judges should not have friends among lawyers, of course, but the question is whether adding a lawyer as a Facebook-defined friend conveys a stronger impression to the outside world (other than ordinary

[75] Para. 8.12.1.

socialising) that the lawyer is in a position to influence the judge. Is there any difference between a judge socialising in person and a judge socialising through a social network?[76] The argument to the effect that there might be, is that the public nature of the information on a judge's friends or connections might give the impression of a bond that goes beyond mere acquaintance and the online connection, alone or in combination with other facts, might been seen as requiring disclosure to the parties in some cases.[77] Further, if the social network is a closed one, limited to the judge's relatives and a few close colleagues, and it is used for exchanging personal information, it is likely that the lawyer might be seen as having a special influence on the judge. In the case of a legal association with a Facebook page, the question is whether the association uses the page to talk about the association's aims or about non-legal matters.

Another question is what information and exchanges might be made available on those networking sites. Here, the general rules on judicial expression outside the courtroom apply: no comment on pending cases or controversial issues – that implies avoiding responding to inquiries from users who might want the judge to discuss their cases or provide some legal advice. *Ex parte* communications are no more permissible on social networks than they are outside social networks. Furthermore, social network pages can be open to others' comments. The judge might be seen as endorsing any comment posted on his page, or lending the prestige of the judicial office to anyone who might post comments or materials there. To prevent this, the judge has to carefully and frequently vet his network page, ensuring that personal information, photographs and comments maintain his impartiality and the dignity of the judicial office. In addition, the other members of his social network may not guard privacy as securely as the judge, and the judge should be aware of the risk that the judge's comments, photographs, etc., might be made public without the judge's permission.

Greater clarity was provided through guidance from the Senior Presiding Judge and the Senior President of Tribunals sent to all judicial office holders in August 2012 warning against blogging by judicial office holders with one main requirement that, although blogging by members

---

[76] For a helpful discussion, see New York Advisory Committee on Judicial Ethics, 'Advisory opinion 08-176' (29 January 2009).

[77] Ethics Committee of the Kentucky Judiciary, 'Ethics opinion JE-119' (10 January 2010); C. Gray, 'The Too Friendly Judge? Social Networks and the Bench' (2010) 93 *Judicature* 236.

of the judiciary is not prohibited, officer holders who blog (or who post comments on other people's blogs) must not identify themselves as members of the judiciary. Thus, the 'Magistrates' Blog' now reads that it is written by a 'group of people interested in magistrates' courts and their work'.

VI.   Professional life after retirement

6.16 Since 1993 the policy has been that judicial office holders should not sit beyond the age of seventy.[78] Provided that this is desirable in the public interest (a business case must be made), the Lord Chief Justice can, however, with the concurrence of the Lord Chancellor, extend beyond retirement date circuit judge appointments, or appoint retired circuit judges as deputy circuit judges.[79] It is currently the policy that recorders cease to serve at the end of the financial year in which they reach the age of sixty-five. Any final decision with regard to potential extensions is usually made before the judicial office holders in question have reached their retirement date.

One may challenge the retirement age for judges of seventy. If a person qualified at the Bar or to be a solicitor at age forty, which is possible, he or she would need twenty years of court work as a barrister before thinking of becoming a judge. These people would then start at the bottom of the court circuits at age sixty and work their way up. By age seventy they may be highly regarded judges at circuit or High Court level but be unable to continue up the ladder. Even for the barrister or solicitor who started young, there is no reason why, if they love their job and are good at it, they should be taken off duty at a set age.[80]

6.17 Judges do not go back to the Bar.[81] There is no specific ruling to this effect with regard to High Court judges, but it is known that in the 1950s, two judges, one of whom later became a Law Lord, asked to return to the

---

[78] Judicial Pensions and Retirement Act 1993, s. 26 and sch. 5; Courts Act 2003, ss. 12(2) and 13(1); the Memorandum on conditions of appointment and terms of service will also clarify the matter. This is subject to transitional provisions under which a judge already serving on the implementation of the Act (31 March 1995) retains his pre-existing retirement age.

[79] Courts Act 1971, s. 24; Judicial Pensions and Retirement Act 1993, ss. 26(5) and (6).

[80] On retirement policy, note *Seldon* v. *Clarkson Wright and Jakes* [2012] UKSC 16.

[81] See, e.g., *Hansard*, HL, vol. 312, col. 1288 (Lord Dilhorne), 1303 (Lord Denning) (19 November 1970); Lord Hailsham, *Hansard*, HL, vol. 313, cols. 733–4 (3 December 1970).

Bar and were refused.[82] There is a formal ruling of the Bar Council to the effect that in principle a county court judge cannot return to practise at the Bar in any capacity.[83] However, the rules are not inflexible. In one exceptional case a stipendiary magistrate was allowed to return to the Bar. An Irish judge who has been a judge in Ireland and retired may practise in England.[84] There is no clearly established tradition against a solicitor judge returning to practise upon resignation. The argument against a judge returning to practise at the Bar upon retirement is that it would give him an unfair advantage over other members of the Bar. It seems, however, that this practice rests not so much upon reason and arguments as upon a long-established tradition which has never been questioned. It would not be surprising if some retiring judges were soon to try to return to the Bar and to challenge the basis for any ban which the Bar Council might wish to enforce, especially if the retired judge wishes to write opinions rather than to appear in court. The established practice cannot be definitely stated in relation to solicitors, very few of them being on the bench still.

Before August 1970 the question of whether a judge could leave the bench and go into business was probably regarded as merely an academic question. At that time it seemed clear that judges were not expected to end their life in the City. In August 1970 Justice Fisher, at the age of fifty-two, resigned from the bench after only two-and-a-half years in office. Upon resignation, he became a director of a merchant bank in the City of London. Fisher's resignation raised two questions: (a) is there a tradition against untimely resignation from the bench? (b) are judges barred from accepting business appointments upon resignation or retirement from the bench? These questions, though not treated separately, received conflicting answers. To the *Solicitors' Journal*, Fisher's resignation 'came as a shock'. It warned that if the bench becomes part of the territory for the head hunters' safari, then the judges' reputation for absolute impartiality and integrity, which is as valuable as the impartiality and integrity themselves, would suffer.[85] It might be added that it would be especially unwelcome if they were to work for companies that they have favoured in their past decisions, notwithstanding that the same has occurred with several retired Cabinet ministers.

---

[82] Sir Winston Churchill referred to this in introducing the Bill increasing judicial salaries, *Hansard*, HC, vol. 525, col. 1063 (23 March 1951).

[83] W.W. Boulton, *Conduct and Etiquette at the Bar*, 5th edn (London: Butterworths, 1971), p. 34.

[84] *Ibid.*   [85] (1970) 114 Solicitors' Journal 593.

On the other hand, it was argued[86] that on being appointed to the bench, a man must inevitably step into what is, for him, comparatively unknown territory. Only when he ascends the bench does a man become aware of the full impact of the step he has taken. If, after some time on the bench, he becomes disenchanted with the judicial life and judicial work, surely it is better for the administration of justice, as well as for the judge concerned, that he leave the bench. The *New Law Journal* saw some advantage to the public in judges going into business:

> The city represents a powerful force in our national life and if its sense of values is sometimes highly questionable, it is on that account all to the good if it occasionally receives an infusion of the qualities of a discipline very different from and in some ways superior to its own.[87]

Judges who have been appointed after Fisher's resignation were told by the Lord Chancellor when he interviewed them before appointment that, on accepting the judicial appointment, they should treat the career as a permanent one and that 'they should approach the Bench with the enthusiasm of a bridegroom approaching marriage or of a priest approaching priesthood'.[88] It is difficult to decide whether Fisher serves as a precedent for a future judge who wishes to follow a similar course, or whether it has reaffirmed, by the adverse reaction it attracted, the tradition against untimely resignation and against judges going into business. There does not seem to be any consensus among judges except to say that the appointment is accepted upon the understanding that it is 'a one-way track'. This would seem to lend support to the view that Fisher helped strengthen the tradition against untimely resignations from the bench and against judges leaving the bench for business. One may also read in that light the decision by Sir Hugh Laddie to resign from the High Court in 1985 because he was 'bored' and felt 'isolated' at the bench. He joined a firm of solicitors (he was a barrister by training) and would not appear in court.

6.18 In general, entering politics after retirement from the bench is regarded as less objectionable than going into business, for it might be viewed as public service. Indeed, it is not clear whether there has been any tradition excluding judges from entering politics after leaving the bench. It is true that, except for Lord Reading, judges have not gone in to

---

[86] (1970) 120 NLJ 746; (1970) 67 *Law Society Gazette*, 588.   [87] (1970) 120 NLJ 747.

[88] Erskine, citing Lord Hailsham, in 'The Selection of Judges in England: A Standard for Comparison' (1953) 39 *American Bar Association Journal* 279, 280.

politics upon resignation from the bench. Lord Reading left the office of the Lord Chief Justice to become the Viceroy of India. As one of his biographers reported, 'on the whole the appointment was received well by the Press and also in the Temple'.[89] Later, Lord Reading served as Foreign Secretary in the Cabinet of Ramsay MacDonald's National Government. This appointment did not attract any criticism on the ground that a former judge should not engage in politics. Lord Hewart was invited by Lloyd George to return to politics and 'revitalise the Liberal Party' but Hewart gave up the idea for personal reasons. No mention, however, was made of any tradition against judges going into politics upon retirement.[90]

Beyond the question of entering politics upon retirement, the *Guide to Judicial Conduct* expresses the view that 'even in retirement a former judge may still be regarded by the general public as a representative and any activity that might tarnish the reputation of the judiciary should be avoided'.[91] In particular, the constitutional conventions on judicial comments, detailed in Chapter 8, apply to retired judges.[92]

Conclusions

6.19 We have expressed some concern over the continuing tradition of English judges acting as chairmen of public inquiries whenever asked to do so. The Lord Chief Justice should have an effective veto on the matter and should exercise it where the subject matter is politically sensitive. Further the Lord Chief Justice should consider whether the court in which the selected judge sits will be able to continue its regular business during the anticipated period of his absence. We noted also that some non-members of the judiciary have had notable successes in chairing public inquiries.

The *Guide to Judicial Conduct* otherwise offers effective advice in extracurricular activities, including requirements that judges avoid involvement in businesses and that even positions of responsibility (especially involving management and finance) with other bodies should

---

[89] H.M. Hyde, *Lord Reading: The Life of Rufus Isaacs, the First Marquess of Reading* (London: Heinemann, 1967), p. 327.

[90] R. Jackson, *The Chief: the Biography of Gordon Hewart, Lord Chief Justice of England 1922–1940* (London: George G. Harrap, 1959).

[91] *Guide to Judicial Conduct*, para. 9.2; Judicial Executive Board, 'Guidance to Judges on Appearances before Select Committees', November 2012, para. 19.

[92] See below, paras. 8.5–8.17.

be avoided due to their complexity and the possible perception that the judge's position is being used in some improper way. The latter concern may apply to some fund-raising activities too. The theme persists in relation to judges who retire; there seems to be less objection to their being politically active than to their being commercially active. The reasons for any restrictions post retirement seem to be in need of much forceful argument.

The major contemporary problem is perhaps the use of social networking sites. The apparently innocuous act of adding another lawyer (most naturally, one from the same chambers) as a 'friend' on a social networking site might arguably convey a stronger impression to the outside world (than ordinary socialising) that the lawyer is in a position to influence the judge. At the same time, there may be a wish for judges to be active in this sphere to dispel the ivory tower image which they still have in some circles. There is no obvious solution to the dilemma.

7

Immunity, discipline and removal of judges

Introduction

7.1 We saw in Chapters 5 and 6 how standards of judicial conduct are now expressly construed as a defining component of public trust in the judiciary. In this chapter we focus upon the process of regulation of judicial conduct. While tenure of judicial office is a fundamental element of judicial independence, disciplinary procedures apply to judges who misbehave in one way or another, albeit that few judges have had charges brought against them. The power to remove and discipline judges directly affects individual judges as well as the judiciary as a whole, thus the grounds and mechanisms for the discipline and removal of judges are of vital importance to the independence of the judiciary. They must be subject to proper safeguards, and their analysis forms the major part of this chapter. Little has been written in recent times about removal and discipline of English judges,[1] no doubt because of the proud record of English judges with regard to their professional behaviour. The separation of powers enshrined in the Constitutional Reform Act 2005 (CRA) invites a renewed scrutiny, however, of the role played by the executive and the legislature in the exercise of the powers of discipline and removal of judges. Until the CRA, the power to discipline was in the hands of the Lord Chancellor, also the head of the judiciary. Following the transfer of the latter responsibility to the Lord Chief Justice in 2005, the power to discipline judges is now shared between the Lord Chief Justice and the Lord Chancellor, placing safeguards upon its use. In addition to disciplinary actions, the procedures of impeachment and address of removal, which can lead to the vacation of senior judicial office, are also considered.

The disciplinary regime must be distinguished from the criminal and civil liability regime that applies to judges in the discharge of their

---

[1] D. Pannick, *Judges* (Oxford University Press, 1987).

judicial duties. Judicial immunity relieves judges from the fear of being sued for speaking and acting openly in the course of judicial proceedings.[2] Judges in the exercise of their judicial function have exemption from all civil liability for anything done or said by them in their judicial capacity. As noted in our introductory chapter, the exclusion of civil liability for judicial acts is granted as a matter of public policy, 'not so much for [the judges'] own sake as for the sake of the public, and for the advancement of justice, that being free from actions, they may be free in thought and independent in judgment, as all who administer justice ought to be'.[3] The rule of judicial immunity also provides finality in litigation: it puts an end to judicial controversies.[4] The case cannot effectively be reopened by suggesting that, if the judge had been less careless, then the claimant would have won. Such claim would only be pursued through the appeal process.

Judicial immunity from liability does not give a judge any privilege to make mistakes or to do wrong,[5] but the remedy for a judicial wrong committed in the course of judicial proceedings does not generally lie in an action for damages. Rather, the appeal system is expected to address a judicial wrong in the exercise of the judicial function, as discussed in our Chapter 5. Appeal is the ordinary way to hold judges accountable to society and to the legal profession, by allowing for wrong, unfair or biased decisions to be overturned.

It has also been said that, without immunity from civil liability for judicial acts, no one would want to be appointed to the bench for fear of 'wasting and harassing persecution'.[6] This argument has some particular force as, at common law, the Crown was not vicariously liable for the torts of its servants and, while it waived its immunity from liability generally in 1947, it maintained it in respect of judges. The Crown or

---

[2] *Dawkins* v. *Lord Rokeby* (1875) LR 7 HL, 744, 753; *Darker* v. *Chief Constable of the West Midlands* [2001] 1 AC 435, 445H–446B [Lord Hope]; *Arthur J S Hall* v. *Simons* [2002] 1 AC 615, 740 G–H [Lord Hobhouse], 679B–C [Lord Steyn], 697B–698H [Lord Hoffmann].

[3] *Garnett* v. *Ferrand* (1827) 6 B & C 611, 625 [Lord Tenterden CJ], adopted by the Court of Appeal in *Sirros* v. *Moore* [1975] QB 118, 132 [Lord Denning MR]; *Arthur JS Hall & Co* v. *Simons* [2002] 1 AC 615.

[4] *Floyd* v. *Barker* (1607) 77 ER 1305.

[5] *Munster* v. *Lamb* (1883) 11 QBD 588, 607 [Fry LJ]. The general principles of liability apply when a judge commits a wrong outside his judicial capacity.

[6] *Floyd* v. *Barker* (1607) 77 ER 1305, 1306; *Taafe* v. *Downes* (1813) 13 ER 15, 20; *Fray* v. *Blackburn* (1863) 122 ER; *Anderson* v. *Gorrie* [1895] 1 QB 668; *Groenvelt* v. *Burwell* (1700) 91 ER 1202, 343, 344 [Holt CJ]; *Haggart's Trustees* v. *Lord President* (1824) 2 Shaws Rep. 125; *Tughan* v. *Craig* [1918] 2 IR 245.

the state[7] assumes primary liability, however, in relation to violation of European Union law and certain provisions of the Human Rights Act 1998 (HRA). Under European Union law, the principle of state liability for breach of European Union law applies to judicial wrongs committed in the exercise of judicial duties. Primary state liability also applies for judicial acts in relation to infringement of the rules laid down in Article 5 of the European Convention on Human Rights (ECHR) (relating to deprivation of liberty) and Article 6 ECHR relating to the guarantees of a fair hearing *in procedendo*. Once the judicial immunity is defeated, general principles apply and the judge is personally liable for the tort committed.

We first discuss judicial immunity and disciplinary proceedings, before considering the mechanisms for removal for the senior courts, available at present and in the past. These include impeachment, *scire facias*, criminal information or criminal prosecution and the address for removal. We focus on the parliamentary power of removal from office. The actual operation of the address to Parliament in the nineteenth century and at the beginning of the twenty-first century shows that Parliament gradually elaborated the sufficient grounds for removal – a high degree of misconduct only – and the constitutional process of disposing of the complaints against judicial conduct. This power remains a necessary mechanism of judicial accountability.

I.   Judicial immunity

7.2 The justifications for and scope of judicial immunity at common law and under statutory law must be examined. The status of the judges also affects the level of protection: a senior judge,[8] such as a judge of the High Court, is protected even though the judge has exceeded his jurisdiction

---

[7] Though references to the Crown can be to the monarch, that term is used here in the broad sense of the apparatus of central government, with the judicature being a unit of that apparatus, see W. Holdsworth, 'Constitutional Position of the Judges' (1932) 48 LQR 25 26–8. With this understanding in mind, the Crown has legal personality and the acts of judges constitute an exercise of the judicial power of the state which can justify the finding of primary liability in the case of judicial wrongs, see Lord Diplock in *Chokolingo* v. *A.-G. of Trinidad and Tobago* [1981] 1 WLR 106, 107.

[8] A 'senior judge' means any of the following, under CRA, s. 109 (5): Master of the Rolls; President of the Queen's Bench Division; President of the Family Division; Chancellor of the High Court; Senior President of Tribunals; Lord Justice of Appeal; puisne judge of the High Court.

provided that the judge has acted judicially and in good faith. Lack of jurisdiction *and* bad faith – the judge knowingly acted outside of jurisdiction – is required for the immunity of superior courts to be waived. Contrary to the position adopted in the United States, the absence of jurisdiction is not enough for the immunity to be waived. By comparison, a judge from a lower court, such as circuit and district courts, who exceeds the court's jurisdiction, is not protected unless the exercise of jurisdiction was caused by an error of fact in circumstances where the court had no knowledge of or means of knowing the relevant facts. Bad faith is not required for the immunity of inferior courts to be lost.[9]

A. The scope of judicial immunity

7.3 Judicial immunity is 'absolute' in the sense that an action against a judge cannot proceed and must be struck out at its outset.[10] Thus judges do not owe a contractual duty or a tortious duty of care to litigants in their courts.[11] The rule has wide application to claims of all sorts[12] but judicial immunity only arises in respect of judicial proceedings. Whether a body may be considered as 'judicial' for the purpose of granting absolute immunity to those involved in its proceedings is a matter of determining the body's similarity or equivalence in function and procedures to those of a court of law.[13] The court will have regard to whether the tribunal is recognised by law, whether the nature of the question is akin to that of a civil or criminal question in the courts, whether the body's procedures are akin to those in civil or criminal courts, and whether the outcome of its procedures leads to a binding determination of the civil rights of a party.[14] The weight given to the various components of similarity is a matter of fact and degree, an exercise in balancing

---

[9] *Re McC (A Minor)* [1985] AC 528.

[10] *Bottomley* v. *Brougham* [1908] 1 KB 584, 587 [Channel J]; *Marrinan* v. *Vibart* [1963] 1 QB 528; *Roy* v. *Prior* [1971] AC 470; *Heath* v. *Metropolitan Police Commissioner* [2004] EWCA 943, 17.

[11] *Sirros* v. *Moore*; *Arenson* v. *Arenson* [1977] AC 405, 431–2 [Lord Kilbrandon].

[12] *Munster* v. *Lamb* (1883) 11 QBD 588, 607–8 [Fry LJ]; *Marrinan* v. *Vibart* [1963] 1 QB 502, 535 [Sellers LJ] and 538–9 [Diplock LJ].

[13] *Royal Aquarium and Summer and Winter Garden Society Ltd* v. *Parkinson* [1892] 1 QB 431, 442 [Lord Esher]; *Quinland* v. *Governor of Swaleside Prison* [2002] EWCA Civ 174.

[14] *Trapp* v. *Mackie* [1979] 1 WLR 377; *O'Connor* v. *Waldron* [1935] AC 76, 81 [Lord Atkin]; *Heath* v. *Metropolitan Police Commissioner* [2004] EWCA Civ 943, 21–2 [Auld LJ].

competing public policies against one another.[15] Thus, absolute immunity is enjoyed not only by judges but also by 'quasi-judicial officers' or officials performing 'quasi-judicial' functions, such as arbitrators,[16] jurors,[17] prosecuting attorneys,[18] a Police Disciplinary Board,[19] prison Visitors,[20] coroners,[21] military tribunals[22] and the participants in a disciplinary tribunal.[23] Justices of the Peace (and their clerks) enjoy immunity for acts or omissions committed within their jurisdiction in execution of their offices,[24] and for acts outside their jurisdiction unless it is proved that they acted in bad faith.[25]

Judicial immunity extends to defamatory words spoken by judges and other judicial officers.[26] In this respect, inferior courts enjoy the same immunity as superior courts.[27] The immunity extends to judicial acts undertaken by officers of the courts but not to administrative acts by Her Majesty's Courts and Tribunals Service (HMCTS). The extension of the absolute immunity rule must be necessary for the administration of justice and any decision in that respect must have regard to the cases in which immunity has been held necessary in the past, so as to form part of a coherent principle.[28]

7.4 As noted above,[29] at common law the degree of judicial immunity varies with the status of the judge. The variation between a 'superior' (now 'senior') and 'inferior' court, has been justified by the jurisdiction of

---

[15] *Trapp v. Mackie* [1979] 1 WLR 377; *Heath v. Metropolitan Police Commissioner* [2004] EWCA 943, para. 22 [Auld LJ]; *Minister of National Revenue v. Coopers and Lybrand* [1979] 1 SCR 495, 504 [Dickson J]; cf. the common Australian test, (a) whether the function is one of a kind normally performed by a judge and (b) whether there is an expectation that the function will be performed by a judge in his or her capacity as a judge, *Yeldham v. Rajski* (1989) 18 NSWLR 48, 61.

[16] *Sutcliffe v. Thackrah* [1974] AC 727; *Arenson v. Casson* [1975] 3 WLR 815; *Stevenson v. Watson* [1879] 4 CPD 148; *R v. Mirza* [2004] 1 AC 1118, para. 6 [Lord Steyn].

[17] *Stowball v. Ansell* 90 ER 377; (1689) Comb. 116; *Floyd v. Barker* (1607) 77 ER 1305; *Sutton v. Johnstone* (1786) 99 ER 1215.

[18] *Hester v. McDonald* [1961] SC 370.

[19] *Heath v. Metropolitan Police Commissioner*; *Bretherton v. Kaye & Winneke* [1971] VR 111.

[20] *O'Reilly v. Mackman* [1982] 3 WLR 604.

[21] *Garnett v. Ferrand* (1827) 6 B & C 611, 625; P. Matthews, 'Costs Against Coroners: an Issue of Principle' [1995] PL 526.

[22] *Dawkins v. Lord Rokeby* [1873] LR 8 QB 255.   [23] *Addis v. Crocker* [1961] 1 QB 11.

[24] Courts Act 2003, s. 31.   [25] Courts Act 2003, s. 33.

[26] *R v. Skinner* (1772) 98 ER 529, 530 [Lord Mansfield].

[27] *Thomson v. Sheriff Kenneth Ross and others* [2000] Scot CS 202.

[28] *Taylor v. Director of the Serious Fraud Office* [1991] 2 AC 177, 21D–E [Lord Hoffmann]; *Mann v. O'Neill* (1997) 71 ALJR 903, 907 [Brennan CJ, Dawson, Toohey and Gaudron JJ].

[29] Para. 7.2.

these courts: a superior court's jurisdiction is not limited by either person, place or subject matter; as a result, it can make a conclusive determination of whether a matter came within its jurisdiction or did not.[30] The distinction is unconvincing, however, and it was rejected as such by the Court of Appeal in *Sirros* v. *Moore*,[31] where an action for damages was brought against a circuit judge. In the words of Lord Denning MR:

> Every judge of the courts of this land – from the highest to the lowest – should be protected to the same degree, and liable to the same degree. If the reason underlying this immunity is to ensure 'that they may be free in thought and independent in judgment', it applies to every judge, whatever his rank ... Each should be able to do his work in complete independence and free from fear. He should not have to turn the pages of his books with trembling fingers, asking himself: 'If I do this, shall I be liable in damages?' So long as he does his work in the honest belief that it is within his jurisdiction, then he is not liable to an action.[32]

Nevertheless, Lord Bridge suggested that the distinction between senior and inferior courts in respect of judicial immunity was 'so deeply rooted in our law that it certainly cannot be eradicated by the Court of Appeal and probably not by your Lordships' House' since 'so fundamental a change would ... require appropriate legislation'.[33] The Supreme Court of Canada has expressed a similar view.[34] By contrast, the New Zealand Court of Appeal has treated *Sirros* v. *Moore* as stating the common law of New Zealand.[35] While it may be desirable that judges at all levels should be granted the same protection from civil liability, the difference in liability between courts still survives and should be addressed by the legislature.[36]

Further, the extent of protection enjoyed by judges at all levels is disputed.[37] At common law, the holder of a judicial office in a lower court who acts in bad faith, doing what he knows he has no power to do,

---

[30] *Sirros* v. *Moore* [1975] QB 118, 138; *Re McC (A minor)* [1985] AC 528, 541 [Lord Bridge].

[31] *Sirros* v. *Moore* [1975] QB 118.   [32] *Ibid.*, 136.

[33] *Re McC (A Minor)* [1985] AC 528, 550; *Maharaj* v. *A.-G. of Trinidad and Tobago (No. 2)* [1979] AC 385 (PC), 409 [Lord Hailsham].

[34] *Morier* v. *Rivard* [1985] 2 SCR 716.

[35] *Nakhla* v. *McCarthy* [1978] 1 NZLR 291; *Moll* v. *Butler* (1985) 4 NSWLR 231; *Rajski* v. *Powell* (1987) 11 NSWLR 522.

[36] *Re Mc (A Minor)* [1985] AC 528, 558–9 [Lord Templeman]; Pannick, *Judges*; C. Gearty, 'Personal Liability of Justices' (1987) 46 CLJ 12, 14.

[37] *Sirros* v. *Moore* [1975] QB 118, 132, 135, 140–1, 150.

is liable in damages.[38] Judicial immunity only extends to judicial activities carried out 'in the honest belief that it is within [the judge's] jurisdiction'.[39] The majority in *Sirros* v. *Moore* considered that all judges should be absolutely immune from personal civil liability in respect of judicial acts done in the bona fide exercise of their office as a judge of that court, within the limits of their jurisdiction. Judicial immunity thus applies where the judge: (i) acts in the bona fide exercise of his office and (ii) in the belief (though mistaken) that he has jurisdiction.

Justices of the Peace were already liable in damages under the Justices Protection Act 1848, presumably for the tort of misfeasance in public office. The Courts Act 2003 preserves the immunity of justices for acts or omissions in the execution of their judicial duties with respect to any matters within their jurisdiction.[40] Actions can lie against a justice in respect of acts or omissions in the purported exercise of his judicial duty, with respect to matters not within his jurisdiction, if it is proved that the justice acted in bad faith.[41]

7.5 An allegation of judicial misconduct by a dissatisfied litigant is often, perhaps even typically, accompanied by an accusation of malice or want of good faith in the exercise of judicial authority. The justices' exception apart, the rule of absolute immunity for judicial acts within jurisdiction, even when the judge acts maliciously, was upheld by Lord Bridge:

> [I] one judge in a thousand acts dishonestly within his jurisdiction to the detriment of a party before him, it is less harmful to the health of society to leave that party without a remedy than that nine hundred and ninety nine honest judges should be harassed by vexatious litigation alleging malice in the exercise of their proper jurisdiction.[42]

Sirros v. *Moore* thus extended the protection of inferior courts to suits alleging malice, yet one may question the high degree of immunity

---

[38] *Marshalsea Case* (1613) 10 Co. Rep. 68b; *Re McC (A Minor)* [1975] QB 118, para. 541 [Lord Bridge]; Cf. *Harvey* v. *Derrick* [1995] 1 NZLR 314, 321 and 326, reversed by the Summary Proceedings Amendment Act (No. 2) 1995, amending s. 193(1) of the Summary Proceedings Act 1957. For the law on senior judges before *Sirros* v. *Moore*, see *Hammond* v. *Howell* (1674) 86 ER 1035, 1037; *Taafe* v. *Downes* (1813) 13 ER 15 at 22; *Mostyn* v. *Fabrigas* (1774) 98 ER 1021; A.A. Olowofoyeku, *Suing Judges: A Study of Judicial Immunity* (Oxford: Clarendon Press, 1993), pp. 20–1.

[39] *Sirros* v. *Moore* [1975] QB 118, 136.

[40] Courts Act 2003, ss. 31–35. This applies to the Justice's clerk or assistant clerk too.

[41] Courts Act 2003, ss. 32 and 35.

[42] *Re McC (A minor)* [1985] AC 528, 541 [Lord Bridge]; *Anderson* v. *Gorrie* [1895] 1 QB 668, 670 [Lord Esher]; cf. *Northern Territory of Australia* v. *Mengel* (1996) 185 CLR 307.

enjoyed by a judge who acts with malice.[43] It is difficult to defend the idea that a man who has an arguable case that a judge has acted corruptly or maliciously to his detriment, should have no cause of action against the judge.[44] A lesser degree of judicial immunity, allowing for the rule that judges who act maliciously or intend to cause harm to a litigant are deprived from judicial immunity, may not affect the free thought or independent judgment of the judiciary.[45] It seems unlikely, however, that the HRA would provide an individual wronged by a judge with a successful challenge of that degree of protection, at least when judges act within their jurisdiction. Judicial immunity has been recognised in some form since 1687 in England,[46] and the European Court of Human Rights appears reluctant to create a substantive civil right that has no basis in domestic law.[47] In addition, the Court has held that the scope of Article 6(1) ECHR includes laws that impose a procedural bar but not laws which extinguish a substantive right,[48] which is what judicial immunity does. If, notwithstanding these two observations, the rule of judicial immunity was said to fall under the scope of Article 6(1) ECHR, then it is open to debate whether judicial immunity in case of malice would be a justified limitation to the right to a fair trial: the relationship of proportionality between the means employed and the aim sought to be achieved, a proper administration of justice, does not seem reasonable.[49]

B.   State liability

7.6 The Crown Proceedings Act 1947 waived the Crown immunity from liability but section 2(5) of the Crown Proceedings Act 1947 underpins the common law immunity of judges by providing that no action can be brought against the Crown in respect of acts or omissions of persons by

---

[43] *Miller* v. *Seare* (1773) 96 ER 673, 674–5 [De Grey CJ]; A. Olowofoyeku, *Suing Judges*, 64.

[44] Pannick, *Judges*, 99.

[45] A. Nicol, 'Judicial Immunity and Human Rights' (2006) 5 EHRLR 558, 563–4; Olowo-foyeku, *Suing Judges*, ch. 7.

[46] *Green and the Hundred of Buccle-Churches* 74 ER 294 (1 Leo. 323), cited by Olowofoyeku, *Suing Judges*, 9–15.

[47] *R (Kehoe)* v. *Secretary of State for Work and Pensions* [2005] UKHL 48; *Matthews* v. *Ministry of Defence* [2003] UKHL 4; *James* v. *UK* (1986) 8 EHRR 123, para. 81; *H* v. *Belgium* (1987) 10 EHRR 339; *Fogarty* v. *UK* (2001) 12 BHRC 132, para. 25; *Pinder* v. *UK* (1985) 7 EHRR 464, para. 5.

[48] *Matthews* v. *Ministry of Defence* [2003] UKHL 4; *James* v. *UK* (1986) 8 EHRR 123, para. 81.

[49] *A* v. *UK* (2003) 36 EHRR 51, para. 77.

any person while discharging or purporting to discharge any responsibility of a judicial nature. One may wonder about the extent to which section 2(5) of the Crown Proceedings Act is compatible with the principle of primary state liability for judicial acts in relation to infringement of the rules laid down in Article 5 ECHR (relating to deprivation of liberty) and Article 6 ECHR relating to the guarantees of a fair hearing *in procedendo.*[50] In addition, in practice, some specific statutes provide for compensation to litigants who have incurred costs as a result of judicial errors.[51] Moreover, section 2(5) has to be disapplied under European Community law where the principle of state liability for breach of European Union law applies to judicial wrongs committed in the exercise of judicial duties. Once the judicial immunity is defeated, general principles apply and the judge is personally liable for the tort committed.

7.7 The immunity granted by the common law to judges is, arguably, preserved in effect by the European Court of Human Rights, at the very least with regard to acts done within jurisdiction.[52] Under section 6(1) HRA, it is unlawful for a public authority, including a court or tribunal, to act in a way which is incompatible with a Convention right. Under section 7(1) HRA, a person who claims that a public authority has acted in such an unlawful manner may bring proceedings against the authority if he is a victim of the unlawful act. Damages may be awarded for the violation of a Convention right pursuant to section 8 HRA where this is necessary to afford just satisfaction, subject to section 9 HRA.[53]

Under section 9(1) HRA, proceedings can only be brought in respect of a judicial act by exercising a right of appeal, by an application for judicial review, or in such other form as may be prescribed by rules. Section 9(3) HRA provides that damages may not be awarded in respect

---

[50] That is, while the judgment is being prepared; it does not apply to the guarantees *in iudicando,* that is those relating to the content of the judgment itself, see Opinion of Advocate General Léger in Case C-224/01 *Gerhard Köbler* v. *Republik Österreich* [2003] ECR I-10239, paras. 77–82; *Dulaurans* v. *France* (2001) 33 EHRR 45; *Kingsley* v. *UK* (2002) 35 EHRR 10.

[51] Criminal Justice Act 1988, s. 133 allows for financial redress from the state for miscarriage of justice. Until 2006 an ex gratia compensation scheme provided compensation at the discretion of the Home Secretary in 'exceptional cases', where 'there had been some misconduct or negligence on the part of the police or some other public authority', see *Hansard* HC, vol. 916, col. 330, 29 July 1976.

[52] *FM* v. *Sir Jan Peter Singer and others* [2004] EWHC 793, para. 37; *Hinds* v. *Liverpool County Court and others* [2008] EWHC 665, para. 18.

[53] HRA s. 8(1) provides that the court may 'grant such relief or remedy, or make such order, within its jurisdiction, as it considers just and appropriate'.

of a judicial act done in good faith otherwise than to compensate a person to the extent required by Article 5(5) ECHR, which concerns the right to liberty or security of the person.[54] Section 9(4) HRA states that any such award of damages is to be made against the Crown. The HRA has thus given the Crown, in the form of a 'public authority', primary liability for infringing certain rights.[55] Under section 9(3) HRA, the presence of good faith means that, unless Article 5(5) ECHR is engaged, no claim in damages lies when a judicial act is found to be in violation of a Convention right. The common law judicial immunity does not seem altered. Nonetheless, the principle of state liability under the HRA has given renewed impetus to the emphasis on speed and timeliness of the judicial process.[56]

When the judge cannot be shown to have acted in bad faith in a civil case, a claimant may still be able to recover some damages under Article 41 (formerly 50) ECHR, which entitles the European Court to order a state to afford just satisfaction to the injured party where the domestic laws of his/her country do not allow full reparation for the infringement of a Convention right, even where that infringement stems from a national court adjudicating at last instance. This provision is narrowly applied in cases where Article 6(1) ECHR has been contravened.[57]

Damages against the state under the HRA appear essentially vindicatory in character,[58] as they are under constitutional instruments in certain states of the Commonwealth, where the right to such remedy remains exceptional.[59]

---

[54] Art. 5(5) ECHR provides that everyone who has been the victim of arrest or detention in contravention of the provisions of this article [the right to liberty and security of person] shall have an enforceable right to compensation.

[55] *Chagos Islanders* v. *The Attorney General, Her Majesty's British Indian Ocean Territory Commissioner* [2004] EWCA Civ 997, para. 20 [Sedley LJ].

[56] See above, para. 3.42.

[57] A.A. Olowofoyeku, 'State Liability for the Exercise of Judicial Power' [1998] PL 444, 460–1; Law Commission, 'Damages under the Human Rights Act 1998', Law Com No. 266; *Anufrijeva* v. *Southwark London Borough Council* [2003] EWCA Civ 1406; *R (Greenfeld)* v. *Secretary of State for the Home Department* [2005] UKHL 14.

[58] *Attorney General of Trinidad and Tobago* v. *Romanoop* [2005] UKPC 15, 18–19 [Lord Nicholls]; *Simpson* v. *Attorney General (Baigent's Case)* [1994] 3 NZLR 667, 678 [Cooke P]; J. Beatson et al., *Human Rights: Judicial Protection in the United Kingdom* (London: Sweet & Maxwell, 2008), paras. 7-169–72.

[59] *Maharaj* v. *Attorney General of Trinidad and Tobago (No. 2)* [1979] AC 385; on exemplary damages, see *Takitota* v. *Attorney General* [2009] UKPC 11; see generally *Harrikissoon* v. *Attorney General of Trinidad and Tobago* [1980] AC 265, 268; *Chokolingo* v. *Attorney General* [1981] 1 WLR 106; *Attorney General of Trinidad and Tobago* v.

7.8 The primary liability of the state has also been established for judicial acts in violation of European Union law: when European Union law applies, no member state is immune from liability to compensate for a judicial wrong in the purported performance of a judicial function. This was set in *Köbler*,[60] where the question was whether the principle of state liability could apply in respect of a supreme court's judgment. The European Court of Justice (now the Court of Justice of the European Union) found a breach of European Community law on the basis that the Austrian Administrative Supreme Court ought to have maintained its request for a preliminary ruling from the European Court (instead of considering the point of law resolved by the settled case law of the European Court), and reached the wrong conclusion as to the application of European Community law in the case of Mr Köbler.[61] The infringement of European Community law, however, was not manifest as to give rise to state liability because the European Community legislation or the Court of Justice case law did not expressly cover the point in dispute; nor was the correct answer obvious.[62] Three conditions must thus be satisfied for liability to arise under *Köbler*: (i) the alleged breach of Community law must be of a rule conferring rights on individuals, (ii) the breach must be 'sufficiently serious' and (iii) there must be a direct causal link between the breach and the loss or damage sustained by the claimant.

The effective protection of the rights which individuals derive from European Union law has been a key concern for the Court of Justice.[63] For the Court, in international law, a state which incurs liability for breach of an international commitment must be viewed as a single entity, irrespective of whether that breach is attributable to the legislature, the judiciary or the executive.[64] A fortiori, in the European legal order where all state authorities are bound to comply with European Union law, which directly governs the situations of individuals, state liability for

---

McLeod [1984] 1 WLR 522, 530; *Hinds* v. *Attorney General of Barbados* [2001] UKPC 56, para. 24 [Lord Bingham]; *Jaroo* v. *Attorney General of Trinidad and Tobago* [2002] UKPC 5.

[60] Case C-224/01 *Köbler* v. *Republik Österreich* [2003] ECR 1-10239, para. 33; Case C-173/03 *Traghetti del Mediterraneo SpA* v. *Repubblica Italiana* [2006] ECR I-5177; cf. *Gestas*, 18 June 2008 (no. 295831), Conseil d'Etat.

[61] Case C-224/01 *Köbler* v. *Republik Österreich* [2003] ECR 1-10239, paras. 117–19.

[62] *Ibid.*, 120–4.

[63] Joined cases C-46/93 and C-48/93 *Brasserie du Pêcheur SA* v. *Federal Republic of Germany, R* v. *Secretary of State for Transport ex parte Factortame Ltd and others* [1996] IRLR 267, para. 42.

[64] Case C-224/01 *Köbler* v. *Republik Österreich* [2003] ECR 1-10239, para. 32.

breach of European Union law arises irrespective of the source of that breach.[65] It also follows that section 2(5) of the Crown Proceedings Act 1947 would have to be disapplied pursuant to the principle of supremacy of European law if, before a domestic court, a claim in damages arises from a judicial act which has resulted in an infringement of Community law.[66]

Against the principle of state liability for judicial acts in violation of European Community law, it was submitted in particular that allowing damages claims in respect of supreme court decisions would undermine the principles of legal certainty and *res judicata*, by encouraging re-litigation of judicial decisions. In response, the Court of Justice emphasised that

> regard must be had to the specific nature of the judicial function and to the legitimate requirements of legal certainty ... State liability for an infringement of Community law by a decision of a national court can be incurred only in the exceptional case where the court has manifestly infringed the applicable law.[67]

In *Cooper v. HM Attorney General*,[68] the first English case considering this form of liability, Lady Justice Arden similarly pointed out that there was no member state liability 'simply because the national court arrives at the wrong answer', because 'regard is [required to be] had to the specific nature of the judicial function'.[69]

It was further argued in *Köbler* that the judicial authority and reputation of judges would be diminished if a judicial mistake could result in state liability for judicial acts; acceptance of state liability for judicial acts would be likely to give rise to the risk that judicial independence might be called into question.[70] The Court of Justice, however, considered that the

---

[65] Breach by the state of obligations imposed upon it by European Union law are generally regarded as actions in the tort of breach of statutory duty.

[66] Case 6/64 *Flaminio Costa v. ENEL* [1964] ECR 585; Case 11/70, *Internationale Handelsgesellschaft mbH v. Einfuhr- und Vorratsstelle für Getreide und Futtermittel* [1970] ECR 1125; Case 106/77 *Amminstrazione delle Finanze dello Stato v. Simmenthal* [1978] ECR 629; Case C-213/89, *R v. Secretary of State for Transport, ex parte Factortame Ltd and Others* [1990] ECRI-2433; *R v. Secretary of State for Transport, ex parte Factortame Ltd* [1990] 2 AC 85; *R v. Secretary of State for Transport, ex parte Factortame Ltd (No. 2)* [1991] 1 AC 603; P. Craig, 'Sovereignty of the United Kingdom Parliament after Factortame' (1991) 11 YEL 221.

[67] Case C-224/01 *Köbler v. Republik Österreich* [2003] ECR 1-10239, para. 53.

[68] *Cooper v. HM Attorney General* [2010] EWCA Civ 464.

[69] Case C-224/01 *Köbler v. Republik Österreich* [2003] ECR 1-10239, para. 70.

[70] *Ibid.*, 27–8.

principle under discussion did not concern the personal liability of the judge, but that of the state,[71] so that judicial independence was not under threat. Besides, the existence of a right to damages to compensate for losses caused by an erroneous judicial decision 'could also be regarded as enhancing the quality of a legal system and thus in the long run the authority of the judiciary'.[72] While a manifest judicial error is unlikely in itself to strengthen public confidence, in the long run, the principle of state liability for judicial breaches of European Community law enhances judicial accountability, quality of justice and therefore public confidence too. Further cases have clarified that the principle applies in exceptional cases.[73]

II.   Disciplinary proceedings

7.9 Judicial immunity does not exclude disciplinary proceedings. We discussed in Chapters 5 and 6 what conduct renders a judge liable to disciplinary proceedings. We now focus on the disciplinary process itself and examine by whom and how such proceedings are initiated and determined, and what sanctions are available for misconduct established in disciplinary proceedings. It is imperative that the grounds and procedures for judicial discipline and removal are stated in clear terms.[74] Judicial tenure must be defined before considering disciplinary proceedings for misconduct short of removal, and misconduct leading to removal.

A.   Disposal of complaints

7.10 Before the CRA, the Lord Chancellor informally resolved complaints.[75] Since the Constitutional Settlement, complaints from anyone about the judicial conduct (i.e., other than against decisions in proceedings) are handled by the Office for Judicial Complaints, which makes recommendations for the Lord Chief Justice and the Ministry of Justice to act upon.[76] Following the CRA 2005, and building on the 2004

---

[71] *Ibid.*, 42.   [72] *Ibid.*, 43.

[73] Case C-173/03 *Traghetti del Mediterraneo SpA* v. *Repubblica Italiana* [2006] ECR I-5177.

[74] Mt. Scopus, 5.3.

[75] The process was rarely invoked, see R. Stevens, *The English Judge* (Oxford University Press, 2002), 166.

[76] CRA, ss. 115–117 provide the Lord Chief Justice with the power to make regulations and rules governing disciplinary cases, with the agreement of the Lord Chancellor.

Concordat, the Lord Chief Justice and the Lord Chancellor drew up the Judicial Discipline (Prescribed Procedures) Regulations 2006 which define the procedures regarding the investigation and determination of allegations by any person of misconduct by judicial office holders.[77] The Office of Judicial Complaints was created under these Regulations, as had been anticipated in the Concordat of 2004. It is to this Office that all complaints relating to judicial misconduct must be made. The performance of the Office for Judicial Complaints in responding to, and investigating, complaints is the subject of review by the Ombudsman. The Ombudsman's role, however, is merely to oversee that the Office for Judicial Complaints has followed its 'prescribed procedures', and to investigate any allegation of 'some other maladministration'; and then to 'recommend' appropriate redress where necessary.[78]

7.11 As mentioned earlier,[79] before 1701 judicial tenure was fixed by the Crown. The Act of Settlement 1701 made judges independent of the Crown by providing that in the future judges' commissions would be made during good behaviour – *quam diu se bene gesserint*.[80] At common law the grant of an office during good behaviour created an office for life determinable only by the death of the grantee or upon his breach of good behaviour.[81] The grantee held the office under the condition that 'he shall behave himself well in it',[82] or, in Hawkins' words, that he shall 'execute it diligently and faithfully'.[83] Upon the breach of this condition the grantor was entitled to terminate the office. Acts which constituted a breach of the good behaviour condition were those done in the exercise of official duties.[84] Unjustifiable

---

[77] CRA, s. 115(a); Judicial Discipline (Prescribed Procedures) Regulations 2006 SI 2006/676, as amended by the Judicial Discipline (Prescribed Procedures) (Amendment) Regulations 2008 SI 2008/2098; see the Complaints (Magistrates) Rules 2008; the Judicial Complaints (Tribunals) Rules 2008 – Roles and Responsibilities; the Judicial Complaints (Tribunals) (No. 2) Rules 2008; Guidance for Handling Complaints Against Judicial Office Holders within Tribunals.

[78] CRA, s. 62 and sch. 1.   [79] See above, paras. 2.6 and 2.7.

[80] Cecil, *Tipping the Scales*, 67–89.

[81] E. Coke, *Institutes of the Laws of England* (W. Clarke & Sons, London, last edn, 1824), vol. I, p. 42 a; *Harcourt v. Fox* (1693) 1 Show KB 425, 506, 536; M. Bacon, *New Abridgment of the Law, Offices and Officers (H)*, vol. III, 6th edn (1793) p. 733; J. Chitty, *A Treatise on the Law of the Prerogatives of the Crown; and the Relative Duties and Rights of the Subject* (London: J. Butterworth and Son, 1820).

[82] W. Blackstone, *Commentaries on the Laws of England* (1765), vol. II, book 4, ch. 18.

[83] W. Hawkins, *A Treatise of the Pleas of the Crown*, 6th edn (London: Leach, 1787), ch. 66, p. 310; Chitty, *Prerogatives of the Crown*, 85.

[84] Coke, *Institutes*, vol. IV, 117; T.R.S. Anson, *The Law and Custom of the Constitution*, 3rd edn (Oxford: Clarendon, 1907), vol. I, 222–3.

absence from duty, neglect of duty or refusal to perform the official duties formed grounds for removal from office.[85]

Today, under the Senior Courts Act 1981 and the Tribunals, Courts and Enforcement Act 2007, High Court and Court of Appeal judges as well as the Senior President of Tribunals hold office until retirement age 'during good behaviour'.[86] The tenure of judges during good behaviour also no longer means life tenure but tenure until retirement age (currently seventy). Under section 108 of the CRA, the disposal of complaints (where the facts are established) lies with the Lord Chief Justice and the Lord Chancellor. While High Court judges and above may be reprimanded or suspended, they can only be removed by the Queen if both Houses of Parliament pass a resolution requiring them to go,[87] and no English judge from a senior court has been removed from office under such procedure. The Lord Chancellor retains his powers to remove circuit judges, but since the passing of the CRA, these powers depend upon the new 'prescribed procedures' having been followed. The Lord Chief Justice has a range of lesser powers in relation to 'misconduct' by any member of the judiciary, which he must exercise too after the 'prescribed procedures' are satisfied, and in consultation with the Lord Chancellor. Thus, besides suspension in cases where a person is subject to criminal proceedings, section 108(3) of the CRA provides that 'The Lord Chief Justice may give a judicial office holder formal advice, or a formal warning or reprimand, for disciplinary purposes (but this section does not restrict what he may do informally or for other purposes or where any advice or warning is not addressed to a particular office holder)'. The Lord Chief Justice may also suspend a senior judge from office for any period during which the person is subject to proceedings for an address.[88] Illness or disability provide a distinct power to the Lord Chancellor of vacating the office, in effect requiring the resignation of the occupant.[89]

---

[85] *The Earl of Shrewsbury's Case*, 9 Coke Rep 42a, 50a; Bacon, *New Abridgment of the Law*, (M), 741–3; Hawkins, *Pleas of the Crown*, 310–11; J. Comyns, *A Digest of the Laws of England*, 5th edn (London: J. Butterworth and Son, 1822), pp. 210–11; Chitty, *Prerogatives*, 85–7; Anson, vol. II, 222–3.

[86] Senior Courts Act 1981, s. 11(2); Tribunals, Courts and Enforcement Act 2007, sch. 1, para. 6.

[87] Senior Courts Act 1981, s. 11(3); see, in the case of illness or disability, Senior Courts Act 1981, s. 11(8) and (9).

[88] CRA, ss. 108(6) and 109(3).   [89] Senior Courts Act 1981, s. 11(8) and (9).

Judges below the High Court are formally less secure. The same retirement age applies,[90] but they can be removed by the Lord Chancellor without following the Act of Settlement procedure, pursuant to statutory powers 'on the grounds of incapacity or misbehaviour' in the exercise of their judicial duties.[91] However, since the formal separation of powers between the executive and the judiciary in 2005, no such removal of members of the circuit and district benches may be carried out without the prior agreement of the Lord Chief Justice.[92] This power of removal has been exercised rarely in England and Wales, and for the first time only in 1983, when a judge was caught smuggling whisky from Guernsey into England.

Similarly, members of the Upper Tribunal or First-tier Tribunal may be removed by the Lord Chancellor on the grounds of inability or misbehaviour, but the exercise of the Lord Chancellor's statutory power of removal usually requires the concurrence of the Lord Chief Justice of England and Wales, the Lord President or the Lord Chief Justice of Northern Ireland as appropriate.[93] The Lord Chancellor's power to remove other tribunal judges is set out in legislation.[94] Magistrates are removable by the Lord Chancellor with the agreement of the Lord Chief Justice on the grounds of incapacity or misbehaviour; of a persistent failure to meet such standards of competence as are prescribed by a direction given by the Lord Chancellor; or if he is satisfied that the magistrate is declining or neglecting to take a proper part in the exercise of his functions as a Justice of the Peace.[95]

---

[90] Judicial Pensions and Retirement Act 1993, s. 26.

[91] The Lord Chancellor's power to remove county court judges (now circuit judges) for misbehaviour was introduced in 1846. Today see Courts Act 1971, s. 17(4) for circuit judges and County Courts Act 1984, s. 11(5) for district judges, both as amended by paras. 68 and 164 of sch. 4 to the CRA; CRA, s. 108(1); Courts Act 1971, s. 21(6) concerning recorders; Courts Act 2003, s. 22(5) for district judges (magistrates' courts); Coroners Act 1988, s. 3. Before then, the Lord Chancellor would exercise his power of removal subject to the principles of natural justice, see *Ex parte Ramshay* (1852) 18 QB 174.

[92] Courts Act 1971, s. 17(4) and County Courts Act 1984, s. 11(5), both as amended by paras. 68 and 164 of sch. 4 to the CRA; CRA, s. 108(1).

[93] Appointed and transferred-in judges and other members of the First-tier Tribunal who are appointed on a salaried as opposed to a fee-paid basis may only be removed by the Lord Chancellor on the grounds of inability or misbehaviour, para. 4, Tribunals Courts and Enforcement Act 2007; sch. 7 concerns the Administrative Justice and Tribunals Council.

[94] Employment Tribunals Act 1996, s. 5B.   [95] Courts Act 2003, s. 11.

7.12 At common law a judge holding office at pleasure could be suspended by the Crown. Thus, Sir Edward Coke had been suspended from office before he was finally removed.[96] At common law prior to the Act of Settlement, the Crown could also suspend judges even if they held office during good behaviour.[97] There can be little doubt that the Act of Settlement abolished this prerogative power in respect of judges.[98] The opposite view would be inconsistent with the object of the Act to render the judges independent of the Crown. While, before the CRA, at law a senior judge could not be suspended, in practice a judge would have been expected to take leave of absence pending a criminal trial or proceedings before Parliament for misbehaviour. The same view was expressed in Parliament on several occasions in the course of the debates on motions for an address. This was considered necessary because permitting him 'to dispense justice as a judge of the land as usual with grave accusations hanging over his head'[99] was likely to destroy public confidence in the impartiality of judicial proceedings before him in particular, and of the judicial process in general.

If the judge refused to take leave of absence (or to resign), it was believed that administrative arrangements would be made to ensure that no cases were assigned to his list.[100] Similar arrangements were made if a judge lost his faculties because of old age or illness but still refused to retire. In the 1950s a judge of the High Court lost his faculties, and pressure was put on him by his brethren to retire from the bench. It is

---

[96] E. Foss, *The Judges of England*, 6 vols. (London: Longman, Brown, Green, and Longmans), vol. VI, p. 118.

[97] For the royal prerogative of suspension of officers holding office during good behaviour, see *Slingsby's Case* (1680) 3 Swans 178, 36 ER 821. There are two recorded cases where the Crown exercised this power. In 1630 King Charles I forbade John Walter, the Lord Chief Baron of the Exchequer, to sit in court, in fact suspending him from office. In 1673 another judge holding office during good behaviour, John Archer, a Justice of the Common Pleas, was suspended under similar circumstances. In both cases the judges continued to receive their emoluments and retained their title. Suspension meant that they could not exercise their official functions.

[98] Moreover, the power was not transferred to any other authority.

[99] *Kenrick's Case* (1825) 13 Parl. Deb., 2nd Ser., 1138, 1149; *Kelly's Case* (1867) 185 Parl. Deb., 3rd Ser., 268–9.

[100] This would probably have been done by the Head of the Division (under his general authority to administer his Division and his general responsibility for the orderly running of the cause lists) instructing the clerk not to prepare any list for the particular judge. Thus, in the Queen's Bench Division the Lord Chief Justice would give the Clerk of the Lists instructions to this effect. In the Court of Appeal the judge would have been excluded by the Master of the Rolls from the panels of the court sitting to hear appeals.

said that, upon his failing to respond to the pressure put upon him, no work was assigned to him. Finally he retired.[101]

The practice of suspension is now enshrined in law under the CRA. The Lord Chief Justice may, with the agreement of the Lord Chancellor, suspend a person, including a senior judge, from a judicial office

> for any period during which the following applies: (a) the person is subject to criminal proceedings; (b) the person is serving a sentence imposed in criminal proceedings; (c) the person has been convicted of an offence and is subject to prescribed procedures in relation to the conduct constituting the offence.

He may also suspend a person from a judicial office

> for any period if (a) the person has been convicted of a criminal offence; (b) it has been determined under prescribed procedures that the person should not be removed from office, and (c) it appears to the Lord Chief Justice with the agreement of the Lord Chancellor that the suspension is necessary for maintaining confidence in the judiciary.[102]

A similar practice of suspension as the one described in the previous paragraph applied to Justices of the Peace and is now similarly enshrined in the Constitutional Reform Act 2005.[103]

7.13 The Office for Judicial Complaints mainly administers and processes complaints. It can initially dismiss a complaint on various grounds including that it is untrue, mistaken, misconceived, not adequately particularised, or raises no question of misconduct. But if there is a matter to be investigated, the investigation is carried out by a judge nominated by the Lord Chief Justice, of at least the same rank as the judge under investigation.[104] The defendant judge is invited to reply to the Office for Judicial Complaints' request for information.[105] The investigating judge will then advise the Lord Chancellor and the Lord

---

[101] After the introduction in 1959 of a compulsory retirement age, such cases are less likely to arise, but are not unthinkable. See also Administration of Justice Act 1973, s. 12.

[102] CRA, ss. 108 and 109(3).   [103] CRA, ss. 108–109.

[104] Where a complaint is made against either a tribunal office holder or a magistrate, it is dealt with in the first instance by the relevant Tribunal President or Magistrates' Advisory Committee.

[105] In 2006 new disciplinary procedures introduced the naming of judges whose conduct was the subject of an investigation, see the Judicial Discipline (Prescribed Procedures) Regulations 2006. These regulations have been recently reviewed: Office of Judicial Complaints, 'Evaluation of the Consultation Exercise Following a Review of The Rules and Regulations Governing Judicial Discipline' (September 2012).

Chief Justice whether there needs to be a judicial investigation by a judge.[106] These procedures and decisions may be reviewed by a review body that comprises two judges and two lay members. Almost equally important is its role in educating the public about its processes. To this end, it publishes brief details of all complaints made to it with the outcomes.

The decision was taken in 2009 by the Lord Chancellor and the Lord Chief Justice that the Office of Judicial Conduct should publish the names of the judicial office holders who have been disciplined during the year, apparently as the direct result of pressure exerted by the media in relation to judicial conduct, following a (failed) attempt by a news-paper to have the Ministry of Justice release the names of judges found guilty of misconduct on the basis of the Freedom of Information Act.[107] In practice, however, only findings of a serious offence leading to sus-pension or removal of a judge were publicised by way of press statement. Although the defendant judge is named, the details of the allegations are often rather elliptic, even though (in some cases) the curious reader would be able to discover them with a Google search, and not all findings of misconduct would be publicised.

This half-way house seemed destined for revision. In June 2012, following an internal review, the Lord Chancellor and the Lord Chief Justice decided that, in the interest of improving the openness and transparency of the complaints system, a press statement would normally be made where a formal disciplinary sanction had been imposed upon a judicial office holder (including magistrates) following a finding of mis-conduct, with deletion of the press statements from the website after one year for statements relating to disciplinary sanctions below suspension or removal from office, and deletion after five years for sanctions of suspen-sion or removal from office.[108] The first to have her formal warning from the Lord Chief Justice and the Lord Chancellor publicised under these new rules was an Employment Tribunal judge, whose conduct was found to be below the standard of service expected of a judicial office following complaints concerning a delayed judgment, failure to meet her minimum

---

[106] Alternatively, the nominated judge may advise that disciplinary action should be taken without the need for any further investigation.

[107] Information Tribunal, *Guardian* v. *Ministry of Justice*, EA/2008/0084, 10 June 2009.

[108] Publication of the finding of misconduct may also arise where a judicial office holder requests the Lord Chief Justice and the Lord Chancellor to do so, see the Office for Judicial Complaints Publication Policy.

sitting requirements in 2009 and failure to respond to correspondence from the Employment Tribunal.[109]

7.14 The establishment of a formal judicial complaints mechanism with disciplinary proceedings needs safeguards.[110] Any complaints-handling mechanism must ensure that judges must be protected from pressure not only from the government, but also from the public. Unsubstantiated allegations are part and parcel of many public sector positions, and being the subject of complaint by itself by no means suggests guilt, nor should it be considered stigmatic or considered by the Judicial Appointments Commission at a later date when considering promotions. In practice, the great majority of complaints before the Office for Judicial Complaints relate to dissatisfaction with the case rather than to judicial conduct. It seems inevitable that some of these complaints will inconvenience judges, even if it is clear that the Office for Judicial Complaints will ultimately decide that no question of misconduct is raised.

Most complaints are indeed unsubstantiated. In 2011–12, of the 1,615 complaints received, 79 resulted in disciplinary action, a very low proportion of the judicial office holders, which comprised 3,700 full- and part-time judiciary, about 278,000 magistrates and several thousand tribunal members.[111] Disciplinary action was undertaken against 49 magistrates, 14 tribunal members, 14 judges and 2 coroners, leading to 30 judicial office holders being removed from office, including 19 magistrates, 9 tribunal members and 3 members of the courts judiciary. In 2010–11, 106 cases resulted in disciplinary action, with 29 judicial office holders being removed from office, including 22 magistrates, 6 tribunal members and 1 coroner.[112] In previous years too, the occasions where misconduct required a disciplinary sanction of any kind, are in proportion very low. Moreover, they mainly concern magistrates.

Traditionally, most judges would 'do the decent thing' and resign[113] if the Lord Chancellor remained dissatisfied at the end of their meeting.

---

[109] Statement from the Office for Judicial Complaints, OJC 13/12, 8 June 2012.

[110] Consultative Council of European Judges, 'On the Principles and Rules Governing Judges' Professional Conduct, in Particular Ethics, Incompatible Behaviour and Impartiality'.

[111] Office for Judicial Complaints, 'Annual Report 2011–12', 13 July 2012, p. 5.

[112] *Ibid.*, 7.

[113] J. Bell, *Judiciaries within Europe, A Comparative Review* (Cambridge University Press, 2006), p. 323.

It is still the case that resignations follow conduct investigations – thus in 2011–12 there were fourteen resignations during conduct investigations.

7.15 The scope for judicial review of the removal of lower judges by the Lord Chancellor was also discussed by Lord Campbell CJ in *Ex parte Ramshay*.[114] In that case the court refused an application for a *quo warranto* against the county court judge who had been appointed to succeed the applicant who had been removed from the office for inability and misbehaviour. From the judgment of Lord Campbell CJ it seems that the court would readily intervene if the judge was removed without notice or hearing, but where an inquiry was duly conducted, only in very exceptional cases would the court review the substantive ground for which the judge was removed.

A lower court judge who has been removed by the Lord Chancellor with the agreement of the Lord Chief Justice and who wishes to challenge the validity of his removal would now turn to the Judicial Appointments and Conduct Ombudsman following concerns about how a complaint for judicial misconduct was handled by the relevant disciplinary body, the Office for Judicial Complaints, the Tribunal President,[115] or the Magistrates Advisory Committees. The Ombudsman's role is to review the handling of the case, examining whether there was a failure to follow prescribed procedures or some other maladministration, and to make recommendations for redress. Where the Ombudsman finds that maladministration led to the original decision being unreliable, he can set aside that decision and direct that a new investigation or review be undertaken (in whole or in part). He can also recommend payment of compensation for loss suffered as a result of maladministration.[116] A minority of complaints were partially or fully upheld in 2011–12, pointing to maladministration of the Office of Judicial Complaints in nine cases.[117]

---

[114] *Ex Parte Ramshay* (1852) 18 QB 174.

[115] Or a judicial office holder designated by the President under rule 4(1) of The Judicial Complaints (Tribunals) (No. 2) Rules 2008.

[116] CRA, sch. 13, para. 15(4); Judicial Appointments and Conduct Ombudsman, 'Annual Report 2011–12'.

[117] Judicial Appointments and Conduct Ombudsman, 'Annual Report 2011–12', 15; see e.g., the case study four, where the Ombudsman found that the Office for Judicial Complaints did not conduct a full and adequate investigation, with poor case management and unnecessary delay; in that particular case the Office of Judicial Complaints re-opened its investigation to consider the matters of concern, Judicial Appointments and Conduct Ombudsman, 'Annual Report 2011–12', 20.

B. Misconduct

7.16 In Chapters 5 and 6, we gave illustrations of some issues of judicial conduct, with a focus on impartiality. There is, however, no statutory definition of misbehaviour or misconduct. By their nature, issues of judicial conduct defy neat categorisation[118] and the reasons for disciplinary action will be varied. It is clear that disciplinary proceedings for misconduct are only possible in relation to non-judicial activities. Judges should not be reprimanded for anything they say in court in pursuance of resolving the case. They have an obligation to ask the hard questions and put challenging observations to counsel. Their immunity for what is said in court is designed to seek the truth. However, the boundary lines are inevitably closely drawn. Falling asleep during a trial might clearly constitute 'misconduct' since the activity, whilst done in court, is clearly not done in the purported furtherance of the trial.

In a letter from the Lord Chancellor to the Lord Chief Justice in 1994, drink driving and offences of violence, dishonesty or 'moral turpitude'[119] were said to constitute 'misbehaviour', and so would behaviour which 'could cause offence, particularly on racial or religious grounds, or amounting to sexual harassment'. The Office for Judicial Complaints adds that the use of insulting, racist or sexist language in court or inappropriate behaviour outside the court, such as a judge using his judicial title for personal advantage or preferential treatment, may constitute personal misconduct.[120] Thus, in 2010 the National Secular Society complained that sentencing remarks by Cherie Booth QC (acting as a recorder) suggested that she would have treated a non-religious defendant more harshly. The Office for Judicial Complaints stated that the observations by the former prime minister's wife did not constitute judicial misconduct. She was, however, to be given informal advice from a senior judge about her comments. It seems that comments which are controversial by nature of their substance might only be dealt with informally, as anticipated in section 108(3) CRA 2005.[121]

---

[118] D. Wood, 'Judicial Ethics. A Discussion Paper' (Melbourne: AIJA, 1996), p. 15. For a further account of 'misconduct', see the debates over an address for removal of a judge, para. 7.47. The analysis in paras. 7.15–7.17 relies upon excerpts from S. Turenne, 'Judicial Misconduct and Disciplinary Procedures – a Brave New World' (2012) 23 *European Law Business Review* 107.

[119] See below, para. 7.44.

[120] Office for Judicial Complaints, 'Annual Report for 2009–2010', 11.

[121] Under CRA, s. 108(3), 'The Lord Chief Justice may give a judicial office holder formal advice, or a formal warning or reprimand, for disciplinary purposes (but this section

As regards wholly 'out of court' behaviour, the Office for Judicial Complaints lists the following grounds for taking disciplinary action in practice, without giving further details: inappropriate behaviour or comments (which led to 5 removals in 2011–12), not fulfilling judicial duty (13 removals in 2011–12), misuse of judicial status (2 removals in 2011–12), motoring offences (1 removal in 2011–12), criminal or other court proceedings/convictions (the cause of 9 removals in 2011–12), breach of professional conduct and conflict of interest.[122] Breach of professional conduct would include complaints about a judicial office holder which are being investigated by an external professional body such as the Bar Standards Board, General Medical Council or the Law Society.[123] Breaches of professional standards of conduct may not always equate with misconduct giving rise to disciplinary sanctions, however, and the standards set in the *Guide to Judicial Conduct* are not statutory duties. As noted by the Consultative Council of European Judges,[124] standards of conduct represent best practice which all judges should aim to develop and to which all judges should aspire; breach of these standards may fall short of misconduct giving rise to disciplinary proceedings. The Consultative Council rightly suggests that misconduct must be serious and flagrant, in a way which cannot be posited simply because there has been a failure to observe professional standards set out in guidelines on judicial conduct. In spite of this, it is fair to say that, in most cases, the *Guide to Judicial Conduct* is highly relevant in the assessment of a breach of professional conduct.

Cases concerning sexual conduct are likely to attract prurient interest in the press, yet they may be quite unrelated to how a judge might be expected to approach his judicial work. As an example, a deputy district judge resigned from the bench after his affair with a married woman led her husband to kill the couple's three-year-old daughter. They had met through a contact website on which the judge appeared naked. According to the Office for Judicial Complaints 'it was felt by the Lord Chancellor and Lord Chief Justice, that although the behaviour of the judge occurred in his private life, his actions had bought the judiciary into disrepute'.[125]

---

does not restrict what he may do informally or for other purposes or where any advice or warning is not addressed to a particular office holder).'

[122] Office for Judicial Complaints, 'Annual Report for 2011–2012', 16.

[123] *Ibid.*, 14 and 29.

[124] Opinion no. 3 of the Consultative Council of European Judges, para. 60.

[125] Statement from the Office for Judicial Complaints, OJC 03/08, August 2008.

He was therefore informed that it was proposed to remove him from office and, after he made some representations, which were dismissed, he then resigned from office.

7.17 Where a judge is found to have committed a criminal offence, the Lord Chief Justice or Lord Chancellor would refer him to the Office for Judicial Complaints in order to establish whether it would be appropriate to remove him from office in the circumstances. Thus, the conviction of assault of a deputy High Court judge and a recorder, in June 2011, led to his removal from his judicial positions in November 2011 by the Lord Chancellor and the Lord Chief Justice, for bringing the judiciary into disrepute.[126]

7.18 A leading case on misconduct or incapacity so serious as to warrant removal is the Privy Council's *Hearing on the Report of the Chief Justice of Gibraltar*,[127] following a domestic tribunal hearing which recommended the removal of the Chief Justice. Section 64(2) of the Gibraltar Constitution Order 2006 provides that 'The Chief Justice ... may be removed from office only for inability to discharge the functions of his office (whether arising from infirmity of body or mind or any other cause) or for misbehaviour.' The term 'misbehaviour' needs to be defined with reference to its context; since it is the criterion for removing a judge, an appropriately high level ought to be set.[128] Accordingly, the majority of the Privy Council endorsed the reasoning of Gray J in the Australian case of *Clark* v. *Vanstone*[129] and identified four 'ingredients' in the conduct under review leading to that conduct being characterised as 'misbehaviour' for the purposes of removal from office. The ingredients are (i) whether it affected the ability of the (judge) to carry out the duties and discharge the functions of his office; (ii) whether it affected the perceptions of others as to the (judge's) ability to carry out those duties and discharge those functions; (iii) whether to allow the (judge) to continue in office and to perform his duties would be perceived as inimical to the public interest; (iv) whether the judicial office would be brought into disrepute as a result of that conduct. Thus the first three factors assume a link between the misbehaviour and a reason why the judge would be less effective to continue his duties on account of it. To

---

[126] Statement from the Office for Judicial Complaints, 2 November 2011, OJC 33/11.
[127] Hearing on the Report of the Chief Justice of Gibraltar [2009] UKPC 43.
[128] *Lawrence* v. *Attorney General of Grenada* [2007] UKPC 18, 23; *Clark* v. *Vanstone* (2004) 81 ALD 21, 78.
[129] *Clark* v. *Vanstone* (2004) 81 ALD 21.

some extent these indicators overlap, but the requirement that the judicial office be brought into disrepute adds a judgment of the gravity of the conduct. However, determining all four of them proved difficult in the case of *Gibraltar*.

Lord Philips, Lord Brown, Lord Judge and Lord Clarke, for the majority, thought that some criticism – but not enough to justify removal, either in isolation or cumulatively – could be levelled at the Chief Justice's decisions to say nothing when his wife attacked various members of the executive and the Bar Council. The majority considered that he ought to have actively dissociated himself from these comments to avoid the impression that his wife might be reflecting his own views.[130] Lady Hale, Lord Hope and Lord Rodger, for the minority, saw no such need, because it should not be assumed by the public that two partners to a marriage necessarily hold the same views or that one is speaking for the two of them and not just for herself.[131] This disagreement reflects the difficult nature of the final test above, whether the judicial office would be brought into disrepute: is it the public at large among whom the office should be brought into disrepute to effect removal from office? One additional difficulty in the case of *Gibraltar* was the presence of a lively media, looking for stories of discord, which would have had the potential to have some effect on public opinion. It was therefore preferable that the Chief Justice was not removed on this ground. One may here echo the concerns of the minority on the impact of judicial independence if a judge were to be subject to removal on the basis of social misjudgements, lack of etiquette or even failure to anticipate what the media might be expected to make of such behaviour.

In contrast to 'misbehaviour', 'incapacity' (or 'inability') refers not only to unfitness through illness but also to unfitness through a defect in character.[132] This broad interpretation was supported by Lord Philips in the case of *Gibraltar* on the ground of the public interest.[133] 'Inability' also covers conduct which, though it does not by itself show the judge to be unfit for office, becomes unacceptable because it is persistent, repeated or continues even after it has been brought to the judge's attention. The accumulation of incidents may make the judge unfit for office, on the basis that such blunders could not be accepted in perpetuity.[134] It should

---

[130] Hearing on the Report of the Chief Justice of Gibraltar [2009] UKPC 43, 36.
[131] *Ibid.*, 257.   [132] *Stewart v. Secretary of State for Scotland* 1998 SC (HL) 81.
[133] Hearing on the Report of the Chief Justice of Gibraltar [2009] UKPC 43, 205.
[134] *Ibid.*, 206.

be emphasised that in the case of removal for 'misbehaviour', the ability of the judge to discharge his functions is assessed in relation to the understandable and natural reactions of others to the misbehaviour; in the case of removal for 'inability' stemming from a perceived character flaw, the emphasis is on the judge's own ability to understand the errors of his ways and to reform himself.

The Privy Council thought that it was proper to consider a character flaw as constituting the 'inability', even though it is not an illness and may not directly impair the lawyerly skills of the judge in open court. A wide interpretation of this sort did not threaten judicial independence because the judge is only liable to removal at the behest of more senior judges, who can be expected to be mindful of the needs of judicial independence and thus unlikely to allow too wide an interpretation of the term.[135]

However, the confidence of the majority may have been misplaced. It did consider that a series of incidents which in isolation did not constitute misconduct, in cumulation over a period of years did constitute 'inability' on the part of a judge to discharge his office.[136] But the minority thought that the majority still did not identify the 'cause' of the Chief Justice's inability. It was unclear what, if any, character defect was thought to be identified. Complaints about his inability to 'control' his wife or to dissociate from her conduct could not be said to show a character flaw as such. Similarly a number of outbursts and displays of distrust towards some member of the executive seemed to stem from a desire to preserve judicial independence, which could hardly be said to be a character flaw. Perhaps the 'character flaw' may be defined as a propensity to overreact or to fail to consider the likely public reaction to his conduct, but here too there are difficulties. An overreaction assumes provocation on the part of others, and might not seem to be a serious flaw. The failure to consider public reaction is not a 'regular' flaw of character either, though judges are expected to anticipate media controversies following a judgment, for example.

There seems to be a further misgiving in the case of *Gibraltar*. If one expects to conclude that a judge is 'unable' to adapt his conduct on account of some flaw because he has failed to adapt after having been made aware of it by more senior judges, then applying this test in *Gibraltar* is difficult. It is unclear when the Chief Justice (as the top

---

[135] *Ibid.*, 204–5.   [136] *Ibid.*, 222–9.

judge), was, or even could, ever have been put on notice of the need to adapt his conduct. It might be noted that even the minority in *Gibraltar* thought the Chief Justice should resign, since there were clearly questions over public confidence in him that could never be resolved.[137] They did, however, think it important to hold that the high threshold for removal had not been satisfied, and it is submitted that their joint opinion is the more convincing. It might be added that it is important to resolve complaints quickly, so that an 'acquitted' judge may resume his office. In the case of *Gibraltar*, the length and well-publicised nature of the proceedings made that difficult.

C.   *The role of the Bar Standards Board*

7.19 Upon appointment, a judge remains a member of his Inn, and it is customary to elect as benchers all members of the Inn appointed to a senior judicial office. The question is whether the Bar Standards Board can institute disciplinary proceedings against a judge for misbehaviour in the exercise of his judicial functions, in his private life, or for acts done by him while at the Bar.

The Inns of Court – Lincoln's Inn, Inner Temple, Middle Temple, and Gray's Inn – are voluntary unincorporated societies of lawyers which are independent of the state and of each other, although they act together in matters of legal education, admission of students, call to the Bar, and discipline.[138] Only the Inns can confer the degree of barrister. Each Inn has a governing body composed of benchers (or Masters of the Bench), who alone have the power to fill up vacancies in their number or add to their number. The composition and the administration of disciplinary tribunals is today the responsibility of the Council of the Inns of Court, which represents the four Inns.[139] Statutory responsibility for the

---

[137] Cf. *Wilson v. Attorney-General* [2011] 1 NZLR 399.

[138] Boulton, Conduct and Etiquette at the Bar, 1–3.

[139] Resolution of the Judges dated 26 November 1986. Following the decision in *Re P (A Barrister)* [2005] 1 WLR 3019, the Council of the Inns of Court is responsible for convening all hearings in relation to the regulation of barristers. Judges, since the reign of His Majesty King Edward I, have been responsible for discipline over the Bar, though in practice discipline is carried out by the benchers. This means that the Disciplinary Tribunal panels' decisions are subject to an appeal before a panel nominated by the Lord Chief Justice, comprising, among others, one judge of the High Court or the Court of Appeal. When sitting in this capacity the judges act as 'Visitors', see Code of Conduct of the Bar of England & Wales, 8th edn, Annex M, 'Hearings before the Visitors Rules'. See the Final Report from the Council of the Inns of Court (COIC) Disciplinary Tribunals

disciplinary proceedings overall, however, is vested in the Bar Standards Board, which regulates the Bar.[140]

It may be argued that the position of judges as benchers or members of one Inn is not different from that of other benchers or members. The Bar Standards Board is a voluntary, unincorporated society, governed by its own rules, and its members may proceed against any of its members or benchers, be they leading barristers, judges, law officers, ordinary barristers or students. But the general view, founded upon a well-established practice, is that upon appointment to judicial office, the judge's misconduct falls within the remit of the Office for Judicial Complaints, and this excludes disciplinary proceedings at the Bar. Part-time fee-paid judges, such as deputy district judges or recorders, who remain practising barristers, are however subject to the Code of Conduct of the Bar, and thus liable to disciplinary proceedings initiated by the Bar Standards Board. These are posts where the judge sits for typically fifteen to thirty days a year only, whereas salaried part-time judicial office holders are permanent office holders and are subject to the same terms and conditions as a full-time judicial office holder, including the requirement of giving up legal practice on appointment.

Thus, a QC who sat as a deputy High Court judge and a recorder was convicted of common assault upon his wife. Having then been expelled by his chambers, he was soon afterwards, in 2011, dismissed by the Lord Chief Justice. The matter was referred by the Bar Standards Board to a disciplinary tribunal arranged by the Council of the Inns of Court. The former judge admitted to engaging in conduct which brought the legal profession into disrepute and was suspended in 2012 for three months with the costs of the proceedings to pay.[141] He also expressed his desire to go back to practise at the Bar. The judge from the disciplinary tribunal panel declared that, in the circumstances, he was not to be punished a second time for things he had already been punished for, thus his sentence to a short period of suspension.

The confirmed practice is underpinned by the principle that the body whose reputation may be discredited by the misconduct may initiate

---

and Hearings Review Group, chaired by Desmond Browne QC, 12 July 2012; *Carron Ann Russell* v. *Bar Standards Board* [2012], The Visitors to the Inns of Court, 12 July 2012.

[140] Legal Services Act 2007.

[141] Disciplinary Tribunal, Decision of 27 June 2012; Code of Conduct of the Bar of England & Wales, 301 (iii).

disciplinary proceedings. Thus the Office for Judicial Complaints has competence for a full-time judicial office holder, who would not hold the annual practising certificate required to exercise rights of audience. Both the Office of Judicial Complaints and the Bar Standards Board may instigate an investigation, however, when the individual is both a part-time judge and a part-time barrister. In that case, it is unlikely that serious misconduct would be sanctioned by the Lord Chief Justice and the Lord Chancellor after investigation from the Office for Judicial Complaints without being sanctioned by the Bar Standards Board. Thus, following a conduct investigation into her conviction of driving with excess alcohol in a public place, a recorder resigned from judicial office. The Lord Chancellor and Lord Chief Justice had indicated their intention to remove her from judicial office.[142] She was shortly afterwards fined and reprimanded by a disciplinary tribunal panel arranged by the Council of the Inns of Court.[143]

While we focus on the disciplinary process followed by the Bar Standards Board, other external professional bodies such as the General Medical Council or the Law Society are expected to investigate allegations of misconduct of, respectively, coroners who are also medical practitioners and solicitors.

III.   Judicial mechanisms for the removal of judges

7.20 In this section the judicial mechanisms for removal are discussed. Judicial proceedings in the form of a writ of *scire facias* are theoretically still available to courts to repeal the royal grant of a judicial office. Criminal prosecution used to be another judicial mechanism for removal. Both would be initiated by the executive, but the final decision rests with the courts.

A.   Scire facias

7.21 The royal grant of a judicial office during good behaviour gives tenure, but the absence of good behaviour results in the forfeiture of the tenure of the judicial office and in the judicial office being declared

---

[142] Statement from the Office for Judicial Complaints, OJC 03/12, 2 February 2012.
[143] Disciplinary Tribunal, Decision 24 February 2012; Disbenchment was once possible, see *Manisty* v. *Kenealy* (1876) 24 WR 918.

vacant.[144] The absence of 'good behaviour' would be established in judicial proceedings commenced by the filing of a writ of *scire facias*,[145] and the writ issued would repeal the letters patent by which the judge held his office.[146] The proceedings could be instituted by the Attorney General in the Court of King's Bench or by an aggrieved individual upon the fiat of the Attorney General. It would seem, however, that even with the very limited discretion that the Attorney General had in giving the fiat for *scire facias*, the protection of judges from vexatious actions by dissatisfied litigants was a legitimate ground for refusal, all the more since otherwise judicial immunity from actions for acts done in the exercise of judicial functions would have been rendered an empty formula.

Scire facias has never been employed for removing a superior judge, though it has been used for forfeiture of offices held during good behaviour.[147] It was frequently mentioned in the course of the debates in Parliament on motions for an address as a possible course for removal of judges, and it was sometimes suggested as the proper form of proceedings to be followed for removal of judges.[148] Cases where those

---

[144] See the Opinion of the Law Officers of Victoria delivered in 1864, quoted in A. Todd, *On Parliamentary Government in England: its Origin, Development and Practical Operation* (London: Longmans, Green & Co., 1867–69), vol. II, ch. 2.

[145] A writ of *scire facias* would be available to terminate public offices, including a judicial office, see the Opinion of the English Law Officers (Sir William Atherton and Sir Roundell Palmer) delivered in 1862; Todd, *Parliamentary Government*, 728; Chitty, *Prerogatives*, 87, 331; G.S. Robertson, *The Law and Practice of Civil Proceedings By and Against the Crown and Departments of the Government* (London: Stevens & Sons, 1908), p. 537; C. Viner, *A General Abridgement of Law and Equity*, 2nd edn 30 vols., with 7 vol. Supplement (London: G.G.J. and J. Robinson, 1792–1795), vol. 19; P.H. Short and F.H. Mellor, *Practice on the Crown Side of the Queen's Bench Division of Her Majesty's High Court of Justice, Founded on Corner's Crown Office Practice. Including Appeals from Inferior Courts. With Appendices of Rules and Forms*, 2nd edn (London: Stevens & Haynes, 1908).

[146] *Bynner v. The Queen* (1846) 9 QB 523, 550; *R v. The Eastern Archipelago Co.* (1854) 43 ER 483, 485–6.

[147] Either *scire facias* or *quo warranto* could be employed for effecting forfeiture of office or revocation of grant, see *Lord Bruce's Case* (1728) 2 Strange 819, 93 ER 870; *Peter v. Kendel* (1827) 6 B & C 703, 108 ER 610. For early cases where *scire facias* was employed to repeal patents of offices, see *R v. Toly* (1561) 73 ER 436; *R v. Biage* (1561) 73 ER 436; *R v. Eston* (1562) 73 ER 437. Recorders holding office during good behaviour who had been removed without *scire facias* challenged the removal by an application for *mandamus* to restore them to office, see *R v. Wells* (1767) 98 ER 41; *R v. Bailiffs of Ipswich* (1706) 2 Salkeld 435, 91 ER 378.

[148] *Fox's Case* (1806) 7 Parl. Deb., 751, 767 [Lord Erskine]; *O'Grady's Case* (1823) 9 Parl. Deb., 2nd Ser., 360, 364–5 [Mr Smith]; *Barrington's Case* (1830) 24 Parl. Deb., 2nd Ser., 1075 [Mr Denman]; I.R. Kaufman, 'Chilling Judicial Independence' (1978–1979) 88 YLJ 681, 694–7.

holding office during good behaviour resisted royal attempts to remove them without *scire facias* were cited in Parliament as precedents supporting such suggestion.[149]

A dominant view is that the Crown Proceedings Act 1947 abolished other forms of *scire facias* concerning the recovery of Crown debts on the Revenue side of the Queen's Bench Division, but not the *scire facias* for the purpose of rescinding royal grants from superior judges[150] on the Crown side of the Queen's Bench Division. Thus the absence of *scire facia* proceedings against a superior judge since the end of the sixteenth century cannot preclude the availability of such procedure. Nonetheless, while it is of the essence of the common law that its remedies, even though fallen into disuse, may be revived if they prove again of value, the writ does appear obsolete. It is unlikely that some satisfactory precedents could be found for its use, and it is suggested that it has been superseded by some other procedural remedies such as declaratory relief or an injunction[151] as well as the right to damages against the state in some specific instances.[152]

B.   Criminal prosecution

7.22 At common law, an officer holding office during good behaviour could be removed from office upon criminal conviction for a misdemeanour in the exercise of his official duties, or for an offence which, though unconnected with his official duties, was in itself so infamous as to render him unfit to hold public office or induced the forfeiture of the office.[153] Criminal conviction resulted in the repeal of the patent by which the office was held and entitled the Crown to seize the office

---

[149] 3 Coke Car. Reports 203, 79 ER 778–9; Foss, *Judges of England*, vol. VI, 372; C.H. McIlwain, 'The Tenure of English Judges' (1913) 7 Am Pol Sci Rev 217, pp. 221, 223; see the arguments from Chief Baron Walter, Ld. Raym. T. 217, (1674) 83 ER 113; Foss, *Judges of England*, vol. VII, 52–3.

[150] Crown Proceedings Act 1947 (10 & 11 Geo. 6, c. 44), sch. I, s. 1(3); *Attorney General* v. *Colchester Corporation* [1955] 2 QB 207, 212 and 217; A de Smith, 'The Prerogative Writs' (1951) CLJ 40, 41; G.L. Williams, *Crown Proceedings: an Account of Civil Proceedings by and against the Crown as Affected by the Crown Proceedings Act, 1947* (London: Stevens, 1948), p. 114.

[151] Section 9 of the Administration of Justice (Miscellaneous Provisions) Act 1938 replaced informations in the nature of *quo warranto* by injunctions; the Attorney General could move for an injunction in the High Court to restrain the judge from continuing to act in an office to which he was no longer entitled.

[152] See above, paras. 7.6–7.8.

[153] *Kenrick's Case II* (1826) 14 Parl. Deb. 2nd Ser., 660 [Mr Denman].

without further proceedings in the form of *scire facias*.[154] This and other common law methods of removal were not excluded by the Act of Settlement and, after its passing, judges could be removed upon criminal conviction without an address of both Houses of Parliament.[155]

The power to bring proceedings by criminal information was abolished by the Criminal Law Act 1967. Today, a judge who has been convicted of a criminal offence in his judicial office or of any offence involving moral turpitude which, though unconnected with his office, renders him unfit to hold public office, would be suspended under the CRA, as noted earlier.[156]

While no case has been recorded of superior judges being prosecuted for misdemeanour in office, in the eighteenth and nineteenth centuries, the Court of King's Bench frequently gave leave to aggrieved individuals to file criminal informations against magistrates and sometimes county court judges.[157] Such leave was normally given to prosecute magistrates for gross neglect of duty or for misbehaviour actuated by corrupt or malicious motives. Only one case is recorded in modern times of a superior judge prosecuted for a criminal offence. In 1805 Robert Johnson, one of the judges of the Court of Common Pleas in Ireland, was prosecuted and tried upon an indictment for criminal libel on the Earl of Hardwicke, Lord Lieutenant of Ireland and other high officials.[158] The words complained of were contained in a series of articles published in England under a false name. The publisher was convicted and revealed the name of the contributor. Since the articles were published in England, Mr Justice Johnson became subject to the jurisdiction of the English courts. After long battles on the procedural issues, Mr Justice Johnson was tried upon an indictment in the Court of the King's Bench in London before Lord Ellenborough CJ with three other judges. The contents of the

[154] Comyns, *Laws of England*, vol. V, 215; *Kenrick's Case II* (1826) 14 Parl. Deb. 2nd Ser., 660.

[155] Anson, Law and Custom, part I, 222–3; H. Hallam, *The Constitutional History of England from the Accession of Henry VII to the Death of George II*, 5th edn (London: John Murray, 1846), vol. II, pp. 357–8; F.W. Maitland, *The Constitutional History of England: a Course of Lectures* (Cambridge University Press, 1908), p. 313; *Fox's Case* (1806) 7 Parl. Deb., 761–2 [Lord Grenville].

[156] CRA, ss. 108, 109(3).

[157] For discussion of criminal informations generally, see Short and Mellor, *Practice on the Crown Side*, 151, 398; J. Shortt, *Informations (Criminal and Quo Warranto) Mandamus and Prohibition* (London: W. Clowes & Sons, 1887), p. 24. Against magistrates, see Short and Mellor, *Practice on the Crown Side*, 26–9; 158–9, 398; against county court judges, see *R v. Marshall* (1855) 4 El. & Bl. 475, 119 ER 174.

[158] See (1805) 29 State Trials 81.

articles for which he was prosecuted were summarised by Lord Ellenborough in his summing up to the jury:

> It [the publication] defames the Lord Lieutenant as a man only fit to be a feeder of sheep, states that his head is made up of particles of a ligneous tendency; and then, comparing it with the Trojan Horse, adds that notwithstanding its supposed innocuousness, its hollowness would be soon filled with instruments of mischief. As to the Lord Chancellor of Ireland, it degrades him in terms no less libellous ... It likewise traduces Mr Justice Osborne and states him to have acted corruptly under the influence of Mr Marsden, the Secretary of State, whom it accuses of having washed his stained hands in the very fountain of justice.[159]

The indulgence of Mr Justice Johnson in political controversy and the use of very strong terms were utterly inconsistent with his judicial office and might have justified his removal from the bench. In those days, the jury needed only fifteen minutes to find him guilty of the charges. The judges were spared the duty of passing sentence, for, following a change of government, as the State Trials reporter records, a *nolle prosequi* between conviction and sentence was entered upon this indictment in Trinity term, 1806, by the new Attorney General, Sir Arthur Pigott, 'and Mr Justice Johnson retired from the bench upon a pension for his life'.[160]

IV.   Parliamentary mechanisms for the removal of judges

7.23 Here we detail the procedures of impeachment and address for removal, which have in common a public discussion in Parliament and the fact that Parliament makes the final decision. While impeachment is an archaic procedure of removal, the power of removal by an address to Parliament has not been ousted by the Act of Settlement 1701 and is still valid today. However, unless it can be attributed to improper motives or a 'decay of mental power', a mistake in fact or in law or any error of judgment will not justify removal by Parliament. These matters are rather within the province of the appellate courts.[161] Further, constitutional

---

[159] *Ibid.*, 499.   [160] *Ibid.*, 502.

[161] Thus, in *Ellenborough's Case* (1816), Mr Ponsonby said that 'it was not enough to prove a mistake in point of fact but some gross error which would only be attributed to improper motives and which give reasons to supposed that the badness of heart had contributed to [the perversion of judgment], *Ellenborough's Case* (1816) 34 Parl. Deb., 1st Ser., 104, at 110. Similarly, in *Kenrick's Case*, Mr Secretary Pell said that 'with respect to any misconduct arising from error of judgment and intemperance the House ought to rest satisfied with the adjudication of a court of justice', *Kenrick's Case* (1825) 13 Parl. Deb.,

constraints shape the grounds and procedures for removal by an address. Parliament will not inquire into the conduct of a judge or pass an address for his removal unless he was charged with misconduct involving 'moral turpitude'. This will be illustrated by a survey of the major cases of removal proceedings taken against senior judges.

A. *Impeachment*

7.24 Impeachment is the most solemn form of trial in English law, reserved for trying 'high crimes and misdemeanours' beyond the reach of the ordinary law of the land or which no other authority of the state will prosecute.[162] Impeachment is in fact a trial by the legislature, wherein the Commons are the prosecutors and the Lords, 'exercising at once the functions of a high court of justice and of a jury'[163] return the verdict and impose the sentence. 'Impeachments are reserved for extraordinary crimes and extraordinary offenders but all persons whether peers or commoners may be impeached for any crime whatever.'[164] In general, impeachment was employed against high public officials[165] for the punishment of 'offences of public nature'.[166] The procedure is now considered obsolete.

Impeachment was essentially a political weapon of Parliament in its struggle with the Crown, and no rigid rules may be found as to the grounds sufficient for initiating proceedings. The articles of charge or articles of impeachment employed terms such as 'high crimes and misdemeanours', 'high treason', 'great misdemeanours', 'high misdemeanours', but the acts covered by these terms varied a great deal. They

---

2nd Ser., 1138, at 1375; in *Torrens' Case*, it was denied that 'because a judge had made a mistake or because there had been a failure of justice, the House was entitled to examine as an appellate tribunal into the conduct of a judge against whom no corruption or misconduct was charged', *Torrens' Case* (1856) 140 Parl. Deb, 3rd Ser., 1544, at 1558. By analogy, Parliament will not interfere with matters of court practice and procedure, such matters also being left to the courts, see *Ellenborough's Case* (1816) 34 Parl. Deb., 1st Ser., 104, at 122 and 207; *McClelland's Case* (1819) 40 Parl. Deb., 1st Ser., 851; *Best's Case* (1821) 4 Parl. Deb., New Ser., 918.

[162] Erskine May, *Parliamentary Practice*, 8th edn (1879), 681.

[163] Erskine May, *Parliamentary Practice*, 7th edn (1964), 39.

[164] Erskine May, *Parliamentary Practice*, 8th edn (1879), 681.

[165] See Holdsworth, *History*, vol. I, 380–2.

[166] See Mr Serjeant Pengelly's Speech, *Trial of the Earl of* Macclesfield, T.B. Howell, A Complete Collection of State Trials (London: Hansard, Bagshaw, 1809–16), vol. XVI; Howell's State Trials (1725), 1330.

included official misconduct such as neglect of duty, abuse of power, oppression of rights, or misapplication of funds. They also included acts which Parliament deemed an encroachment upon its prerogatives, bribery and corruption, and subversive activities, such as treason.[167] There had been some doubt whether a commoner could be impeached for any capital offence,[168] but it was later settled that the Commons have the undoubted right 'to impeach before the Lords, any Peer or Commoner for Treason, or any other crime or misdemeanour'.[169]

The Crown cannot affect impeachment proceedings by exercise of its power of prorogation, which terminates sessions of Parliament, or dissolution, which brings to an end the very existence of a Parliament.[170] Nor may the Crown grant a pardon to the person accused.[171] But while a pardon is not pleadable against an impeachment, after the Lords have pronounced their verdict and imposed the sentence, the Crown may commute the sentences or grant a full pardon.[172]

Impeachment has not been resorted to since 1805.[173] The Select Committee of the House of Commons on Parliamentary Privilege has twice proposed that impeachment should be abolished by legislation.[174] The Joint Committee on Parliamentary Privilege has also recently stated that 'the circumstances in which impeachment has taken place are now so remote from the present that that the procedure may be considered obsolete'.[175]

---

[167] For cases of impeachment. see generally J. Hatsell, *Precedents of Proceedings in the House of Commons, with Observations* (London: Printed for L. Hansard and Sons, 1818), particularly the list of cases in vol. IV, 105–7, and Appendix 10 at 423–8. For the meaning of the term 'high crimes and misdemeanours', see R. Berger, 'Impeachment for "High Crimes and Misdemeanors"' (1971) 44 *Southern California Law Review* 395, 400–15.

[168] Blackstone, *Commentaries*, vol. IV, 259. For discussion of this point, see Erskine May, *Parliamentary Practice*, 8th edn (1879), 681–3; Hatsell, *Precedents*, vol. IV, 83–4.

[169] So resolved the House of Commons on 26 March 1681, quoted in Hatsell, *Precedents*, vol. IV, 83.

[170] Hatsell, *Precedents*, vol. II, 335; Hatsell, *Precedents*, vol. IV, 273–4.

[171] *Lord Danby's Case* (1679), see Hatsell, *Precedents*, vol. IV, 208; resolution to the same effect was passed by the Commons in 1689; finally, it was enacted by the Act of Settlement, Hatsell, *Precedents*, vol. IV, 299, 308.

[172] Erskine May, *Parliamentary Practice*, 8th edn (1879), 687.

[173] The last two impeachment trials were those of Warren Hastings (1788) and Lord Melville (1805); see generally C.L. Black, *Impeachment: A Handbook* (New Haven: Yale University Press, 1974, reissued in 1998).

[174] 'Report from Select Committee on Parliamentary Privilege', HC 34 (1967–68), para. 115; 'Third Report from the Select Committee on Privileges', HC 41 (1976–77), para. 16.

[175] Joint Committee on Parliamentary privilege, HL Paper 43-1 HC 214-1 (1998–99), para. 16; see the motion calling for impeachment of Tony Blair, tabled on 25 November 2004,

Course of the proceedings

7.25 The right to institute proceedings for impeachment is exclusively within the province of the House of Commons.[176] The proceedings may originate with a petition of an aggrieved person,[177] with a report of a committee imputing misconduct on the part of some public official[178] or with relevant information which is brought to the attention of the House by any member. No proceedings for impeachment may commence unless a motion to that effect is passed. A member presents the charges and accusations against the person accused, and the House, after consideration, resolves either to refer the matter to a committee for further inquiry,[179] or to impeach the accused. Before final resolution, the House may hear the accused at the Bar either in person or by counsel.[180] When a motion to impeach is passed, the member who made the motion is instructed to go to the Bar of the House of Lords and to impeach the accused. The formal impeachment at the Bar having been made, a committee is appointed to draw up the articles of impeachment; when the articles are agreed upon, they are delivered to the House of Lords and sent to the accused; his answers are communicated to the Commons. Managers are appointed to conduct the trial on behalf of the Commons. In order to secure his presence at the trial, the accused person may be put into custody by the Commons, if a commoner, or, by the Lords, if a peer. He remains in custody unless admitted to bail.[181]

At a date fixed by the Lords the trial begins, the managers present the charges and evidence and witnesses in support, and the accused, in person or by counsel, presents his defence and, if necessary, evidence and witnesses in support. The Lords, after hearing the evidence and arguments, pass a verdict of 'guilty' or 'not guilty'. Each peer is asked for his opinion on each charge separately whether the accused is 'guilty' or 'not guilty'. If found not guilty (by a simple majority), the Lords dismiss the impeachment. If found guilty, the Lords may not pass

---

'Conduct of the Prime Minister in relation to the War against Iraq'. The Iraq Inquiry, established later by the following Prime Minister Gordon Brown, may be seen as a more appropriate response to this motion.

[176] For the procedure of impeachment, see generally Hatsell, *Precedents*.

[177] E.g., *Lord Mordaunt's Case* (1666); Hatsell, *Precedents*, vol. IV, 120–1.

[178] E.g., *Commissioner Pett's Case* (1667), Hatsell, *Precedents*, vol. IV, 122.

[179] E.g., *Lord Chief Justice Kuling's Case* (1667), Hatsell, Precedents, vol. IV, 123.

[180] *Sir John Bennet's Case* (1621), see Hatsell, *Precedents*, vol. IV, 131–2.

[181] Hatsell, *Precedents*, vol. IV, 276–7, 285 (Commons' power of committal and bail), 192–4 (Lords' power). See also Erskine May, *Parliamentary Practice*, 8th edn (1879), 684.

judgment unless the Commons demand it.[182] Upon the demand made by the Speaker on behalf of the Commons, the Lords impose sentence upon the convicted person. He may be imprisoned, fined, removed and disqualified from office, or otherwise punished, and if the offence is capital, he may be sentenced to death. Thus, Bacon LC (Viscount St. Albans) was heavily fined, imprisoned, and 'was rendered incapable of any office, or place, or employment in the state of commonwealth; never to sit in Parliament, or come within the verge of the court'.[183]

The Commons may at any stage put an end to the proceedings by failing to take the necessary steps, such as non-appearance in the trial.[184] Even after the accused is convicted, the Commons can in effect pardon him by failing to demand a sentence.

Rights of the accused under the law and custom of Parliament

7.26 The law applicable to impeachment is not the law of the land; rather it is the law of Parliament. As was resolved by the Lords, 'these matters when brought before them shall be discussed and adjudged by the course of Parliament, and not by the civil law nor by the common law of the land used in other inferior courts'.[185] However, it does not follow from this that the rights of the accused are less secure. Procedural safeguards have been laid down by Parliament. It was resolved by the House of Commons 'that it is the undoubted right of every subject of England under any accusation either by impeachment or otherwise to be brought to speedy trial in order to be acquitted or condemned'.[186] It was also resolved that when an impeached person is committed to custody, 'the Lords may limit a convenient time to bring his particular charge before them, for avoiding delay in justice'.[187]

The rights of defendants tried before the Lords were particularly specified in an order providing

> that in all cases of moment, the defendant shall have copies of all depositions, both pro and contra, after publication; a convenient time before the

---

[182] Erskine May, *Parliamentary Practice*, 8th edn (1879), 681, 685–6.

[183] *Dr Sacheverell's Case* (1709), Hatsell, *Precedents*, vol. IV, 265, 230. Later, he was granted full pardon by the King.

[184] As in *Lord Somer's Case* (1701), Hatsell, *Precedents*, vol. IV, 300–1.

[185] Quoted in *Dr Sacheverell's Case* (1709), Hatsell, *Precedents*, vol. IV, 272.

[186] Resolution of Commons on 26 February 1701, quoted in *Dr Sacheverell's Case* (1709), Hatsell, *Precedents*, vol. IV, 265, 301 n. 29.

[187] Quoted in *Dr Sacheverell's Case* (1709), Hatsell, *Precedents*, vol. IV, 193.

hearing, to prepare themselves; and also, that the defendants, if they shall demand it of the House in due time, shall have their learned counsel to assist them in their defence, whether they be able by reason of health to answer in person or not.[188]

Another procedural safeguard to secure justice is that all the Lords must be present at the trial, and absence from trial, if without due excuse, was deemed 'a great and wilful neglect of duty'.[189] It seems that the hearing of the evidence and arguments could not be delegated to a committee, for 'in cases of impeachments . . . all the Lords must judge'.[190] In conducting the trial, the managers are confined to the charges contained in the articles of impeachment.[191] The Commons can exhibit other charges but the accused person must then be given an opportunity of putting his answers to them.

The law applicable to impeachment is the law of Parliament. However, when in doubt about a question of law the Lords would consult the judges before making a final decision on the matter. Thus, the Lords sought the opinion of the judges on points of evidence, on the appropriate form of the indictment or information, and on the question whether the charges had been brought in regularly and legally.[192] It was laid down that the opinion of the judges should be delivered in the presence of the managers and the accused person.[193] When the Lords found it necessary, the judges were ordered to attend the House of Lords until the trial was over.[194] On the whole, it appears that impeachment is criminal in nature and the Lords considered it as such.[195]

---

[188] These rules were included in an order of the Lords on 28 May 1624, Hatsell, *Precedents*, vol. IV, 171–2.

[189] Lords' resolution on 23 June 1701, Hatsell, *Precedents*, vol. IV, 301.

[190] *Dr Sacheverell's Case* (1709), Hatsell, *Precedents*, vol. IV, 369–70 (Appendix 3: Report of Conference of both Houses on 13 January 1691).

[191] Erskine May, *Parliamentary Practice*, 8th edn (1879), 684.

[192] On evidence, see *Warren Hasting's Case* (1788), Hatsell, *Precedents*, vol. IV, 304; on the appropriate form of the indictment or information, see, e.g., *Dr Sacheverell's Case* (1709), Hatsell, *Precedents*, vol. IV, 305 and, on whether the charges had been brought in regularly and legally, see *Lord Chancellor Clarendon's Case* (1663), Hatsell, *Precedents*, vol. IV, 166. The judges were also consulted by the Lords on the question whether treason was a bailable offence, see *Lord Danby's Case* (1678), Hatsell, *Precedents*, vol. IV, 194.

[193] Hatsell, *Precedents*, vol. IV, 304, particularly the notes.   [194] *Ibid.*, 305.

[195] Berger, 'Impeachment for "High Crimes and Misdemeanors"', 400–15; R. Berger, 'Impeachment of Judges and "Good Behavior" Tenure' (1970) 79 *Yale Law Journal* 1475, 1518–19.

The use of impeachment against judges

7.27 Throughout the period of English history when impeachment was in vogue and frequently exercised, many judges, among them Lord Chancellors and Lord Chief Justices, were impeached in Parliament. A short survey of cases in which proceedings for impeachment were instituted against judges is given below. In reading this survey it should be borne in mind, as has already been indicated, that impeachment was a political weapon exercised by Parliament against political opponents. In many cases judges were impeached for supporting the Crown against Parliament, either in the exercise of their judicial functions or in advice given extra-judicially. Even when the activities of the impeached judges were improper or corrupt, the motives for instituting the proceeding were not confined to purifying the administration of justice. Thus, much as one could condemn the behaviour of Bacon, who was convicted on his own confession of accepting numerous bribes, it is to be admitted that in English society of that period 'gifts' to judges and other public officials were commonplace, and that Bacon was attacked for his role in support-ing the Crown in the constitutional struggle with Parliament. Nor was it surprising that Sir Edward Coke, who had been dismissed from the bench in 1616, and now served in the Commons, was overzealous in the proceedings against his long-time opponent. Along the same lines, it is safe to say that the impeachment of Lord Macclesfield a century later was politically motivated, although the final judgment passed on him may be sustained.

The charges presented against judges in impeachments represent a good cross-section of the grounds deemed sufficient for initiating such proceedings. As early as 1384 a Lord Chancellor was accused in Parlia-ment of bribery. In that year a petition was presented against Sir Michael de la Pole (later Earl of Suffolk), the Lord Chancellor, by a fishmonger of London, who alleged that he could not obtain justice in his case before the Chancellor and that he was 'wickedly delayed'. Much worse, he charged the Lord Chancellor of accepting bribes from him. The Lords acquitted the Lord Chancellor of the charges, and the accuser was later convicted of defamation and ordered to pay heavy damages.[196] In 1386 Sir Michael de la Pole was impeached by Parliament upon various charges of a political nature: that he had purchased valuable lands of

---

[196] For a detailed account of this case, see Cecil, *Tipping the Scales*, 93–9.

the King for less than they were worth, and that he applied appropriated funds to purposes other than those specified.[197]

In 1388 Parliament resorted to impeachment for punishing Sir Robert Belknap, late Chief Justice of the Common Pleas, and other judges for having given false answers on the law of treason upon questions put to them by the King. Upon their conviction the Lords ordered that 'they should be drawn and hanged as traitors'.[198]

After a long disuse the impeachment was revived in 1620 when Bacon, the Lord Chancellor, was impeached and convicted upon his own confession of accepting numerous bribes. He was heavily fined and imprisoned and disqualified from office for life. Later the King pardoned him.[199] A year later another case of bribery was discussed in Parliament. Sir John Bennet, a judge of the prerogative court of Canterbury, was charged with bribery and corruption.[200] The trial was not pursued in the Lords but proceedings in the Star Chamber resulted in a conviction and heavy fine.

In 1641 Lord Chief Justice Bramston, Lord Chief Baron Davenport, Mr Justice Berkeley, and others, were impeached[201] for their opinion in the case of *Ship Money*,[202] upholding the power of the King to levy taxation for ships without the consent of Parliament. Proceedings were instituted against Sir John Kelyng CJ in 1667 for illegal and arbitrary discharge of his judicial functions, particularly for oppressive behaviour toward juries. The matter was dropped after the judge addressed the House 'with reverence and humility'.[203]

In 1680 Sir Francis North CJ was accused of assisting, advising and drawing of a proclamation to suppress petitions to the King to call a Parliament.[204] In the same period, Sir William Scroggs CJ was impeached for discharging a grand jury before they made their presentment,

---

[197] Hatsell, *Precedents*, vol. IV, 57–8; Howell, State Trials, vol. I, 91.

[198] Hatsell, *Precedents*, vol. IV, 59–61; their lives were spared, Howell's State Trials, vol. I, 120.

[199] Howell's State Trials, vol. II, 1087 et seq.; Campbell, *Lives*, 388 et seq.; A.D. Gibb, *Judicial Corruption in the United Kingdom* (Edinburgh: Green & Son, 1957), I et seq.; Cecil, *Tipping the Scales*, 99–113.

[200] Cecil, *Tipping the Scales*, 74–81; Hatsell, *Precedents*, vol. I, 131–132; Howell's State Trials, vol. II, 1145; (1547–1628) 1 Commons Journal 580, 583, 584, 586–8, 590, 59.

[201] Hatsell, *Precedents*, vol. IV, 145; Howell's State Trials, vol. III, 1283, 1301. Bramston and Davenport were accused but not convicted; Berkeley was convicted.

[202] R v. *Hampden* (1637), Howell's State Trials, vol. III, 825, Howell's State Trials, vol. II, p. 825; Keir, 'The Case of the Ship-Money'.

[203] 9 Commons Journal 4, 18, 20, 29, 35–7; Howell's State Trials, p. 992; J. Campbell, *Lives of the Chief Justices* (London: John Murray, 1849), 509–10; Hatsell, *Precedents*, vol. IV, 123–4.

[204] Hatsell, *Precedents*, vol. IV, 123–4.

arbitrarily granting general warrants in blank, and illegally refusing bail.[205] Baron Weston was impeached for saying in a charge to a jury: 'For my part I know no representative of the nation but the King: all power centres in him.'[206]

In 1725 the Earl of Macclesfield, the Lord Chancellor, was impeached for and convicted of the sale of offices of Masters in Chancery. Despite legislation prohibiting the sale of offices, Lord Chancellors continued to profit from the sale of Masters in Chancery, and possibly other offices too, until the eighteenth century. However, the immediate cause for instituting the proceedings against Lord Macclesfield was the bursting of the South Sea Bubble which uncovered a major judicial scandal, the common practice for Masters in Chancery to speculate with the funds placed under their care and to put the profits in their pockets.[207] When the South Sea stock collapsed, ruining several Masters in Chancery, the public was not content with their punishment but felt also that the Lord Chancellor had to pay a heavy price for the misdeeds of the Masters who worked under his supervision. Parliament, with the reluctant consent of the government, impeached and convicted Macclesfield, sending him to the Tower and fining him £50,000. There are conflicting views in final judgment of his impeachment, one view being that 'he suffered less for his own faults, than for the evil results of a bad system'.[208] Others believe that he was guilty of serious misbehaviour even by the standards of his times, failing to exercise the necessary control over the Masters and, in eagerness to give the offices to the highest bidders, paying insufficient attention to the competence and personal integrity of the men who took the offices.[209]

B.   Address from Parliament

7.28 We turn to the power of removal by address, which has been exercised once, when Sir Jonah Barrington was removed from office as a judge of the Irish High Court of Admiralty in 1830 for corruption, after

---

[205] (1680–1692) 2 Parl. Deb. 1, 22–5, Hatsell, *Precedents*, vol. IV, 127–8; Howell's, State Trials, 163 et seq.

[206] Hatsell, *Precedents*, vol. IV, 127–8 and notes. Sir Thomas Jones, one of the judges of the King's Bench, was also impeached there, Hatsell, *Ibid.*, 128.

[207] L.C.B. Gower, 'A South Sea Heresy?' (1952) 68 LQR 214; Foss, *Judges of England*, vol. VIII, 2–3.

[208] J.C. Jeafferson, *A Book About Lawyers* (London: Hurst and Blackett, 1867), vol. I, p. 256.

[209] Campbell, *Precedents*, vol. IV, 554–6; Foss, *Judges of England*, vol. VIII, 3–4; A. Denning, *The Road to Justice* (London: Stevens, 1955), 20–2.

he misappropriated funds due to litigants. While Parliament has established some general principles as to what will justify inquiry into the conduct of a judge, his censure or removal from office, whether or not Parliament will interfere will depend on the circumstances of the case. As Mr Denman (later Lord Chief Justice) said, in *Kenrick's Case*, 'the question before the House [in that case and in other similar cases] must be questions of degree and it was entirely for the House to consider whether the case was of sufficient magnitude, and whether it brought a sufficient scandal on the administration of justice to require the interference of Parliament'.[210] In the course of the debates on judicial conduct, Lords and Members of Parliament have frequently employed public confidence in the administration of justice as a yardstick for measuring the magnitude of the misconduct complained of.[211]

An addition to existing procedures for removal

7.29 At common law, prior to the Act of Settlement 1700, judicial office held during good behaviour could be terminated by impeachment, by judicial proceedings commenced by a writ of *scire facias* to repeal the letters patent or upon criminal conviction. The Act of Settlement, establishing the security of judicial tenure, provided that judges should hold office during good behaviour, 'but upon the address of both Houses of Parliament it may be lawful to remove them'. Upon an address for the removal of a judge, passed by each House of Parliament and presented to the Crown, the Crown may lawfully remove the judge. The effect of this provision of the Act on the availability of the mechanisms of removal at common law prior to the Act remains a controversial issue almost three centuries after the passing of the Act.

One view is that the Act, by establishing security of judicial tenure and a new mechanism of removal, excluded all other methods of removal existing prior to the Act, and that only Parliament can take the initiative by passing an address for removal for breach of good behaviour. The other view is that the Act only established an additional power of removal by address which 'may be invoked upon occasions when the

---

[210] *Kenrick's Case* (1826) 14 Parl. Deb., 3rd Ser., 660.

[211] See Lord John Russell in *Kenrick's Case* (1826) 14 Parl. Deb., 3rd Ser., 367; (1867) 185 Parl. Deb., 3rd Ser., 269 [per Lord St Leonards, a former Lord Chancellor] and 271–2 [Earl Russell, a former Prime Minister]; *Grantham's Case* (1906) 160 Parl. Deb., 4th Ser., 369, at 396 [per the Attorney General], 410 [per Prime Minister Campbell-Bannerman] and 388 [Mr Dewar]; these cases are considered below, para. 7.44.

misbehaviour complained of would not constitute a legal breach of the conditions on which the office is held'. According to this view, 'the liability to this kind of removal is, in fact, a qualification of, or exception from, the words creating a tenure during good behaviour, and not an incident or legal consequence thereof'.[212]

The exclusive argument, namely that the Act of Settlement established an exclusive method of removal, rests upon the proposition that the proviso establishing the address does not limit the tenure during good behaviour but describes the process by which the breach of the good behaviour is to be ascertained. By establishing this process, it was provided that misbehaviour amounting to a breach of the good behaviour condition should be established not by judicial proceedings but by a resolution of both Houses of Parliament.[213] This construction of the provision establishing the address, say the proponents of the exclusive argument, is consistent with the substance of the section creating tenure during good behaviour.

If the opposite view is accepted and

> the power, of removal [by address] is to be regarded as an unqualified power, to be exercised for any cause, or without the existence of any cause, the office is held during the pleasure of the legislative and executive branches of the government, and not during the official good conduct of the incumbent. In [the opposite] view, therefore, the provision is inconsistent with the declared tenure of the commission.[214]

It clearly appears that the Act of Settlement did not exclude the power to impeach judges. The object of the Act, which was entitled in part 'an Act for the further limitation of the Crown', was to secure the independence of the judges of the Crown but not to render them independent of Parliament or to restrict the powers of Parliament over them. Apart from this, it would be unsound to believe that at a time of struggle for power between Parliament and the Crown, Parliament would give up a strong and efficient power over judges (which enabled Parliament not only to remove a judge or disqualify him from public office but also to sentence him severely) merely in order to assume the

---

[212] Todd, *Parliamentary Government*, vol. II, 729.

[213] L.R. Wooddeson, *Elements of Jurisprudence Treated of in the Preliminary Part of a Course of Lectures on the Laws of England* (Dublin: printed by H. Fitzpatrick for J. Moore, 1792), pp. 88 and 121; Chitty, *Prerogatives*, 83.

[214] G.T. Curtis, *History of the Origin, Formation and Adoption of the Constitution of the United States* (New York: Harper, 1860), vol. II, p. 69.

milder power of removal by address. Indeed, some of the proponents of the exclusive argument admit that Parliament retained the power to impeach judges.[215] The real issue, therefore, is whether the Act of Settlement excluded all methods of removal which had been available to the Crown prior to the Act. Since it was in accord with the legislative object to provide judges with adequate protection from Royal interference, the argument that the Act 'virtually [repealed] all previous powers which the Crown might have possessed over judicial officers'[216] cannot be easily cast aside.

7.30 Prior to the Act of Settlement the Crown could have proceeded against judges holding office during good behaviour by filing a writ of *scire facias* to repeal their letters patent, or by criminal information. If the rationale of the exclusive argument is accepted, it should follow that both *scire facias* and criminal information were excluded by the Act and subsequently could not be used to remove judges. In light of this, the view expressed by some authorities[217] that a judge can be removed only by an address, but upon conviction for 'some criminal offence' he may be removed without an address, gives rise to some difficulties. To reconcile these difficulties it may be argued that while Parliament cannot reasonably be said to have intended to leave on the bench a judge who had been convicted of a criminal offence until after an address is presented to the Crown, it is perfectly sound to assume that it was the intention of Parliament that, short of criminal offence, judges may only be removed upon an address. This argument, however, does not settle the matter, for it is still inconsistent with the premise upon which the exclusive argument is based. This point does not merit further discussion for, as will be shown, neither criminal information nor *scire facias* were excluded by the Act of Settlement.

The generally accepted interpretation of the Act is that while judges should hold office during good behaviour and cannot be removed by the Crown except for breach of good behaviour, established in *scire facias* proceedings, Parliament itself enjoys an unqualified power of removal. The wording of the Act supports this interpretation. The first phrase of the relevant section provides for tenure during good behaviour (and establishes judicial salaries), then the second phase beginning with 'but'

---

[215] *Ibid.*
[216] *O'Grady's Case* (1823) 9 Parl. Deb., 2nd Ser., 360, 365 [Mr Wetherell MP].
[217] Hallam, *Constitutional History*, vol. II, 357–8; Maitland, *Constitutional History of England*, 313.

(and in subsequent statutes with 'subject to'),[218] establishes the power of removal by address. This wording points strongly against regarding the power of removal by address as incidental to tenure during good behaviour established by the opening sentence.[219]

The principle of construction that judicial process is not abolished except by clear words likewise supports the view that *scire facias* was not excluded by the Act.[220] This interpretation is not inconsistent with the object of the Act of Settlement to render the judges independent of the Crown, nor is it incompatible with tenure during good behaviour. Under this interpretation, the Crown acting alone and without an address cannot remove a judge. It has to establish the breach of good behaviour for which the judge is to be removed in *scire facias* proceedings before a court of law. The Crown is only responsible for initiating the proceeding; the ultimate decision rests with the court.

The fact that this interpretation gives an unqualified power of removal to Parliament should not give rise to difficulties. The problem should be examined in the historical context of the struggle between Parliament and the Crown. Bearing in mind that Parliament came out of the constitutional conflict as the winner, it was only natural for it to assert full control over the judges[221] In order to exercise full parliamentary control over the judges, impeachment was not enough, for it could only be used for 'high crimes and misdemeanours'. Whatever its exact meaning, this term did not cover the broad area of improper behaviour (such as gross immorality), or physical or mental inability for which it was justifiable to remove a judge. To remedy this situation, an additional power of removal was established which can be exercised in appropriate cases.

Likewise, after the establishment of judicial tenure during good behaviour a power of removal, which is not subject to the technical condition of good behaviour, was necessary. Before the Act of Settlement when judges held office at pleasure, the Crown could remove them for improper behaviour, or physical or mental inability, which although not amounting to a breach of the good behaviour condition nor to a criminal act was a justifiable cause for removal from office. The Act established tenure during good behaviour and stripped the Crown of this

---

[218] No significance is attached to the change of these words.
[219] Todd, *Parliamentary Government*, vol. II, 729.   [220] *Ibid.*
[221] W.E. Hearn, *The Government of England: its Structure and its Development*, 2nd edn (London: Longmans, Green & Co., 1886), 87.

power; thus a gap was created where neither Parliament by impeachment nor the Crown by *scire facias* or criminal information could remove a judge who fell within this gap. In order to fill the gap an additional method of removal by address was established, which made it possible for Parliament to remove a judge for improper behaviour or inability who otherwise, after the tenure during good behaviour had been established, could not have been removed.

The prevailing view among legal scholars is that the Act did not exclude other mechanisms of removal existing prior to the Act and that in exercising the power of removal by address, Parliament is not limited to considerations of 'good behaviour' in its technical sense.[222] This view finds support also in statements made in the course of the debates in Parliament on motions for an address for removal of judges,[223] where some Lords and members argue about *scire facias* or impeachment as the proper or constitutional mode of removal of judges.[224]

It thus clearly appears from statements in Parliament and from the language of the Act of Settlement and its aims that, after the Act, judges holding office during good behaviour could have been proceeded against by address, impeachment, *scire facias* or criminal information.

---

[222] Lord Sankey, 90 HL Deb., 77 (23 November 1933); Todd, *Parliamentary Government*, vol. II, 729; Anson, *Law and Custom*, vol. II, part I, 222–3; Holdsworth, *A History*, v. X, 415; Heuston, *Lives*, 518–19; McIlwain, 'Tenure of English Judges', 225; Berger, 'Impeachment for "High Crimes and Misdemeanors"', 1479–82. See the opinion of the Law Officers (Sir William Atherton and Roundel Palmer) presented to Parliament in 1862, and the opinion of the Law Officers of Victoria (1862) quoted in Todd, *Parliamentary Government*, vol. II, 727–8; *McCawley* v. *R* (1918) 26 CLR 9, 58–9; see also *Shell Co. Australia* v. *Federal Commissioner of Taxation* [1931] AC 275 (PC) 280.

[223] *Barrington's Case* (1830) 24 Parl. Deb., 2nd Ser. 965, 966; some minority views were these of Mr Wetherell and Mr Canning in *O'Grady's Case* (1823) 9 Parl. Deb., 2nd Ser. 360, 364–5.

[224] In support of *scire facias*, see *O'Grady's Case* (1823) 9 Parl. Deb., 2nd Ser., 360, 364–5 [Mr Smith]; see also Lord Erskine LC in the earlier case of Mr Justice Luke Fox, judge of the Common Pleas in Ireland, (1806) 7 Parl. Deb., 751, 767 and 770, quoted by Campbell in *Lives*, 60. In support of impeachment, see *O'Grady's Case* (1823) 9 Parl. Deb., 2nd Ser., 360, 1010 [Mr Secretary Peel], though see Mr Secretary Peel's later view that a judge could only be removed upon an address from Parliament, in *Kenrick's Case* (1826) 14 Parl. Deb., 3rd Ser., at 501; *O'Grady's Case* (1823) 9 Parl. Deb., 2nd Ser., 360, 361 [Mr Canning]; *Best's Case* (1821) 4 Parl. Deb., New Ser., 918, 930 [Mr Wynn]. Articles of impeachment were brought against Lord Ellenborough CJ in 1816 although they were dismissed after a discussion on the merits, 32 Parl. Deb., 1st Ser., 1145 (1816). The terminology used in the Parliamentary Reports was 'articles of charge' but see J. Hatsell, *Precedents*, vol. IV, who uses the term 'Articles of Impeachment'.

Address is exclusive in practice

7.31 The question is not put to rest here. The generally accepted view today is, and probably has been for more than the last century, that judges cannot be removed except upon an address. The arguments for this are overwhelming.

The heated debates on the reduction of judicial salaries in the 1930s presented a good opportunity for discussion of the constitutional position of the judges. Of particular importance is the collective memorandum submitted to the prime minister by all the judges of the High Court and Court of Appeal in protest against the reduction of their salaries.[225] In that memorandum the judges, after quoting the Act of Settlement, wrote: 'The judges hold office as expressed above during good behaviour and are removable only on an Address to the Crown by both Houses of Parliament.'[226] In the course of the debates on the reduction of judicial salaries, Lord Buckmaster, a former Lord Chancellor, said that the judges of the Supreme Court were irremovable except by an address from both Houses of Parliament, his words meeting with the concurrence of Lord Cecil of Chelwood and Lord Reading, the former Lord Chief Justice.[227] In the same debate Lord Sankey LC expressed the view that the Act of Settlement did not exclude *scire facias*, but, on the other hand, he admitted that, at present, Lord Buckmaster's proposition that 'judges are irremovable except on an address' is a 'principle upon which we are all agreed'.[228] The preamble of the Judiciary (Safeguarding) Bill, presented in the House of Lords in the wake of the judicial salaries crisis, read in part: 'Whereas it is provided by the Act of Settlement 1700 that His Majesty's judges shall not be removed from their office save in pursuance of a resolution of both Houses of Parliament'.[229] A similar statement was included in the Status of Judges Bill, presented at the same time in the House of

---

[225] The following judges sat on the Bench in December 1931 when the collective memorandum was presented: Lord Hewart CJ, Lord Hanworth MR, Lord Merrivale, P. Scrutton, Lawrence, Greer, Slesser and Romer LJJ, Avory, Horridge, Rowlatt, McCardie, Roche, Swift, Acton, Branson, Talbot, MacKinnon, Finlay, Wright, Hawke, Charles, Humphreys and MacNaghten JJ.

[226] The memorandum was read by the Lord Chancellor in the House of Lords, *Hansard*, HL, vol. 88, cols 1209–11 (29 July 1933).

[227] *Hansard*, HL, vol. 90, cols. 66, 73, 85, 94 (23 November 1933).

[228] *Hansard*, HL, vol. 90, cols. 75 and 77 (23 November 1933).

[229] *Hansard*, HL, vol. 91, col. 228 (15 March 1934). The Bill was passed by the House of Lords four times but never came into law.

Commons by six eminent MPs.[230] In the course of the debates in the House of Lords on the Judiciary (Safeguarding) Bill, Lord Carson, a former Law Lord, was of the opinion that judges could be removed only by an address from the two Houses of Parliament.[231] In the same debate, neither the memorandum of the judges nor the preambles of the Bills nor the other statements quoted above were disputed; the memorandum of the judges, including the passage that judges can only be removed by address, was in fact quoted with approval.[232]

Ten years before the judicial salaries crisis a flagrant violation of the principle of the independence of the judiciary took place. Mr Justice A.T. Lawrence, aged seventy-seven, was appointed Lord Chief Justice upon the understanding that he would retire when called upon to do so. In a letter to Prime Minister Lloyd George, Lord Birkenhead, the Lord Chancellor, strongly opposed this disgraceful arrangement. After quoting the terms of the Act of Settlement, Lord Birkenhead wrote that the arrangement

> violates the letter of the Statute ... and defeats the object for which the enactment was passed. That object was to secure that the judges should hold office independently of any political or other influence and should be removable only for the most serious judicial misbehaviour and then in the most public and open manner.[233]

This language clearly suggests that Lord Birkenhead thought that judges could only be removed by an address.

Lord Denning has on several occasions written that 'the accepted view is that in England judges are not to be removed except for misconduct and then only on the petition of both Houses of Parliament'.[234] Many eminent authorities have expressed the same view.[235]

---

[230] House of Commons Bill No. 61, Parl. Papers 1933–1934, vol. IV, 251. The Bill did not go further than the First Reading.

[231] *Hansard*, HL, vol. 90, col. 1057 (1 March 1934).

[232] *Hansard*, HL, vol. 90, col. 1053 (1 March 1934).

[233] Lord Birkenhead, *The Life of F.E. Smith, First Earl of Birkenhead* (London: Eyre & Spottiswoode, 1960), p. 403.

[234] A. Denning, *The Changing Law* (London: Stevens, 1953), 5; Denning, *The Road to Justice*, 13–15.

[235] See, inter alia, Lord Brougham, *The British Constitution: Its History, Structure and Working* (London: Richard Griffin & Co., 1861); Lord Cranworth LC, 189 Parl. Deb. 4th Ser., 1213 (9 August 1867); Lord Kilmuir LC, 'Individual Freedom under an Unwritten Constitution' (1959) 45 *Virginia Law Review* 629, 642; Lord Scarman, 'The English Judge' (1967) 30 MLR 1, 3; Hallam, *Constitutional History*, vol. II, 357–8; Maitland, *Constitutional History*, 313; Dicey, *Law of the Constitution*, 10th edn (London: Macmillan, 1959), 132.

Introducing the bill for increasing judicial salaries in 1954, Sir Winston Churchill supported the same proposition, joined a few months later by Lord Salisbury.[236] Sir Winston Churchill and Lord Salisbury only declared an established constitutional practice. In 1891, in an answer to a parliamentary question on a mentally ill judge who still sat on the bench, Mr W.H. Smith, Leader of the House and First Lord of the Treasury, speaking for the government, said:

> It is the policy of the Government, of Parliament and I might also say the Constitution, to respect the absolute independence of the Judicial Bench. The Government has no authority whatever over a judge of the land . . . if [the Hon. Member] has reason to believe that there is a failure of justice it is in his power . . . to move an address to the Crown for the removal of the judge in question. That is the only course open to any honourable Member whether he be a Member of the Government or Parliament.[237]

So far as our research could reveal, no reference has been made in Parliament since 1830 to *scire facias* as a mechanism of removal. On the other hand, at the same period one can find statements to the effect that judges can only be removed by an address.[238]

The Act of Settlement has never been directly considered by the courts,[239] but statements made by judges in several decisions tend to support the generally accepted view that an address of both Houses of Parliament is the exclusive method of removal of judges.[240]

A Constitutional Convention

7.32 It has been shown that the Act, properly construed, did not exclude removal by *scire facias* but that, in practice, address has been firmly regarded for almost two centuries as the exclusive mechanism of

---

[236] *Hansard*, HC, vol. 525, col. 1061 (23 March 1954); *Hansard*, HL, vol. 188, col. 1018 (6 April 1954).

[237] 351 Parl. Deb., 3rd Ser., 487 (9 March 1891).

[238] See e.g., (1842) 60 Parl. Deb., 3rd Ser., 267 [Lord Russell]; (1856) 140 Parl. Deb., 3rd Ser., 760 [Sir John Shelly] and 782 [Sir George Grey, Home Secretary]; (1867) 189 Parl. Deb., 4th Ser., 1214 [Lord Clanricarde].

[239] Lord Birkenhead LC refused to offer any conclusion upon the construction of the Act of Settlement, see *McCawley* v. *R* [1920] AC 691, 713 (PC). That case was an appeal from *McCawley* v. *R* (1918) 26 CLR 9 where Isaacs and Rich JJ (in the Australian Supreme Court) suggested that the address was added to the common law methods of removing judges, *McCawley* v. *R* (1918) 26 CLR 9, 58–9.

[240] *Terrell* v. *Secretary of State for the Colonies* [1953] 2 QB 482, 493 [Lord Goddard CJ]; *Ex parte Ramshay* (1852) 18 QB 174, 192 [Lord Campbell]; *Anderson* v. *Gorrie* [1895] 1 QB 668, 670 [Lord Esher MR].

removal. The legal construction of the Act and the accepted practice can, however, be reconciled. On the true construction of the Act of Settlement, it did not exclude judicial removal, but subsequently a constitutional practice has been established that senior courts judges can only be removed by an address of Parliament.[241]

The statements cited to the effect that the address is exclusive, although made in reference to the Act of Settlement, were not made in the context of discussion of the legal construction of the Act. They were not necessarily part of a focused discussion on whether the Act excluded other mechanisms of removal. For these reasons they have a limited value, if any, in the construction of the Act of Settlement. They constitute, however, a most significant illustration of the constitutional practice governing the matter. Such constitutional practice supports the wider constitutional principle of judicial independence, itself first pronounced through statute before being supplemented, fortified and slightly modified by 'the accumulated tradition of the country'.[242] That the independence of the judges depends not only upon statutes but also upon 'the accumulated tradition of the country' hardly needs to be demonstrated. As Lord Sankey put it, 'the independence and prestige which our judges have enjoyed in their position have rested far more upon the great tradition and long usage with which they have always been surrounded, than upon any statute'.[243]

Without attempting to offer a final judgment on the matter, it is submitted that this constitutional practice arguably constitutes a constitutional convention. It is not proposed here to go into a lengthy discussion on how and when a constitutional convention becomes established, but some arguments are tentatively offered. First, the wording of the

---

[241] In the course of our discussion, statements made in Parliament have been quoted in support of the view that the Act did not exclude *scire facias*. It is accepted since 1993 that the courts may refer to reports of proceedings in Parliament in order to discover parliamentary intentions in cases of ambiguity or obscurity in a statute or, where giving words their literal meaning would lead to absurdity, see *Pepper (Inspector of Taxes)* v. *Hart* [1992] 1 All ER 42, 64, 67–9 [Lord Browne-Wilkinson]. Any statement on the Bill for the Act in question, as set out in the official report or record of debates, may be referred to when it is clear, was made by or on behalf of the minister or other person who was the promoter of the Bill, and discloses the legislative intention underlying its words; importantly, the court may also have regard to such other material (if any) of the legislature as is relevant for understanding that statement and its effect, see *Halsbury's Laws of England*, 5th edn (2012), vol. 96, pp. 1121–2.

[242] Lord Cecil, *Hansard*, HL, vol. 95, cols. 124 and 127 (28 November 1934).

[243] Lord Sankey, *Hansard*, HL, vol. 90, col. 124 (23 November 1933).

statements of ministers, Lord Chancellors and judges, Lords and Members of Parliament, to the effect that judges are only removable by an address, clearly suggests that they all regarded the exclusive power of removal by Parliament as a constitutional principle binding upon them. Indeed, those principles have sometimes been alluded to as 'conventions'. Thus, during the debates on judicial salaries in the 1930s, Lord Cecil submitted that the principle that judges can only be removed by an address, and other principles securing judicial independence, were 'constitutional principles of the utmost importance' which ought not to be infringed in order to preserve the separation of powers between the executive and the judiciary.[244] The rules regarding the procedure and standard for removal have also not been regarded as mere internal rules of parliamentary procedure but as constitutional principles, emanating from the fundamental principle of judicial independence.

Thus, discussing the grounds for an address, Mr Denman (later Lord Chief Justice) said that it 'had now become a constitutional principle that no judge should be removed from his situation unless a clear charge of malversation could be made out against him',[245] and Lord John Russell stated that 'it was a principle of the constitution that judges should only be removable for partial and improper conduct'.[246] In another case Prime Minister Ramsay MacDonald said: 'However unfortunate the words have been, they clearly do not constitute the kind of fault amounting to a moral delinquency which constitutionally justifies an address.'[247]

As to the procedure to be followed upon a motion for an address, Sir Charles Wetherell said: 'As a constitutional question, the [address] for the removal of a judge from his office, ought to be founded on evidence taken at [the] bar.'[248] The Solicitor General in another case thought it was 'unconstitutional to condemn a judge of rank and character without giving him an opportunity of being heard'.[249] Mr MacNeil argued in the case of *Mr Justice Grantham* that 'it had been held to be in accordance with constitutional practice that such procedure [for address] should not be instituted unless the *prima facie* case against the judge was so strong as

---

[244] Lord Cecil, *Hansard*, HL, vol. 90, cols. 73, 84–5 (23 November 1933); Lord Rankeillour, *Hansard*, HL, vol. 90, col. 101 (23 November 1933).

[245] *Barrington's Case* (1830) 24 Parl. Deb., 2nd Ser., 965.

[246] *Kenrik's Case* 14 Parl. Deb., 3rd Ser., 366–7 (1826).

[247] Upon the complaint of Mr Justice McCardie's behaviour in *General O'Dwyer's Case*, see *Hansard*, HC, vol. 175, col. 7 (23 June 1924).

[248] *Barrington's Case* (1830) 24 Parl. Deb., 2nd Ser., 965, 978.

[249] *O'Grady's Case* (1823) 9 Parl. Deb., 2nd Ser., 360, 1006.

to justify an address' and in the same case the Attorney General thought the *prima facie* case 'was the first constitutional step' for proceedings for an address.[250]

In the light of this, it is suggested that some basic principles governing the procedure and grounds for an address have arguably become constitutional conventions: 'A long series of precedents all pointing in the same direction is very good evidence of a convention.'[251] This would apply to the procedural safeguards of hearing, notice, distinct charges, prima facie case and to the grounds for removal such as the requirement of a moral element in the misconduct, insufficiency or error of judgment or of matter of court practice. These principles have been referred to as binding upon Parliament and with full approval in every case which was discussed in Parliament. Whether the principles by which Parliament has considered itself bound amount to constitutional conventions or whether they are only part of the 'law and custom of Parliament',[252] it is safe to say that although there are no statutory limits on Parliament's power, as a matter of long-established practice, the judges are adequately protected from arbitrary action both as to the procedure and the grounds for removal by address. Thus Professor de Smith wrote in 1971 that 'in practice no Judge is likely to be removed except upon a parliamentary address based on the judge's misbehaviour'.[253]

Is the address mandatory upon the Crown?

7.33 At the present time there is little doubt that the address for removal is mandatory upon the Crown. As Professor Hood Phillips[254] said, 'the Queen would be bound by convention to act on an address from both Houses'. However, it is not clear whether at the time of the passing of the Act of Settlement and subsequently in the eighteenth and nineteenth

---

[250] *Grantham's Case* (1906) 160 Parl. Deb., 4th Ser., 370 and 393; *Kelly's Case* (1867) 185 Parl. Deb., 368 (Lord St Leonards).

[251] Hood Phillips, Constitutional and Administrative Law, 82.

[252] G. Marshall, *Constitutional Conventions: the Rules and Forms of Political Accountability* (Oxford: Clarendon Press, 1984); I. Jennings, *The Law and the Constitution*, 5th edn (London: University of London Press, 1959), ch. III.

[253] S.A. de Smith, *Constitutional and Administrative Law* (Englewood Cliffs, NJ: Prentice Hall, 1971), 374; Hearn, *Government of England*, 83.

[254] Hood Phillips, *Constitutional and Administrative Law*, 335; see also E.W. Ridges, *Constitutional Law*, 8th edn, ed. G.A. Forrest (London: Stevens and Sons, 1950), 336. The Crown could not refuse to act upon such an address.

centuries the address for removal was mandatory or merely directory upon the Crown.

It was argued that an address was no more than a form of communication from Parliament to the King with no mandatory power over him, and the reference to an address in a statute does not change its nature.[255] However, it seems doubtful that in passing the Act of Settlement establishing a new mechanism for removal in which the Crown takes the final step, Parliament intended to leave it to the King to decide whether the judge would be removed, after both Houses had found him unfit to remain in office. The only (non-English) case in which a motion for an address was passed seems to support this view. Not only did the King act upon the address, but even beforehand it was taken for granted that the King would do so. The only question debated was whether the King himself or his ministers would sign the removal.[256] Indeed, in no case has anyone expressed doubt as to whether the King would act upon the address if passed. Lord Brougham wrote in the middle of the nineteenth century that judges were removable by 'joint address of the two Houses of Parliament, to which the sovereign *must* assent'.[257]

Constitutional constraints

7.34 According to our suggested construction of the Act of Settlement, judges hold office during good behaviour and cannot be removed by the Crown unless they break that condition, but Parliament itself enjoys an unqualified power of removal. Parliament could remove a judge from the bench for any other reason which might induce both Houses of Parliament to pass the necessary address to the sovereign.[258] Nor does the Act of Settlement, nor the statutes replacing it, provide for any procedure to be followed by Parliament in passing an address. Parliament is thus neither required to follow certain procedures nor to apply any standards

---

[255] This is in essence the argument advanced by McIlwain, 'Tenure of English Judges', 226; see also Berger, 'Impeachment for "High Crimes and Misdemeanors"', 1500–1.

[256] *Sir Jonah Barrington's Case* (1830) 24 Parl. Deb., 2nd Ser., 1075, 1088.

[257] Lord Brougham, *The British Constitution*, 357 (emphasis added); but see Hearn, *Government of England*, 84: 'the Crown is not bound to act upon that address'; *contra* Bagehot: 'the sovereign ... has three rights ... the right to be consulted, the right to encourage, the right to warn', *The English Constitution* (London: C.A. Watts, 1964), part III. The right to refuse seems deliberately to have been excluded.

[258] E.S.C Wade and G. Phillips, *Constitutional Law. An Outline of the Law and Practice of the Constitution Including Central and Local Government and the Constitutional Relations of the British Commonwealth and Empire*, 4th edn, ed E.C.S. Wade (London: Longmans, Green and Co, 1950), p. 663.

in determining whether the alleged misconduct justifies removal from office. In practice, however, the procedure for removal by an address was applied in such a manner as to safeguard the independence of the judges and to protect them from unjustifiable public indignity and procedural injustice. From the voluminous debates on motions for an address, the clear principle has emerged that it is incumbent upon Parliament to protect the independence of the judiciary, and this principle sets adequate constraints on the procedures and standards of misbehaviour required in practice for an address of Parliament. Thus the constitutional history and the culture of judicial independence distinctively restrict this unqualified power of removal from Parliament.

A few instructive illustrations will suffice. In *Lord Ellenborough's Case*, the Solicitor General said:

> The House on the one hand should watch with jealousy over the conduct of the judges, so on the other it should protect them while deserving protection not only as a debt of justice to the judges but as a debt due to justice herself, in order that the public confidence in the purity of the administration of our laws [would not be impaired].[259]

In *Lord Abinger's Case*, Lord John Russell stated: 'Independence of judges is so sacred that nothing but the most imperious necessity should induce the House to adopt a course that might weaken their standing or endanger their authority.'[260] This view can be found beyond debates on motions for an address, in almost every debate on the administration of justice or on judicial salaries until the twenty-first century. One oft-quoted statement of Sir Winston Churchill illustrates the degree of commitment of the English system to the principle of independence of the judiciary:

> The complete independence of the Judiciary ... is the foundation of many things in our island life ... It is perhaps one of the deepest gulfs between us and all forms totalitarian rule ... The British Judiciary with its tradition and record is one of the greatest living assets of our race and people and the independence of the Judiciary is part of our message to the ever-growing world which is rising so swiftly around us.[261]

---

[259] 34 Parl. Deb., 1st Ser., 110 (1816).
[260] (1843) 66 Parl. Deb., 3rd Ser., 1124, 1129 [Sir James Graham]; *Baron Smith's Case* (1834) 21 Parl. Deb., 3rd Ser., 272, 322 [Mr Hakombe]; *Grantham's Case* (1906) 160 Parl. Deb., 4th Ser., 370, 379 [Mr Buckmaster], 408 [Mr Balfour].
[261] *Hansard*, HC, vol. 525, col. 1061 (23 March 1951).

Parliament's duty to protect the judges from public indignity, procedural injustice and unjustifiable charges has translated into an elaborate body of rules and principles set in the course of determining cases of judicial misbehaviour brought before Parliament. The proceedings in Parliament upon a motion for an address have been deemed judicial, and procedural safeguards to protect the accused judge have been firmly established. The series of historical precedents in Parliament setting the procedure and grounds for an address will be now examined.

C.   The process of the address

7.35 This section investigates the process of the address for removal and some of the issues connected with this procedure.[262] The discussion will be followed by a survey of the cases in which the mechanism of removal by address has operated.

Initiating the proceedings

7.36 Although proceedings for an address for removal may originate in either House of Parliament, proceedings have always originated in the House of Commons except for a few cases, in particular *Fox's Case*.[263] In that case, proceedings for an address for removal originated in the House of Lords but were subsequently abandoned upon a resolution that the House of Lords could not institute proceedings against a judge before the House of Commons had looked into the matter. Such discussion would be prejudgment of the case, should it subsequently come before the Lords on proceedings for impeachment. The resolution, however, was passed over the protest of the strong minority opinion of Lord Eldon and others, which weakened the authoritative value of the

---

[262] The cases of Mr Justice Fox, Lord Chief Justice Ellenborough, Baron Smith, and Sir Jonah Barrington were relied upon in *Abinger's Case*; there the Attorney General distinguished *Abinger's Case* from *Smith's Case*, see *Abinger's Case* (1843) 66 Parl. Deb., 3rd Ser., 1129, 1071–3. In *Barrington's Case* (1830) 24 Parl. Deb., 2nd Ser., 965, 967, *O'Grady's Case* (1823) 9 Parl. Deb., 2nd Ser., 360 was distinguished and relied upon for other grounds. In *Grantham's Case*, the cases of *Smith, Lord Abinger* and *Torrens* were referred to, see *Grantham's Case* (1906) 160 Parl. Deb., 4th Ser., 393–4. Parliament's adherence to precedent is also shown by case of impeachment: committees were appointed 'to look into precedents relating to questions arising in the course of the debate', see Hatsell, *Precedents*, vol. IV, 149.

[263] (1806) 7 Parl. Deb., 751; *Grantham's Case* (1906), 160 Parl. Deb., 4th Ser., 370 [Mr MacNeill]; Todd, *Parliamentary Government*, vol. II, 730, 741.

case.[264] An examination of the cases further shows that the case of *Fox* did not stand in the way of motions and petitions presented to the House of Lords charging a judge with misconduct.[265] The better view therefore is that although proceedings may originate in either House of Parliament, 'preferably they should be commenced in the House of Commons'.[266]

Proceedings for an address for removal may be initiated by a motion for inquiry into the conduct of a judge. The motion may be based on the petition of an aggrieved individual, on a report of a commission imputing misconduct to a judge, or on an investigation conducted by the MP who moves that proceedings be initiated against the judge.[267] Parliament may then pass a resolution for an address to the Crown praying that a commission of inquiry shall investigate the administration of a certain court presided over by a particular judge,[268] thereby, in fact, ordering the government to make an appropriate investigation into the conduct of the judge which will eventually serve as a basis for debate in Parliament.

Referring the matter for inquiry

7.37 A motion for an inquiry into the conduct of a judge would be made upon previous notice,[269] to allow the accused to meet the charges by communicating his defence to other MPs. In the period between the notice and the debate on the motion the government and other Members would conduct some inquiries and would form their view upon the matter.[270]

---

[264] *Fox's Case* (1806) 7 Parl. Deb., 751, 758-9; 788-9; accord *Halsbury's Laws of England*, 4th edn (1974), vol. 8, 681 n. 5.

[265] *Kelly's Case* (1867) 185 Parl. Deb., 3rd Ser., 257; *Ellenborough's Case* (1813), 25 Parl. Deb. 1st Ser., 207.

[266] *Halsbury's Laws of England* (4th edn, reissue LexisNexis, 1996), vol. VIII (II), para. 905.

[267] For motions based on a petition, see *Fox's Case* (1805) 45 Lords Journal 181, 203, 204; *Kenrick's Case* (1825) 13 Parl. Deb., 2nd Ser., 1138; *Kenrick's Case II* (1826)14 Parl. Deb., 2nd Ser., 362, 500; *Kelly's Case* (1867) 185 Parl. Deb., 3rd Ser., 260, 268-9; *Best's Case* (1821) 4 Parl. Deb., New Ser., 918; for motions based on a commission's report, see *O'Grady's Case* (1823) 9 Parl. Deb., 2nd Ser., 360; *Barrington's Case* (1830) 24 Parl. Deb., 484; (1830) 85 Commons Journals 196; for motions based on an MP's investigation, see, e.g., *McClelland's Case* (1819) 40 Parl. Deb., 1st Ser., 851.

[268] See such an address of the House of Commons in the case of Sir Jonah Barrington, (1828) 2 *Mirror of Parliament*, 1577.

[269] *Kenrick's Case* (1825) 13 Parl. Deb., 2nd Ser., 1138, 1140 [Mr Secretary Peel]; *Smith's Case* (1834), 21 Parl. Deb., 3rd Ser., 272, 333.

[270] See *Gurney's Case* (1843) 69 Parl. Deb., 3rd Ser., 189, 196-9, 202; *Kelly's Case* (1867) 185 Parl. Deb., 3rd Ser., 260, 270.

After due notice has been given, the Member at a later date would state the alleged misconduct. Sometimes the complaint would be incorporated into articles of charge.[271] Upon presenting the charges, the Member would move for referring the matter to a Select Committee or to a Committee of the whole House, for further inquiry.

Before the matter could be referred for further inquiry, the charges would have had to be specific and distinct,[272] with specific and reliable evidence in support.[273] Charges which were presented against an individual judge, but tended to impute improper conduct to other members of the court, not party to the proceedings, would have been dismissed at the outset.[274] It has been an established 'constitutional practice that such procedure [for an address] should not be instituted unless the prima facie case against a judge was so strong as to justify an address'.[275]

If the charges were duly introduced and the procedural requirements met, other considerations were still to be examined. First, only such misconduct as would warrant an address for removal should be referred for further inquiry.[276] As Sir Robert Peel suggested, before referring the matter for inquiry, they should ask themselves 'was the accusation a grave one? Did it affect the impartiality, the integrity, or the moral character of the judge?'[277] In order to answer these questions, they would have had to form their judgment as to the standards of conduct required from a judge under the circumstances and the standards of judicial misbehaviour which justify an address for removal. At this point the fate of the proceedings would have been decided.

In principle, therefore, unless the prima facie case against the judge is strong and unless the charges, if proved, would justify an address for his removal, Parliament will not interfere. Given this principle, it seems that Parliament does not exercise any disciplinary function over judges short of removal by an address, and that it cannot pursue a course with the

---

[271] *McClelland's Case* (1819) 40 Parl. Deb., 1st Ser., 851. But such procedure has been so long out of use that it is doubtful whether it is still available, *Hansard*, HC, vol. 865, col. 42 (10 December 1973) [the Speaker].

[272] *Kenrick's Case* (1825) 13 Parl. Deb., 2nd Ser., 1138, 1248; *Abinger's Case*, 66 Parl. Deb. 3rd Ser., 1130, 1140; *Smith's Case* (1834) 21 Parl. Deb. 3rd Ser., 272, 327.

[273] *Abinger's Case* (1843) 66 Parl. Deb. 3rd Ser. 1129–30; *Smith's Case* (1834) 21 Parl. Deb. 3rd Ser. 272, 311.

[274] *Ellenborough's Case* (1816), 33 Parl. Deb., 1st Ser., 709.

[275] *Grantham's Case* (1906) 160 Parl. Deb., 4th Ser., 370; *Abinger's Case* (1843) 66 Parl. Deb., 3rd Ser., 1043.

[276] *Smith's Case* (1834) 21 Parl. Deb. 3rd Ser., 272, 706, 741, 745 [Sir Robert Peel].

[277] *Ibid.*, 741.

final aim not of an address for removal but of censure, criticism or condemnation of judicial conduct. This view has been expressed many times in Parliament. In the case of *Smith*, it was suggested that Parliament had no right to institute an inquiry into the conduct of a judge 'with any other view than to address the Crown for his removal'. Otherwise, 'the independence of the judicial bench was a mockery and [the Act of Settlement] was no better than waste paper'.[278]

Gladstone when prime minister advanced the same view in the course of the debates on a vote of censure of the government for engineering the appointment of Sir Robert Collier to the Judicial Committee of the Privy Council. Gladstone argued that if such a vote of censure were passed, it would affect the judge, contrary to established principles:

> At present you are strictly restrained from interference except in one most solemn and formal manner. You are not to tamper with the question whether the judges are on this or that particular assailable. You are not to inflict upon them a minor punishment. You have never thought it wise to give opinions in criticism or in reprobation of their conduct when they have casually gone astray. [If] the act [of a judge] was not an act with respect to which it would be right to ask Parliament to address the Crown for his removal, it was not an act of which hostile notice should be taken at all. Are you prepared to [break] that fence [which] prevents you from intermeddling with the character of the judges by means of votes, which . . . dare not aim at their removal, but which, at the same time, have a certain credit and authority?[279]

In more recent times, in the case of *Grantham*, the Attorney General (Sir John Walton) strongly opposed any disciplinary measures short of an address for removal, arguing that 'Such a course would leave the learned judge in the occupation of his eminent position, but discredited and disgraced in his administration of justice by the censure of the House of Commons'.[280] The same view was again advanced in 1959, when a motion was tabled in the House of Commons criticising the conduct of Mr Justice Stable in a case. Shortly thereafter an amendment to that motion was tabled. It read: 'That this House is of the opinion that unless

---

[278] (1834) 21 Parl. Deb., 3rd Ser., 713; (1834) 1 *Mirror of Parliament* 304. This view was affirmed by Mr Napier in 1856. Opposing parliamentary discussion of the state of the judicial bench in Ireland, he said that the 'House could not constitutionally interfere in a matter of that importance, unless it was prepared to follow up its interference by an Address to the Crown' (1856) 140 Parl. Deb., 3rd Ser., 772; see to the same effect Lord Chancellor Chelmsford (1866) 182 Parl. Deb., 3rd Ser., 1637.

[279] (1872) 209 Parl. Deb., 3rd Ser., 757.   [280] (1906) 160 Parl. Deb., 4th Ser., 392, 395.

the motion explicitly asks for the removal from office of the person concerned, assessment and correction of errors committed by judges in the course of judicial proceedings is better left to courts of appeal.'[281]

7.38 In practice, however, judicial misconduct was referred to a Select Committee for further inquiry, and subsequently the matter was dropped on the ground that the alleged misconduct did not justify an address for removal.[282] The further inquiry normally resulted in the revelation of new relevant facts and considerations which tipped the scales in favour of the judge and led the House to abandon the proceedings against him.

Second, the harm that such an inquiry might bring to the accused judge would have played a part in the decision if the nature of the case was such that subsequent non-parliamentary proceedings were possible.[283] Moreover, there is a real danger of harm in such an inquiry because of the rule that a witness testifying before the Select Committee which inquires into the conduct of a judge, 'is bound to answer all questions which the committee see fit to put to him, and cannot excuse himself, for example on the ground that it will incriminate him or that it would prejudice him as defendant in litigation'.[284]

An inquiry into the conduct of a judge, no matter how it terminates, is of itself a form of punishment, and this will also be carefully considered by Parliament in deciding whether or not to refer the matter for inquiry.[285]

Course of proceedings

7.39 If the House decided to refer the case for further inquiry, it may have referred it to a Select Committee or to a Committee of the whole House.[286]

---

[281] *The Times*, 27 November 1959.

[282] Thus the practice runs counter to the view that Parliament cannot exercise any checking measure short of removal by address.

[283] *Kenrick's Case* (1825) 13 Parl. Deb., 2nd Ser., 1138, 1409 [Mr Secretary Peel]. The judge has absolute immunity in the exercise of his judicial functions, so subsequent proceedings outside Parliament may be feasible only when the misconduct outside his judicial functions gives rise to civil action or criminal prosecution against the judge.

[284] Erskine May, *Parliamentary Practice*, 8th edn (1879), 702. See, however, R. Gordon QC and Amy Street, 'Select Committees and Coercive Powers – Clarity or Confusion?' (London: Constitution Society, 2012).

[285] *Smith's Case* (1834) 21 Parl. Deb., 3rd Ser., 272, 311.

[286] For a Select Committee, see *O'Grady's Case* (1823) 9 Parl. Deb., 2nd Ser., 360; *Smith's Case* (1834) 21 Parl. Deb. 3rd Ser., 272; *Barrington's Case* (1830) 24 Parl. Deb., 2nd Ser., 965; for a Committee of the whole House, see *Kenrick's Case* (1825) 13 Parl. Deb., 2nd Ser., 1138; *Kenrick's Case II* (1826) 14 Parl. Deb., 2nd Ser., 363.

The Select Committee would investigate the alleged misconduct, gather evidence and hear witnesses, including the accused judge. Upon completing its work, the committee would have reported its recommendation and this is discussed in the House, sitting as a Committee of the whole House. Alternatively, the House may have referred the matter directly to a Committee of the whole House. The Committee of the whole House was confined to the taking of evidence which may be reported without any declaration of opinion, this being reserved to the House. Otherwise, and this was the course followed in most cases, the Committee of the whole House heard evidence and arguments and decided what further steps were to be taken in the matter.[287] The Committee of the whole House consists of all the Members and is in fact the House in less formal guise, presided over by a chairman instead of by the Speaker, and conducting its business according to more flexible rules.[288]

The judge is given due notice of the intended proceedings. When the charges or petitions are presented, the judge will be provided with a copy as well as with any orders and resolutions of the House on the matter. He may appear before the House by counsel, in person, or both, and introduce evidence in his defence. As a general rule, the whole House will hear evidence at the Bar notwithstanding that the Select Committee had previously heard the same evidence.[289] However, when the charges mainly depend on documentary evidence, or when the party has been given sufficient opportunity to be heard before committees inquiring into his conduct, but deliberately failed to appear, this may result in a denial of an application for hearing evidence at the Bar of the House. Upon these grounds, Sir Jonah Barrington was denied a hearing on the merits at the Bar of the House, although his counsel was allowed to address the House. The resolutions arrived at in the Committee of the whole House are reported to the House, where they are debated. If a resolution calling for an address for removal is reported by the committee and agreed upon in the House, a committee to draft the address will be appointed. The draft of the committee will be considered by the House of Commons, and upon its approval it will be carried to the Lords.

The whole process is repeated again in the House of Lords, including setting up a Committee, hearing evidence at the Bar, debates and deliberation. If the Lords come to the same decision to present an address for

---

[287] *Kenrick's Case II* (1826) 14 Parl. Deb., 2nd Ser., 500–2.
[288] Erskine May, *Parliamentary Practice*, 8th edn (1879), 628, 701.
[289] *Barrington's Case* (1830) 24 Parl. Deb., 2nd Ser., 965, 977, 978.

removal, they insert their title in the blank left for them by the Commons in the address. After the Lords return a message, acquainting the House of Commons with their concurrence and that the blank has been filled, the address is presented to Her Majesty. The complete process has been carried to its ultimate conclusion only once in the United Kingdom, in the case of Sir Jonah Barrington, a judge of the High Court of Admiralty in Ireland.[290]

Procedural safeguards

7.40 There are no clear statutory provisions regulating the procedure for an address for removal. Doubts might therefore be entertained as to the nature of the proceedings in Parliament upon a motion for an inquiry into conduct of a judge with a view to passing an address for removal. On the whole, however, in spite of divisions between MPs on procedural questions, it is clear that the proceedings have been deemed judicial in nature and procedural safeguards protecting the accused judge, as well as public confidence in the courts, have been followed. It is settled that the charges presented to the House against a judge should be in writing.[291] The judge should be duly advised of the intended proceedings against him and copies of the petitions or the charges, as the case may be, and the orders of the House relating to the matter should be promptly sent to him.[292] The judge is heard and allowed to cross-examine witnesses and call witnesses in support of his defence.

The House will not alter the language of charges against a judge at a late stage of the proceedings, since this is deemed to be a denial of due notice and a denial of the opportunity to meet the charge.[293] Delay in the proceedings against a judge in Parliament is avoided.[294] Speedy proceedings secure that the charges will not hang too long over the judge's head. For the same reasons and for ensuring that the defence will be heard soon after the charges are brought, the proceedings against the judge should be initiated early at the beginning of Parliament's session.[295] The concern of the House to protect judges from public indignity resulting from false

---

[290] *Barrington's Case* (1830) 24 Parl. Deb., 2nd Ser., 965.
[291] *Baron Page's Case* (1722) 7 Parl. Hist., 962; *Kenrick's Case* (1825) 13 Parl. Deb., 2nd Ser., 1138, 1149 [Mr Secretary Peel].
[292] *Kenrick's Case* (1825) 13 Parl. Deb., 2nd Ser., 1138.
[293] *Barrington's Case* (1830) 24 Parl. Deb. 2nd Ser., 965, 978.
[294] *O'Grady's Case* (1823) 9 Parl. Deb., 2nd Ser., 360, 981.
[295] *Kenrick's Case* (1825) 13 Parl. Deb., 2nd Ser., 1138, 1410; *O'Grady's Case* (1823) 9 Parl. Deb., 2nd Ser., 360, 978 [Mr Scarlett].

charges is illustrated in the order issued by the Commons that the charges against Lord Ellenborough CJ be erased from the Journals of the House.[296] So anxious has Parliament been to protect the judiciary from unnecessary exposure to public indignity that it has been willing to qualify the constitutional right of aggrieved individuals to lay their grievances before Parliament. Parliament twice refused to entertain petitions against judges: Earl Russell and Mr Denman, who brought up the petitions believing that 'if a petition is couched in respectful terms to the House, no Member ought to refuse to present it', were criticised in the House of Lords and House of Commons respectively for failing to exercise their discretion and to decline to present the petition.[297]

That the proceedings for an address have been deemed judicial also appears from the frequent reference by Members to proceedings for impeachment in support of their views of the proper procedural course which should be followed by the House upon a motion for an address for removal.[298]

The role of government

7.41 It is an established principle that the 'Government ought not to support a motion [for an inquiry into the conduct of a judge], without having themselves instituted some preliminary investigations, and been prepared to say, that there was a fit occasion for following it up by an address to the Crown'.[299] This principle derived from the government's responsibility for the 'due administration of justice throughout the Kingdom' and from the 'obligation which they owe to the dispensers of justice to preserve them from injurious attack or calumnious accusations'.[300] In practice, the government has conducted independent inquiries into the allegations before forming their view on the matter. The judges have been approached, normally by the Lord Chancellor, and given an opportunity to refute the charges.

---

[296] (1816) 34 Parl. Deb., 1st Ser., 131; *Kelly's Case* 1867) 185 Parl. Deb. 3rd Ser., 268.

[297] *Kelly's Case* (1867) 185 Parl. Deb. 3rd Ser., 268; *Mr Justice Best's Case* (1821) 4 Parl. Deb., New Ser., 918.

[298] *Barrington's Case* (1830) 24 Parl. Deb., 2nd Ser., 965, 970; the mode of proceedings by address was essentially the same as proceedings by impeachment. See also *Smith's Case* (1834) 21 Parl. Deb., 3rd Ser., 272, 324; *O'Grady's Case* (1823) 9 Parl. Deb., 2nd Ser., 360, 361.

[299] Sir James Scarlett (later Lord Abinger); *Smith's Case* (1834) 21 Parl. Deb., 3rd Ser., 518, quoted with approval in *Abinger's Case* (1843) 66 Parl. Deb., 3rd Ser., 1102.

[300] Todd, *Parliamentary Government*, vol. II, 742.

In spite of expressions to the contrary, the general view was that the government ought not to institute proceedings in Parliament against judges; this should be done by ordinary members of the House.[301] Underlying this view is the desire to prevent unnecessary interference by the executive with the independence of the judiciary. Also, if the government takes up the case, it might be treated in Parliament as a party question, creating irrelevant considerations and partisanship rather than impartiality. However, in cases where misconduct of a judge justified the institution of proceedings in Parliament against him and no private Member undertakes to initiate such proceedings, it clearly appeared that it would be the duty of the government to initiate such proceedings. As Mr Denman, later Lord Chief Justice, put it:

> Suppose it should prove a case of an officer of high judicial rank acting in a manner utterly derogatory from his station and dignity, were they to be told that government would not then take some step in the business, and that it must drop, unless some private member undertook the ulterior course, of moving for parliamentary impeachment?[302]

One may infer from the case of Mr Justice Grantham that sometimes the government will be expected to take the initiative.[303] In that case, the Prime Minister (Mr Asquith) stated that, as the conduct of the judge was universally condemned, the government 'does not propose to invite Parliament on this occasion to take the extreme step of addressing the Crown for the removal of the judge'.

In practice, whatever position the government takes in the proceedings for an address, and whether they are instituted by the government or by a private Member, it is very likely to have an important effect on the final result.[304] Considering also the government's control over the majority in Parliament, it is not surprising that, except in one case, the final result in all cases was that supported by the government.

In some cases the government and the prime minister were visibly involved. In the case of *Barrington*,[305] the government initiated the proceedings and actively supported an address for removal in both

---

[301] *O'Grady's Case* (1823) 9 Parl. Deb., 2nd Ser., 360, 362, 364. For views to the contrary, see *Kenrick's Case* (1825) 13 Parl. Deb., 2nd Ser., 1138, 1139 and 1148; *O'Grady's Case* (1823) 9 Parl. Deb., 2nd Ser., 360.

[302] *O'Grady's Case* (1823) 9 Parl. Deb., 2nd Ser., 363.

[303] 22 HC Deb. 366 (1 March 1911).

[304] *O'Grady's Case* (1823) 9 Parl. Deb., 2nd Ser., 360, 362 [Mr Abercromby].

[305] *Barrington's Case* (1830) 24 Parl. Deb., 2nd Ser., 965.

Houses. Indeed, the Attorney General and the Solicitor General conducted the case against Sir Jonah Barrington in the House of Lords, after a resolution for an address for his removal had been passed by the House of Commons. Conversely, except for the case of *Smith*,[306] the government opposed the inquiry or the passing of an address for removal in all other cases and in all those cases the attempt to remove the judge failed. In the case of *Smith*, the ministers first objected to the inquiry but later changed their minds. This move was strongly criticised, and probably had an adverse effect on their stand, for no more than eight days after the matter had been referred to a Select Committee the order was discharged and proceedings against the judge were abandoned, although supported by the ministers.[307]

Not only did the government have considerable control over the final outcome of the proceedings, but through its far-reaching control over parliamentary time it could prevent debates on motions for inquiries into judicial misconduct by refusing requests for time for the discussion of such motions. Thus in 1924 the prime minister (Ramsay MacDonald) refused a request for time for discussing a motion for an inquiry into Mr Justice McCardie's conduct in the *General O'Dwyer* case with a view to passing an address for his removal.[308] Whether time would be granted for discussion of motions for an address for removal mainly depended on the number of MPs who would support the motion after it was put down on the Order Paper. Thus in the case of *Grantham*, the prime minister (Sir H. Campbell-Bannerman), having been criticised for granting time for discussing the judge's misconduct, replied: 'The Right Hon. Gentleman attached some blame to me for having given a day for the discussion of this question. I think he forgets the memorial that was presented to me signed by 347 members of this House asking for an opportunity.'

Effect of dissolution, prorogation and pardon

7.42 Unlike proceedings for impeachment, dissolution or prorogation of Parliament terminates the proceedings on a motion for an address for removal. This appears from the case of *Fox*[309] where a special statute was passed by Parliament 'to continue the proceedings in the House of Lords

---

[306] *Smith's Case* (1834) 21 Parl. Deb., 3rd Ser., 272.
[307] *Smith's Case* (1834) 21 Parl. Deb., 3rd Ser., 272, 337, 752.
[308] *Hansard*, HC, vol. 175, cols. 6–7 (23 June 1924).
[309] (1805) 45 Lords Journal 181, 359, 366, 370.

touching the conduct of Luke Fox ... notwithstanding any prorogation or dissolution of Parliament'.[310]

The effect that a pardon may have upon proceedings for an address raises more difficult questions. It would seem that proceedings for an address cannot be deemed criminal, for the most extreme measure which may follow is an address for removal of the judge. On this view, a pardon has no application. Even though the judge cannot be prosecuted in the ordinary criminal courts for the offence pardoned, Parliament is free to pass an address for his removal on account of that offence.

However, it may be suggested that the nature of the proceedings for an address is such that it would be affected by a pardon. Certain expressions uttered in the course of debates on motions for an address,[311] and the frequent references to impeachment in those debates, lend some support to such suggestion. The question then is whether the rule that a pardon is not pleadable against impeachment is also applicable to proceedings for an address. It may be said that unless a statute or precedent ruled to the contrary, the prerogative of pardon cannot be affected, and while it was settled in *Lord Danby's Case* and later enacted by statute, that pardon is not pleadable against impeachment proceedings, no rule has been laid down in Parliament, nor has it been enacted by statute, that pardon may not be pleaded in proceedings for an address.

Furthermore, from the case of *Fox*, where a special statute was passed to continue proceedings for an address for removal notwithstanding dissolution or prorogation, it seems that the analogy existing between address and impeachment is not sufficient to apply to an address the same rules as those applicable to impeachment. Nevertheless, the report of the Committee of the House of Commons which investigated Lord Danby's pardon lends support to the view that a pardon may not be pleaded against proceedings for an address.[312]

Whether or not in law a pardon is pleadable against proceedings for an address, it is extremely unlikely that the Home Secretary, who is now

---

[310] 45 Geo. III. c.117.

[311] In *Fox's Case* (1806) 7 Parl. Deb., 755–66, the following expressions were employed to refer to proceedings for an address: 'complaint of criminal matter', 'criminal complaint', 'criminal jurisdiction'.

[312] It can be argued that the rationale behind the invalidation of Lord Danby's pardon ('the setting up a pardon to be a bar of an impeachment, defeats the whole use and effect of impeachment') is equally applicable to a pardon in bar of an address for removal, see The Report of the Committee of the House of Commons), cited in Hatsell, *Precedents*, vol. IV, 404.

responsible for the exercise of the prerogative of pardon, would ever attempt to exercise that power in such a way as to affect proceedings against a judge in Parliament or elsewhere.

Judicial review of the removal of judges by an address of Parliament

7.43 Whatever the true construction of the Act of Settlement may be, it is suggested that the action of Parliament upon a motion for an address is unlikely to oust the jurisdiction of the court.[313] This reading of section 11 (3) of the Senior Courts Act 1981, which enshrines the power of removal, may, at first sight, seem unlikely. Parliament has unquestioned authority over the procedures it employs as legislator: 'to determine for itself what the procedures shall be, whether there has been a breach of its procedures and what then should happen'.[314] In practice, the courts exercise 'a self-denying ordinance in relation to interfering with the proceedings of Parliament'.[315] The effective working of the constitution, however, relies upon a long-standing comity between Parliament and the courts such that each takes care not to intrude on the other's province, or to undermine the other's authority. Bradley further commented that, notwithstanding that parliamentary privilege 'stems from the "lex et consuetudo parliament" rather than from the common law courts, it is definitely part of the law'.[316] The courts' recognition of Parliament's province is not one way. Parliament has also shown respect for the courts' province. Matters pending before the courts are not to be discussed in Parliament; likewise, it has been firmly established that Parliament will not intervene when the complaints against a judge concerned matters of court practice and procedure or when the decision complained of was discussed in the appellate court.[317]

---

[313] But removal of a judge by impeachment is not judicially reviewable in the United States, see *Nixon* v. *US* 1993 508 US 927.

[314] Joint Committee on Parliamentary Privilege, 'Parliamentary Privilege – First Report', vol. I (HL 43-I / HC 214-I, April 1999), para. 13.

[315] This was said in relation to Article IX of the Bill of Rights, see *R.* v. *Parliamentary Commissioner for Standards, ex parte Al Fayed* [1998] 1 WLR 669, 670 [Lord Woolf].

[316] A. Bradley, Memorandum on 'Parliamentary Privilege – The Relationship between Courts and Parliaments', in Joint Committee on Parliamentary Privilege, 'Parliamentary Privilege – First Report', vol. II (24 February 1998) (HL 43-II / HC 214-II, April 1999), para. 8; also citing Holt CJ in *Paty's Case* ((1704) 2 Ld. Raym. 1105): 'The privileges of the House of Commons are well known, and are founded upon the law of the land, and are nothing but the law.'

[317] See, e.g., *Best's Case* (1821) 4 Parl. Deb. New Ser., 918.

But section 11(3) Senior Courts Act 1981 may now fall to be interpreted by reference to section 3 HRA. Since any judge subject to removal proceedings would face dismissal, the proceedings would warrant classification as civil and attract the protection guaranteed by a right to a fair trial, under Article 6 ECHR.[318] If a judge challenged the constitutional proceedings for removal of a judge before the courts, it is therefore suggested that, under section 6(1) ECHR, these proceedings would be amenable to domestic judicial scrutiny. The courts would be required to read section 11(3) Senior Courts Act 1981 in a way that is compatible with Article 6 ECHR. Then the rules relating to the finding or hearing of evidence, and the rules relating to the standard of proof required, would fall within the remit of the courts.[319] However, one might expect that Parliament itself is likely to adopt procedures which are compliant with Article 6 ECHR, thus rendering any judicial review proceedings unnecessary.[320]

Parliamentary proceedings are certainly not beyond the reach of the European Court of Human Rights, as illustrated by the case of *Demicoli* v. *Malta*, though this applied to a journalist in criminal proceedings before Parliament.[321] In this case, the Constitutional Court of Malta deemed it inappropriate to intervene in the House of Representative proceedings. The editor of a political satirical magazine had been found guilty of contempt of Parliament, but the two members whose conduct was criticised by the editor participated throughout the investigatory proceedings. The European Court held that the editor had the right to a fair hearing by an independent and impartial tribunal, and that this right was violated by the participation of these two members of the Maltese House of Representatives. Since the editor could either be imprisoned or fined for breach of parliamentary privilege, the proceedings attracted the protection guaranteed by Article 6 ECHR.

There might arise situations in which misbehaviour for which a judge has been removed will be tried by a court of law. There is no reason to

[318] *Demicoli* v. *Malta* (1992) 14 EHRR 47; Joint Committee on Parliamentary Privilege, 'Parliamentary Privilege – First Report', paras. 29 and 283.
[319] Hearn, Government of England, 85; Cf. Nixon v. US (1993) 508 US 927; *Justice* v. *Ramaswami (Sub-Committee on Judicial Accountability* v. *Union of India)* (1991) 4 SCC 699.
[320] Joint Committee on Parliamentary Privilege, 'Parliamentary Privilege – First Report', para. 29; *Demicoli* v. *Malta* (1992) 14 EHRR 47, Joint Committee on Parliamentary Privilege, 'Parliamentary Privilege – First Report' vol. I (HL 43-I / HC 214-I, April 1999), para. 29.
[321] *Demicoli* v. *Malta* (1992) 14 EHRR 47.

doubt that a court of law may try a judge for an act that amounts to a criminal offence for which he had been removed upon an address. Likewise, situations might arise in which judicial misbehaviour short of a criminal offence, and outside the judge's judicial duties, have been discussed by Parliament and are then the subject of an action in the courts. Thus, if a judge in his private capacity attacks a man, in a circumstance which induced an MP to move for an address, and later on an action in tort is brought by or against the judge, the court would have full jurisdiction. In such a situation it is not inconceivable that the findings of fact will be different. In *Kenrick's Case*, Mr Scarlett (later Lord Abinger CB) urged this situation as a reason for the House not entertaining a petition against a judge for misbehaviour in his private capacity. Mr Scarlett argued that '[should the House] find the accusation true, and the [aggrieved individual] should bring his action; the jury might find a verdict for the defendant, and thus the decision of the House and of a court of justice would be in direct opposition'.[322] Rejecting this argument, Mr Denman said: 'If that argument were valid there would be an end altogether to parliamentary control; for in almost every case in which their jurisdiction could be called for, the parties might possibly have legal remedy elsewhere.'[323]

D.   The mechanism in operation

7.44 The major cases of proceedings taken against judges after the Act of Settlement with a view to considering an address for their removal from office may now be surveyed. In most cases it is abundantly clear that the proceedings were aimed at removal by address. Sometimes, however, doubts remain whether the motion for inquiry into the conduct of the judge was to be followed by impeachment, address for removal, or merely by a general censure of the judge in the ensuing debates.[324] This is mainly due to the similarity in the ways of instituting different forms of procedure in Parliament and in the terminology employed by Members in the various modes of proceedings against judges. As the cases below illustrate, it is firmly established that misconduct involving moral turpitude is a sufficient ground for removing a judge from office, although the principle has normally been expressed in negative terms: Parliament will

---

[322] *Kenrick's Case* (1825) 13 Parl. Deb., 2nd Ser., 505.   [323] *Ibid.*, 506.

[324] See *Page's Case* (1722) 7 Parl. Hist. 962; *Ellenborough's Case* (1813) and (1816) 34 Parl. Deb. 1st Ser., 104.

not inquire into the conduct of a judge or pass an address for his removal unless he was charged with misconduct involving moral turpitude. In almost every case debated in Parliament this principle has been reaffirmed. What is meant by the phrase 'conduct involving moral turpitude' can be best explained by examining the terms employed to describe 'conduct involving moral turpitude', justifying an inquiry into the conduct of a judge and an address for his removal from office.

In the majority of cases, the concepts of corruption or corrupt motives have been used.[325] One can also find references to mental and physical disabilities,[326] neglect of duty,[327] partiality,[328] dishonest motives,[329] misconduct in private life,[330] perversion of justice[331] and other 'gross misconducts which all persons would admit to deserve serious reprehension'.[332]

The first recorded case of proceedings against a judge in Parliament after the Act of Settlement was the case of *Page* in 1722.[333] Sir Francis Page, one of the Barons of the Exchequer, was charged with endeavouring to corrupt the borough of Banbury by offering them a bribe to induce them to choose a certain person as a candidate in a coming election. It was charged that 'Mr Baron Page not only offered to the borough to forgive them six or seven hundred pounds they owed to him for their new charter but likewise to give them another large sum in ready money'.[334] The suggestion advanced by some Members that the Baron

---

[325] *Ellenborough's Case* (1816) 34 Parl. Deb., 1st Ser., 104; *McClelland's Case* (1819) 40 Parl. Deb., 1st Ser., 851; *O'Grady's Case* (1823) 9 Parl. Deb., 2nd Ser., 360; *Kenrick's Case* (1825) 13 Parl. Deb., 2nd Ser., 1138; *Smith's Case* (1834) 21 Parl. Deb., 3rd Ser., 694; *Abinger's Case* (1843) 66 Parl. Deb., 3rd Ser., 1129; *Torrens' Case* (1856) 140 Parl. Deb, 3rd Ser., 1544; *Monahan's Case* (1861) 163 Parl. Deb., 3rd Ser., 984. The principles behind the grounds for removal by address are similar to those applied by the Court of King's Bench in considering applications for criminal informations against county court judges and magistrates for misconduct, see Short and Mellor, *Practice on the Crown Side*; J. Shortt, *Informations (Criminal and Quo Warranto) Mandamus, and Prohibition* (London: W. Clowes and Sons, 1887), pp. 26–9. The same general principles would seem to apply in disciplinary proceedings, see above, para. 7.16.

[326] *Torrens' Case* (1856) 140 Parl. Deb, 3rd Ser., 1544; *Fox's Case* (1806) 7 Parl. Deb., 752; *Grantham's Case* (1906) 160 Parl. Deb., 4th Ser., 369.

[327] *Barrington's Case* (1830) Parl. Deb., 2nd Ser., 484.

[328] *Smith's Case* (1834) 21 Parl. Deb., 3rd Ser., 694.

[329] *Abinger's Case* (1843) 66 Parl. Deb., 3rd Ser., 1129.

[330] *Kenrick's Case* (1825) 13 Parl. Deb., 2nd Ser., 1138.

[331] *Torrens' Case* (1856) 140 Parl. Deb, 3rd Ser., 1544.

[332] *Monahan's Case* (1861) 163 Parl. Deb., 3rd Ser., 984.

[333] (1722) 7 Parl. Hist. 961.   [334] *Ibid.*, 962.

be censured immediately was rejected upon the ground that 'it was unreasonable to arraign, condemn, and censure a man, especially one in so high a station, before they heard what he had to say in his own vindication'.[335] The complaint against the judge was put into writing, and a copy of it was delivered to Baron Page. At a later date witnesses were examined at the Bar of the House, and Baron Page was represented by counsel who addressed the House on his behalf. After hearing the evidence, the question was put whether the mover 'had made good his charges against Sir Francis Page'. After a long debate the charge was dismissed by a vote of 128 to 124.

In 1725, as seen above, Lord Macclesfield, the Lord Chancellor, was impeached and convicted of selling Masterships in Chancery.[336] Almost a century passed before proceedings were initiated against another judge. Then, in 1805, on three petitions presented to the House of Lords against Luke Fox, a judge of the Common Pleas in Ireland, it was moved that a humble address be presented to His Majesty to remove the judge from his office.[337] Mr Justice Fox was alleged to have introduced political topics into his instructions to the grand jury at the Assizes. It was said that he told them that it was their duty to address His Majesty to have the Lord Lieutenant of Ireland removed. He was also charged with having tried to persuade the commanding officer of a regiment to do the same. Likewise, he was accused of imposing a fine of £500 on the High Sheriff for being late in meeting him when he went to the Assizes, and with insulting a petty jury. For almost two years the case was debated and evidence heard in the House, in a Select Committee and in the House sitting as a Committee of the whole House. Upon a petition of the judge, Lord Grenville, the prime minister, moved that the proceedings against the judge be abandoned on the ground that the House of Lords could not entertain an inquiry into the conduct of a judge before the House of Commons had looked into the matter. For if the House of Lords passes a resolution for an address of removal, and then the matter goes to the House of Commons, the Commons may constitutionally resolve that the charges against the judge ought to be brought by way of impeachment. In such a case, the Lords, having prejudged the case, would not be able to try it. Over the objection of a strong minority opinion of Lord Eldon and others, Lord Grenville's motion was agreed to, and there the matter ended.[338] Mr Justice Fox remained on the bench until his resignation in 1816.

---

[335] *Ibid.*   [336] See above, para. 7.27.   [337] (1805) 45 Lords Journal 181.
[338] *Mr Justice Fox's Case* (1806) 7 Parl. Deb., 751–71, 788–9.

Lord Ellenborough, the Lord Chief Justice, had to face charges of misconduct both in the House of Lords and in the House of Commons. In 1813, he was charged before the Lords that as a Member of the Commission appointed in 1805 to inquire into the conduct of Caroline Princess of Wales, he misstated certain points of evidence given by one of the witnesses.[339] In 1816, thirteen articles of charge were presented against Lord Ellenborough in the House of Commons by Lord Cochrane, charging him with judicial misconduct in a criminal case heard before him in which Lord Cochrane was a defendant.[340] Inter alia, Lord Ellenborough was charged with improperly compelling counsel for the defendant to enter in the defence at midnight despite the fatigue of counsel and the defendant, with misdirecting the jury as to the evidence and with manifesting partiality, injustice and oppression in the course of the trial. In both cases the Houses dismissed the charges.

In 1819 an article of charge in respect of certain crimes and misdemeanours was presented in the House of Commons against James McClelland, one of the Barons of the Court of the Exchequer of Ireland.[341] The Baron was charged with ordering soldiers to clear out his court, barring access to the court, refusing on improper grounds to postpone a trial and other alleged misconduct. It was agreed that there was no allegation of corrupt motives, and the matters brought up involved questions of pure procedure which were within the Judge's discretion. Therefore the House refused to interfere and the article of charge was rejected.

In 1821 a petition was presented to the House of Commons against Mr Justice Best.[342] In the course of a trial for blasphemous libel the judge fined the defendant for contempt three times. First, the defendant was fined £20 and then £40 twice. Upon these facts the judge was charged with misconduct in the discharge of his judicial functions. As the fines for contempt were unanimously upheld by the Court of the King's Bench on a motion for a new trial, the House refused to 'assume the power of acting as a court of appeal from the Court of the King's Bench',[343] and the petition was rejected by a vote of 64 to 37.

---

[339] (1813) 25 Parl. Deb., 1st Ser., 207.
[340] *Ellenborough's Case* (1816) 34 Parl. Deb., 1st Ser., 103, 104, 114; (1816) 33 Parl. Deb., 1st Ser., 706.
[341] *McClelland's Case* (1819) 40 Parl. Deb., 1st Ser., 851.
[342] *Best's Case* (1821) 4 Parl. Deb. New Ser., 918.
[343] *Ibid.*, 923 [the Attorney General].

The next judge against whom proceedings were initiated in Parliament was Standish O'Grady, Chief Baron of the Irish Court of Exchequer.[344] In 1821, in their ninth report, the Commissioners on the courts of justice in Ireland accused Chief Baron O'Grady of illegally increasing his judicial fees above 'the ancient fees to which he was by law entitled'.[345] Thus, Chief Baron O'Grady increased his remuneration when he doubled his fees and introduced new ones. The charges were investigated by two Select Committees of the House of Commons, which confirmed the charges, and again by the Commissioners to whom the government referred the reports of the Select Committees. Later, all the reports were debated in a Committee of the whole House, which resolved that the increase of judicial fees by the Chief Baron was 'inconsistent with the laws and constitution of the realm'.[346] This resolution was subsequently agreed to by the House. At this stage the government and Members of the House strongly objected to the proceedings upon various grounds. The judge was not heard at the Bar of the House, and it was '[illegal, unjust and unconstitutional] to condemn a judge of rank and character without giving him an opportunity of being heard in his defence'.[347]

The Commission's report was no substitute for hearing at the Bar, for the Commissioners did not have the witnesses cross-examined on the part of the judge nor had the judge been allowed to call his witnesses to rebut the evidence against him. Likewise, doubts had been entertained upon the question whether it was illegal for the judge to increase the fees, which meant that no case of 'criminality or corruption had been made out against the chief baron'.[348] Finally, it was agreed in mitigation of the charges, that the receipt of fees by judges in the Court of Common Law and Exchequer had been recently abolished, making the type of misbehaviour in question a matter of the past. Upon these grounds, it was resolved, by a vote of 38 to 16, that 'this House, under all the circumstances above stated, does not deem it necessary to adopt any further proceedings in the case of the Chief Baron O'Grady'.[349] Thus came to an end the proceedings which were initiated two years earlier.

William Kenrick, who was a magistrate in England and a judge of the Great Sessions in Wales (an office equal in rank and tenure to that of a

---

[344] *O'Grady's Case* (1823) 9 Parl. Deb. 2nd Ser. 360, 938, 977, 1421, 1423, 1429, 1506.

[345] *Ibid.*, 996. Until 1825 judges received the judicial fees paid by suitors as part of their remuneration, see above, para. 2.8.

[346] *Ibid.*, 1425.   [347] *Ibid.*, 1006.   [348] *Ibid.*, 1510.   [349] *Ibid.*, 1510–15.

judge of the King's Bench),[350] faced charges of misconduct in the House of Commons on two different occasions. In 1825, upon the petition of one Mr Canfor, Judge Kenrick was charged with abuse of power, improper exercise of his judicial duties as a magistrate, and suppressing a charge of felony. The House inquired into this matter upon the ground that misconduct of Judge Kenrick in his capacity as Justice of the Peace, if proved, might warrant removal from his higher judicial office, that of a judge of the Great Sessions. After hearing evidence and counsel for the judge, and after much debate and deliberation in the House sitting as a Committee of the whole House, it was resolved that it was not necessary 'to recommend to the House the institution of any further proceedings with reference to the petition of Mr Canfor'.[351]

Upon another petition, Judge Kenrick, in his private capacity, was charged with prosecuting a poor man for theft in order that he might get possession of his house, which upon conviction would be forfeited to the Crown. It was further charged that after the man was committed, Judge Kenrick tried to persuade him to plead guilty, promising to ask for leniency for him. Ultimately, the theft charge was dropped as Judge Kenrick withdrew his prosecution. It was settled in that case that misconduct of a judge in his private life may justify his removal from the bench. There, Lord John Russell said that 'when a serious stain was thrown on the character of a person in a judicial situation it was the duty of that House to inquire whether the individual was fit to exercise the important functions attached to his situation'.[352] Mr Denman formulated the principle in these words: 'by the Act of Settlement it was the duty of the House to examine the conduct of the judges, if notoriously improper, even on matters that affected their private character. If open scandal arose from private conduct of a judge which would be prejudicial to the administration of justice in his person, the House was bound to inquire into the affair.'[353] Although it was generally agreed that misconduct of a judge in his private life may justify an address for removal, in the absence of clear evidence of corrupt motives, the House refused to interfere. After hearing witnesses and the judge's counsel and after much debate and deliberation, the House rejected without division a motion that the charges against the judge were fully established. Judge Kenrick then resigned his office.

---

[350] See (1826) 14 Parl. Deb., 3rd Ser., 659 [Mr Denman]. The office was abolished in 1830.
[351] (1825) 14 Parl. Deb., 2nd Ser., 1138, 1247, 1350, 1407, 1408, 1410, 1425.
[352] (1830) 24 Parl. Deb., 2nd Ser., 974.
[353] *Kenrick's Case II* (1826) 14 Parl. Deb., 2nd Ser., 363, 366–7, 500, 507, 658.

As *Barrington's Case* shows, unjustified absence from office or neglect of official duties in some other respect may justify removal of a judge from the bench. The case of Sir Jonah Barrington, a judge of the High Court of Admiralty in Ireland, is the first and only case of a judge being removed upon an address of both Houses of Parliament.[354] It was charged that Sir Jonah Barrington on several occasions had appropriated for his own use money paid into court. The sums were £682, £200 and £40, not small in those days. Sir Jonah flew to France and appointed deputies to carry on his judicial duties. Sir Jonah's embezzlement was exposed by the eighteenth report of the Commissioners on the courts of justice in Ireland. The report was laid before the House of Commons and referred to a Select Committee, which investigated the matter and confirmed the charges against the judge. Sir Jonah did not accept the Committee's invitation to appear before them or to state the persons whom he wished to be examined by the Committee. The House sitting as a Committee of the whole House considered the charges. Sir Robert Peel, noting that 'there were many sufficient grounds for an address for the removal of a judge, though no legal crime could be proved against him', said that 'the absence of a judge from the realm [and] pretended indisposition on the part of a judge ... would justify the House in addressing the Crown to remove [him].[355] Sir Robert reasoned: 'Was it to be endured that a judge, who performed no duty, should be allowed to draw his salary from the public funds? Would it become them, the guardians of the public purse, to suffer this?'[356] Mr Denman, supported by several Members, argued that the judge should be heard at the Bar of the House notwithstanding that a Select Committee had already heard evidence.[357] However, the general opinion in the House was that as Sir Jonah had refused to appear before the Committee, and since the evidence against him was documentary and founded upon his own admissions, it was not necessary to take further evidence at the Bar. Thus, without further hearings, the House agreed upon a motion for an address for removal, and a committee was appointed to draft the address to the Crown, which was approved by the House. The address recapitulated the

---

[354] *Barrington's Case* (1830) 24 Parl. Deb., 2nd Ser., 484, 965, 1075.
[355] (1830) 24 Parl. Deb., 2nd Ser., 974.
[356] *Ibid.* In *Smith's Case*, Sir Robert Peel again suggested that 'gross and grievous neglect of duty' would warrant a removal from the bench, *Smith's Case* (1834) 21 Parl. Deb., 3rd Ser., 694, at 744.
[357] *Ibid.*, 966.

acts of which Sir Jonah had been found guilty and concluded: 'It is unfit and would be of bad example, that he should continue to hold the said office. We therefore humbly pray your Majesty that your Majesty will be pleased to remove Sir Jonah Barrington from the office which he holds, Judge of the High Court in Admiralty in Ireland.'[358]

The address was delivered to the Lords in a conference. In the House of Lords the whole process was repeated.[359] Unlike the Commons, the Lords heard the judge and his counsel, and they were allowed to cross-examine witnesses. The Attorney General and the Solicitor General conducted the case against the judge. After the hearings the address was considered and agreed upon. A message was carried to the House of Commons informing them of the approval, and certain Members were appointed by both Houses to present the address to His Majesty. His Majesty replied that he would give directions that Sir Jonah Barrington be removed from his judicial office.[360]

Four years after Sir Jonah's removal, charges of judicial misconduct were made against another Irish judge in Parliament. Sir William Smith, one of the Barons of the Exchequer in Ireland, was charged in the House of Commons with keeping his court very late at night (sometimes until 6:00 a.m.), coming very late to court (after 12:30 p.m.), and introducing political topics in charges to grand juries.[361] The matter was referred to a Select Committee, but eight days later, against the views of the ministers, the order was discharged and the proceedings were abandoned upon the ground that there was no corruption in the alleged misconduct and that the House should not interfere in questions of procedure and the administration of courts.

In 1843 Lord Abinger, Lord Chief Baron of the Exchequer, was charged in the House of Commons with using highly political language on the bench. In his instructions to the jury on a trial of defendants who participated in demonstrations and strikes for further reform of the right to vote, Lord Abinger made long speeches condemning their political ideas. The following passage is a good illustration of Lord Abinger's expressions for which he was accused of unconstitutional, partial and oppressive conduct:

> You will find that there is a society of persons who go by the name of Chartists ... what is the object of the charter which these men are

---

[358] *Ibid.*, 1075.   [359] (1830) 62 Lords Journal 162, 166, 583, 597, 602, 716, 873, 879, 901.
[360] See *Ibid.*, 915.   [361] (1834) 21 Parl. Deb., 3rd Ser., 272, 695.

seeking? What are the points of the charter? Annual Parliaments, universal suffrage and vote by ballot. What a strange effect then would the
establishment of a system of universal suffrage produce! Under it every
man though possessing no property would have a voice in the choice of
the representation of the people. The necessary consequences of this
system would be that those who have no property would make laws for
those who have property and the destruction of the monarchy and the
aristocracy must necessarily ensue.[362]

The language used by Lord Abinger was deemed objectionable even in
1843 and was strongly criticised by the press and in Parliament during
the debates on the motion for an inquiry into his conduct. The Tory
government objected to the motion. The Attorney General (Sir
F. Pollock) argued that 'a judge not only might allude, but that it
sometimes became his duty to allude, to political affairs'.[363] It was also
urged that in the absence of 'badness of heart and a corrupt intention',[364]
a motion for an inquiry should not be sustained. The proponents of an
inquiry pressed their view, asserting that 'no judge ought to travel out of
the record immediately before him', and that 'the people abhorred
political judges'.[365] At the end, the motion was rejected by a large
majority: 228 to 73.

Mr Duncombe, who moved for an inquiry into the conduct of Lord
Abinger, was also responsible for the debate on the conduct of Baron
Gurney later in the same year.[366] Upon a petition from a man who had
been convicted of sedition and was then in prison, Mr Duncombe
alleged that during the trial before Baron Gurney, constant interruptions by the judge deprived the defendant of an opportunity of vindi-
cating his innocence before the jury. As the law afforded no remedy,
and an application for the remission of the sentence was refused, Mr
Duncombe moved that an address should be presented to Her Majesty
to take the case into her merciful consideration. The Home Secretary
(Sir James Graham), relying on the replies he received from the judge,
dismissed the charges against him and asserted that there was no
sufficient ground for impugning the conduct of the judge. Nor did he
think that there were special circumstances warranting an address
calling for the exercise of the prerogative of pardon. Finally, the motion
was withdrawn.

---

[362] *Abinger's Case* (1843) 66 Parl. Deb., 3rd Ser., 1037, 1048.
[363] *Ibid.*, 1071, 1100, 1103.   [364] *Ibid.*, 1129 [Sir James Graham].
[365] *Ibid.*, 1097–8.   [366] *Gurney's Case* (1843) 69 Parl. Deb., 3rd Ser., 189.

In 1856 a Member who appeared to have been shocked by an alleged injustice to a poor woman resulting from a matrimonial case in Ireland charged Mr Justice Torrens, one of five judges who affirmed the decision on appeal, with misconduct in the discharge of his judicial duties. The judge, who was singled out for no particular reason, was accused of admitting hearsay evidence, relying on a statement of a witness, which the witness denied that he ever made, and of similar charges. In the absence of any charge of corruption or incapacity and the decision having been upheld on appeal, the House refused to 'take upon itself the duties of a court of review of the proceedings of the ordinary courts of law'.[367] The charges were dismissed and the motion to inquire into the conduct of the judge was rejected.

It appears from that case that, if a judge became unable to discharge his judicial duties properly because of 'the decay of his mental power',[368] sufficient ground for an address for his removal from office would arise. Thus, Lord Palmerston, the Prime Minister, said in *Torrens' Case* that the 'gross perversion of the law...by incapacity' would justify removal.[369] Commenting on Palmerston's statement, the Attorney-General in *Grantham's Case* remarked:

> By 'incapacity' I think Lord Palmerston had in his mind physical [or mental] incapacity not mere aberration, not mere error in the exercise of the judicial function, but the incapacity of a judge who continues so long on the Bench that he is physically [or mentally] unable to discharge his duties.[370]

Similarly, in *Fox's Case*, Lord Grenville, the Prime Minister, said:

> A judge may be in a situation of notorious incapacity from age, and yet it may happen that through the peevishness natural to age, or ill humour, or some other cause, he may wish to adhere to his situation after he has been rendered unfit for its duties. That this would be a painful necessity for the interference of parliament no one would doubt.[371]

In 1865 the conduct of Lord Westbury, the Lord Chancellor, was censured both by the House of Lords and the House of Commons. In the

---

[367] *Torrens' Case* (1856) 140 Parl. Deb., 3rd Ser., 1544, 1561 (Lord Palmerston, the Prime Minister).

[368] (1866) 182 Parl. Deb., 3rd Ser., 1633; A. Paterson, 'The Infirm Judge' (1974) *British Journal of Law and Society* 83, 86.

[369] *Torrens' Case* (1856) 140 Parl. Deb, 3rd Ser., 1544.

[370] *Grantham's Case* (1906) 160 Parl. Deb., 4th Ser., 369.

[371] *Fox's Case* (1806) 7 Parl. Deb., 752.

House of Lords, he was accused of recommending a clerk for retirement on pension, knowing that he had embezzled large sums of public money. Upon the clerk's retirement Lord Westbury appointed one of his sons to the vacated office. The Lords vindicated His Honour but his judgment was condemned.[372] A charge of similar nature was presented against the Lord Chancellor in the House of Commons.[373] He was said to have helped a bankruptcy registrar to retire with a pension notwithstanding that the registrar was suspected of official misconduct, and to have appointed in his position someone who, it seemed, bribed the Lord Chancellor's son in order to convince his father to appoint him to office. In the House of Commons it was resolved that his conduct in both cases,

> shows a laxity of practice and want of caution with regard to the public interest on the part of the Lord Chancellor in sanctioning the grant of retiring pensions to public officers against whom grave charges were pending, which in the opinion of this House are calculated to discredit the administration of his great office.[374]

As a result of this vote of censure, the Lord Chancellor resigned immediately.[375] The Lord Chancellor being removable at the pleasure of the prime minister, this case cannot fall into the category of proceedings for an address for removal and is included here to give a complete picture of the proceedings against judges, including the Lord Chancellor in his (then) capacity of head of the judiciary.

The next complaint was made in 1867 against Lord Chief Baron Kelly in the House of Lords.[376] The circumstances giving rise to the complaint took place 32 years before the complaint was presented. It was charged that Sir Fitzroy Kelly, as the judge was then, had made a false statement before a committee of the House of Commons which was investigating whether he was guilty of bribery or illegal practice at an election. The committee unseated him on the ground that he had committed bribery by his agents and friends, but no lack of integrity was attributed to him. A petition alleging that the judge had pledged his honour as a gentleman to the truth

---

[372] (1856) 177 Parl. Deb., 3rd Ser., 1203; (1865) 178 Parl. Deb., 3rd Ser., 1573; (1865) 179 Parl. Deb., 3rd Ser., 6.

[373] (1865) 180 Parl. Deb., 3rd Ser., 1045.   [374] (1865) 180 Parl. Deb., 3rd Ser., 1135.

[375] (1865) 180 Parl. Deb., 3rd Ser., 1142; T.A. Nash, *The Life of Richard, Lord Westbury, Formerly Lord High Chancellor, with Selections from his Correspondence* (London: R. Bentley and Sons, 1888), vol. II, p. 110; J.B. Atlay, *The Victorian Chancellors* (London: Smith Elder, 1906-1908), vol. II, pp. 268-78; Gibb, *Judicial Corruption*, 42-51; Cecil, *Tipping the Scales*, 126-42.

[376] *Kelly's Case* (1867) 185 Parl. Deb., 3rd Ser., 257.

of a statement in order to deceive the committee, was presented by Earl Russell, who moved that the House of Lords should appoint a committee to inquire into the complaint and if the charge were proved, that an address for removal be presented to the Crown. Earl Russell sent a copy of the petition to the Lord Chancellor, so that he could obtain the answers of the judge to the charge against him. In fact, the answers given by the judge, supported by the shorthand writer's notes, refuted the charges.

In the debate that followed, the conduct of the Lord Chief Baron was completely vindicated by the Lord Chancellor and other peers. It was unanimously felt that Earl Russell should not have presented a petition containing an unfounded charge relating to a matter which had taken place years earlier and never before been raised. The long time which had passed since the alleged misconduct took place weakened the charge. Moreover, before his elevation to the bench, Sir Fitzroy had been Solicitor General and twice Attorney General, but no objection had been made then, although these offices were regarded as 'a direct road to promotion to the office of a Judge'.[377] Earl Russell, acceding to the sense of the House, withdrew the petition.

In 1906 the conduct of Sir William Grantham, a judge of the King's Bench Division, was the subject of discussion and condemnation in the House of Commons. He was charged with having displayed partisan political bias during a trial of an election petition. The nature of partisanship or partiality which would justify removal was carefully defined by the Attorney General:

> I understand partisanship to mean a conscious partiality leading a judge to be disloyal even to his own honest convictions. I understand it to mean that the Judge knows that justice demands that he should take one course but that his political alliance or political sympathies may be such that he deliberately chooses to adopt the other. In such case the moral element undoubtedly enters into the definition of misconduct and cannot be excluded.[378]

Mr Justice Grantham, who was 'a dyed-in-the-wool Conservative'[379] and whom the prime minister called 'an outspoken and intemperate partisan',[380] set aside the election of a Liberal and upheld the election of a

---

[377] *Grantham's Case* (1906) 160 Parl. Deb., 4th Ser., 369; Cecil, *Tipping the Scales*, 194–208.
[378] *Grantham's Case* (1906) 160 Parl. Deb., 4th Ser., 369, at 394.
[379] Cecil, *Tipping the Scales*, 195.
[380] *Grantham's Case* (1906) 160 Parl. Deb., 4th Ser., 409.

Conservative in circumstances that gave rise to allegations of political bias. The Conservative candidate at Great Yarmouth had held a party in October 1905 where alcohol as well as other refreshments were supplied. At the elections held in January 1906 the Conservative was elected. The losing Liberal candidate petitioned to have the election of the Conservative at Great Yarmouth set aside on the ground, inter alia, that the party held by him was a corrupt treating. Mr Justice Grantham rejected the allegation of treating on the ground that an election was not then imminent. The other judge sitting on the petition would have unseated the Conservative but because the judges were equally divided the petition failed.

In another election petition, similar circumstances arose. In September 1905 the father and mother of the Liberal candidate at Bodmin held a garden party where no alcoholic drink was served. Upon the election of the Liberal, the Conservative petitioned to set aside the election for corrupt treating. Holding that the party was held 'on the eve of the election', the election of the Liberal candidate was set aside. Thus, a judge unseated a Liberal for a party held in September 1905, which he deemed 'on the eve' of an election, while upholding the election of a Conservative who held a party in October of that year, holding that 'the election was not then imminent'.

Another charge adduced against the judge was that he had made undesirable and biased remarks about the trial at a dinner party given by the mayor during the hearing of the petition to set aside the election of the Conservative at Great Yarmouth. The feelings against the conduct of the judge were so high that 347 MPs backed a motion for inquiry into his conduct. The motion being so strongly supported, the government was constrained to allot a day for debate on the matter. In the lengthy debate the general view was that no corrupt motive was shown and, in the absence of corruption or moral turpitude, the House should not resort to the extreme penalty of passing an address for removal. However, the judge was condemned in the strongest terms by almost every Member who participated in the debate. As one Member put it: 'There had been such a practically unanimous condemnation of the course that had been pursued that he could hardly conceive existing in the mind of any judge worthy to occupy a place on the English Bench a wish for the retention of office.'[381] In spite of the outspoken criticism in Parliament and clear invitations for his resignation, Mr Justice Grantham did not resign.

---

[381] *Ibid.*, 410 [Mr Blake].

In 1911 Mr Justice Grantham's conduct again came before Parliament. Having kept his rage under strict control for five years, Mr Justice Grantham felt that he should vindicate himself and 'expose the falsity of the charges' made against him. In a speech delivered on 7 February 1911, before the Bar at Liverpool, he violently attacked the House of Commons. A month later two MPs asked the prime minister what steps the government proposed to take with reference to the speech made by Mr Justice Grantham. Mr Asquith, the prime minister, noted 'with satisfaction and without surprise that the speech referred to has been universally and emphatically condemned by professional and public opinion', and he added:

> In the hope and belief that this unanimous verdict of censure may prevent the recurrence of an incident so inconsistent with the judicial character and the best traditions of the Bench, they do not propose to invite Parliament on this occasion to take the extreme step of addressing the Crown for the removal of the judge.[382]

In 1924, Mr George Lansbury put down a motion for an address for the removal of Sir Henry McCardie, a judge of the King's Bench Division. Mr Justice McCardie was trying a libel case. An issue arising in that case was the conduct of General Dyer, who had been dismissed by the government for ordering troops to fire at a mob during disturbances at Amritsar in India. In his instructions to the jury, the judge said: 'Speaking with full deliberation and knowing the whole of the evidence in the case I express my view that General Dyer, in the grave and exceptional circumstances, acted rightly, and in my opinion, he was wrongly punished by the Secretary of State for India.'[383]

The motion for an address having been put down on the Order Paper, Mr Lansbury asked the prime minister whether the government would grant time for the discussion of the motion. Mr Ramsay MacDonald, the prime minister, replied that 'a discussion on this subject would only add to the harm that has been done in India by the words complained of'.[384] In addition to this political reason for refusing time, he added, significantly: 'However unfortunate the words have been, they clearly do not constitute the kind of fault amounting to a moral delinquency which constitutionally justifies an Address as proposed.'[385]

---

[382] *Hansard*, HC, vol. 22, col. 366 (1 March 1911).
[383] *Hansard*, HC, vol. 175, cols. 6–7 (23 June 1924).
[384] *Hansard*, HC, vol. 175, col. 6 (23 June 1924).
[385] For an account of this case, rather favourable to the judge, see G. Pollock, *Mr Justice McCardie: A Biography* (London: John Lane, 1934), 132–9.

The prime minister, however, did not fail to observe that the judiciary should guard itself against pronouncements upon issues involving grave political consequences which are not themselves being tried. Being 'perfectly satisfied' with this statement, Mr Lansbury withdrew his motion.

More recently, at the end of 1973, the question of an address for removal of a judge again came to the fore. In October of that year, the now defunct Industrial Relations Court exercised its power of sequestration against certain assets held in the 'political fund' of a large trade union (the Amalgamated Union of Engineering Workers), which refused to obey the Court's order. This evoked a campaign of criticism undertaken by trade unionists and Labour backbenchers against Sir John Donaldson, the President of the Court. A motion was put down in Parliament, calling for Donaldson's removal from office for, inter alia, 'political prejudice and partiality'. The motion attracted the signatures of 187 Labour MPs. The judge took the unusual step of defending the decision of his Court in public and of 'setting the record straight'. Donaldson J explained that 'neither the sequestrators nor the Court had any knowledge that this £100,000 was earmarked for a political or any other purpose'.[386]

Lord Hailsham LC strongly criticised the proponents of the motion for an address to remove Donaldson J. Speaking as head of the judiciary in a public speech, Lord Hailsham said that the public should note the identity and party of the Members concerned and 'strike a blow for the integrity and independence of the judges of this country, and the immunity of each one of us from being traduced by an abuse of privilege'. The Lord Chancellor's speech invoked violent reactions from Labour MPs and a motion was tabled in the Commons condemning the Lord Chancellor for improperly attempting to influence the proceedings of the House and the course of a particular debate and describing his behaviour as a 'regrettable breach of the long-standing convention of respect between the two Houses and a gross contempt of the House of Commons'.[387] Despite the important questions raised by this controversy, neither of the motions was ever debated in Parliament. The Speaker refused to give priority to a debate on the Lord Chancellor's speech, and parliamentary time for debating the motion for an address to remove

---

[386] See Mr Justice Donaldson's speech in Glasgow, (1973) 123 *New Law Journal* 1111.
[387] G. Drewry, 'The Privilege of Parliament' (1974) 124 *New Law Journal* 489; *Hansard*, HC, vol. 865, cols. 1089–91 (4 December 1973), 1291–7 (5 December 1973); *Hansard*, HC, vol. 866, cols. 1141–2 (18 December 1973) [Lord Hailsham].

Sir John Donaldson was not available.[388] The matters fell into abeyance when Parliament rose for the Christmas recess.

Conclusions

7.45 In *Sirros* v. *Moore*, the Court of Appeal removed the absolute immunity enjoyed by judges of the superior courts. Judges may be liable in tort and to judicial review proceedings where they act without or in excess of their jurisdiction, unless the exercise of jurisdiction was caused by an error of fact in circumstances where the court had no knowledge of or means of knowing the relevant facts.[389] Other models are possible – civil liability might be incurred in cases of wilful default of the judge[390] – but there is no reason to prefer them, at least not in a system with independent appointments on merit, and where judges are typically appointed after a successful career in practice. The concern that complaints about judges will lead to satellite litigation also supports treating such complaints through the appeal system.

The Office of Judicial Complaints now has jurisdiction to hear complaints on matters not directly related to the substance of judicial decisions, although, unsurprisingly, many such complaints are nonetheless received. Challenges that lie ahead for this body may be as follows. First, fuller explanations would be preferred of cases where a judge's (legal) activities in his private life are the subject of complaint and one may also wonder whether a refusal to recuse, made in good faith, should be a disciplinary matter. A fuller disclosure of cases that were put to the Lord Chief Justice and Lord Chancellor for consideration, especially where some disciplinary action resulted, might be desirable. In principle, however, we approve of the point that such decisions are taken jointly and that they may apply at all levels of the judiciary. In practice, judges in lower courts prefer to resign if it is clear that they may otherwise be dismissed.

However those at the level of High Court and above cannot be dismissed by the Lord Chancellor and Lord Chief Justice alone and

---

[388] *Hansard*, HC, vol. 865, cols. 1291–7 (5 December 1973); *Hansard*, HC, vol. 864, col. 1560 (22 November 1973); *Hansard*, HC, vol. 865, cols. 42–4 (10 December 1973).

[389] Re McC (A Minor) [1985] AC 528.

[390] Opinion No. 3 of the Consultative Council of European Judges (CCJE) to the attention of the Committee of Ministers of the Council of Europe on the principles and rules governing judges' professional conduct, in particular ethics, incompatible behaviour and impartiality, CCJE (2002) Opinion No. 3, 53, 55, 57.

indeed any such procedure will bypass the Office of Judicial Complaints altogether. In theory the House of Commons may pass a motion to impeach a judge for 'high crimes and misdemeanours' which will then be considered by the House of Lords, but this is certainly obsolete. There may be a continued power of the Attorney General to issue *scire facias* to revoke the judge's appointment on the basis that he has not held his office 'during good behaviour'; if this is not so, it is likely due to the Crown Proceedings Act 1947. But the most likely avenue seems to be by address to both Houses of Parliament on the basis of incapacity or that the judge has not been of good behaviour, and practice seems to suggest that this is regarded as the exclusive procedure – though it was last used successfully in 1830 over financial irregularities. It may be a requirement that the matter be laid by a MP acting privately rather than on behalf of the government or indeed any political party.

We have considered the history in some detail on the laying of motions in the House of Commons with a view to an address for removal of a judge or where preliminary proceedings have been initiated with such a view. It seems that in practice removal from office of a senior judge would only take place upon the ground of misconduct, with the need to show a 'moral element in the misconduct', such as moral turpitude. We have thought it important to preserve the historical references in anticipation of a time when the address of removal may need to be employed. One further observation may be made however. The address was introduced to protect the judges from executive interference. An examination of the cases where a motion for an address was presented shows that, except for the case of *Smith*, in which the government changed its mind, in all cases the result was one supported by the government. It may be said that the party-bound Parliament of today would prevent the proper exercise of the power of removal by address, and that this power would be better transferred to another body.[391] The actual operation of the address in the nineteenth century and at the beginning of the twenty-first century seems, however, satisfactory, with the elaboration by Parliament of the sufficient grounds for removal and process of disposing of the complaints against judicial conduct. But if a judge challenged the constitutional proceedings for removal of a judge before the courts, it is suggested that, under Article 6(1) ECHR, these

---

[391] Cf. National Commission on Judicial Discipline and Removal, *Report* (Washington: West Company Publishing, 1993), 152 FRD265, pp. 291–2.

proceedings would be amenable to domestic judicial scrutiny. The courts would be required to read section 11(3) Senior Courts Act 1981 in a way that it compatible with Article 6 ECHR. Parliament itself is likely to adopt procedures which are compliant with Article 6 ECHR, thus rendering any judicial review proceedings unnecessary.[392] In light of these procedural safeguards, it is therefore suggested that the very existence of a parliamentary power of removal provides a necessary mechanism for the removal of judges in case of misconduct. Public proceedings would also, in practice, protect senior judges from any executive interference.

---

[392] *Green Paper on Parliamentary privilege* (Cm 8318, April 2012); Lord Judge LCJ and Beatson LJ, corrected oral evidence taken before the Joint Committee on Parliamentary Privilege (5 March 2013), HC JCPP-OE-V.

8

Freedom of expression and public confidence in the judiciary

Introduction

8.1 We consider, in this chapter, the interrelated subjects of judicial freedom of expression outside the courtroom, the freedom of the media (the press and any other form of public communication) to criticise the judiciary and the protection of public confidence in the judiciary. As we shall see, the underlying values easily come into conflict. Judicial decisions that are made by trained, unbiased figures after a careful attempt to apply the law to the supposed facts should command respect, but they should not be immune from criticism. What constitutes unfair criticism, and when, how and by whom should such criticism be properly met?

We first discuss the policy, since 1987, of free judicial speech outside the courtroom, subject to preserving judicial impartiality and the dignity of the judicial office. It is now accepted that judges have a wider responsibility to dispel misconceptions and to promote access to justice and inform the public on legal matters of general public interest. An educative role introduces a form of social accountability without compromising judicial independence. In turn, this helps the wider community to discuss, endorse, criticise or applaud the conduct of their courts on an informed basis.[1] This also contributes to shaping public support, which depends, in part, upon public perception, and which is a condition of judicial independence – it is easier to resist an assault on judicial independence with public support than in a context of public apathy.[2] The boundaries for these extra-judicial comments, however, are difficult to draw, and it seems that there is no better substitute for the word 'circumspection'.

---

[1] *South Africa* v. *Mamabolo* (2001) 10 BHRC 493.
[2] J. Doyle, 'The Well-Tuned Cymbal', in H. Cunningham (ed.), *Fragile Bastion. Judicial Independence in the Nineties and Beyond* (Sydney: Judicial Commission of New South Wales, 2000), pp. 40–1.

Second, we examine the impact of the media scrutiny on the administration of justice. Judges are public figures. They must not be too susceptible or of too fragile a constitution while the media checks for flaws in the legal process or in the judge's behaviour; or when the media acts as a watchdog for justice. Moreover, a free press or media goes hand in hand with an independent judiciary.[3] There has accordingly been, over the years, an important shift in the relationship between the judiciary and the media, such that, per Lord Judge LCJ in 2011, 'the days when the possibility of communication between the judiciary and the media was regarded as anathema, and wholly wrong in principle have gone forever'.[4] The growth of judicial review, the constitutional role given under the Human Rights Act 1998 (HRA) and the formal separation of powers under the 2005 settlement explain a persistent public scrutiny of the justice system over the years. To some extent the key questions are about the wider responsibility of media within society, a subject beyond the scope of this book. We should, however, discuss the role of the judiciary in correcting the media and the long-standing convention that ministers should not criticise individual judges in the media for individual decisions.

Lastly, we discuss the proportionality of invoking the traditional protections of the judiciary from improper criticism outside[5] court, namely the offence of scandalising the court. There has not been any such prosecution in England since 1931, and the greater willingness of the judiciary to respond to public criticism makes this prosecution an implausible mechanism to protect public confidence in the judiciary.

8.2 As we will see, the balance can shift between the right of the public to engage in the criticism of judges as public officials, the value of protecting the functions of the institution of justice and the freedom of judges to engage in public debate on matters relating to the functioning of justice.

---

[3] *Pennekamp* v. *State of Florida* 328 US 331 (1946), 335 [F. Frankfurter]; I. Judge, 'The Judiciary and the Media', speech delivered at the Lionel Cohen memorial lecture, Jerusalem (28 March 2011); A.W. Bradley, 'Press Freedom, Governmental Constraints and the Privy Council' [1990] PL 453.

[4] Judge LCJ, 'The Judiciary and the Media'.

[5] We assume that it is relatively uncontentious that there should be punishment for contempt of court when a judge is insulted by a witness or member of public during court proceedings themselves. This is unproblematic under Art. 10 ECHR, since Art. 10(2) would permit such state interference as punishment for contempt provided that it were necessary and proportionate for maintaining the authority and impartiality of the judiciary.

We shall offer some specific arguments, however. Extra-judicial comments in the media should be confined to points of law reform, provided that it remains clear that the judge will faithfully apply the existing law if called on to do so, and to factors which make the administration of justice easier and more efficient. It may not be necessary for such comments to be screened or in any way pre-approved but there should nonetheless be a central body with responsibility for speaking for the judiciary in the media. Comments about the merits of individual decisions in the media cannot be made or addressed by any judge but the convention that ministers should not criticise judges over any decisions must be maintained and strengthened. If the media wish to report ministerial criticism of a judge's decision, they should remind the public of the convention of non-criticism and that similarly, by convention, the judge will not defend his decision in public.

I.   Judicial speech outside the courtroom

A.   The basic regulating principles

8.3 We now sketch the principles governing the self-regulation of judicial expression. For a long time judicial silence was considered necessary to avoid the politicisation of judges,[6] and to a lesser extent to reduce the risk that their expressed views might be taken by future litigants as indicting possible bias against their case. Thus the judiciary was banned, under the Kilmuir Rules dating from 1955, from speaking to the media outside the courtroom: 'So long as a judge keeps silent, his reputation for wisdom and impartiality remains unassailable: but every utterance which he makes in public, except in the course of the actual performance of his judicial duties, must necessarily bring him within the focus of criticism.'[7] But the Kilmuir Rules never applied to retired judges, and so retired judges have played an important role in voicing the judiciary's concerns on some occasions.

The Kilmuir Rules always co-existed, however, with a long-standing practice of public lectures and comments off the bench on existing law or proposed legal reforms. Some exceptions could also be found, such as

---

[6] '... an overspeaking judge is no well-tuned cymbal', Sir F. Bacon, 'Essays: Of Judicature', in J. Spedding, R. Ellis and D. Heath (eds.), *Works of Francis Bacon*, vol. VI (New York: Hurd and Houghton, 1861 reprint), p. 3.

[7] A. W. Bradley, 'Judges and the Media – the Kilmuir Rules' [1986] PL 383, 384.

Lord Widgery LCJ and Lord Denning, who gave press interviews on their work and attitudes to the law.[8] Shortly after passing the Kilmuir Rules, Lord Kilmuir spoke publicly in 1956 to the Holdsworth Club about the Nuremberg trials. Just before, in 1955, at the first Commonwealth Law Conference, Lord Radcliffe had spoken on the work of the Judicial Committee of the Privy Council. Judges have always been in high demand for judicial lectures before members of the profession, learned societies and universities in England and abroad. Some well-established judicial lectures, such as the Hamlyn lectures, the Holdsworth Club, the Commonwealth Law Conference and the annual conventions of the American and Canadian Bar Associations have given judges the opportunity to make statements on legal matters of public interest.

It seems that the coexistence of public lectures and the Kilmuir Rules was never comfortable. Arguments in support of an absolute interpretation of the Kilmuir Rules were that the press and television would not invite judges to give neutral, academic lectures; they would rather press for comments on controversial matters, for 'newsworthy' comments; they would also naturally approach those judges thought to be most likely to say something 'interesting', such as Lord Denning. Public comments from judges on various issues might mean that many more judges would have to disqualify themselves because of the appearance of bias, due to their having made comments on a matter which later came before them in court.

When Lord Denning published his lectures in 1949, the Lord Chancellor, Viscount Jowitt, wrote to him:

> I always hold my thumbs, as the children say, when I hear that a judge has written a book and I am old-fashioned enough to think that the less they write the better it is for all concerned. I feel this for two reasons. Firstly because a judge is so likely to commit himself to some proposition of law with regard to which he has not had the advantage of hearing argument and which may therefore be too widely stated, and secondly because he may so easily slip over the borderline which separates controversial and uncontroversial matters.

It is arguable that the fear of appearing partisan only justifies circumspection and moderate language today. But the second reason remains a valid concern.

---

[8] Lord Widgery, *The Times*, 7 August 1972; A. Denning, *The Sunday Times*, 17 and 24 June 1973.

8.4 As time went by, the discretion that was once seen as serving impartiality came to be seen as excessive remoteness from the public. Miscarriages of justice and the lack of diversity in the social composition of the judiciary partly triggered that change of perception. The turn now taken by the relationship between the judiciary, the public and the media in England and Wales is also explained in the following statement (originally applying to the Australian judiciary):

> There is a lively debate about the proper relations between the judiciary and the political branches. Senior judges have talked more openly about the inevitable judicial choices confronting them. They have dismissed the fairy tale of the declaratory theory. Debating contentious ... decisions, judges have spoken of giving effect to the contemporary values of the [English] people. They have talked of the ever-greater impact of international law on [English] law. They have said parliaments sometimes prefer to leave the hard policy questions to the courts. They have warned that parliaments are less able to stand between the people's liberties and the power of the executive government ... These statements invite supplementary questions ... They are part of debates that seem open-ended.[9]

'In the absence of fairy tales',[10] it has become accepted that judges must earn public confidence. It is suggested that judicial independence is not supported by too great a distance from the public; it requires a necessary but rather delicate engagement with the public on appropriate occasions. Thus it is the judiciary's responsibility to enhance the public understanding of their work. Those who want judicial independence must not be afraid to explain their work and to gain the trust that underlies independence.[11] On matters relating to the administration of justice, judges are allowed, even expected, to be responsive communicators outside their courts.[12]

8.5 In 1987, the Kilmuir Rules were abolished. The Lord Chancellor, Lord Mackay, considered that it should be left to each individual judge to decide whether or not to speak publicly.[13] On his understanding, judicial

---

[9] B. Lane, 'The Role of the Judiciary in a Modern Democracy', Second Annual Symposium of the Judicial Conference of Australia, Sydney (8–9 November 1997).

[10] Lord Reid, 'The Judge as Lawmaker' (1972) 12 *Journal of the Society of Public Teachers of Law* 22.

[11] HL Select Committee on the Constitution, 'Relations between the Executive, the Judiciary and Parliament', 6th Report of Session 2006–07, HL paper 151 (11 July 2007), para. 140.

[12] Art. 9 of the United Nations Basic Principles on the Independence of the Judiciary, GA Res. 40/32 and GA Res. 40/146 (1995).

[13] Similarly, T. Bingham, 'Judicial Ethics', in R. Cranston (ed.), *Legal Ethics and Professional Responsibility* (Oxford: Clarendon Press, 1995), p. 35 (also published in T. Bingham, *The Business of Judging. Selected Essays and Speeches* (Oxford University Press, 2000), p. 69.

independence ultimately rests on the good judgement of the judges themselves. The bias argument was thought to have been overplayed as even a
secretly biased judge would still be a biased judge,[14] and it might be for the
best that a litigant would have a proper opportunity to air concerns which
may have been raised by extra-judicial comments.[15] Lord Mackay argued
that in some cases the media can secure a wider public understanding of
the working of the law, and the participation of judges would enhance the
value of such programmes.[16] He later said that since the judiciary were an
important part of the community, he did not understand why 'they should
be mute when everybody else can say what they like'.[17]

The abolition of the Kilmuir Rules emphasised the need to clarify the
principles regulating when judges may or may not speak out. The cardinal
(self-regulated) principle is that of circumspection: the reticence to speak
out, as opposed to an absolute silence, is what the judicial office requires.[18]
Some clear boundaries remain in principle, and as a matter of convention[19] a judge will not offer public endorsement to a politician standing for
election, or express public criticism of the fitness of a colleague appointed
to the bench.[20] A judge should refrain from answering public criticism of a
judgment or decision, whether from the bench or otherwise. Judges should
not air disagreements over judicial decisions in the press.[21] Beyond this,
and still subject to circumspection, the limits on the substance of judicial
free speech appear constrained by the constitutional cultures of the various
stakeholders in the judiciary. Lord Mackay reiterated the long-standing
principles that judges must avoid public statements 'either on general
issues or particular cases which might cast any doubt on their complete
impartiality' and 'they should avoid any involvement, either direct or
indirect, in issues which are or might become politically controversial'.[22]

---

[14] *Re JRL; Ex parte CJL* (1986) 161 CLR 342, 352.

[15] Lord Mackay, Lord Mackay, *The Administration of Justice* (London: Stevens & Sons/
Sweet & Maxwell, 1994), p. 26.

[16] Lord McKay, 'The Judiciary and Non-judicial Activities' (1970) 35 *Law and Contemporary Problems* 9, 21.

[17] HL Select Committee on the Constitution, 'Relations between the Executive, the Judiciary
and Parliament', 38.

[18] Lord Hope, 'What Happens When a Judge Speaks Out?', Holdsworth Club Presidential
Address (19 February 2010), p. 11.

[19] Judicial Executive Board, 'Guidance to Judges on Appearances before Select Committees',
November 2012.

[20] *Ibid.*, paras. 3, 8 and 9.   [21] Guide to Judicial Conduct, 8.1.1.

[22] Letter to the Lord Chief Justice dated 16 October 1989, copied to all judges and full-time
judicial officers in England and Wales.

8.6 The principle in force today remains one of free but circumspect judicial speech. There cannot be any objection on the ground of bias based on the judge's extracurricular utterances per se, whether in textbooks, lectures, speeches, articles, interviews, reports or responses to consultation papers.[23] Impartiality is what regulates judicial speech outside the courtroom. The *Guide to Judicial Conduct* warns of the greatest circumspection in language and tone when judges talk to the media.[24] Judges should not comment or criticise the government on policy issues, for fear of being perceived as political and thus losing public confidence in them.[25]

Thus the *Guide to Judicial Conduct* provides that propriety, and the appearance of propriety, are essential to the performance of all of the activities of a judge:

> 5.1(2) As a subject of constant public scrutiny, a judge must accept personal restrictions that might be viewed as burdensome by the ordinary citizen and should do so freely and willingly. In particular, a judge shall conduct himself or herself in a way that is consistent with the dignity of the judicial office.
>
> . . .
>
> 5.1(6) A judge, like any other citizen, is entitled to freedom of expression, belief, association and assembly, but in exercising such rights, a judge shall always conduct himself or herself in such a manner as to preserve the dignity of the judicial office and the impartiality and independence of the judiciary.

As to what the judge might say outside the courtroom on judicial matters:

> 5.1(11) Subject to the proper performance of judicial duties, a judge may:
>> 5.1(11.1) Write, lecture, teach and participate in activities concerning the law, the legal system, the administration of justice or related matters;
>> 5.1(11.2) appear at a public hearing before an official body concerned with matters relating to the law, the legal system, the administration of justice or related matters;
>> 5.1(11.3) serve as a member of an official body, or other government commission, committee or advisory body, if such membership is not inconsistent with the perceived impartiality and political neutrality of a judge; or

---

[23] *Locabail* [2000] QB 451, 77–8.   [24] Guide to Judicial Conduct, 8.1.1.

[25] Judicial Executive Board, 'Guidance to Judges on Appearances before Select Committees', paras. 3, 10–13; HL Select Committee on the Constitution, 'Relations between the Executive, the Judiciary and Parliament', 52.

> 5.1(11.4) engage in other activities if such activities do not detract from the dignity of the judicial office or otherwise interfere with the performance of judicial duties.

The Supreme Court's *Guide to Judicial Conduct* similarly states:

> 3.1 Each Justice will strive to ensure that his or her conduct, both in and out of court, maintains and enhances the confidence of the public, the legal profession and litigants in the impartiality of the individual Justice and of the Court.
>
> 3.2 Each Justice will seek to avoid extra-judicial activities that are likely to cause him or her to have to refrain from sitting on a case because of a reasonable apprehension of bias or because of a conflict of interest that would arise from the activity.

This illustrates that judicial governance is dominated by conventions, expressed by the Judges' Council, the representative sounding board for the judiciary, rather than by legal rules. The range of restraints, and a degree of social isolation inherent in the acceptance of the judicial office, are significant, and recognised as such by the *Guide to Judicial Conduct*:

> Any social activity or involvement in a community organisation, particularly, but not exclusively, educational, charitable and religious organisations must be assessed in the light of the judge's duty to maintain the dignity of the office and the judge's ability to discharge his or her duties. Engagement with non-political issues, such as arts, culture or history, can be acceptable, provided that no particular agenda is being promoted.[26]

The *Guide* also offers advice on internet interviews, and warns judges of putting personal information or photographs on the web which might compromise their judicial independence, reminding them that while newspaper and broadcast interviews are relatively ephemeral, web versions remain permanently available to potentially millions of people worldwide.

There can be a fine line between informing the public on matters relating to the administration of justice and the judge's participation in a public controversy which might be of a political nature, which would then affect the reputation and career of the judge.[27] We have seen in previous chapters that ill-advised public statements may be treated as judicial misconduct and dealt with according to the extent the judge's actions are thought to have compromised the perception of his impartiality.

---

[26] *Guide to Judicial Conduct*, paras 8.4.1 and 8.8.8.
[27] Lord Irvine, *Hansard*, vol. 572, cols. 1259–60, 5 June 1996.

B.   Individual speech

No comments on individual cases

8.7 Some further principles are well established. There should be no comment from judges on individual cases, which also requires that a judge must avoid associating himself with a particular cause, group or organisation. Judges do not discuss pronouncements on individual cases, whether or not the matter has finally been disposed of on appeal. The golden convention is that they do not comment on pending cases, either in their court or in another judge's court.[28] Despite this, at the beginning of the twenty-first century or so, the practice of journalists 'doorstepping' judges who had given a controversial decision developed. 'Doorstepping' is 'the situation where reporters call out questions to you as you enter or leave a building or a car'.[29] It has mostly disappeared, with the assistance of the Press Complaints Commission. Lord Woolf commented on the press's practice:

> One of the first times I came to the notice of the press was when I was called upon to decide a case in which a man claimed damages for a personality change caused by an accident. The medical evidence supported his claim that the personality change had resulted in him committing rape. I awarded him damages, aware that he was being sued by his victim and that she would be the ultimate recipient of a large proportion of the compensation he received. This subtlety was lost on the press, who greeted my decision with uproar. My wife was door-stepped (I believe that is the technical term) and was asked for a reaction to my judgment. She replied, 'I can't say a word – my husband will kill me'. Her remarks were not reported. The term 'the gentlemen of the press' is not entirely archaic.[30]

Another aspect of the 'no comment' policy is that associating oneself with a particular cause, group or organisation must be avoided.[31] This cannot

---

[28] *Guide to Judicial Conduct*, para. 8.1.1; HL Select Committee on the Constitution, 'Relations between the Executive, the Judiciary and Parliament', paras. 126 and 150; Lord Woolf, *Hansard*, HL, col. 882 (21 May 2003).

[29] Lord Chief Justice and Senior President of Tribunals, 'Media Guidance for the Judiciary' (February 2012), p. 11.

[30] Lord Woolf, 'Should the Media and the Judiciary be on Speaking Terms?', Eighth RTÉ/UCD Law Faculty Lecture, Dublin (22 October 2003), in C. Campbell-Holt (ed.), *The Pursuit of Justice* (Oxford University Press, 2008), p. 149; Lord Irvine, '"Reporting the Courts": The Media's Rights and Responsibilities', 4th RTÉ\UCD Lecture, UCD, Dublin (14 April 1999).

[31] Guide to Judicial Conduct, 8.2.2.; UK Supreme Court Guide to Judicial Conduct, 3.3.

be taken lightly in a context of rising applications for bias. Thus Lord Phillips was challenged following an interview given to the press where he said, among other things, that he had considerable sympathy for those who found themselves in a situation similar to Mrs Purdy. Mrs Purdy had asked for an order requiring the Director of Public Prosecutions to clarify his policy for the controversial prosecution of assisted suicide, and her case had recently been decided by the House of Lords, with Lord Phillips sitting on that case.[32] A group opposed to the legalisation of assisted suicide applied to the (now) Supreme Court for the (then) House of Lords' decision on Purdy to be set aside, on the ground that Lord Phillips, as one of the members of the Appellate Committee that heard that case, was apparently biased.[33] A panel of justices, none of whom had been a member of the Appellate Committee in the case of Mrs Purdy, dismissed their application. They held that the fair-minded and informed observer, having considered the facts, would not have concluded that there was a reasonable possibility that when he heard the case Lord Phillips was biased.[34]

8.8 Some degree of freedom exists within lectures to derogate from the rule that judges should not comment on others' judgments. Thus, in a lecture published in 2005, Lord Hoffmann criticised certain judgments of his colleagues in the House of Lords.[35] In 2007 a High Court judge criticised the Court of Appeal's decision of *Halsey v Milton Keynes NHS Trust* on mediation as 'clearly wrong and unreasonable' during a lecture at a City law firm.[36] He claimed that the 2004 ruling has created a barrier to mediation that should be removed. In rare cases, judges seem able to comment extra-judicially on decisions in which they were involved. Thus, in discussing extra-judicially the limits of parliamentary sovereignty, Lord Bingham refers to the three judges' *obiter dicta* (Lords Steyn and Hope, Lady Hale) in *Jackson*,[37] and declares himself unable 'to accept that [his] colleagues' observations are correct'.[38] It was already

---

[32] *R (Purdy)* v. *Director of Public Prosecutions* [2009] UKHL 45.

[33] Application in *R (Purdy)* v. *Director of Public Prosecutions* [2009] UKHL 45, 8 December 2009.

[34] Decision of 12 December 2009.

[35] L. Hoffman, 'Tax Avoidance' (2005) 2 British *Tax Review* 197. We are indebted to Grant Hammond for this example, see G. Hammond, 'Free Speech and Judges in New Zealand', in H.P. Lee (ed.), *Judiciaries in Comparative Perspective* (Cambridge University Press, 2011), p. 195.

[36] *Law Society Gazette*, 18 July 2007.   [37] *R (Jackson)* v. *Attorney General* [2005] UKHL 56.

[38] T. Bingham, *The Rule of Law* (London: Penguin, 2010).

clear from the judgment, however, that Lord Bingham did not share his colleagues' views. In this context, his arguments can be seen as part of an ongoing discussion in academic and judicial circles about what the law is on a particular point; thus it is of public benefit.[39]

Moderate language

8.9 The editorship of a journal is generally seen as incompatible with holding judicial office since it involves a regular commitment and as the editor might be seen as endorsing the opinions expressed in such journal. By comparison, writing books and articles, or editing legal textbooks, is not incompatible with holding judicial office and the discharge of judicial functions; this is indeed a long and well-established tradition within the English judiciary.[40] Contributing to legal publications, for example as a recorder, is appropriate and furthers rather than hinders the administration of justice. So recalled the Court of Appeal in *Timmins* v. *Gormley*.[41] The recorder had published extensively on personal injury topics in almost all the publications devoted to that subject. It was submitted before the Court of Appeal that there was a real danger that the recorder was subject to unconscious but settled prejudice against insurers, and that his findings supported the allegation of bias. The Court found that the case turned on the statements made in those articles. Noting that there is nothing improper in the recorder being engaged in his writing activities, the Court held:

> It is the tone of the recorder's opinions and the trenchancy with which they were expressed which is challenged here. Anyone writing in an area in which he sits judicially has to exercise considerable care not to express himself in terms which indicate that he has preconceived views which are so firmly held that it may not be possible for him to try a case with an open mind.[42]

The Court allowed the appeal and ordered a retrial on the basis that, from some of the articles he had written, the recorder held pronounced pro-claimant anti-insurer views with a real danger of bias as a consequence.

---

[39] Hammond, 'Free Speech and Judges in New Zealand'.
[40] In the 1940s MacKinnon LJ used to contribute 'notes and queries' on law and judges in many issues of the *Law Quarterly Review*.
[41] *Timmins* v. *Gormley* [2000] 1 All ER 65.
[42] *Ibid.*, para. 85; reference is made to the decision of the High Court of Australia in the case of *Vakauta* v. *Kelly* (1989) 167 CLR 568; see also *Buscemi* v. *Italy*, ECtHR, 1999-VI, paras. 67–8; *Newcastle City Council* v. *Lindsay* [2004] NSWCA 198.

The importance of moderate language in considering, for example, the drawbacks of incorporating the European Convention on Human Rights (ECHR) into UK law was asserted in the Scottish case *Hoekstra*, in which four defendants were convicted of drug offences in Scotland in March 1997. The appeals before the Appeal Court, invoking the appellants' rights under the ECHR, were rejected in January 2000. Leave to appeal to the Privy Council was also refused but a further stage of the appeal before the Appeal Court remained to be heard in March 2000. Before that time, the judge (who had formally retired but had been appointed to sit as a retired judge) published articles in the press criticising the incorporation of the ECHR into UK law, suggesting that it would provide 'a field-day for crackpots, a pain in the neck for judges and legislators and a goldmine for lawyers'.[43] The case then went before a differently consti-tuted appellate court, which set aside the decision of the court of which that judge had been a member, on the basis of apprehended bias on his part. The Appeal Court recalled that:

> Judges, like other members of the public and other members of the legal profession, are entitled to criticise developments in our law, whether in the form of legislation or in the form of judicial decisions. Indeed criti-cism of particular legislative provisions or particular decisions is often to be found in judges' opinions. Similarly, judges may welcome particular developments in our law. It is well known that in their extra-judicial capacity many prominent judges – not only in England – publicly advo-cated incorporation of the Convention and equally publicly welcomed the Government's decision to incorporate. But what judges cannot do with impunity is to publish either criticism or praise of such a nature or in such language as to give rise to a legitimate apprehension that, when called upon in the course of their judicial duties to apply that particular branch of the law, they will not be able to do so impartially.[44]

The restriction on judicial speech is thus one of manner, when the forceful manner of speech gives the appearance of prejudgment or bias on a particular issue. Lord Hope's unequivocal condemnation of torture in a scholarly article in 2004, combined with a criticism of the US government's conduct at Guantanamo Bay, only superficially stands against the rule: it is right that Lord Hope authoritatively recalls the position at law, that evidence which has been obtained by the use of any form of inducement or pressure is inadmissible.[45] The fundamental

---

[43] *Hoekstra* v. *HM Advocate (No. 3)* [2000] HRLR 410.   [44] *Ibid.*
[45] Lord Hope, 'Torture' (2004) 53 ICLQ 803, 807.

nature of that rule justifies its clear assertion in a legal writing. In addition, if anything, transparency also justified Lord Hope's reference to this scholarly piece in sitting in a case about the admissibility of torture evidence.[46] A committed view, thus, can and must be expressed in a considerate tone, in order for its proponent to stay within the remit of freedom of expression, without appearing biased to a reasonable observer.

8.10 In recent times, Judge James Pickles took part, without the Lord Chancellor's permission, in some BBC broadcasts and he also wrote for the *Daily Telegraph* in 1985 about sentencing and parole. Having been threatened with the sack, he nonetheless wrote a second article for *The Listener* in 1986. He then gave a verbal undertaking to Lord Lane, the then Lord Chief Justice, that he would contact him before speaking to the press, but he rescinded the agreement when, according to him, the Lord Chief Justice proved tardy in answering his letters. He gave press interviews and criticised the judiciary in a book published in 1987.[47] He was again been threatened with dismissal for calling Lord Hailsham, the then Lord Chancellor, a 'brooding quixotic dictator', 'born with a golden spoon in his mouth'.[48]

Pickles's public confrontations with the Lord Chancellor and Lord Chief Justice ended with the relaxation, detailed above, of the Kilmuir Rules. Judge Pickles was not slow to take advantage of this newly found freedom. In 1990 he tried a young mother for helping shoplifters and sent her to prison for six months. The Court of Appeal, headed by Lord Chief Justice Lord Lane, freed the mother on probation, holding that she should not have been sentenced to youth custody. Pickles called an impromptu press conference in a pub in which he described Lord Lane as 'a dinosaur living in the wrong age'.[49] Lord Woolf observed in 2003, though without express reference to Judge Pickles, that the public soon tired of a certain circuit judge with 'a penchant for self-publicity'.[50] Today it seems likely that some sanctions, though possibly short of removal, would have been undertaken.

---

[46] *A v. Home Secretary (No. 2)* [2005] UKHL 71.

[47] J. Pickles, *Straight from the Bench: Is Justice Just?* (London: Phoenix House, 1987); *The Guardian*, 26 May 1986.

[48] D. Woodhouse, *The Office of the Lord Chancellor* (Oxford University Press, 2001), p. 28.

[49] *The Guardian*, 28 November 1990.

[50] Woolf, 'Should the Media and the Judiciary be on Speaking Terms?', 8.

8.11 It is inappropriate for judges to accept fees or honoraria for lectures,[51] though they can receive their expenses. Judges cannot teach regularly at a university or other educational institution for a salary. A judge may teach regularly for no remuneration, provided it does not interfere with his official functions – but it is likely to prove too heavy a burden. Judges receive royalties for their writings, many of the books published being edited collections of the lectures they have given.[52]

Speeches on the administration of justice

8.12 In the 1970s, apart from the Lord Chief Justice, who sometimes made public statements on matters affecting the administration of justice or judges (normally in his annual speech at the Lord Mayor of London's banquet for the judges), judges did not normally offer public statements. Statements of judges on various aspects of the administration of justice from the bench or in a lecture before a learned society would only occasionally be reported in the press.

In recent times, the frequency of speeches has increased, and they are systematically published on the judiciary website. There are too many significant speeches one way or another for us to consider, but one lecture must be mentioned. In 2003 Lord Woolf LCJ delivered an exceptionally critical lecture at Cambridge on 'The Rule of Law and a Change in the Constitution'. Lord Woolf underlined the failures of the Blair government to appreciate the role of the Lord Chancellor in representing the judiciary through his membership of the Cabinet, arguing that the Lord Chancellor could act as 'lightning conductor at times of high tension between the executive and the judiciary'.[53] He spoke against the constitutional changes, such as the abolition of the role of the Lord Chancellor, being made without any consultation of the judiciary and being announced in a mere government press release. He also expressed concerns at the creation of a Supreme Court, and raised a concern, reiterated by Lord Phillips in 2011, that the running costs of the Supreme Court would be recouped by imposing a surcharge on court fees. Lord

---

[51] *Guide to Judicial Conduct*, 8.8.2. The *Guide* also suggests that where a judge gives a lecture for a commercial undertaking there is no objection, if he considers that it would be appropriate, to his requesting that any fee otherwise payable be paid to a charity of his choice.

[52] Examples are scattered throughout the footnotes of this work.

[53] Lord Woolf, 'The Rule of Law and a Change in the Constitution' (2004) 63 CLJ 317, 320.

Woolf finally spoke against the creation of a specific Asylum and Immigration Tribunal, which he considered went against the rule of law.

There is a fine line between commenting on matters of expertise and interest and entering the realm of political controversy. The topics addressed – the constitutional reform of the Appellate Committee of the House of Lords, the administration of justice through a new tribunal, the abolition of the role of representation of the judiciary by the Lord Chancellor in Cabinet – all fall within the remit of judicial free speech. They are matters upon which the judiciary should be able legitimately to comment, given its expertise and the fact that the changes considered have a substantial impact upon its constitutional and practical structure. The depth of the changes and the casual approach to them by the government, previously discussed,[54] justify the strong terms used by Lord Woolf in that lecture, which was widely commented upon in the press.

The trend in public speeches is an expansive one. Between January and December 2010 senior judges gave forty speeches, including fourteen given by the Master of the Rolls, six given by the Lord Chief Justice and one by the Senior President of Tribunals. By comparison, between January and December 2003 there were twenty judicial speeches, including eleven given by the Lord Chief Justice, and one by the Master of the Rolls. This enhanced engagement with the legal community, the public and the media illustrates the awareness of the judiciary that people should understand how rulings are reached and the constraints under which they work.[55] Judges increasingly take part in radio programmes – such as Clive Anderson's series on BBC Radio 4, 'Unreliable Evidence' – where judges comment on matters of general interest, such as the impact of funding shortages and high staff turnover on the civil justice system.[56]

8.13 Occasionally, judges write obituaries on their late colleagues. They sometimes write letters to newspaper editors, upon which the sensible advice is now to consider whether it is appropriate to include any reference to the writer's judicial position; to ensure that the writer not seen to be commenting on a particular case or a politically sensitive issue; and to ask a colleague to read the draft in advance.[57]

---

[54] See Chapter 2.
[55] HL Select Committee on the Constitution, 'Relations between the Executive, the Judiciary and Parliament', 152.
[56] BBC, 13 February 2007.
[57] The Lord Chief Justice and the Senior President of Tribunals, 'Media Guidance', 14.

8.14 Judges are not only excluded from taking part in politically partisan activities in any form, they must not state their views on political matters. It is often said that judges do not comment on public policy within the courtroom, unless it is legally relevant to deciding the case, as it may be when construing the intention of a statute or regulation. Sir Alfred Denning (as he then was) took up the issue. He agreed that judges should carry out faithfully the intentions of Parliament and should not enter into any captious or irresponsible criticism of what Parliament had done, nor display a want of confidence in Parliament. However, continued Denning, there were circumstances where judges were entitled to comment:

> Parliament's policies may have results it did not foresee. Its enactments may not work out in practice in the way in which it had intended. The drafts-manship may be obscure and give rise to unexpected difficulties. When this happens, the judges have the right and indeed the duty to point it out; and in the past they have often done so without being accused of impropriety.[58]

He may equally point to defects in the law or in the workings of an Act, as appears in particular cases before him. That view remains applicable today.

In practice, judges sometimes offer comments and suggestions on law and policy within the courtroom. Courts or trial judges can question the wisdom of legislation, and point out that a particular statute is creating what most people would regard as an injustice. In 2009 a Crown Court judge criticised sentencing laws which he said left the courts unable to protect women from domestic abuse.[59] The judge had passed a prison sentence with an extended parole licence provision on a man for assault on his partner occasioning actual bodily harm. He had to change the sentence because the total of the prison term and the extended sentence went beyond the legal maximum of five years. Saying that the man represented a serious risk to women, the judge said:

> I make it clear that this sentence is not consistent with my public duty, only consistent with the law of the land ... The fact that the court is unable to discharge its function to protect women might be considered by some as a worrying aspect of this case ... the current state of the law means I am prevented from passing a sentence which properly reflects the facts of this case.

While these criticisms are not common practice, and the above examples tend to be part of the reasons that the judge must give for his decision, they nonetheless blur the line on what is acceptable or not acceptable

---

[58] Denning, *The Changing Law*, 12–14.   [59] *The Daily Telegraph*, 6 September 2009.

speech: 'If it is accepted that a judge can comment on the operation of the law within a case, on what basis is it to be said that the fundamental value of free speech is to be confined *outside* the courtroom?'[60] Indeed, it may often be supposed that when a judge goes to lengths to explain why he is not passing the sort of sentence that he would have liked to pass, he is aware that this will draw public attention to the case, beyond explaining the good or bad fortune to the defendant himself.

Criticisms of rules or policies that a judge is obliged to give effect to in any event are legitimate provided that they are of potential educational value for the lay public. Judges have always had the ability to comment on the law: unless a penalty for an offence is fixed by law, a judge can give an absolute discharge on the conviction of any defendant and that may entail an implicit comment that there was no merit in applying the law to that defendant. One recent example is the prosecution of Mrs Gilderdale in 2010 for the attempted murder of her daughter who was bed-bound and had tried to take her own life by injecting an excess of morphine into her system. The factual allegation, which was not disputed, was that Mrs Gilderdale had afterwards administered some sleeping pills and anti-depressants to ensure that her daughter's attempt would be successful. The trial judge tried unsuccessfully to persuade the Crown Prosecution Service to drop the charge of attempted murder in favour of one of assisted suicide, and after the jury acquitted, this was the offence of which Mrs Gilderdale was convicted. Even then she received only a conditional discharge for one year, which was widely taken to be a criticism of the law and the decision to prosecute. The judge had also paid tribute to the jury, saying: 'I do not normally comment on the verdicts of juries but in this case their decision, if I may say so, shows that common sense, decency and humanity which makes jury trials so important in a case of this kind.'[61] The role of judges is always to seek to explain the law as they apply it to the instant case, and that entails some freedom to comment on the values underpinning the law.

Indeed, speaking out may sometimes constitute a moral duty in extreme circumstances, for example in applying laws relating to racial segregation at certain troubled times in history.[62]

---

[60] Hammond, 'Free Speech and Judges in New Zealand'.

[61] *R v. Kay Gilderdale*, unreported, Lewes Crown Court (January 2010); *The Guardian*, 25 January 2010.

[62] D. Dyzenhaus, *Hard Cases in Wicked Legal Systems: South African Law in the Perspective of Legal Philosophy* (Oxford: Clarendon Press, 1991); 2nd edn, published as *Hard Cases in*

Influencing legal developments

8.15 Some judges interviewed strongly believed in the necessity to engage with proposals relating to the administration of justice, in particular on criminal matters and sentencing, in order to make the law work. The Judicial Executive Board itself recognises two qualifications to the convention against comment on bill provisions or government policy. They apply 'where the Bill or policy directly affects the operation of the courts or aspects of the administration of justice within the judge's particular area of judicial responsibility or expertise'. First, 'the judge may comment on the practical operation or technical aspects of the Bill or policy'.[63] This is underpinned by the principle of joint responsibility (with the Lord Chancellor) for the operation of the courts. Second, 'in these circumstances, a judge may properly comment on the merit of a Bill or policy which affects the independence of the judiciary'.[64]

Other judges interviewed thought that the only proper channel for influencing proposals was through the Law Commission, where traditionally judges have been appointed as Law Commissioners (though this is less noticeable in recent times) and whose proposals are frequently open to consultation, including consultation with individual judges. Judges also sit on bodies with responsibility for the justice system, for example the Sentencing Council for England and Wales, which provides guidance that statute requires the sentencing judge to take into account.

In addition, formal responses given by the judiciary to particular government proposals constitute another transparent and formal mechanism for engaging with legal development. They tend to be widely reported, and while they may create a tension with the executive, Sir Igor Judge (as he was then) emphasised that 'we do not expect our response to carry the day' and 'in the end Parliament legislates, and then it does not really matter what the judges think' because 'the judges apply the law that Parliament has produced'.[65] Hence the Council of Her Majesty's Circuit Judges gave a negative response to the Home Office's

---

Wicked Legal Systems: Pathologies of Legality (Oxford University Press, 2010); S. Turenne, *Le juge face à la désobéissance civile. Etude en droits américains et français comparés* (Paris: Librairie Générale de Jurisprudence, Paris, 2007).

[63] Judicial Executive Board, 'Guidance to Judges on Appearances before Select Committees', para. 13.

[64] *Ibid.*; Lord Judge CJ, 'Judicial Independence and Responsibilities', 16th Commonwealth Law Conference, Hong Kong (9 April 2009).

[65] HL Select Committee on the Constitution, 'Relations between the Executive, the Judiciary and Parliament', 55.

paper 'Convicting Rapists and Protecting Victims – Justice for Victims of Rape' in January 2007. Less usual, but perhaps typical is the Judges' Council letter to Justice Secretary Kenneth Clarke in June 2011, where the judges denounce the waste of the court's time in immigration appeals, claiming that 85 per cent of cases did not have any merit.[66] The letter was leaked in the press, and no official reaction to it is known.

Since the Constitutional Reform Act 2005 (CRA), which separated very clearly the judiciary from the executive, judges have been greatly involved in the administration of justice, a task substantially done until then by the Lord Chancellor's Department. Yet this is not felt to be acknowledged by the public at large nor even by the executive itself, and so judges do not seem to have any peculiar authority when speaking of matters affecting the administration or delivery of justice. According to Alan Moses, engaging with the public in this administrative capacity only confuses their public image, and 'what provides the mark of recognition is the mask'.[67] Some interviewees referred us to this speech and concurred that judicial authority – symbolised by the 'mask' – is perceived only to exist in respect to decision making.

8.16 Moreover, private meetings take place between ministers and judges, especially the Attorney General, the Justice Secretary and the Lord Chief Justice's office. The discussions are and must be limited to the impact of particular policies in terms of the administration of justice. Judges cannot formally, or even informally, anticipate the courts' view on the lawfulness of any proposed measure. They cannot discuss whether a specific proposal would be ruled by the courts to be in breach of the HRA; this would make it difficult for them to judge in their courts the new legislation they would have helped to draft. That has not always been understood, and in 2004, the former Home Secretary, Charles Clarke, expressed his 'frustration' 'at the inability to have general conversations of principle with the law lords'.

When, in 2004, the House of Lords found disproportionate and discriminatory the indefinite detention of suspected foreign terrorists under post-9/11 anti-terrorism laws, the government introduced control orders. Charles Clarke's frustration referred to his hope to learn from meetings with judges what sort of restrictions on terrorist suspects a

---

[66] The letter says: 'Most claims fail, most of the claims which fail are without merit, and many are abusive of the court's process.'

[67] Moses LJ, 'The Mask and the Judge', Margaret Howard Lecture Speech (15 May 2006).

court might find lawful. Lord Bingham, the senior Law Lord, recalled that he had been told that the Home Secretary wanted a 'purely social meeting' with the Law Lords. 'One was, perhaps, a little sceptical.'[68] Charles Clarke repeated his criticisms of the Law Lords' refusal to meet before the House of Lords Select Committee on the Constitution during its inquiry into relations between the executive, the judiciary and Parliament in 2006–07.[69] The Committee rightly pointed out that such a meeting 'risks an unacceptable breach of the principle of judicial independence',[70] but that did not prevent Charles Clarke from asserting similar views in 2011, when giving evidence before the Joint Committee on the Draft Detention of Terrorist Suspects (Temporary Extension) Bills.[71]

8.17 Can there be a more explicit dialogue between judges, Parliament and the government about the way in which legal rules, such as the ones deriving from the ECHR, are interpreted? The traditional objection would be that ministers, like anyone else, should seek independent legal advice about the viability of any of their proposals – starting, in the government's case, with their chief legal adviser, the Attorney General. The counter-argument is that, on some matters, which will clearly be litigated at Supreme Court level, the judges alone might know what they are likely to decide. Such discussions would without doubt compromise judicial independence; should the government amend its proposals after any such discussion, there would be immense pressure on a future court to approve the amended version. One might also be sceptical as to what extent the government would be concerned in proposing sound laws and to what extent it was trying to avert the political consequences of failure in the courts, for it is no part of the judiciary to help to pre-empt the latter.

The Lord Chief Justice confirmed in 2008 that the judiciary's role in any pre-legislative scrutiny exercise is to comment only on the practicality of the drafting and the workability of policy for the Courts: 'Judges must not risk collusion with the executive when they are likely to be required to adjudicate on challenges to the actions of the executive . . . the

---

[68] J. Rozenberg, *Standpoint*, October 2010.

[69] HL Select Committee on the Constitution, 'Relations between the Executive, the Judiciary and Parliament', Oral Evidence, 26.

[70] HL Select Committee on Constitution, 'Relations between the Executive, the Judiciary and Parliament', Oral Evidence, 97.

[71] Oral Evidence taken before the Joint Committee on the Draft Detention of Terrorist Suspects (Temporary Extension) Bills (4 April 2011), Q162, HC 893 (2010–2011).

Law Lords should not even be perceived to have prejudiced an issue as a result of communication with the executive.'[72]

The same reservations apply to post-legislative scrutiny, where Select Committees make inquiries into the way in which the courts are interpreting and applying legislation. This may be done from time to time, however, such as when the Joint Committee on Human Rights investigated the courts' interpretation of section 6 HRA and concluded that their interpretation had been too narrow.[73] The Lords Select Committee on the Constitution considers post-legislative scrutiny highly desirable: it 'should be undertaken far more generally', as a way to 'boost the level of constructive dialogue between Parliament and the courts'.[74]

More widely, it is now perceived that concerns about the administration of justice and the impact of legislation and other policy proposals upon the courts and the judiciary should be addressed by Select Committees, in addition to the opportunity provided annually to the Lord Chief Justice to appear before the House of Lords Select Committee on the Constitution.[75] This parliamentary forum provides for the oversight of the judiciary, with evidence taken from the Lord Chief Justice or some other senior judges on specific topics. This more recent form of judicial accountability remains subject to the conventions regulating judicial speech outlined in this chapter. They have recently been affirmed by the Judicial Executive Board in the context of Select Committee appearances.[76] While it seems legitimate to encourage judges 'to discuss their views on key legal issues in the cause of transparency and better understanding of such issues amongst both parliamentarians and the public',[77] this is likely to have a limited impact, for reasons already outlined.

---

[72] Lord Phillips, 'The Supreme Court and Other Constitutional Changes in the UK', Address to Members of the Royal Court, The Jersey Law Society and Members of the States of Jersey, Jersey (2 May 2008), p. 7.

[73] Joint Committee on Human Rights, Ninth Report of Session 2006–07, 'The Meaning of Public Authority under the Human Rights Act' (HL Paper 77/HC 410) and Seventh Report of Session 2003–04, 'The Meaning of Public Authority under the Human Rights Act' (HL Paper 39/HC 382); HL Constitution Committee, 'Fourteenth Report of Session 2003–04, Parliament and the Legislative Process' (HL 173-I); Sixth Report of Session 2004–05, 'Parliament and the Legislative Process: The Government's Response' (HL 114); Law Commission, 'Post-legislative Scrutiny' (Cm 6945).

[74] HL Select Committee on the Constitution, 'Relations between the Executive, the Judiciary and Parliament', para. 130.

[75] Ibid., para. 120.

[76] Judicial Executive Board, 'Guidance to Judges on Appearances before Select Committees'.

[77] HL Select Committee on the Constitution, 'Relations between the Executive, the Judiciary and Parliament', para. 125.

C.   Who speaks for the judiciary?

8.18 Prior to the CRA, it was the practice for chief justices to be made members of the House of Lords when or shortly after they were appointed. This gave them the right to speak publicly in the chamber on issues relating to the independence of the judiciary. The judges have always had the view that, in relation to the administration of justice, and in relation to sentencing, where the expertise of the judges is obvious, they are entitled to express their views in Parliament and, with their legislative hats on, to seek to influence Parliament. It seems part of a good administration of justice that judges highlight the dangers of particular government or legislative proposals before they are passed by Parliament and prove to be unworkable or to have an undesirable impact on the administration of justice in practice. Under the CRA, however, the Lord Chief Justice is disqualified from sitting in the House of Lords. In practice, the Lord Chief Justice speaks publicly if a particular government policy is likely to have an adverse impact upon the administration of justice, assuming that ministers have failed to provide a satisfactory response during private consultations.[78]

The Lord Chief Justice can also make his views known to a Select Committee such as the Lords Select Committee on the Constitution.[79] Criticism in this political forum is regarded as an 'ultimate weapon'[80] to be resorted to as seldom as possible. One interviewee considered 'the nuclear option'[81] of the Lord Chief Justice refusing to sign the budget, on the ground (for example) that he had asked for five years for an increase in the number of judges and that it had not happened yet and created difficulties in the administration of justice. The judge suggested that no one wanted to consider a 'show down' before Parliament and yet that this may become a necessity. But such a show down would be played out in the media, and as we shall see, the judiciary feel that they have been under-protected from criticism in recent years in the media. Further, participation in a public debate would create the risk that they will be

---

[78] *Ibid.*, paras. 52–3.
[79] CRA, s. 5 allows the Lord Chief Justice (and the Lord Chief Justice of Northern Ireland and the Lord President of the Court of Session in Scotland) to 'lay before Parliament written representations on matters that appear to him to be matters of importance relating to the judiciary, or otherwise to the administration of justice'.
[80] Lord Hope, 'What Happens When a Judge Speaks Out?', 11.
[81] An expression used by the Lord Chief Justice, (then Lord Phillips), see HL Select Committee on the Constitution, 'Relations between the Executive, the Judiciary and Parliament', Appendix 8: Evidence by the Lord Chief Justice (3 May 2006), QQ. 48–50.

drawn into wider debates which risk undermining public confidence in their impartiality in future cases. Debates about legal aid, maximum and minimum sentences and the size of the prison population all concern the administration of justice but they are also issues of deep political controversy.[82]

The Lord Chief Justice has clarified that this 'nuclear option' might be used in a constitutional crisis, 'if something was proposed by way of legislation that was so contrary to the rule of law that judges would feel: "We have got to step in and make plain our objection to this"'.[83] The Lord Chief Justice admitted considering this option in relation to the failure (as he saw it) of the then Lord Chancellor to provide safeguards following the creation of the Ministry of Justice.[84] The then Lord Chancellor, Lord Falconer, also suggested that representations should only be made when the judiciary failed to obtain satisfaction through prior discussions, and on issues relating to judicial independence, such as undue interference in judicial appointments or inadequate resourcing of the court system.[85]

8.19 Yet judges have had to adjust to the increased challenges of securing an effective response to unwarranted criticisms. They must strengthen the ways to engage in and influence debates about matters relating to the administration of justice without laying themselves open to the accusation of entering some areas of deep political controversy.[86] The legal profession itself may play an active role in sustaining public confidence in the judiciary. Similarly to the media, it may act as a check on the judiciary. Thus, the May 1992 issue of *Legal Business* published a ranking

---

[82] Lord Irvine, *Hansard*, HC, vol. 572, cols. 1259–60, 5 June 1996.

[83] HL Select Committee on the Constitution, 'Relations between the Executive, the Judiciary and Parliament', para. 118, QQ. 48, 50. The Select Committee has suggested a protocol for addressing any representation made by the Lord Chief Justice under s. 5 of the CRA. A prompt formal and written response to the Lord Chief Justice's concerns is expected, 'probably in the form of a written ministerial statement', and 'before the bill has progressed too far in either House' if the Lord Chief Justice's concerns relate to a particular bill, *Ibid.*, paras. 117–19; Lord Falconer Q. 63. The Select Committee also recommended the publication of such representations in Hansard and a debate on the bill or policy in question on the floor of the House, *Ibid.*, paras. 118–19. A hearing before a committee, perhaps the House of Lords Select Committee on the Constitution and the Constitutional Affairs Select Committee in the House of Commons, might be appropriate, *Ibid.*, para. 118.

[84] HL Select Committee on the Constitution, 'Relations between the Executive, the Judiciary and Parliament', Q. 61.

[85] *Ibid.* [86] Lord Irvine, *Hansard*, HC, vol. 572, cols. 1259–60, 5 June 1996.

order of High Court judges called 'The most respected and the least respected' which it claimed was the result of a survey it had conducted among members of the legal profession. Of the judge who came bottom of the poll, the editor wrote:

> The judge should be seen to be even-handed, fair and reasonable. . . . it is my submission that, on this test, X fails abysmally – and his conduct should therefore disqualify him from being a High Court judge . . . sheer bloody-mindedness and rudeness . . . his behaviour in court . . . undermines the very credibility of English law and he does a disservice to all involved in the legal process . . . the behaviour of X is unacceptable. He is not suited for the bench . . . he holds a public office and his behaviour reflects upon the integrity of that office . . . X is an embarrassment to the Bench.

The comments from lawyers about one of the five most disliked judges included the following: '[he] is incapable of making up his mind. It is said that if his wife puts out two bowls of cereal for him, he never gets to work.' He is 'very wimpish when it comes to making decisions because he has a fear of offending anyone', and is accused of trying 'to run cases without truly having grasped what it is about'; he is also said to be 'slow as a hearse'.[87] Only one of the judges at the bottom of the popularity ranking, Mr Justice Cresswell, responded, saying that he did not accept the alleged criticisms of his decision-making or other judicial abilities; 'ill-informed and unjust criticism in whatever tone will never deter me from taking care with my work'. In a similar exercise in 2006, *The Lawyer* attempted to defuse some of the criticism by claiming that the harshest criticism was not for judges but for the court system as a whole, pointing that good case management was a key element in assessing judges.[88]

But legal professionals could also support the judiciary in facing excessive media criticism – most obviously, by intervening to point out facts of a case which the media have ignored but which play an important part in explaining the decision. In some countries, such as the United States or New Zealand, the American Bar Association (ABA), the Law Society and Bar Association have reaffirmed their role in respect to criticisms of judges. In the English context, this may have some impact too, at least in responding to media criticisms, all the more since the senior judges have themselves regularly spoken as advocates for the legal

---

[87] *The Independent*, 7 April 1994.   [88] *The Lawyer*, 9 October 2006.

profession, in particular in relation to proposals to change legal aid.[89] The ABA Commission on Separation of Powers and Judicial Independence recommended that state bar associations intervene in specific circumstances: when the criticism is serious and will most likely have more than a passing or de minimis negative effect in the community; when the criticism displays a lack of understanding of the legal system or the role of the judge and is based at least partially on such misunderstanding; and when the criticism is materially inaccurate, the inaccuracy should be a substantial part of the criticism so that the response does not appear to be nit-picking.

8.20 The Council of Europe recommends that communication to the press of issues of public interest is made by a judge responsible for communication or some spokesman for the judiciary.[90] The Judicial Communications Office created in 2005, now known as the Press Office (a part of the Judicial Office) actively corrects inaccurate statements made about the courts. It is not to spin, but to provide the media with the basic facts they need. This office follows the judiciary's involvement in the public forum, either in providing information to the community at large or in working with the media to enhance the coverage of the administration of justice.

8.21 Subject to the above, it is the responsibility of the Lord Chief Justice and the Heads of Divisions that all judges adhere to this principle of non-partisan judgment. In addition, since the creation of the Office for Judicial Complaints in 2005, judicial speech, whether in court or outside the court, can also be the subject of disciplinary procedures. Insulting, racist or sexist language certainly amounts to misconduct.[91] Two examples may suffice. One judge was given formal advice by the Lord Chief Justice in 2010, following the Office of Judicial Complaints' finding that his comments represented an inappropriate judicial comment. As he jailed an illegal immigrant and drug runner, the judge said the case illustrated how a 'lax' immigration policy had led to 'hundreds and hundreds of thousands' of immigrants arriving in Britain to claim generous welfare benefits. Not only was this an inflammatory remark made

---

[89] See, e.g., Lord Ackner reacting in 1988 to the proposals to change legal aid and reducing the role of barristers, and recently, Lady Hale, 'Equal Access to Justice in the Big Society', Sir Henry Hodge Memorial Lecture 2011 (27 June 2011).

[90] Art. 19, Council of Europe, Recommendation no. 12 of 2010.

[91] Judicial Studies Board, 'Equal Treatment Bench Book'.

without statistical foundation, it was also the case that the immigrant had arrived in Britain on a visitor's visa but claimed asylum when the visa ran out.[92] Second, another judge received a formal reprimand following some of his observations during the trial of some pro-Palestinian campaigners and his summing up. The Office of Judicial Complaints found that his comparison of Israel to the Nazi regime did not arise directly from the evidence at trial and could be seen as an expression of the judge's personal views on a political question.[93]

II.   Media scrutiny under check

8.22 A robust and informed public debate about judicial affairs promotes judicial accountability. Media scrutiny must be welcomed, but its limits considered too, given the threat to judicial independence caused by excessive media or ministerial criticism. The possible responses from the judiciary are examined.

A.   The development of media scrutiny

8.23 Public scrutiny is perhaps the most of important of all checks on the judiciary: 'Without publicity, all other checks are insufficient: in comparison to publicity, all other checks are of small account ... It is the keenest spur to exertion and the surest guard against improbity. It keeps the judge himself, while trying, under trial.'[94] The media sometimes acts as the first check on judicial conduct. It also conveys to the judiciary the sense of the community on matters of general public interest. Hence the press, lawyers and members of the public are entitled to criticise the court, even if the language used is intemperate, or the terms of the criticism, in some respects, erroneous. Courts ought to be able to bear trenchant criticism directed at all aspects of the administration of justice, including judicial decision making, judicial conduct, judicial appointments or court procedures and management.

In 1969, the Salmon Committee observed that 'the right to criticise judges ... may be one of the safeguards which helps to insure their high standard of performance, and also that the same meticulous care which

---

[92] *Daily Mail*, 5 August 2009.
[93] Office for Judicial Complaints, Statement OJC/25/10, 7 October 2010.
[94] J. Bentham, *Rationale of Judicial Evidence, Specially Applied to English Practice. From the Manuscript*, ed. J.S. Mill (London: Hunt and Clarke, 1827).

has always been taken in appointing them in the past will continue to be taken in the future'.[95] In an address to magistrates, Lord Hailsham LC gave this advice to the justices:

> So long as you do not find your private home invaded or your personal privacy intruded upon do not treat the Press as your enemy. What goes on in court is public property and it is not merely their right but their duty to report, and it is their right and very often their duty to comment. Private justice is almost always a denial of justice.[96]

Lord Denning said in later years: 'Justice has no place in darkness and secrecy. When a judge sits on a case, he himself is on trial ... If there is any misconduct on [his] part, any bias or prejudice, there is a reporter to keep an eye on him.'[97]

It is not difficult to find examples of media scrutiny improving the delivery of justice. Media pressure played a part in exposing some of the notorious miscarriages of justice in the 1970s. The media might also be able to signal flaws in the legal process, as it did on the use of expert evidence in court in relation to cot death. The two wrongful convictions of Sally Clark and Angela Cannings[98] for murdering their babies had, each time, partly relied on the expert evidence at the original trials of Professor Sir Roy Meadow, an experienced paediatrician, who refuted the proposition that Sally Clark's two sons may have died from cot death. The prosecution of Sally Clark for murdering her two babies partly relied on his flawed statistical calculations, that the probability of the two deaths having been incidences of cot death was 1 in 73 million. Aside from the fact that the calculation underlying this probability is incorrect, this calculation was never compared with an estimate of the probability that the two deaths were the result of a double murder.[99] Professor Sir Roy Meadow was vilified through the extensive media reports of the proceedings, but the media pressure showed more generally a failure of the system,[100] since not just the experts but the lawyers and judges involved may have been able to prevent the miscarriage of justice but

---

[95] Salmon LJ, 'Report of the Interdepartmental Committee on the Law of Contempt as it affects Tribunals of Enquiry', Cmnd 4078 (London: HMSO, 1969), p. 15.

[96] Lord Hailsham, 'Presidential Address' (1971) 27 *The Magistrate* 185, 186.

[97] Lord Denning, Address before the High Court Journalists Association, *The Times*, 3 December 1964.

[98] *R v. Cannings* [2004] 1 WLR 2607.

[99] HC Select Committee on Science and Technology, 'Scientific Advice, Risk and Evidence Based Policy Making', Seventh Report (2005–06) (16 March 2005), p. 168.

[100] *Meadow v. General Medical Council* [2007] 1 All ER 1, paras. 168–70.

failed to do so. In particular, the same expert evidence had been used in family courts for some time, but they were not open to the public or media, and thus its flaws only came about with the criminal trials of Angela Cannings and Sally Clark.

The media pressure has been key in making the family courts more open and accessible, with, for example, a campaign by *The Times* starting in July 2008 to open up the family courts to the press, so that experts and social services would be more accountable for the childcare system. This was done, following Sir Mark Potter, 'not for the purposes of currying favour with the press', but because of 'the harm' being done 'both to the child care system and the reputation of family judges by the complaints of aggrieved parties to which they could not reply and the consequent allegations of secret justice'.[101] Accordingly, a Practice Direction and Guidance were issued in 2009 permitting wider press access to family proceedings.

8.24 The media have become more or less consistently outspoken over the years. Their criticism may sometimes be unfair, though the risk of misunderstanding is 'just part of the job – one of the consequences of the fact that trials are heard in public'.[102] It is fair to suggest that in years gone by, much criticism was aimed at appointees who had little to show by way of legal pedigree and who owed their position to contacts with the Lord Chancellor, though such criticism would often only emerge in newspaper obituaries ('it is possible that party claims were considered as much as legal qualifications. There were at least a dozen men with better credentials').[103] Contemporary criticism would more likely be offered to some judges who arguably should, but had not, been removed for misconduct or infirmity. In 1891 *The Times* emphatically called for the retirement of Mr Justice Fitzjames Stephen, who had been afflicted with mental illness but still remained in office, writing that the capacity of the judge was 'the universal topic of conversation whenever lawyers meet', 'a subject of wonder and regret to the whole profession'.[104] The

---

[101] Potter LJ, 'Do the Media Influence the Judiciary', The Foundation for Law, Justice and Society in Affiliation with the Centre for Socio-Legal Studies, University of Oxford (2011), p. 7.

[102] Lord Hope, 'What Happens When a Judge Speaks Out?', 9–10.

[103] *The Times*, 1 December 1911, quoted in S.W. Durran. *The Lawyer, Our-Old-Man-of-the-Sea* (London: Kegan Paul & Co., 1913), p. 225.

[104] *The Times*, 6 March 1891, quoted in H. Cecil, *Tipping the Scales* (London: Hutchinson, 1964), pp. 179–80.

Profumo scandal in 1963 gave rise to allegations against judges and criticism of the courts.[105] In 1968 Lord Avonside, a Scottish judge, was strongly criticised for accepting an invitation from Edward Heath, then the Leader of the Opposition, to serve on a committee of the Conservative Party which was appointed to consider party proposals for a Scottish Assembly. Lord Avonside resigned from the committee under public pressure. In 1970 Sir Henry Fisher also came under fire for having resigned from the High Court after only two-and-a-half years on the bench. He was particularly criticised for joining a firm of merchant bankers upon his resignation, as it was believed that he broke an established tradition that, upon retirement from the bench, judges do not take business appointments.

However, such scrutiny was of rather an ad hominem nature. It is hard to see a similar tendency of the media to criticise judges over the merits of individual decisions. Some fifty years ago, the press was criticised for failing to discharge properly its public duty to bring to light the shortcomings in the administration of justice. Mr Blom-Cooper (as he then was) wrote that:

> criticism of the judiciary over the last fifty years has been confined to conversations over the coffee cups and to the seclusion of private solicitors' offices and barristers' chambers ... The English have cloaked their judges with an immunity from public criticism which tends only to diminish the quality of justice administered by those so privileged.[106]

Professor Griffith complained that 'judges are treated as though they were Caesar's wives and we should be unsuspicious'.[107] The JUSTICE Report on Law and the Press also expressed some dissatisfaction with the role of the press in checking the judges. It recommended that 'the newspapers [should] devote more continual and serious attention to matters concerning the administration of justice and employ more experienced reporters and editorial staff for this purpose'.[108] Some suggested that in fact newspapers were afraid to criticise judges for fear of being punished for contempt. In the course of a debate in the House of Lords on the law and the press, Lord Gardiner LC observed that 'unfortunately, the administration of justice in this country is insufficiently

---

[105] For an account of the Profumo scandal see Cecil, *Tipping the Scales*, 188.
[106] L. Blom-Cooper, 'The Judiciary in an Era of Law Reform' 37 *Political Quarterly* 378 (1966).
[107] J. Griffith, 'Conspiracy and the Judges', *New Statesman*, 17 October 1971, p. 854.
[108] JUSTICE, 'The Law and the Press' (1966), p. 17.

criticised'.[109] But in fact much may have been owed to the inherent tendency of many editors to avoid criticism of judges. In 1971, upon the death of Lord Goddard (Lord Chief Justice 1947–58), the *Times* columnist Bernard Levin had made vitriolic comments[110] on Lord Goddard's shortcomings. He attacked Goddard in the strongest terms for his conduct in the Craig-Bentley Trial and in the Laski libel action and for his campaign against penal reform.[111] Today, his criticism of Lord Goddard seems simply 'orthodox'[112] and in 1993 Bentley was granted a posthumous pardon in relation to the sentence of death, following a Divisional Court judgment to that effect. In 1998 the Court of Appeal allowed a posthumous appeal against conviction because Lord Goddard's summing up was so prejudiced that it denied him that fair trial which is 'the birthright of every British citizen'.[113] Yet among the numerous letters written in June 1971 to *The Times* commenting on Bernard Levin's' article, one Mr Peter Black perceptively wrote that 'had Goddard still been among us, Levin's perfectly justified expression of opinion on a matter of public importance would probably not have been printed as it stood'.[114]

The controversy surrounding the publication, in 1971, of the Report on the Judiciary of a JUSTICE subcommittee offered another example of the reluctance to criticise the bench. The report proposed reforms in the appointment and removal of judges as well as other reforms in the training of judges and the eligibility of solicitors and academic lawyers for higher judicial posts. The Report divided the Council of JUSTICE which could not reach an agreement on its recommendations, and a number of its eminent members objected to its publication on the ground that it might 'shake public confidence in the Judiciary' or might engender 'mistrust of the Judiciary in those who without reading the full Report might draw unjustified inferences from recommendations above'.[115] Ultimately, after the report was 'leaked' to the general press, JUSTICE decided to publish it as a report of the subcommittee which prepared it, and not as a JUSTICE report.

It is difficult to understand why a serious study on the appointment, retirement and removal of judges should be suppressed only because the

---

[109] *Hansard*, HL, vol. 274, cols. 1371, 1439, 25 May 1966.
[110] *The Times*, 8 June 1971.
[111] D. Yallop, *To Encourage Others* (London: W.H. Allen, 1972); E. Grimshaw and G. Jones, *Lord Goddard: His Career and Cases* (London: Allan Wingate, 1958), pp. 40–60, 129–50.
[112] *The Times*, 7 September 2004.
[113] *R* v. *Bentley* [2001] 1 Cr App R 307, para. 68; see above para. 5.23.
[114] *The Times*, 12 June 1971.   [115] JUSTICE, 'The Judiciary'.

reforms proposed imply that the existing system is defective. As one critic wrote, 'the system loses far more than it gains by continuing to shield the judiciary from public scrutiny, and the public can only gain from the exposure of possible defects in the system'.[116] The JUSTICE Report affair has nothing to do with fear of the contempt power, but with a then long-established tradition to avoid outspoken criticism of judges and the administration of justice.

8.25 Deference started to become unfashionable in the 1980s. In more recent times, in 1986, the *Daily Mirror* responded to the *Spycatcher* injunction with upside-down photographs of the Law Lords who had upheld the injunction, below the headline 'YOU FOOLS!'.[117] No action was taken, and Sedley LJ (as he was then) observed that since that day, 'not only deference but civility towards the bench has become unmodish'.[118] Miscarriages of justice, such as those involving the Birmingham Six[119] and the Guildford Four in the 1980s, triggered personal criticisms of the judges involved in those miscarriages.

In 1989, Lord Lane quashed the convictions of the Guildford Four.[120] But he was to be 'haunted'[121] by the words he used when he presided in January 1988 in the three-judge Court of Appeal which rejected the appeals of the Birmingham Six: 'As with many cases referred by the Home Secretary to the Court of Appeal, the longer the case has gone on the more this court has been convinced the jury was correct.' The same year, Lane turned down the appeal of the Tottenham Three, wrongly jailed for the murder of PC Keith Blakelock, after finding that there was 'no lurking doubt' in spite of the flimsiness of the prosecution case. The Three's successful appeal in 1991 brought criticism of the Lord Chief Justice and an apology from the Presiding Judges.

When the Birmingham Six returned to the Court of Appeal in 1991, Lloyd LJ defended Lane, saying: 'The scientific issues before the court (in the earlier appeal) were not the same as they are now.' Nonetheless, the acquittal of the Six brought renewed calls for Lane's resignation. Bernard Levin wrote in *The Times*, under the title 'Hoist by their own

---

[116] *Ibid.*, Foreword.

[117] *Attorney-General* v. *Guardian Newspapers Ltd (No. 2)* [1990] AC 109.

[118] S. Sedley, 'Foreword', in I. Cram (ed.), *Borrie and Lowe: the Law of Contempt*, 4th edn (London: LexisNexis Butterworths, 2010), p. viii.

[119] *R* v. *McIlkenny* [1992] 2 All ER 417.

[120] *R* v. *Richardson*, *R* v. *Conlon*, The Times, 20 October 1989.

[121] Obituary, *The Times*, 24 August 2005.

arrogance',[122] that the 'narcissistic arrogance' of Lane's 'worthless certainty' was a danger to justice, and he urged him to go. A Commons'
motion to that effect was signed by 140 MPs. When he retired in 1992,
Bernard Levin wrote 'the odious nature of Lord Lane's retirement bun-
fight suggests that many of them [the judiciary] still don't know why
they are distrusted and even despised'.[123]

When Lane retired in 1992, Lord Donaldson, the Master of the Rolls,
denounced the attempts to make the Lord Chief Justice a 'scapegoat',
saying that he could now break the traditional silence of judges about their
colleagues and 'give voice to the anger and disgust which we have felt at the
campaign of calumny waged against you in recent months'. Nonetheless,
in 1993, a journalist in the *Sunday Times* commented: 'Corruption is
almost unknown in the brotherhood of judges, but stupidity, crassness
and blatant prejudice especially against women are not.'[124]

8.26 Today the overall picture has evolved once more. Aided by more
transparent appointment and disciplinary processes, there is less criticism of the competence and integrity of the English judges. Further, the
media stereotype of the English judges as being overwhelmingly upper
class and remote from society is markedly less pronounced and certainly
they are less consistently portrayed as conservative establishment figures.
However, the advent of the HRA, which allows and sometimes arguably
requires, judges to quash administrative decisions or policies which
violate a protected human right, calls for judgments of a more 'evaluative'
kind,[125] prompting complaints that the judges are striking down policies
of the democratically elected. Sir Mark Potter observes with irony that
the High Court judge was, in the late 1980s, typically portrayed in some
parts of the media, as a 'portsoaked reactionary, still secretly resentful of
the abolition of the birch and hostile to liberal influences of any kind'.
The same judge is now, in the same parts of the media, 'an unashamedly
progressive member of the chattering classes, spiritually if not actually
resident in Islington or Hampstead, out of touch with "ordinary people",
and diligently engaged in frustrating the intentions of Parliament with
politically correct notions of Human Rights'.

8.27 Thus, much of the English media criticises judges for leniency or
inconsistency in sentencing. In 1995 the Chairman of the Conservative

---

[122] 18 March 1991.   [123] *The Times*, 15 June 1992.
[124] *The Sunday Times*, 10 June 1993.
[125] T. Bingham, 'The Human Rights Act' (2010) EHRLR 568, 570.

Party urged members of the public to write to judges and magistrates and complain about lenient sentencing.[126] Giving evidence before the Constitution Committee in 2006, Paul Dacre, editor of the *Daily Mail*, stated that 'whilst the public still have huge faith in the independence and integrity and incorruptibility of the British judiciary', they are becoming 'slightly confused' because they see 'political judgments being made by judges which fly in the face of what they perceive as national interests' and 'an increasingly lenient judiciary, handing down lesser and lesser sentences'.[127] Perhaps the best-known example, and the one always cited by the judges interviewed, is the low sentence given to a convicted paedophile where the judge had correctly applied existing sentencing guidelines. Regrettably, the Home Secretary of the day joined in the attack on the trial judge, and the incident heightened concerns among the judiciary that the Lord Chancellor is not in a sufficiently strong position to remind his Cabinet colleagues of their duties to respect the decisions of the judiciary.[128] The Select Committee on the Constitution, in its Sixth Report (2006–07) regretted the 'misleading and wholly inappropriate' rhetoric developed by some newspapers, such as the *Daily Mail* in a 2003 editorial: 'Britain's unaccountable and unelected judges are openly, and with increasing arrogance and perversity, usurping the role of Parliament, setting the wishes of the people at nought and pursuing a liberal, politically correct agenda of their own, in their zeal to interpret European legislation.'[129] In 2006 Clare Dyer, the legal editor of the *Guardian*, confirmed the critical trend in giving evidence before the House of Lords Constitution Select Committee, saying that judges were increasingly seen as 'too left wing, too bleeding liberal, too wet' and 'too pro-human rights and too soft'.[130]

8.28 We note these trends not in order to criticise them but as necessary background to discussing how judges should anticipate and respond to media criticism, not all of which will be well founded. We were struck, however, by how many judges interviewed thought that their public image had never been worse, and criticism had been more forthcoming

---

[126] A. Lester, 'Judges and Ministers', 18 LRB, vol. 18, n. 8, 18 April 1996, p. 10.

[127] *Ibid.*, 143.

[128] HL Select Committee on the Constitution, 'Relations between the Executive, the Judiciary and Parliament', para. 45.

[129] *Daily Mail*, 20 February 2003.

[130] HL Select Committee on the Constitution, 'Relations between the Executive, the Judiciary and Parliament', 142.

than ever before, notwithstanding that they still compare well with most other professionals in England. The media rhetoric contrasts with the relatively high opinion of the justice system in the UK compared with other European countries. Thus the November 2010 Eurobarometer survey indicates that 50 per cent of the individuals surveyed tend to trust the justice system/the UK legal system, against 47 per cent of individuals who tend not to trust it.[131]

B. *Judicial anticipation and response to media criticism*

8.29 The harm to individual judges and the threat to judicial independence caused by excessive media or ministerial criticism do require a response from the judiciary. Given that judges are not elected in this country, we can quite safely suggest that no judge would consciously do that which his conscience tells him is wrong for gaining media praise, nor fail to do 'what is right' in fear of media criticism. Lord Mansfield CJ, in an oft-quoted passage, said:

> I will not do that which my conscience tells me is wrong, upon occasion, to gain the huzzas of thousands or the daily praise of all the papers which come from the press: I will not avoid doing what I think is right, though it should draw on me the whole artillery of libels.[132]

Upon this point Mr Justice Cardozo, has also spoken:

> Historic liberties and privileges are not to bend from day to day because of some accident of immediate overwhelming interest which appeals to the feelings and distorts judgment ... A community whose judges would be willing to give it whatever law might gratify the impulse of the moment would find that it had paid too high a price for relieving itself of the bother of awaiting a session of the Legislature and the enactment of statute in accordance with established forms.[133]

Judges' decisions may still be subconsciously or subliminally influenced by the anticipated views of media commentators. The particular difficulty is that media opinions cannot be equated with the opinion of the public at large. The press or media constructs public opinion as much as it

---

[131] The Public Opinion Analysis sector of the European Commission, Eurobarometer survey of November 2010.

[132] *R v. Wilkes* (1770) 4 Burr. 2527. 2561. 98 ER 327, 346; H. McCardie, *The Law, the Advocate and the Judge, A Reading Delivered before the Honourable Society of the Middle Temple* (19 May 1927), p. 26.

[133] *Doyle v. Hofstader* 257 NY 244, 268 (1931).

channels 'public opinion'. The message conveyed does not even have to be true: while the media have reflected concerns about a 'compensation culture', research done in 2004 showed that the existence of such culture was a myth, but a myth which fuelled wide misperceptions, and nurtured changes in the law of damages.[134] So it is for the benefit of the legal system itself that judges have developed two strategies for dealing with the press without compromising their independence and professional distance by constantly engaging with the media.

One strategy is educational and essentially prophylactic: potential misconceptions or misreporting of their decisions may be anticipated and incorporated in the decision. The other strategy is reactive: where, despite all due caution, a decision has been misreported and is causing public disquiet, moves may be made to correct the mistake, but without entering into argument over the merits of the decision. If two solutions were possible, no action will be taken to counter criticism that the judges preferred the worse solution, but a correction may be made if it is popularly suggested that a judge could have done something which he had no power, or lacked jurisdiction, to do.

The anticipation of media storm

8.30 The prophylactic strategy is relatively recent and depends on an understanding that law reports are now available freely online and by no means read only by professionals and by law students. Lord Neuberger recalled in 2011 the ever more important duty of judges to communicate the law through their judgments as clearly as possible, as the law, reflecting society as well as legislation, becomes ever more complicated.[135] In cases involving difficult moral and ethical issues, such as in the assisted suicide cases (*Pretty* and *Purdy*),[136] the courts have ignored the strong media tide in support of Ms Purdy's call for clarification of the law in respect of assisted suicide. Both the Court of Appeal and the House of Lords instead clearly emphasised the limits of their remit – it is for Parliament to change the law on a difficult issue such as the one raised in *Purdy*.[137]

---

[134] HC Constitutional Affairs Committee, 'Compensation Culture: Third Report of Session 2005–06', vol. 2, report HC 754-II (10 March 2006), example cited by Potter LJ, 'Do the Media Influence the Judiciary'.

[135] Lord Neuberger, 'Open Justice Unbound', Judicial Studies Board Annual Lecture (16 March 2011), para. 14.

[136] R (Purdy) v. Director of Public Prosecutions [2009] UKHL 45; Pretty v. Director of Public Prosecutions and Secretary of State for the Home Department [2001] UKHL 61.

[137] R (Purdy) v. Director of Public Prosecutions [2009] UKHL 45, para. 26 [Lord Hope].

Judges are encouraged to anticipate the storm and assist the press, in an attempt to avoid misreporting, especially in relation to sentencing. Summaries of complex judgments are expected to be handed down to assist the media, explaining why a particular sentence has been imposed, and pointing out any statutory restrictions that may have prevented them from imposing a higher one. They are provided in the media releases which now regularly accompany judgments in particularly high-profile or complex cases. Beyond assisting the media, this is enhancing transparency of justice. Similarly, if the media is running a story based on a single out-of-context comment, an accurate account of what actually happened in court should be provided with the full transcript. Public information officers attached to the Lord Chief Justice are expected to anticipate media storms and to prepare appropriate press releases for immediate effect, thus reducing the risk of misreporting. Judges have a system in place before attacks are launched.[138]

Thus, for the first time, the intense media coverage of the trial of Rosemary West in 1995 was managed by the Lord Chancellor's press office. West was tried and eventually convicted of the murder of eleven people in Gloucester. This was the first trial in the United Kingdom where reporters covering it were provided with a media annexe adjacent to the trial courtroom, with sound links from the trial courtroom being relayed into other courtrooms. More than 150 reporters were accommodated when it came to the summing up and sentencing at the end of the trial. Media management for the West trial became the template for future high-profile trials and for major public inquiries headed by a judge, such as Lord Hutton's Inquiry into the death of Dr David Kelly in 2004, or for high-profile inquests, such as those into the death of Diana Princess of Wales and Dodi al Fayed.

8.31 The House of Lords Constitution Committee emphasised, in 2007, that individual judges should make 'every effort to explain the reasoning behind their judgments or sentencing decisions in the clearest possible manner in order to avoid any misunderstanding of the true position by either the media or the public'.[139] Indeed, the inaccuracy of the reporting of sentencing prevents an open debate, itself a precondition for sensible

---

[138] Compare with the United States ABA guidelines, 'Rapid Response to Unfair and Unjust Criticism of Judges' (2008).

[139] HL Select Committee on the Constitution, 'Relations between the Executive, the Judiciary and Parliament', 150; C. Sunstein, 'If People Would Be Outraged by Their Rulings, Should Judges Care?' (2007) 60 *Stanford Law Review* 155.

sentencing.[140] The report recognises that individual judges and the judiciary as a whole can be treated as 'fair game' by columnists and headline writers in the tabloid press. The judgment of Foskett J in an application for judicial review in relation to the *Baby P* case is rightly cited as 'an impeccable exercise in judicial distancing from the views and influence of the media, as well as the politics of the matter',[141] while addressing the need for clarity with a thorough judgment on an issue that was widely publicised. The judge introduced his judgment in these terms:

> Almost anything that happens in connection with the Baby P case, or with its wider implications, occasions comment. That is entirely to be expected and is, of course, a welcome feature of any informed and balanced public debate about how tragedies of the nature that occurred in relation to Peter can be avoided in the future. Whether the outcome of the present court case has anything to contribute to that important debate will be for others to judge.
>
> However, any informed and balanced view of the consequences of the case before the court needs an understanding of the precise issues for consideration and the way in which the court deals with those issues. It does also require a clear appreciation of what this case is not about.[142]

The judge then carefully circumscribed the scope of his judgment, excluding some matters of interest to the press and clarifying that the judgment concerned the fairness of the procedures followed by the public authorities to dismiss the applicant. He later stated:

> 48. Second, the Claimant is undoubtedly of the view that she has been subject to press and media interest and intrusion that has gone beyond an acceptable threshold, a view that appears to be shared by others and, at least to some extent at some stage, according to an interview in the papers before me, by the Secretary of State himself. Again, I cannot avoid reference to the involvement of the press in relation to some parts of the background since it forms a significant feature of that background and may have a bearing on at least one important feature in the case. However, anything I say about the press interest should not be seen as either condemning or condoning what has occurred. There will be those who consider the press interest in the Claimant to have been entirely appropriate and called for; there will be those who consider it to have been unfairly personalised and unnecessarily and aggressively intrusive. That is a matter of personal opinion and taste. My position on this issue must be one of neutrality. No issue of law arises from it ...

---

[140] Lord Woolf, 'Should the Media and the Judiciary be on Speaking Terms?'.
[141] Potter LJ, 'Do the Media Influence the Judiciary', 4–5.
[142] *Sharon Shoesmith* v. *OFSTED and others* [2010] EWHC 852 (Admin), para. 24.

> 49. Third, I can deal with the issues and arguments in this case only on the basis of the evidence put before me.[143]

In the Court of Appeal, Maurice Kay LJ further emphasised the role of the press in this case:

> 134. I cannot leave this case without commenting on the way in which Ms Shoesmith was treated. In another case, Sedley LJ was moved to say:
> 'It seems that the making of a public sacrifice to deflect press and public obloquy, which is what happened to the appellant, remains an accepted expedient of public administration in this country. (*Gibb v Maidstone & Tunbridge Wells NHS Trust* [2010] EWCA Civ 678, (at paragraph 42)'
> 135. In my view, it is also what happened in the present case.[144]

8.32 This educational strategy does not have to be pursued only in judgments. Other local initiatives to educate the press about the administration of justice may be appropriate too. Lord Judge LCJ placed a strong emphasis in 2011 on the need for practical cooperation between the judiciary and media representatives:

> In England, judges with administrative responsibilities, for example, the senior judge in the Crown Court of, say, Leeds or Manchester is encouraged to have a working relationship with the editor of the local newspapers, so that if for example it appears that a judge in his sentencing remarks has said something outrageous or absurd, at least before this goes into print, it can be checked that he has indeed said that which was attributed to him, or that if he did, there was a context which explains it. A record of what the judge actually said should be made available. In that way what might be a misguided headline is avoided. On the other hand, if the judge did indeed utter a remark which, whatever the context, was absurd or stupid or revealing a prejudice, why then, it should be reported, and criticised for absurdity, stupidity or prejudice.[145]

Thus the guidance on 'Family Courts: Media Access & Reporting July 2011', was, for the first time, drafted by a group of lawyers and journalists, both from the print and broadcast media. This guidance is a further step in the established cooperation between the Society of Editors, lawyers and the judiciary for the production of guides to reporting restrictions in the Crown Court and the Magistrates Court. A newspaper reporter can draw the attention of the court to the contents

---

[143] *Ibid.*, paras. 48–9.
[144] *Shoesmith (on the application of)* v. *OFSTED and others* [2011] EWCA Civ 642, paras. 134–5.
[145] Judge LCJ, 'The Judiciary and the Media', 7.

of these guides, so as to avoid the expense of employing lawyers for the purpose. The result is fewer inappropriate reporting restrictions, or, if such restictions are imposed, their prompt removal, without, in the words of the Lord Chief Justice, the independence of the judiciary or the media being diminished.[146]

The same public consultation exercise is underway regarding live text-based communications in relation to the proceedings – mainly tweeting – of hearings by journalists, while practice guidance has been provided by the Lord Chief Justice on this subject.[147] A similar increased transparency exists in relation to super-injunctions.[148]

Senior judges can now be given television and radio interview training; it has become possible for judges to take part in their local court 'open days' and talk to their local reporters. The first media guidance for judges was provided in 2000 by Lord Irvine's office on how to handle the media while dealing with cases attracting major press coverage.

Correcting misreporting from the media

8.33 The second strategy alluded to above is the reactive one of making corrections. We referred, in our introduction, to the convention that judges do not respond to criticism in individual cases. As Lord Denning said, 'from the nature of our office we cannot reply to criticism. We cannot enter into public controversy. We must rely on our conduct itself to be its own vindication.'[149] Even when they are misreported, individual judges traditionally do not publicly put right the inaccuracies, though they may refer to the matter in open court.[150] The principle has always, rightly, been that a judgment speaks for itself, for better or for worse.[151] Sir Igor Judge, then President of the Queen's Bench Division,

---

[146] *Ibid.*

[147] Lord Chief Justice, 'Practice Guidance: The use of live text-based forms of communication (including Twitter) from Court for the purposes of fair and accurate reporting', 14 November 2011.

[148] The report of a committee chaired by Lord Neuberger on that matter addressed media concern by distinguishing between the rare super-injunction and other cases, and by emphasising the need to improve the procedures/practice of parties proposing to seek anonymity in case of high media interest.

[149] *Ex parte Blackburn (No. 2)* [1968] 2 WLR 1201, 1207.

[150] Cecil, *The English Judge.* For two early cases of a judge writing a letter to the press in matters concerning his judicial conduct, see L. Radzinowicz, 'Sir James Fitzjames Stephen', Selden Society Lecture 1957, p. 41; *The Times*, 21 August 1975.

[151] Hammond, 'Free Speech and Judges in New Zealand'.

told the Constitution Committee in 2006 that 'enhancing public confidence is a most difficult concept and it is particularly difficult ... for judges who actually are not in the business of trying to sell themselves to anyone. If our judgments do not speak for themselves there is nothing that the Communications Office or the press office can do.'[152]

In the United States, where public criticism is rife and no restraints similar to England and Wales apply, a 'Prohibition on Judicial Response' can be found in the Code of Conduct.[153] However, judges should be prepared to correct factual errors (as opposed to entering into argument or debate over the merits of their decisions) and to inform the public of the limits of their powers in certain cases, for example when criticised for not doing something which was in fact outside their jurisdiction or otherwise legally impossible. Given that most people draw their knowledge of the judiciary and the justice system from the media, the judiciary must also ensure that the media criticisms also reflect an understanding of the limits or obligations imposed by the law on the judge.[154] A summary or a statement of the merits or the meaning of a decision is a convenient way to meet those expectations.

Some cases involve repeated visits to the courts, and these provide ideal opportunities for judges to set the record straight. A High Court judge criticised a *Sunday Telegraph* journalist over his reporting of a case heard in the family courts in 2010.[155] The journalist had written two articles about a case involving a one-year-old child taken into care and its mother, father, grandmother and guardian, and a city council. In his ruling, the judge said that the two articles written by the journalist about the case were 'unbalanced', 'inaccurate' and 'wrong'. The journalist's second article criticised the council for basing its decision to place the child in care on the evidence of an unnamed paediatrician, and referred to the judge being 'so excoriatory' about the paediatrician's evidence. But the judge in his ruling corrected the journalist about his reporting, saying that that paediatrician had had no involvement in the case at all; the journalist was also criticised for failing to attend the hearings and relying on one of the parties only in his account of the proceedings:

> Parents involved in court proceedings cannot always be relied upon to be unbiased and dispassionate. More often ... they are partisan and

---

[152] HL Select Committee on the Constitution, 'Relations between the Executive, the Judiciary and Parliament', 148.
[153] Canon 3 (A)(6).   [154] Judge LCJ, 'The Judiciary and the Media', 7.
[155] *The Guardian*, 17 May 2011.

tendentious. It is not only judges that need to recognise that but journalists too. As this case has shown, to rely uncritically upon what a parent says can lead to reporting that is unbalanced, inaccurate and just plain wrong.[156]

8.34 Support for media relations has been available from 1987 onwards, from the Lord Chancellor's Press Office, in relation in particular to high-profile trials. The press office, first staffed in 1987 by one professional communicator, progressively expanded and gained responsibility for managing not just media issues but also internal communications as well as a departmental website and an intranet. The Lord Chancellor's press office gained full strength when Lord Taylor, who was appointed as new Lord Chief Justice in 1992, heralded a new relationship with the media with regular press conferences for legal correspondents and interviews. He was also the first head of the judiciary to appear on the BBC's *Question Time*. Lord Taylor supported a greater public engagement of judges on the ground of judicial accountability:

> It is simply no longer sensible to remain silent when so much attention, much of it highly critical, is focused on courts and the judicial process. In the absence of any reply it would be assumed against the judges that they were so arrogant and complacent as to believe that they could ignore criticism, or that they had no good answer to it. I think that it is gradually gaining acceptance that the judiciary has a duty not only to defend itself, but also to be accountable. Some countries even have public relations' departments, for example Australia. Lord Woolf told me that once a year he held a press conference to inform the public about the work of the judiciary. He certainly demonstrated that it is possible to maintain judicial independence from the executive and at the same time be accountable to the public.[157]

8.35 While misreporting is often unintentional, it can be repeated and become an accepted fact in the media. The judiciary's policy is to obtain retractions from the press, and a correction of the archives. In a rare case, the *Sun*'s front page on 28 July 2011 carried a single column panel saying 'Judge is cleared – see page 2'. The original story, on the front page, ran under the headline 'Paedo trial judge "drunk in court"'. This was a rather sensational interpretation of a Press Association report in April 2011 that that a Crown Court judge was under investigation by the Office of

---

[156] In response, the journalist in question complained about the obstacles to reporting cases in family courts.
[157] *Daily Telegraph*, 24 April 1996.

Judicial Complaints. He had been accused of being 'influenced by alcohol' at a trial in Swindon in which he acquitted a man of raping an eight-year-old girl after the jury failed to reach a verdict. When the Office of Judicial Complaints, having investigated the matter, rejected the mother's claim,[158] the judge asked for some front page reference to his exoneration, and the Press Complaints Commission negotiated on his behalf to obtain the publication of the retraction of the original story. The retraction concluded with a quote from the judge pointing to the effect of this damaging and unfounded allegation on him and his family, adding that 'It was a slur on the judiciary as a whole. I'm pleased it has been thoroughly investigated and rejected.'[159]

Corrections can also be made to protect the name of one who has been wrongly accused in the media. This can occur in the Family Court where the decisions themselves typically omit the names of the parties. Thus the President of the Family Division issued in August 2011 a press release in a paedophile allegations case even before giving two judgments in open court.[160] In the press release, the judge explained that in two previous hearings the High Court had found that the father had not sexually abused his daughter, and that the mother had manufactured the 'evidence'. His first public judgment (omitting only the name of the child) would explain why he had reached the same conclusion as the two previous judges. His second judgment would explain why he had found a woman in contempt of court. The press releases stated that the child's mother, with the assistance of another woman, had unlawfully and in breach of court orders put into the public domain via email and the internet a series of unwarranted and scandalous allegations about the father and others. This was accompanied by some poor press reporting, and even an MP publicly taking the defence of the mother and breaking a super-injunction under parliamentary privilege for that purpose. The judge made the judgment public in order for the father to publicly clear his name:

> I have read all the papers in the case carefully. The father of the child, who may be named, is *not* a paedophile and he has *not* sexually abused his daughter . . . These proceedings have had a serious effect on the life of the

[158] Office for Judicial Complaints, Statement OJC 25/11 (27 July 2011).

[159] *The Guardian*, 28 July 2011. The PCC has been criticised for failing to regulate the press's conduct and its powers have come under review under the Leveson inquiry into phone-hacking.

[160] *Re X (a child)*, 25 August 2011, not yet reported.

father, and have threatened the stability of the child. Her mother's actions are wholly contrary to her interests. The father is entitled to tell the world, and the world is entitled to know, that he is not a paedophile; that he has not sexually abused his daughter, and that the allegations made against him are false.

8.36 There is a growing consensus as to who – the individual judge, the Judicial Communications Office or even the Lord Chief Justice or the Lord Chancellor themselves – should correct mistaken media reporting. Although much depends on the nature of the criticism, judges should pre-empt possible misunderstandings in their own judgments and they should not seek to clarify their judgments in the press when they have failed to do so in their judgments. Here later clarification might only be sought by other means, from the Judicial Communications Office or even some informed academic commentary. Persistent factual errors in reporting the facts of the case or their own reasons are corrected that way.

Where the matter is not so much one of the details of a particular case, but one of a wider legal misunderstanding about the powers and responsibilities of judges, then the Judicial Communications Office should intervene. For example, in murder cases, the judge's sentence may comply with the sentencing guidelines, and yet the victim or the victim's family may regard it as too lenient, and the media will criticise the judgment instead of the guidelines.[161] The Judicial Communications' Office should correct such misconceptions, if they are thought liable to mislead the public on an important matter. We note that, in 2008, the Judicial Communications Office set a judges' media panel, with a few judges being deployed, after media training, to take part in interviews or media discussions so that a judicial viewpoint can be clearly stated. They do not comment on specific cases but they can, for instance, explain how sentencing policy works in relation to a type of crime. Moreover, the Lord Chancellor, who, under section 3 CRA, must uphold judicial independence, should be prepared to speak where the very independence of judges is potentially undermined by misinformed criticism.

Recently, a High Court judge, Mr Justice Eady, gave a series of controversial rulings in defamation cases brought against the media. The *Daily Mail* editor, in a series of attacks, described him as unaccountable and hostile to freedom of speech. Lord Pannick QC used his maiden speech in the Lords in 2008 to defend him.[162] He suggested that, in the

---

[161] Criminal Justice Act 2003, ss. 172–74.   [162] *The Times*, 24 November 2008.

face of ill-informed attacks, an independent judiciary should be seen, where necessary, to defend itself and respond to those attacks. Mr Justice Eady was further criticised by the editor of the *Daily Mail* when the latter gave evidence to the Parliamentary Select Committee on Culture, Media and Sport in 2009. The judge was accused of 'moral and social nihilism' and 'arrogance', though the editor added that this was not intended to be anything personal.[163] In a rare public speech some months later, the judge responded, without giving names, that 'The media have nowhere to vent their frustrations other than through personal abuse of the particular judge who happens to have made the decision.'[164] He suggested that 'letting off steam' that way was an inevitable consequence of adopting, under the HRA, the balancing approach and an 'intense focus' on the particular facts of the case.

8.37 Ensuring accurate and fair media reporting does not, however, justify privileged press relationships, that is, off-the-record briefings or unattributable comments to journalists by judges, a phenomenon on the increase according to the House of Lords Constitution Committee in 2007.[165] That view was firmly made by Lord Mackay and Sir Igor Judge (as he was then) and endorsed by the same Constitution Committee.

C. *Executive criticism in the media*

8.38 When commenting upon judicial decisions, the executive must avoid criticism that would undermine the independence of or public confidence in the judiciary, and avoid actions which may call into question their willingness to abide by judges' decisions, other than stating their intention to appeal.[166] Ministers can disagree with the outcome of individual judgments and express their intention to appeal, but express or implied personal attacks on judges are not acceptable, nor can intemperate and inaccurate comments be tolerated.[167]

---

[163] Oral evidence to the Parliamentary Select Committee on Culture, Media and Sport, 23 April 2009.

[164] Eady J, 'Privacy and the Press: Where Are We Now?', Judiciary of England and Wales Justice Conference (1 December 2009), p. 4.

[165] HL Select Committee on the Constitution, '6th Report', 154–5.

[166] Article 18, Recommendation CM/Rec (2010) 12 of the Committee of Ministers of the Council of Europe to member states on judges: independence, efficiency and responsibilities, adopted by the Committee of Ministers on 17 November 2010.

[167] HL Select Committee on the Constitution, 'Relations between the Executive, the Judiciary and Parliament', Oral Evidence, para. 41.

Under Section 3 CRA, the Lord Chancellor and other Ministers of the Crown must uphold the continued independence of the judiciary. This provision reflects the concerns of the Judges' Council that, with the abolition of the traditional role of the Lord Chancellor, there would not be anyone to protect the judiciary from politicians' attacks. The sooner the Lord Chancellor speaks out, privately and, if necessary, publicly, to defend the independence of the judges, the better it is.[168] The Lord Chief Justice commented in 2010 upon the 'imperceptible threat' to the independence of the judiciary created by the ministerial criticism of a judicial decision:

> There was a time when it became a habit of government Ministers who were unhappy with a decision reached by the courts not merely to say, 'I intend to appeal', which is a perfectly reasonable response to a decision that you disagree with, but, in effect, to go to the media to criticise the individual judge on a personal basis and to explain why, spinning fast, the judgment was absolutely daft. That I did regard as an imperceptible threat because the independence of the judiciary, when all is said and done, depends on the public will that the judiciary should be independent. If judges are constantly criticised by Ministers for their decisions, it undermines the principle and the perception.[169]

We noted earlier the breakdown in the relationship between the judiciary and the Cabinet in 2006 in the *Sweeney* case, where the judge had correctly applied existing sentencing guidelines.[170] The Home Secretary of the day (John Reid MP) joined the media in the attack on the trial judge as 'unduly lenient'.[171] The Select Constitution Committee pointed to a 'systemic failure'[172] as the Lord Chancellor was too slow to defend judges against his colleagues in the Cabinet, raising doubts as to whether the Lord Chancellor is in a sufficiently strong position to remind his Cabinet colleagues of their duty to respect the decisions of the judiciary.[173] One judge interviewed commented that the Lord Chancellor was a politician and had to face his own battle on the budget, as well as dealing with prisons. She expressed concern about what would happen

---

[168] HL Select Committee on the Constitution, 'Relations between the Executive, the Judiciary and Parliament', Oral Evidence, 97 (Lord MacKay).
[169] HL Select Committee on the Constitution, 'Meetings with the Lord Chief Justice and the Lord Chancellor', 9th Report of 2010–2011, HL Paper 89, 16.
[170] Sentencing Remarks, T20067014, 12 June 2006.   [171] *Daily Telegraph*, 20 June 2006.
[172] HL Select Committee on the Constitution, 'Relations between the Executive, the Judiciary and Parliament', 49.
[173] *Ibid.*, 45.

when a non-lawyer becomes Lord Chancellor, doubting that they would understand the requirements of judicial independence.[174]

The Lord Chancellor did not publicly defend the judge in question until appearing on the BBC's *Question Time* programme three days after the sentence was handed down. Even then, he claimed that the Home Secretary did not attack the judge. The following day, his junior minister further criticised the judge in a radio programme, but the Lord Chancellor extracted an apology from her. The Attorney General decided not to appeal the sentence imposed by the trial judge, concluding that it was not 'unduly lenient'. The Lord Chief Justice later labelled the attacks 'intemperate, offensive and unfair', while the Secretary of the Council of HM Circuit Judges, told the BBC that 'some of the judges felt that there was quite a silence, and there was no-one actually speaking on behalf of the judges ... We are thinking that we must perhaps change that.'[175] The senior judiciary was also too slow in heading off the inflammatory press coverage which followed the sentencing decision. The Lord Chancellor, giving evidence to the House of Commons Constitutional Affairs Committee one month later, accepted that the *Sweeney* case had an impact on undermining confidence in the judiciary, and some interviewees prompted that example in the course of discussing the relationship of judges with the media.

The *Sweeney* episode is by no means isolated. To some extent, tolerance of executive criticism seems to have come from the very top of British politics. The prime minister's comments following the decision to grant indefinite leave to remain in the UK to the nine Afghan nationals were an improper interference with the administration of justice, as the decision was in the process of being appealed. The prime minister remarked that 'it's not an abuse of justice for us to order their deportation, it's an abuse of common sense frankly to be in a position where we can't do this'. But the judgment was upheld with the words that 'Judges and adjudicators have to apply the law as they find it, and not as they might wish it to be.'[176] In that case, the public criticism of judges clashes with the protection of the functioning of the institutions of justice.

---

[174] Chris Grayling, who became Lord Chancellor in September 2012, is the first non-lawyer acceding to this position in modern times.

[175] For a summary of the events, see HL Select Committee on the Constitution, 'Relations between the Executive, the Judiciary and Parliament', 46.

[176] *R (S)* v. *Secretary of State for the Home Department* (2006) EWHC 111. There was no public reaction from the Lord Chancellor.

The relationship between judges and the Cabinet took another turn when David Blunkett, then Home Secretary, criticised a judge in 2003 for upholding the right of six asylum seekers to receive support from the National Asylum Support Service, writing in a tabloid under the headline 'It's time for judges to learn their place'.[177] He said that he was 'personally fed up' with judges overturning his decisions in asylum cases.[178] The Lord Chancellor, Lord Irvine, pointed out that 'maturity requires that, when you get a decision that favours you, you do not clap. And when you get one that goes against you, you don't boo.' The Lord Chancellor retired from office soon afterwards. Lord Woolf, then Lord Chief Justice, also responded before Parliament that 'unfortunately there are times when the judiciary are left with the impression that their efforts are neither appreciated nor welcomed'. Lord Woolf wrote privately to David Blunkett protesting at his attacks on judges in the case of asylum seekers,[179] before speaking publicly in 2004 in response to the extraordinary proposal of the Home Secretary and the Lord Chancellor that, under the ouster Clause 11 of the Asylum and Immigration (Treatment of Claimants etc) Bill, the courts would be prevented from considering a legal challenge to a decision of an immigration tribunal.[180] The – failed – attempt to restrict the jurisdiction of the courts blatantly undermined judicial independence. In such a case, as pointed out by Lord Lloyd, a former Law Lord, to the Select Committee on the Constitution, 'the Lord Chancellor's duty is absolute; he must point out in Cabinet that this would undermine the independence of the judiciary'.[181]

More recently, after assuming that the criticism under New Labour might be a thing of the past, the Lord Chief Justice's expressed optimism in 2010 was undermined by the unusually robust criticism from not just the Home Secretary but also the prime minister. The Home Secretary (Theresa May) said, in a statement to the House of Commons, that the government was 'disappointed and appalled' by the UK Supreme Court

---

[177] *News of the World*, 23 February 2003; *R (Q)* v. *Secretary of State for the Home Department* [2004] QB 36. No public reaction from the Lord Chancellor is known.

[178] This followed a Court of Appeal decision requiring state support for genuinely destitute asylum seekers, see *R (Q, D, J, M, F & B)* v. *Secretary of State for the Home Department* (2003) EWHC 195 (Admin).

[179] D. Blunkett, *The Blunkett Tapes: My Life in the Bear Pit* (London: Bloomsbury, 2006), p. 267.

[180] *The Times*, 24 February 2004.

[181] HL Select Committee on the Constitution, 'Relations between the Executive, the Judiciary and Parliament', 39.

judgment on the right of convicted sex offenders to have lifetime restrictions on their freedoms reviewed from time to time to ensure that they remain necessary. The Lord Chancellor (Kenneth Clarke) wrote to the Home Secretary to remind her of the government's duty to uphold the independence of the judiciary.[182] The prime minister recently reacted to a judgment of the European Court of Human Rights on prisoners' voting rights, declaring: 'It makes me physically ill even to contemplate having to give the vote to anyone who is in prison.'[183] These criticisms only underline the need for the Lord Chancellor to ensure that his Cabinet colleagues respect judicial decisions. Yet this is not happening. In a statement presenting the draft Bill on voting eligibility for prisoners to Parliament, the Lord Chancellor outlined three possible options for reform, including re-enacting the current general ban on prisoner voting, with a few minor changes. The Explanatory Notes (from the Lord Chancellor's Department) flatly state that 'the Government is unable to say that the provisions are compatible with [the ECHR]'.[184] The Lord Chancellor is, arguably knowingly, putting forward a proposal that breaches an ECHR right. The two other options for reform, however, would be compliant with the ECHR.

8.39 It has been suggested that a convention that ministers should not criticise adverse decisions ought to have been included in the Concordat.[185] The House of Lords Constitution Select Committee recommended the insertion in the Ministerial Code of a reference to the 'constitutional conventions which ought to govern public comment by ministers on judges'.[186] One may doubt the effectiveness of such measure in the light

---

[182] *R (F and Thomson)* v. *Secretary of State for the Home Department* [2010] UKSC 17.

[183] *Hansard*, HC, vol. 517, col. 921, 3 November 2010; the Grand Chamber of the European Court of Human Rights gave six months to the UK to bring forward measures to repeal the blanket ban on prisoners' rights, see *Scoppola* v. *Italy (No. 3)* [2012] ECHR 868; the prime minister responded saying that 'No one should be in any doubt, prisoners are not getting the vote under this government'. See also *Greens and M.T.* v. *UK*, Applications nos. 60041/08 & 60054/08 ECtHR 23 November 2010; *Hirst* v. *UK (No. 2)* [2005] ECHR 681; T. May, *Hansard*, HC, vol. 523, cols. 959–60, 16 February 2011: at the 2011 Conservative Party conference, she disparaged a tribunal judge who, she claimed, had ruled that an illegal immigrant could not be removed from the UK because of a pet cat, see above, para. 2.13.

[184] Explanatory Notes, Voting Eligibility (Prisoners) Draft Bill, November 2012, paras. 58 and 88.

[185] Bradley, 'Judges and the Media', 478–80.

[186] See HL Select Committee on the Constitution, 'Relations between the Executive, the Judiciary and Parliament', paras. 41 and 50.

of the New Zealand experience, where the insertion of such principle in the equivalent Ministerial Code was not seen as sufficient hindrance from unfair and improper criticisms.[187] It was there further suggested that judges ought to be able to make a complaint to the Judicial Conduct Commissioner about what had been said about them, with a power given to that Commission to require the publication of correction.[188] This would be similar to the power already given to the Press Complaints Commission.

One similar proposal which may be considered in the various contemporary reviews into media governance is that when a minister lambasts an adverse decision, the press should add that the minister is breaking convention in criticising the judge, and that judges themselves will not respond to public debates about their decisions. This does at least inform the public that they are only hearing one side of the story, and that they ought not to be hearing from the minister at all. The point is one of public information, not one of deterring such statements. Indeed, effective deterrence seems very difficult, and even when some ministers have remembered the protocol not to attack individual judges, they have instead criticised the HRA, while meaning their audience to understand that the individual judgment is the real cause of their ire. The Joint Committee on Human Rights found that ministers are making 'unfounded assertions about the Act' and using the Act as 'a scapegoat for administrative failings in their departments'.[189] Tension between the judiciary and the executive is likely to continue, despite the reminder from the House of Lords Constitution Committee that this kind of comment is unacceptable.[190]

III. Scandalising the court and defamation

8.40 Given the unfair reception of some judicial decisions, and the potential of some such criticism to undermine confidence in the justice system, is there a case for having criminal sanctions against bad-faith criticism, even if they are to be deployed only in extreme cases? If not, is it proper that judges should be able to sue their critics in defamation – typically by suing the newspaper in which the offending comments were published?

---

[187] New Zealand Cabinet Manual, para. 4; the Standing Orders of the House of Representatives also prohibit Members of Parliament from criticising judges, Standing Orders of the House of Representatives, 1999, No. 114.

[188] Hammond, 'Free Speech and Judges in New Zealand'.

[189] HL Select Committee on the Constitution, 'Relations between the Executive, the Judiciary and Parliament', para. 147.

[190] Ibid.

Scandalising a court, or murmuring judges in Scotland,[191] can be defined as 'any act done or writing published calculated to bring a court or a judge of the court into contempt or to lower his authority'.[192] It applies any time, by contrast with the *sub judice* rule which applies to pending legal proceedings only.[193] The offence requires publication in the print, broadcast or electronic media, or acts akin to publication, such as statements to the media.[194] The publication must be voluntary, and the publisher must know that the publication contains the allegations in question[195] and that the allegations reflect on the courts.[196] The Privy Council confirmed in *Ahnee* v. *DPP* that no additional element of *mens rea* was required when the publication is intentional and the defence of fair criticism in good faith does not apply.[197]

8.41 The offence of scandalising the court was in disuse in England even before the recognition of the right to free speech under the HRA. The Phillimore Committee[198] recommended 'a new and strictly defined criminal offence'. It proposed that the offence should be constituted by the publication, in whatever form, of matter imputing improper or corrupt judicial conduct with the intention of impairing public confidence in the administration of justice, that it would be triable only on indictment, and that prosecution should only be at the instance of the Attorney General.[199]

---

[191] *Stair Memorial Encyclopaedia*, vol. VI, p. 117, para. 320.

[192] *R* v. *Gray* [1900] 2 QB 36, 40 [Lord Russell CJ]; *Skipworth's Case* (1873) LR 9 QB 230; *Onslow's and Whalley's Case* (1873) LR 9 QB 219; *In the Matter of a Special Reference from the Bahama Islands* [1893] AC 138; *Bennett* v. *Southwark London Borough Council (Bennett)* [2002] ICR 881, para. 27 [Sedley LJ]. Scandalising the court is one form of contempt among others, such as 'contempt in the face of the court', for example, throwing missiles at the judge, insulting persons in court, demonstrating in court; 'contempt out of court', such as reprisals against witnesses after the conclusion of proceedings, disobedience to court orders, or conduct, whether intentional or not, liable to interfere with the course of justice in particular proceedings', see the Contempt of Court Act 1981; Cram (ed.), *Borrie and Lowe*, 401. The boundaries between the various forms of contempt can be blurry: it is possible for contempt by scandalising to be committed by what is said or done in court, see e.g. *Lewis* v. *Judge Ogden* [1984] 153 CLR 682; Cram (ed.), Borrie and Lowe, 11.18.

[193] It falls outside the strict liability rule under the Contempt of Court Act 1981, and is not confined to a particular medium, see Cram (ed.), *Borrie and Lowe*, 11.10.

[194] Law Commission, 'Consultation Paper No 207', p. 6.

[195] *McLeod* v. *St Aubyn* [1899] AC 549.   [196] *Perera* v. *R* [1951] AC 482 (PC).

[197] *Ahnee* v. *DPP* [1999] 2 AC 294, p. 307.

[198] The Phillimore Committee, 'Report of the Committee on Contempt of Court', Cmnd 5794 (1974).

[199] The Phillimore Committee, 'Report', 164–6.

It should be emphasised that the purpose of this offence (an instance of the law of contempt) is to uphold judicial authority or the process of the administration of justice, and not the private interest of the judges acting in a personal or extra-judicial capacity.[200] Thus, in *In the Matter of a Special Reference from the Bahama Islands*, the Privy Council held that criticisms of the Chief Justice which were not directed at him in his official capacity as a judge were not contempt.[201] In such case, the judge can only sue in defamation or libel to remedy any damage to his personal reputation.[202]

Although the 'scandalising' form of contempt has not been found by an English court since 1931, prosecutions and convictions continue to take place in other jurisdictions such as Australia, New Zealand, Hong Kong and Singapore[203] and have resulted in some appeals to the Privy Council. The surprising grant of leave to prosecute, in Northern Ireland, an MP who criticised a judge's handling of a judicial review application, in March 2012, put the offence on the agenda of the Law Commission, which recommended its abolition in December 2012.[204] The House of Lords has now accepted the abolition of that offence, and our account below provides some background to this position.[205]

8.42   In the leading authority, *R v. Editor of The New Statesman, ex parte DPP*, Mr Clifford Sharp, the editor of *The New Statesman*, was punished for contempt after the journal published an article implying that the religious beliefs of the judge, Mr Justice Avory, made it inevitable that he

---

[200]   *R v. Almon* (1765) Wilm 243, 97 ER 94; *Badry v. DPP of Mauritius* [1982] 3 All ER 973; *R v. Metropolitan Police Commissioner ex parte Blackburn (No. 2)* [1968] 2 QB 150, 154 [Lord Denning].

[201]   In the Matter of a Special Reference from the Bahama Islands [1893] AC 138.

[202]   *Ibid.*; *McLeod v. St Aubyn* [1899] AC 549, 561 [Lord Morris].

[203]   See *In re Phelan* (1877) 5, 7 [Kotzé]; *S v. Harber and another* [1988] ZASCA 34; *S v. Kaakunga* 1978 (1) SA 1190 (SWA); *Ahnee and others v. Director of Public Prosecutions* [1999] 2 WLR 1305 (PC); *R v. Koptyo* (1987) 47 DLR (4th) 213 (Ont. CA); *Narmada Bachao Andolan v. Union of India and others* (1999) 8 SCC 308; *Attorney-General for New South Wales v. Mundey* [1972] 2 NSWLR 887; *Solicitor-General v. Radio Avon Ltd* [1978] 1 NZLR 225 (CA); *Wong Yeung Ng v. Secretary for Justice* [1999] 2 HKLRD 293 (CA); M. Chesterman, 'Contempt: in the Common Law, but not the Civil Law' (1997) 46 ICLQ 521.

[204]   The prosecution was discontinued in Northern Ireland in May 2012 following a preliminary hearing and after Hain wrote to the Attorney General to explain and clarify his remarks; UK Law Commission, 'Contempt of Court: Scandalising the Court. A Consultation Paper', Law Commission Consultation Paper No. 207 (London, 2012), p. 6.

[205]   *Hansard*, HL, cols. 871–9 (10 December 2012).

would rule against a woman who was a birth control advocate.[206] Lord Hewart CJ rejected the argument of the defence, that the article was not intended to bring the judge into contempt but to convey that the subject was so controversial that no one who held strong views on one side could prevent his judgment from being unconsciously influenced by them. The Court found that the imputation of unfairness and lack of impartiality to a judge in the discharge of his judicial duties lowered the judge's authority and interfered with the performance of his judicial duties. The apology of Mr Sharp was accepted, and he was ordered to pay the costs of the proceedings.[207]

A.   A defence of truth and fair comment

8.43 Should a defence of truth, for statements of facts, and a defence of fair comments, for value judgments, be made available to a person charged with scandalising the court, as applies in defamation law? For a long time the weight of authority at common law seems to have gone against justification of truth as a defence to the charge of scandalising the court. In New Zealand, William J agreed upon the basic principle of a defence of truth, but rejected it as lacking a basis in law, commenting that the court does not sit to try the conduct of the judge.[208] *R* v. *Colsey* is the last case in which the power of contempt was exercised for criticism of judges in England and Wales, and it shows the court overreacting.[209] The editor of *Truth* was punished for contempt because of comments on a decision of the Court of Appeal dealing with trade union law. Commenting on the judgment of Lord Justice Slesser,[210] who had once been a law officer in a Labour government, *Truth* wrote: 'Lord Justice Slesser, who can hardly be altogether unbiased about legislation of this type, maintained that really it was a very nice provisional order or as good a one as can be expected in this vale of tears.' Lord Hewart CJ, for the Court, ruled

---

[206] *R* v. *Editor of The New Statesman, ex parte Director of Public Prosecutions* (1928) 44 TLR 300.

[207] *Attorney General* v. *Barry Wain* [1991] 2 MLJ 525; *Attorney-General* v. *Lingle* [1995] 1 SLR 696. The 'scandalising' form of contempt is there a constitutionally recognised qualification to the free speech clause.

[208] *Attorney-General* v. *Blomfield* (1914) 33 NZLR 545, 563; *S-G* v. *Radio Avon Ltd* [1978] 1 NZLR 225, 231.

[209] *R* v. *Colsey, ex parte Director of Public Prosecutions*, The Times, 9 May 1931; Cram (ed.), *Borrie and Lowe*, 426. The Privy Council has been the source of the most recent case law, see e.g., *Vidyasagara* v. *The Queen* [1963] AC 589.

[210] *R* v. *Minister of Labour, ex parte National Trade Defence Association* (1931) 47 TLR 364.

that these comments constituted contempt and ordered the editor of *Truth* to pay a fine of £100 and costs.

Nonetheless, as was suggested in New Zealand, the imputation of bias to judges may sometimes be justified: 'if then the judge shows bias, should the honest critic, who says that he has done so, be fined or imprisoned?'[211] Similarly, suppose that a person alleged that Sir Francis Bacon was accepting bribes and offered proof for his allegation. Would he be quite properly committed for contempt by Bacon and forbidden to produce any evidence in support of his charges?

The need for public scrutiny of judicial conduct must therefore limit the scope of application of the offence of scandalising the court. In 1969 the Salmon Committee underlined that if there is a just cause for challenging the integrity of a judge, it could not be contempt of court to do so.[212] The JUSTICE report on Contempt of Court recommended, in 1959, that there should be the opportunity of making bona fide charges of partiality or corruption against a judge. It considered, however, that the appropriate means for this purpose was not the press but a letter to the Lord Chancellor or the complainant's Member of Parliament.[213] In addition to a defence of truth, the Phillimore Committee added an important proviso that public interest requires that normally allegations of judicial corruption or lack of impartiality should first be submitted to the Lord Chancellor.[214]

The Law Commission's opinion in 1979, however, was that only false allegations should be subject to sanctions at all.[215] Since the 2005 settlement, the Office for Judicial Complaints provides an effective channel for complaints of partiality or corruption (the latter being a rather unlikely event) against a judge. The concern underlying JUSTICE's proposals remains strong and can be seen in the conclusion of the Law Commission of Canada[216] in 1982 that truth should not be available as a defence as it may result in 'guerrilla warfare' against the judiciary.

The authoritative answer to the question of a defence of truth seems to have been provided by the European Court of Human Rights. In *De Haes and Gijsels* v. *Belgium*, the Court refers to the necessity of protecting the

---

[211] Mr Justice McKenna, 'The Judge and the Common Man' 32 MLR 601, 604.
[212] Salmon LJ, 'Report', 421.   [213] JUSTICE, 'Contempt of Court' (1959), p. 15.
[214] The Phillimore Committee, 'Report', 166.
[215] Law Commission, 'Offences Relating to Interference with the Courts of Justice', Law Com. No. 96 (1979), paras. 3.64–3.70.
[216] Law Commission, 'Contempt of Court' (1982), p. 26.

judiciary from 'destructive attacks that are unfounded'.[217] When allegations are excessive, some factual basis for making criticisms would provide them some protection.[218] Conversely, in the absence of a sufficient factual basis, some accusations will have an excessive breadth which may appear unnecessarily prejudicial and will thus justify a domestic conviction for criminal defamation.[219] This suggests that a defence of justification must be available in English law for the European Court to uphold the offence of scandalising the court in compliance with the ECHR.[220]

8.44 In some common law jurisdictions an allegation of bias or corruption is automatically contempt. Thus, in a Malaysian case in 1999, an appeals court upheld the contempt conviction of a Canadian journalist for scandalising the court, for imputing that a court had been influenced, at least in part, by outside pressures. The appellant had written an article which stated that a case where the plaintiff was the wife of a judge had moved through the judicial system with unusual speed. The appellant became the first journalist in fifty years to be jailed for contempt of court in the Commonwealth.[221] Similarly, in the Indian case of *EMS Namboodiripad* v. *TN Nambiar*,[222] the content of the allegations alone, without considering its context, constitutes contempt. The Supreme Court upheld the conviction for contempt by the Chief Minister of Kerala, who accused judges of class bias in a public statement, commenting that judges are 'guided and dominated by class hatred, class interests and class prejudices and where the evidence is balanced between a well-dressed pot-bellied man and a poor ill-dressed and illiterate person the Judge instinctively favours the former'. The Court found that 'the likely effects of his words must be seen and they have clearly the effect of lowering the prestige of Judges and Courts in the eyes of the people'.[223]

By comparison, following the European Court of Human Rights, depending on their contents, tone and context, allegations of bias from the judges can constitute an expression of opinion which raises matters of public interest. In *Kyprianou* v. *Cyprus*, the European Court confirmed

---

[217] *De Haes and Gijsels* v. *Belgium* (1998) 25 EHRR 1, para. 37.

[218] E. Barendt, *Freedom of Speech*, 2nd edn (Oxford University Press, 2007), p. 224.

[219] *Prager and Oberschlick* v. *Austria* (1995), Series A No. 313, (1996) 21 EHRR 1, paras. 34–7.

[220] Cram (ed.), *Borrie and Lowe*, 11.27; C.J. Miller, *Contempt of Court*, 2nd edn (Oxford University Press, 2000), ch. 12; Arlidge, Eady and Smith, paras. 5-258 et seq.

[221] 'Justice in Malaysia', *The Wall Street Journal*, 13 September 1999.

[222] AIR 1970 SC 2015, para. 699.   [223] *Ibid.*, para. 713.

that public confidence in the courts underpins the protection of the authority of the judiciary with criminal sanctions against those making unfounded criticisms against the judiciary.[224] This was to be balanced with the lawyer's freedom of expression in defending his clients. The Court held that the 'disproportionately severe' penalty imposed on counsel was 'capable of having a "chilling effect" on the performance by lawyers of their duties as defence counsel':[225]

> [Lawyers] might for instance feel constrained in their choice of pleadings, procedural motions and the like during proceedings before the courts, possibly to the potential detriment of their client's case. For the public to have confidence in the administration of justice they must have confidence in the ability of the legal profession to provide effective representation. The imposition of a prison sentence on defence counsel can in certain circumstances have implications not only for the lawyer's rights under Article 10 but also the fair trial rights of the client under Article 6 of the Convention ... It follows that any "chilling effect" is an important factor to be considered in striking the appropriate balance between courts and lawyers in the context of an effective administration of justice.[226]

B.   Is the offence necessary?

8.45 The key question now is whether any offence of scandalising the court, even one which recognises some kind of 'justified comment' defence, is 'necessary' for upholding respect for the English judiciary – which is the question raised by Article 10(2) of the ECHR. Though criticisms of judges constitute political speech which requires the highest protection under the ECHR,[227] in *The Sunday Times* v. *The UK*, the European Court of Human Rights held that some limits to freedom of expression can be found in the law of contempt where the purpose to be served is the maintenance of the authority and impartiality of the judiciary.[228] The European Court stated:

> If the issues arising in litigation are ventilated in such a way as to lead the public to form its own conclusion thereon in advance, it may lose its respect for and confidence in the courts. Again, it cannot be excluded that the public's becoming accustomed to the regular spectacle of pseudo-trials

---

[224] (2007) 44 EHRR 27, para. 528.   [225] *Ibid.*, paras. 531 and 537.

[226] *Ibid.*, para. 531; *Skalka* v. *Poland* (2004) 38 EHRR 1.

[227] *Wingrove* v. *UK* (1996) 24 EHRR 1; *Lingens* v. *Austria* (1986) 8 EHRR 103; *Thorgeirson* v. *Iceland* (1992) 14 EHRR 843.

[228] *Sunday Times* v. *UK (No. 1)* (1979–80) 2 EHRR 245, para. 55; C. Walker, 'Scandalising in the Eighties' (1985) 101 LQR 359, 365.

in the news media might in the long run have nefarious consequences for the acceptance of the courts as the proper forum for the settlement of legal disputes.[229]

However, this decision has received some criticism and notably depends on some substantial margin of appreciation. It need not apply today to the offence of scandalising the court and should the question arise, then it ought to be noted that the 'necessity' to protect judges in this way is not perceived to be strong in England and Wales or in other major Commonwealth countries. In the Australian case of *Attorney-General for NSW* v. *Mundey*, Hope J said:

> There is no more reason why the acts of courts should not be trenchantly criticized than the acts of public institutions, including parliaments. The truth is of course that public institutions in a free society must stand upon their own merits: they cannot be propped up if their conduct does not command the respect and confidence of the community. If [the judiciary's] conduct justifies the respect and confidence of a community they do not need the protection of special rules to protect them from criticism.[230]

One may add to that the desirability of not deterring good-faith criticism, which may be an unintended consequence of the law even if it is limited to 'bad-faith' criticism.[231] In *Ambard* v. *Attorney-General for Trinidad and Tobago*, a local newspaper was found in contempt by the Supreme Court for criticising discrepancies in sentencing in two attempted murder cases. The Privy Council overturned the ruling:

> The path of criticism is a public way; the wrong-headed are permitted to err therein: provided that members of the public abstain from imputing improper motives to those taking part in the administration of justice, and are genuinely exercising a right of criticism, and not acting in malice or attempting to impair the administration of justice, they are immune. Justice is not a cloistered virtue: she must be allowed to suffer the scrutiny and the respectful even though outspoken comments of ordinary men.[232]

While in Canada the offence of scandalising the court is not incompatible with the Charter of Rights' protection of the right to freedom of

---

[229] *Sunday Times* v. *UK (No. 1)* (1979–80) 2 EHRR 245, para. 64.

[230] *Attorney-General for NSW* v. *Mundey* [1972] 2 NSWLR 887, 908 [Hope J]; Walker, 'Scandalising in the Eighties', 377–84.

[231] On discerning 'good faith', see *R* v. *Metropolitan Police Commissioner, ex parte Blackburn (No. 2)*, 155–6 [Lord Salmon].

[232] *Ambard* v. *Attorney-General for Trinidad and Tobago* [1936] AC 322, 335.

expression, the emphasis, as in England, is on the broad shoulders that judges should have or, as Cory JA said in *R v. Koptyo*, 'The courts are not fragile flowers that will wither in the hot heat of controversy. They [judges] are well-regarded in the community because they merit respect. They need not fear criticism nor need to sustain unnecessary barriers to complaints about their operations or decisions.'[233]

Statements of a sincerely held belief on a matter of public interest, even if intemperately worded, are thus protected under the Canadian Charter of Rights.

8.46 We should consider too the various elements which shape the way the balance tilts between freedom of expression and the need to protect the authority and the impartiality of the judiciary. The robustness of the judiciary must be assessed, and the general context of scurrilous allegations against judges is equally relevant. While in England such proceedings of scandalising the court are rare and none have been successfully brought since 1931, '. . . on a small island such as Mauritius the administration of justice is more vulnerable than in the United Kingdom. The need for the offence of scandalising the court on a small island is greater.'[234] The proximity between judges and the government in some countries constitutes another relevant factor, which however points to the offence being equally used as an instrument to silence honest criticism of biased judges.[235]

The context of the allegations is a prominent consideration. In the civil libel suit *De Haes and Gijsels v. Belgium*, the European Court found that the restraint on defamation was not justified on the facts.[236] The applicants, one editor and one journalist, had been ordered to pay damages to certain judges for accusing them, in several articles, of bias. The Court held that defamatory criticism based on the past history of the father of one of the judges criticised was inadmissible. It also reasoned that the allegations of bias were the expression of an opinion, rather than a matter of fact, in the context of serious debate taking place in Belgium. The Court continued:

---

[233] *R v. Koptyo* (1987) 47 DLR (4th) 213 (Ont. CA), 469.

[234] *Ahnee and others* v. *Director of Public Prosecutions* [1999] 2 WLR 1305, 1313; R. Sackville, 'How Fragile Are the Courts? Freedom of Speech and Criticism of the Judiciary', 13th Lucinda Lecture, Monash University (29 August 2005), pp. 5–6.

[235] G. Robertson and A. Nicol, *Media Law*, 5th edn (London: Sweet and Maxwell, 2007), paras. 7-054–7-055.

[236] *De Haes and Gijsels v. Belgium* (1998) 25 EHRR 1.

> Although Mr De Haes and Mr Gijsels' comments were without doubt severely critical, they nevertheless appear proportionate to the stir and indignation caused by the matters alleged in their articles. As to the journalists' polemical and even aggressive tone, which the Court should not be taken to approve, it must be remembered that Article 10 protects not only the substance of the ideas and information expressed but also the form in which they are conveyed.[237]

It seems to us that even the prospect of prosecution is disproportionate today, given the lesser deference afforded to figures in authority, the potential to deter even good-faith criticism and the increasing number of ways in which the judiciary is defending itself from unfair criticism.

C.   Defamation

8.47   The Media Guidance for the Judiciary advises judges that suing the media for libel is a matter of last resort.[238] Whatever damages the judge may receive would go towards repayment of the legal costs and any money left over is expected to be donated to charity. Defamation actions are in fact rare and they should remain so. Successful actions against the media criticising judges in the performance of their duties may have an undesirable 'chilling' effect on media criticism which, for the most part, acts as a healthy check on the judiciary's conduct. The status and dignity of the judicial office also prima facie goes against the judge's initiation of legal proceedings – judges should be able to cope with robust criticism, however provocative the comments may be. Moreover, legal proceedings sustain attention to words which would otherwise have been largely ignored by the public or quickly forgotten, and judges are invited to consider any implications for the reputation and standing of the judiciary collectively as well as for the judge.[239] Finally, judges suing for defamation could be construed as an example of the courts looking after their own interest.[240]

In 1992 Mr Justice Popplewell won a public apology and damages against the *Today* newspaper for suggesting that he 'appeared to nod off' during a murder trial.[241] In 1996 a Crown Court judge won a public

---

[237] *Ibid.*, 47–8; for a similar emphasis on the public interest of a publication, see *Amihalachioaie* v. *Moldova* (2004) 17 BHRC 689; see also *Jersild* v. *Denmark*, 23 September 1994, Series A no. 298, p. 23, para. 31, and *Goodwin* v. *UK*, 27 March 1996, *Reports of Judgments and Decisions* 1996-II, p. 500, para. 39.

[238] 'Media Guidance', 16.   [239] 'Media Guidance', 16.

[240] Law Reform Commission of Australia, 'Contempt', Report No. 35 (1987), para. 452.

[241] *The Times*, 22 and 24 July 1992.

apology and damages from a news agency over distorted reports of a sex assault case he presided over. The misleading reports of the judge's remarks stated the defendant had been told that 'he would not be in the dock if he had sent his victim a bunch of flowers'. Some media published that account, leading to calls for the immediate resignation of the judge.[242] In 2011 Sedley LJ also successfully sued for libel, winning an apology in court from the *Daily Telegraph* for the false statements it had made about Lord Justice Sedley's conduct of a particular case in an article entitled 'Judge "hastened deaths of elderly"'. The *Daily Telegraph*'s article was based on a complaint made to the Office for Judicial Complaints. The complaint was fed to the newspaper before the Office of Judicial Complaints reached the conclusion (after three months) that the allegations were without substance.

In all the cases mentioned, the accusations were so severe that the judges could have been said to be unfit to practise as a result.[243] The legal action was commensurate with the damage caused.[244] Swift action is required – the judge's reputation is damaged while the Office for Judicial Complaints' investigation goes on and some alternative tracks to defamation proceedings are available. If, as in the case of Lord Justice Sedley, the false statements come from a law practitioner, a complaint could be filed with the Law Society or Bar Council and one interviewee suggested that this would normally be the first port of call. The Press Complaints Commission could be an alternative port of call if its membership were reformed (there currently are seven newspaper editors out of seventeen commissioners) and if it were given the power to fine.[245]

Conclusions

8.47 The principles of freedom of expression and judicial accountability permit extra-judicial comments to the extent that they preserve public confidence in the judiciary and the administration of justice. It is suggested that the current rule of circumspection in judicial speech outside

---

[242] *The Lawyer*, 7 February 1996.

[243] Cf. *Herald and Weekly Times Ltd* v. *Popovic* (2003) 9 VR 1; *John Fairfax Publications Pty Ltd* v. *O'Shane* [2005] NSWCA 164; *John Fairfax Publications Pty Ltd* v. *O'Shane (No. 2)* [2005] NSWCA 291.

[244] 'Media Guidance', 15–16.

[245] A new press watchdog backed by statute has recently been recommended, see Leveson LJ, 'An Inquiry into the Culture, Practices and Ethics of the Press Report', HC 780-I (2012).

the courtroom is as good as it can get. It is better that judges should speak out from time to time rather than remain for ever silent.[246] Judges must speak with reticence and moderation, for fear of a politicisation of their words, fear of compromising their impartiality in future cases, and fear of damaging the dignity and political independence of the judicial office by their words.[247] The increasing practice of individual judges speaking out calls, however, for greater monitoring in the coming years, and communication based on a greater exposure of judges *outside* the courtroom should be seen as a priority for the Judicial Communications Office, this in order to strengthen judicial independence.[248]

It is right that judges speak out with circumspection on matters concerning 'the law, the legal system, the administration of justice or related matters'. In the absence of an effective guardian as the Lord Chancellor used to be before 2005, channels for expressing the judiciary's views or responses, when appropriate, must also be strengthened. As in many other Commonwealth countries such as Australia, the judicial response, if such a response is deemed appropriate, must be prompt, clear and concise.

Future respect for the judiciary also depends upon a long-term goal of education of the public about the judiciary and the importance of judicial independence with a great number of judicial speeches from its senior judges, and greater information made accessible to the public. But the Judicial Office could perhaps consider having a greater number of media-trained judges speaking with the media, and it could perhaps further consider the 'fire brigade' style of some American states, in which judges enlist a series of individuals, such as law professors, editorial board members and other select persons to quickly speak out to clear up distortions when judge-bashing has started.[249] Third-party commentary from such 'fire brigade' would limit the impact of the damage done to public confidence.

Further, if English judges are not the 'remote sphinx type figures as the judge used to be thought of in the past',[250] one wonders how close to the

---

[246] Hope, 'What Happens When a Judge Speaks Out?', 11.

[247] Lord Irvine, *Hansard*, HC, vol. 572, 5 June 1996, cols. 1259–60.

[248] HL Select Committee on the Constitution, 'Relations between the Executive, the Judiciary and Parliament', 153.

[249] C.P. Danos, 'Responding to the Unwarranted Criticism of Judges', National Center for State Courts (19 May 1997, revised March 2003); see P.D. Schulz, *Courts and Judges on Trial, Analysing and Managing the Discourses of Disapproval* (Berlin: Lit Verlag, 2010).

[250] Clare Dyer, cited in HL Select Committee on the Constitution, 'Relations between the Executive, the Judiciary and Parliament', 153.

ordinary citizen they should be, that is, how much about their lives and their activities in the local community we could or should know. Clare Dyer from the *Guardian* told the Constitution Committee in 2006–07 that 'people want to know more about the people they are reading about'. Professor Dame Hazel Genn also pointed that, as judges get involved on their initiative in their local communities, 'there is scope for them to do more', and 'It is important that somebody has responsibility for projecting positive images of the judiciary'. Indeed, judges who do not speak out outside the courtroom may choose to speak out on matters that interest them. Their engagements in charities may or may not be controversial. The recent guidance relating to blogging and the use of Twitter by judicial office holders (magistrates, in practice) sends a necessary strong message of circumspection but it fails to acknowledge how a responsible use of social media can also foster a better understanding of the machinery of justice.[251]

As a benign illustration, and a break from tradition, in January 2011 a BBC documentary showed four of the UK Supreme Court Justices, including the President of the Court and its Deputy President, in their everyday life.[252] The synopsis claimed to reveal a 'glimpse of the human characters behind the judgments and explores why the Supreme Court and its members are fundamental to our democracy'. The documentary offered some basic information about the court, addressing what happens when judges cannot agree on a judgment, raising also the issue of diversity. It showed how judges did not think that they had the freedom to decide according to their personal opinions. We also saw the justices at home, providing us some minimal information about them. This was a rather enjoyable educational programme for those who knew little about the UK Supreme Court. But will this glimpse of the justices' humanity lead to a more intrusive scrutiny of their private lives? Those questions would seem to constitute another ground for the Judicial Communications Office to consider the proper extent of judicial exposure outside the courtroom as a priority.[253]

8.48 Attacks on the judiciary should be distinguished from similar attacks on politicians and other public figures on the basis of the practical

---

[251] Lord Chief Justice and Senior President of Tribunals, 'Guidance for the Judiciary – Blogging by Judicial Office Holders', August 2012.

[252] BBC, 'The Highest Court in the Land: Justice Makers'.

[253] HL Select Committee on the Constitution, 'Relations between the Executive, the Judiciary and Parliament', 153.

difficulty of the judge's bringing a civil action to clear his name and the tradition that judges do not reply to criticism.[254] Judges cannot respond to criticisms and engage in public debate to the same extent as other victims of newspaper libel.[255] Lord Judge LCJ said:

> It is difficult if not impossible for the judge to answer, because inevitably it would mean commenting on a case which he had tried or decided, when everything that needs to be said about the decision should have been dealt with in the judgment, so that for the judge that must be the end of it; and finally, and perhaps in the end most importantly if we are discussing the independence of the media and the judiciary, because of its corrosive long-term effect on the public's view of the judiciary and the exercise of its functions.[256]

But the greater willingness of the judiciary to respond to public criticism, which we have already scrutinised, 'reflects the reality that the traditional stoic silence in the face of an ill-informed or even malicious attack is by no means the most effective way of maintaining confidence in the judicial system'.[257] It is also arguable that the press can be limited in action, and be more likely to err on the basis of the rules allowing proceedings to take place in camera or enabling the judges not to disclose particular facts. In general, those rules have been wisely applied, and the principle of open justice, 'a sound and very sacred part of the constitution of the country and the administration of justice',[258] limits the scope of these rules to some very specific cases.

It seems to us that the offence of scandalising the court is unnecessary. The value of public scrutiny of the judiciary supports the view that a comment about the competence or integrity of the court that is fairly made but would yet impair the confidence of the public is for the public benefit. Judges must have broad shoulders, so that the test for prosecution under the offence of scandalising the court has a higher threshold. It could require a real and compelling threat which, viewed contextually, is likely to cause a sufficiently serious and substantial prejudice upon the administration of justice for criminal prosecution to be brought for scandalising the court.[259] Bringing the judiciary into disrepute, whether for alleged ineffectiveness, incompetence, or lack of probity or impartiality falls short of that threshold.

---

[254] The Phillimore Committee, 'Report', 162.
[255] *Prager and Obserschlick* v. *Austria* (1996) 21 EHRR 1, para. 34.
[256] Judge, 'The Judiciary and the Media', 5.
[257] Sackville, 'How Fragile Are the Courts?', 11.
[258] *Scott* v. *Scott* [1913] AC 417, 473 [Lord Shaw].
[259] *South Africa* v. *Mamabolo* (2001) 10 BHRC 493, para. 75 [Sachs J].

9

Conclusions

9.1 Judicial independence has carried different meanings throughout history, just as social standards differ with the economic and political environment. This book has focused on the importance of the institutional checks and balances over the judiciary and their practice in England, with the purpose of exploring the modern meaning of judicial independence. Our analysis is developed in the context of England and Wales. This does not imply that any meaning of judicial independence is deeply entrenched in any given society and cannot be measured under a common standard. Rather, judicial independence is perhaps best understood in relation to the background of any given society. It will have a different meaning in a jurisdiction where judges are appointed from the ranks of practising lawyers in comparison to a jurisdiction where there is no distinction between barristers and solicitors, and where judges are appointed and trained for their roles from graduation. Thus, the contemporary features of the English judiciary are its constitutionalisation under the Constitutional Reform At 2005 (CRA), the managerialism that is now attached to the judicial office and its professionalisation.

Beyond the particular scrutiny of the English judiciary, the analysis of this book would confirm the insight that judicial independence is underpinned by a cluster of principles whose weight varies against the history and constitutional background of any given society. These principles have been examined in turn, through successive chapters, and in relation to each other. Separation of powers, merit and fair reflection of society in appointments, and impartiality in the exercise of the judicial function are core values which sustain judicial independence; judicial tenure, an adequate salary and the principle of immunity from civil liability in the discharge of the judicial office complete this set of constraints upon judges and others in the name of judicial independence.

Constitutionalisation of the judiciary

9.2 Only in the CRA has the long-standing convention that government ministers must uphold the continued independence of the judiciary been formalised. Although there had been a tradition of independence, with the Lord Chancellor avoiding sitting in a judicial capacity, there were anxieties that England would be found in violation of Article 6 ECHR. This, combined with personal tensions within the Cabinet, led to the abolition of the Lord Chancellor's position as head of the judiciary in the CRA. We have welcomed the thrust of the CRA. It better satisfies any interpretation of the separation of powers that judges should be appointed by an independent commission, that a politician should not be mainly concerned with judicial discipline and that the highest court of appeal, also a quasi-federal court for the UK, should be housed separately from the higher chamber of the legislature.

The independence of the judiciary is conceived within the realm of boundaries between the courts and Parliament and, in this respect, the development of judicial review and constitutional adjudication under the Human Rights Act 1998 (HRA) has shifted demarcation lines. The modern remedy of judicial review acknowledges a right to official decisions that are lawful, reasonable and fair, and its development has added too to the growth in judicial power. Yet judicial review affords the protection of the rule of law, and while the exercise of judicial review may strain the relationship between the executive and the judiciary, it cannot be interfered with lightly. But the political context rather explains much of the political role played by the English judiciary over the last ten years: a wealth of anti-terrorist legislation has been enacted in response to major events, in particular the 11 September 2001 attacks in the United States and the 7 July 2005 bombings in London, and the courts have had to engage with the protection of fundamental rights under the European Convention on Human Rights (ECHR). The incorporation of the European Convention into domestic law with the HRA has strengthened the position of the judiciary but it has also led to the realisation of the political impact of judicial decisions, under the courts' obligation to declare primary legislation incompatible if it does not admit of a reading compliant with the European Convention. Executive action may be declared unlawful outright. Perhaps symbolically, the first case to be heard by the new Supreme Court in 2009 led to quashing governmental orders to freeze the assets of al-Qaeda suspects as they had been taken without parliamentary approval.

9.3 The UK Supreme Court is at the forefront in accommodating the demands of international law while maintaining the coherence of the UK quasi-federal legal order. Its unique feature, by comparison with the US Supreme Court, is that its human rights review jurisdiction preceded devolution, or quasi-federal review, when devolution preceded the human rights review in the United States or even Canada. The incorporation and interpretation of the HRA has been largely complementary to the common law, and it is hoped that the future of the Act will be determined by a mature inquiry into its effects.

While political attention is turned to the judicial interpretation of the HRA, English judges also have the power to set aside primary legislation which does not comply with the law of the European Union and, with the development of European criminal law in particular, tensions are also expected in the judicial efforts to make European Union law fit in domestic law. The Europeanisation of procedures, rules and standards in the judicial workings is here to stay however. In substance and procedure, the right to a fair trial under Article 6 ECHR has stimulated the development of the English judicial system. It made delay in judicial proceedings justiciable; it has influenced the substance of judicial impartiality at common law, and quality of justice is a goal strongly promoted by the Council of Europe.

9.4 Separation of powers fosters the culture of judicial independence but the continuation of judicial independence is not a matter of course. It is constantly subject to challenges, by other branches of government and as a result of different types of internal development. In England, the enhancement of judicial independence in practice, since the institutional separation of the judiciary from the executive under the CRA, has, to some extent, been subdued. This is partly as the value of judicial independence was already firmly established as a matter of convention before 2005. The independence of the judiciary still rests not on formal constitutional guarantees and prohibitions but upon a mixture of statutory and common law rules, constitutional conventions and parliamentary practice, fortified by professional tradition and public opinion.

The trust in tradition and popular opinion must nevertheless be sustained, however, so that judicial decisions are complied with or can be defended against unwarranted criticism from the media and from government ministers. The policy considerations that surface in some decisions under the HRA rightly expose judges to greater scrutiny, and the value of public scrutiny must be balanced with the need to protect public confidence in the courts. Judges do not traditionally reply to criticisms and do not engage in public debate to the same extent as others. If the convention that ministers do not criticise judges is to fall by the wayside, then the role of the Lord Chancellor becomes more important. Yet the office of Lord Chancellor today may not be the 'buffer' between the judiciary and the government and/or Parliament that it once was,[1] in spite of its constitutional duty to uphold judicial independence. The silence beyond a statement from the Lord Chief Justice's Judicial Office to correct the misreporting of a case may not be sufficient to enhance public trust in the courts and judges, and the elaboration of further means of response may be needed from the Judicial Office.

Should judges be able to have unfair and misleading criticisms addressed in some suitable manner, then it would seem that the offence of scandalising the court is unnecessary. But judges can only expect institutional support in respect of their decisions when they are applying the law, as they understand it to be, to the cases in front of them. Any other comment, including off-the-cuff remarks about policy and remarks about persons which are unnecessary to explain the verdict, does not enjoy any such protection and may give rise to disciplinary proceedings. Equally, we have expressed concern over the continuing tradition of English judges acting as chairmen of public inquiries at the behest of the government. It is difficult to dissociate the figure of the appointed judge in the exercise of his judicial functions from the figure of the judge acting as a fact-finder for the purpose of a public inquiry. In the latter case, the judge acts outside his judicial capacity and is not subject to the judicial oath; this must be emphasised as the line between law and politics is easily blurred in the conduct of inquiries. We suggest that the Lord Chief Justice should have an effective veto on the matter and should exercise it where the subject matter is politically sensitive. The Lord Chief Justice should also be able to take account of the needs of judicial business, which should not be disrupted by such an extra-judicial function.

It seems right, however, that judges speak outside the courtroom with circumspection on matters of expertise concerning the law, the legal system, the administration of justice or related issues. It is better that judges should speak out from time to time rather than remain for ever silent. Nonetheless, they must speak with reticence and moderation, for

---

[1] G. Drewry, 'Lord Haldane's Ministry of Justice – Stillborn or Strangled at Birth?' (1983) 61 *Public Administration* 396, 407.

fear of damaging the dignity and independence of the judicial office by their words. The increasing practice of individual judges speaking out therefore calls for greater monitoring, as well as greater clarity as to who shall speak publicly on behalf of the judiciary to uphold judicial independence. Public confidence in the courts and in the administration of justice also relies upon educating the public about the judiciary, and the recent guidance relating to blogging by judicial office holders, while it sends a necessary message of circumspection, fails to acknowledge how a responsible use of social media can also develop a better understanding of the machinery of justice.

Accountability to Parliament

9.5 The separation of powers and constitutionalisation of the judiciary call for renewed mechanisms of judicial accountability. One tool for accountability that has been increasingly used consists in the appearance of judges before Select Committees in Parliament. This has brought greater transparency of judicial business, as information appears in the public domain through the work of these Committees. Thus, the debates on the Constitutional Reform Bill, leading to the CRA, reflected the full engagement of Parliament with these constitutional matters. However, legislative time is limited, and so are the resources and expertise available to Select Committees. The discipline of the party whip has also maintained the executive grip over the legislature, and this also leads us to suggest that, while accountability to Parliament is required, the equilibrium reached by the CRA in the appointment process should be maintained and the concern for a non-partisan process – as well as a concern for the costs of such confirmation hearings – must prevail. The greater involvement of the Lord Chancellor in the appointment process, suggested by the Crime and Courts Bill 2012, cannot be supported. But the presentation by the Chairman of the Judicial Appointments Commission to Parliament of the process behind the appointments made at the UK Supreme Court is a welcome development. The duty upon the UK Supreme Court, under the CRA to produce an annual report to Parliament is another mechanism of accountability. The Supreme Court Annual Report and Accounts for 2011–2012, however, fall short of engaging with a substantive review of its legal activity, in contrast not only with some other European supreme courts such as the German *Bundesgerichtshof* or the French *Cour de cassation* and *Conseil d'Etat*, but also with the Annual Report from the Senior President of Tribunals, whose latest report to the Lord Chancellor developed in some respects a review of the case law. Greater emphasis on substance would be appropriate, not least because some parliamentarians seem genuinely ignorant of much of the business of the courts, and similarly, the Lord Chief Justice who produces an annual review, could include a brief coverage of the more important decisions in the Court of Appeal.

Managerialism

9.6 The development of judicial independence since the CRA has also been restricted under the administrative and financial pressures exerted upon judges. While the individual independence of judicial office holders is not affected, the development of institutional independence is burdensome and amplified by the enlargement of the 'judicial family' to tribunals since 2011. The administration of justice since 1971 has supported the progressive formalisation of the chains of commands within the judiciary, with governance arrangements made visible and further streamlined with the integration of the administration of magistrates' courts and the Tribunals' Service into Her Majesty's Courts and Tribunals Service in 2011. The administration of justice was gradually aligned with the administration of other public services in the 1980s, and its 'normalisation' was supported by reforms of the machinery of justice such as the Woolf reforms. Upon reading the accumulated quantitative data on judicial business (without any attempt to provide a substantial or qualitative analysis of the complexity of proceedings) one may ask whether the Courts and Tribunals Service is simply an enforcement agency for the executive; some margin of appreciation or greater flexibility must exist to preserve the quality of justice and give due consideration to the complexity of some proceedings. Greater resources will ensure effectiveness in the conduct of judicial business and support judicial independence.

Shared administration of justice between the Lord Chief Justice and the Lord Chancellor is a bare minimum to ensure the proper delineation of the exercise of the judicial function and the prerogatives of good administration. While the Courts and Tribunals Service sets out agency standards, the senior judges must be able to influence these standards or targets in order to ensure the fine tuning of procedural fairness with efficiency and economy in the conduct of judicial business. Nevertheless, even in times of greater prosperity, shared administration of justice through an executive agency is a reasonable model, as it provides for greater accountability for the workings of the judicial system and fits in well with a context of constitutional transition.

The more overt pressures on the judiciary remain financial. The number of judges remains static but caseloads only increase, and the savings to be found by better case management are limited. Cuts in legal aid, possibly regarded as one solution in some quarters, are no more than a panacea. In addition, there is no right that any judicial pay increase which may be recommended by the Senior Salaries Review Body will be acted upon and recently such recommendations have been disregarded. Given that the judges' pay reflects the higher income bracket – as indeed it should, if they are to be regarded as independent in their decision making – there is little prospect of this situation changing.

A fair reflection of society

9.7 The main achievement of the CRA towards judicial independence lies in the Judicial Appointments Commission. In a firm departure from the system of 'secret soundings' that applied to the recruitment of a small pool of practitioners, the transparency promoted by the Commission and its outreach efforts enhance appointments on merit, and the Commission has had no hesitation in wrestling with the executive on the matter of appointments. A forthcoming challenge for the Judicial Appointments Commission is also to engage with the appointments to the European Court of Justice and the shortlisting process for the English judge at the European Court of Human Rights.

Yet the current concern regarding appointments is one of enhancing diversity. The lack of women as well as black and Asian minorities in the composition of the senior judiciary is striking. While this reflects the wider difficulties in the legal profession that too few women and ethnic-minority lawyers hold senior positions, the debate looks set to continue as to whether the criterion of 'merit' might legitimately include consider-ation of a candidate's gender, ethnic origin or other background factors; we have argued that at the level of the Supreme Court at least, where decisions relate to policy or principle, a broader range of experience and expertise in the court, from both judicial and non-judicial backgrounds, would enhance the decision-making process, but the arguments are less likely to apply at the lower levels of the judiciary. Here, the argument might be made that gender or race might be a legitimate tie-breaker if the candidates in question are of sufficient and equal merit but this too may make little difference; our interviewees thought that it was rare that two candidates could not be separated at all after their CV, references, interview and test performances are taken into account. It may be that targets will be introduced until such time as the profile of the judiciary is considered suitably diverse. In so far as targets could shift, in practice, into quotas, we have expressed reservations about this measure. It certainly would need to be complemented by other measures to promote applications from the very best minority candidates. We have also drawn attention to the difficulties that solicitors in top firms might have in seeking time off to work as recorders, and have suggested that some outstanding academics might be suitably deployed at High Court or appellate level. In the case of solicitors at least, the wider pool would be expected to include a relatively large proportion of female and ethnic-minority candidates.

Professionalisation

9.8 Whether or not these measures regarding diversity are adopted, but especially if they are, it would be prudent to consider other aspects of what has been loosely termed the 'judicial career'. It is a historical fact that senior judges come from practice at the Bar; the idea of a 'judicial career' does not exclude such appointment to the bench in middle age. Indeed, the emergence of 'some semblance of a career judiciary', in the sense of some career patterns being developed, was noted in the 1990s.[2] Thus, the Judicial Appointments Commission and the Association of Her Majesty's District Judges have now developed a process of using appraisal information for deputy district judges in the reference process for selection exercises. If promotions were to be heavily based on appraisals by peers, however, it may trigger a concern of abdication of responsibility from the appraiser, although this could be monitored by the Judicial Appointments Commission.[3]

Appraisal goes with training, which has contributed to the modernisation of the attitude of the judiciary.[4] Some further rationalisation of judicial training is taking place so that, for example, tribunal and court judges are expected, in the near future, to be trained together in generic skills for judicial office holders. Training serves, too, the further purpose of

---

[2] The Home Affairs Select Committee Report in 1996, and Sir Robin Auld in 2001.
[3] J. Bell, *Judiciaries within Europe, A Comparative Review* (Cambridge University Press, 2006).
[4] Lord Chief Justice, 'The Judicial Studies Board Lecture 2010' (March 2010).

supporting progression and mobility within the various groups of judges; indeed training may be necessary to make such progression and mobility a reality. Here again, financial constraints mean that ongoing professional development is currently limited but training is certainly a feature of a professional judiciary. The professionalisation of the judiciary is best supported by the establishment of the Judicial Appointments Commission, as it seeks to remove patronage from the appointment system and to enhance the value of transparency necessary to judicial independence.

There is nevertheless a gap between developing professionalisation and a career judiciary, where appointment is confirmed after training in a judicial school, and that frontier needs to be clearly marked. The current system should be cultivated while encouraging diversity in the composition of the judiciary with reforms in the legal profession. There too, one may point to the dominance of the executive in the Legal Services Board, which regulates the legal profession – and any change there would in due course influence the character of the judiciary.

9.9 Another modern development that affects judicial independence lies in the establishment of the Office for Judicial Complaints, which has now assumed responsibility for investigating complaints about judges, although the outcome, where the alleged facts have been sustained, is in the hands of the Lord Chancellor and the Lord Chief Justice. A distinction is made between anything necessarily connected with the delivery of a judgment and any other conduct of the judge, though in the area of complaints this distinction is easily blurred. It is suggested that a decision by a judge not to recuse himself in the face of a plausible suggestion of apparent bias should be outside the remit of the Office of Judicial Complaints and remain addressed by the Court of Appeal. Where the complaint clearly concerns extra-judicial business, it seems that two contentious areas concern online opinions and activity, and indiscreet sexual activity. There are no easy answers as to what should be the exact standards in order to maintain the reputation of the judiciary but they cover the judge's official and non-official spheres of activities, and shield judicial independence from dependencies, associations, and even less intensive involvements which might cast doubts on judicial neutrality. The standards of conduct in the exercise of the judicial office have traditionally been high and continue to be so, under the strong supervision of the Court of Appeal in addition to the new regulatory framework introduced in the CRA.

However, those at the level of the High Court and above cannot be dismissed by the Lord Chancellor and Lord Chief Justice alone and indeed any such procedure will bypass the Office of Judicial Complaints altogether. The most likely avenue for removal seems to be by address to both Houses of Parliament on the basis of misconduct involving moral turpitude. The address was introduced to protect the judges from executive interference, as the acceptable way to check judicial behaviour. In modern times, however, the executive control over the legislature means that the address may, in practice, be inconsistent with the independence of judges. It is significant that an examination of the cases where a motion for an address was presented shows that, except for *Baron Smith's case*, in which the government changed its mind, in all cases the result was one supported by the government. Yet the actual operation of the address in the nineteenth century and at the beginning of the twentieth century seems satisfactory, with the elaboration by Parliament of the sufficient grounds for removal and the general considerations weighed in the process of disposing of the complaints against judicial conduct which have, arguably, become conventions today.

The meaning of judicial independence

9.10 Our analysis of judicial independence in England has reflected upon the core tenets of judicial independence. Judges should have security of tenure and only be removed for specific grounds and by means of an adequate procedure. The process of selection of judges should be free from any politicisation, personal or other irrelevant considerations. Upon appointment, a judge should receive adequate remuneration, which requires a regular pension scheme and should be adequately safeguarded against being used as a means of asserting control over judges. A judge must also be free from political or other pressures. A judge must first be immune from such risks of distorting justice as direct pressure, bribery or approaches by the litigant, a friend or counsel; he must also be removed from any sophisticated entanglements, be they political, personal or financial, that might appear to influence him in the exercise of his judicial functions, let alone entanglements that might actually influence him. The judiciary should also be representative of the society which it judges. Whatever social background a judge comes from he or she should endeavour to ensure that their background and prejudices do not influence their decisions.

Judicial independence sets constraints upon judges and others in order to serve the demand of impartiality in the judicial evaluation at the heart of the rule of law. The contribution of this book would also be to suggest that one additional constraint applies to judges, to the extent that the judiciary must account for its conduct of judicial business in the broadest sense, and, in doing so, must visibly demonstrate its independence. Judicial accountability is no longer simply construed as accountability to other judges as a group sharing an ethos, particular values and skills, and through decision making, by way of appeal and review.[5] This ends a traditionally fairly comfortable relationship between the judiciary, Parliament and the executive in England and Wales. Nonetheless, the proper relationship between the judiciary and the other branches of the government will be based on dialogue of respect and the judiciary and the executive must work together in a proper relationship as a part of the total government of the country: judicial accountability is now inextricably interwoven with judicial independence.

Judicial independence, as an essential safeguard of fundamental rights, is also intertwined with some other fundamental values underpinning the judicial system, and common standards of judicial independence can only be drawn in relation to them. The value of constitutionality provides adequate protection of the values of the justice system, assuring fairness and justice in adjudication, efficiency of the judicial process, securing access to justice, public confidence in the courts – and the safeguarding of judicial independence. A proper legal system is one which advances each of these values on its own, and achieves a suitable balance between them whenever they conflict with one another. As we identified, the values at play in the practice of judicial independence today in England showed a judiciary in tune with the cultural, social and political realities of its jurisdiction, adjusting to the formidable changes introduced by the constitutional settlement. But the challenges faced in seeking judicial independence are similar among jurisdictions. On the key facets of judicial independence – appointments, tenure, salaries, removal – judges at different levels and from different backgrounds share remarkably similar concerns. We have offered a view of what the elements of judicial independence should be, its significance in ensuring the rule of law, and the strains it faces from the executive, the legislature or others, with the hope of providing a framework for our readers to develop their own analysis, and so that our readers beyond England can for themselves establish and develop the standards of judicial independence in their own jurisdictions.

---

[5] V. Bogdanor, 'Parliament and the Judiciary: The Problem of Accountability', Third Sunningdale Accountability Lecture, 2006.

Annex 1

Courts and tribunals structure

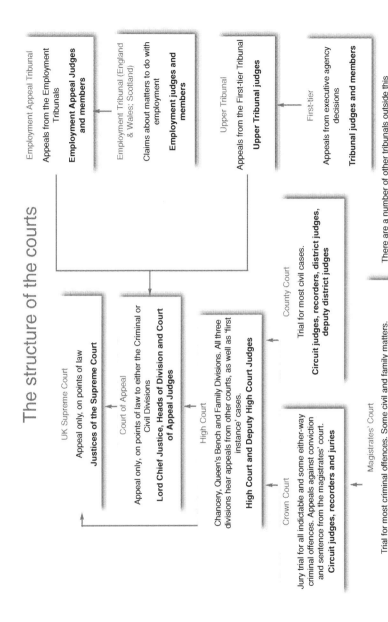

Figure 1. Court structure
Source: Judicial Office

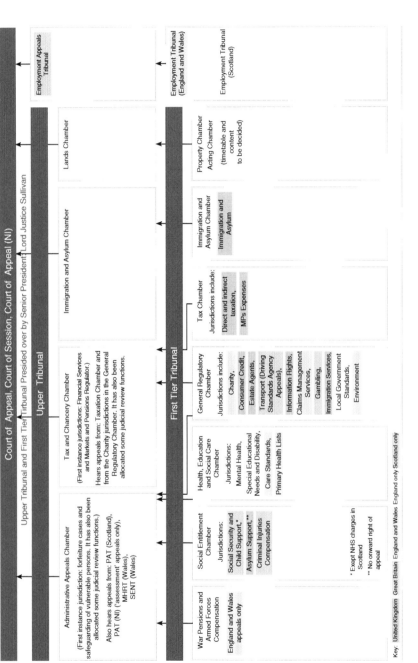

Figure 2. Tribunal structure
Source: Judicial Office

INDEX

Note: Documents and entries in a foreign language are given in italics.

Printed in Great Britain
by Amazon